500 BUDGET RECIPES

500 BUDGET RECIPES

Easy-to-cook and delicious dishes for all the family, offering fabulous recipes that make the most of a thrifty food budget

EDITED BY LUCY DONCASTER

southwater

This edition is published by Southwater,
an imprint of Anness Publishing Ltd,
108 Great Russell Street, London WC1B 3NA; info@anness.com

www.southwaterbooks.com; www.annesspublishing.com;
twitter: @Anness_Books

If you like the images in this book and would like to investigate using them for publishing, promotions or advertising, please visit our website www.practicalpictures.com for more information.

A CIP catalogue record for this book is available from the British Library.

Publisher: Joanna Lorenz
Executive Editor: Joanne Rippin
Designer: Adelle Morris
Photographers: Karl Adamson, Edward Allwright, Peter Anderson, David Armstrong, Tim Auty, Caroline Barty, Steve Baxter, Martin Brigdale, Nicki Dowey, James Duncan, Gus Filgate, John Freeman, Iain Garlick, Michelle Garrett, Will Heap, Peter Henley, John Heseltine, Amanda Heywood, Ferguson Hill, Janine Hosegood, David Jordan, Andrea Jones, Maris Kelly, Dave King, Don Last, William Lingwood, Patrick McLeary, Michael Michaels, Steve Moss, Thomas Odulate, Debby Patterson, Juliet Piddington, Peter Reilly, Craig Robertson, Simon Smith, Sam Stowell, Polly Wreford.
Recipe Writers: Pepita Aris, Catherine Atkinson, Josephine Bacon, Jane Baforth, Alex Barker, Ghillie Basan, Judy Bastyra, Michelle Berriedale-Johnson, Angela Boggiano, Janet Brinkworth, Georgina Campbell, Carla Capalbo, Lesley Chamberlain, Kit Chan, Jacqueline Clark, Maxine Clark, Frances Cleary, Carole Clements, Andi Clevely, Jan Cutler, Trish Davies, Roz Denny, Patrizia Diemling, Stephanie Donaldson, Coralie Dorman, Matthew Drennan, Sarah Edmonds, Joanna Farrow, Rafi Fernandez, Maria Filippelli, Jenni Fleetwood, Christine France, Silvano Franco, Yasuko Fukuoka, Sarah Gates, Shirley Gill, Brian Glover, Nicola Graimes, Rosamund Grant, Carole Handslip, Juliet Harbutt, Rebekah Hassan, Shaun Hill, Simona Hill, Deh-Ta Hsiung, Shehzad Husain, Jessica Houdret, Christine Ingram, Judy Jackson, Becky Johnson, Bridget Jones, Manisha Kanini, Sheila Kimberley, Soheila Kimberley, Lucy Knox, Masaki Ko, Elizabeth Lambert Ortez, Ruby Le Bois, Clare Lewis, Sara Lewis, Patricia Lousada, Gilly Love, Lesley Mackley, Norma MacMillan, Sue Maggs, Kathy Man, Sally Mansfield, Maggie Mayhew Norma Miller, Jane Milton, Sallie Morris, Anna Mosesson, Janice Murfitt, Annie Nichols, Suzannah Olivier, Maggie Pannell, Katherine Richmond, Keith Richmond, Rena Salaman, Jennie Shapter, Anne Sheasby, Ysanne Spevack, Marlena Spieler, Jenny Stacey, Liz Trigg, Christopher Trotter, Linda Tubby, Sunil Vijayakar, Hilaire Walden, Laura Washburn, Steven Wheeler, Jenny White, Biddy White-Lennon, Kate Whiteman, Rosemary Wilkinson, Carolo Wilson, Elizabeth Wolf-Cohen, Jeni Wright, Annette Yates.
Production Controller: Rosanna Anness

NOTES
Bracketed terms are intended for American readers.

For all recipes, quantities are given in both metric and imperial measures and, where appropriate, in standard cups and spoons. Follow one set of measures, but not a mixture, because they are not interchangeable.

Standard spoon and cup measures are level.
1 tsp = 5ml, 1 tbsp = 15ml, 1 cup = 250ml/8fl oz.

Australian standard tablespoons are 20ml. Australian readers should use 3 tsp in place of 1 tbsp for measuring small quantities.

American pints are 16fl oz/2 cups. American readers should use 20fl oz/2.5 cups in place of 1 pint when measuring liquids.

Electric oven temperatures in this book are for conventional ovens. When using a fan oven, the temperature will probably need to be reduced by about 10–20°C/20–40°F. Since ovens vary, you should check with your manufacturer's instruction book for guidance.

The nutritional analysis given for each recipe is calculated per portion (i.e. serving or item), unless otherwise stated. If the recipe gives a range, such as Serves 4–6, then the nutritional analysis will be for the smaller portion size, i.e. 6 servings. The analysis does not include optional ingredients, such as salt added to taste.

Medium (US large) eggs are used unless otherwise stated.

PUBLISHER'S NOTE
Although the advice and information in this book are believed to be accurate and true at the time of going to press, neither the authors nor the publisher can accept any legal responsibility or liability for any errors o omissions that may have been made nor for any inaccuracies nor for any loss, harm or injury that comes about from following instructions or advice in this book.

Contents

Introduction

Feeding a hungry family can be an expensive business, and with today's hectic lifestyle it is all too easy to spend much more than you need to. At the same time it is easy to disregard the importance of fresh, healthy home-made food, and focus simply on getting a meal on the table as quickly as possible. Lack of planning can result in huge amounts of food being thrown away, wasting both money, time and resources. However, with just a little bit of thought, forward planning, some simple shopping tips and a wealth of inspiring recipes, you can create delicious meals without breaking the bank.

Above: Buying fresh produce to cook at home is cheaper, healthier and better tasting than ready-made meals.

Weekly planning

For many people, the thought of planning an evening meal simply never crosses their minds until dinner-time arrives. This lack of forethought often results in eating fast food or buying ready meals, both of which can be very costly and not particularly nutritious. A little bit of planning not only saves money, but it also ensures greater variety in the diet and can save time at the end of a busy day.

The easiest way to plan a weekly menu is to fill in a simple chart that shows at a glance which courses and dishes are going to be served, and makes sticking to a budget much easier. If you are cooking for a household, involve everyone in this planning process, making everyone feel that their food preferences are being acknowledged and that they are taking an active role in deciding what they eat.

Clever shopping

Before you go shopping, you should have a list of the items you want to buy, which should be written when you are planning the weekly menu. This ensures that you don't forget anything as well as helping to prevent you from impulse buying and going over budget. The cost of produce varies from store to store, as well as from season to season, and it is important that you shop around to get the best deal and the best quality. Many stores have multi-buy offers, as well as bargain bins and reduced-to-clear items, and it is a good idea to find out when stores do their stock turn-over, as this is the time when they are most like to drastically reduce the cost of items in order to clear the stock. By finding out this information, you can pick up great bargains on a weekly basis and reduce your overall shopping bill. Buying in bulk, in conjunction with shopping around, is often the best way to reduce the relative cost of foods. It is, however, important to take several factors into consideration. If you are buying fresh produce, you will need to use it quickly, freeze it or preserve it as jams, pickles or chutneys. If you are buying canned, bottled or packet goods, you will need space to store them.

Left: A well-stocked storecupboard can save you time and money when cooking, but don't let it become too full of out-of-date items.

ɨow to make the most of leftovers

.eftovers account for a large proportion of the food that is vasted every day, but this waste is completely unnecessary, s they can easily be transformed into a wide range of lelicious new dishes. As part of the planning process you can nake more than you need for one meal, so that the leftovers an be converted into something else. Here are some udget-friendly ideas for ways in which you can make the nost of the food you buy.

A surprising amount of flesh can be stripped from a carcass fter a roast meal, and this cooked meat can be converted nto a wide range of pies, curries, soups or even simply fried vith onions and rice to create a tasty and very quick supper. The carcass can then be converted into home-made stock or use in any number of recipes. Leftover vegetables can be ombined with the stock and flesh, if you like, to create a asty soup, or fried up to make a quick and easy supper.
: is a good idea to make more Bolognese and pasta sauces nan you actually need, as they freeze very well and form the asis of many dishes, such as lasagne, moussaka, cottage pie nd chilli con carne. The same applies for meat stews, which re easily made into pies with the addition of a potato or astry topping. Leftover boiled or steamed potatoes can be liced and transformed into a Spanish omelette, or cubed nd combined with corned beef, onions and tomato sauce. Other boiled or steamed vegetables make an almost instant

Above: Canned beans are cheap and versatile and can be used in stews, healthy salads or quick-and-easy tasty dips and pâtés.

ragu or curry when combined with a can of chopped tomatoes and a few storecupboard flavourings.

Leftover pasta and rice is often thrown away because it is cheap. This is a waste, as it can be used to create a cold pasta salad, or to bulk out omelettes and soups. Stale bread also has many uses: it can be made into breadcrumbs and frozen, then used for crunchy savoury toppings, or cut it into cubes to be brushed with oil and fried to make home-made croûtons, added to soups, dipped in egg and made into French toast, or used in recipes such as Autumn Pudding or Bread and Butter Pudding. Use the hard rind from cheeses such as grano padano to add flavour to soups and sauces. Simply add it at the start of cooking and remove to serve.

The recipes

In the pages of this book you will find 500 budget recipes designed to make your weekly spend go as far as possible. Use them to plan ahead, compile shopping lists, and make the most of seasonal ingredients. Choose recipes that use what you already have in the storecupboard and try new ideas so that the meals you cook have variety and new flavours for friends and family to try.

Left: Leftovers shouldn't be thrown away, but used to create new meals, such as these crêpes stuffed with roast turkey and cranberry sauce.

Basic Recipes

A well-flavoured stock or gravy can really affect the final taste of a dish. Good-quality ready-made stocks and gravies – either cube, powders or liquid concentrate – are readily available, but stocks are easy and cheap to make. Always ask for the meat bones when buying from a butcher, and trimmings if you have fish prepared by the fishmonger, as these are perfect for making good stock. The basic tomato sauce included here is not really a stock, but is another great recipe to cook in bulk and use as a base for soups, casseroles or sauces.

Vegetable Stock

Vegetable stocks are very good for soups, adding a depth of flavour to non-meat recipes, especially when they are simple soups made of three or four ingredients. Make this stock in double quantities and freeze in smaller portions so it is easy to use when you need it.

Makes about 1 litre/ 1¾ pints/4 cups

3 unpeeled onions, quartered
200g/7oz large open mushrooms
300–400g/11–14oz mixed vegetables, such as broccoli, carrots, celery, tomatoes and/or spring onions (scallions), roughly chopped
45ml/3 tbsp green or brown lentils

1 Place the onions in a heavy pan with the mushrooms, mixed vegetables and green or brown lentils.

2 Add 2.5ml/½ tsp salt, 10ml/2 tsp peppercorns and 1.7 litres/ 3 pints/7½ cups water to the pan. Bring to the boil, then reduce the heat and simmer, partially covered, for 50–60 minutes.

3 Leave the stock to cool slightly, then strain into a bowl and leave to cool completely. Store the cold stock in the refrigerator for up to 24 hours, or you can freeze it for up to 6 months. Use the stock in soups and sauces or vegetarian recipes, such as pilaffs, casseroles, curries or stews.

Beef Stock

Beef bones should be easy to obtain from your local butcher, and you should find that they will cost nothing, or very little. Any type of bone will do, but make sure they are small enough to fit into your pan, or ask your butcher to cut them down.

Makes about 1 litre/1¾ pints/4 cups

900g/2lb beef bones
2 unpeeled onions, cut into quarters
1 bouquet garni
2 large carrots, roughly chopped
1 stick celery

1 Preheat the oven to 220°C/425°F/Gas 7. Put the bones in a roasting pan and roast for about 45 minutes, or until well browned, turning two or three times.

2 Transfer the roasted bones and any juices to a large, heavy pan. Add the onion quarters, leaving the skins on, the bouquet garni and chopped carrots. Add 5ml/1 tsp salt and 5ml/1 tsp black peppercorns.

3 Pour over about 1.7 litres/3 pints/7½ cups cold water and bring just to the boil. Using a slotted spoon, skim off any scum on the surface of the stock.

4 Reduce the heat and partially cover the pan. Simmer the stock on the lowest heat for about 3 hours, then leave to cool.

5 Strain the stock into a large bowl and leave to cool completely, then remove any fat from the surface. Store the stock in the refrigerator for up to 3 days or freeze in batches for up to 6 months.

Cook's Tip
If you don't have time to make stock straight after eating fish or roasted meats, you can freeze the main ingredients – meat bones, fish trimmings or a cooked chicken carcass – until you are ready to make it at a later date.

Chicken Stock

A good chicken stock turns a soup or rice dish into a feast.

Makes about 1 litre/1¾ pints/4 cups

1 large roast chicken carcass
2 unpeeled onions, quartered
3 bay leaves
1 leek, washed and chopped
2 large carrots, roughly chopped

1 Put the chicken carcass and bones and roasting juices into a heavy pan. Add the onion, bay leaves and chopped carrots and leek, 2.5ml/½ tsp salt and 5ml/1 tsp black peppercorns, and pour over 1.7 litres/3 pints/7½ cups cold water. Bring to the boil.

2 Reduce the heat, partially cover the pan and cook on the lowest setting for 1½ hours. Using a large spoon, carefully turn the chicken in the stock and crush the carcass occasionally.

3 Strain into a large bowl and leave to cool completely. When cool, remove any fat from the surface. Store the stock in the refrigerator for up to 2 days or freeze for up to 6 months.

Fish Stock

The excellent thing about fish stock is you can use the trimmings that are usually thrown away.

Makes about 600ml/1 pint/2½ cups

500g/1¼lb fish bones and trimmings, without heads and gills
1 bouquet garni
1 onion or 3–4 shallots, peeled and quartered
2 celery sticks, roughly chopped

1 Pack the bones and trimmings into a heavy pan with the rest of the ingredients, 2.5ml/½ tsp salt and 2.5ml/½ tsp peppercorns. Pour in 1 litre/1¾ pints/4 cups water.

2 Bring to the boil. Reduce the heat, cover and cook on low heat for 30 minutes. Cool, then strain into a bowl. Store in the refrigerator for up to 24 hours or freeze for up to 3 months.

Onion Stock

Use this onion stock as the base for a great gravy with sausages or roast meat.

Makes about 300ml/½ pint/1¼ cups

30ml/2 tbsp olive oil
25g/1oz/2 tbsp butter
8 onions, sliced
pinch of caster (superfine) sugar
300ml/½ pint/1¼ cups boiling water and 1 beef stock cube

1 Put the oil and butter in a large pan and add the onion stirring so it is all coated. Cover and cook on low heat, stirring frequently, for 30 minutes.

2 Add the sugar and cook for 5 minutes more. Add the stock and bring to the boil. Boil for 10–15 minutes until the liquid is reduced by half. Cool and freeze.

Basic Tomato Sauce

This rich tomato sauce has a sweet, intense flavour, and is perfect for soup, pasta sauce or pizza topping. It can also be used in various stews and casseroles. Freeze it in small quantities for use later.

Makes about 300ml/½ pint/1¼ cups

15ml/1 tbsp olive oil
1 medium onion, chopped
1 small carrot, peeled and diced
1 stick celery, finely sliced
1 clove garlic, peeled and crushed
400g/14oz can chopped tomatoes
100ml/3½ fl oz/scant ½ cup red or white wine
5ml/1 tsp herbes de Provence
salt and ground black pepper

1 Put the oil in a large pan and add the onion, carrot, celery and garlic. Cook on medium heat, stirring, until the onions are transluscent and the celery and carrot are starting to soften.

2 Stir in the tomatoes, wine and herbs. Season with salt and pepper. Cover and simmer for 15–20 minutes until the vegetables are completely tender and the liquid reduced. Blend the sauce until smooth. Cool and freeze.

Leek and Potato Soup

This is a hearty staple and a widely travelled soup, served as everything from a warming lunch to a hot drink from a flask on a cold winter's walk. The chopped vegetables produce a chunky soup. If you prefer a smooth texture, press the mixture through a strainer or blend in a processor.

Serves 4
50g/2oz/¼ cup butter
2 leeks, chopped
1 small onion, finely chopped
350g/12oz potatoes, peeled and chopped
900ml/1½ pints/3¾ cups vegetable stock
salt and ground black pepper
chopped fresh parsley, to garnish
warmed bread, to serve

1 Heat 25g/1oz/2 tbsp of the butter in a large pan over medium heat. Add the leeks and onion and cook gently, stirring occasionally, for about 7 minutes, until the vegetables are softened but not browned.

2 Add the potatoes to the pan and cook for approximately 2–3 minutes, then add the stock and bring to the boil. Reduce the heat, cover and simmer for 30–35 minutes.

3 Season the soup to taste and remove the pan from the heat. Dice the remaining butter and stir it into the soup until it has just melted. Ladle the soup into bowls. Serve immediately, garnished with the chopped parsley, with generous chunks of warm, fresh bread.

Cook's Tips

- *Don't use a food processor or blender to purée this soup as it can give the potatoes a gluey consistency. The potatoes should be left to crumble and disintegrate naturally as they boil, making the consistency of the soup thicker the longer you leave them.*
- *Make a full-flavoured vegetable stock by simmering peelings and trimmings, as well as onions, celery, carrots and other vegetables in water for 2 hours and straining the liquid.*

Summer Minestrone

This brightly coloured, fresh-tasting soup makes the most of delicious summer vegetables and fresh basil and is a meal in itself. Chop the vegetables to small dice.

Serves 4
45ml/3 tbsp olive oil
1 large onion, finely chopped
15ml/1 tbsp sun-dried tomato purée (paste)
450g/1lb ripe Italian plum tomatoes, peeled and finely chopped
225g/8oz green courgettes (zucchini), trimmed and roughly chopped
225g/8oz yellow courgettes, trimmed and roughly chopped
3 waxy new potatoes, washed and diced
2 garlic cloves, crushed
about 1.2 litres/2 pints/5 cups vegetable stock or water
60ml/4 tbsp fresh basil, chopped with scissors or torn
50g/2oz/⅔ cup grated grano padano cheese
salt and ground black pepper

1 Heat the oil in a large, heavy pan, add the onion and cook gently for about 5 minutes, stirring constantly, until softened but not browned.

2 Stir in the sun-dried tomato purée, chopped tomatoes, courgettes, diced potatoes and garlic. Mix well and cook gently for 10 minutes, uncovered, shaking the pan frequently to stop the vegetables sticking to the base.

3 Pour in the stock or water. Bring to the boil, lower the heat, half-cover the pan and simmer gently for 15 minutes or until the vegetables are just tender. Add more stock if necessary.

4 Remove from the heat, stir in the basil and half the cheese, and serve hot sprinkled with the remaining cheese.

Cook's Tip
Grano padano cheese is similar in taste and texture to Parmesan, but has a slightly milder taste. It is usually cheaper than Parmesan, and makes an economical alternative.

Leek and Potato Energy 179kcal/747kJ; Protein 3.2g; Carbohydrate 17.9g, of which sugars 4g; Fat 11g, of which saturates 6.7g; Cholesterol 27mg; Calcium 32mg; Fibre 3g; Sodium 88mg
Summer Minetrone Energy 254kcal/1059kJ; Protein 10.2g; Carbohydrate 24.3g, of which sugars 11.1g; Fat 13.5g, of which saturates 4.1g; Cholesterol 13mg; Calcium 211mg; Fibre 4.1g; Sodium 167mg

;arrot and Orange Soup

This traditional light and :ummery soup is always ›opular for its wonderfully reamy consistency and 'ibrantly fresh citrus flavour. : is also a good winter tandby when carrots are arge and less tender than he summer harvest. Use a :ood, home-made chicken or 'egetable stock if you can.

;erves 4

;0g/2oz/¼ cup butter
3 leeks, sliced
450g/1lb carrots, sliced
1.2 litres/2 pints/5 cups chicken or vegetable stock
rind and juice of 2 oranges
2.5ml/½ tsp freshly grated nutmeg
a splash of dry sherry (optional)
150ml/¼ pint/⅔ cup Greek (US strained plain) yogurt
salt and ground black pepper
fresh sprigs of coriander (cilantro), to garnish
bread, to serve

Melt the butter in a large pan. Add the leeks and carrots and tir well, coating the vegetables with the butter.

: Cover and cook for about 10 minutes, until the vegetables are ›eginning to soften but not colour.

; Pour in the stock and the orange rind and juice. Add the ˌutmeg and season to taste with salt and pepper.

4 Bring to the boil, lower the heat, cover and simmer for about 0 minutes, or until the vegetables are tender.

Leave to cool slightly, then purée the soup in a food ›rocessor or blender until smooth.

Return the soup to the pan, add a splash of dry sherry if you ⁄ish, then add 30ml/2 tbsp of the yogurt. Taste the soup and djust the seasoning, if necessary. Reheat gently.

' Ladle the soup into warmed individual bowls and use a spoon ɔ put a swirl of yogurt in the centre of each. Sprinkle the fresh ɔrigs of coriander over each bowl to garnish, and serve nmediately with fresh bread.

Cream of Onion Soup

This wonderfully satisfying and low-cost soup has a deep, buttery flavour that is complemented by the addition of crisp croûtons or chopped chives, sprinkled over just before serving.

Serves 4

115g/4oz/½ cup unsalted (sweet) butter
1kg/2¼lb yellow onions, sliced
1 fresh bay leaf
105ml/7 tbsp dry white vermouth or dry sherry
1 litre/1¾ pints/4 cups chicken or vegetable stock
150ml/¼ pint/⅔ cup double (heavy) cream
a little lemon juice (optional)
salt and ground black pepper
day-old French bread, sliced and toasted and chopped fresh chives, to garnish

1 Melt 75g/3oz/6 tbsp butter in a large pan. Set about 200g/7oz of the onions aside and add the rest to the pan with the bay leaf. Stir the onions to coat in the butter, then cover and cook very gently for about 30 minutes. The onions should be soft and tender, but not browned.

2 Add the vermouth or sherry, increase the heat and boil rapidly until the liquid has evaporated. Add the stock, 5ml/1 tsp salt and pepper to taste. Bring to the boil, lower the heat and simmer gently for 5 minutes, then remove from the heat.

3 Leave the mixture to cool, then discard the bay leaf and process the soup in a blender or food processor. Return the soup to the rinsed pan.

4 Melt the remaining butter in another pan. Add the remaining onions, cover, and cook gently until soft but not browned. Uncover and continue to cook until golden yellow.

5 Add the cream to the soup and reheat gently until hot, but without boiling as this may curdle the cream. Season to taste, adding lemon juice if using.

6 Add the onions and warm through for 1 minute. Garnish with chopped chives and serve with slices of toasted French bread.

arrot and Orange Energy 206kcal/856kJ; Protein 5g; Carbohydrate 15.8g, of which sugars 14.2g; Fat 14.4g, of which saturates 8.3g; Cholesterol 27mg; Calcium 111mg; Fibre 5.8g; Sodium 131mg
ream of Onion Energy 522kcal/2151kJ; Protein 4g; Carbohydrate 21.5g, of which sugars 15.6g; Fat 44.5g, of which saturates 27.5g; Cholesterol 113mg; Calcium 90mg; Fibre 3.5g; Sodium 397mg

Spiced Parsnip Soup

This lightly spiced, creamy soup is perfect for a cold winter day. Parsnips are a cold-weather vegetable and when in season are an extremely economical ingredient, so this soup is not only filling, easy to make and packed with flavour, it is also very cheap.

Serves 6

900g/2lb parsnips
50g/2oz/¼ cup butter
1 onion, chopped
2 garlic cloves, crushed
10ml/2 tsp ground cumin
5ml/1 tsp ground coriander
about 1.2 litres/2 pints/5 cups hot chicken stock
150ml/¼ pint/⅔ cup single (light) cream
salt and ground black pepper, to taste
chopped fresh chives and/or croûtons, to garnish

1 Peel and thinly slice the parsnips. Heat the butter in a large heavy pan and add the peeled parsnips and chopped onion with the crushed garlic.

2 Cook over low heat until the vegetables are softened but not coloured, stirring occasionally.

3 Add the ground cumin and ground coriander to the vegetable mixture and cook, stirring, for 1–2 minutes, and then gradually blend in the hot chicken stock and mix well.

4 Cover the pan and simmer the soup for about 20 minutes, or until the parsnip is soft. Remove the pan from the heat and leave to cool slightly.

5 Purée the soup in a food processor or blender. Check the texture, and adjust with a little extra stock or water if it seems too thick.

6 Check the seasoning and adjust as required. Add the cream and reheat without boiling.

7 Serve immediately, sprinkled with chopped chives or parsley and/or croûtons, to garnish.

Curried Cauliflower Soup

A simple yet delicious soup, which is perfect for lunch or as a light meal, served with warm, crusty bread and garnished with fresh coriander. Take advantage of any offers in your store of cauliflower bulk deals; make caulifower cheese with some and this soup with others.

Serves 4

750ml/1¼ pints/3 cups full-fat (whole) milk
1 large cauliflower
15ml/1 tbsp garam masala
salt and ground black pepper, to taste
fresh coriander (cilantro) leaves, to garnish (optional)

1 Pour the milk into a large pan and place over medium heat. Remove the leaves from the cauliflower and break into florets. Don't throw away the stalk, trim and chop it into small pieces.

2 Add the chopped cauliflower and florets to the milk with the garam masala and season to taste with salt and pepper.

3 Bring the milk to the boil, then reduce the heat, partially cover the pan with a lid and simmer for about 20 minutes, or until the cauliflower is tender.

4 Let the mixture cool for a few minutes, then transfer to a food processor and process until smooth (you may have to do this in two separate batches).

5 Return the purée to the pan and heat through gently without boiling, checking and adjusting the seasoning to taste. Serve immediately, garnished with fresh coriander, if you like.

Cook's Tip

If you don't have garam masala in your kitchen, use 5ml/1 tsp each of ground cumin and coriander, or 15ml/1 tbsp mild curry powder. You don't have to use full fat (whole) milk, if you have semi-skimmed (low-fat) in the refrigerator then use that, but whole milk does give a lovely creamy flavour.

Spiced Parsnip Energy 215kcal/899kJ; Protein 3.9g; Carbohydrate 21.3g, of which sugars 10.6g; Fat 13.3g, of which saturates 7.7g; Cholesterol 32mg; Calcium 92mg; Fibre 7.3g; Sodium 74mg
Curried Cauliflower Energy 143kcal/601kJ; Protein 12g; Carbohydrate 13.9g, of which sugars 12.6g; Fat 4.8g, of which saturates 2.3g; Cholesterol 11mg; Calcium 271mg; Fibre 3.2g; Sodium 104mg

'lushroom Soup with Tarragon

'he rich, earthy flavour of rown cap mushrooms is ubtly enhanced with fresh arragon to create a hearty et economical appetizer or ınch. Serve with fresh bread nd cold meats for a tasty ght meal.

erves 6

shallots
5g/½oz/1 tbsp butter
450g/1lb/6 cups brown cap (cremini) mushrooms, finely chopped
300ml/½ pint/1¼ cups vegetable stock
300ml/½ pint/1¼ cups semi-skimmed (low-fat) milk
15–30ml/1–2 tbsp chopped fresh tarragon
salt and ground black pepper, to taste
sprigs of fresh tarragon, to garnish

Finely chop the shallots. Melt the butter in a large pan, add ıe shallots and cook for 5 minutes, stirring occasionally.

. Add the mushrooms and cook gently for 3 minutes, stirring, ıen the stock and milk. Bring to the boil, then cover the pan nd simmer for about 20 minutes until the vegetables are soft.

Stir in the chopped tarragon and season to taste with salt and round black pepper.

Allow the soup to cool slightly, then purée in a blender or ood processor, in batches if necessary, until smooth.

Return the processed soup to the rinsed-out pan and reheat ently. Ladle into warmed bowls and serve garnished with prigs of tarragon.

Cook's Tip
Brown cap (cremini) mushrooms have a more robust flavour than cultivated mushrooms, such as button (white), cap and flat mushrooms. Field (portobello) mushrooms are similar in appearance to cultivated flat mushrooms, but they are simply large brown cap mushrooms.

Potato Soup

This incredibly economical soup is not only excellent as it is, but it is very versatile too, as it can be used as a base for numerous other soups. Use a floury potato, such as Golden Wonder or russet, as waxy pototes won't give the right texture. The chicken stock can be replaced with vegetable stock if you wish, but fresh chicken stock gives it added depth of flavour and richness.

Serves 8

50g/2oz/¼ cup butter
2 large onions, peeled and finely chopped
675g/1½lb potatoes, peeled and diced
about 1.75 litres/3 pints/7½ cups hot chicken stock
a little milk, if necessary
a few chopped fresh chives, to garnish (optional) and rustic bread, to serve
salt and ground black pepper, to taste

1 Melt the butter in a large heavy pan and add the onions, turning them in the butter until well coated. Cover and leave to cook over very low heat for about 10 mintues.

2 Add the potatoes to the pan, and mix with the butter and onions until well combined. Season with salt and pepper to taste, cover and cook without colouring over low heat for about 10 minutes.

3 Add most of the stock, bring to the boil and simmer for 25 minutes, or until the vegetables are tender.

4 Remove from the heat and allow to cool slightly. Purée the soup in batches in a blender or food processor for really smooth, silky consistency, or crush and beat with a wooden spoon if you prefer a more rustic-textured soup.

5 Reheat over low heat and adjust the seasoning to taste if necessary. If the soup seems too thick, add extra stock to achieve the right consistency.

6 Serve the soup in warmed bowls, sprinkled with chopped chives with warm rustic bread, such as soda bread.

ushroom with Tarragon Energy 58kcal/242kJ; Protein 3.4g; Carbohydrate 3.7g, of which sugars 3.3g; Fat 3.4g, of which saturates 1.9g; Cholesterol 8mg; Calcium 84mg; Fibre 1.4g; Sodium 44mg
tato Energy 167kcal/699kJ; Protein 2.9g; Carbohydrate 23.5g, of which sugars 5.3g; Fat 7.5g, of which saturates 4.5g; Cholesterol 18mg; Calcium 26mg; Fibre 2.1g; Sodium 201mg

Cream of Celeriac Soup

Celeriac is a very economical vegetable and has a wonderful flavour that is reminiscent of celery, but adds a slightly nutty taste.

Serves 6

1 leek, thickly sliced
500g/1lb celeriac, diced
1.2 litres/2 pints/5 cups vegetable stock
250ml/8fl oz/1 ¼ cup dry white wine
freshly grated nutmeg
salt and ground black pepper

1 Place the leek and celeriac in a large pan and add the stock and wine. Bring to the boil, reduce the heat and simmer for 10–15 minutes until the vegetables are soft.

2 Blend the soup until smooth, in batches if necessary, return to the rinsed-out pan and season to taste with nutmeg, salt and pepper. Reheat gently and serve in warm bowls.

Cabbage and Potato Soup

This soup is ideal at any time of the year, and as befits a peasant recipe from Eastern Europe, it is a very frugal dish indeed.

Serves 4

30ml/2 tbsp olive oil
2 small onions, sliced
6 garlic cloves, halved
350g/12oz/3 cups cut shredded cabbage
4 potatoes, unpeeled
5ml/1 tsp caraway seeds
1.2 litres/2 pints/5 cups water
5ml/1 tsp salt

1 Pour the olive oil into a large pan, add the sliced onion and cook gently for about 5 minutes to soften. Add the garlic and the shredded cabbage to the pan and cook over low heat for 10 minutes, stirring occasionally.

2 Add the potatoes, caraway seeds, salt and water. Bring to the boil, then simmer until all the vegetables are cooked through, about 20–30 minutes. Blend the soup and serve.

Corn, Potato and Bean Chowder

A chunky soup, which combines creamy potatoes and flageolet beans with the sweet taste of corn, this is excellent served with thick crusty bread and topped with some melted strong Cheddar cheese.

Serves 4

30ml/2 tbsp sunflower or vegetable oil
25g/1oz/2 tbsp butter
1 onion, chopped
1 garlic clove, crushed
1 medium baking potato, chopped
2 celery sticks, sliced
1 small green (bell) pepper, seeded, halved and sliced
600ml/1 pint/2½ cups stock or water
300ml/½ pint/1¼ cups milk
200g/7oz can flageolet or cannellini beans
300g/11oz can corn kernels
good pinch dried sage
salt and ground black pepper, to taste
grated Cheddar cheese and crusty bread, to serve

1 Heat the oil and butter in large heavy pan, then add the onion, garlic, potato, celery and green pepper. Cook gently for about 10 minutes, shaking the pan occasionally.

2 Pour in the stock or water, season with salt and pepper to taste and bring to the boil.

3 Reduce the heat, cover again and simmer gently for about 15 minutes until the vegetables are tender.

4 Add the milk, beans and corn, including their liquids, and the sage. Simmer, uncovered, for 5 minutes.

5 Taste and adjust the seasoning if necessary. Sprinkle with grated Cheddar cheese and serve immediately.

Variation
You can use other types of canned beans instead of flageolet beans, including pinto beans, butter (lima) beans or broad (fava) beans. Alternatively, add a can of mixed beans.

Celeriac Energy 25kcal/101kJ; Protein 2g; Carbohydrate 3g, of which sugars 2g; Fat 1g, of which saturates 0g; Cholesterol 0mg; Calcium 39mg; Fibre 5g; Sodium 412mg
Cabbage Energy 144kcal/601kJ; Protein 3.1g; Carbohydrate 20.4g, of which sugars 8.1g; Fat 6g, of which saturates 0.9g; Cholesterol 0mg; Calcium 60mg; Fibre 3.3g; Sodium 507mg
Corn Chowder Energy 346kcal/1454kJ; Protein 10.3g; Carbohydrate 48.4g, of which sugars 19.6g; Fat 13.7g, of which saturates 5.1g; Cholesterol 18mg; Calcium 150mg; Fibre 6.5g; Sodium 487mg

ʾumpkin Soup with Yogurt

ʾhis simple puréed soup is a reat winter treat and makes comforting lunch served ⁄ith bread, or a flavoursome ppetizer. It tastes especially ood with some melted utter and yogurt drizzled ver the top. Save the umpkin seeds, wash 1oroughly, and dry fry them ɔr a crunchy soup topping.

Serves 4

1kg/2¼lb pumpkin flesh, cut into cubes
1 litre/1¾ pints/4 cups chicken stock
10ml/2 tsp sugar
25g/1oz/2 tbsp butter
60–75ml/4–5 tbsp thick and creamy natural (plain) yogurt
salt and ground black pepper, to taste

Put the pumpkin cubes into a pan with the stock, and bring ıe liquid to the boil. Reduce the heat, cover the pan, and mmer for about 20 minutes, or until the pumpkin is ɔmpletely tender.

Process the soup in a blender, or use a potato masher to ·eak up the flesh. Return the soup to the pan and bring it to ıe boil again.

Add the sugar to the pan and season to taste with salt and epper. Keep the soup gently simmering while you melt the ɹtter in a small pan over low heat.

Ladle the hot soup into individual serving bowls. Swirl a little ɔgurt on to the surface of the soup and drizzle the melted ɹtter over the top.

Serve immediately, offering extra yogurt so that you can enjoy e contrasting burst of sweet and tart in each mouthful.

Variation

Pumpkins are usually only available in the autumn, but you can use butternut squash for this recipe instead if you wish, as it is available all year round.

Pumpkin Soup with Rice

This fragrant, creamy pumpkin soup is subtly spiced with cinnamon and is made into a more substantial and economical dish with the addition of a small amount of rice. For a lighter and less creamy version of the soup you can increase the amount of chicken stock to milk, if you wish – just make sure that the total amount of liquid is the same.

Serves 4

about 1.1kg/2lb 7oz pumpkin
750ml/1¼ pints/3 cups chicken stock
750ml/1¼ pints/3 cups full-fat (whole) milk
10–15ml/2–3 tsp sugar
75g/3oz/½ cup cooked white rice
salt and ground black pepper, to taste
5ml/1 tsp ground cinnamon, to garnish
fresh crusty bread, to serve

1 Remove any seeds or strands of fibre from the pumpkin, cut off the skin and chop the flesh. Put the prepared pumpkin in a pan and add the stock, milk, sugar and seasoning.

2 Bring to the boil, then reduce the heat and simmer for about 20 minutes, until the pumpkin is tender.

3 Drain the pumpkin, reserving the liquid, and purée it in a blender or food processor, then return it to the pan.

4 Bring the soup back to the boil again, throw in the rice and simmer for a few minutes, until the grains are reheated.

5 Check the soup for seasoning and add salt and pepper to taste, pour into bowls and dust with cinnamon. Serve piping hot, with chunks of fresh, crusty bread.

Variation

If you would like to make a spicy variation of this soup, simply add 5ml/1 tsp mild curry powder to the soup at step 1, and replace the cinnamon for dusting with a pinch of cayenne pepper for a touch of heat.

ımpkin with Yoghurt Energy 97kcal/406kJ; Protein 2.6g; Carbohydrate 9.3g, of which sugars 8g; Fat 5.8g, of which saturates 3.6g; Cholesterol 14mg; Calcium 104mg; Fibre 2.5g; Sodium 51mg
ımpkin with Rice Energy 148kcal/627kJ; Protein 8.8g; Carbohydrate 20.7g, of which sugars 13.5g; Fat 4g, of which saturates 2.3g; Cholesterol 11mg; Calcium 308mg; Fibre 2.8g; Sodium 81mg

Cappelletti in Broth

This simple broth contains cappelletti, which are little stuffed pasta shapes that resemble hats. If you are unable to find them, you could use stuffed tortellini or any pasta shapes, such as fusilli, penne or orechiette. Dried pasta is almost always cheaper than fresh, so use that to make this recipe even more economical.

Serves 4

1.2 litres/2 pints/5 cups chicken stock
90–115g/3½–4oz/1 cup fresh or dried cappelletti
45ml/3 tbsp chopped fresh flat leaf parsley (optional)
30ml/2 tbsp grated grano padano cheese
salt and ground black pepper, to taste
crusty bread, to serve

1 Pour the chicken stock into a large pan and bring to the boil. Add a little salt and ground black pepper to taste, then drop in the dried cappelletti. Stir the pasta well and bring the chicken stock back to the boil.

2 Lower the heat to a simmer and cook according to the instructions on the packet, until the pasta is al dente, that is, tender but still firm to the bite. Stir occasionally to prevent the pasta sticking together.

3 Swirl the finely chopped fresh flat leaf parsley in to the stock, if using, then taste and adjust the seasoning, adding more salt and ground black pepper if necessary.

4 Ladle the broth into four warmed soup plates, then sprinkle with the freshly grated grano padano cheese and serve immediately. Add some crusty bread to make this lovely soup into a substantial meal.

Variation
There are as many variations of this soup as there are types of filled or dried pasta shapes, and you can also make beef stock or vegetable stock variations.

Tiny Pasta in Broth

This Italian soup is ideal for a light supper served with ciabatta bread and also makes a delicious first course for an al fresco supper. A wide variety of different types of pastina, or soup pasta, are available including stellette (stars), anellini (tiny thin rounds), risoni (rice-shaped) and farfalline (little butterflies). Choose just one shape or a combination of different varieties for an interesting result. You can also use spaghetti, just break it into little strands before dropping in to the water.

Serves 4

1.2 litres/2 pints/5 cups beef stock
75g/3oz/¾ cup dried tiny soup pasta
2 pieces bottled roasted red (bell) pepper
shaved Parmesan cheese
salt and ground black pepper

1 Bring the beef stock to the boil in a large pan. Add seasoning to taste, then drop in the dried soup pasta. Stir well and bring the stock back to the boil.

2 Reduce the heat so that the soup simmers and cook for 7–8 minutes, or according to the packet instructions, until the pasta is tender but still firm to the bite.

3 Drain the pieces of roasted pepper and dice them finely. Place them in the base of four warmed soup plates.

4 Taste the soup for seasoning and adjust if necessary, then ladle it into the soup plates. Serve immediately, topped with shavings of Parmesan.

Cook's Tip
This is an ideal dish to serve for a children's tea, as it is so quick and easy to throw together. The children will love the miniature pasta shapes floating in the soup, and they will also be entertained watching the Parmesan shavings slowly melt into the warm liquid.

Cappelletti in Broth Energy 111kcal/469kJ; Protein 5.9g; Carbohydrate 16.7g, of which sugars 0.8g; Fat 3g, of which saturates 1.6g; Cholesterol 8mg; Calcium 96mg; Fibre 0.7g; Sodium 265mg
Tiny Pasta in Broth Energy 135kcal/567kJ; Protein 7.8g; Carbohydrate 16.7g, of which sugars 3.3g; Fat 4.7g, of which saturates 2.7g; Cholesterol 13mg; Calcium 159mg; Fibre 1.3g; Sodium 321mg

:hunky Tomato Soup with Noodles

'his full-flavoured Moroccan oup is given a warming kick y the ras el hanout, a spicy aste that you can buy in ıost supermarkets. Noodles re a great way to eke it out.

erves 4

5–60ml/3–4 tbsp olive oil
–4 cloves
onions, chopped
butternut squash, peeled, seeded and cut into small chunks
celery stalks, chopped
carrots, peeled and chopped
large, ripe tomatoes, skinned and chopped
5–10ml/1–2 tsp sugar
15ml/1 tbsp tomato purée (paste)
5–10ml/1–2 tsp store-bought ras el hanout
2.5ml/½ tsp ground turmeric
a big bunch of fresh coriander (cilantro), chopped (reserve a few sprigs for garnish)
1.75 litres/3 pints/7½ cups vegetable stock
a handful dried egg noodles or capellini, broken into pieces
salt and ground black pepper, to taste
60–75ml/4–5 tbsp creamy yogurt and fresh bread, to serve

In a deep, heavy pan, heat the oil and add the cloves, onions, quash, celery and carrots. Fry until they begin to colour, then ir in the tomatoes and sugar. Cook the tomatoes until the ater reduces and they begin to pulp. Stir in the tomato purée, as el hanout, turmeric and chopped coriander.

Pour the stock into the vegetable and tomato mixture, stir nd then bring to the boil. Reduce the heat and simmer the oup for 30–40 minutes, until the vegetables are tender and the quid has reduced a little.

To make a puréed soup, leave the liquid to cool slightly before rocessing in a food processor or blender, then pour back into ie pan and add the pasta. Alternatively, to make a chunky soup, mply add the pasta to the unblended soup and cook for a ırther 8–10 minutes, or until the pasta is al dente.

Season the soup to taste and ladle it into bowls. Spoon a virl of yogurt into each one, garnish with the extra coriander nd serve with freshly baked bread.

Carrot and Cabbage Soup with Omelette

A very satisfying low-cost soup that is quick and easy to prepare. It is versatile, too, in that you can vary the vegetables according to what is the most affordable in the store. The strips of omelette help to make the soup a little more sustaining.

Serves 4

1 egg
15ml/1 tbsp groundnut (peanut) oil
900ml/1½ pints/3¾ cups vegetable stock
2 large carrots, finely diced
4 outer leaves from a Savoy cabbage, very finely shredded
30ml/2 tbsp soy sauce
2.5ml/½ tsp sugar
2.5ml/½ tsp ground black pepper
fresh coriander (cilantro) leaves, to garnish
prawn crackers, to serve

1 Beat the egg in a bowl. Heat the oil in a small frying pan until it is hot, but not smoking. Pour in the egg and swirl the pan so that it coats the base evenly.

2 Cook the omelette over medium heat until it has all set and the underside is golden.

3 Slide the omelette out of the pan and roll it up like a pancake. When cool enough to handle slice very finely to make thin noodle-like strips, and set aside for the garnish.

4 Put the stock into a large pan. Add the carrots and cabbage and bring to the boil. Reduce the heat and simmer gently for 5 minutes until the vegetables are just tender.

5 Add the soy sauce, sugar and pepper to the pan, stir, then pour the soup into warmed bowls.

6 Lay a few omelette strips on the surface of each soup bowl, and complete the garnish with the coriander leaves before serving. Serve with prawn crackers, if you wish, to complete the Asian influence of this soup.

hunky Tomato Energy 258kcal/1086kJ; Protein 7.6g; Carbohydrate 36.3g, of which sugars 18.3g; Fat 10.2g, of which saturates 1.7g; Cholesterol 0mg; Calcium 175mg; Fibre 6.9g; Sodium 72mg
arrot and Cabbage Energy 87kcal/360kJ; Protein 3.2g; Carbohydrate 9g, of which sugars 8.6g; Fat 4.4g, of which saturates 0.8g; Cholesterol 48mg; Calcium 58mg; Fibre 2.8g; Sodium 569mg

Cannellini Bean, Tomato and Parsley Soup

Healthy, hearty and deeply satisfying, this stunning soup is great on its own or especially delicious when served with bread and olives as a light supper.

Serves 4

275g/10oz/1½ cups dried cannellini beans, soaked overnight in cold water
1 large onion, thinly sliced
1 celery stick, sliced
2 or 3 carrots, sliced
400g/14oz can tomatoes
15ml/1 tbsp tomato purée (paste)
150ml/¼ pint/⅔cup olive oil
5ml/1 tsp dried oregano
30ml/2 tbsp finely chopped fresh flat leaf parsley
salt and ground black pepper, to taste

1 Drain the beans, rinse them under cold water and drain them again. Transfer them into a large pan, pour in enough water to cover the beans and bring to the boil over medium heat. Cook for about 3 minutes, then drain.

2 Return the beans to the pan, pour in fresh water to cover them by about 3cm/1¼in, then add the sliced onion, celery and carrots, and the tomatoes, and stir in.

3 Stir in the tomato purée, olive oil and oregano. Season with a little ground black pepper, but don't add salt at this stage, as it will toughen the skins of the beans.

4 Bring to the boil, lower the heat and cook the soup for about 1 hour, or until the beans are just soft and tender. Season with salt, you may find the soup needs more seasoning than usual because it is not made with stock. Stir in the parsley and serve.

Variation

If you do not want to soak dried cannelini beans, you can use ready-to-use canned ones instead. Omit step 1 as they don't need to be cooked for as long.

Tuscan Bean Soup

A classic Italian recipe, this bean soup is typical peasant food, simple but delicious. It is packed with flavour, healthy and – because of the beans – very sustaining. Cavolo nero is a very dark green cabbage with a nutty flavour that is available during the winter months. Don't, however, splash out on cavolo nero if it is expensive, or out of season, instead choose any leafy greens that are local and in season, such as Swiss chard, curly kale, spring greens or Savoy cabbage.

Serves 4

2 x 400g/14oz cans chopped tomatoes with herbs
250g/9oz cavolo nero leaves, or Savoy cabbage
400g/14oz can cannellini beans, drained and rinsed
60ml/4 tbsp extra virgin olive oil
salt and ground black pepper, to taste

1 Pour the tomatoes into a large pan and add a can of cold water. Season with salt and pepper to taste and bring to the boil, then reduce the heat to a simmer.

2 Roughly shred the cabbage leaves and add them to the pan. Partially cover the pan and simmer gently for about 15 minutes or until the cabbage is tender.

3 Add the cannellini beans to the pan and warm through over low heat for a few minutes.

4 Check and the seasoning, and add salt and pepper to taste if required, then ladle the soup into bowls, drizzle each one with a little olive oil and serve.

Cook's Tip

Extra virgin olive oil may seem an expensive storecupboard ingredient, but if you buy it in bulk and decant it yourself into bottles it is more cost effective. It is also worth using good quality olive oil in a recipe such as this, as the flavour of it is an important part of the soup.

Cannellini Bean Energy 490kcal/2,051kJ; Protein 17.9g; Carbohydrate 47.8g, of which sugars 11.3g; Fat 26.6g, of which saturates 4.1g; Cholesterol 0mg; Calcium 89mg; Fibre 8.4g; Sodium 45mg
Tuscan Bean Energy 227kcal/950kJ; Protein 8.2g; Carbohydrate 22.3g, of which sugars 10.4g; Fat 12.2g, of which saturates 1.9g; Cholesterol 0mg; Calcium 60mg; Fibre 7.9g; Sodium 443mg

3road Bean and Potato Soup

˜his elegant and economical oup tastes best if you use resh broad beans, when they re in season in the summer nonths, rather than dried ›nes. Fresh coriander adds a listinctive, fragrant note to he creamy mixture, while nanaging to not overpower he subtle and delicious taste ›f the beans.

ierves 4

'0ml/2 tbsp olive oil
2 onions, chopped
3 large floury potatoes, peeled and diced
450g/1lb fresh shelled broad (fava) beans
1 bunch fresh coriander (cilantro), roughly chopped
1.75 litres/3 pints/7½ cups vegetable stock
150ml/¼ pint/⅔ cup single (light) cream, plus a little extra, to garnish
salt and ground black pepper, to taste

Heat the oil in a large pan, add the onions and cook gently or 5 minutes until soft.

Add the potatoes, most of the beans (reserving a few for the arnish) and the stock to the pan, and bring the mixture to the oil. Simmer for 5 minutes, then add the coriander and simmer or a further 10 minutes.

Blend the soup in batches in a food processor or blender, nen return to the rinsed pan.

Stir the cream in to the soup, season with salt and pepper taste, and bring to a gentle simmer, but don't boil. Serve nmediately, garnished with coriander, the reserved beans and drizzle of cream.

Cook's Tip

When broad beans are out of season stock up on frozen beans as, like peas, they freeze well and retain almost all of their fresh-picked goodness and vitamins. If you keep a bag in the freezer this soup makes a great standby lunch.

Chickpea Soup

This nutritious soup is enjoyable at any time of year. Compared to other usually hearty soups based on beans, peas and lentils, this has a unique lightness in both flavour and texture. Serve as an appetizer, or with pitta bread and feta cheese.

Serves 4

150ml/¼ pint/⅔ cup olive oil, plus extra for drizzling and serving
1 large onion, chopped
350g/12oz/1¾ cups dried chickpeas, soaked in cold water overnight, or for at least 8 hours, then drained
15ml/1 tbsp plain (all-purpose) flour
juice of 1 lemon, or to taste
45ml/3 tbsp chopped fresh flat leaf parsley
salt and ground black pepper, to taste

1 Heat the olive oil in a heavy pan, add the onion and cook gently until it starts to colour.

2 Meanwhile, rinse the chickpeas and drain again. Add to the pan, coat in the oil, then pour in enough hot water to cover them by about 4cm/1½ in. Slowly bring to the boil.

3 Skim off and discard any white froth that rises to the surface. Lower the heat, and add some ground black pepper.

4 Cover the pan and cook for about 1–1¼ hours, or until the chickpeas are soft.

5 Combine the flour and lemon juice. When the chickpeas are soft, add this mixture to them. Mix, then add seasoning to taste. Cover and cook for 5–10 minutes more, stirring occasionally.

6 To thicken the soup, take out about two cupfuls of the chickpeas and process them in a food processor or blender, until the chickpeas are broken up, then stir into the soup.

7 Add the chopped parsley to the soup, then taste and add more lemon juice if bland. Serve in heated bowls with a drizzle of olive oil on top.

road Bean Energy 187kcal/784kJ; Protein 8.1g; Carbohydrate 19.2g, of which sugars 3.5g; Fat 9.2g, of which saturates 3.7g; Cholesterol 14mg; Calcium 89mg; Fibre 6.1g; Sodium 22mg
hickpea Energy 544kcal/2,274kJ; Protein 20.1g; Carbohydrate 51.6g, of which sugars 6.1g; Fat 30g, of which saturates 4g; Cholesterol 0mg; Calcium 184mg; Fibre 10.9g; Sodium 40mg

American Red Bean Soup

This soup is in Tex-Mex style, and it is served with a deliciously cooling avocado and lime salsa. If you relish the spicy heat of this soup, add a little more cayenne pepper for a truly fiery and filling experience.

Serves 6

30ml/2 tbsp olive oil
2 onions, chopped
2 garlic cloves, chopped
10ml/2 tsp ground cumin
1.5ml/¼ tsp cayenne pepper
15ml/1 tbsp paprika
15ml/1 tbsp tomato purée (paste)
2.5ml/½ tsp dried oregano
400g/14oz can chopped tomatoes
2 x 400g/14oz cans red kidney beans, drained and rinsed
salt and ground black pepper
Tabasco, to serve

For the guacamole salsa

2 avocados
1 small red onion, finely chopped
1 green chilli, seeded and finely chopped
15ml/1 tbsp chopped fresh coriander (cilantro)
juice of 1 lime

1 Heat the oil in a large pan and add the onions and garlic. Cook for about 4–5 minutes, until softened. Add the cumin, cayenne and paprika, and cook for 1 minute, stirring

2 Stir in the tomato purée and cook for a few seconds, then stir in the oregano. Add the chopped tomatoes, kidney beans and 900ml/1½ pints/3¾ cups water.

3 Bring the tomato and bean mixture to the boil. Reduce the heat and cover the pan, then simmer for 15–20 minutes. Cool the soup slightly, then purée it in a food processor or blender until smooth. Return to the rinsed-out pan and season to taste.

4 To make the guacamole salsa, halve, stone (pit) and peel the avocados, then dice them finely. Place in a small bowl and gently, but thoroughly, mix with the finely chopped red onion and chilli, and the coriander and lime juice.

5 Reheat the soup and ladle it into bowls. Spoon a little guacamole salsa into the middle of each and serve, offering Tabasco for those who want to spice up their soup.

Lentil and Bacon Soup

Ready-prepared, puréed versions of this winter warmer are sometimes so thick you could stand your spoon in them. This version isn't blended, and is delightful served with chunks of warm, crusty wholemeal bread. The addition of bacon and herbs helps to boost the otherwise mild flavour of this popular budget classic.

Serves 4

450g/1lb thick-sliced bacon, cubec
1 onion, roughly chopped
1 small turnip, roughly chopped
1 celery stick, chopped
1 potato, roughly chopped
1 carrot, sliced
75g/3oz/scant ½ cup lentils
1 bouquet garni
ground black pepper
fresh flat leaf parsley, to garnish

1 Heat a large pan and add the bacon. Cook for a few minutes, allowing the fat to run out.

2 Add the onion, turnip, celery, potato and carrot. Cook for about 4 minutes, stirring from time to time.

3 Add the lentils, bouquet garni, seasoning and pour in enough water to cover the ingredients. Bring to the boil, then reduce the heat and cover the pan. Simmer for 1 hour or until the lentils are tender.

4 Taste the soup and adjust the seasoning. Ladle into warmed bowls, garnish with the parsley and serve with crusty bread.

Variation

If you have a little more time to invest in cooking, and want to create a heartier, main-course dish, you can substitute the sliced bacon with a whole piece of bacon. Simmer the joint in enough water to cover, adding a sliced onion, carrot and bay leaf. The usual cooking time is 20 minutes per 450g/1lb, plus 20 minutes extra. Use the stock for the soup and cube some of the cooked bacon. Cook the vegetables in a little oil in step 2, then add the cooked meat before serving.

American Bean Energy 302kcal/1265kJ; Protein 11.7g; Carbohydrate 33.2g, of which sugars 11.8g; Fat 14.5g, of which saturates 2.8g; Cholesterol 0mg; Calcium 125mg; Fibre 11.8g; Sodium 537mg
Lentil and Bacon Energy 260kcal/1091kJ; Protein 14.8g; Carbohydrate 24.6g, of which sugars 3.9g; Fat 12.1g, of which saturates 3.8g; Cholesterol 29mg; Calcium 42mg; Fibre 3.2g; Sodium 370mg

›picy Red Lentil Soup with Onion and Parsley

‾his light lentil soup is subtly ›piced with cumin, fenugreek ›nd coriander. Served with a ›retty and flavoursome ›arnish of chopped red onion ›nd flat leaf parsley and a ›queeze of lemon juice, it ›akes a refreshing appetizer ›t any time of the year.

›erves 4–6

0–45ml/2–3 tbsp olive or sunflower oil
large onion, finely chopped
garlic cloves, finely chopped
fresh red chilli, seeded and finely chopped
5–10ml/1–2 tsp cumin seeds
5–10ml/1–2 tsp coriander seeds
1 carrot, finely chopped
scant 5ml/1 tsp ground fenugreek
5ml/1 tsp sugar
15ml/1 tbsp tomato purée (paste)
250g/9oz/generous 1 cup split red lentils
1.75 litres/3 pints/7½ cups chicken stock
salt and ground black pepper

To serve

1 small red onion, finely chopped
1 large bunch of fresh flat leaf parsley, finely chopped
4–6 lemon wedges

Heat the oil in a heavy pan and stir in the onion, garlic, chilli, ›umin and coriander seeds. When the onion begins to colour, ›ss in the carrot and cook for 2–3 minutes. Add the fenugreek, ›ugar and tomato purée and stir in the lentils.

Pour in the stock, stir well and bring to the boil. Lower the ›eat, partially cover the pan and simmer for 30–40 minutes, until ›e lentils have broken up.

If the soup is too thick, thin it down with a little water. Season ›ith salt and pepper to taste.

Serve the soup straight from the pan or, if you prefer a ›mooth texture, process it in a blender, then reheat if necessary.

Ladle the soup into bowls and sprinkle liberally with the ›hopped onion and parsley. Serve with a wedge of lemon to ›queeze over the soup.

Creamy Red Lentil Soup with Cumin

Lentil and grain soups, often containing chunks of meat or vegetables, are common fare throughout the Middle East, but every so often you come across a simple, puréed soup, flavoured with a single ingredient such as mint or cumin, which is not only pleasantly refreshing, but with such a minimum of ingredients is also incredibly economical to make.

Serves 4

225g/8oz/1 cup red lentils
30ml/2 tbsp olive oil
40g/1½oz butter
10ml/2 tsp cumin seeds
2 onions, chopped
1 litre/1¾ pints/4 cups chicken stock
5–10ml/1–2 tsp ground cumin
sea salt and ground black pepper
1 lemon, cut into wedges, to serve
60ml/4 tbsp strained yogurt, to serve (optional)

1 Rinse the lentils and leave to drain. Heat the oil and butter in a large, heavy pan and stir in the cumin seeds. Cook, stirring, until the seeds begin to emit a nutty aroma, making sure you don't burn them.

2 Add the chopped onions to the pan, and cook, stirring for 3–4 minutes. When they begin to turn golden brown add in the lentils and stir in to the onions.

3 Pour the stock into the pan and bring to the boil. Reduce the heat, cover the pan and simmer for about 30 minutes, topping up with water if necessary.

4 When the lentils are completely soft and beginning to break down, ladle the mixture into a food processor or blender and whizz to a smooth purée.

5 Return the soup to the rinsed-out pan and reheat. Season with salt and pepper if needed, and ladle into bowls. Dust with a little ground cumin and serve with lemon wedges to squeeze over. Add a spoonful of thick creamy yogurt to each bowl of soup, if you like.

›icy Red Lentil Energy 203kcal/856kJ; Protein 11.1g; Carbohydrate 31.8g, of which sugars 7.3g; Fat 4.4g, of which saturates 0.6g; Cholesterol 0mg; Calcium 45mg; Fibre 3.5g; Sodium 26mg
›reamy Red Lentil Energy 235kcal/991kJ; Protein 13g; Carbohydrate 28.4g, of which sugars 3.7g; Fat 8.9g, of which saturates 2.2g; Cholesterol 0mg; Calcium 66mg; Fibre 2.9g; Sodium 40mg

Green Lentil Soup

High in fibre and superbly cheap, green lentils make a particularly tasty and low-cost soup. If you prefer a smoother soup, blend it in a processor or blender instead of mashing in step 5.

Serves 4–6

225g/8oz/1 cup green lentils
75ml/5 tbsp olive oil
3 onions, finely chopped
2 garlic cloves, finely sliced
10ml/2 tsp cumin seeds, ground, or 5ml/1 tsp ground cumin
1.5ml/¼ tsp ground turmeric
600ml/1 pint/2½ cups vegetable stock
salt and ground black pepper
30ml/2 tbsp roughly chopped fresh coriander (cilantro), to garnish
warm crusty bread, to serve

1 Put the lentils in a pan and cover with cold water. Bring to the boil and boil rapidly for 10 minutes. Drain.

2 Heat 30ml/2 tbsp of the oil in a pan and fry two of the onions with the garlic, cumin and turmeric for approximately 3 minutes, or until golden brown, stirring.

3 Add the lentils, stock and 600ml/1 pint/2½ cups water. Bring to the boil, reduce the heat, cover and simmer gently for 30 minutes until the lentils are soft.

4 Heat the remaining oil and fry the third onion until golden brown, stirring frequently.

5 Use a potato masher to lightly mash the lentils and make the soup pulpy in texture. Reheat gently and season with salt and ground black pepper to taste.

6 Pour the soup into bowls. Stir the coriander into the fried onion and sprinkle over the soup. Serve with warm bread.

Cook's Tip
Unlike other dried beans and legumes, green lentils, like red, do not need to be soaked before cooking.

Brown Lentil Soup

Brown lentils do not need soaking, so they make an easy option for a quick meal based on storecupboard ingredients. The secret of a good brown lentil soup is to be generous with the olive oil, as the peppery taste complements the earthy flavour of the lentils. This soup can be served either as a substantial appetizer, or as a warming lunch dish when it is accompanied by plenty of freshly baked bread. If you prefer a soup with a smooth texture, simply blend it before serving.

Serves 8

275g/10oz/1¼ cups brown-green lentils, preferably the small variety
150ml/¼ pint/⅔ cup extra virgin olive oil
1 onion, thinly sliced
2 garlic cloves, sliced into thin matchsticks
1 carrot, sliced into rounds
400g/14oz can chopped tomatoes
15ml/1 tbsp tomato purée (paste)
2.5ml/½ tsp dried oregano
1 litre/1¾ pints/4 cups hot water
salt and ground black pepper, to taste
30ml/2 tbsp chopped fresh herbs, to garnish

1 Rinse the brown-green lentils thoroughly, drain them and put them in a large pan with cold water to cover.

2 Bring the water to the boil and boil for 3–4 minutes. Strain, discarding the liquid, and set the lentils aside.

3 Wipe the pan clean and add the olive oil. Place it over medium heat until hot and then add the thinly sliced onion and sauté until translucent.

4 Stir in the sliced garlic, then, as soon as it becomes aromatic, return the lentils to the pan. Add the carrot, tomatoes, tomato purée and oregano. Stir the hot water into the pan, and add black pepper to taste.

5 Bring the soup to the boil, then lower the heat, cover the pan and cook gently for 20–30 minutes, until the lentils feel soft but have not begun to disintegrate. Add salt, if required. Serve the soup garnished with the chopped herbs.

Green Lentil Energy 220kcal/921kJ; Protein 9.5g; Carbohydrate 25.1g, of which sugars 3.7g; Fat 9.8g, of which saturates 1.4g; Cholesterol 0mg; Calcium 32mg; Fibre 2.5g; Sodium 15mg
Brown Lentil Energy 462kcal/1,935kJ; Protein 18.4g; Carbohydrate 40g, of which sugars 6.6g; Fat 26.6g, of which saturates 3.7g; Cholesterol 0mg; Calcium 86mg; Fibre 8g; Sodium 64mg

moked Mackerel and Tomato Soup

his Thai-inspired soup uses
noked mackerel, a very
conomical and widely
vailable cured fish.

erves 4

)0g/7oz smoked mackerel fillets
tomatoes
litre/1¾ pints/4 cups vegetable stock
lemon grass stalk, finely chopped
:m/2in piece fresh galangal, finely diced
4 shallots, finely chopped
2 garlic cloves, finely chopped
2.5ml/½ tsp dried chilli flakes
15ml/1 tbsp Thai fish sauce
5ml/1 tsp light muscovado (brown) sugar
45ml/3 tbsp thick tamarind juice, made by mixing tamarind paste with warm water
small bunch of fresh chives or spring onions (scallions), to garnish, (optional)

Prepare the smoked mackerel fillets. Remove and discard the
in, if necessary, then chop the flesh into large pieces. Remove
ny stray bones with your fingers or a pair of tweezers.

Cut the tomatoes in half, squeeze out most of the seeds with
our fingers, then finely dice the flesh with a sharp knife. Set
side until required.

Pour the stock into a large pan and add the lemon grass,
alangal, shallots and garlic. Bring to the boil, reduce the heat
nd simmer for 15 minutes.

Add the fish, tomatoes, chilli flakes, fish sauce, muscovado
ugar and tamarind juice.

Simmer the soup for 4–5 minutes, then serve garnished with
nives or spring onions, with plain noodles for a substantial meal.

Variation
For a spicier soup, you could use smoked peppered mackerel fillets. They are available in many large supermarkets, and add a delicious peppery flavour.

Crab, Coconut, Chilli and Coriander Soup

You may be lucky to live on the coast and be able to find fresh crab quite easily, but although fresh crab meat has a better flavour, you can use canned crab meat in this sensational soup to keep the cost down. Palm oil is a favourite South American ingredient; use virgin olive oil if you can't obtain it.

Serves 4

30ml/2 tbsp olive oil
1 onion, finely chopped
1 celery stick, chopped
2 garlic cloves, crushed
1 fresh red chilli, seeded and chopped
1 large tomato, peeled and chopped
45ml/3 tbsp chopped fresh coriander (cilantro)
1 litre/1¾ pints/4 cups fresh crab or fish stock
500g/1¼lb crab meat
250ml/8fl oz/1 cup coconut milk
30ml/2 tbsp palm oil or olive oil
juice of 1 lime
salt, to taste
hot chilli oil and lime wedges, to serve

1 Heat the olive oil in a pan over medium heat. Stir in the chopped onion and celery, and sauté gently for 5 minutes, until the onion is soft and translucent.

2 Add the garlic and chilli, mix to combine the ingredients well, and cook for a further 2 minutes.

3 Add the tomato and half the coriander and increase the heat. Cook, stirring, for 3 minutes, then add the stock. Bring to the boil, then simmer for 5 minutes.

4 Stir the crab, coconut milk and palm oil or olive oil into the pan and simmer over a very low heat for a further 5 minutes. The consistency should be thick, but not stew-like, so add some water if needed.

5 Stir in the lime juice and remaining coriander, then season with salt to taste. Serve in warmed bowls with the chilli oil and lime wedges on the side.

noked Mackerel Energy 203kcal/845kJ; Protein 10.3g; Carbohydrate 5.3g, of which sugars 5g; Fat 15.8g, of which saturates 3.3g; Cholesterol 53mg; Calcium 21mg; Fibre 1.2g; Sodium 385mg
rab, Coconut, Chilli Energy 228kcal/951kJ; Protein 23.6g; Carbohydrate 5.4g, of which sugars 5g; Fat 12.6g, of which saturates 3.7g; Cholesterol 90mg; Calcium 199mg; Fibre 1.1g; Sodium 767mg

Pumpkin, Rice and Chicken Soup

This comforting soup is a complete meal in itself, served with warm, crusty bread for scooping up the delicious liquid. For an even more substantial budget meal, add a little more rice.

Serves 4

1 wedge of pumpkin, about 450g/1lb
15ml/1 tbsp sunflower oil or vegetable oil
25g/1oz/2 tbsp butter
6 green cardamom pods
2 leeks, chopped
750ml/1¼ pints/3 cups chicken stock
115g/4oz/generous ½ cup basmati rice, soaked
350ml/12fl oz/1½ cups milk
salt and ground black pepper
strips of pared orange rind, to garnish
granary or wholemeal (wholewheat) bread, to serve

1 Skin the pumpkin and remove all the seeds and pith, so that you have about 350g/12oz flesh. Cut the flesh into small cubes.

2 Heat the oil and butter in a pan and fry the cardamom pods for 2–3 minutes, until slightly swollen.

3 Add the leeks and pumpkin. Cook, stirring, for 3–4 minutes over medium heat, then lower the heat, cover and sweat for 5 minutes, until the pumpkin is soft.

4 Pour 600ml/1 pint/2½ cups of the stock into the pan. Bring to the boil, then lower the heat, cover and simmer gently for 10–15 minutes, until the pumpkin is soft.

5 Pour the remaining stock into a measuring jug and make up with water to 300ml/½ pint/1¼ cups. Drain the rice and put it into a pan. Pour in the stock, bring to the boil, then simmer for about 10 minutes until the rice is tender. Add seasoning to taste.

6 Remove the cardamom pods, then process the soup in a blender or food processor until smooth. Pour back into a clean pan and stir in the milk, chicken and rice (with any stock that has not been absorbed). Heat until simmering. Garnish with the orange rind and extra black pepper, and serve with bread.

Chicken, Egg and Lemon Soup

This simple soup is a classic recipe from Greece, and is a great example of how a few ingredients can make a marvellous dish if carefully chosen and cooked. It is essential to use a well-flavoured stock. Add as little or as much rice as you like. It is important not to overheat the soup when adding the eggs and lemon.

Serves 4

900ml/1½ pints/3¾ cups chicken stock, preferably home-made
50g/2oz/generous ⅓ cup long grain rice
3 egg yolks
30–60ml/2–4 tbsp lemon juice
30ml/2 tbsp finely chopped fresh flat leaf parsley
lemon slices and parsley sprigs, to garnish
salt and ground black pepper

1 Pour the chicken stock into a large pan, bring to simmering point, then add the drained rice.

2 Half cover the pan and cook for about 12 minutes until the rice is just tender. Season with salt and pepper to taste.

3 Whisk the egg yolks in a bowl, then add about 30ml/2 tbsp o the lemon juice, whisking constantly until the mixture becomes smooth and bubbly.

4 Add a ladleful of soup to the egg and lemon mixture, and whisk briskly again. This is an important part of the method; adding a ladle of warm soup means the egg mixture is less likel to coagulate when added to the pan.

5 Remove the pan from the heat and slowly add the egg mixture to the soup, whisking all the time. The soup will turn a pretty lemon colour and will thicken slightly.

6 Taste the soup and add more lemon juice and salt and peppe if necessary. Add the chopped parsley and stir in.

7 Serve the soup immediately, without reheating it, in four warmed bowls. Garnish each serving with a lemon slice and a sprig of flat leaf parsley.

Pumpkin Energy 315kcal/1320kJ; Protein 24.6g; Carbohydrate 29.9g, of which sugars 6.3g; Fat 10.8g, of which saturates 4.9g; Cholesterol 71mg; Calcium 140mg; Fibre 2.1g; Sodium 122mg
Chicken, Egg Energy 96kcal/404kJ; Protein 3.3g; Carbohydrate 10.9g, of which sugars 0.2g; Fat 4.7g, of which saturates 1.2g; Cholesterol 151mg; Calcium 39mg; Fibre 0.4g; Sodium 10mg

:hicken, Leek and Celery Soup

'his makes a substantial main ourse soup in winter. Serve vith fresh crusty bread for a 'rugal feast.

erves 4–6

.3kg/3lb chicken pieces
small head of celery, trimmed
onion, coarsely chopped
fresh bay leaf
a few fresh parsley stalks
a few fresh tarragon sprigs
3 large leeks
2 potatoes, cut into chunks
150ml/¼ pint/⅔ cup white wine
30–45ml/2–3 tbsp single (light) cream
90g/3½oz pancetta
olive oil, for frying
salt and ground black pepper

Place the chicken in a large pan or stockpot. Chop four or five ›f the outer sticks of the head of celery and add to the pan vith the onion and herbs. Just cover with water and bring to ne boil. Reduce the heat, cover the pan, and simmer for 1 hour.

: Remove the chicken from the pan using a slotted spoon and ut off and reserve the meat. Strain the stock through a sieve strainer), then return it to the cleaned pan and boil rapidly until : has reduced in volume to about 1.5 litres/2½ pints/6¼ cups.

Set aside about 150g/5oz of the leeks. Slice the remaining eeks and the remaining celery.

Heat a little olive oil in a large, heavy pan. Add the sliced leeks nd celery, cover and cook over low heat for about 10 minutes, r until the vegetables are softened but not browned.

Add the potatoes, wine and 1.2 litres/2 pints/5 cups of stock. ring to the boil, then reduce the heat, part-cover the pan and immer for 15–20 minutes, or until the potatoes are cooked.

Slice the reserved leeks, place in a frying pan with the ancetta and fry for 3–5 minutes until the pancetta is crispy.

Blend the soup with a blender or in a food processor, return ɔ the pan, stir in the cream and reheat the soup gently. Serve in varmed bowls, topped with the pancetta and leeks.

Moroccan Lamb Soup

A cheaper cut of lamb, such as scrag end, middle neck or knuckle, would be ideal for this substantial meat and vegetable soup, which is a meal in itself.

Serves 4

25g/1oz/2 tbsp butter
225g/8oz lamb, cut into 1cm/½in pieces
1 onion, chopped
450g/1lb tomatoes
60ml/4 tbsp chopped fresh coriander (cilantro)
30ml/2 tbsp chopped fresh parsley
2.5ml/½ tsp ground turmeric
2.5ml/½ tsp ground cinnamon
50g/2oz/¼ cup red lentils
75g/3oz/½ cup dried chickpeas, soaked overnight
600ml/1 pint/2½ cups cold water
4 baby onions or small shallots, peeled
25g/1oz/¼ cup soup noodles
salt and ground black pepper, to taste

For the garnish

chopped fresh coriander (cilantro)
lemon slices
ground cinnamon

1 Heat the butter in a large pan or flameproof casserole and fry the lamb and onion for 5 minutes, stirring frequently, until they are beginning to brown slightly.

2 Peel the tomatoes, if you wish, by plunging them into boiling water to loosen the skins. Wait for them to cool a little before peeling off the skins. Cut them into quarters and add to the lamb with the herbs and spices.

3 Place the lentils in a sieve (strainer) and rinse under cold running water, then drain the chickpeas. Add the lentils and chickpeas to the pan with the water. Season with salt and pepper to taste. Bring to the boil, cover and simmer gently for about 1½ hours.

4 Add the baby onions or small shallots to the pan and cook for a further 30 minutes. Add the noodles 5 minutes before the end of the cooking time.

5 Serve the soup when the noodles are tender, garnished with the coriander, lemon slices and cinnamon.

:hicken Energy 253kcal/1056kJ; Protein 16.5g; Carbohydrate 10.3g, of which sugars 2.4g; Fat 14.7g, of which saturates 3.4g; Cholesterol 48mg; Calcium 31mg; Fibre 2g; Sodium 231mg
loroccan Lamb Energy 303kcal/1271kJ; Protein 19.8g; Carbohydrate 27.6g, of which sugars 6.2g; Fat 13.2g, of which saturates 6.4g; Cholesterol 56mg; Calcium 78mg; Fibre 4.7g; Sodium 113mg

Beef and Barley Soup

This traditional Irish farmhouse soup makes a wonderfully restorative dish for little cost. The flavours will develop particularly well if the soup is made in advance and then reheated before serving.

Serves 6–8

450–675g/1–1½lb rib steak, or other stewing beef on the bone
2 large onions
50g/2oz/¼ cup pearl barley
50g/2oz/¼ cup green split peas
3 large carrots, chopped
2 white turnips, peeled and chopped into dice
3 celery stalks, chopped
1 large or 2 medium leeks, thinly sliced
salt and ground black pepper, to taste
chopped fresh parsley, to garnish

1 Bone the meat and put the bones and half an onion, roughly sliced, into a large pan. Cover with cold water, season and bring to the boil. Skim if necessary, then simmer until needed.

2 Meanwhile, trim any fat or gristle from the meat and cut into small pieces. Chop the remaining onions finely.

3 Drain the stock from the bones, make it up with water to 2 litres/3½ pints/8 cups, and return to the rinsed pan with the meat, onions, barley and split peas.

4 Season, bring to the boil, and skim if necessary. Reduce the heat, cover and simmer for about 30 minutes.

5 Add the rest of the vegetables and simmer for 1 hour, or until the meat is tender. Check the seasoning and adjust if necessary. Serve in large warmed bowls, generously sprinkled with parsley.

Cook's Tip

Pearl barley has had all the husk removed so that it not only adds bulk to soups, it also has a slightly thickening effect. If you want a more fibre-rich barley, used hulled (covered) barley, which only has the very outer husk removed.

Oxtail Soup

This hearty soup is an English classic, stemming from the days when it was natural to make use of every part of an animal. Long slow cooking produces a rich flavour and tender meat.

Serves 4–6

1 oxtail, cut into joints, about 1.3kg/3lb weight, trimmed
25g/1oz/2 tbsp butter
2 medium onions, chopped
2 medium carrots, chopped
2 celery sticks, sliced
1 bacon rasher (strip), chopped
2 litres/3½ pints/8 cups good beef stock
1 bouquet garni
2 bay leaves
30ml/2 tbsp flour
squeeze of fresh lemon juice
60ml/4 tbsp sherry or Madeira
salt and ground black pepper

1 Melt the butter in a large pan, and when foaming, add the oxtail a few pieces at a time and brown quickly on all sides. Lift the meat out on to a plate.

2 To the same pan, add the onions, carrots, celery and bacon. Cook over medium heat for 5–10 minutes, stirring occasionally, until the vegetables are softened and golden brown.

3 Return the oxtail to the pan and add the stock, bouquet garn bay leaves and seasoning. Bring just to the boil and skim off any foam. Cover and simmer gently for about 3 hours or until the meat is so tender that it is falling away from the bones. Strain the mixture, discarding the vegetables, bouquet garni and bay leaves, and leave to stand.

4 When the oxtail has cooled sufficiently to handle, pick all the meat off the bones and cut it into small pieces.

5 Skim off any fat on the surface of the stock, then transfer the stock into a large pan. Add the pieces of meat together with the flour mixed to a smooth paste with a little cold water.

6 Bring to the boil, stirring, until the soup thickens slightly. Season with salt, pepper and lemon juice to taste. Just before serving, stir in the sherry or Madeira.

Beef and Barley Energy 167kcal/705kJ; Protein 16g; Carbohydrate 21.4g, of which sugars 7.8g; Fat 2.6g, of which saturates 0.8g; Cholesterol 34mg; Calcium 54mg; Fibre 3.6g; Sodium 58mg
Oxtail Energy 459kcal/1914kJ; Protein 45.4g; Carbohydrate 6.5g, of which sugars 2.6g; Fat 26.8g, of which saturates 11.8g; Cholesterol 176mg; Calcium 36mg; Fibre 0.7g; Sodium 403mg

ᵓork and Rice Soup

ᴵ1ade with tender chunks of ork, this aromatic and ɹstaining rice soup from the hilippines is an ideal choice ɔr a special low-cost lunch r supper. It is a complete ɿeal in itself, but tastes articularly good served ʾith spring onions, garlic and aw chilli.

erves 4–6

5–30ml/1–2 tbsp palm oil or groundnut (peanut) oil
large onion, finely chopped
garlic cloves, finely chopped
5g/1oz fresh root ginger, finely chopped
350g/12oz pork rump or tenderloin, cut widthways into bitesize slices
5–6 black peppercorns
115g/4oz/1 cup plus 15ml/1 tbsp short grain rice
2 litres/3½ pints/8 cups pork or chicken stock
30ml/2 tbsp patis (fish sauce)
salt, to taste

To serve

2 garlic cloves, finely chopped
2 spring onions (scallions), white parts only, finely sliced
2–3 green or red chillies, seeded and quartered lengthways (optional)

Heat the oil in a wok or deep, heavy pan that has a lid. Stir in ɿe onion, garlic and ginger and fry until fragrant and beginning ɔ colour. Add the pork and fry, stirring frequently, for –6 minutes, until lightly browned. Stir in the peppercorns.

Meanwhile, put the rice in a sieve (strainer), rinse under cold ɹnning water until the water runs clear, then drain. Toss the rice ıto the pan, making sure that it is coated in the mixture.

Pour in the stock, add the patis and bring to the boil. Reduce ɿe heat and partially cover with a lid. Simmer for 40 minutes, :irring ocassionally to make sure that the rice doesn't stick to ɿe bottom of the pan. Season with salt to taste.

Just before serving, dry-fry the garlic in a small, heavy pan, ntil golden brown, then stir it into the soup.

Ladle the soup into warmed bowls and sprinkle spring onions ver the top. Serve the chillies separately, if you like.

Leek and Bacon Soup

This simple yet attractive soup makes good use of winter vegetables, combining them with tender chunks of flavoursome bacon to create a refreshing broth that makes an ideal light lunch.

Serves 6

1 unsmoked bacon joint, such as corner or collar, weighing about 1kg/2¼lb
500g/1¼lb/4½ cups leeks, washed and finely sliced
1 large carrot, peeled and finely chopped
1 large main-crop potato, peeled and sliced
15ml/1 tbsp fine or medium oatmeal
salt and ground black pepper
handful of fresh parsley, finely chopped, to garnish

1 Trim the bacon of any excess fat, put into a large pan and pour over enough cold water to cover it. Bring to the boil, then discard the water. Add 1.5 litres/2½ pints/6¼ cups cold water, bring to the boil, then cover and simmer gently for 30 minutes.

2 Meanwhile, thickly slice the white and pale green parts of the leeks, reserving the dark green leaves. Add to the pan together with the carrot, potato and oatmeal, then bring back to the boil. Cover and simmer gently for a further 30–40 minutes until the vegetables and bacon are tender.

3 Lift the bacon out of the pan and either slice it and serve separately or cut it into bitesize chunks and return it to the pan.

4 Taste and adjust the seasoning as required. Bring the soup just to the boil once more. Finely slice the reserved dark green part of the leeks, add to the soup and simmer gently for 5 minutes before serving, garnished with parsley.

Cook's Tip
For a quicker version, fry 4 finely chopped bacon rashers in butter. Omit step 1. Add the bacon to a pan with 1.5 litres/2½ pints ham stock and the vegetables. Continue as in the recipe.

ɔrk and Rice Energy 195kcal/813kJ; Protein 14.8g; Carbohydrate 19.9g, of which sugars 3.4g; Fat 6.2g, of which saturates 1.3g; Cholesterol 37mg; Calcium 24mg; Fibre 0.8g; Sodium 399mg
eek and Bacon Energy 273kcal/1135kJ; Protein 18.8g; Carbohydrate 10.9g, of which sugars 3.5g; Fat 17.3g, of which saturates 6.3g; Cholesterol 53mg; Calcium 33mg; Fibre 2.7g; Sodium 1550mg

Bacon and Chickpea Soup

This silky-smooth nutty soup is absolutely delicious and so easy to make. Served with a bowl of warm and spicy tortilla chips and dip, it makes an economical midweek supper dish and will be enjoyed by all the family.

Serves 6

400g/14oz/2 cups dried chickpeas, soaked overnight in cold water
115g/4oz/½cup butter
150g/5oz streaky (fatty) bacon, roughly chopped
2 onions, finely chopped
1 carrot, chopped
1 celery stick, chopped
15ml/1 tbsp chopped fresh rosemary
2 fresh bay leaves
2 garlic cloves, halved
salt and ground black pepper, to taste

For the tortilla chips
75g/3oz/6 tbsp butter
2.5ml/½ tsp sweet paprika
1.5ml/¼ tsp ground cumin
175g/6oz plain tortilla chips

1 Drain the chickpeas, put in a pan and cover with water. Bring to the boil and simmer for 20 minutes. Strain and set aside.

2 Melt the butter in a large pan and add the pancetta or bacon. Fry over medium heat until just beginning to turn golden. Add the chopped vegetables and cook for 5–10 minutes until soft.

3 Add the chickpeas to the pan with the rosemary, bay leaves, garlic cloves and enough water to cover completely. Bring to the boil, half cover with a lid, turn down the heat and simmer for 45–60 minutes, stirring occasionally. Leave to cool slightly.

4 Process the soup until smooth in a blender or food processor. Return to the rinsed-out pan, taste and season. Reheat gently.

5 To make the chips, preheat the oven to 180°C/350°F/Gas 4. Melt the butter with the paprika and cumin in a pan, then brush over the tortilla chips. Reserve any leftover butter. Spread the chips on a baking sheet and warm in the oven for 5 minutes. Ladle the soup into bowls, pour a little reserved butter over each and sprinkle with paprika. Serve with warm tortilla chips.

Mediterranean Sausage and Pesto Soup

This delicious soup makes a satisfying one-pot meal that brings the summery flavour of fresh basil to midwinter meals. The earthy red lentils enhance the flavour of the smoked sausage. It's a cheap and filling soup packed with plenty of slow-release carbs which help to keep you full for longer – thus reducing costs even further.

Serves 4

15ml/1 tbsp olive oil, plus extra for frying
1 red onion, chopped
450g/1lb good quality smoked pork sausages
225g/8oz/1 cup red lentils
400g/14oz can chopped tomatoes
1 litre/1¾ pints/4 cups water
fresh basil sprigs
salt and ground black pepper
60ml/4 tbsp pesto, to serve

1 Heat the olive oil in a large pan and cook the red onion until softened but not coloured. Coarsely chop all but one of the sausages and add them to the pan. Cook for 5 minutes, stirring, or until they are cooked.

2 Stir in the lentils, tomatoes and water, and bring to the boil. Reduce the heat, cover and simmer for about 20 minutes.

3 Cool the soup slightly before puréeing it in a blender. Return the soup to the rinsed pan.

4 Heat some oil in a frying pan and fry the basil leaves until crisp, remove from the pan and set aside.

5 Slice the remaining sausage into rounds, then fry in the same pan, turning the pieces often, for 10 minutes, until browned and crispy on both sides.

6 Gently reheat the soup, adding seasoning to taste, then ladle into four warmed soup bowls. Sprinkle with the sausage slices and crispy basil leaves, and swirl a little pesto through each portion. Serve with lots of warm crusty bread for an even more sustaining meal, if you wish.

Bacon and Chickpea Energy 996kcal/4154kJ; Protein 31.4g; Carbohydrate 80.1g, of which sugars 6.6g; Fat 63.3g, of which saturates 30.1g; Cholesterol 126mg; Calcium 252mg; Fibre 14.3g; Sodium 1186mg
Sausage and Pesto Energy 656kcal/2741kJ; Protein 30.9g; Carbohydrate 46.7g, of which sugars 8.2g; Fat 39.7g, of which saturates 13.1g; Cholesterol 75mg; Calcium 250mg; Fibre 4.8g; Sodium 1109mg

‹ale, Chorizo and Potato Soup

his hearty, warming soup as a lovely spicy kick to it, ʼhich comes from the noked paprika-enriched horizo sausage. The soup's avour becomes more otent if it is chilled vernight. When buying the horizo select the whole ausage rather than pre-acked sliced kind.

Serves 8

225g/8oz kale, stems removed
225g/8oz chorizo sausage
675g/1½lb red potatoes
1.75 litres/3 pints/7½ cups vegetable stock
pinch cayenne pepper (optional)
salt and ground black pepper, to taste
12 slices French baguette, lightly toasted

Place the kale in a food processor and process for a few econds to chop it finely.

Prick the chorizo sausages and place in a pan with enough ater to cover. Simmer for 15 minutes. Drain, and when cool nough to handle, cut into thin slices.

Cook the potatoes in a pan of boiling water for 15 minutes r until tender. Drain and place in a bowl, then mash, adding a tle of the cooking liquid to form a thick paste.

Bring the vegetable stock to the boil and add the kale. Add e chorizo and simmer for 5 minutes. Add the mashed potato adually, and simmer for 20 minutes.

Season the soup with black pepper and a little cayenne epper, if you wish to add a little extra heat.

Place the toasted baguette slices in each bowl, and pour over e soup. Serve, generously sprinkled with black pepper.

Variation
Any kind of dark green kale can be used, when it isn't in season use spring greens (collards) or Swiss chard instead.

Split Pea Soup

This recipe dates to Victorian England, when it was called London Particular; named after the thick winter fog, known as a 'pea-souper' because it had the beige colour and thick consistency of pea soup. The original version of this soup would probably have included cheap cuts such as pig's trotters and a marrow bone for really lip-smacking sticky richness. Dried split peas are very cheap, and sustaining, making this soup a real budget recipe.

Serves 4–6

350g/12oz/1½ cups dried split yellow or green peas
25g/1oz/2 tbsp butter
6 rashers (strips) rindless lean streaky (fatty) bacon, finely chopped
1 medium onion, finely chopped
1 medium carrot, thinly sliced
1 celery stick, thinly sliced
1.75 litres/3 pints/7½ cups ham or chicken stock
60ml/4 tbsp double (heavy) cream
salt and ground black pepper
croûtons and fried chopped bacon, to garnish

1 Put the split peas into a large bowl, cover well with boiling water and leave to stand for 5–10 minutes.

2 Meanwhile, melt the butter in a large pan. Add the bacon, onion, carrot and celery and cook over medium heat for about 10–15 minutes, stirring, until beginning to turn golden brown.

3 Drain the peas and add them to the pan. Stir in the stock. Bring to the boil, cover and simmer gently for about 1 hour or until the peas are very soft.

4 Process or blend until smooth and return the soup to the pan. Season to taste and stir in the cream. Heat until just bubbling and serve with croûtons and crispy bacon on top.

Cook's Tip
Soaking the split peas in boiling water reduces the cooking time, but you can just add them unsoaked at step 3 and increase the soup cooking time by 10–15 minutes.

ale and Potato Energy 290kcal/1228kJ; Protein 11.6g; Carbohydrate 49.3g, of which sugars 3.4g; Fat 6.5g, of which saturates 1.8g; Cholesterol 32mg; Calcium 120mg; Fibre 3.4g; Sodium 619mg
lit Pea Energy 378kcal/1584kJ; Protein 20.2g; Carbohydrate 34.9g, of which sugars 3.1g; Fat 18.5g, of which saturates 8.7g; Cholesterol 47mg; Calcium 45mg; Fibre 3.4g; Sodium 527mg

Chilled Vichyssoise

This classic, chilled summer soup is made from the simplest of ingredients and is very economical to make. Served garnished with fresh chives, it makes an elegant opening course to a special meal, or serve it as a light lunch with plenty of freshly baked bread.

Serves 6

50g/2oz/¼ cup unsalted (sweet) butter
450g/1lb leeks, white parts only, thinly sliced
3 large shallots, sliced
250g/9oz floury potatoes (such as King Edward or Idaho), peeled and cut into chunks
1 litre/1¾ pints/4 cups light chicken stock
300ml/½ pint/1¼ cups double (heavy) cream
iced water (optional)
a little lemon juice (optional)
salt and ground black pepper
chopped fresh chives, to garnish

1 Melt the butter in a large, heavy pan. Add the leeks and shallots and cook gently, covered, for 15–20 minutes, until soft.

2 Stir the potato chunks into the pan. Pour in the stock and stir to combine all the ingredients.

3 Bring to the boil, then reduce the heat and partly cover the pan. Simmer for 15 minutes, or until the potatoes are soft.

4 Process the soup in a blender or food processor. Strain into a bowl and add the cream. Adjust the seasoning, if necessary, and add water if too thick. Chill for at least 4 hours or until very cold.

5 Taste the soup for seasoning and add a squeeze of lemon juice, if required. Pour the soup into bowls and sprinkle with chopped chives. Serve immediately.

Variation
For a hot version, increase the quantity of potatoes to 450g/1lb. Halve the quantity of double (heavy) cream and reheat the soup, adding milk if it seems too thick, to serve.

Cucumber and Yogurt Soup

Cucumber and yogurt make a refreshing cold soup, perfect for a summer lunch on a hot day.

Serves 6

1 cucumber
4 garlic cloves
2.5ml/½ tsp salt
75g/3oz/¾ cup walnut pieces
40g/1½oz day-old bread, torn into pieces
30ml/2 tbsp sunflower oil
400ml/14fl oz/1⅔ cups natural (plain) yogurt
120ml/4fl oz/½ cup cold water
5–10ml/1–2 tsp lemon juice
25ml/1½ tbsp olive oil

For the garnish
40g/1½oz/scant ½ cup walnuts, coarsely chopped
sprigs of fresh dill

1 Cut the cucumber in half and peel one half of it. Dice the cucumber flesh and set aside.

2 Using a large mortar and pestle, crush the garlic and salt together until thoroughly combined, then add the walnut and bread pieces to the mortar.

3 When the mixture is smooth, slowly add the sunflower oil and mix until the ingredients are well combined.

4 Transfer the mixture to a large bowl and beat in the yogurt. Fold in the diced cucumber, then add the cold water and lemon juice to taste.

5 Pour the soup into chilled soup bowls. Garnish with the chopped walnuts and drizzle with the olive oil. Finally, arrange the sprigs of dill on top and serve immediately.

Variations
• *If you prefer your soup smooth, purée it in a food processor or blender before serving.*
• *For a creamier version, you could subsitute Greek (US strained plain) yogurt for the natural (plain) yogurt.*

Chilled Vichyssoise Energy 547kcal/2260kJ; Protein 4.6g; Carbohydrate 17.7g, of which sugars 6.8g; Fat 51.4g, of which saturates 31.7g; Cholesterol 129mg; Calcium 79mg; Fibre 3.6g; Sodium 103mg
Cucumber and Yogurt Energy 77kcal/322kJ; Protein 6.9g; Carbohydrate 10.3g, of which sugars 10.1g; Fat 1.3g, of which saturates 0.6g; Cholesterol 2mg; Calcium 255mg; Fibre 0.3g; Sodium 106mg

old Beetroot Soup

l year around, soup is at
e heart of every Russian
eal. In the summer the
ups are often served
illed, as in this budget
cipe, to be enjoyed in the
mmer heat.

rves 4

0g/1¾lb small raw beetroot (beets)
litres/2 pints/5 cups water
medium potatoes
3 eggs
2–3 cucumbers, total weight 300g/11oz
1 bunch spring onions (scallions)
15ml/1 tbsp mustard
60ml/4 tbsp smetana or crème fraîche
15–30ml/1–2 tbsp fresh lemon juice
5–15ml/2–3 tsp sugar
salt
60–75ml/4–5 tbsp finely chopped fresh dill, to garnish

Put the beetroot in a pan, add the water and 5ml/1 tsp salt d bring to the boil. Boil for about 50 minutes, until soft. Leave cool in the stock.

Put the potatoes in a pan of salted water. Bring to the boil d cook for 20 minutes, until soft. Drain.

Put the eggs in a pan, cover with cold water and bring to the il. Reduce the heat, and simmer for 10 minutes. Drain and put der cold running water. Remove the shells and chop the eggs.

When the beetroots are cold, pour the beetroot stock into a g (pitcher) or bowl and put in the refrigerator. Remove the n from the beetroots, and coarsely grate or cut into thin ips. Dice the cold potatoes. Cut the cucumbers into strips d finely chop the spring onions.

Put the beetroot in a tureen or serving bowl. Mix in the tatoes, cucumbers, eggs, spring onions and the mustard.

To serve, pour the beetroot stock over the beetroots in the rving bowl, add the smetana or crème fraîche and mix gently gether. Season with the lemon juice, sugar and salt to taste. rinkle the chopped dill on top to garnish.

Chilled Gazpacho

This Mediterranean soup is deeply rooted in the region of Andalusia, southern Spain, but is eaten throughout the country. The soothing blend of tomatoes, sweet peppers and garlic is sharpened with sherry vinegar, and enriched with olive oil. Serving it with saucerfuls of garnishes makes it into a light meal rather than an appetizer, and it is perfect for a summer lunch.

Serves 4

1.3–1.6kg/3–3½lb ripe tomatoes
1 green (bell) pepper, seeded and roughly chopped
2 garlic cloves, finely chopped
2 slices day-old bread, crusts removed
60ml/4 tbsp extra virgin olive oil
60ml/4 tbsp sherry vinegar
150ml/¼ pint/⅔ cup tomato juice
300ml/½ pint/1¼ cups iced water
salt and ground black pepper
ice cubes, to serve (optional)

For the garnishes
30ml/2 tbsp olive oil
2–3 slices day-old bread, diced
1 small cucumber, peeled and finely diced
1 small onion, finely chopped
1 red (bell) and 1 green (bell) pepper, seeded and finely diced
2 hard-boiled eggs, chopped

1 Skin the tomatoes, then quarter them and remove the cores and seeds, saving the juices. Put the pepper in a food processor or blender and process for a few seconds. Add the tomatoes, reserved juices, garlic, bread, oil and vinegar and process. Add the tomato juice and blend to combine.

2 Season the soup, then pour into a large bowl, cover with clear film (plastic wrap) and chill for at least 12 hours.

3 Prepare the garnishes. Heat the olive oil in a frying pan and fry the bread cubes for 4–5 minutes until golden brown and crisp. Drain well on kitchen paper, then arrange in a small dish. Place each of the remaining garnishes in separate small dishes.

4 Just before serving, dilute the soup with the ice-cold water. The consistency should be thick but not too stodgy. If you like, stir a few ice cubes into the soup, then spoon into bowls and serve with the garnishes.

ld Beetroot Energy 215kcal/908kJ; Protein 11.8g; Carbohydrate 28.9g, of which sugars 19.9g; Fat 6.8g, of which saturates 2.3g; Cholesterol 147mg; Calcium 122mg; Fibre 6.3g; Sodium 311mg
illed Gazpacho Energy 356kcal/1494kJ; Protein 7.6g; Carbohydrate 41.9g, of which sugars 21.5g; Fat 18.8g, of which saturates 2.9g; Cholesterol 0mg; Calcium 90mg; Fibre 6.7g; Sodium 346mg

Salmon Mousse

This deliciously creamy mousse makes a little salmon go a long way. It is equally good made with sea trout.

Serves 6

250g/9oz salmon fillet
120ml/4fl oz/½ cup fish stock
2 sheets leaf gelatine, or 15ml/1 tbsp powdered gelatine
juice of ½ lemon
30ml/2 tbsp dry sherry or dry vermouth
30ml/2 tbsp freshly grated grano padano cheese
300ml/½ pint/1¼ cups whipping cream
2 egg whites
sunflower oil, for greasing
salt and ground white pepper

For the garnish

5cm/2in piece cucumber, with peel left on, cut into thin slices and then halved
fresh dill or chervil

1 Put the salmon in a shallow pan. Pour in the fish stock and heat to simmering point. Poach the fish for about 3–4 minutes, until it is lightly cooked.

2 Strain the stock into a jug (pitcher) and leave the fish to cool. Add the gelatine to the hot stock and stir until it has dissolved. Set the stock aside until required.

3 Remove the skin from the fish and flake the flesh. Pour the stock into a food processor or blender. Process briefly, then add the salmon, lemon juice, sherry or vermouth and grano padano, and process until smooth. Scrape into a bowl and leave to cool.

4 Lightly whip the cream, then fold it into the salmon mixture. Season, then cover with clear film (plastic wrap) and chill until just beginning to set; with the consistency of mayonnaise.

5 In a grease-free bowl, beat the egg whites with a pinch of salt until they form soft peaks. Using a metal spoon, stir one-third into the mixture to slacken it, then fold in the rest.

6 Grease six ramekins, divide the mousse among them and level the surface. Chill for 2–3 hours, until set. Arrange slices of cucumber and a little chopped dill or chervil on each and serve.

Smoked Salmon Roulade

Make the most of a small amount of smoked salmon by using it to flavour the filling for this delicately flavoured roulade. Salmon trimmings are more economical than premium sliced. The roulade makes a luxurious appetizer for a supper party, or nibbles with apperitifs.

Serves 6–8

25g/1oz/2 tbsp butter
25g/1oz/¼ cup plain (all-purpose) flour
175ml/6fl oz/¾ cup milk, warmed
3 large eggs, separated
50g/2oz/⅔ cup freshly grated grano padano cheese
30ml/2 tbsp chopped fresh flat leaf parsley
60ml/4 tbsp chopped fresh basil or dill
115g/4oz smoked salmon trimmings, chopped
150ml/¼ pint/⅔ cup full fat crème fraîche or sour cream
salt and ground black pepper, to taste

1 Melt the butter in a heavy pan, stir in the flour and cook over low heat to a thick paste. Gradually add the milk, whisking constantly until it boils, then cook for 1–2 minutes more. Stir in the egg yolks, two-thirds of the grano padano cheese, the chopped parsley and half the dill. Add salt and ground black pepper to taste.

2 Prepare a 33 x 28cm/13 x 11in Swiss roll tin (jelly roll pan) and preheat the oven to 180°C/350°F/Gas 4. Whisk the egg whites and fold into the yolk mixture, then pour into the tin and bake for 12–15 minutes.

3 Cover with baking parchment and set aside for 10–15 minutes then tip out on to another sheet of parchment, sprinkled with little grano padano. Leave to cool.

4 Mix the smoked salmon with the crème fraîche or sour cream and remaining chopped dill. Season to taste.

5 Peel off the lining paper from the roulade, spread the filling evenly over the surface and roll up, then leave to firm up in a cold place. Sprinkle with the remaining cheese and serve.

Salmon Mousse Energy 285kcal/1183kJ; Protein 12.6g; Carbohydrate 5.8g, of which sugars 3.2g; Fat 22.7g, of which saturates 8.7g; Cholesterol 57mg; Calcium 73mg; Fibre 0.2g; Sodium 103mg
Salmon Roulade Energy 196kcal/814kJ; Protein 10.4g; Carbohydrate 4.1g, of which sugars 1.6g; Fat 15.5g, of which saturates 9g; Cholesterol 119mg; Calcium 144mg; Fibre 0.4g; Sodium 402mg

·gg and Salmon Puff Parcels

hese elegant parcels hide a
ıouthwatering mixture of
ıvours, and make a delicious
ɔpetizer or lunch dish.
ɜrve with curry-flavoured
ıayonnaise or hollandaise
ıuce and a green salad.

ɜrves 6
50g/12oz tail pieces of salmon
5g/3oz/scant ½ cup long grain rice, cooked according to pack instructions, and cooled
juice of ½ lemon
15ml/1 tbsp chopped fresh dill
15ml/1 tbsp chopped fresh flat leaf parsley
10ml/2 tsp mild curry powder
6 small (US medium) eggs, soft-boiled and cooled
425g/15oz flaky or puff pastry, thawed if frozen
1 egg, beaten
salt and ground black pepper, to taste

Preheat the oven to 220°C/425°F/Gas 7. Place the salmon tail eces in a large pan and cover with water. Gently heat until most at a simmer and cook the fish pieces for 8–10 minutes ntil they flake easily.

Lift the salmon out of the pan and remove the bones and ɪin. Flake the fish into the cooled rice, add the lemon juice, ɜrbs, curry powder and seasoning, and mix well. Shell the eggs.

Roll out the pastry and cut into six 15cm/6in squares. Brush ıe edges with the beaten egg. Place a spoonful of the rice ıixture in the middle of each square, push an egg into the ɜntre and top with a little more of the rice mixture.

Pull over the pastry corners to the middle to form a neat, ıuare parcel, pressing the joins together with your fingers to seal.

Brush the parcels with more beaten egg, place on a baking ıeet and bake for 20 minutes, then reduce the oven ımperature to 190°C/375°F/Gas 5.

Cook the parcels for 10 minutes more, until golden and ɪisp. Let the parcels cool slightly before serving, or serve cold ı part of a picnic feast.

Crispy Whitebait

Whitebait are the small fry of herring and sprats, and are especially delicious when fried and eaten whole. Here, they are served with an intensely flavoured tomato, salsa and wedges of zesty lemon to squeeze over the hot, crispy fish.

Serves 4
225g/8oz whitebait, thawed if frozen
30ml/2 tbsp seasoned plain (all-purpose) flour

For the salsa
1 shallot, finely chopped
2 garlic cloves, finely chopped
4 ripe tomatoes, chopped
1 small red chilli, seeded and finely chopped
90ml/6 tbsp olive oil
60ml/4 tbsp sweet sherry
30–45ml/2–3 tbsp chopped mixed fresh herbs, such as parsley or basil
25g/1oz/½ cup stale white breadcrumbs
60ml/4 tbsp sunflower oil
salt and ground black pepper

1 Preheat the oven to 150°C/300°F/Gas 2. Wash the fresh or thawed whitebait thoroughly, drain well and dry on kitchen paper, then dust in the seasoned flour.

2 To make the salsa, place the chopped shallot, garlic, tomatoes, chilli and 30ml/2 tbsp olive oil in a pan. Cover with a lid and cook gently for about 10 minutes.

3 Pour the sherry into the pan and season with salt and pepper to taste. Stir in the herbs and breadcrumbs, then cover and keep the salsa hot until the whitebait are ready.

4 Heat the remaining oil in a heavy frying pan and cook the fish in batches until crisp and golden. Drain the fish on kitchen paper and keep warm until all batches are cooked. Serve the whitebait with salsa and bread.

Cook's Tip
Frozen whitebait are good value for money if you are unable to buy fresh ones from your supermarket or local fishmonger.

ıff Parcels Energy 494kcal/2063kJ; Protein 23.4g; Carbohydrate 36.9g, of which sugars 1.1g; Fat 29.7g, of which saturates 2.7g; Cholesterol 219mg; Calcium 112mg; Fibre 0.8g; Sodium 326mg
ʳispy Whitebait Energy 722kcal/2989kJ; Protein 26.8g; Carbohydrate 7.3g, of which sugars 0.2g; Fat 65.3g, of which saturates 0g; Cholesterol 0mg; Calcium 1183mg; Fibre 0.3g; Sodium 316mg.

Crispy Salt and Pepper Squid

Squid are very economical, and these delicious crunchy morsels look stunning skewered on small or large wooden sticks. The crisp, golden coating contrasts with the succulent squid inside.

Serves 4

750g/1lb 10oz fresh or frozen squid, cleaned (see Cook's Tip) and thawed, if frozen
juice of 4–5 lemons
15ml/1 tbsp ground black pepper
15ml/1 tbsp salt
10ml/2 tsp caster (superfine) sugar
115g/4oz/1 cup cornflour (cornstarch)
3 egg whites, lightly beaten
skewers, to serve
sunflower oil, for frying
sweet-and-sour or chilli sauce, for dipping

1 Cut the squid into large bitesize pieces and score a diamond pattern on each piece. Trim the tentacles.

2 Place in a large mixing bowl and pour over the lemon juice. Cover and marinate for 10–15 minutes. Drain well and pat dry.

3 In a separate bowl mix together the pepper, salt, sugar and cornflour. Dip the squid pieces in the egg white and then toss lightly in the seasoned flour, shaking off any excess.

4 Fill a wok or large, heavy pan one-third full of sunflower oil and heat to 180°C/350°F. (A cube of bread, dropped into the oil, should brown in 15 seconds.)

5 Working in batches, deep-fry the squid for 1 minute, until crispy. Drain on kitchen paper and serve threaded on to skewers with sweet-and-sour or chilli sauce.

Cook's Tip
To clean the squid, pull the head and tentacles, intestines and quill away from the body. Discard the head and innards. Gripping firmly with your fingers, pull off the purplish membrane, then slit the body open and wash under cold water.

Crab Cakes

Canned crab meat is a good tasty alternative to fresh, and is often a more economical option. These mini fish cakes are popular with adults and children alike but are definitely one for younger members of the family who like flavourful fish cakes. They may even help you make some fish-shaped cakes.

Serves 4

450g/1lb canned crab meat
30ml/2 tbsp mayonnaise
2.5–5ml/½–1 tsp mustard powd
1 egg, lightly beaten
Tabasco sauce
45ml/3 tbsp chopped fresh pars
4 spring onions (scallions), finely chopped (optional)
50–75g/2–3oz/½–¾ cup dried breadcrumbs
chopped spring onions (scallions), to garnish
sunflower oil, for frying
salt, ground black pepper and cayenne pepper
red onion marmalade, to serve

1 Put the crab meat in a large bowl and stir in the mayonnaise with the mustard and egg. Season to taste with a dash of Tabasco, more if you want your crab cakes to be spicy, and salt pepper and cayenne.

2 Stir in the chopped parsley, spring onions, if using, and 50g/2oz/½ cup of the breadcrumbs. The mixture should be jus firm enough to hold together; you may need to add some mo breadcrumbs.

3 Divide the mixture into eight portions, roll each into a ball and flatten slightly to make a thick flat disc. Spread out the cra cakes on a platter and place them in the refrigerator for about 30 minutes before frying.

4 Pour the oil into a heavy pan to a depth of about 5mm/¼in. When the oil is hot, cook the crab cakes, in two batches, until golden brown on both sides.

5 As the crab cakes are cooked, remove from the pan, drain o kitchen paper and keep warm. Serve with a spring onion garni and red onion marmalade.

Crispy Squid Energy 346kcal/1462kJ; Protein 31.2g; Carbohydrate 31.3g, of which sugars 2.6g; Fat 11.6g, of which saturates 1.8g; Cholesterol 422mg; Calcium 32mg; Fibre 0g; Sodium 1741mg
Crab Cakes Energy 285kcal/1187kJ; Protein 23.9g; Carbohydrate 10.3g, of which sugars 0.9g; Fat 16.7g, of which saturates 2.4g; Cholesterol 134mg; Calcium 178mg; Fibre 0.8g; Sodium 768mg

ocaccia with Sardines

resh sardines not only have lovely flavour and texture, ut are also cheap to buy so ake an economical yet tterly delicious lunch in ext to no time. Use plump, pe vine cherry or plum omatoes when they are in eason for a fuller flavour, or ou can use well-drained canned tomatoes during the winter months.

Serves 4

20 cherry tomatoes
45ml/3 tbsp olive oil
12 fresh sardine fillets
1 focaccia loaf, one-day old if possible
salt and ground black pepper

Preheat the oven to 190°C/375°F/Gas 5. Put the cherry omatoes in a small roasting pan and drizzle 30ml/2 tbsp of ne olive oil over the top.

Season the tomatoes with salt and pepper and roast for bout 10–15 minutes, shaking the pan gently once or twice uring cooking so that the tomatoes cook evenly on all sides. Vhen they are tender and slightly charred, remove from the ven and set aside.

While the tomatoes are cooking, preheat the grill (broiler) to gh. Brush the sardine fillets with the remaining oil and lay them n a baking sheet. Grill (broil) for 4–5 minutes on each side, ntil cooked through.

Split the focaccia in half horizontally and cut each piece in half give four equal pieces. Toast the cut side under the grill.

Top the toasts with the sardines and tomatoes and an extra izzle of oil. Season with black pepper and serve.

Variation

If you have some left-over boiled potatoes in the refrigerator, slice them and fry them in oil, then pile the sardines and tomatoes on top.

Barbecued Sardines

Sardines are ideal for the barbecue but they are equally delicious cooked under a grill. The marinade starts the cooking process as well as helping to keep the fish succulent.

Serves 6

6 whole sardines, gutted
1 orange, sliced
a small bunch of fresh flat leaf parsley, chopped
60ml/4 tbsp extra virgin olive oil
salt and ground black pepper

1 Arrange the sardines and orange slices in a single layer in a dish. Sprinkle over the chopped parsley, salt and pepper, and drizzle the oil over. Cover and chill for 2 hours.

2 Prepare the barbecue or preheat the grill (broiler) to high. Place the sardines and orange slices on to a grill rack.

3 Cook on the barbecue or under the hot grill for 4–5 minutes on each side, until the fish are cooked. Serve immediately.

Chicken Liver Pâté

This pâté really could not be simpler to make, and tastes so much better than anything you can buy ready-made. Serve with lightly toasted bread, or baguette for an elegant appetizer.

Serves 4

350g/12oz chicken livers, trimmed and roughly chopped
50g/2oz/¼ cup butter
30ml/2 tbsp brandy
30ml/2 tbsp double (heavy) cream
salt and ground black pepper

1 Fry the chopped chicken livers in the butter for 3–4 minutes, or until they are browned and cooked through. Add the brandy and allow it to bubble for a few minutes. Transfer into a food processor with the cream and some salt and pepper to taste.

2 Process the mixture until smooth and spoon into ramekin dishes. Level the surface and chill overnight to set. Serve the pâté garnished with sprigs of parsley and some toast.

ocaccia with Sardines Energy 301kcal/1262kJ; Protein 15.8g; Carbohydrate 27.6g, of which sugars 3.1g; Fat 15g, of which saturates 2.9g; Cholesterol 0mg; Calcium 106mg; Fibre 1.7g; Sodium 334mg
arbecued Sardines Energy 156kcal/649kJ; Protein 13.1g; Carbohydrate 1.7g, of which sugars 1.7g; Fat 10.8g, of which saturates 2.3g; Cholesterol 0mg; Calcium 73mg; Fibre 0.3g; Sodium 72mg
hicken Liver Pâté Energy 227kcal/942kJ; Protein 15.7g; Carbohydrate 0.2g, of which sugars 0.2g; Fat 16.3g, of which saturates 9.6g; Cholesterol 369mg; Calcium 13mg; Fibre 0g; Sodium 144mg

Creamy Chicken Livers

Cheap, versatile, nutritious and packed with flavour, chicken livers are a much under-rated ingredient and a good choice for budget dining. Here, they are combined with onion, garlic, sherry and cream and served with lightly toasted sliced baguette to make a quick-and-easy appetizer, light lunch or snack. You could also serve this dish with polenta for a delicious and low-cost main meal.

Serves 4

225g/8oz chicken livers, washed and trimmed
15ml/1 tbsp olive oil
1 small onion, finely chopped
2 small garlic cloves, finely chopped
5ml/1 tsp fresh thyme leaves, chopped
30ml/2 tbsp sweet oloroso sherry
30ml/2 tbsp crème fraîche or double (heavy) cream
2.5ml/½ tsp paprika
salt and ground black pepper
fresh thyme, to garnish
1 baguette, sliced into 12, to serve

1 Using a sharp knife, carefully remove any green spots and sinews from the chicken livers.

2 Heat the oil in a frying pan, then add the onion, garlic, chicken livers and thyme leaves and fry for 3 minutes.

3 Stir the sherry into the pan, then add the cream and cook briefly to warm through.

4 Preheat the grill (broiler) and lightly toast the slices of baguette on both sides.

5 Season the liver mixture to taste with salt and pepper and add paprika. Garnish with fresh thyme and serve immediately with the toasted baguette slices.

Cook's Tip

Chicken livers go off quickly, so buying frozen is a good idea, and is even more economical. If you are using frozen for this recipe, make sure they are thoroughly defrosted before cooking.

Chargrilled Spicy Chicken Wings

Chicken wings, thighs and drumsticks have a very good flavour and are often excellent value for money. Here, the wings are marinated in a spicy paste and then grilled over charcoal or fried. They can be served on their own with a few sprigs of coriander as an appetizer at a barbecue, or include them as part of a selection of dishes at a buffet or informal lunch.

Serves 4

12 chicken wings
salt and ground black pepper
fresh coriander (cilantro) leaves, roughly chopped, and 2–3 green chillies, seeded and quartered lengthways, to garnish

For the spice paste

4 shallots, chopped
4 garlic cloves, chopped
25g/1oz fresh root ginger, chopped
8 fresh red chillies, seeded and chopped
1 lemon grass stalk, trimmed and chopped
30ml/2 tbsp sesame or groundnut (peanut) oil
15ml/1 tbsp tomato purée (paste)
10ml/2 tsp sugar
juice of 2 limes

1 First make the spice paste. Using a mortar and pestle, grind the shallots, garlic, ginger, chillies and lemon grass to a paste. You can also use a small food processor.

2 Bind the spices mixture with enough oil to make a loose paste, then stir in the tomato purée, sugar and lime juice. Season with salt and pepper.

3 Rub the spice paste into the chicken wings, cover and leave to marinate in the refrigerator for at least 2 hours.

4 Prepare and light the barbecue or preheat a grill (broiler). Lift the wings out of the marinade and place them on the rack.

5 Cook the wings on the barbecue or grill for about 5 minutes each side until cooked through and with the skins slightly charred in places. Brush the wings with the marinade occasionally while they are cooking. Serve immediately, garnished with the fresh coriander and green chillies.

Chicken Livers Energy 436kcal/1846kJ; Protein 21.1g; Carbohydrate 69.2g, of which sugars 4.9g; Fat 9.4g, of which saturates 3.2g; Cholesterol 222mg; Calcium 158mg; Fibre 3.1g; Sodium 785mg
Chargrilled Wings Energy 350kcal/1455kJ; Protein 30.7g; Carbohydrate 2.6g, of which sugars 2.6g; Fat 24.1g, of which saturates 5.9g; Cholesterol 134mg; Calcium 11mg; Fibre 0.1g; Sodium 99mg

entil and Meat Patties

)therwise known as shami ebabs, these lentil and lamb atties are from Malaysia. hey make a delicious ppetizer served with a iqant sambal or some emon wedges, or they can e eaten as a snack between hunks of bread with tomato etchup, like a burger.

erves 4

0ml/2 tbsp vegetable oil
onions, finely chopped
garlic cloves, finely chopped
green chilli, seeded and chopped
25g/1oz fresh root ginger, finely chopped
150g/5oz/generous ½ cup red, brown, or green lentils, cooked
250g/9oz lean minced (ground) lamb
10ml/2 tsp Indian curry powder
5ml/1 tsp turmeric powder
4 eggs
vegetable oil, for frying
salt and ground black pepper
fresh coriander (cilantro) leaves, roughly chopped, to garnish (optional)
1 lemon, quartered, to serve

Heat the oil in a heavy pan and stir in the onions, garlic, chilli nd ginger. Fry until they begin to colour, then add the cooked ntils and minced lamb.

. Cook for a few minutes, then add the curry powder and ırmeric. Season and cook over high heat until the moisture has vaporated. Remove from the heat and leave until the mixture cool enough to handle. Beat one of the eggs in a bowl and nix it into the meat.

Using damp hands, take small portions of the mixture and roll nem into balls about the size of a plum or apricot. Press each all in the palm of your hand to form thick, flat patties.

Beat the remaining eggs in a bowl. Heat enough oil in a heavy an for shallow frying. Dip each patty in the egg and place them l into the oil.

Fry the patties for about 3–4 minutes each side, until golden. Garnish with the fresh coriander and serve with lemon wedges ɔ squeeze over.

Flatbreads with Spicy Lamb

These tasty Middle Eastern flatbreads are delicious and good value for money.

Serves 2–4

5ml/1 tsp active dried yeast
17.5ml/3½ tsp sugar
350g/12oz/3 cups strong white bread flour
150ml/¼ pint/⅔ cup warm water
15ml/1 tbsp olive oil
15ml/1 tbsp butter
1 onion, finely chopped
2 garlic cloves, chopped
225g/8oz/1 cup finely minced (ground) lean lamb
30ml/2 tbsp tomato purée (paste)
1 fresh red chilli, finely chopped
5ml/1 tsp dried mint
5–10ml/1–2 tsp sumac or paprika
1 bunch of fresh flat leaf parsley, roughly chopped
1 lemon, halved
salt and ground black pepper

1 Make the dough. Put the yeast and 2.5ml/½ tsp sugar into a bowl with half the water. Set aside for about 15 minutes until frothy. Sift the flour and 2.5ml/½ tsp salt into a large bowl, make a well in the middle and add the creamed yeast and the rest of the water. Using your hand, draw in the flour and work the mixture to a dough, adding more water if necessary.

2 Turn the dough on to a lightly floured surface and knead until it is smooth and elastic. Place in a lightly oiled bowl, cover with a damp dish towel and leave in a warm place for about 1 hour or until the dough has doubled in size.

3 Heat the oil and butter in a heavy pan and gently fry the onion and garlic until soft. Transfer to a bowl, with the lamb, tomato purée, remaining sugar, chilli and mint. Season, and mix and knead with your hands. Cover with clear film (plastic wrap). Place two baking sheets in the oven. Preheat the oven to 220°C/425°F/Gas 7.

4 Knock back (punch down) the risen dough, knead, then divide into four. Roll each into a thin round. Oil the hot baking sheets, place the rounds on them, and spread thinly with meat mixture.

5 Bake for 15–20 minutes, until the meat is browned. Sprinkle with sumac or paprika, parsley and lemon juice and serve.

entil Patties Energy 488kcal/2033kJ; Protein 28g; Carbohydrate 25.7g, of which sugars 3.7g; Fat 31.2g, of which saturates 7.4g; Cholesterol 238mg; Calcium 87mg; Fibre 3.1g; Sodium 140mg
atbreads with Lamb Energy 496kcal/2092kJ; Protein 20g; Carbohydrate 75.2g, of which sugars 8.1g; Fat 14.9g, of which saturates 6.1g; Cholesterol 51mg; Calcium 167mg; Fibre 3.8g; Sodium 333mg

Spiced Lamb Poppadums

Crisp, melt-in-the-mouth mini poppadums make a great base for these divine little bites. Top them with a drizzle of yogurt and a spoonful of mango chutney, then serve immediately. To make an equally tasty variation, you can use chicken or pork in place of the lamb.

Makes 25

30ml/2 tbsp sunflower oil
4 shallots, finely chopped
30ml/2 tbsp medium curry paste
300g/11oz minced (ground) lamb
90ml/6 tbsp tomato purée (paste)
5ml/1 tsp sugar
200ml/7fl oz/scant 1 cup coconut cream
juice of 1 lime
60ml/4 tbsp chopped fresh mint leaves
vegetable oil, for frying
25 mini poppadums
salt and ground black pepper, to taste

To serve

natural (plain) yogurt and mango chutney, to drizzle
red chilli slivers and mint leaves, to garnish

1 Heat the oil in a wok or large, heavy pan over medium heat and add the shallots. Stir-fry for 4–5 minutes, until softened.

2 Add the curry paste, stir-fry for 1–2 minutes, then add the lamb. Stir-fry over high heat for a further 4–5 minutes, then stir in the tomato purée, sugar and coconut cream.

3 Cook the lamb over low heat for 25–30 minutes, or until the meat is tender and all the liquid has been absorbed.

4 Season to taste and stir in the lime juice and mint leaves. Remove from the heat and keep warm.

5 Fill a separate wok one-third full of oil and deep-fry the mini poppadums for 30–40 seconds, until puffed up and crisp. Drain on kitchen paper.

6 Place the poppadums on a serving platter. Put a spoonful of spiced lamb on each, then top with a little yogurt and mango chutney. Serve, garnished with slivers of chilli and mint leaves.

Golden Beef and Potato Puffs

These crisp, golden pillows of pastry filled with fragrant spiced beef and creamy mashed potato are delicious served piping hot, straight from the wok, with tangy tomato ketchup on the side for dipping.

Serves 4

15ml/1 tbsp sunflower oil
½ small onion, finely chopped
3 garlic cloves, crushed
5ml/1 tsp finely grated fresh ginger
1 red chilli, seeded and chopped
30ml/2 tbsp curry powder
75g/3oz minced (ground) beef
115g/4oz mashed potato
60ml/4 tbsp chopped fresh coriander (cilantro)
2 sheets ready-rolled, puff pastry
1 egg, lightly beaten
vegetable oil, for frying
salt and ground black pepper
fresh coriander leaves, to garnish
tomato ketchup, to serve

1 Heat the oil in a wok or large, heavy pan, then add the onion garlic, ginger and chilli. Stir-fry gently for 2–3 minutes. Add the curry powder and beef and stir-fry over high heat for a further 4–5 minutes, until the beef is browned.

2 Transfer the beef mixture to a large bowl and add the mashed potato and coriander. Add salt and pepper, and then stir thoroughly, or mix with your hands, then set aside.

3 Lay the pastry sheets on a clean, dry surface and cut out eight rounds, using a 7.5cm/3in pastry (cookie) cutter.

4 Place a large spoonful of the beef mixture in the centre of each pastry round. Brush the edges of the pastry with the beaten egg and fold each round in half to enclose the filling. Press and crimp the edges with the tines of a fork to seal.

5 Fill a wok one-third full of oil and heat to 180°C/350°F (or until a cube of bread, dropped into the oil, browns in 15 seconds). Deep-fry the puffs, in batches, for 2–3 minutes until they rise to the top, and are puffed up and golden brown.

6 Remove from the pan and drain on kitchen paper until all are cooked. Serve hot with tomato ketchup for dipping.

Spiced Lamb Poppadums Energy 63kcal/260kJ; Protein 2.7g; Carbohydrate 2.7g, of which sugars 1.3g; Fat 4.7g, of which saturates 1.4g; Cholesterol 9mg; Calcium 7mg; Fibre 0.3g; Sodium 45mg
Golden Puffs Energy 408kcal/1695kJ; Protein 9g; Carbohydrate 24.2g, of which sugars 1.8g; Fat 31.8g, of which saturates 4.2g; Cholesterol 67mg; Calcium 46mg; Fibre 0.5g; Sodium 202mg

ried Black Pudding on Toast

lack pudding is a traditional nglish bloody sausage, specially enjoyed in the orth of the country. It is avoured with spices and erbs, including garlic and regano, and has a vonderfully rich, spicy taste. lthough more usually eaten s part of an English reakfast, black pudding can lso be used to make electable but economical avoury snacks that are erfect for serving as nibbles t a party.

Serves 4

15ml/1 tbsp olive oil
1 onion, thinly sliced into rings
2 garlic cloves, thinly sliced
5ml/1 tsp dried oregano
5ml/1 tsp paprika
225g/8oz black pudding (blood sausage), cut into 12 thick slices
1 thin baguette, cut into 12, lightly toasted
30ml/2 tbsp fino sherry
sugar, to taste
salt and ground black pepper
chopped fresh oregano, to garnish

Heat the olive oil in a large frying pan, add the sliced onion, arlic, oregano and paprika and fry for 7–8 minutes until the nion is softened and has turned golden brown.

Add the slices of black pudding to the pan, then increase the eat and cook them for 3 minutes, without stirring.

Turn the pieces of black pudding over carefully with a spatula nd cook for a further 3 minutes, until crisp. Keep warm.

Arrange the rounds of toasted bread on a large serving plate nd top each with a slice of still warm black pudding.

Stir the sherry into the onions and add a little sugar to taste. leat, swirling the mixture around the pan until bubbling, then eason with a little salt and black pepper.

Spoon a little of the sherry and onion mixture on top of each ice of black pudding. Sprinkle the oregano over and serve. on't assemble the toasts too far in advance, otherwise they vill become soft, cold and much less appetizing.

Crunchy Salad with Black Pudding

Highly flavoured black pudding is a spicy sausage enriched with blood. This puts some people off, which is a pity as it has a great flavour. It is the star of this simple salad.

Serves 4

250g/9oz black pudding (blood sausage), sliced
1 focaccia loaf, plain or flavoured with sun-dried tomatoes, garlic and herbs, cut into chunks
45ml/3 tbsp olive oil
1 cos or romaine lettuce, torn into bitesize pieces
250g/9oz cherry tomatoes, halved

For the dressing

juice of 1 lemon
90ml/6 tbsp olive oil
10ml/2 tsp French mustard
15ml/1 tbsp clear honey
30ml/2 tbsp chopped fresh herbs, such as coriander (cilantro), chives and parsley
salt and ground black pepper

1 Dry-fry the black pudding in a large, non-stick frying pan for 5–10 minutes, or until browned and crisp, turning occasionally.

2 Remove the black pudding from the pan using a slotted spoon and drain on kitchen paper. Set the black pudding aside and keep warm.

3 Cut the focaccia into chunks. Add the oil to the juices in the frying pan and cook the focaccia cubes in two batches, turning often, until golden on all sides. Lift out the focaccia chunks and drain on kitchen paper.

4 Mix together all the focaccia, black pudding, lettuce and cherry tomatoes in a large bowl. Mix together the dressing ingredients and season with salt and pepper. Pour the dressing over the salad. Mix well and serve immediately.

Cook's Tip

If black pudding (blood sausage) isn't your thing, try this recipe with spicy chorizo or kabanos sausages instead. Cut them into thick diagonal slices before cooking.

ried Black Pudding Energy 506kcal/2137kJ; Protein 18.4g; Carbohydrate 77.8g, of which sugars 4.7g; Fat 14.8g, of which saturates 5.2g; Cholesterol 38mg; Calcium 171mg; Fibre 3.1g; Sodium 1422mg
runchy Salad Energy 641kcal/2674kJ; Protein 15.1g; Carbohydrate 55g, of which sugars 8.1g; Fat 41.6g, of which saturates 9.4g; Cholesterol 43mg; Calcium 196mg; Fibre 3.2g; Sodium 1001mg

Poached Eggs Florentine

In this indulgent appetizer, soft poached eggs are served on a bed of wilted spinach and topped with a lovely creamy, cheese sauce.

Serves 4
675g/1½lb spinach, washed
30ml/2 tbsp butter
60ml/4 tbsp double (heavy) cream
pinch of freshly grated nutmeg
salt and ground black pepper
30ml/2 tbsp grano padano cheese, grated

For the topping
30ml/2 tbsp butter
25g/1oz/¼ cup plain (all-purpose) flour
300ml/½ pint/1¼ cups hot milk
pinch of ground mace
115g/4oz/1 cup Gruyère cheese, grated
4 eggs

1 Place the spinach in a large pan with very little water. Cook for 3–4 minutes or until tender, then drain, squeeze, and chop finely. Return to the pan and reheat with the butter, cream, nutmeg and seasoning. Divide between four small gratin dishes.

2 To make the topping, heat the butter in a small pan, add the flour and cook for 1 minute into a paste. Gradually blend the hot milk into the butter and flour, beating well as it thickens to break up any lumps. Cook for 1–2 minutes, stirring. Remove from the heat and stir in the mace and three-quarters of the Gruyère cheese.

3 Preheat the oven to 200°C/400°F/Gas 6. Bring a pan of water to the simmer, then carefully drop in the eggs. Poach gently for 3–4 minutes, then lift out of the water with a slotted spoon.

4 Place a poached egg in each dish. Cover with cheese sauce and sprinkle with the remaining Gruyère, and the grated grano padano. Bake for 10 minutes, until golden and serve hot.

Cook's Tip
The term 'à la Florentine' means 'in the style of Florence' and refers to baked dishes that are topped with rich mornay sauce.

Baked Eggs with Creamy Leeks

This simple but elegant appetizer is perfect for last-minute entertaining or quick dining. It is economical, as well as being nourishing, sustaining and delicious.

Serves 4
15g/½oz/1 tbsp butter, plus extra for greasing
225g/8oz small leeks, cut into thin slices
75–90ml/5–6 tbsp whipping cream
4 small–medium (US medium–large) eggs
salt and ground black pepper, to taste
crisp, fried sage leaves, to garnish

1 Preheat the oven to 190°C/375°F/Gas 5. Butter the base and sides of four small ramekins or individual soufflé dishes.

2 Melt the butter in a frying pan and cook the leeks over medium heat, stirring frequently, for 3–5 minutes, until softened and translucent, but not browned.

3 Add 45ml/3 tbsp of the cream and cook over low heat for 5 minutes, until the leeks are very soft and the cream has thickened a little. Season to taste.

4 Place the ramekins in a small roasting pan and divide the cooked leek mixture among them. Break an egg into each, spoon over the remaining cream and season to taste with salt and pepper.

5 Pour boiling water into the roasting pan to come about halfway up the sides of the ramekins.

6 Transfer the pan to the oven and bake for about 10 minutes, until just set. Garnish with fried sage leaves and serve.

Variation
If you don't have any fresh sage leaves, try garnishing with a few chopped chives instead.

Eggs Florentine Energy 459kcal/1901kJ; Protein 21.7g; Carbohydrate 11.5g, of which sugars 6.5g; Fat 36g, of which saturates 20.3g; Cholesterol 270mg; Calcium 636mg; Fibre 3.7g; Sodium 626mg
Baked Eggs Energy 149kcal/614kJ; Protein 4.4g; Carbohydrate 2.2g, of which sugars 1.8g; Fat 13.7g, of which saturates 7.5g; Cholesterol 123mg; Calcium 39mg; Fibre 1.3g; Sodium 64mg

Deep-fried Tamarind Eggs

his tasty salad, full of hinese flavours, combines rispy fried eggs with runchy, refreshing eansprouts and salad leaves, nd a deliciously sweet and angy tamarind dresssing.

erves 4

large (US extra large) eggs
unflower oil, for frying
75g/3oz/scant ½ cup palm sugar (jaggery)
90ml/6 tbsp tamarind juice
75ml/5 tbsp Thai fish sauce
6 shallots, finely sliced
4 garlic cloves, thinly sliced
2 red chillies, seeded and sliced
115g/4oz salad leaves
a small handful of coriander (cilantro) leaves
25g/1oz beansprouts

Place the eggs in a pan and cover with cold water. Bring to ne boil and cook for 4 minutes. Remove with a slotted spoon, nen drain and rinse in cold water. Shell and set aside.

Fill a wok one-third full of oil and heat to 180°C/350°F or until a cube of bread, dropped into the oil, browns in 5 seconds).

Using a slotted spoon, lower the eggs, one at a time, into the ot oil. Deep-fry for 2–3 minutes, or until lightly golden. Remove nd drain on kitchen paper. Keep warm.

Place the palm sugar, tamarind juice and fish sauce in a clean vok with 30ml/2 tbsp of water and bring to the boil, stirring ntil the sugar dissolves. Reduce the heat, then simmer gently r 3–4 minutes. Transfer the mixture to a bowl and set aside.

Wipe out the wok and add 30ml/2 tbsp oil. When hot, fry the nallots, garlic and chillies until they are all lightly browned.

In a large bowl, toss together the salad leaves, coriander leaves nd beansprouts with the tamarind mixture. Divide this among ur plates.

Cut the fried eggs in half and and divide among the prepared lates. Sprinkle over the shallot mixture and serve immediately.

Potato, Onion and Broad Bean Tortilla

The classic tortilla is simple and cheap to make yet tastes fabulous. Serve it as a light summer lunch dish with a green leafy salad, or cut it into pieces, thread on to cocktail sticks and serve as an appetizer or as nibbles at a party.

Serves 6

45ml/3 tbsp olive oil
2 Spanish (Bermuda) onions, thinly sliced
300g/11oz waxy potatoes, cut into 1cm/½ in dice
250g/9oz/1¾ cups shelled broad (fava) beans
5ml/1 tsp chopped fresh thyme or summer savory
6 large (US extra large) eggs
45ml/3 tbsp chopped mixed fresh chives and flat leaf parsley
salt and ground black pepper

1 Heat 30ml/2 tbsp of the oil in a deep 23cm/9in non-stick frying pan. Add the onions and potatoes and season with salt and pepper to taste. Stir to mix, then cover and cook gently, stirring, for 20–25 minutes.

2 Meanwhile, cook the beans in lightly salted, boiling water for 5 minutes. Drain well and set aside to cool. When the beans are cool enough to handle, peel off the grey outer skins. Add to the frying pan, together with the thyme or summer savory. Stir and cook for a further 2–3 minutes.

3 Beat the eggs with salt and pepper to taste and the mixed fresh herbs, then pour over the potatoes and onions and increase the heat slightly. Cook gently until the egg on the base sets and browns.

4 Carefully invert the tortilla on to a large plate. Add the remaining oil to the pan and heat.

5 Slip the tortilla back into the pan, uncooked side down, and cook for another 3–5 minutes. Slide the tortilla out on to a plate. Divide it as you like, and serve it warm rather than when it is still piping hot.

eep-fried Eggs Energy 351kcal/1462kJ; Protein 13g; Carbohydrate 23.3g, of which sugars 21.5g; Fat 23.8g, of which saturates 4.4g; Cholesterol 333mg; Calcium 117mg; Fibre 1.3g; Sodium 165mg
otato Tortilla Energy 673kcal/2812kJ; Protein 34.9g; Carbohydrate 59.2g, of which sugars 18.1g; Fat 35.2g, of which saturates 7.3g; Cholesterol 571mg; Calcium 272mg; Fibre 14.3g; Sodium 252mg

Pimiento Tartlets

Originally from Spain, these pretty little tartlets are filled with strips of roasted sweet peppers and a deliciously creamy, cheesy custard.

Serves 4

1 red (bell) pepper
1 yellow (bell) pepper
175g/6oz/1½ cups plain (all-purpose) flour
75g/3oz/6 tbsp butter, diced
30–45ml/2–3 tbsp cold water
60ml/4 tbsp double (heavy) cream
1 egg
15ml/1 tbsp freshly grated grano padano cheese
salt and ground black pepper

1 Preheat the oven to 200°C/400°F/Gas 6, and heat the grill (broiler). Place the peppers on a baking sheet and grill for 10 minutes, turning occasionally, until blackened. Cover with a dish towel and leave for 5 minutes. Peel away the skin, then discard the seeds and cut the flesh into very thin strips.

2 Sift the flour and a pinch of salt into a bowl. Add the butter and rub it in until the mixture resembles fine breadcrumbs. Stir in enough of the water to make a firm, not sticky, dough.

3 Roll the dough out on a floured surface and line 12 individual moulds or a 12-hole tartlet tin (muffin pan). Prick the bases and fill the pastry cases with crumpled foil. Bake for 10 minutes.

4 Remove the foil from the pastry cases and divide the pepper strips among the pastry cases.

5 Whisk the cream and egg in a bowl. Season and pour over the peppers. Sprinkle with grano padano and bake for about 20 minutes. Cool for 2 minutes. Serve warm or cold.

Variations

To ring the changes, you could use strips of grilled aubergine (eggplant) mixed with chopped sun-dried tomatoes, or drained and chopped marinated artichoke hearts, in place of the strips of roasted (bell) peppers.

Red Onion and Goat's Cheese Tarts

Made with ready-bought puff pastry, these attractive little tartlets couldn't be easier to make. Garnish them with fresh thyme sprigs and serve with a selection of salad leaves and a tomato and basil salad for a light lunch or quick supper. A wide variety of goat's cheeses are available, the creamy log-shaped types without a rind are most suitable for these pastries. Make sure the pastry you buy is all-butter.

Serves 4

15ml/1 tbsp olive oil
450g/1lb red onions, sliced
425g/15oz packet all-butter puff pastry
115g/4oz/1 cup goat's cheese, cubed
a few thyme sprigs, to garnish (optional)
salt and ground black pepper

1 Heat the oil in a large, heavy frying pan, add the onions and cook over low heat for 10 minutes, or until softened, stirring occasionally to prevent them from browning.

2 Add seasoning to taste and cook for a further 2 minutes. Remove the pan from the heat and leave to cool. Preheat the oven to 220°C/425°F/Gas 7.

3 Roll out the puff pastry on a lightly floured board or work surface and cut out four rounds, using a 15cm/6in plate as a cutting guide to go around.

4 Place the pastry rounds on a dampened baking sheet and, using the point of a sharp knife, score a border, 2cm/¾in inside the edge of each pastry round.

5 Divide the cooked onions among the pastry rounds and top with the cubed goat's cheese.

6 Bake the pastries for 25–30 minutes, until the pastry is golden brown and the goat's cheese has melted.

7 Serve the tarts immediately, garnished with the sprigs of thyme, if you like.

Pimiento Tartlets Energy 427kcal/1778kJ; Protein 8.4g; Carbohydrate 40g, of which sugars 6.4g; Fat 27g, of which saturates 16.1g; Cholesterol 112mg; Calcium 131mg; Fibre 2.8g; Sodium 180m
Red Onion Tarts Energy 554kcal/2308kJ; Protein 13.5g; Carbohydrate 48.5g, of which sugars 8g; Fat 36.4g, of which saturates 5.6g; Cholesterol 27mg; Calcium 128mg; Fibre 1.6g; Sodium 506m

Iushroom Caviar

'egetable 'caviars' are little ussian tapas-style dishes. 'he name was given to udget vegetable versions of he luxurious delicacy that nly the rich could afford. erve it Russian style, with oasted rye bread, and hopped hard-boiled egg, pring onion and parsley.

Serves 4

45ml/3 tbsp olive or vegetable oil
450g/1lb mushrooms, finely chopped
5–10 shallots, chopped
4 garlic cloves, chopped
salt and ground black pepper, to taste
parsley, and hard-boiled egg, chopped, to serve

Heat the oil in a large pan, add the chopped mushrooms, hallots and garlic, and cook gently for about 5 minutes, stirring ccasionally, until browned.

: Season the mixture with salt and pepper to taste, then ontinue cooking, until the mushrooms give up their juices.

Continue cooking, stirring frequently, until the liquor from the nushrooms has evaporated and they are evenly brown and dry.

Set aside the mixture to cool slightly, then scrape it in to a ood processor or blender and process briefly until a chunky aste is formed.

Spoon the mushroom caviar into small serving dishes, top ach one with a little chopped hard-boiled eggs and sprinkle vith the chopped fresh parsley. Serve immediately with plenty f toasted bread.

Variation

For a rich wild mushroom caviar, soak 10–15g/¼–½oz dried porcini in about 120ml/4fl oz/½ cup water for approximately 30 minutes. Remove the mushrooms from the liquid, chop roughly, and add, together with their soaking liquid, to the browned mushrooms in step 2. Continue as above.

Mushrooms with Garlic Chilli Sauce

These spicy, garlic-flavoured mushrooms make an ideal vegetarian appetizer for a dinner party, they are also great cooked on a barbecue.

Serves 4

12 large field (portobello), brown cap (cremini) or oyster mushrooms, or a mixture of the three, halved
4 garlic cloves, coarsely chopped
6 fresh coriander (cilantro) sprigs, chopped
ground black pepper, to taste

For the dipping sauce

30ml/2 tbsp sugar
90ml/6 tbsp rice vinegar
5ml/1 tsp salt
1 garlic clove, crushed
1 small fresh red chilli, seeded and finely chopped
30ml/2 tbsp light soy sauce

1 If using wooden skewers, soak eight of them in cold water for at least 30 minutes before making the kebabs. This will prevent them from burning on the barbecue or grill (broiler).

2 Make the dipping sauce by heating 15ml/1 tbsp of the sugar, rice vinegar and salt in a small pan, stirring occasionally until the sugar and salt have dissolved. Add the garlic and chilli, pour into a serving dish and keep warm.

3 Thread three mushroom halves on to each skewer. Lay the skewers side by side in a shallow dish.

4 In a mortar or spice grinder, pound or blend the garlic and coriander to form a rough paste. Scrape the paste into a bowl and mix with the remaining sugar, soy sauce and a little pepper. Brush the soy sauce mixture over the mushrooms and leave to marinate for 15 minutes.

5 Prepare the barbecue or grill, and cook the mushrooms for 2–3 minutes on each side. Serve with the dipping sauce.

Cook's Tip

If you like hot food, do not remove the seeds from the red chilli.

Iushroom Caviar Energy 116kcal/479kJ; Protein 2.9g; Carbohydrate 6.4g, of which sugars 4.4g; Fat 9g, of which saturates 1.3g; Cholesterol 0mg; Calcium 26mg; Fibre 2.3g; Sodium 8mg
Iushrooms with Sauce Energy 78kcal/329kJ; Protein 5.8g; Carbohydrate 11.5g, of which sugars 9.1g; Fat 1.3g, of which saturates 0.3g; Cholesterol 0mg; Calcium 23mg; Fibre 3.3g; Sodium 1039mg

Mushrooms on Spicy Toast

This recipe uses a technique called dry-panning, which is a quick way of cooking mushrooms that makes the most of their flavour. The juices run when the mushrooms are heated, and then act as the cooking liquid, so they become really moist and tender.

Serves 4

8–12 large flat field (portobello) mushrooms
50g/2oz/¼ cup butter
5ml/1 tsp curry powder
salt, to taste
4 slices thickly-sliced white or brown bread, lightly toasted, to serve

1 Preheat the oven to 200°C/400°F/Gas 6. Peel the mushrooms, if necessary, and remove the stalks. Heat a dry frying pan until very hot.

2 Place the mushrooms in the hot frying pan, with the gills on top. Using half the butter, add a piece the size of a hazelnut to each one, then sprinkle all the mushrooms lightly with salt.

3 Cook over medium heat until the butter begins to bubble and the mushrooms are juicy and tender.

4 Meanwhile, mix the remaining butter with the curry powder. Spread on the bread. Bake in the oven for 10 minutes, pile the mushrooms on top and serve.

Variations

Using a flavoured butter makes these mushrooms even more special. Try one of the following:
- *Herb butter – mix softened butter with chopped fresh herbs, such as parsley and thyme, or marjoram and chopped chives.*
- *Olive butter – mix softened butter with diced green olives and spring onions (scallions).*
- *Tomato butter – mix softened butter with sun-dried tomato purée (paste).*
- *Garlic butter – mix softened butter with chopped garlic.*

Seven-spice Aubergines

Crisp, fragrant and very moreish, these tasty bites make a delicious low-cost appetizer. The Chinese seven-spice powder imbues a warm flavour that goes well with the light, curry batter. If you are unable to find it, you can use five-spice powder instead. You can also use courgettes for this recipe.

Serves 4

500g/1¼lb aubergines (eggplant)
2 egg whites
90ml/6 tbsp cornflour (cornstarch, or plain (all-purpose) flour
5ml/1 tsp salt
15ml/1 tbsp seven-spice powder
15ml/1 tbsp mild chilli powder
sunflower oil, for frying
noodles and chilli sauce, to serve

1 Using a large, sharp knife, slice the aubergines into thin discs. Pat dry with kitchen paper.

2 Whisk the egg whites in a large bowl until they are light and foamy, but not dry.

3 Combine the cornflour or flour, salt, seven-spice powder and chilli powder and spread evenly on to a large plate.

4 Fill a wok or large, heavy pan one-third full of sunflower oil and heat to 180°C/350°F (or until a cube of bread, dropped into the oil, browns in 15 seconds).

5 Working in batches, dip the aubergine slices in the egg white and then into the spiced flour. Deep-fry for 3–4 minutes, or unt crisp and golden. Remove the aubergines with a wire skimmer or slotted spoon and drain well on kitchen paper.

6 Serve the aubergines immediately, accompanied by noodles, and hot chilli dipping sauce.

Cook's Tips

Choose small, firm aubergines with shiny, unblemished skins, and avoid any that feel soft or that are beginning to wrinkle.

Mushrooms on Toast Energy 230kcal/966kJ; Protein 6.1g; Carbohydrate 25.1g, of which sugars 1.6g; Fat 12.5g, of which saturates 6.7g; Cholesterol 27mg; Calcium 63mg; Fibre 1.9g; Sodium 341m
Seven-spice Aubergines Energy 203kcal/850kJ; Protein 2.7g; Carbohydrate 23.5g, of which sugars 2.5g; Fat 11.7g, of which saturates 1.4g; Cholesterol 0mg; Calcium 17mg; Fibre 2.5g; Sodium 45mg

Courgette Tempura

This quick-and-easy dish is a twist on the classic Japanese tempura, using gram flour in the batter. Also known as besan, gram flour is produced from chickpeas and is more commonly used in Indian cooking to make various snacks. It gives a wonderfully crisp texture on the outside while the courgette inside becomes meltingly tender.

Serves 4

600g/1lb 6oz courgettes (zucchini)
5ml/1 tsp baking powder
90g/3½oz/¾ cup gram flour
2.5ml/½ tsp turmeric
10ml/2 tsp ground coriander
5ml/1 tsp ground cumin
5ml/1 tsp chilli powder
250ml/8fl oz/1 cup beer
sunflower oil, for frying
salt, to taste
steamed basmati rice, natural (plain) yogurt and pickles, to serve

1 Using a large, sharp knife, slice the courgettes into thick batons about the size of a finger and set aside.

2 Sift the baking powder, gram flour, turmeric, ground coriander, cumin and chilli powder into a large bowl. Season the mixture with salt and mix to combine. Gradually mix in the beer to make a thick batter.

3 Fill a wok or large, heavy pan one-third full of sunflower oil and heat to 180°C/350°F (or until a cube of bread, dropped into the oil, browns in 15 seconds).

4 Dip the courgette batons in the batter and then deep-fry for 1–2 minutes, or until crisp and golden. Carefully lift out of the wok or pan using a slotted spoon and drain on kitchen paper.

5 Serve the courgette tempura immediately with steamed basmati rice, yogurt, pickles and chutney.

Variations
You can cook all kinds of vegetables in this way. Try using onion rings, aubergine (eggplant) slices, cauliflower or broccoli.

Courgette Fritters with Chilli Jam

Chilli jam is hot, sweet and sticky – rather like a thick chutney. It adds a delicious piquancy to these light fritters, which are always popular with adults and children alike.

Serves 6

450g/1lb/3½ cups coarsely grated courgettes (zucchini)
50g/2oz/⅔ cup freshly grated grano padano cheese
2 eggs, beaten
60ml/4 tbsp plain (all-purpose) flour
vegetable oil, for frying
salt and ground black pepper

For the chilli jam

75ml/5 tbsp olive oil
4 large onions, diced
4 garlic cloves, chopped
1–2 green chillies, seeded and sliced
30ml/2 tbsp soft dark brown sugar

1 First make the chilli jam. Heat the olive oil in a frying pan until hot, then add the onions and the garlic. Reduce the heat to low, then cook for 20 minutes, stirring frequently, until the onions are very soft.

2 Leave the onion mixture to cool, then transfer to a food processor or blender. Add the chillies and sugar and blend until smooth, then return the mixture to the pan.

3 Cook for a further 10 minutes, stirring, until the liquid evaporates and the mixture has the consistency of jam. Cool.

4 To make the fritters, squeeze the courgettes in a dish towel to remove any excess liquid, then combine with the grano padano, eggs, flour and salt and pepper.

5 Pour enough oil to cover the base of a large frying pan, and heat. When hot, add 30ml/2 tbsp of the mixture for each fritter and cook three fritters in batches. Cook for 2–3 minutes on each side until golden, then keep warm while you cook the rest of the fritters.

6 Drain the fritters on kitchen paper and serve warm with a spoonful of the chilli jam.

Courgette Tempura Energy 241kcal/999kJ; Protein 7.3g; Carbohydrate 15.3g, of which sugars 4.6g; Fat 15.6g, of which saturates 1.9g; Cholesterol 0mg; Calcium 83mg; Fibre 3.8g; Sodium 15mg
Courgette Fritters Energy 326kcal/1355kJ; Protein 10g; Carbohydrate 22.3g, of which sugars 13.2g; Fat 22.6g, of which saturates 4.7g; Cholesterol 103mg; Calcium 177mg; Fibre 2.6g; Sodium 131mg

Mini Baked Potatoes with Sour Cream

These attractive miniature baked potatoes are packed with flavour and can be eaten with the fingers. They provide an economical and unusual way of starting off an informal supper party. They are also great finger food for a bonfire night party.

Makes 20

20 small new potatoes or salad potatoes
60ml/4 tbsp vegetable oil
120ml/4fl oz/½ cup sour cream
25g/1oz blue cheese, crumbled
salt
30ml/2 tbsp chopped fresh chives, to garnish

1 Preheat the oven to 180°C/350°F/Gas 4. Wash and dry the potatoes, and pierce each one two or three times with the tip of a sharp knife. Toss the potatoes with the oil in a large bowl until evenly coated.

2 Dip the potatoes in the salt to coat lightly, then spread them out on a large baking sheet. Bake for 45–50 minutes in the oven until they are tender.

3 In a small bowl, combine the sour cream and blue cheese, mixing together well to combine thoroughly.

4 Cut a cross in the top of each potato. Press gently with your fingers to open the potatoes. Top each one with a dollop of the blue cheese mixture.

5 Place the potatoes on a serving dish and garnish with the chives, serve immediately.

Variations

- *You can use the cheese mixture to top larger baked potatoes, if you like.*
- *If you don't have any blue cheese, use a strongly flavoured Cheddar cheese instead.*

Potato Skewers with Mustard Dip

Tender new potatoes cooked on the barbecue have a great flavour and deliciously crisp skin, but you could also cook the skewers under the grill if the weather is bad.

Serves 4

200g/7oz shallots
1kg/2¼lb small new potatoes
salt and ground black pepper, to taste, plus 15ml/1 tbsp salt

For the dip

4 garlic cloves, crushed
2 egg yolks
30ml/2 tbsp lemon juice
350ml/12fl oz/1½ cups extra virgin olive oil
10ml/2 tsp wholegrain mustard

1 Prepare and light the barbecue or preheat the grill (broiler) t high. To make the dip, place the garlic, egg yolks and lemon juice in a blender or a food processor and process for a few seconds until the mixture is smooth.

2 Keep the blender motor running and add 300ml/½ pint/1¼ cups of the olive oil very gradually, pouring it in a thin stream, until the mixture forms a thick, glossy cream. Add the mustard and stir the ingredients together, then season with salt and pepper. Chill until ready to use.

3 Skin the shallots and then cut them in half. Par-boil the potatoes in their skins in a pan of boiling water for 5 minutes. Drain well and then thread the potatoes on to metal skewers, alternating with the shallots.

4 Brush the skewers with the remaining olive oil and sprinkle with 15ml/1 tbsp salt. Cook over a barbecue or under a hot gri for 10–12 minutes, turning occasionally. Serve the skewers immediately with the dip.

Cook's Tip

Early or 'new' potatoes, and salad potatoes have the firmness and waxy texture that is necessary for the potatoes to stay on the skewer. Don't be tempted to use floury types of potato.

Mini Baked Potatoes Energy 71kcal/299kJ; Protein 1.3g; Carbohydrate 8.3g, of which sugars 0.9g; Fat 3.9g, of which saturates 1.3g; Cholesterol 5mg; Calcium 15mg; Fibre 0.5g; Sodium 23mg
Potato Skewers Energy 2731kcal/11338kJ; Protein 28g; Carbohydrate 181.3g, of which sugars 25g; Fat 215.4g, of which saturates 32.8g; Cholesterol 403mg; Calcium 174mg; Fibre 14.3g; Sodium 297m

otato Skins with Cajun Dip

ivinely crisp and decadent, ese potato skins are great ı their own, or served with is piquant dip as a garnish · on the side. They are licious as a snack, or as accompaniment to a rbecued feast.

rves 2
large baking potatoes
vegetable oil, for deep frying

For the dip
120ml/4fl oz/½ cup natural (plain) yogurt
1 garlic clove, crushed
5ml/1 tsp tomato purée (paste)
2.5ml/½ tsp green chilli purée or ½ small green chilli, chopped
1.5ml/¼ tsp celery salt
salt and ground black pepper

Preheat the oven to 180°C/350°F/Gas 4. Bake the potatoes r 45–50 minutes until tender. Remove from the oven and set ide to cool slightly.

When the potatoes have cooled down enough to handle, cut em in half and scoop out the flesh, leaving a thin layer on the ins. Keep the flesh for another meal.

To make the dip, mix together all the ingredients and chill in e refrigerator until the skins are ready.

Heat a 1cm/½in layer of oil in a large pan or deep-fat fryer. ıt each potato half in half again, then fry them until crisp and lden on both sides.

Drain on kitchen paper, sprinkle with salt and black pepper d serve with a bowl of dip or a dollop of dip in each skin.

Cook's Tip
- *If you prefer, you can microwave the potatoes to save time. This will take about 10 minutes.*
- *The scooped-out flesh from the potatoes is delicious if mixed with leftover vegetables such as peas or cabbage, then formed into small cakes and fried in a little oil until golden.*

Spicy Chickpea Samosas

A blend of crushed chickpeas and coriander sauce makes an interesting alternative to the more familiar meat or vegetable fillings in these crisp little pastries. The samosas look pretty garnished with fresh coriander leaves and finely sliced onion and are delicious served with a simple dip such as fresh tomato, hummus or a mixture of Greek yogurt and chopped fresh mint leaves. Hara masala is a green spice mix that can be found in specialist food stores and large supermarkets.

Makes 18
2 x 400g/14oz cans chickpeas, drained and rinsed
120ml/4fl oz/½ cup hara masala or coriander (cilantro) sauce
275g/10oz filo pastry
60ml/4 tbsp chilli and garlic oil

1 Preheat the oven to 220°C/425°F/Gas 7. Process half the chickpeas to a paste in a food processor.

2 Transfer the chickpea paste into a bowl and add the whole chickpeas, the hara masala or coriander sauce, and a little salt. Mix until well combined.

3 Cut a sheet of filo pastry into three strips. Brush with a little of the oil. Place 10ml/2 tsp of the filling at one end of a strip.

4 Turn one corner diagonally over the filling to meet the long edge. Continue folding the filling and the pastry along the length of the strip, keeping the triangular shape.

5 Transfer to a baking sheet and repeat with the remaining filling and pastry. Brush the samosas with any remaining oil and bake for 15 minutes. Serve immediately, garnished with coriander and sliced red onion.

Variation
You can substitute the chickpeas with cannellini beans if that's what you have in the storecupboard.

tato Skins Energy 211kcal/873kJ; Protein 2.7g; Carbohydrate 12.5g, of which sugars 3.3g; Fat 17g, of which saturates 2.2g; Cholesterol 0mg; Calcium 62mg; Fibre 0.7g; Sodium 35mg
icy Chickpea Samosas Energy 119kcal/499kJ; Protein 4.1g; Carbohydrate 13.7g, of which sugars 0.4g; Fat 5.7g, of which saturates 0.8g; Cholesterol 0mg; Calcium 36mg; Fibre 2.2g; Sodium 99mg

Falafel with Tahini Dip

Sesame seeds give a delightfully crunchy coating to these spicy patties, served with a creamy dip.

Serves 6

250g/9oz/1⅓ cups dried chickpeas
2 garlic cloves, crushed
1 fresh red chilli, seeded and finely sliced
5ml/1 tsp ground coriander
5ml/1 tsp ground cumin
15ml/1 tbsp chopped fresh mint
15ml/1 tbsp chopped fresh parsley
2 spring onions (scallions), finely chopped
1 large egg, beaten
sesame seeds, for coating
sunflower oil, for frying
salt and ground black pepper

For the tahini yogurt dip

30ml/2 tbsp light tahini
200g/7oz/scant 1 cup natural (plain) yogurt
5ml/1 tsp cayenne pepper
15ml/1 tbsp chopped fresh mint
1 spring onion (scallion), finely sliced

1 Place the chickpeas in a large bowl, cover with cold water and leave to soak overnight. Drain and rinse the chickpeas, then place them in a large pan and cover with cold water. Bring to the boil and boil rapidly for 10 minutes. Reduce the heat and simmer for 1¼–2 hours until the chickpeas are tender.

2 To make the tahini yogurt dip, mix together the tahini, yogurt, cayenne pepper and mint in a small bowl. Sprinkle the spring onion and extra cayenne pepper on top and chill until required.

3 Combine the chickpeas with the garlic, chilli, ground spices, herbs, spring onions and seasoning, then mix in the egg. Place in a food processor and blend until the mixture forms a coarse paste. If the paste seems too soft, chill it for 30 minutes.

4 Form the chilled chickpea paste into 12 patties with your hands, then roll each one in the sesame seeds to coat evenly.

5 Heat enough oil to cover the base of a large frying pan. Fry the falafel, in batches if necessary, for 6 minutes, turning once. Drain on kitchen paper, and serve warm with the tahini yogurt dip garnished with fresh herbs.

Pea and Potato Pakoras

These inexpensive golden bites are sold as street food throughout India.

Makes 25

15ml/1 tbsp sunflower oil
20ml/4 tsp cumin seeds
5ml/1 tsp black mustard seeds
1 small onion, chopped
10ml/2 tsp grated fresh root ginger
2 green chillies, chopped
600g/1lb 6oz potatoes, peeled, cooked and diced
200g/7oz peas
juice of 1 lemon
90ml/6 tbsp chopped fresh coriander (cilantro) leaves
salt and ground black pepper
vegetable oil, for frying

For the batter

115g/4oz/1 cup gram flour
25g/1oz/¼ cup plain (all-purpose) flour
40g/1½oz/⅓ cup rice flour
350ml/12fl oz/1½ cups water
large pinch of turmeric
10ml/2 tsp dried coriander

1 Heat a wok or large frying pan over medium heat and add the sunflower oil. When hot, add the cumin and mustard seeds and stir-fry for 1–2 minutes. Add the onion, ginger and chillies to the wok or large pan and cook for 3–4 minutes, stirring constantly to prevent the onion from burning.

2 Add the cooked potatoes and peas, stir well to combine and stir-fry for 3–4 minutes. Season to taste, then stir in the lemon juice and coriander leaves. Leave the mixture to cool slightly, then divide into 25 portions. Using damp hands, shape each portion into a small ball and chill in the refrigerator.

3 To make the batter, put the gram flour, plain flour and rice flour in a large bowl. Season with salt and pepper and add the turmeric and coriander. Gradually whisk in the water.

4 Fill a wok or large, heavy pan one-third full of vegetable oil and heat to 180°C/350°F. Working in batches, dip the chilled pea and potato balls in the batter, then carefully slip into the hot oil. Fry for 1–2 minutes, or until golden, drain and keep warm.

5 Drain on kitchen paper and keep warm while you cook the rest of the balls. Serve hot.

Falafel Energy 372kcal/1557kJ; Protein 19.3g; Carbohydrate 35.3g, of which sugars 5.8g; Fat 18.1g, of which saturates 2.6g; Cholesterol 48mg; Calcium 280mg; Fibre 8g; Sodium 89mg
Pea and Potato Pakoras Energy 126kcal/525kJ; Protein 4.1g; Carbohydrate 8.3g, of which sugars 2.6g; Fat 8.8g, of which saturates 5.2g; Cholesterol 0mg; Calcium 35mg; Fibre 1.3g; Sodium 16m

piced Onion Koftas

ɪese spicy Indian onion tters are made with gram ɔur, otherwise known as ickpea flour or besan. ɛrve with spicy chutney or herby yogurt dip.

ɛrves 4–5

'5g/1½lb onions, halved and thinly sliced
nl/1 tsp salt
nl/1 tsp ground coriander
5ml/1 tsp ground cumin
2.5ml/½ tsp ground turmeric
1–2 green chillies, seeded and finely chopped
45ml/3 tbsp chopped fresh coriander (cilantro)
90g/3½oz/¾ cup gram flour
2.5ml/½ tsp baking powder
vegetable oil, for deep-frying
lemon wedges and fresh coriander sprigs, to garnish
yogurt and herb dip, to serve

Place the onions in a colander, add the salt and toss. Place on plate and leave to stand for 45 minutes, tossing once or twice. nse the onions, then squeeze out any excess moisture.

Place the onions in a bowl. Add the ground coriander, cumin, rmeric, chillies and fresh coriander. Mix well.

Add the gram flour and baking powder, then use your hand to ix all the ingredients thoroughly. Shape the mixture by hand to 12–15 koftas about the size of golf balls.

Heat the oil for deep-frying to 180–190°C/350–375°F or ɪtil a cube of day-old bread browns in about 30–45 seconds. y the koftas, four or five at a time, until deep golden brown all ver. Drain each batch on kitchen paper and keep warm until all e koftas are cooked. Serve with lemon wedges and coriander rigs and a yogurt dip (see Cooks tip).

Cook's tips

To make a yogurt and herb dip, stir 30ml/2 tbsp each of chopped fresh coriander and mint into 250ml/8fl oz/1 cup set yogurt. Season with salt, ground toasted cumin seeds and a pinch of muscovado (molasses) sugar.

Spicy Pumpkin Dip

This spicy dip is a beautiful warm orange colour and its flavour, spiced with paprika and ginger, is equally warming. It is great to serve at a Thanksgiving feast. It can be stored for at least a week in the refrigerator. Serve with chunks of crusty bread or a selection of raw vegetables to dip into it.

Serves 6–8

45–60ml/3–4 tbsp olive oil
1 onion, finely chopped
5–8 garlic cloves, roughly chopped
675g/1½lb pumpkin, peeled and diced
5–10ml/1–2 tsp ground cumin
5ml/1 tsp paprika
1.5–2.5ml/¼–½ tsp ground ginger
1.5–2.5ml/¼–½ tsp curry powder
75g/3oz chopped canned tomatoes or diced fresh tomatoes
15–30ml/1–2 tbsp tomato purée (paste)
½–1 red jalapeño or serrano chilli, chopped, or cayenne pepper, to taste
pinch of sugar, if necessary
juice of ½ lemon, or to taste
salt
30ml/2 tbsp chopped fresh coriander (cilantro) leaves, to garnish

1 Heat the oil in a frying pan, add the onion and half the garlic and fry until softened. Add the pieces of pumpkin, then cover the pan and cook for about 10 minutes, or until the pumpkin is half tender.

2 Add the spices to the pan and cook for 1–2 minutes. Stir in the tomatoes, tomato purée, chilli, sugar and salt and cook over medium-high heat until the liquid has evaporated.

3 When the pumpkin is tender, mash to a coarse purée. Add the remaining garlic and taste for seasoning, then stir in the lemon juice to taste. Serve at room temperature, sprinkled with the chopped fresh coriander.

Variation

Use butternut squash, or any other winter squash, in place of the pumpkin, if you like.

iced Onion Koftas Energy 207kcal/861kJ; Protein 5.4g; Carbohydrate 19.8g, of which sugars 8.2g; Fat 12.3g, of which saturates 1.4g; Cholesterol 0mg; Calcium 84mg; Fibre 4.3g; Sodium 14mg
icy Pumpkin Dip Energy 54kcal/224kJ; Protein 0.9g; Carbohydrate 2.9g, of which sugars 2.3g; Fat 4.4g, of which saturates 0.7g; Cholesterol 0mg; Calcium 37mg; Fibre 1.3g; Sodium 3mg

Baba Ganoush with Crispy Pittas

Baba Ganoush is a delectable aubergine dip, with a smoky flavour, from the Middle East. It makes a very good appetizer served with raw vegetable crudités or bread for a party, or serve it at a barbecue as a side dish.

Serves 6

2 small aubergines (eggplants)
1 garlic clove, crushed
60ml/4 tbsp tahini
25g/1oz/¼ cup ground almonds
juice of ½ lemon
30ml/2 tbsp fresh mint leaves
salt, to taste

For the crispy pittas
4 pitta breads
45ml/3 tbsp sesame seeds
45ml/3 tbsp fresh thyme leaves, chopped
45ml/3 tbsp poppy seeds
175ml/6fl oz/¾ cup olive oil
2.5ml/½ tsp ground cumin

1 Start by making the crispy pittas. Split the pitta breads through the middle and carefully open them out.

2 Mix the sesame seeds, chopped thyme and poppy seeds in a mortar. Work them lightly with a pestle to release the flavour.

3 Stir in 150ml/¼ pint/⅔ cup olive oil. Spread the mixture over the cut sides of the pitta bread. Grill (broil) until golden brown and crisp. Cool on a wire rack. When cool, break into large pieces and set aside.

4 Grill the aubergines, turning them frequently, until the skin is blackened and blistered. Remove the peel, chop the flesh roughly and leave to drain in a colander.

5 Squeeze out as much liquid from the aubergine as possible. Place the flesh in a blender or food processor, then add the garlic, tahini, ground almonds, lemon juice and cumin, with salt to taste. Process to a smooth paste, then roughly chop half the mint and stir into the dip.

6 Spoon the paste into a bowl, sprinkle the remaining mint leaves on top and drizzle with the remaining olive oil. Serve with the crispy pittas.

Hummus

Blending chickpeas with garlic and oil creates a surprisingly creamy purée that is delicious as part of a Turkish-style mezze, but is now known and enjoyed all over the world. Eat as a dip with bread, cucumber and carrot sticks and cherry tomatoes. Make a double quantity as it keeps well in the refrigerator, and any leftovers make a good sandwich filler.

Serves 4–6

150g/5oz/¾ cup dried chickpeas
juice of 2 lemons
2 garlic cloves, sliced
30ml/2 tbsp olive oil
pinch of cayenne pepper
150ml/¼ pint/⅔ cup tahini paste
salt and ground black pepper, to taste
extra olive oil and a little extra cayenne pepper, for sprinkling
crispy toast or warm pitta bread, to serve

1 Put the dried chickpeas in a large bowl with plenty of cold water and set aside to soak overnight, or for at least 8 hours.

2 Thoroughly rinse and drain the chickpeas, then place them in a large pan and cover with fresh water. Bring to the boil and boil rapidly for 10 minutes.

3 Reduce the heat, cover the pan, and simmer the chickpeas gently for 1¼–2 hours until soft. Keep an eye on the water level and top up if necessary.

4 Drain the chickpeas in a colander, then purée in a food processor until they form a smooth paste.

5 Add the lemon juice, garlic, olive oil, cayenne pepper and tahini paste and blend until creamy, scraping the mixture down from the sides of the bowl.

6 Season the purée with plenty of salt and ground black pepper and transfer to a serving dish.

7 Sprinkle with a little olive oil and cayenne pepper, and garnish with a few parsley sprigs. Serve with toasted pitta bread and olives, if you like.

Baba Ganoush Energy 129kcal/535kJ; Protein 3.3g; Carbohydrate 1.9g, of which sugars 1.6g; Fat 12.2g, of which saturates 1.6g; Cholesterol 0mg; Calcium 85mg; Fibre 2.5g; Sodium 4mg
Hummus Energy 453kcal/1887kJ; Protein 15.7g; Carbohydrate 32.1g, of which sugars 13.8g; Fat 30g, of which saturates 4.2g; Cholesterol 0mg; Calcium 345mg; Fibre 10.5g; Sodium 49mg

Cannellini Bean Dip

'his soft bean dip or pâté is ood spread on wheaten rackers or toasted muffins. can also be eaten with rudites, such as sliced ucumber, carrot or red epper. Alternatively, it can be erved as a light meal, with vedges of tomato and a risp green salad.

Serves 4

400g/14oz can cannellini beans
grated rind and juice of 1 lemon
30ml/2 tbsp olive oil
1 garlic clove, finely chopped
30ml/2 tbsp chopped fresh parsley
red Tabasco sauce, to taste
cayenne pepper
salt and ground black pepper

Drain the beans in a sieve (strainer) and rinse them well nder cold water. Transfer to a shallow bowl.

If you want a rough dip, use a potato masher to roughly urée the beans, then stir in the lemon juice and grated rind, ien add the olive oil. For a smoother dip, place the beans in a od processor and process, add the lemon juce and rind, then our in the olive oil, while pulsing the machine, until you have a lky purée. You can also do half the mixture smooth and half ough, the mix together, if you prefer a contrast.

Stir the chopped garlic and parsley into the mashed beans, or ansfer the purée from the processor into a bowl, and then dd the garlic and parsley. Add Tabasco sauce and salt and ound black pepper to taste.

Spoon the mixture into a serving bowl and dust lightly with ayenne pepper. Chill until ready to serve.

Variation
Other canned beans can be used for this dip, for example butter (lima) beans or kidney beans. You can also use dried beans for a more cost-effective version, soaking them overnight and then cooking them as recommended on the packet. Allow the beans to cool before making the dip.

Feta and Roast Pepper Dip with Chillies

This is a familiar dish in Greece, called htipiti, often eaten as a snack with a glass of ouzo. Its Greek name means 'that which is beaten' and lemon and feta give it a lovely spicy flavour. If you chill the dip before serving the texture will be firmer.

Serves 4

1 yellow or green (bell) pepper
1–2 fresh green chillies
200g/7oz feta cheese, rinsed and cubed
60ml/4 tbsp extra virgin olive oil, plus extra for drizzling
juice of 1 lemon
45–60ml/3–4 tbsp milk
ground black pepper
finely chopped fresh flat leaf parsley, to garnish
slices of toast or toasted pitta bread, to serve

1 Scorch the pepper and chillies by threading them on to metal skewers and turning them over a flame or under the grill (broiler), until blackened and blistered all over.

2 Put the pepper and chillies into a plastic bag to loosen the skin and set aside until cool enough to handle.

3 Peel off as much of the skins as possible and wipe off the blackened parts with kitchen paper. Slit the pepper and chillies and discard the seeds and stems.

4 Put the pepper and chilli flesh into a food processor. Add the feta cheese, olive oil, lemon juice and milk, and blend well. Add a little more milk if the mixture is too stiff.

5 Season with black pepper, drizzle with olive oil, sprinkle a little fresh parsley over the top, and serve with slices of toast.

Variation
The dip is also excellent served with vegetable crudités, such as cauliflower, green or red (bell) pepper and celery.

annellini Bean Energy 314kcal/1317kJ; Protein 11.3g; Carbohydrate 32.7g, of which sugars 2.2g; Fat 16.3g, of which saturates 2.3g; Cholesterol 0mg; Calcium 50mg; Fibre 7.9g; Sodium 17mg
eta and Pepper Dip Energy 245Kcal/1,014kJ; Protein 8.7g; Carbohydrate 4.5g, of which sugars 4.3g; Fat 21.5g, of which saturates 8.6g; Cholesterol 36mg; Calcium 198mg; Fibre 0.8g; Sodium 727mg

Orange, Black Olive and Red Onion Salad

Thinly sliced oranges can be used to make unusual and refreshing salads. In this Spanish version, dating back to the times of the Moorish kingdoms, the oranges are partnered with thinly sliced red onions and black olives, and flavoured with those classic Middle Eastern flavourings: cumin seeds and fresh mint.

Serves 6

6 oranges
2 red onions
15ml/1 tbsp cumin seeds
5ml/1 tsp coarsely ground black pepper
15ml/1 tbsp chopped fresh mint
90ml/6 tbsp olive oil
salt, to taste
fresh mint sprigs and black olives, to garnish

1 Using a sharp knife, slice the oranges thinly, working over a bowl to catch any juice. Then, holding each orange slice in turn over the bowl, cut round the middle fleshy section with scissors to remove the peel and pith. Reserve the juice.

2 Slice the two red onions as thinly as possible and separate into individual rings.

3 Arrange the orange and onion slices in layers in a shallow dish, sprinkling each layer with cumin seeds, pepper, mint, olive oil and salt. Pour in the reserved orange juice. Leave to marinate in a cool place for about 2 hours.

4 Just before serving, sprinkle the oranges and onions with the mint sprigs and black olives.

Cook's Tip
It is important to let the salad stand before serving. This allows the flavours to develop and the pungent taste of the onion to soften slightly. Don't make it too far in advance, however, as the onions will lose their bite if left too long.

Mixed Salad with Capers

Colourful salads are a great start to a summer meal, and can be an enjoyably communal affair, with everyone helping themselves with a fork from a large serving bowl placed in the middle of the table.

Serves 4

4 large tomatoes
½ cucumber
1 bunch spring onions (scallions)
1 bunch watercress or rocket (arugula), washed
8 pimiento-stuffed olives
30ml/2 tbsp drained pickled capers

For the dressing
1 garlic clove, crushed
30ml/2 tbsp red wine vinegar
5ml/1 tsp paprika
2.5ml/½ tsp ground cumin
75ml/5 tbsp extra virgin olive oil
salt and ground black pepper

1 To peel the tomatoes, place them in a heatproof bowl, cover with boiling water and leave to stand for 1 minute.

2 Plunge the tomatoes into a bowl of cold water. Leave for 1 minute, then drain. Slip off the skins and dice the flesh finely. Put in a salad bowl.

3 Peel the cucumber, dice finely and add to the tomatoes. Trim and chop half the spring onions, and add to the bowl.

4 Toss the vegetables together, then break the watercress or rocket into sprigs. Add to the tomato mixture, with the olives and capers.

5 Make the dressing. Put the garlic in a bowl and mix in the vinegar and spices. Whisk in the oil and taste for seasoning. Pou the dressing over the salad, toss to mix, then garnish with the remaining spring onions.

Cook's Tip
This is a great way to use up jars of capers and olives in the refrigerator. Use baby gerkins or silverskin onions instead.

Orange Salad Energy 157kcal/652kJ; Protein 1.9g; Carbohydrate 12.8g, of which sugars 11.3g; Fat 11.3g, of which saturates 1.6g; Cholesterol 0mg; Calcium 70mg; Fibre 2.6g; Sodium 11mg
Mixed Salad with Capers Energy 162Kcal/670kJ; Protein 1.9g; Carbohydrate 4.3g, of which sugars 4.2g; Fat 15.4g, of which saturates 2.3g; Cholesterol 0mg; Calcium 49mg; Fibre 2g; Sodium 243mg

Watermelon and Feta Cheese Salad

This delicious dish combines the contrasting flavours and textures of sweet and juicy watermelon with salty feta cheese, resulting in a stunning salad that is perfect for the hot summer months.

Serves 4

4 large slices of watermelon, chilled
1 frisée lettuce, core removed
130g/4½oz feta cheese, preferably sheep's milk feta, rinsed, and cut into bitesize pieces
handful of lightly toasted pumpkin seeds
handful of sunflower seeds
10–15 black olives

For the dressing

30–45ml/2–3 tbsp extra virgin olive oil
juice of ½ lemon
5ml/1 tsp vinegar of choice, or to taste
sprinkling of fresh thyme
pinch of ground cumin

1 Pour the extra virgin olive oil, lemon juice and vinegar into a bowl or jug (pitcher).

2 Add the fresh thyme and ground cumin to the bowl, and whisk until well combined. Set the dressing aside until you are ready to serve the salad.

3 Cut the rind off the watermelon and remove as many seeds as possible. Cut the flesh into triangular-shaped chunks.

4 Put the lettuce leaves in a bowl, pour over the dressing and toss together to combine thoroughly.

5 Arrange the leaves on a serving dish or individual plates and add the watermelon, feta cheese, pumpkin and sunflower seeds and black olives. Serve the salad immediately.

Cook's Tip

Make sure you wait until watermelon is in season, so that you are making the most of the economical glut. Feta cheese is also a reasonably priced cheese, and a little goes a long way.

Vegetable Salad with Aioli Dressing

This colourful salad, often called Russian salad, contains a range of diced summer vegetables, including new potatoes, green beans, peas and red pepper, which are tossed in a pungent dressing.

Serves 4

8 new potatoes, washed and diced
1 large carrot, diced
115g/4oz fine green beans, cut into 2cm/¾in lengths
75g/3oz/¾ cup peas
½ red onion, chopped
4 baby gherkins, sliced
1 small red (bell) pepper, seeded and diced
50g/2oz/½ cup pitted black olives
15ml/1 tbsp drained capers
15ml/1 tbsp freshly squeezed lemon juice
30ml/2 tbsp chopped fresh parsley, to garnish

For the aioli

2 garlic cloves, finely chopped
150ml/¼ pint/⅔ cup mayonnaise, home-made or store-bought
salt and ground black pepper

1 Make the aioli. Crush the garlic with a pinch of salt in a mortar and whisk or stir into the mayonnaise.

2 Cook the potatoes and diced carrot in a pan of boiling lightly salted water for 5–8 minutes, until almost tender. Add the beans and peas to the pan and cook for 2 minutes, or until all the vegetables are tender. Drain well.

3 Transfer the vegetables into a large bowl. Add the onion, gherkins, red pepper, olives and capers. Stir in the aioli and season to taste with pepper and lemon juice.

4 Toss the vegetables and aioli together until well combined, check the seasoning and chill well. Serve garnished with parsley.

Variation

This delicious and colourful salad can be made using any combination of chopped, cooked vegetables, such as broad (fava) beans, courgette (zucchini), marrow (large zucchini), aubergine (eggplant) sweet potato or pumpkin.

Watermelon Salad Energy 256kcal/1066kJ; Protein 7.7g; Carbohydrate 12.9g, of which sugars 11.6g; Fat 19.7g, of which saturates 6.2g; Cholesterol 23mg; Calcium 165mg; Fibre 1.4g; Sodium 616mg
Vegetable Salad Energy 395kcal/1636kJ; Protein 5.2g; Carbohydrate 25.6g, of which sugars 8.1g; Fat 30.9g, of which saturates 4.8g; Cholesterol 28mg; Calcium 68mg; Fibre 4.9g; Sodium 472mg

Beetroot Salad with Oranges and Cinnamon

The combination of sweet beetroot, zesty orange and warm cinnamon is both unusual and delicious.

Serves 6

675g/1½lb beetroot (beet), steamed or boiled, then peeled
1 orange, peeled, pith and skin removed, and sliced
30ml/2 tbsp orange flower water
15ml/1 tbsp sugar
5ml/1 tsp ground cinnamon
salt and ground black pepper, to taste

1 Quarter the cooked beetroot, then slice the quarters. Arrange the beetroot on a plate with the orange slices or toss them together in a bowl.

2 Gently heat the orange flower water with the sugar, stir in the cinnamon and season to taste. Pour over the beetroot and orange salad and chill for at least 1 hour before serving.

Beetroot and Apple Salad

This is a pretty salad, in which the pieces of apple turn pink.

Serves 4

30ml/2 tbsp mayonnaise
30ml/2 tbsp natural (plain) yogurt
2 crisp eating apples
6 medium beetroot (beet), steamed or boiled, then peeled
handful chives, chopped
salt and ground black pepper, to taste
salad leaves, to serve

1 In a large bowl, stir together the mayonnaise and yogurt. Peel the apples, remove their cores and cut into small pieces.

2 Dice the peeled beetroot. Stir the apple, beetroot and two-thirds of the chives into the mayonnaise mixture. Season to taste with salt and pepper. Leave to stand for 10–20 minutes. Serve with salad leaves, garnished with the remaining chives.

Grated Beetroot Salad with Yogurt and Garlic

Beetroot is a wonderfully inexpensive root vegetable when in season. Its earthy flavour is perfectly balanced in this recipe by creamy yogurt and a hint of garlic in this stunning and simple salad. It is delicious served on its own with pitta bread, or as an accompaniment to grilled meat or chicken.

Serves 4

4 raw beetroot (beets), washed and trimmed
500g/1¼lb/2¼ cups thick and creamy natural (plain) yogurt
2 garlic cloves, crushed
a few fresh mint leaves, shredded, to garnish
salt and ground black pepper, to taste

1 Add the beetroot to a large pan of boiling water and cook fo 35–40 minutes until tender, but the flesh is not soft or mushy. Alternatively, roast the beetroot, uncut, in an oven you are using to bake another dish, so you save on the cost of fuel.

2 When cooked, if boiling, drain the beetroot in a sieve (strainer) and refresh immediately under cold running water to prevent it from cooking further.

3 Peel off the skins and grate the beetroot on to a plate. Squeeze it with your hands or press through a sieve to drain of excess water.

4 In a bowl, beat the yogurt with the garlic and season to taste with salt and pepper.

5 Add the beetroot, reserving a little to garnish the top, and mi well. Garnish with mint leaves.

Variation
You can use golden beetroot (beet) for this salad, if you wish. It has bright golden-yellow flesh and a sweeter flavour.

Beetroot Salad with Oranges Energy 58kcal/247kJ; Protein 2.2g; Carbohydrate 12.9g, of which sugars 12.2g; Fat 0.1g, of which saturates 0g; Cholesterol 0mg; Calcium 33mg; Fibre 2.5g; Sodium 75mg
Beetroot and Apple Salad Energy 191kcal/793kJ; Protein 4.1g; Carbohydrate 9.5g, of which sugars 8.8g; Fat 15.5g, of which saturates 1.6g; Cholesterol 0mg; Calcium 54mg; Fibre 2.7g; Sodium 58m
Grated Beetroot Salad Energy 95kcal/403kJ; Protein 7.8g; Carbohydrate 14.4g, of which sugars 13g; Fat 1.4g, of which saturates 0.6g; Cholesterol 2mg; Calcium 249mg; Fibre 1.3g; Sodium 137mg

Warm Leafy Salad with Soft Poached Eggs

ggs, chilli oil, hot crunchy roûtons and cool, crisp alad leaves make a lively and nusual combination. This elicious salad will provide n attractive first course or a ustaining lunch or supper, erved with bread.

erves 2

5ml/1½ tbsp chilli oil
1 slice wholegrain bread, crusts removed and cubed
2 eggs
115g/4oz mixed salad leaves
45ml/3 tbsp extra virgin olive oil
2 garlic cloves, crushed
15ml/1 tbsp balsamic vinegar or sherry vinegar
ground black pepper
50g/2oz grano padano cheese, shaved

Heat the chilli oil in a large, heavy frying pan. Add the cubes f bread and cook for 5 minutes, tossing the cubes occasionally, ntil they are crisp and golden. Remove from the pan and drain n a sheet of kitchen paper.

Bring a large pan of water to a gentle boil. Break each egg to a jug (pitcher) and slide it carefully into the water. Poach or 3–4 minutes.

Meanwhile, divide the salad leaves equally between two small erving plates. Sprinkle the croûtons over the mixed salad leaves.

Wipe the frying pan clean, then add the olive oil and heat ently. Add the crushed garlic and balsamic or sherry vinegar nd cook over high heat for about 1 minute, stirring or shaking e pan occasionally, until the aromas are released. Pour the arm dressing over the salad leaves and toss.

Remove the poached eggs from the pan with a slotted spoon, nd pat them dry on kitchen paper.

Place an egg on top of each plate, top with shavings of grano adano cheese. Season with salt and plenty of ground black epper, and serve immediately.

Gado Gado Salad

This Indonesian salad combines steamed vegetables and hard-boiled eggs with a richly flavoured peanut and soy sauce dressing.

Serves 6

225g/8oz new potatoes, scrubbed and halved
2 carrots, cut into sticks
115g/4oz green beans
½ small cauliflower, broken into florets
¼ firm white cabbage, shredded
200g/7oz bean or lentil sprouts
4 eggs, hard-boiled, shelled and quartered

For the sauce

90ml/6 tbsp crunchy peanut butter
300ml/½ pint/1¼ cups cold water
1 garlic clove, crushed
15ml/1 tbsp dry sherry
15ml/1 tbsp fresh lemon juice
5ml/1 tsp anchovy extract
30ml/2 tbsp dark soy sauce
10ml/2 tsp caster (superfine) sugar

1 Place the halved potatoes in a metal colander or steamer and set over a pan of gently boiling water. Cover the pan or steamer with a lid and cook the potatoes for 10 minutes.

2 Add the rest of the vegetables to the steamer and steam for a further 10 minutes, until tender.

3 Quickly douse the vegetables in cold running water to halt the cooking process, cool and arrange on a platter with the peeled egg quarters.

4 Beat together the peanut butter, water, garlic, sherry, lemon juice, anchovy extract, soy sauce and sugar in a large mixing bowl until smooth. Drizzle a little sauce over each portion then pour the rest into a small bowl and serve separately.

Cook's Tip

There is a range of nut butters available in health-food stores and supermarkets. Alternatively, you can make your own peanut butter by blending 225g/8oz/2 cups roasted peanuts with 120ml/4fl oz/½ cup oil in a food processor.

arm Leafy Salad Energy 697kcal/2907kJ; Protein 25.9g; Carbohydrate 41.3g, of which sugars 2.8g; Fat 49g, of which saturates 11.5g; Cholesterol 215mg; Calcium 408mg; Fibre 6.3g; Sodium 914mg
ado Gado Salad Energy 235kcal/979kJ; Protein 12.7g; Carbohydrate 18.3g, of which sugars 10.6g; Fat 12.5g, of which saturates 3.2g; Cholesterol 127mg; Calcium 91mg; Fibre 4.8g; Sodium 494mg

Fried Egg Salad

Chillies and eggs may seem unlikely partners, but they actually work very well together. The peppery flavour of the watercress complements the spicy eggs perfectly in this tasty, tangy and unusual salad. Serve with warmed flat bread.

Serves 2

1 garlic clove, thinly sliced
4 eggs
2 small fresh red chillies, seeded and thinly sliced
2 shallots, thinly sliced
½ small cucumber, finely diced
1cm/½in piece fresh root ginger, peeled and grated
juice of 2 limes
30ml/2 tbsp soy sauce
5ml/1 tsp caster (superfine) sugar
small bunch coriander (cilantro)
bunch watercress, coarsely chopped
15ml/1 tbsp groundnut (peanut) oil

1 Heat the oil in a frying pan. Add the garlic and cook over low heat until it starts to turn golden.

2 Crack the eggs into the frying pan. Break the yolks with a wooden spatula, then fry until the eggs are almost firm. Remove from the pan and set aside.

3 Add the sliced red chillies, shallots, cucumber and ginger into a large bowl. Toss the mixture to combine well.

4 In a separate bowl, whisk the lime juice with the soy sauce and sugar. Pour this dressing over the chilli, shallot and cucmber mixture, and toss lightly.

5 Set aside a few coriander sprigs for the garnish. Chop the rest of the coriander and add it to the salad. Toss all the ingredients again. Reserve a few watercress sprigs and arrange the remainder on to two plates.

6 Cut the fried eggs into slices and divide them between the watercress mounds.

7 Spoon the shallot mixture over the eggs and serve, garnished with the reserved coriander and watercress.

Aubergine Salad with Egg

This appetizing and unusual salad combines grilled aubergines, salty shrimp, hard-boiled eggs and sweet shallots with a zesty lime dressing and slivers of chilli.

Serves 4–6

2 aubergines (eggplants)
30ml/2 tbsp dried shrimp, soaked in warm water for 10 minutes
15ml/1 tbsp chopped garlic
1 hard-boiled egg, chopped
4 shallots, thinly sliced into rings
fresh coriander (cilantro) leaves and 2 fresh red chillies, seeded and sliced, to garnish

For the dressing

30ml/2 tbsp fresh lime juice
5ml/1 tsp light muscovado (brown) sugar
30ml/2 tbsp Thai fish sauce
15ml/1 tbsp vegetable oil

1 Preheat the grill (broiler) to medium. Prick the aubergines several times arrange on a baking sheet, and cook under the grill for 30–40 minutes, until charred and tender. Remove the aubergines and set aside until they are cool enough to handle.

2 Meanwhile, make the dressing. Put the lime juice, muscovado sugar and fish sauce into a small bowl. Whisk, then cover with clear film (plastic wrap) and set aside until required.

3 When the aubergines are cool enough to handle, peel off the skin and cut the flesh into medium slices.

4 Heat the oil in a small frying pan. Drain the dried shrimp and add to the pan with the garlic. Cook over medium heat for 3 minutes, until golden. Remove from the pan and set aside.

5 Arrange the aubergine slices on a serving dish. Top with the hard-boiled egg, shallots and dried shrimp mixture. Drizzle over the dressing and garnish with the coriander and red chillies.

Variation
For a special occasion, use salted duck's or quail's eggs, cut in half, instead of hen's eggs.

Fried Egg Salad Energy 235kcal/977kJ; Protein 14.8g; Carbohydrate 6.4g, of which sugars 5.6g; Fat 17.2g, of which saturates 3.9g; Cholesterol 381mg; Calcium 154mg; Fibre 1.2g; Sodium 1234mg
Aubergine Salad with Egg Energy 58kcal/242kJ; Protein 4.6g; Carbohydrate 3.1g, of which sugars 2.8g; Fat 3.2g, of which saturates 0.6g; Cholesterol 57mg; Calcium 74mg; Fibre 1.5g; Sodium 230mg

Spiced Aubergine Salad with Yogurt and Parsley

The delicate flavours of aubergine, tomatoes and cucumber are lightly spiced with cumin and coriander in this fresh-tasting salad, with a Middle Eastern flavour. Make the salad in the summer, when the vegetables are at their seasonal best, and serve with fresh flat bread.

Serves 4

2 small aubergines (eggplants), thickly sliced
75ml/5 tbsp extra virgin olive oil
50ml/2fl oz/¼ cup red wine vinegar
2 garlic cloves, crushed
15ml/1 tbsp lemon juice
2.5ml/½ tsp ground cumin
2.5ml/½ tsp ground coriander
½ cucumber, thinly sliced
2 well-flavoured tomatoes, thinly sliced
30ml/2 tbsp natural (plain) yogurt
salt and ground black pepper
chopped fresh flat leaf parsley, to garnish

1 Preheat the grill (broiler). Lightly brush the aubergine slices on with oil and cook them under high heat, turning once, until they are golden and tender. Alternatively, cook them on a griddle pan.

2 When they are done, remove the aubergine slices to a chopping board and cut them into quarters.

3 Mix together the remaining oil, the vinegar, garlic, lemon juice, cumin and coriander in a small bowl. Season with salt and pepper to taste and whisk thoroughly.

4 Add the warm aubergines to the bowl of dressing, stir well, leave to cool and then chill for at least 2 hours so that all the flavours penetrate the aubergine.

5 Remove the aubergine from the refrigerator and add the sliced cucumber and tomatoes.

6 Pile the salad on to a large serving dish and spoon the yogurt over the top. Sprinkle with chopped parsley and serve with warm or toasted flat bread.

Roasted Shallot and Squash Salad with Feta

This sustaining salad combines sweet chunks of squash and roasted shallots with salty feta cheese and spicy red chillies. It is especially good for lunch or a picnic, served with plenty of crusty bread to mop up the juices.

Serves 4–6

75ml/5 tbsp olive oil
15ml/1 tbsp balsamic vinegar, plus a little extra, if you like
15ml/1 tbsp sweet soy sauce
350g/12oz shallots, peeled but left whole
3 fresh red chillies
1 butternut squash, peeled, seeded and cut into chunks
5ml/1 tsp finely chopped fresh thyme
15g/½oz flat leaf parsley
1 small garlic clove, finely chopped
75g/3oz/¾ cup walnuts, roughly chopped
150g/5oz feta cheese
salt and ground black pepper

1 Preheat the oven to 200°C/400°F/Gas 6. Beat the olive oil, balsamic vinegar and soy sauce together in a large bowl, then season to taste with a little salt and plenty of black pepper.

2 Toss the shallots and two of the chillies in the oil mixture and transfer into a large roasting pan or ovenproof dish. Roast in the oven for 15 minutes, stirring once or twice.

3 Add the squash and roast for a further 30–35 minutes, stirring once, until the squash is tender and browned. Remove from the oven, stir in the thyme and leave to cool.

4 Chop the parsley and garlic together and mix with the walnuts. Seed and finely chop the remaining chilli.

5 Stir the parsley, garlic and walnut mixture into the vegetables. Add chopped chilli to taste and adjust the seasoning, adding a little extra balsamic vinegar, if you like.

6 Crumble the feta into small pieces, and add to the salad. Transfer to a serving dish and serve immediately.

Spiced Aubergine Salad Energy 155kcal/642kJ; Protein 1.9g; Carbohydrate 4.9g, of which sugars 4.7g; Fat 14.4g, of which saturates 2.2g; Cholesterol 0mg; Calcium 35mg; Fibre 2.7g; Sodium 14mg
Roasted Shallot and Squash Salad Energy 275kcal/1136kJ; Protein 7.7g; Carbohydrate 9.3g, of which sugars 7g; Fat 23.2g, of which saturates 5.6g; Cholesterol 18mg; Calcium 165mg; Fibre 2.9g; Sodium 541mg

Hot and Sour Noodle Salad

Noodles are very economical when bought dried, and they make the perfect basis for a salad, adding bulk to the meal, and absorbing the dressing and providing a contrast in texture to the crisp vegetables. Here, they are served with a piquant sauce made from chillies, lime juice and soy sauce.

Serves 2

200g/7oz thin rice noodles
small bunch fresh coriander (cilantro)
2 tomatoes, seeded and sliced
130g/4½oz baby corn cobs, sliced lengthways
4 spring onions (scallions), thinly sliced
1 red (bell) pepper, seeded and finely chopped
juice of 2 limes
2 small fresh green chillies, seeded and finely chopped
10ml/2 tsp sugar
115g/4oz/1 cup peanuts, toasted and chopped
30ml/2 tbsp soy sauce
salt, to taste

1 Bring a large pan of lightly salted water to the boil. Snap the rice noodles into short lengths, add to the pan and cook for 3–4 minutes. Drain, then rinse under cold water and drain again.

2 Set aside a few coriander leaves for the garnish. Chop the remaining leaves and place them in a large serving bowl.

3 Add the noodles to the bowl, with the tomato slices, corn cobs, spring onions, red pepper, lime juice, chillies, sugar and toasted peanuts. Season with the soy sauce, then taste and add a little salt if you think the mixture needs it.

4 Toss the salad lightly but thoroughly, then garnish with the reserved coriander leaves and serve immediately.

Cook's Tip

Thin rice noodles are very delicate, if you prefer a more substantial meal, use the same amount of egg noodles – or use if they're what you have in the storecupboard.

Fried Tofu Salad

Tofu is extremely nutritious and is ideal for use in salads made with strong flavours, such as spring onions, coriander, garlic and chilli. This delicious Asian version can be served on its own or with stir-fried noodles.

Serves 4

450g/1lb firm rectangular tofu, rinsed, patted dry and cut into rectangular blocks
1 small cucumber, partially peeled in strips, seeded and shredded
2 spring onions (scallions), trimmed, halved and shredded
2 handfuls of fresh beansprouts rinsed and drained
fresh coriander (cilantro) leaves (optional), to garnish

For the sauce

30ml/2 tbsp tamarind pulp, soaked in water until soft
vegetable oil, for deep-frying
4 shallots, finely chopped
4 garlic cloves, chopped
2 red chillies, seeded
2.5ml/½ tsp shrimp paste
115g/4oz/1 cup roasted peanuts, crushed
30–45ml/2–3 tbsp kecap manis, or soy sauce mixed with 2.5ml/½ tsp brown sugar
15ml/1 tbsp sesame or groundnut (peanut) oil
15ml/1 tbsp tomato ketchup

1 First make the sauce. Squeeze the tamarind pulp to soften it in the water, and then strain through a sieve (strainer). Measure out 120ml/4fl oz/½ cup tamarind pulp.

2 Heat the oil in a wok or heavy pan, add the shallots, garlic and chillies, and cook until fragrant. Stir in the shrimp paste and the peanuts, and cook until they emit a nutty aroma.

3 Add the kecap manis, sesame or groundnut oil, tomato ketchup and tamarind pulp and blend to form a thick sauce. Set aside and leave to cool.

4 Heat enough oil for deep-frying to 180°C/350°F in a wok or heavy pan. Slip in the blocks of tofu and fry until golden brown all over. Pat dry on kitchen paper and cut each block into slices.

5 Arrange on a plate with the cucumber, spring onions and beansprouts. Drizzle over the sauce and garnish with coriander.

Hot and Sour Noodle Salad Energy 783kcal/3269kJ; Protein 24.7g; Carbohydrate 106.4g, of which sugars 20.4g; Fat 27.9g, of which saturates 5.2g; Cholesterol 0mg; Calcium 129mg; Fibre 8.5g; Sodium 1845mg
Fried Tofu Salad Energy 423kcal/1749kJ; Protein 17.9g; Carbohydrate 7.8g, of which sugars 4.5g; Fat 35.8g, of which saturates 5.3g; Cholesterol 0mg; Calcium 607mg; Fibre 2.8g; Sodium 296mg

Grilled Aubergine, Mint and Couscous Salad

Packets of flavoured couscous are available in most supermarkets – you can use whichever you like, but garlic and coriander is particularly good for this recipe. If you already have a bag of plain couscous in the kitchen, however, use that. One of the secrets of budget cooking is to utilize and adapt the ingredients you already have. Serve with a crisp green salad.

Serves 2

1 large aubergine (eggplant)
30ml/2 tbsp olive oil
110g/4oz packet flavoured, or plain (see Cook's Tip below) couscous
30ml/2 tbsp fresh mint, roughly chopped
½ lemon
salt and ground black pepper, to taste

1 Preheat the grill (broiler) to high. Cut the aubergine into large chunky pieces and toss them with the olive oil.

2 Season with salt and pepper to taste and spread the aubergine pieces on a non-stick baking sheet.

3 Grill the aubergine pieces for 5–6 minutes, turning occasionally, until they are golden brown.

4 Meanwhile, prepare the couscous according to the instructions on the packet.

5 Stir the grilled aubergine and chopped mint into the couscous, squeeze over some lemon juice, toss thoroughly and serve immediately with a crisp green salad.

Cook's Tip
If using a plain, unflavoured couscous, add a knob of butter and some salt and pepper to the water when soaking.

Quinoa Salad with Zesty Citrus Dressing

Quinoa is quick to prepare and reasonably priced. It is packed with protein and is also gluten free, making it ideal for those with intolerances. Here it is combined with strong flavours, including chilli and citrus juice.

Serves 6

175g/6oz/1 cup quinoa
90ml/6 tbsp olive oil
juice of 2 limes
juice of 1 large orange
2 fresh green chillies, seeded and finely chopped
2 garlic cloves, crushed
½ cucumber, peeled
1 large tomato, seeded and cubed
4 spring onions (scallions), thinly sliced
30ml/2 tbsp chopped fresh mint
15ml/1 tbsp chopped fresh flat leaf parsley
salt, to taste

1 Put the quinoa in a sieve (strainer), rinse thoroughly under cold water, then transfer into a large pan. Pour in enough cold water to cover and bring to the boil.

2 Lower the heat and simmer the quinoa for 10–12 minutes, until tender. Drain and leave to cool.

3 Make a dressing by whisking the oil with the citrus juices. Stir in the chillies and garlic and season with salt to taste.

4 Cut the cucumber in half lengthways and scoop out and discard the seeds. Cut into 5mm/¼in slices and toss with the quinoa with the tomato, spring onions, fresh mint and parsley.

5 Pour the dressing over the salad and toss again until well mixed. Check the seasoning and serve.

Variation
Quinoa comes in white, red and black varieties, you can use any for this recipe. Couscous makes a good substitute.

Grilled Aubergine Salad Energy 251kcal/1044kJ; Protein 4.8g; Carbohydrate 32.5g, of which sugars 2g; Fat 12.1g, of which saturates 1.7g; Cholesterol 0mg; Calcium 53mg; Fibre 2g; Sodium 5mg
Quinoa Salad Energy 213kcal/885kJ; Protein 3.4g; Carbohydrate 24.3g, of which sugars 2g; Fat 11.6g, of which saturates 1.6g; Cholesterol 0mg; Calcium 26mg; Fibre 0.5g; Sodium 5mg

Simple Rice Salad

Sometimes called confetti salad, this stunning dish features brightly coloured chopped vegetables served in a well-flavoured dressing. It makes an ideal budget lunch at home or at a picnic.

Serves 6

275g/10oz/1½ cups long grain rice
75ml/5 tbsp mixed olive oil and extra virgin olive oil
15ml/1 tbsp sherry vinegar
5ml/1 tsp strong Dijon mustard
1 bunch spring onions (scallions), finely sliced
1 green (bell) pepper, seeded and finely diced
1 yellow (bell) pepper, seeded and finely diced
225g/8oz tomatoes, peeled, seeded and chopped
30ml/2 tbsp chopped fresh flat leaf parsley or fresh coriander (cilantro)
salt and ground black pepper

1 Cook the long grain rice in a large pan of lightly salted boiling water for about 10–12 minutes, until just tender. Be careful not to overcook it.

2 Drain the rice in a sieve (strainer), rinse thoroughly under cold running water and drain again. Leave the rice to cool.

3 Make the dressing by whisking together the olive oil, sherry vinegar and mustard in a small bowl.

4 Transfer the rice to a large bowl, add half the dressing, stir to moisten the rice, then leave to cool further.

5 Add the spring onions, peppers, tomatoes and parsley or coriander with the remaining dressing, and toss well to mix. Season with salt and pepper to taste.

Cook's Tip
To peel the tomatoes, place them in a heatproof bowl, cover with boiling water and leave to stand for 1 minute. Plunge into a bowl of cold water. Leave for 1 minute, then drain. Slip off the skins, then slice them in half, scoop out the seeds and dice.

Thai Rice Salad

This recipe is infinitely adaptable, as you can use whatever fruit, vegetables and even left-over meat that you might have. Simply mix with cooked rice and pour over the fragrant dressing, for a sustantial salad.

Serves 4–6

350g/12oz/3 cups cooked rice
1 Asian pear, cored and diced
50g/2oz dried shrimp, chopped
1 avocado, peeled, stoned (pitted) and diced, tossed in a little lemon juice to prevent browning
½ medium cucumber, finely diced
2 lemon grass stalks, finely chopped
1 fresh green or red chilli, seeded and finely sliced
115g/4oz/1 cup flaked (sliced) almonds, toasted
small bunch fresh coriander (cilantro), chopped
fresh Thai sweet basil leaves, torn, to garnish

For the dressing
300ml/½ pint/1¼ cups water
10ml/2 tsp shrimp paste
15ml/1 tbsp light muscovado (brown) sugar
2 kaffir lime leaves, torn into small pieces
½ lemon grass stalk, sliced or well bruised
30ml/2 tbsp sweet chilli sauce

1 First, make the dressing, put the measured water in a small pan together with the shrimp paste, sugar, kaffir lime leaves and lemon grass.

2 Heat gently, stirring, until the sugar dissolves, then bring to boiling point and simmer for 5 minutes. Strain into a bowl and set aside until cold.

3 Put the cooked rice in a large salad bowl and fluff up the grains with a fork. Add the diced Asian pear, chopped dried shrimp, diced avocado and cucumber, lemon grass and sweet chilli sauce. Mix well.

4 Add the sliced green or red chilli, almonds and coriander to the bowl and toss well to combine.

5 Garnish with the torn Thai basil leaves and serve with the bowl of dressing to spoon over the top of individual portions.

Simple Rice Salad Energy 276kcal/1150kJ; Protein 4.6g; Carbohydrate 41.9g, of which sugars 5.2g; Fat 9.9g, of which saturates 1.4g; Cholesterol 0mg; Calcium 29mg; Fibre 1.7g; Sodium 8mg
Thai Rice Salad Energy 125kcal/523kJ; Protein 2.6g; Carbohydrate 20.9g, of which sugars 1.4g; Fat 4.1g, of which saturates 0.6g; Cholesterol 0mg; Calcium 38mg; Fibre 1.3g; Sodium 7mg

ulgur Salad

his Turkish meze dish of ulgur and tomato is easy to ake and very tasty. Packed ith fresh mint and parsley, it both filling and refreshing. is good served at room mperature as part of a uffet or barbecue spread, ith lemon wedges.

erves 4–6

75g/6oz/1 cup bulgur wheat, rinsed and drained
5–60ml/3–4 tbsp olive oil
juice of 1–2 lemons
30ml/2 tbsp tomato purée (paste)
10ml/2 tsp sugar
2 small red onions, cut in half lengthways, in half again crossways, and sliced
10ml/2 tsp Turkish red pepper, or 1–2 fresh red chillies, seeded and finely chopped
1 bunch each of fresh mint and flat leaf parsley, finely chopped
salt and ground black pepper
a few fresh mint and parsley leaves, to garnish

Put the drained bulgur wheat into a wide bowl, pour over ough boiling water to cover it by about 2.5cm/1in, and give it quick stir.

Cover the bowl with a plate or pan lid and leave the bulgur steam for about 25 minutes, until it has soaked up the water d doubled in quantity.

Pour the oil and lemon juice over the bulgur and toss to mix, en add the tomato purée and toss the mixture again until the lgur is well coated.

Add the sugar, onion, Turkish red pepper or chillies, and the erbs. Season with salt and pepper. Serve at room temperature, rnished with a little mint and parsley.

Cook's Tip
This salad should be light and lemony, packed full of the refreshing flavours of parsley and mint, with a slight tang of chilli, so be liberal with these ingredients. The sugar intensifies the tomato flavour of the purée.

Tabbouleh

This is a wonderfully refreshing, tangy salad of soaked bulgur wheat and masses of fresh mint, parsley and spring onions. Serve as an appetizer or an accompaniment to a main course of grilled meat.

Serves 4–6

250g/9oz/1½ cups bulgur wheat
1 large bunch spring onions (scallions), thinly sliced
1 cucumber, finely diced
3 tomatoes, chopped
1.5–2.5ml/¼–½ tsp ground cumin
1 bunch fresh parsley, chopped
1 large bunch fresh mint, chopped
juice of 2 lemons, or to taste
30ml/2 tbsp extra virgin olive oil
salt, to taste
6 olives, lemon wedges, tomato wedges, cucumber slices and mint sprigs, to garnish (optional)
cos or romaine lettuce and natural (plain) yogurt, to serve (optional)

1 Place the bulgur wheat in a bowl, cover with cold water and leave to soak for about 30 minutes.

2 Transfer the bulgur wheat into a sieve (strainer) and drain, shaking to remove any excess water, then return it to the bowl.

3 Add the spring onions to the bulgur wheat, then mix and squeeze together with your hands to combine.

4 Add the cucumber, tomatoes, cumin, parsley, mint, lemon juice, oil and salt to the bulgur wheat and toss to combine.

5 Heap the tabbouleh on to a bed of lettuce on a serving platter or large bowl and garnish with the olives, lemon wedges, tomato wedges, cucumber and mint sprigs. Serve with a bowl of natural yogurt, if you like.

Variations
• You can use couscous soaked in boiling water in place of the bulgur wheat, if you prefer.
• Using chopped fresh coriander (cilantro) instead of the parsley will give the salad a zesty citrus flavour.

lgur Salad Energy 149kcal/620kJ; Protein 3g; Carbohydrate 21.6g, of which sugars 5.4g; Fat 6.1g, of which saturates 0.8g; Cholesterol 0mg; Calcium 54mg; Fibre 1.7g; Sodium 19mg
bbouleh Energy 232kcal/965kJ; Protein 5.2g; Carbohydrate 34.6g, of which sugars 2.7g; Fat 8.4g, of which saturates 1.1g; Cholesterol 0mg; Calcium 51mg; Fibre 1.4g; Sodium 12mg

White Bean and Tomato Salad

Tender white beans are delicious served in a spicy sauce with the bite of fresh, crunchy green pepper. Using canned beans means that the salad is very quick and easy to make. Satisfying and economical, the salad is perfect for eating with pitta bread for lunch or at a picnic. Make sure the canned beans are tender, and, if not, cook them in unsalted boiling water for 5–10 minutes before making the salad.

Serves 4

750g/1lb 10oz tomatoes
1 onion
½–1 mild fresh chilli
1 green (bell) pepper
4 garlic cloves
pinch of sugar
400g/14oz can cannellini beans, drained
45–60ml/3–4 tbsp olive oil
grated rind and juice of 1 lemon
15ml/1 tbsp white wine vinegar
salt and ground black pepper
chopped fresh parsley, to garnish
pitta bread, to serve

1 Finely chop the tomatoes, onion, mild chilli, green pepper and garlic cloves, then place in a large bowl.

2 Add the sugar, and mix. Rinse the drained cannellini beans and add to the bowl, together with salt and plenty of ground black pepper. Toss together until everything is well combined.

3 Add the olive oil, grated lemon rind, lemon juice and vinegar to the salad and toss lightly to combine.

4 For the best flavour, cover the bowl with clear film (plastic wrap) and chill in the refrigerator for at least an hour, to allow the flavours to mingle and intensify. Cut the pitta bread into wedges, and lightly toast.

5 Garnish the salad with fresh parsley and serve immediately accompanied by wedges of pitta bread.

Variation
Use fresh coriander (cilantro) instead of parsley if you prefer.

Bean Salad with Red Onion, Eggs, Olives and Anchovies

Colourful, good value for money and packed with flavour, this versatile salad can be made with a wide range of beans – whatever you have in your kitchen. It makes a nutritious snack or light meal when served with crusty bread, or as an accompaniment to roasted meat or fried fish.

Serves 4

225g/8oz/1¼ cups dried haricot (navy), soya or black-eyed beans (peas), soaked overnight
1 red onion, cut in half lengthways, in half again crossways, and sliced along the grain
45–60ml/3–4 tbsp black olives, drained
1 bunch of fresh flat leaf parsley, roughly chopped
60ml/4 tbsp olive oil
juice of 1 lemon
3–4 eggs, boiled until just firm, shelled and quartered
12 canned or bottled anchovy fillets, rinsed and drained
salt and ground black pepper
lemon wedges, to serve

1 Drain the beans, place them into a pan and fill the pan with plenty of cold water. Bring to the boil and boil for 1 minute, then lower the heat and partially cover the pan.

2 Simmer the beans for about 45 minutes, until they are cooked but still firm – they should have a bite to them, and not be too soft and mushy.

3 Drain the beans, rinse well under cold running water and remove any loose skins.

4 Mix the beans in a wide shallow bowl with the red onion slices, olives and most of the parsley. Add in the oil and lemon juice, and mix well to combine. Season to taste with salt and ground black pepper.

5 Place the eggs and anchovy fillets on top of the salad and sprinkle with the remaining parsley. Serve with lemon wedges for squeezing over the salad.

White Bean and Tomato Energy 226kcal/947kJ; Protein 8.8g; Carbohydrate 27.6g, of which sugars 12.9g; Fat 9.6g, of which saturates 1.5g; Cholesterol 0mg; Calcium 92mg; Fibre 9g; Sodium 409mg
Bean Salad Energy 402kcal/1674kJ; Protein 28g; Carbohydrate 10.4g, of which sugars 4.2g; Fat 28g, of which saturates 4.4g; Cholesterol 149mg; Calcium 221mg; Fibre 10g; Sodium 696mg

Narm Black-eyed Bean Salad with Rocket and Black Olives

'his is an easy dish, as black-
yed beans do not need to
e soaked overnight. By
dding spring onions and dill,
: is transformed into a
efreshing and healthy meal.
: can be served hot or cold.

erves 4
75g/10oz/1½ cups black-eyed beans (peas)
50ml/¼ pint/⅔ cup extra virgin olive oil
5 spring onions (scallions), sliced into rounds
a large handful of fresh rocket (arugula) leaves, chopped if large
45–60ml/3–4 tbsp chopped fresh dill
juice of 1 lemon, or to taste
10–12 black olives
salt and ground black pepper, to taste
small cos or romaine lettuce leaves, to serve

Thoroughly rinse the beans and drain them well. Transfer into pan and pour in cold water to just about cover them. Slowly ring to the boil over low heat. As soon as the water is boiling, emove from the heat and drain immediately.

. Put the beans back in the pan with fresh cold water to cover nd add a pinch of salt – this will make their skins harder and top them from disintegrating when they are cooked.

Bring the beans to the boil over medium heat, then lower the eat and cook them until they are soft but not mushy. They will ake 20–30 minutes only, so keep an eye on them.

Drain the beans, reserving 75–90ml/5–6 tbsp of the cooking quid. Transfer the beans into a large salad bowl.

Immediately add the remaining ingredients, including the eserved liquid, and mix well, if dressed warm, the beans take up nore of the dressing and the salad has much more flavour.

Serve immediately, piled on the lettuce leaves, or leave to cool ghtly and serve later.

Lentil and Spinach Salad

This earthy and sustaining salad combines Puy lentils with onions, bay, thyme, parsley and cumin in a tangy mustard, garlic and lemon dressing.

Serves 6
225g/8oz/1 cup Puy lentils
1 fresh bay leaf
1 celery stick
fresh thyme sprig
1 onion or 3–4 shallots, finely chopped
10ml/2 tsp crushed toasted cumin seeds
400g/14oz young spinach
30–45ml/2–3 tbsp chopped fresh parsley
toasted baguette, to serve

For the dressing
105ml/7 tbsp olive oil
5ml/1 tsp Dijon mustard
15–25ml/1–1½ tbsp red wine vinegar
1 small garlic clove, finely chopped
2.5ml/½ tsp finely grated lemon rind
salt and ground black pepper, to taste

1 Rinse the lentils and place them in a large pan. Add enough water to cover. Tie the bay leaf, celery and thyme into a bundle and add to the pan, then bring to the boil. Reduce the heat and cook the lentils for 30–45 minutes, or until just tender.

2 Meanwhile, to make the dressing, mix 75ml/5 tbsp of the olive oil, the mustard and 15ml/1 tbsp red wine vinegar with the garlic and lemon rind, and season well with salt and pepper.

3 Thoroughly drain the lentils and turn them into a bowl. Add most of the dressing and toss well, then set the lentils aside.

4 Heat the remaining olive oil in a deep frying pan and sauté the onion or shallots over low heat for 4–5 minutes, then add the cumin and cook for a further 1 minute. Add the spinach and season to taste with salt and pepper, then cover and cook until wilted. Stir the spinach into the lentils and leave to cool.

5 Stir in the remaining dressing and chopped parsley. Adjust the seasoning, and add extra red wine vinegar, if necessary. Transfer the salad to a serving dish and serve with toasted baguette.

arm Black-eyed Bean Salad Energy 434kcal/1,811kJ; Protein 16.6g; Carbohydrate 31.4g, of which sugars 2.7g; Fat 27.8g, of which saturates 4g; Cholesterol 0mg; Calcium 149mg; Fibre 12.5g; Sodium 334mg
ntil and Spinach Salad Energy 248kcal/1037kJ; Protein 11.2g; Carbohydrate 20.3g, of which sugars 2.1g; Fat 14.1g, of which saturates 2g; Cholesterol 0mg; Calcium 150mg; Fibre 5.1g; Sodium 102mg

Summer Pasta Salad

Ripe tomatoes, creamy mozzarella and juicy olives make a good base for a fresh pasta salad that is perfect for a light summer lunch.

Serves 4

350g/12oz/3 cups dried penne
150g/5oz packet buffalo mozzarella, drained and diced
3 ripe tomatoes, diced
10 pitted black olives, sliced
10 pitted green olives, sliced
1 spring onion (scallion), thinly sliced on the diagonal
1 handful fresh basil leaves
salt and ground black pepper, to taste

For the dressing

90ml/6 tbsp olive oil
15ml/1 tbsp balsamic vinegar or lemon juice

1 Cook the pasta for 10–12 minutes, or according to the instructions on the packet. Transfer it into a colander and rinse briefly under cold running water, then shake the colander to remove as much water as possible and leave to drain.

2 Make the dressing. Whisk the olive oil and balsamic vinegar or lemon juice in a jug (pitcher) with a little salt and ground black pepper to taste.

3 Place the pasta, mozzarella, tomatoes, olives and spring onion in a large bowl, pour the dressing over and toss together well. Taste for seasoning before serving, sprinkled with basil leaves.

Variations

- *For a tuna and corn salad, omit the mozzarella and olives, and at step 3 stir 175g/6oz can tuna in olive oil in to the cooked pasta, flaking with a fork to break up the chunks. Then stir in a 175g/6oz can corn.*
- *For roasted cherry and tomato rocket salad arrange 225g/8oz cherry tomatoes in a roasting pan, sprinkle with olive oil, slivers of garlic, salt and a pinch of sugar, and roast in the oven at 190°c/375°F/Gas 5 for 20 minutes. Mix the tomatoes into the pasta, together with 2 handfuls of rocket.*

Country Pasta Salad

Colourful, tasty and nutritious, this is the ideal all-in-one dish pasta salad for a summer picnic or an al fresco lunch. This salad will keep for up to 2 hours in the refrigerator, if you wish to make in advance.

Serves 6

300g/11oz/2¾ cups dried fusilli
150g/5oz fine green beans
1 potato, cooked in salted water, cooled and diced
200g/7oz cherry tomatoes
2 spring onions (scallions)
90g/3½oz/scant 1¼ cups grano padano cheese, shaved
6–8 pitted black olives, cut into rings
15–30ml/1–2 tbsp capers
salt and ground black pepper, to taste

For the dressing

90ml/6 tbsp extra virgin olive oil
15ml/1 tbsp balsamic vinegar
15ml/1 tbsp chopped fresh flat leaf parsley

1 Cook the pasta according to the instructions on the packet. When tender, but still with a little bite, drain it into a colander, rinse under cold running water until cold, then shake the colander to remove as much water as possible. Leave to drain and dry.

2 Trim the green beans and cut them into 5cm/2in lengths, and place in a pan of boiling water for about 5–6 minutes or steam for 8–10 minutes, until cooked through but still retaining a little bite. Drain the beans, refresh under running cold water, and leave to cool.

3 To make the dressing, put the olive oil, balsamic vinegar and parsley in a large bowl with a little salt and ground black peppe to taste and whisk well to mix.

4 Halve the tomatoes, finely chop the spring onions, and add tc the dressing with the grano padano, olive rings and capers.

5 Stir in the cold pasta, beans and potato. Toss well to mix. Cover and leave to stand for about 30 minutes. Taste for seasoning before serving.

Summer Pasta Salad Energy 577kcal/2420kJ; Protein 18.2g; Carbohydrate 67.2g, of which sugars 5.3g; Fat 28g, of which saturates 8.1g; Cholesterol 22mg; Calcium 175mg; Fibre 3.9g; Sodium 580r
Country Pasta Salad Energy 381kcal/1600kJ; Protein 13.3g; Carbohydrate 44.4g, of which sugars 3.8g; Fat 18g, of which saturates 5g; Cholesterol 15mg; Calcium 212mg; Fibre 2.9g; Sodium 341mg

ʼasta Salad with Salami

his pasta dish, enlivened ,ith tasty salami and .oquefort cheese, is easy to nake and would be perfect ɔr a picnic or packed lunch. ake the dressing and salad ,aves separately and mix ɔgether at the last moment r the leaves will wilt.

erves 4
25g/8oz pasta twists
75g/10oz jar charcoal-roasted peppers in oil
115g/4oz/1 cup pitted black olives
4 drained sun-dried tomatoes in oil, quartered
115g/4oz Roquefort cheese, crumbled
10 slices peppered salami, cut into strips
115g/4oz packet mixed leaf salad
30ml/2 tbsp white wine vinegar
30ml/2 tbsp chopped fresh oregano
2 garlic cloves, crushed
salt and ground black pepper, to taste

Cook the pasta in a large pan of lightly salted boiling water ɔr 12 minutes, or according to the instructions on the packet, ntil tender but not soft. Drain thoroughly and rinse with cold ater, then drain again.

Drain the peppers and reserve 60ml/4 tbsp of the oil for the essing. Cut the peppers into long, fine strips and mix them ith the olives, sun-dried tomatoes and Roquefort cheese in a rge bowl. Add the pasta and peppered salami to the bowl and ɔss well to combine the ingredients.

Divide the salad leaves among four individual bowls and ɔoon the pasta salad on top. Whisk the reserved oil with the negar, oregano, garlic and seasoning to taste. Spoon this essing over the salad and serve immediately.

Variation
This salad makes a little salami and cheese go a long way, but If Roquefort cheese is a little outside your budget, try making this salad with the very economical feta cheese instead, and reducing the amount to 75g/2oz.

Tangy Fish Salad

Flakes of white fish are deep-fried until crispy and make a wonderful topping for this refreshing main course salad. The combination of crispy, crunchy textures and fragrant, spicy flavours is unbeatable. Choose the fish depending on your budget.

Serves 4
250g/9oz white fish fillet, skinned
sunflower oil, for frying
1 cucumber, seeded and thinly sliced
2 plum tomatoes, seeded and diced
1 red onion, halved and thinly sliced
1 bunch fresh coriander (cilantro) leaves
1 bunch fresh mint leaves
45ml/3 tbsp roasted peanuts, chopped

For the dressing
30ml/2 tbsp sweet chilli sauce
30ml/2 tbsp Thai fish sauce
juice of 2 limes
15ml/1 tbsp soft light brown sugar

1 Place the fish in a wok or heavy pan and cover with cold water. Place over a medium heat and bring to the boil. Reduce the heat and cook gently for 6–8 minutes, or until the fish is cooked.

2 Carefully remove the fish from the wok or pan and pat dry on kitchen paper. Break up the flesh into large flakes. Place in a food processor or blender and pulse until the mixture resembles coarse breadcrumbs.

3 Fill a wok or pan one-third full with oil and heat to 180°C/350°F (or until a cube of bread, dropped into the oil, browns in about 15 seconds). Working in batches, deep-fry the fish mixture for 1–2 minutes until browned and crispy. Drain well and then set aside.

4 Place the sliced cucumber, tomatoes, red onion and herbs in a bowl and toss to combine.

5 Mix together the sweet chilli sauce, fish sauce, lime juice and sugar and pour this over the salad. Sprinkle over the deep-fried fish and chopped peanuts. Serve immediately.

ısta Salad Energy 429kcal/1797kJ; Protein 17.8g; Carbohydrate 46.7g, of which sugars 6.6g; Fat 20.3g, of which saturates 8.9g; Cholesterol 37mg; Calcium 188mg; Fibre 3.9g; Sodium 1341mg
ngy Fish Salad Energy 252kcal/1050kJ; Protein 17.9g; Carbohydrate 11.9g, of which sugars 10.6g; Fat 15g, of which saturates 2.2g; Cholesterol 22mg; Calcium 70mg; Fibre 2.4g; Sodium 705mg

Bean Salad with Tuna

This makes a great main meal dish if served with a green salad and crusty bread. Using good-quality canned tuna brings the overall cost of the dish right down, making it affordable and delicious.

Serves 4

250g/9oz/1⅓ cups dried haricot (navy) or cannellini beans, soaked overnight in plenty of cold water
1 bay leaf
200–250g/7–9oz fine green beans, trimmed
1 large red onion, sliced
45ml/3 tbsp chopped fresh flat leaf parsley
200–250g/7–9oz good-quality canned tuna in olive oil, drained
200g/7oz cherry tomatoes, halved
salt and ground black pepper, to taste

For the dressing

90ml/6 tbsp olive oil
15ml/1 tbsp tarragon vinegar
5ml/1 tsp tarragon mustard
1 garlic clove, finely chopped
5ml/1 tsp finely grated lemon rind
a little lemon juice
pinch of caster (superfine) sugar (optional)

1 Drain the soaked beans and bring them to the boil in fresh water with the bay leaf. Boil for 10 minutes, then reduce the heat and simmer for 1–1½ hours, until tender. Drain.

2 Meanwhile, place the olive oil, tarragon vinegar and mustard, and garlic in a jug (pitcher) and whisk until mixed. Season to taste with salt, pepper, lemon juice and a pinch of caster sugar, if you like. Leave to stand.

3 Blanch the green beans in boiling water for 3–4 minutes. Drain, refresh under cold water and drain thoroughly again.

4 Place both types of beans in a bowl. Add half the dressing and toss to mix. Stir in the onion and half the chopped parsley, then season to taste with salt and pepper.

5 Flake the tuna into large chunks with a knife and toss it into the beans with the tomato halves. Arrange the salad on four individual plates. Drizzle the remaining dressing over the salad and sprinkle the remaining chopped parsley on top.

Salad Niçoise

Made with the freshest of seasonal ingredients, this classic Provençal salad makes a simple yet unbeatable summer dish. Serve with warm country-style bread for a nutritious and sustaining main meal.

Serves 4

115g/4oz green beans, trimmed and cut in half
115g/4oz mixed salad leaves
½ small cucumber, thinly sliced
4 ripe tomatoes, quartered
50g/2oz can anchovies, drained
4 eggs, hard-boiled
1 tuna steak, about 175g/6oz
½ bunch radishes, trimmed
50g/2oz/½ cup small black olives

For the dressing

2 garlic cloves, crushed
90ml/6 tbsp extra virgin olive oil,
30ml/2 tbsp white wine vinegar
salt and ground black pepper

1 To make the dressing, whisk together the olive oil, the garlic and the vinegar in a bowl and season to taste with salt and pepper. Alternatively, shake together in a screw-top jar. Set aside

2 Cook the green beans in a pan of boiling water for 2 minutes until just tender, then drain.

3 Mix together the salad leaves, sliced cucumber, tomatoes and green beans in a large, shallow bowl. Halve the anchovies lengthways and shell and quarter the eggs.

4 Preheat the grill (broiler). Brush the tuna with olive oil and sprinkle with salt and black pepper. Grill (broil) for 3–4 minutes on each side until cooked through. Cool, then flake with a fork.

5 Sprinkle the flaked tuna, sliced anchovies, quartered eggs, radishes and olives over the salad. Pour over the dressing and toss together lightly to combine. Serve immediately.

Variations

Include a handful of small cooked new potatoes for a more substantial salad.

Bean Salad Energy 461kcal/1929kJ; Protein 29.9g; Carbohydrate 37g, of which sugars 8.7g; Fat 22.6g, of which saturates 3.3g; Cholesterol 25mg; Calcium 131mg; Fibre 13g; Sodium 167mg
Salad Niçoise Energy 351kcal/1457kJ; Protein 21.7g; Carbohydrate 5.3g, of which sugars 5g; Fat 27.3g, of which saturates 5g; Cholesterol 210mg; Calcium 114mg; Fibre 2.6g; Sodium 876mg

piced Trout Salad

'ost of the preparation for
is delicious salad is done in
dvance, so it makes an ideal
idweek supper, as you can
ave the fish marinating
uring the day. The trout is
arinated in a mixture of
oriander, ginger and chilli
nd served with cold baby
oast potatoes.

erves 4

5cm/1in piece fresh root ginger, peeled and finely grated
1 garlic clove, crushed
5ml/1 tsp hot chilli powder
15ml/1 tbsp coriander seeds, lightly crushed
grated rind and juice of 2 small lemons
60ml/4 tbsp olive oil
450g/1lb trout fillet, skinned
900g/2lb new potatoes, washed but not peeled
5–10ml/1–2 tsp salt
ground black pepper, to taste
15ml/1 tbsp whole or chopped fresh chives, to garnish

Mix the ginger, garlic, chilli powder, coriander seeds and lemon nd in a bowl. Whisk in the lemon juice with 15ml/1 tbsp of the ive oil to make a marinade.

Place the trout in a shallow, non-metallic dish and cover with e marinade. Turn the fish to make sure they are well coated, over with clear film (plastic wrap) and chill for at least 2 hours overnight. You could also do this stage in the morning, before ou to to work, and leave in the refrigerator until the evening.

Preheat the oven to 200°C/400°F/Gas 6. Place the potatoes a roasting pan, toss them in 30ml/2 tbsp olive oil and season ith salt and pepper. Roast for 45 minutes or until tender. emove from the oven and set aside to cool.

Reduce the oven temperature to 190°C/375°F/Gas 5. emove the trout from the marinade and place in a roasting an. Bake for 20 minutes or until cooked through. Remove from e oven and leave to cool.

Cut the potatoes into chunks, flake the trout into bitesize eces and toss them together in a serving dish with the maining olive oil. Sprinkle with the chives and serve.

Ham and New Potato Salad

Combining warm new potatoes, young spinach leaves, cooked ham and hard-boiled eggs with a lightly spiced, nutty dressing, this delicious warm salad is an excellent choice for a casual, cost-effective summer supper with friends.

Serves 4

225g/8oz new potatoes, halved if large
50g/2oz green beans
115g/4oz young spinach leaves
2 spring onions (scallions), sliced
4 eggs, hard-boiled and quartered
50g/2oz cooked ham, cut into strips
juice of ½ lemon
salt and ground black pepper, to taste

For the dressing
60ml/4 tbsp olive oil
5ml/1 tsp ground turmeric
5ml/1 tsp ground cumin
50g/2oz/⅓ cup shelled hazelnuts

1 Cook the potatoes in boiling salted water for 10–15 minutes, or until tender. Meanwhile, cook the beans in boiling salted water for 2 minutes.

2 Drain the cooked potatoes and beans. Toss together with the spinach and spring onions.

3 Arrange the hard-boiled egg quarters on the salad and sprinkle the strips of ham over the top. Drizzle with the lemon juice and season with plenty of salt and pepper.

4 To make the dressing, put the oil, turmeric, cumin and hazelnuts in a large, heavy frying pan and cook, stirring frequently, until the nuts turn golden.

5 Pour the hot dressing over the salad and serve immediately.

Variation
An even quicker salad can be made by using a 400g/14oz can of mixed beans and pulses instead of the potatoes. Drain and rinse the beans and pulses, then drain again.

iced Trout Salad Energy 365kcal/1535kJ; Protein 26g; Carbohydrate 37.1g, of which sugars 2.9g; Fat 13.5g, of which saturates 1.5g; Cholesterol 0mg; Calcium 28mg; Fibre 2.3g; Sodium 580mg
am and Potato Salad Energy 318kcal/1319kJ; Protein 12.4g; Carbohydrate 11g, of which sugars 2.2g; Fat 25.4g, of which saturates 4g; Cholesterol 198mg; Calcium 106mg; Fibre 2.3g; Sodium 268mg

Chicken and Tomato Salad with Hazelnut Dressing

This simple, warm salad combines pan-fried chicken and spinach with a light, nutty dressing. Serve it with bread for a sustaining main meal. You can use thigh fillets rather than breast for a cheaper meal.

Serves 4

225g/8oz baby spinach leaves
250g/9oz cherry tomatoes, halved
1 bunch of spring onions (scallions), chopped
2 skinless chicken breast fillets, cut into thin strips
salt and ground black pepper

For the dressing

45ml/3 tbsp olive oil
30ml/2 tbsp hazelnut oil
15ml/1 tbsp white wine vinegar
1 garlic clove, crushed
15ml/1 tbsp chopped fresh herbs

1 First make the dressing: place 30ml/2 tbsp of the olive oil, the hazelnut oil, vinegar, garlic and chopped herbs in a small bowl or jug (pitcher) and whisk together until mixed. Set aside.

2 Trim any long stalks from the spinach leaves, then place in a large serving bowl with the tomatoes and spring onions, and toss together to mix.

3 Heat the remaining olive oil in a frying pan, and stir-fry the chicken over high heat for 7–10 minutes, until it is cooked, tender and lightly browned.

4 Arrange the cooked chicken pieces over the salad. Give the dressing a quick whisk to blend, then drizzle it over the salad. Add salt and pepper to taste, toss lightly and serve immediately.

Variation

It is much cheaper to buy a whole chicken than just the breast fillets. If you do this, joint the chicken, use the breasts for this recipe, roast the legs for another meal, and use the carcass to make stock for a delicious soup.

Rice Salad with Chicken

With their tangy flavour, orange segments are the perfect partner for tender chicken in this tasty and wholesome rice salad.

Serves 4

3 large seedless oranges
175g/6oz/scant 1 cup long grain rice
450g/1lb cooked chicken, diced
45ml/3 tbsp chopped fresh chives
75g/3oz/¾ cup almonds or cashew nuts, toasted
mixed salad leaves, to serve

For the dressing

175ml/6fl oz/¾ cup home-made vinaigrette (see Cook's Tip)
10ml/2 tsp strong Dijon mustard
2.5ml/½ tsp sugar
salt and ground black pepper

1 Pare one of the oranges thinly, removing only the rind, not th white pith. Put the pieces of rind in a pan and add the rice.

2 Pour in 475ml/16fl oz/2 cups water and bring to the boil. Cover and cook over very low heat for about 15 minutes, or until the rice is tender and all the water has been absorbed.

3 Meanwhile, peel the oranges, removing all the white pith. Working over a plate to catch the juices, separate them into segments. Transfer the juices into a small bowl and add the vinaigrette with the mustard and sugar, whisking to combine.

4 When the rice is cooked, remove it from the heat and discar the pieces of orange rind. Spoon into a bowl, let it cool slightly, then add half the dressing. Toss well, then set aside to cool.

5 Add the chicken, chives, toasted nuts and orange segments tc the cooled rice. Pour over the remaining dressing and toss gently to combine. Serve on a bed of mixed salad leaves.

Cook's Tip

To make a simple vinaigrette, whisk 45ml/3 tbsp wine vinegar with 90ml/6 tbsp olive oil. Add 60ml/4 tbsp extra virgin olive oil and season well.

Chicken Salad Energy 247kcal/1029kJ; Protein 23.5g; Carbohydrate 3.6g, of which sugars 3.5g; Fat 15.5g, of which saturates 2.1g; Cholesterol 61mg; Calcium 114mg; Fibre 2.2g; Sodium 139mg
Rice Salad Energy 668kcal/2785kJ; Protein 35.9g; Carbohydrate 47.8g, of which sugars 12.3g; Fat 37.2g, of which saturates 4.8g; Cholesterol 79mg; Calcium 141mg; Fibre 4.1g; Sodium 80mg

'angy Chicken Salad

his fresh and lively dish ᐟpifies the character of Thai uisine, with its sweet and ot tang. It is ideal for a light nch on a hot and lazy ummer's day.

erves 4-6

skinless, boneless chicken breast portions
garlic cloves, crushed
0ml/2 tbsp soy sauce
0ml/2 tbsp vegetable oil
15g/4oz/½ cup water chestnuts, sliced
0g/2oz/½ cup cashew nuts, roasted and coarsely chopped
shallots, thinly sliced
kaffir lime leaves, thinly sliced
1 lemon grass stalk, thinly sliced
5ml/1 tsp chopped fresh galangal
1 large fresh red chilli, seeded and finely chopped
2 spring onions (scallions), thinly sliced
10–12 fresh mint leaves, torn
1 lettuce, separated into leaves, to serve
2 fresh red chillies, seeded and sliced, to garnish

For the dressing

120ml/4fl oz/½ cup coconut cream
30ml/2 tbsp Thai fish sauce
juice of 1 lime
30ml/2 tbsp light muscovado (brown) sugar

Place the chicken in a large dish. Rub with the garlic, soy sauce nd 15ml/1 tbsp of the oil. Cover with clear film (plastic wrap) nd leave to marinate for 1–2 hours.

Heat the remaining oil in a wok or frying pan and stir-fry the hicken for 3–4 minutes on each side, or until cooked. Remove nd set aside to cool.

In a pan, heat the coconut cream, fish sauce, lime juice and gar. Stir until the sugar has dissolved; set aside.

Tear the cooked chicken into strips and put it in a bowl. Add e water chestnuts, cashew nuts, shallots, kaffir lime leaves, mon grass, galangal, red chilli, spring onions and mint leaves.

Pour the coconut dressing over the mixture and toss well. erve the chicken on a bed of lettuce leaves and garnish with ced red chillies.

Beef and Mushroom Salad

This flavoursome and nourishing salad combines tender strips of beef and earthy mushrooms with fresh vegetables and a lovely zesty sauce.

Serves 4

675g/1½lb fillet (tenderloin) or rump (round) steak
30ml/2 tbsp olive oil
2 small mild red chillies, seeded and sliced
225g/8oz/3¼ cups fresh shiitake mushrooms, stems removed and caps sliced
1 romaine lettuce, torn into strips
175g/6oz cherry tomatoes, halved
5cm/2in piece cucumber, peeled, halved and thinly sliced
45ml/3 tbsp sesame seeds, lightly toasted or dry fried

For the dressing

3 spring onions (scallions), finely chopped
2 garlic cloves, finely chopped
juice of 1 lime
30ml/2 tbsp chopped fresh coriander (cilantro)
15–30ml/1–2 tbsp Thai fish sauce
5ml/1 tsp soft light brown sugar

1 Preheat the grill (broiler) to medium, then cook the steak for 2–4 minutes on each side, depending on how well done you like it. Leave to cool for at least 15 minutes. Slice the meat as thinly as possible and place the slices in a bowl.

2 Heat the olive oil in a small frying pan. Add the seeded and sliced red chillies and the sliced shiitake mushroom caps. Cook for 5 minutes, stirring occasionally.

3 Turn off the heat and add the steak slices to the pan. Stir well until the beef slices are evenly coated in the chilli and mushroom mixture.

4 To make the dressing mix the spring onion, garlic and lime juice in a bowl, stir in the coriander, fish sauce and sugar until the sugar dissolves, then pour the dressing over the meat mixture and toss gently.

5 Arrange the lettuce, tomatoes and cucumber on a serving plate. Spoon the steak mixture in the centre and sprinkle the sesame seeds over. Serve immediately.

ngy Chicken Energy 349kcal/1453kJ; Protein 24.3g; Carbohydrate 11.5g, of which sugars 9.8g; Fat 23.2g, of which saturates 12.3g; Cholesterol 43mg; Calcium 49mg; Fibre 1.7g; Sodium 200mg
ef Energy 441kcal/1834kJ; Protein 42.3g; Carbohydrate 3.9g, of which sugars 3.8g; Fat 28.5g, of which saturates 8.3g; Cholesterol 98mg; Calcium 110mg; Fibre 2.6g; Sodium 119mg

Potato and Garlic Pizza

This simple pizza uses a flavoursome and unusual combination of sliced new potatoes, smoked mozzarella and garlic.

Serves 2–3

225g/8oz/2 cups strong white bread flour, sifted, plus extra for dusting
5ml/1 tsp salt
2.5ml/½ tsp easy-blend (rapid-rise) dried yeast
75ml/5 tbsp olive oil, plus extra for greasing
350g/12oz small new or salad potatoes, cooked
2 garlic cloves, crushed
1 red onion, thinly sliced
150g/5oz/1¼ cups smoked mozzarella cheese, grated
10ml/2 tsp chopped fresh rosemary or sage
salt and ground black pepper
30ml/2 tbsp freshly grated grano padano cheese, to garnish

1 To make the pizza base, place the flour, salt and easy-blend dried yeast in a large bowl. Make a well in the centre and add 45ml/3 tbsp oil and 150ml/¼ pint/⅔ cup warm water. Mix with a round-bladed knife to form a soft dough. Turn out on to a lightly floured work surface and knead for 5 minutes.

2 Cover the dough and leave to rest for about 5 minutes, then knead for a further 5 minutes, until smooth and elastic. Place in a lightly oiled bowl and cover with clear film (plastic wrap). Leave for 45 minutes, or until doubled in size.

3 Preheat the oven to 220°C/425°F/Gas 7. Peel the cooked potatoes and slice thinly. Heat 30ml/2 tbsp of the oil in a frying pan. Add the potatoes and garlic and fry for 5–8 minutes.

4 Knead the risen dough lightly, then roll out to form a rough 30cm/12in round. Place on a lightly oiled baking sheet.

5 Brush the pizza base with the remaining oil. Sprinkle the onion over, then arrange the potatoes on top. Sprinkle over the mozzarella and rosemary or sage and plenty of black pepper.

6 Bake for 15–20 minutes until golden. Remove from the oven, sprinkle with grano padano and more black pepper.

Rocket and Tomato Pizza

Simple, colourful and irresistible, this stunning pizza will be loved by all the family. Rocket, with its pronounced flavour, adds the final peppery taste and fresh texture after the pizza is cooked.

Serves 2

225g/8oz/2 cups strong white bread flour, sifted
5ml/1 tsp salt
2.5ml/½ tsp easy-blend (rapid-rise dried yeast
90ml/6 tbsp olive oil
1 garlic clove, crushed
150g/5oz canned chopped tomatoes
2.5ml/½ tsp sugar
30ml/2 tbsp torn fresh basil leave
2 tomatoes, seeded and chopped
150g/5oz mozzarella cheese,
salt and ground black pepper
25g/1oz rocket (arugula) leaves

1 To make the pizza base, place the flour, salt and easy-blend dried yeast in a large bowl. Make a well in the centre and add 45ml/3 tbsp oil and 150ml/¼ pint/⅔ cup warm water. Mix with round-bladed knife to form a soft dough. Turn out on to a light floured work surface and knead for 5 minutes.

2 Cover the dough and leave to rest for about 5 minutes, then knead for a further 5 minutes, until smooth and elastic. Place in a lightly oiled bowl and cover with clear film (plastic wrap). Leave for 45 minutes, or until doubled in size.

3 Preheat the oven to 220°C/425°F/Gas 7. To make the topping, heat 15ml/1 tbsp oil in a frying pan and fry the garlic for 1 minute. Add the canned tomatoes and sugar, and cook fo 5–7 minutes, until reduced and thickened. Stir in the basil and seasoning to taste, then set aside.

4 Knead the risen dough lightly, then roll out to form a rough 30cm/12in round. Place on a lightly oiled baking sheet and push up the edges of the dough to form a shallow, even rim.

5 Spoon the tomato mixture over the base, then top with the chopped fresh tomatoes, slice or tear the mozzarella and add to the pizza. Season, then drizzle with olive oil. Bake in the top of the oven for 10–12 minutes. Sprinkle with rocket and serve.

Potato Pizza Energy 690kcal/2899kJ; Protein 24.8g; Carbohydrate 85.2g, of which sugars 6.4g; Fat 30.1g, of which saturates 10.6g; Cholesterol 39mg; Calcium 410mg; Fibre 4.2g; Sodium 620mg
Rocket Pizza Energy 690kcal/2899kJ; Protein 24.8g; Carbohydrate 85.2g, of which sugars 6.4g; Fat 30.1g, of which saturates 10.6g; Cholesterol 39mg; Calcium 410mg; Fibre 4.2g; Sodium 620m

Fiorentina Pizza

An egg adds the finishing touch to this classic Italian spinach pizza. Don't cook the pizza for too long, so that the yolk remains runny.

Serves 2–3

225g/8oz/2 cups strong white bread flour, sifted
5ml/1 tsp salt
2.5ml/½ tsp easy-blend (rapid-rise) dried yeast
90ml/6 tbsp olive oil
1 garlic clove, crushed
150g/5oz canned chopped tomatoes
2.5ml/½ tsp sugar
30ml/2 tbsp torn fresh basil leaves
1 small red onion, thinly sliced
175g/6oz fresh spinach leaves
150g/5oz mozzarella cheese, torn
1 egg
25g/1oz/¼ cup Gruyère cheese, grated
freshly grated nutmeg
salt and ground black pepper

1 Make the pizza dough, following steps 1–2 in the recipe for Rocket and Tomato Pizza, opposite.

2 To make the topping, heat 15ml/1 tbsp oil in a frying pan and fry the garlic for 1 minute. Add the canned tomatoes and sugar, and cook for 5–7 minutes, until thickened. Season to taste.

3 Heat 15ml/1 tbsp of the oil and fry the onion until soft. Add the spinach and fry until wilted. Drain any excess liquid.

4 Knead the risen dough lightly, then roll out to form a rough 30cm/12in round. Place on a lightly oiled baking sheet.

5 Preheat the oven to 220°C/425°F/Gas 7. Brush the base with half the remaining olive oil.

6 Spread the tomato sauce over the base, then top with the spinach. Sprinkle over a little nutmeg and arrange the mozzarella on top. Drizzle over the remaining oil. Bake for 10 minutes, then remove from the oven.

7 Make a small well in the centre of the topping and break the egg into the hole. Sprinkle over the Gruyère cheese and return to the oven for a further 5–10 minutes until crisp and golden.

Aubergine Shallot Calzone

This tasty filling makes an unusual filling for a calzone – a pizza that is folded over to make an enclosed pasty-like pocket. Add more or less chilli flakes, to taste.

Serves 2

1 x quantity of pizza dough (see page 70)
45ml/3 tbsp olive oil
3 shallots
4 baby aubergines
1 garlic clove, chopped
50g/2oz sun-dried tomatoes, chopped
1.25ml/ tsp dried chilli flakes
10ml/2 tsp chopped fresh thyme
75g/3oz mozzarella, cubed
salt and ground black pepper
30ml/2 tbsp Parmesan cheese, grated

1 Make the pizza dough, following steps 1–2 in the recipe for Rocket and Tomato Pizza, opposite. Preheat the oven to 220°C/425°F/Gas 7.

2 Heat the oil and cook the shallots until soft in a frying pan. Add the aubergines, garlic, sun-dried tomatoes, chilli flakes, thyme and seasoning. Cook for 4–5 minutes, stirring frequently, until the aubergine is beginning to soften.

3 Divide the risen pizza dough in half and roll out each piece on a lightly floured surface, to an 18cm/7in circle.

4 Spread the aubergine mixture over half of each circle, leaving a 2.5cm/1in border, then sprinkle over the mozzarella.

5 Dampen the edges with water, then fold over the other half of the dough to enclose the filling. Press the edges firmly together to seal. Place on two greased baking sheets.

6 Brush with half the remaining oil, and make a small hole in the top of each, to allow the steam to escape.

7 Bake the calzones for 15–20 minutes until golden. Remove from the oven and brush with the remaining oil. Quickly sprinkle half the Parmesan over each calzone, and serve. The filling will be hot, so be careful.

Fiorentina Pizza Energy 503kcal/2100kJ; Protein 20.8g; Carbohydrate 40.3g, of which sugars 5.9g; Fat 29.7g, of which saturates 10.9g; Cholesterol 101mg; Calcium 417mg; Fibre 2.8g; Sodium 668mg
Aubergine Calzone Energy 805kcal/3380kJ; Protein 28g; Carbohydrate 95g, of which sugars 11g; Fat.37g, of which saturates12g; Cholesterol 36mg; Calcium 485mg; Fibre 10g; Sodium 1265mg

Feta and Roasted Garlic Mini Pizzas

These little pizzas are for garlic-lovers. Garlic loses much of its pungency when roasted, becoming sweet and delicious. Simply squeeze the roasted flesh out of the skins and onto your pizza.

Serves 2

1 medium garlic bulb, unpeeled
45ml/3 tbsp olive oil
1 red (bell) pepper, quartered and seeded
1 yellow (bell) pepper, quartered and seeded
2 plum tomatoes
1 x quantity of pizza dough (see page 70)
175g/6oz feta cheese, crumbled
ground black pepper
20ml/2 tbsp fresh oregano, chopped to garnish

1 Preheat the oven to 220°C/425°F/Gas 7. Break the garlic bulb into cloves, discarding the outermost papery layers. Toss in 15ml/1 tbsp of the oil in a shallow roasting pan.

2 Place the peppers skin side up on a baking sheet and place in the oven, or grill, until the skins are evenly charred. Roast the pan of garlic cloves at the same time for about 10 minutes, or until just starting to soften slightly. Set aside.

3 Place the charred peppers in a covered bowl for 10 minutes, then peel off the skins. Cut the flesh into strips.

4 Put the tomatoes in a bowl and pour over boiling water. Leave for 30 seconds then plunge into cold water. Peel, seed and roughly chop the flesh.

5 Divide the dough into four pieces and roll out each one on a lightly floured surface to a 13cm/5in circle. Place them on to greased baking sheets.

6 Brush the dough circles with half the remaining oil, and sprinkle over the chopped tomatoes. Top with the pepper strips, crumbled feta and a few garlic cloves. Drizzle the remaining oil over the tops and season with plenty of black pepper. Bake for 15–20 minutes until the tops are crisp and golden. Sprinkle with chopped oregano and serve.

Butternut Squash and Sage Pizza

The combination of the sweet butternut squash, sage and sharp goat's cheese works wonderfully on this pizza. Pumpkin and winter squashes are popular in northern Italy.

Serves 2

15g/½oz/1 tbsp butter
30ml/2 tbsp olive oil
2 shallots, finely chopped
1 butternut squash, peeled, seeded and cubed, about 450g/1lb prepared weight
16 sage leaves
1 x quantity of pizza dough (see page 70)
1 x quantity of tomato sauce (see page 70)
115g/4oz/1 cup mozzarella cheese, sliced
115g/4oz/½ cup firm goat's cheese
salt and ground black pepper

1 Preheat the oven to 200°C/400°F/ Gas 6. Oil two baking sheets. Put the butter and oil in a roasting pan and heat in the oven for a few minutes. Add the shallots, squash and half the sage leaves. Toss to coat. Roast for 15–20 minutes until tender.

2 Raise the oven temperature to 220°C/425°F/Gas 7. Divide the pizza dough into two equal pieces and roll out each piece on a lightly floured surface to a 26cm/12in round.

3 Transfer each round to a baking sheet and spread with the tomato sauce, leaving a 1cm/½in border all around. Spoon a quarter of the squash and shallot mixture over the top of each pizza, you won't need all of it, the remainder can be frozen.

4 Arrange the slices of mozzarella over the squash mixture and crumble the goat's cheese over. Sprinkle the remaining sage leaves over and season with plenty of salt and pepper. Bake for 15–20 minutes until the cheese has melted and the crust on each pizza is golden. Serve immediately.

Cook's Tip
The remaining butternut and shallot mixture can be frozen or used as the base of a soup.

Mini Pizzas Energy 889kcal/3730kJ; Protein 30g; Carbohydrate 102g, of which sugars 17g; Fat 43g, of which saturates 16g; Cholesterol 61mg; Calcium 498mg; Fibre 9g; Sodium 2266mg
Butternut Squash Pizza Energy 1084kcal/4544kJ; Protein 40g; Carbohydrate 110g, of which sugars 17g; Fat 57g, of which saturates 26g; Cholesterol 103mg; Calcium 569mg; Fibre 5g; Sodium 1643mg

·tuffed Baked Potatoes

ɔtatoes baked in their skins ıake a frugal and nourishing ıeal, and are even more ɹstaining with one of these ısty, easy and equally conomical stuffings.

erves 4

medium baking potatoes
ive oil
lt and ground black pepper

tir-fried vegetable

5ml/3 tbsp sunflower oil
leeks, thinly sliced
carrots, cut into sticks
1 courgette, thinly sliced
115g/4oz baby corn, halved
115g/4oz/1½ cup button mushrooms, sliced
45ml/3 tbsp soy sauce
15ml/1 tbsp sesame oil
30ml/2 tbsp dry sherry
sesame seeds, to garnish

Cheese and creamy corn

425g/15oz can creamed corn
115g/4oz/1 cup strong hard cheese, grated
5ml/1 tsp mixed dried herbs
fresh flat leaf parsley sprigs, to garnish

Preheat the oven to 200°C/400°F/Gas 6. Score the potatoes ·ith a cross and rub all over with the olive oil.

Place on a baking sheet and cook for 45 minutes to 1 hour, ıtil soft in the middle.

Meanwhile prepare the fillings. For the stir-fry vegetable, heat ıe sunflower oil in a wok or large frying pan, then add the ıopped leeks, carrots, courgette and baby corn, and stir-fry ɔgether for about 2 minutes. Add the mushrooms and stir-fry ɔr a further minute.

Mix together the soy sauce, sherry and sesame oil and pour ·ver the vegetables. Heat through until just bubbling and ɔrinkle the sesame seeds over the top.

For the cheese and creamy corn filling, heat the corn gently ·ith the cheese and mixed herbs until well blended.

Cut the potatoes open along the score lines and push up the ɘsh. Season to taste and fill with your chosen filling.

Layered Vegetable Terrine

This attractive terrine is a delicious combination of vegetables and herbs. Serve it hot or warm with a simple salad garnish.

Serves 6

3 red (bell) peppers, halved
115g/4oz spinach leaves, trimmed
450g/1lb waxy potatoes, peeled and cooked in salted water
25g/1oz/2 tbsp butter
pinch grated nutmeg
115g/4oz/1 cup Cheddar cheese, grated
1 medium courgette, sliced lengthways and blanched
salt and ground black pepper

1 Preheat the oven to 180°C/350°F/Gas 4. Place the peppers in a roasting pan and roast, cores in place, for 30–45 minutes until charred. Remove from the oven. Place in a plastic bag to cool. Peel the skins and remove the cores.

2 Blanch the spinach for a few seconds in boiling water. Drain and pat dry on kitchen paper. Line the base and sides of a 900g/2lb loaf tin (pan), making sure the leaves overlap slightly.

3 Slice the cooked potatoes thinly and lay one-third of the slices over the base, dot with a little of the butter and season with salt, pepper and nutmeg. Sprinkle a little cheese over.

4 Arrange three of the peeled pepper halves on top. Sprinkle a little cheese over and then a layer of blanched courgette slices. Repeat the layers, seasoning as you go. Lay the final layer of potato on top and sprinkle over any remaining cheese. Fold the spinach leaves over. Cover with foil, place in roasting pan and pour in enough water to come halfway up the sides of the tin.

5 Bake for 45 minutes–1 hour. Remove from the oven, allow to cool slightly in the tin, then turn the loaf out, slice and serve.

Variations
Other seasonal additions to this terrine could include lightly steamed green beans, peas and corn.

uffed Baked Potatoes Energy 223kcal/941kJ; Protein 7.3g; Carbohydrate 38.6g, of which sugars 8.3g; Fat 4.5g, of which saturates 0.8g; Cholesterol 0mg; Calcium 55mg; Fibre 5.4g; Sodium 1150mg
ıyered Vegetable Terrine Energy 205kcal/854kJ; Protein 8.3g; Carbohydrate 19.2g, of which sugars 7.7g; Fat 10.6g, of which saturates 6.6g; Cholesterol 27mg; Calcium 196mg; Fibre 3g; Sodium 203mg

Potato Gnocchi with Grano Padano Cheese

Gnocchi make a substantial and tasty alternative to pasta. Serve with a green salad for a simply delicious light meal.

Serves 6

1kg/2¼lb waxy potatoes
250–300g/9–11oz/2¼–2¾ cups plain (all-purpose) flour
1 egg
generous pinch of freshly grated nutmeg
25g/1oz/2 tbsp butter
a pinch of salt
grano padano cheese, cut in shavings, to garnish
fresh basil leaves, kept whole, to garnish

1 Cook the potatoes in their skins in a large pan of boiling water until tender but not falling apart. Drain, cool slightly, and peel while warm.

2 Spread a layer of flour on a work surface. Pass the hot potatoes through a food mill, dropping them directly on to the flour. Sprinkle with half of the remaining flour and mix in very lightly. Break the egg into the mixture. Add the nutmeg and knead, adding more flour if the mixture is too loose.

3 Divide the dough into four pieces. On a lightly floured surface, form each into a roll about 2cm/¾in in diameter. Cut the rolls crossways into pieces about 2cm/¾in long. One by one, press and roll the gnocchi lightly along the prongs of a fork towards the points, making ridges on one side, and a depression from your thumb on the other.

4 Bring a large pan of salted water to a fast boil, then drop in half the gnocchi. When they rise to the surface, they are done.

5 Remove the gnocchi from the pan with a slotted spoon, and place in a warmed serving bowl. Cook the rest of the gnocchi.

6 Melt the butter in a large pan, add the cooked gnocchi, toss gently, sprinkle over some black pepper, garnish with grano padano shavings and basil leaves, and serve immediately.

Bubble and Squeak

Whether you have leftovers or cook this old-fashioned classic from fresh, be sure to give it a really good 'squeak', pressing it down in the pan so it turns a rich honey brown. Serve with warm bread for a low-cost supper, or with grilled pork chops.

Serves 4

60ml/4 tbsp vegetable oil
1 medium onion, chopped
450g/1lb floury potatoes, cooked and mashed
225g/8oz cooked cabbage or Brussels sprouts, finely chopped
salt and ground black pepper, to taste

1 Heat 30ml/2 tbsp of the oil in a heavy frying pan. Add the onion and cook over medium heat, stirring frequently, until softened but not browned.

2 In a large bowl, mix together the potatoes and cooked cabbage or Brussels sprouts and season with salt and plenty of ground black pepper to taste.

3 Add the potato and greens mixture to the pan with the cooked onions, stir well, then press the vegetable mixture into a large, even cake.

4 Cook over medium heat for about 15 minutes, until the cake has browned underneath. Invert a large plate over the pan and turn it over so the potato cake is on the plate.

5 Return the pan to the heat and add the remaining oil. When hot, slide the cake back into the pan, browned side uppermost. Cook until the bottom is golden. Cut the cake into wedges and serve immediately.

Variations

- *Add any leftover gravy from a roast dinner for a really delicious flavour.*
- *Bacon fat can be used in place of the vegetable oil for a non-vegetarian version.*

Potato Gnocchi Energy 302kcal/1279kJ; Protein 7.8g; Carbohydrate 59.2g, of which sugars 2.8g; Fat 5.4g, of which saturates 2.7g; Cholesterol 41mg; Calcium 74mg; Fibre 3g; Sodium 57mg
Bubble and Squeak Energy 205kcal/857kJ; Protein 3.5g; Carbohydrate 23.3g, of which sugars 4.2g; Fat 11.5g, of which saturates 1.2g; Cholesterol 0mg; Calcium 34mg; Fibre 3g; Sodium 15mg

Baked Polenta with Tomato Sauce

Polenta, or cornmeal, is real Italian peasant food, and like pasta is a great frugal staple. It is prepared like a sort of oatmeal, and eaten soft, or left to set, cut into shapes, then cooked. Prepare the polenta in advance, so it has time to cool and set.

Serves 4

5ml/1 tsp salt
250g/9oz/1½ cups quick-cook polenta
25ml/1 tsp paprika
2.5ml/½ tsp ground nutmeg
30ml/2 tbsp extra virgin olive oil
1 large onion, finely chopped
2 garlic cloves, crushed
2 x 400g/14oz cans chopped tomatoes, or 450g/1lb fresh tomatoes
15ml/1 tbsp tomato purée (paste)
5ml/1 tsp sugar
75g/3oz Gruyère cheese, grated
salt and ground black pepper

1 Preheat the oven to 200°C/400°F/ Gas 6. Line a 28 x 18cm/11 x 7in tin (pan) with clear film (plastic wrap). Boil 1 litre/1¾ pints/4 cups water in a large pan.

2 Add the salt and pour in the polenta in a steady stream and cook, stirring constantly, for 5 minutes.

3 Beat the paprika and nutmeg into the mixture. Pour into the pan and smooth the surface. Leave to cool and set

4 Heat the oil in a pan and cook the onion and garlic until soft. Add the tomatoes, tomato purée and sugar. Season. Simmer for 20 minutes until thickened and reduced.

5 When the polenta has set completely, cut it into squares, of about 5cm/2in in size.

6 Place a layer of tomato sauce in the bottom of a buttered ovenproof dish. Place the polenta squares on top, and finish with the remainder of the tomato sauce.

7 Sprinkle the polenta with the cheese and bake for 25 minutes, until golden. Serve immediately.

Vegetable Hot-pot

Make this healthy one-dish meal in the summer, when the seasonal vegetables are cheaper, and serve with Italian bread.

Serves 4

60ml/4 tbsp extra virgin olive oil
1 large onion, finely chopped
2 small or medium aubergines (eggplants), cut into small cubes
4 courgettes (zucchini), cut into small chunks
2 red, yellow or green (bell) peppers, seeded and chopped
115g/4oz/1 cup frozen peas
115g/4oz green beans
450g/1lb new or salad potatoes, peeled and cubed
200g/7oz can flageolet beans, rinsed and drained
2.5ml/½ tsp ground cinnamon
2.5ml/½ tsp ground cumin
5ml/1 tsp paprika
4–5 tomatoes, peeled
400g/14oz can chopped tomatoes
30ml/2 tbsp chopped fresh parsley
3–4 garlic cloves, crushed
350ml/12fl oz/1½ cups vegetable stock
salt and ground black pepper
black olives to garnish

1 Preheat the oven to 190°C/375°F/Gas 5. Heat 45ml/3 tbsp of the oil in a heavy pan, and cook the onion until golden.

2 Add the aubergines, sauté for 3 minutes, then add the courgettes, peppers, peas, beans and potatoes, and stir in the spices and seasoning. Cook for 3 minutes, stirring constantly.

3 Cut the tomatoes in half and scoop out the seeds. Chop the tomatoes finely and place them in a bowl.

4 Stir in the canned tomatoes with the chopped fresh parsley, crushed garlic and the remaining olive oil.

5 Spoon the aubergine mixture into a shallow ovenproof dish and level the surface.

6 Pour the stock over the aubergine mixture and then spoon over the prepared tomato mixture. Cover the dish with foil and bake for 30–45 minutes, until the vegetables are tender.

7 Serve hot, garnished with black olives and parsley.

Baked Polenta Energy 425kcal/1777kJ; Protein 13.1g; Carbohydrate 59.4g, of which sugars 12g; Fat 14.5g, of which saturates 5.1g; Cholesterol 18mg; Calcium 175mg; Fibre 4.5g; Sodium 165mg
Vegetable Hot Pot Energy 386kcal/1618kJ; Protein 15.4g; Carbohydrate 51.7g, of which sugars 22.6g; Fat 14.5g, of which saturates 2.5g; Cholesterol 0mg; Calcium 142mg; Fibre 14.3g; Sodium 234mg

Leek, Squash and Tomato Gratin

You can use virtually any kind of squash for this colourful and succulent gratin, from patty pans and acorn squash to pumpkins. Buy whichever is in season in order to reduce the costs.

Serves 6

450g/1lb peeled and seeded squash, cut into 1cm/½in slices
60ml/4 tbsp olive oil
450g/1lb leeks, cut into thick, diagonal slices
675g/1½lb tomatoes, thickly sliced
2.5ml/½ tsp toasted cumin seeds
300ml/½ pint/1¼ cups single (light) cream
1 fresh red chilli, seeded and sliced
1 garlic clove, finely chopped
15ml/1 tbsp chopped fresh mint
30ml/2 tbsp chopped fresh parsley
60ml/4 tbsp white breadcrumbs
salt and ground black pepper

1 Steam the prepared squash in a steamer set over boiling salted water for 10 minutes. Heat half the oil in a frying pan and cook the leeks gently for 5–6 minutes, until golden. Try to keep the slices intact. Preheat the oven to 190°C/375°F/Gas 5.

2 Layer the squash, leeks and tomatoes in a 2-litre/3¾-pint/8-cup gratin dish, in rows. Season with salt, pepper and cumin.

3 Pour the cream into a small pan and add the chilli and garlic. Bring to the boil over low heat, then stir in the mint. Pour the mixture evenly over the layered vegetables.

4 Cook for 50–55 minutes, or until the gratin is bubbling and tinged brown. Sprinkle the parsley and breadcrumbs on top and drizzle over the remaining oil.

5 Bake for another 15–20 minutes until the breadcrumbs are browned and crisp. Serve immediately.

Variations
For a curried version of this dish, use ground coriander as well as cumin seeds, and coconut milk instead of cream. Use fresh coriander (cilantro) instead of mint and parsley.

Courgette and Potato Bake

Cook this delicious dish in early autumn, at the end of the courgette season, and the aromas spilling from the kitchen will recall the rich summer tastes and colours just past. The dish is baked for over an hour, giving an intense flavour.

Serves 4

675g/1½lb courgettes (zucchini)
450g/1lb potatoes, peeled and cut into chunks
1 onion, finely sliced
3 garlic cloves, chopped
1 large red (bell) pepper, seeded and cubed
400g/14oz can chopped tomatoes
150ml/¼ pint/⅔ cup extra virgin olive oil
5ml/1 tsp dried oregano
150ml/¼ pint/⅔ cup hot water
45ml/3 tbsp chopped fresh flat leaf parsley, plus a few extra sprigs, to garnish
salt and ground black pepper, to taste

1 Preheat the oven to 190°C/375°F/Gas 5. Scrape the courgettes lightly under running water to dislodge any grit and then slice them into thin rounds.

2 Put the courgettes in a large baking dish and add the chopped potatoes, onion, garlic, red pepper and tomatoes.

3 Using your hands mix in the olive oil and dried oregano so each vegetable is coated, and then spread out into a single layer. Pour on the hot water.

4 Season with plenty of salt and ground black pepper and cover. Bake for 30 minutes in the centre of the preheated oven, then stir in the parsley and a little more water.

5 Return the baking dish to the oven and cook for a further 30 minutes, uncovered, increasing the temperature to 200°C/400°F/Gas 6 for the final 10–15 minutes, so that the potatoes brown and all the liquid has been absorbed.

6 Serve the bake immediately, garnished with the remaining parsley. You could also serve this for non-vegetarians with grilled meats, such as sausages, pork chops or steak.

Leek and Tomato Gratin Energy 248kcal/1032kJ; Protein 5.7g; Carbohydrate 16.7g, of which sugars 7.8g; Fat 18g, of which saturates 7.4g; Cholesterol 28mg; Calcium 126mg; Fibre 3.8g; Sodium 104mg
Courgette Bake Energy 374kcal/1,554kJ; Protein 6.6g; Carbohydrate 28.6g, of which sugars 11.2g; Fat 26.7g, of which saturates 4g; Cholesterol 0mg; Calcium 86mg; Fibre 5.1g; Sodium 29mg

‹lediterranean Bake

eppers, tomatoes and nions are baked together › make a colourful, soft egetable dish, studded with lives, that makes the most f bounty from the garden. he vegetables can also be ooked on the barbecue.

erves 8

red (bell) peppers
yellow (bell) peppers
1 red onion, sliced
2 garlic cloves, halved
50g/2oz/¼ cup black olives
6 large ripe tomatoes, cut into quarters
5ml/1 tsp soft light brown sugar
45ml/3 tbsp amontillado sherry
3–4 fresh rosemary sprigs
30ml/2 tbsp olive oil
salt and ground black pepper, to taste
fresh bread, to serve

Cut the peppers in half lengthways with a large knife and emove the seeds. Cut each pepper lengthways into 12 strips. reheat the oven to 200°C/400°F/Gas 6.

Place the pepper strips, onion, garlic, olives and tomatoes in a rge roasting pan.

Sprinkle the vegetables with the brown sugar, then pour in the nerry. Season well with salt and black pepper, cover with foil nd bake for 45 minutes.

Remove the foil from the pan and stir the mixture well. Add ne rosemary sprigs and drizzle with the olive oil.

Return the roasting pan to the oven and cook for a further 0 minutes, uncovered, until the vegetables are very tender. erve hot or cold with plenty of chunks of fresh crusty bread.

Cook's Tips

- *Good quality Spanish olives are best for this dish, although you can use other ones if you prefer.*
- *Amontillado sherry has a dry to medium, slightly nutty flavour that perfectly complements the saltiness of the olives.*

Peppers with Spiced Vegetables

Indian spices season the potato and aubergine stuffing in these baked peppers.

Serves 6

6 large red or yellow (bell) peppers
500g/1¼lb waxy potatoes, cooked
1 small onion, chopped
4–5 garlic cloves, chopped
5cm/2in piece fresh ginger, grated
1–2 fresh green chillies, chopped
105ml/7 tbsp water
90–105ml/6–7 tbsp vegetable oil
1 aubergine (eggplant), diced
10ml/2 tsp cumin seeds
10ml/2 tsp black mustard seeds
2.5ml/½ tsp ground turmeric
5ml/1 tsp ground coriander
5ml/1 tsp ground cumin
pinch of cayenne pepper
about 30ml/2 tbsp lemon juice
salt and ground black pepper

1 Cut the tops off the (bell) peppers then remove and discard the seeds. Bring a large pan of lightly salted water to the boil. Add the peppers and cook for 5–6 minutes. Drain and leave the peppers upside down in a colander to drain completely. Cut the cooked potato into 1cm/½in dice.

2 Blend the onion, garlic, ginger and green chillies in a food processor with 60ml/4 tbsp of the water to a purée.

3 Heat 45ml/3 tbsp of the oil in a large, deep frying pan and cook the aubergine, stirring occasionally, until browned. Remove from the pan and set aside. Add another 30ml/2 tbsp of the oil to the pan and cook the potatoes until lightly golden.

4 Add another 15ml/1 tbsp oil to the pan, then add the cumin and black mustard seeds. Cook briefly, add the turmeric, coriander and ground cumin and stir in the onion purée.

5 Cook until it begins to brown. Return the aubergines to the pan, season with salt, pepper and cayenne. Add the remaining water and half the lemon juice and then cook, stirring, until the liquid evaporates. Preheat the oven to 190°C/375°F/Gas 5.

6 Fill the peppers with the potato mixture and place on a baking sheet. Bake for 30–35 minutes. Leave to cool a little, then sprinkle with a little more lemon juice, and serve.

editterranean Bake Energy 151kcal/635kJ; Protein 6.3g; Carbohydrate 23g, of which sugars 7.9g; Fat 4.4g, of which saturates 1.2g; Cholesterol 35mg; Calcium 113mg; Fibre 2.5g; Sodium 37mg
eppers with Veg Energy 267kcal/1116kJ; Protein 13.9g; Carbohydrate 26.1g, of which sugars 15.3g; Fat 12.5g, of which saturates 4.7g; Cholesterol 37mg; Calcium 81mg; Fibre 4.4g; Sodium 84mg

Roasted Aubergines Stuffed with Feta Cheese and Fresh Coriander

Aubergines in season are not expensive, and they have a substantial, almost meaty texture that makes them perfect for a main course ingredient. They also take on a lovely smoky flavour when grilled on a barbecue, although you could also char the skin in a hot oven.

Serves 6

3 medium to large aubergines (eggplant)
400g/14oz feta cheese
a small bunch of fresh coriander (cilantro), roughly chopped, plus extra sprigs to garnish
60ml/4 tbsp extra virgin olive oil
salt and ground black pepper

1 Prepare and light a barbecue. When the flames have died down and the charcoals have turned grey, cook the aubergines for 20 minutes, turning occasionally, until they are slightly charred and soft. Remove and cut in half lengthways.

2 Carefully scoop the aubergine flesh into a bowl, reserving the skins. Mash the flesh roughly with a fork.

3 Crumble the feta cheese, and then stir it into the mashed aubergine with the chopped coriander and olive oil. Season with salt and ground black pepper to taste.

4 Spoon the feta mixture back into the skins and return to the barbecue for 5 minutes to warm through.

5 Serve immediately with a fresh green salad coated with fruity extra virgin olive oil, garnished with sprigs of fresh coriander.

Cook's Tip

If you don't have a barbecue, you can char the aubergine in a preheated oven at 200°C/400°F/Gas 6. Alternatively, if you have a gas stove, you can carefully hold the peppers in metal tongs over the flame to create the same charring.

Onions Stuffed with Goat's Cheese

Roasted onions and tangy cheese are a winning combination. They make an excellent main course when served with rice.

Serves 4

4 large onions
150g/5oz goat's cheese, crumbled or cubed
50g/2oz/1 cup fresh breadcrumbs
8 sun-dried tomatoes in oil, drained and chopped
1–2 garlic cloves, chopped
2.5ml/½ tsp chopped fresh thyme
30ml/2 tbsp chopped fresh parsley
1 small (US medium) egg, beaten
45ml/3 tbsp pine nuts, toasted
30ml/2 tbsp oil from the sun-dried tomatoes
salt and ground black pepper, to taste

1 Bring a large pan of lightly salted water to the boil. Add the whole onions in their skins and boil for 10 minutes. Drain and cool, then cut each onion in half horizontally and peel.

2 Using a teaspoon, remove the centre of each onion, leaving a thick shell around the outside.

3 Reserve the flesh and place the shells in an oiled ovenproof dish. Preheat the oven to 190°C/375°F/Gas 5.

4 Chop the scooped-out onion flesh and place in a bowl. Add the goat's cheese, breadcrumbs, sun-dried tomatoes, garlic, thyme, parsley and egg. Mix well, then season with salt and pepper and add the toasted pine nuts.

5 Divide the stuffing among the onions and cover with foil. Bake for about 25 minutes.

6 Uncover the onions, drizzle with the oil and cook for another 30–40 minutes, basting occasionally. Serve immediately.

Variations

Use feta cheese in place of the goat's cheese and substitute mint, currants and pitted black olives for the other flavourings.

Roasted Aubergines Energy 257kcal/1,066kJ; Protein 12g; Carbohydrate 4.2g, of which sugars 3.9g; Fat 21.5g, of which saturates 10.3g; Cholesterol 47mg; Calcium 286mg; Fibre 3.3g; Sodium 968mg
Onions with Cheese Energy 402kcal/1669kJ; Protein 14.8g; Carbohydrate 25.1g, of which sugars 11.7g; Fat 27.7g, of which saturates 8.8g; Cholesterol 82mg; Calcium 120mg; Fibre 3.2g; Sodium 346mg

pinach Pancakes with Salsa

ɪinach and egg pancakes e tasty, inexpensive and ɪtritious. Serve with ɪvoursome sun-dried ·mato salsa and bread for a ·ht snack, or with boiled ɜw potatoes for a more ɪstaining main meal.

ɜrves 4
ʾ.5g/8oz spinach
small leek
few sprigs of fresh coriander (cilantro) or parsley
ɹlarge (US extra large) eggs
ɪg/1oz/⅓ cup freshly grated Parmesan cheese
50g/2oz/½ cup plain (all-purpose) flour, sifted
vegetable oil, for frying
salt, ground black pepper and freshly grated nutmeg

For the salsa
2 tomatoes, peeled and chopped
¼ fresh red chilli, seeded and chopped
2 pieces sun-dried tomato in oil, drained and chopped
1 small red onion, chopped
1 garlic clove, crushed
60ml/4 tbsp olive oil
30ml/2 tbsp sherry
2.5ml/½ tsp soft light brown sugar

Prepare the tomato salsa: place the tomatoes, chilli, sun-dried matoes, onion, garlic, olive oil, sherry and brown sugar in a ɔwl and toss together to combine. Cover and leave to stand a cool place for 2–3 hours.

To make the pancakes, finely chop the spinach, leek and ɪriander or parsley, then place in a bowl and beat in the eggs, ɪrmesan cheese and seasoning. Blend in the flour and)–45ml/2–3 tbsp water and leave to stand for 20 minutes.

In batches if necessary drop spoonfuls of the batter into a htly oiled frying pan and cook until golden underneath. Using metal spatula, turn the pancakes over and cook on the other de. Remove from the pan and keep warm until all the batter is ɪished. Serve with the tomato salsa.

Cook's Tip
Use sun-ripened tomatoes, as these have the best flavour.

Baked Herb Crêpes

Turn light herb crêpes into something special. Fill with a spinach, cheese and pine nut filling, then bake and serve with a tomato sauce.

Serves 4
25g/1oz/1 cup chopped herbs
15ml/1 tbsp sunflower oil, plus extra for frying
120ml/4fl oz/½ cup milk
3 eggs
25g/1oz/¼ cup plain (all-purpose) flour
salt and ground black pepper

For the sauce
30ml/2 tbsp olive oil
1 small onion, chopped
400g/14oz can chopped tomatoes
pinch of soft light brown sugar

For the filling
450g/1lb fresh spinach, cooked and drained
175g/6oz/¾ cup ricotta cheese
25g/1oz/¼ cup pine nuts, toasted
5 sun-dried tomatoes, chopped
30ml/2 tbsp shredded fresh basil
4 egg whites
grated nutmeg

1 To make the crêpes, place the herbs and sunflower oil in a food processor and process until smooth. Add the milk, eggs, flour and salt and process again. Leave to rest for 30 minutes.

2 Heat a small non-stick frying pan and add a small amount of sunflower oil. Pour in a ladleful of the batter. Swirl around until the batter covers the base evenly. Cook for 2 minutes, turn over and cook for a further 1–2 minutes. Make seven more crêpes.

3 Make the sauce: heat the olive oil in a pan, add the onion and cook for 5 minutes. Stir in the tomatoes and sugar, and cook for 10 minutes until thickened. Process in a blender, then strain. Preheat the oven to 190°C/375°F/ Gas 5.

4 To make the filling, mix together the spinach and the ricotta, pine nuts, tomatoes, basil, nutmeg and black pepper. Whisk the egg whites until they are stiff. Stir one-third into the spinach mixture, then gently fold in the rest.

5 Place each crêpe on a lightly oiled baking sheet, add a spoonful of filling and fold into quarters. Bake for 12 minutes. Reheat the tomato sauce and serve with the hot crêpes.

inach Pancakes Energy 153kcal/634kJ; Protein 4.6g; Carbohydrate 6.2g, of which sugars 2.1g; Fat 11.8g, of which saturates 2.2g; Cholesterol 63mg; Calcium 92mg; Fibre 1.3g; Sodium 84mg
ɪked Crêpes Energy 434kcal/1800kJ; Protein 14.9g; Carbohydrate 15.1g, of which sugars 9.8g; Fat 35.4g, of which saturates 8.3g; Cholesterol 161mg; Calcium 251mg; Fibre 5g; Sodium 229mg

Carrot and Apricot Rolls

Served with a dollop of yogurt flavoured with mint and garlic, these sweet, herby carrot rolls make a delicious light lunch or supper with a green salad and crusty bread.

Serves 4

8–10 carrots, just cooked
2–3 slices of day-old bread, ground into crumbs
4 spring onions (scallions), chopped
150g/5oz/generous ½ cup dried apricots, chopped
45ml/3 tbsp pine nuts
1 egg
1 fresh red chilli, finely chopped
1 bunch of fresh dill, chopped
1 bunch of fresh basil, shredded
plain (all-purpose) flour
lemon wedges, to serve
sunflower oil, for shallow frying
salt and ground black pepper

For the mint yogurt

about 225g/8oz/1 cup natural (plain) yogurt
juice of ½ lemon
1–2 garlic cloves, crushed
1 bunch of mint, finely chopped

1 First make the mint yogurt. Beat the yogurt in a bowl with the lemon juice and garlic, season to taste with salt and pepper and stir in the mint. Set aside, or chill in the refrigerator.

2 Mash the cooked carrots to a paste while they are warm. Add the breadcrumbs, spring onions, apricots and pine nuts and mix well with a fork. Beat in the egg and stir in the chilli and herbs. Season to taste with salt and pepper.

3 Tip a small heap of flour on to a flat surface. Take a plum-sized portion of the carrot mixture in your fingers and mould it into an oblong roll. Coat in the flour and put it on a plate. Repeat with rest of the mixture, to make 12–16 rolls altogether.

4 Heat enough sunflower oil for shallow frying in a heavy frying pan. Place the carrot rolls in the oil and fry over medium heat for 8–10 minutes, turning them from time to time, until they are golden brown.

5 Remove the rolls from the pan as they are cooked with a slotted spoon and drain on kitchen paper. Serve hot, with lemon wedges and the mint yogurt.

Vegetarian Sausages

These flavoursome cheese and leek sausages are a delicious meat-free alternative for all the family. A traditional recipe from Wales, also known as Glamorgan sausages, they are quick and easy to cook, for a light meal served with a crisp salad and a fruit-based sauce or chutney. For a more substantial meal, serve in a bread roll with ketchup.

Serves 4

150g/5oz/3 cups fresh breadcrumbs, plus extra for coating
100g/3¾oz/1 cup mature (sharp) Caerphilly or Cheddar cheese, grated
1 small leek or 6 spring onions, washed, trimmed and very thinly sliced
15–30ml/1–2 tbsp finely chopped fresh herbs, such as flat leaf parsley, thyme and a very little sage
5ml/1 tsp mustard powder
2 eggs
plain (all-purpose) flour, for coating
milk to mix, if necessary
oil, for deep-frying
salt and ground black pepper, to taste

1 In a large mixing bowl, stir together the breadcrumbs, cheese, leek or spring onions, herbs, mustard and seasoning to taste.

2 Separate one egg and lightly beat the yolk with the whole egg, reserving the white.

3 Stir the beaten eggs into the breadcrumb mixture. You need to add sufficient milk to make a mixture that can then be gathered together into a sticky, but not wet, ball.

4 Using your hands, divide the mixture into eight and shape into sausages of equal size. Cover and refrigerate for about 1 hour, or until needed.

5 Lightly whisk the reserved egg white. Coat each sausage in flour, egg white and then in fresh breadcrumbs.

6 Heat enough oil for deep-frying in a large pan to 180°C/350°F. Lower the sausages into the oil and cook for 5 minutes until crisp and brown. Drain on kitchen paper and serve.

Carrot Rolls Energy 401kcal/1673kJ; Protein 8.7g; Carbohydrate 46g, of which sugars 29.1g; Fat 21.5g, of which saturates 2.5g; Cholesterol 48mg; Calcium 144mg; Fibre 8.5g; Sodium 145mg
Vegetarian Sausages Energy 202kcal/844kJ; Protein 7.6g; Carbohydrate 17.6g, of which sugars 1g; Fat 11.5g, of which saturates 3.8g; Cholesterol 60mg; Calcium 134mg; Fibre 1g; Sodium 251mg

heesy Aubergine Bake

ıis warming and nourishing sh is sure to be a hit with the family, and especially ith children, who might not ually be the greatest of bergine fans. Cook the ke when aubergines are at eir lowest price, and, as ere aren't many other gredients, enjoy a real dget meal.

Serves 4

2 large aubergines (eggplants)
50g/2oz/¼ cup butter
30ml/2 tbsp plain (all-purpose) flour
600ml/1 pint/2½ cups milk
115g/4oz Cheddar cheese, grated
3 handfuls each of white breadcrumbs and finely grated grano padano cheese
salt and ground black pepper

Preheat the oven to 200°C/400°F/ Gas 6. Put the aubergines the gas flame on top of the stove, or under a grill (broiler), d turn them until the skin is charred on all sides and the flesh els soft. Place in a plastic bag and leave for a few minutes.

Hold each aubergine under cold running water and peel off e charred skin. Squeeze the flesh to get rid of any excess ater, remove the stalks and chop the flesh to a pulp.

To make the sauce, melt the butter in a heavy pan, remove m the heat and stir in the flour. Slowly beat in the milk, then turn the pan to medium heat and cook, stirring constantly, til the sauce is smooth and thick.

Beat in the grated Cheddar cheese a little at a time, then beat the aubergine pulp and season to taste with salt and pepper. ansfer the mixture into a baking dish.

Mix together the breadcrumbs and grano padano cheese with generous grind of black pepper.

Sprinkle the breadcrumb mixture over the top of the bergine mixture, smooth the top with a spatula or knife and ke in the preheated oven for about 25 minutes, until the top nicely browned and crunchy. Serve immediately with a crisp een salad and fresh bread.

Cheese Pudding

This light, soufflé-like pudding is simply made with cheese, breadcrumbs, milk and eggs, but has a lovely creamy richness that makes it the perfect foil to freshly cooked vegetables, such as beans or broccoli and carrots, or with a crisp salad tossed in an oil and vinegar dressing. Serve any leftovers on toast with some grilled tomatoes.

Serves 4

225g/8oz/2 cups grated mature (sharp) Cheddar-style cheese
115g/4oz/2 cups fresh breadcrumbs
5ml/1 tsp mustard (such as wholegrain or English) or 2.5ml/½ tsp mustard powder
600ml/1 pint/2½ cups milk
40g/1½oz/3 tbsp butter
3 eggs, beaten
salt and ground black pepper

1 Preheat the oven to 200°C/400°F/Gas 6. Butter the insides of a 1.2 litre/2 pint/5 cup ovenproof soufflé dish.

2 Mix together three-quarters of the grated Cheddar cheese with the breadcrumbs.

3 Put the remaining ingredients into a pan and stir well. Heat gently, stirring, until the butter has just melted. Take care because if the mixture gets too hot then the eggs will start to set.

4 Stir into the cheese mixture and transfer into the prepared dish. Sprinkle the remaining cheese evenly over the top.

5 Put into the hot oven and cook for about 30 minutes or until golden brown and just set – a knife inserted in the centre should come out clean.

6 Serve immediately, with some lightly cooked vegetables as a foil to the rich, creamy pudding.

Cook's Tip
This is a great frugal recipe for using up oddments of leftover cheese, after Christmas, for example.

eesy Bake Energy 322kcal/1344kJ; Protein 14.1g; Carbohydrate 15.2g, of which sugars 9.3g; Fat 22.7g, of which saturates 14.5g; Cholesterol 63mg; Calcium 415mg; Fibre 2.2g; Sodium 350mg
eese Pudding Energy 534kcal/2232kJ; Protein 27.5g; Carbohydrate 29.5g, of which sugars 7.9g; Fat 33.9g, of which saturates 20.2g; Cholesterol 227mg; Calcium 656mg; Fibre 0.6g; Sodium 803mg

Cheese and Tomato Soufflés

Guests are always impressed by a home-made soufflé and this recipe for little individual ones is the ultimate in effortless inexpensive entertaining. Serve with a crisp green salad and some warm bread.

Serves 6

25g/1oz/2 tbsp butter
25g/1oz/2 tbsp plain (all-purpose) flour
350ml/12fl oz/1½ cups full-fat (whole) milk
115g/4oz/1 cup grated Cheddar cheese
50g/2oz sun-dried tomatoes in olive oil, drained, plus 10ml/2 tsp of the oil
130g/4½oz/1½ cups grated grano padano cheese
4 large (US extra large) eggs, separated
salt and ground black pepper, to taste

1 Melt the butter in a pan, then stir in the flour to form a paste and cook for 1 minute. Gradually pour in the milk and mix in until smooth, then bring to the boil, stirring continuously. Stir in the Cheddar and mix until the cheese has melted and the sauce is smooth and thickened.

2 Preheat the oven to 200°C/400°F/Gas 6. Transfer the cheese sauce into a bowl. Thinly slice the sun-dried tomatoes and add them to the sauce with 90g/3½oz/generous 1 cup of the grano padano cheese and the egg yolks. Season well and stir.

3 Brush the base and sides of six 200ml/7fl oz/scant 1 cup ramekins or individual soufflé dishes with the oil, then coat the insides with half of the remaining cheese, tilting them until evenly covered. Tip out any excess cheese and set aside.

4 Whisk the egg whites in a clean, grease-free bowl until stiff. Use a large metal spoon to stir one-quarter of the egg whites into the sauce, then fold in the remaining egg whites.

5 Spoon the mixture into the ramekins or soufflé dishes and sprinkle with the reserved cheese. Place on a baking sheet and bake for about 15–18 minutes, or until the soufflé is well risen and golden. Serve immediately with a mixed green salad.

Frittata with Sun-dried Tomatoes

This Italian-style omelette, flavoured with tangy Parmesan cheese, can be eaten warm or cold. It is perfect as a light vegetarian meal when served with a large mixed salad.

Serves 4

6 sun-dried tomatoes
60ml/4 tbsp olive oil
1 small onion, finely chopped
pinch of fresh thyme leaves
6 eggs
25g/1oz/⅓ cup freshly grated Parmesan cheese, plus shavings to serve
thyme sprigs, to garnish
salt and ground black pepper, to taste

1 Place the tomatoes in a bowl and pour over hot water to cover. Leave to soak for 15 minutes, then remove from the water and pat dry on kitchen paper. Reserve the soaking water. Cut the tomatoes into strips.

2 Heat the olive oil in a large non-stick frying pan. Cook the onion for 5–6 minutes. Add the thyme and tomatoes and cook for a further 2–3 minutes.

3 Break the eggs into a bowl and beat lightly. Stir in 45ml/3 tbsp of the tomato water with the Parmesan, salt and pepper.

4 Raise the heat under the pan. When the oil is sizzling, add the eggs. Mix quickly into the other ingredients, then stop stirring.

5 Lower the heat to medium and cook for 4–5 minutes, or until the base is golden and the top puffed.

6 Take a large plate, invert it over the pan and, holding it firmly with oven gloves, turn the pan and the frittata over on to it.

7 Slide the frittata back into the pan, and continue cooking for 3–4 minutes until golden brown on the second side. Remove the pan from the heat.

8 Cut the frittata into wedges, garnish with thyme sprigs and Parmesan, and serve immediately.

Cheese Soufflés Energy 328kcal/1364kJ; Protein 20g; Carbohydrate 6.2g, of which sugars 3g; Fat 24.7g, of which saturates 13.6g; Cholesterol 184mg; Calcium 497mg; Fibre 0.2g; Sodium 473mg
Frittata Energy 170kcal/705kJ; Protein 5.7g; Carbohydrate 3g, of which sugars 2.6g; Fat 15.2g, of which saturates 4.1g; Cholesterol 13mg; Calcium 158mg; Fibre 0.6g; Sodium 167mg

ouffle Omelette with Mushrooms

ourishing and flavoursome, soufflé omelette makes an eal meal. It is very quick d easy to make, ideal for hen you are in a hurry or e too tired to spend a long ne in the kitchen.

erves 1

eggs, separated
g/½oz/1 tbsp butter
lt and ground black pepper
flat leaf parsley or coriander (cilantro) leaves, to garnish

For the mushroom sauce

15g/½oz/1 tbsp butter
75g/3oz/generous 1 cup button (white) mushrooms, thinly sliced
15ml/1 tbsp plain (all-purpose) flour
85–120ml/3–4fl oz/⅓–½ cup full-fat (whole) milk
5ml/1 tsp chopped fresh parsley

Make the mushroom sauce: melt the butter in a pan or frying in and add the mushrooms. Fry gently for 4–5 minutes, stirring :casionally. The liquid exuded will rapidly be reabsorbed.

Stir in the flour, then gradually add the milk, stirring all the ne. Cook until the sauce boils and thickens.

Add the parsley to the sauce and season to taste with salt d ground black pepper. Keep warm.

Make the omelette. Beat the egg yolks with 15ml/1 tbsp ater and season with a little salt and pepper.

Whisk the egg whites until stiff, then fold into the egg yolks. eheat the grill (broiler).

Melt the butter in a large frying pan and pour in the egg ixture. Cook over low heat for 2–4 minutes.

Place the frying pan under the grill and cook for a further 4 minutes until the top is golden brown.

Slide the omelette on to a warmed serving plate, pour the ushroom sauce over the top and fold the omelette in half. rve, garnished with parsley.

Spicy Omelette

Packed with vegetables and flavoured with chilli and coriander, this tasty omelette is a treat for all the senses – as well as the weekly food budget, especially if you're using up some vegetable leftovers from a previous meal the day before.

Serves 4–6

30ml/2 tbsp vegetable oil
1 onion, finely chopped
1 garlic clove, crushed
1 or 2 fresh green chillies, finely chopped
a few coriander (cilantro) sprigs, chopped, plus extra, to garnish
2.5ml/½ tsp ground cumin
1 firm tomato, chopped
1 small potato, cubed and boiled
25g/1oz/¼ cup cooked peas
25g/1oz/¼ cup cooked corn, or drained canned corn
2 eggs
25g/1oz/¼ cup grated Cheddar cheese
salt and ground black pepper

1 Heat the vegetable oil in a large pan, add the chopped onion and garlic, the green chillies, coriander, cumin, tomato, potato, peas and corn and fry for 2–3 minutes until they are well blended but the potato and tomato are still firm. Season to taste with salt and black pepper.

2 Increase the heat, beat the eggs and pour in to the pan. Reduce the heat, cover the pan and cook until the bottom of the omelette is golden brown.

3 Sprinkle the omelette with the grated cheese. Place the pan under a hot grill (broiler) and cook until the egg has set and the cheese has melted.

4 Garnish the omelette with sprigs of coriander and serve with salad for a light lunch or supper.

Variation

You can use any type of vegetable with the potatoes. Try adding thickly sliced mushrooms instead of the corn if that's what you have in the refrigerator.

ufflé Omelette Energy 838kcal/3514kJ; Protein 45.5g; Carbohydrate 53.7g, of which sugars 42.1g; Fat 51.4g, of which saturates 28.3g; Cholesterol 497mg; Calcium 1150mg; Fibre 1.3g; Sodium 707mg
cy Omelette Energy 93kcal/388kJ; Protein 4g; Carbohydrate 3.7g, of which sugars 1.2g; Fat 7.1g, of which saturates 1.9g; Cholesterol 67mg; Calcium 46mg; Fibre 0.6g; Sodium 104mg

Cheesy Baked Eggs

This delicious dish of potatoes, leeks, eggs and cheese sauce is perfect for a cold day. Serve with boiled potatoes and green vegetables, if you like.

Serves 4

500g/1¼lb potatoes, peeled
3 leeks, sliced
6 eggs
600ml/1 pint/2½ cups milk
50g/2oz/3 tbsp butter, cut into small pieces
50g/2oz/½ cup plain (all-purpose) flour
100g/3¾oz/1 cup Caerphilly or Cheddar cheese, grated
salt and ground black pepper, to taste

1 Cook the peeled potatoes in boiling, lightly salted water for about 15 minutes or until soft. Cook the leeks in a little water for about 10 minutes until soft. Hard-boil the eggs, drain and put under cold running water to cool.

2 Preheat the oven to 200°C/400°F/Gas 6. Drain and mash the potatoes. Drain the leeks and stir into the potatoes with a little black pepper to taste. Remove the shells from the eggs and cut in half or into quarters lengthways.

3 Pour the milk into a pan and add the butter and flour. Stirring continuously with a whisk, bring slowly to the boil and bubble gently for 2 minutes, until thickened and smooth. Remove from the heat, stir in half the cheese and season to taste.

4 Arrange the eggs in four shallow ovenproof dishes. Spoon the potato and leek mixture around the edge of the dishes.

5 Pour the cheese sauce over and top with the remaining cheese. Bake in the hot oven for about 15–20 minutes, until bubbling and golden brown.

Variation
Add a little grated nutmeg into the mixture at the end of step 3, and over the top of the dish before baking, to add flavour.

Goat's Cheese Soufflé

This simple, elegant soufflé makes an ideal appetizer.

Serves 6–8

4 large heads of garlic
6 fresh thyme sprigs
30ml/2 tbsp olive oil
475ml/16fl oz/2 cups milk
2 fresh bay leaves
4 × 1cm/½in thick onion slices
4 cloves
115g/4oz/½ cup butter
75g/3oz/⅔ cup plain (all-purpose) flour, sifted
cayenne pepper
6 eggs, separated, plus 1 egg whit[e]
300g/11oz goat's cheese, crumble[d]
115g/4oz/1⅓ cups freshly grate[d] Parmesan cheese
10ml/2 tsp chopped fresh thyme
5ml/1 tsp cream of tartar
salt and ground black pepper

1 Preheat the oven to 180°C/350°F/Gas 4. Place the garlic and thyme sprigs on a piece of foil. Sprinkle with the oil and close the foil. Bake for 1 hour, until the garlic is soft. Leave to cool. Squeeze the garlic out of its skin. Discard the thyme and garlic skins, then purée the garlic flesh with the oil.

2 Meanwhile, boil the milk, bay leaves, onion and cloves in a pan. Remove from the heat, cover and leave for 30 minutes. Melt 75g/3oz/6 tbsp of the butter in another pan. Stir in the flour and cook gently for 2 minutes. Reheat and strain the milk, then gradually stir it into the flour and butter.

3 Cook the sauce gently for 10 minutes, stirring. Season with salt, pepper and a little cayenne. Cool slightly. Preheat the oven to 200°C/400°F/Gas 6. Beat the egg yolks into the sauce, then beat in the goat's cheese, all but 30ml/2 tbsp of the Parmesan and the thyme. Grease eight small ramekins.

4 Whisk the egg whites and cream of tartar in a clean, grease-free bowl until firm. Stir 90ml/6 tbsp of the whites into the sauce, then gently fold in the remainder using a rubber spatula.

5 Pour the mixture into the ramekins. Run a knife around the edge of each to push the mixture away from the rim. Sprinkle with the reserved Parmesan. Place on a baking sheet and cook for 20 minutes until risen. Serve immediately.

Cheesy Baked Eggs Energy 540kcal/2259kJ; Protein 26.6g; Carbohydrate 41.3g, of which sugars 12.3g; Fat 30.6g, of which saturates 16.2g; Cholesterol 345mg; Calcium 471mg; Fibre 5g; Sodium 443m[g].
Soufflé Energy 563kcal/2339kJ; Protein 28.8g; Carbohydrate 16.5g, of which sugars 5.8g; Fat 42.9g, of which saturates 24.1g; Cholesterol 294mg; Calcium 422mg; Fibre 0.7g; Sodium 710mg.

'arsnip and Chickpea Curry

'he sweet flavour of parsnips oes very well with the romatic spices in this hearty nd healthy Indian-style stew. erve with naan bread.

erves 4

00g/7oz dried chickpeas, soaked overnight in cold water
garlic cloves, chopped
small onion, chopped
cm/2in piece fresh root ginger, chopped
green chillies, seeded and finely chopped
0ml/4 tbsp vegetable oil
5ml/1 tsp cumin seeds
10ml/2 tsp ground coriander seeds
5ml/1 tsp ground turmeric
2.5–5ml/½–1 tsp chilli powder or mild paprika
50g/2oz cashew nuts, toasted and ground
250g/9oz tomatoes, chopped
900g/2lb parsnips, cut into chunks
450ml/¾ pint/scant 2 cups plus 75ml/5 tbsp water
juice of 1 lime, to taste
cashew nuts, toasted and 5ml/1 tsp ground roasted cumin seeds, to garnish
salt and ground black pepper

Put the chickpeas in a pan, cover with fresh water and bring ɔ the boil. Boil for 10 minutes, then reduce the heat and cook ɔr 1–1½ hours until the chickpeas are tender. Drain well.

Set 10ml/2 tsp of the garlic aside, then place the remainder in food processor or blender with the onion, ginger and half the nillies. Add 75ml/5 tbsp water and process to make a paste.

Heat the oil in a large, deep, frying pan and cook the cumin nd coriander seeds for 30 seconds. Stir in the turmeric, chilli owder or paprika and the ground cashew nuts. Add the ginger nd chilli paste and cook, stirring, until the water evaporates. dd the tomatoes and stir-fry until the mixture turns red-brown.

Mix in the chickpeas and parsnips with the rest of the water, ie lime juice, 5ml/1 tsp salt and black pepper. Bring to the boil, ien simmer, uncovered, for 15–20 minutes, until the sauce is iick. Stir in the reserved garlic and chilli.

Sprinkle the roasted cumin seeds and cashew nuts over the urry, and serve with naan bread.

Pumpkin and Peanut Curry

Rich, sweet, spicy and fragrant, the flavours of this delicious Thai-style curry really come together with long, slow cooking.

Serves 4

30ml/2 tbsp vegetable oil
4 garlic cloves, crushed
4 shallots, finely chopped
30ml/2 tbsp yellow curry paste
2 kaffir lime leaves, torn
15ml/1 tbsp galangal, finely chopped
450g/1lb pumpkin, diced
225g/8oz sweet potatoes, diced
400ml/14fl oz/1⅔ cups near-boiling vegetable stock
300ml/½ pint/1¼ cups coconut milk
90g/3½oz/1½ cups chestnut mushrooms, sliced
15ml/1 tbsp soy sauce
15ml/1 tbsp lemon juice
90g/3½ oz/scant 1 cup peanuts, roasted and chopped
50g/2oz/⅓ cup pumpkin seeds, dry roasted, and shredded green chillies (optional) to garnish

1 Heat the oil in a large heavy pan. Add the garlic and shallots and cook over medium heat, stirring occasionally, for 10 minutes, until softened and beginning to turn golden.

2 Add the yellow curry paste to the pan and stir-fry over medium heat for 30 seconds, until fragrant.

3 Add the lime leaves, galangal, pumpkin and sweet potatoes to the pan. Pour the stock and 150ml/¼ pint/⅔ cup of the coconut milk over the vegetables, and stir to combine. Cover with the lid and cook for 30–45 minutes.

4 Stir the mushrooms, soy sauce and lemon juice into the curry, then add the chopped peanuts and pour in the remaining coconut milk.

5 Cover the pan again and cook on high for 20–30 minutes more, or until the vegetables are very tender but not disintegrating, and the sauce has thickened.

6 Spoon the curry into warmed serving bowls, garnish with the pumpkin seeds and chillies, and serve immediately.

ırsnip Curry Energy 506kcal/2124kJ; Protein 18.4g; Carbohydrate 60.1g, of which sugars 18.2g; Fat 23.1g, of which saturates 3.4g; Cholesterol 0mg; Calcium 192mg; Fibre 17.1g; Sodium 86mg
ımpkin Curry Energy 337kcal/1404kJ; Protein 10.3g; Carbohydrate 21.7g, of which sugars 10.8g; Fat 23.8g, of which saturates 4g; Cholesterol 0mg; Calcium 168mg; Fibre 5.1g; Sodium 554mg

Potato Curry with Yogurt

Combining an aromatic mixture of herbs and spices with creamy yogurt and potatoes, this simple Indian curry is a one-pot feast for all the senses with very little expense.

Serves 4

6 garlic cloves, chopped
25g/1oz fresh root ginger, peeled and chopped
30ml/2 tbsp ghee, or 15ml/1 tbsp oil and 15g/½oz/1 tbsp butter
6 shallots, halved lengthways and sliced along the grain
2 green chillies, seeded and sliced
10ml/2 tsp sugar
a handful of fresh or dried curry leaves
2 cinnamon sticks
5–10ml/1–2 tsp ground turmeric
15ml/1 tbsp garam masala
500g/1¼lb waxy potatoes, cut into bitesize pieces
2 tomatoes, peeled, seeded and quartered
250ml/8fl oz/1 cup Greek (US strained plain) yogurt
salt and ground black pepper
5ml/1 tsp red chilli powder, fresh coriander (cilantro) and mint leaves, finely chopped, to garnish
1 lemon, quartered, to serve

1 Using a mortar and pestle or a food processor, grind the garlic and ginger to a coarse paste.

2 Heat the ghee in a heavy pan, add the shallots and chillies and cook until fragrant. Add the garlic and ginger paste with the sugar, and stir until the mixture begins to colour.

3 Stir in the curry leaves, cinnamon sticks, turmeric and garam masala, and toss in the potatoes, making sure they are coated in the spice mixture.

4 Pour just enough cold water to cover the potatoes in to the pan. Bring to the boil, then reduce the heat and simmer until the potatoes are just cooked – they should still have a bite to them. Season with salt and pepper to taste.

5 Add the tomatoes and heat them through. Fold in the yogurt, then sprinkle with the chilli powder, coriander and mint. Serve immediately with lemon wedges to squeeze over it and flatbread for scooping it up.

Hot and Spicy Thai Vegetable Curry

This curry uses coconut milk to cook the vegetables, which gives it a creamy richness that contrasts wonderfully with the heat of the chilli. Thai yellow curry paste is available in supermarkets, but you will really taste the difference when you make it yourself.

Serves 4

30ml/2 tbsp sunflower oil
200ml/7fl oz/scant 1 cup coconut cream
300ml/½ pint/1¼ cups coconut milk
150ml/¼ pint/⅔ cup vegetable stock
200g/7oz green beans, cut into 2cm/¾in lengths
200g/7oz baby corn
4 baby courgettes (zucchini), sliced
1 small aubergine (eggplant), cubed or sliced
30ml/2 tbsp mushroom ketchup
10ml/2 tsp palm sugar (jaggery)
fresh coriander (cilantro) leaves, to garnish
noodles or rice, to serve

For the yellow curry paste
10ml/2 tsp hot chilli powder
10ml/2 tsp ground coriander
10ml/2 tsp ground cumin
5ml/1 tsp turmeric
15ml/1 tbsp chopped galangal
10ml/2 tsp finely grated garlic
30ml/2 tbsp finely chopped lemon grass
4 red Asian shallots, finely chopped
5ml/1 tsp finely chopped lime rind

1 To make the curry paste, place all the ingredients in a food processor and blend with 30–45ml/2–3 tbsp of cold water to make a smooth paste. Add a little more water if the mixture seems too dry.

2 Heat a large wok or deep frying pan over medium heat and add the sunflower oil. When hot add 30–45ml/2–3 tbsp of the curry paste and fry for 1–2 minutes, stirring constantly. Add the coconut cream and cook gently for 8–10 minutes, or until the mixture starts to separate.

3 Add the coconut milk, stock and vegetables and cook gently for 8–10 minutes, until the vegetables are just tender.

4 Stir in the mushroom ketchup and palm sugar, garnish with coriander leaves and serve with noodles or rice.

Potato Curry Energy 231kcal/967kJ; Protein 6.7g; Carbohydrate 26.2g, of which sugars 7.4g; Fat 12.4g, of which saturates 4.1g; Cholesterol 0mg; Calcium 110mg; Fibre 2g; Sodium 63mg
Hot Thai Curry Energy 279kcal/1161kJ; Protein 9.8g; Carbohydrate 17.4g, of which sugars 13.3g; Fat 19.4g, of which saturates 3.6g; Cholesterol 5mg; Calcium 99mg; Fibre 3.3g; Sodium 824mg

Tofu and Green Bean Red Curry

'his is one of those versatile ecipes that should be in very cook's repertoire. This ersion uses green beans, but ther types of vegetable vork equally well, depending n what is available. The tofu akes on the flavour of the pice paste and also boosts he nutritional value.

erves 4

00ml/1 pint/2½ cups canned coconut milk
5ml/1 tbsp Thai red curry paste
45ml/3 tbsp Thai fish sauce
10ml/2 tsp light muscovado (brown) sugar
225g/8oz/3⅓ cups button (white) mushrooms
115g/4oz/scant 1 cup green beans, trimmed
175g/6oz firm tofu, rinsed, drained and cut in 2cm/¾in cubes
4 kaffir lime leaves, torn
2 fresh red chillies, seeded and sliced
fresh coriander (cilantro) leaves, to garnish
boiled rice, to serve

Pour about one-third of the coconut milk into a wok or large ying pan. Cook gently until it starts to separate and an oily heen appears on the surface.

2 Add the red curry paste, fish sauce and sugar to the coconut nilk. Mix thoroughly, then add the mushrooms. Stir and cook for minute. Stir in the remaining coconut milk.

3 Bring back to the boil, then add the green beans and tofu ubes. Simmer gently for 4–5 minutes more until the beans are ıst tender, but still have a little bite.

4 Stir the kaffir lime leaves and sliced red chillies in to the wok r frying pan. Spoon the curry into a warmed serving dish, arnish with the coriander leaves and serve immediately, with oiled rice for a complete meal.

Cook's Tip
If the tofu is a bit wet, wrap it in a clean dish towel and place a weight on it for 10 minutes to remove some moisture.

Vegetable Tofu Burgers

These soft golden patties are stuffed full of mixed frozen vegetables, which are economical and easy to use. The burgers are very quick and easy to make and very popular with kids. Serve in sesame seed buns with salad and ketchup.

Serves 4

4 potatoes, peeled and cubed
250g/9oz frozen mixed vegetables, such as corn, green beans, (bell) peppers
45ml/3 tbsp vegetable oil
2 leeks, coarsely chopped
1 garlic clove, crushed
250g/9oz firm tofu, drained and crumbled
30ml/2 tbsp soy sauce
15ml/1 tbsp tomato purée (paste)
115g/4oz/2 cups fresh breadcrumbs
small bunch fresh coriander (cilantro) or parsley (optional)
salt and ground black pepper
sesame buns, sliced tomatoes, salad and ketchup, to serve

1 Cook the potatoes in salted, boiling water for 10–12 minutes, until tender, then drain. Mash the potatoes in the pan.

2 Meanwhile, cook the frozen vegetables in a separate pan of salted, boiling water for 5 minutes, until tender, then drain well.

3 Heat 15ml/1 tbsp of the oil in a large frying pan. Add the leeks and garlic and cook over low heat, stirring occasionally, for about 5 minutes, until softened and golden. Add to the mashed potatoes, together with the drained vegetables, tofu, soy sauce, tomatoe purée, breadcrumbs, herbs, if using, and plenty of salt and pepper. Mix well until combined. Shape into eight burgers.

4 Heat another 15ml/1 tbsp oil in the frying pan. Cook four burgers at a time over low heat for 4–5 minutes on each side, until golden brown and warmed through.

5 Repeat with the remaining four burgers, using the remaining oil. Keep the first batch warm in a low oven.

6 To serve, tuck a burger inside each sesame bun, top with salad and sliced tomatoes, and serve with ketchup on the side.

ofu Curry Energy 59kcal/250kJ; Protein 3.8g; Carbohydrate 7.5g, of which sugars 7.1g; Fat 1.8g, of which saturates 0.4g; Cholesterol 0mg; Calcium 188mg; Fibre 0.8g; Sodium 291mg
egetable Tofu Burgers Energy 412kcal/1713kJ; Protein 14g; Carbohydrate 57g, of which sugars 7g; Fat 16g, of which saturates 2g; Cholesterol 0mg; Calcium 400mg; Fibre 8g; Sodium 788mg

Vegetable and Marinated Tofu Pasta

Feel inspired to change this recipe to suit the ingredients you have to hand – the more colourful, the better. Make sure the vegetables are cut in even pieces so that they all cook by the same time.

Serves 4

4 carrots, halved lengthways and thinly sliced diagonally
1 butternut squash, peeled, seeded and cut into small chunks
2 courgettes (zucchini), thinly sliced diagonally
1 red onion, cut into wedges
1 red (bell) pepper, seeded and sliced into thick strips
1 garlic bulb, cut in half horizontally
4 rosemary sprigs
60ml/4 tbsp olive oil
60ml/4 tbsp balsamic vinegar
30ml/2 tbsp soy sauce
500g/1¼lb marinated deep-fried tofu
10–12 cherry tomatoes, halved
250g/9oz dried pasta, such as papardelle, fusilli or conchiglie
sea salt and ground black pepper

1 Preheat the oven to 220°C/425°F/Gas 7. Place the carrots, butternut squash, courgettes, onion wedges and pepper in a large, deep roasting pan, spreading them out well. Add the garlic, cut side down, and rosemary. Drizzle over the olive oil, balsamic vinegar and soy sauce.

2 Season to taste with sea salt and pepper and toss to mix together and coat evenly with the oil. Roast the vegetables for 50–60 minutes, until they are tender and lightly browned at the edges. Toss the vegetables around once or twice during the cooking to expose different sides and cook evenly.

3 Add the tofu and cherry tomatoes to the roasting pan about 10 minutes before the end of the roasting time. Meanwhile, bring a large pan of lightly salted water to the boil, add the pasta, bring back to the boil and cook for 10 minutes. Drain the pasta and return to the pan with a little of the cooking water.

4 Remove the roasting pan from the oven and squeeze the garlic out of the baked skins using a wooden spoon. Toss the pasta with the vegetables, tofu and garlic, taste and adjust the seasoning, if necessary, and serve immediately.

Chickpea Rissoles

This is one of the classic meze dishes that are typically found on a Greek table. It is an inexpensive dish, but very appetizing.

Serves 4

300g/11oz/scant 1½ cups chickpeas, soaked overnight in water to cover
105ml/7 tbsp extra virgin olive oil
2 large onions, chopped
15ml/1 tbsp ground cumin
2 garlic cloves, crushed
3–4 fresh sage leaves, chopped
45ml/3 tbsp chopped fresh flat leaf parsley
1 egg, lightly beaten
45ml/3 tbsp self-raising (self-rising) flour
50g/2oz/½ cup plain (all-purpose) flour
salt and ground black pepper
radishes and olives, to serve

1 Drain the chickpeas, rinse under cold water and drain again. Transfer them to a large pan, cover with plenty of fresh cold water and bring them to the boil. Skim the froth from the surface of the water with a slotted spoon until the liquid is clea

2 Cover the pan and cook for 1¼–1½ hours, or until the chickpeas are very soft. Set aside a few tablespoons of cooking liquid, then strain the chickpeas, discarding the rest of the liquid. Transfer them to a food processor, add 30–45ml/2–3 tbsp of the reserved liquid and process to a velvety mash.

3 Heat 45ml/3 tbsp of the olive oil in a large frying pan, add the onions, and sauté until they are light golden. Add the cumin and the garlic and stir for a few seconds until their aroma rises. Stir in the chopped sage leaves and the parsley, and set aside.

4 Scrape the chickpea mash into a large bowl and add the egg the self-raising flour, and the fried onion and herb mixture. Season and mix well. Take large walnut-size pieces and flatten them so that they look like thick, round mini-hamburgers.

5 Coat the rissoles lightly in the plain flour. Heat the remaining olive oil in a large frying pan and fry them in batches until they are crisp and golden on both sides. Drain on kitchen paper and serve hot with the radishes and olives.

Vegetable Pasta Energy 807kcal/3380kJ; Protein 42g; Carbohydrate 75g, of which sugars 21g; Fat.39g, of which saturates 3g; Cholesterol 0mg; Calcium 1987mg; Fibre 8g; Sodium 595mg
Chickpea Rissoles Energy 532Kcal/2231kJ; Protein 19.7g; Carbohydrate 63.6g, of which sugars 8.1g; Fat 23.9g, of which saturates 3.2g; Cholesterol 0mg; Calcium 222mg; Fibre 10.7g; Sodium 77mg

ofu and Pepper Kebabs

oak the wooden skewers in old water for 30 minutes, to revent scorching.

erves 4

50g/9oz firm tofu, drained
50g/2oz/½ cup dry-roasted peanuts
2 red and 2 green (bell) peppers, halved and seeded
60ml/4 tbsp sweet chilli dipping sauce, to serve

Pat the tofu dry on kitchen paper, then cut it into small cubes. inely grind the peanuts in a blender or food processor and ansfer to a plate. Coat the tofu in the ground nuts.

Preheat the grill (broiler) to medium. Cut the peppers into arge chunks, and thread on to four large skewers with the tofu ubes and place on a foil-lined grill rack. Grill (broil) the kebabs, urning them, for 10–12 minutes, or until the peppers and eanuts are beginning to brown. Serve with the dipping sauce.

ried Garlic Tofu

simple but delicious egetarian appetizer. Soak the vooden skewers as above.

erves 4

00g/1¼lb firm tofu, sliced
50g/2oz/¼ cup butter
2 garlic cloves, thinly sliced
200g/7oz enoki or other mushrooms
45ml/3 tbsp soy sauce
30ml/2 tbsp sake or lemon juice

Melt one-third of the butter in a frying pan. Add the garlic nd cook, stirring, until golden. Remove from the pan. Add half e remaining butter to the pan and cook the mushrooms and or 3–4 minutes, until softened, then remove from the pan.

Place the tofu in the pan with the remaining butter and cook n both sides over medium heat. until golden. Return the garlic o the pan, add the soy sauce and sake or lemon juice and immer for 1 minute. Transfer to warm serving plates and serve mmediately with the mushrooms.

Peanut and Tofu Cutlets

These delicious, high-protein patties make a filling and satisfying vegetarian meal served with lightly steamed green vegetables or a crisp salad, and a tangy salsa or tomato ketchup.

Serves 4

90g/3½oz/½ cup brown rice
15ml/1 tbsp vegetable oil
1 onion, finely chopped
1 garlic clove, crushed
200g/7oz/1¾ cups unsalted peanuts
250g/9oz firm tofu, drained and crumbled
small bunch of fresh coriander (cilantro) or parsley, chopped (optional)
30ml/2 tbsp soy sauce
30ml/2 tbsp olive oil, for shallow frying

1 Cook the rice according to the instructions on the packet until tender, then drain.

2 Heat the vegetable oil in a large, heavy frying pan and cook the onion and garlic over low heat, stirring occasionally, for about 5 minutes, until softened and golden.

3 Meanwhile, spread out the peanuts on a baking sheet and toast under the grill (broiler) for a few minutes, until browned.

4 Place the toasted peanuts, onion, garlic, rice, tofu, fresh coriander or parsley, if using, and soy sauce in a blender or food processor and process until the mixture comes together in a thick paste.

5 Divide the paste into eight even mounds and form each mound into a cutlet shape or square.

6 Heat the olive oil for shallow frying in a large, heavy frying pan. Add the cutlets, in two batches if necessary, and cook for 5–10 minutes on each side, until golden and heated through.

7 Remove from the pan with a metal spatula and drain on kitchen paper. Keep warm while you cook the remaining batch, then serve immediately.

ofu Kebabs Energy 175kcal/730kJ; Protein 10g; Carbohydrate 12.9g, of which sugars 11.4g; Fat 9.6g, of which saturates 1.6g; Cholesterol 0mg; Calcium 339mg; Fibre 3.6g; Sodium 108mg
ried Garlic Tofu Energy 198kcal/819kJ; Protein 12g; Carbohydrate 2g, of which sugars 2g; Fat 16g, of which saturates 7g; Cholesterol 27mg; Calcium 645mg; Fibre 2g; Sodium 884mg
eanut Cutlets Energy 495kcal/2059kJ; Protein 20.2g; Carbohydrate 27.1g, of which sugars 5.3g; Fat 34.7g, of which saturates 5.9g; Cholesterol 0mg; Calcium 381mg; Fibre 4.4g; Sodium 543mg

Spaghetti with Garlic and Oil

This very quick and easy dish is a great kitchen standby for rushed evenings or a very quick lunch.

Serves 4

400g/14oz dried spaghetti
90ml/6 tbsp olive oil
3 garlic cloves, chopped
60ml/4 tbsp fresh flat leaf parsley, chopped
salt and ground black pepper
Parmesan cheese, grated, to serve (optional)

1 Cook the pasta in a large pan of lightly salted boiling water for 10–12 minutes, until it is just tender.

2 Heat the oil in a frying pan and gently fry the garlic until just golden. Stir in the parsley and salt and pepper. Set aside.

3 Drain the pasta, retaining a little of the cooking water, mix in the garlic and parsley. Serve with Parmesan if you wish.

Spaghetti with Lemon

Another simple dish, which combines flavoursome ingredients, this is ideal for when you need a quick bite. Try sprinkling over fried breadcrumbs before serving if you wish, for added crunch.

Serves 4

350g/12oz dried spaghetti
90ml/6 tbsp olive oil
juice of 1 large lemon
2 garlic cloves, cut into thin slivers
salt and ground black pepper, to taste

1 Cook the pasta in a large pan of salted boiling water for 10–12 minutes, until it is just tender. Drain the cooked pasta thoroughly in a colander, then return it to the pan.

2 Pour the olive oil and lemon juice over the pasta, sprinkle in the slivers of garlic and add seasoning to taste.

3 Toss the pasta over medium to high heat for 1–2 minutes. Serve immediately in four warmed bowls.

Speedy Spaghetti with Fresh Tomato Sauce

This is an ideal dish to make in the summer when you have a glut of ripe, juicy tomatoes. If you have under-ripe tomatoes, however, you could roast them in a hot oven, with a pinch of sugar sprinkled on top and olive oil drizzled over, for 10–15 minutes to develop the flavour.

Serves 4

675g/1½lb ripe Italian plum tomatoes or sweet cherry tomatoes
60ml/4 tbsp extra virgin olive oil
1 onion, finely chopped
350g/12oz dried spaghetti
a small handful of fresh basil leaves
salt and ground black pepper
coarsely shaved Parmesan cheese, to serve

1 Cut a cross in the base end of each tomato, and cover with boiling water. Leave for 1–2 minutes, then lift them out with a slotted spoon and when cool enough to handle, remove and discard the skins. Place on a chopping board and cut them into quarters, then eighths.

2 Heat the oil in a large pan, add the onion and cook gently for 5 minutes, until softened and lightly coloured.

3 Add the tomatoes to the pan, season with salt and ground black pepper, bring to a simmer, then turn the heat down to low and cover. Cook, stirring occasionally, for 10–15 minutes, until the mixture is thick.

4 Meanwhile, cook the pasta according to the instructions on the packet. Shred the basil leaves or tear them into small pieces.

5 Remove the sauce from the heat, chop or tear the basil into the sauce and check the seasoning.

6 Drain the pasta lightly so it retains some moisture, then transfer into a warmed bowl. Pour the sauce over and toss the mixture well. Serve immediately, with shaved Parmesan handed round in a separate bowl.

Spaghetti with Garlic Energy 505kcal/2126kJ; Protein 12.8g; Carbohydrate 76.4g, of which sugars 3.5g; Fat 18.6g, of which saturates 2.6g; Cholesterol 0mg; Calcium 27mg; Fibre 3.3g; Sodium 3mg
Spaghetti with Lemon Energy 448kcal/1886kJ; Protein 10.5g; Carbohydrate 64.9g, of which sugars 3g; Fat 18.1g, of which saturates 2.5g; Cholesterol 0mg; Calcium 22mg; Fibre 2.6g; Sodium 3mg
Spaghetti with Tomato Sauce Energy 436kcal/1840kJ; Protein 12.2g; Carbohydrate 71.5g, of which sugars 9.2g; Fat 13.2g, of which saturates 1.9g; Cholesterol 0mg; Calcium 58mg; Fibre 4.9g; Sodium 22m

Warm Penne with Green Vegetable Sauce

.ightly cooked fresh green egetables are tossed with asta to create this low-fat talian dish, ideal for a light unch or supper.

erves 4

5ml/1 tbsp olive oil
carrots, finely diced
small leek, washed and thinly sliced
.5ml/½ tsp sugar
1 courgette (zucchini), finely diced
75g/3oz green beans, topped and tailed and cut into 2cm/¾in lengths
115g/4oz/1 cup frozen peas
350g/12oz/3 cups dried penne
1 handful fresh flat leaf parsley, finely chopped
2 ripe plum tomatoes, skinned and diced
salt and ground black pepper, to taste

Heat the oil in a medium frying pan. Add the carrots and leek hen sprinkle the sugar over and cook, stirring frequently, for bout 5 minutes.

2 Stir in the courgette, green beans, peas and plenty of salt nd pepper. Cover and cook over low to medium heat for –8 minutes until the vegetables are tender, stirring occasionally.

3 Meanwhile, cook the pasta in a large pan of boiling salted vater, according to the packet instructions, until it is tender or l dente. Drain the pasta thoroughly and keep it hot until t is ready to be served.

4 Stir the parsley and chopped plum tomatoes into the egetable mixture and adjust the seasoning to taste. Toss vith the cooked pasta and serve immediately.

Variation

Change this recipe to reflect seasonal ingredients, for example you could use a mixture of shredded spring greens (collards) or baby spinach together with basil instead of the parsley.

Pasta with Roast Tomatoes and Goat's Cheese

Roasting tomatoes brings out their flavour and sweetness, which contrasts perfectly with the sharp taste and creamy texture of goat's cheese. Serve with a crisp green salad flavoured with matching herbs.

Serves 4

8 large ripe tomatoes
60ml/4 tbsp garlic-infused olive oil
450g/1lb any dried pasta shapes
200g/7oz firm goat's cheese, crumbled
salt and ground black pepper, to taste

1 Preheat the oven to 190°C/375°F/Gas 5.

2 Place the tomatoes in a roasting pan and drizzle over 30ml/2 tbsp of the oil. Season well with salt and pepper and roast for 20–25 minutes, or until soft and slightly charred.

3 Meanwhile, cook the pasta in plenty of salted, boiling water, according to the instructions on the packet. Drain well and return to the pan.

4 Roughly mash the tomatoes with a fork, and then transfer the contents of the roasting pan into the pasta, including any oily juices. Stir to mix, then gently stir in the goat's cheese and the remaining oil and serve.

Cook's Tip

A good goat's milk cheese tastes as though it has absorbed the herby aromas of tarragon, thyme or marjoram. Include one or all of these herbs in a salad to accompany the dish.

Variation

For a quick version of this dish, replace the roasted tomatoes with sun-dried tomatoes. Choose the ones preserved in olive oil and use their oil instead of garlic-infused oil.

Warm Penne Energy 401Kcal/1698kJ; Protein 15.5g; Carbohydrate 76.7g, of which sugars 11.3g; Fat 5.7g, of which saturates 0.9g; Cholesterol 0mg; Calcium 99mg; Fibre 8.1g; Sodium 26mg
Pasta with Tomatoes Energy 682kcal/2873kJ; Protein 25.6g; Carbohydrate 90.9g, of which sugars 11.2g; Fat 26.6g, of which saturates 11g; Cholesterol 47mg; Calcium 111mg; Fibre 5.5g; Sodium 324mg

Fusilli with Smoked Trout

Smoked trout has a lovely delicate flavour, and mixed with other ingredients a little goes a long way. Here, it is combined with a rich, creamy sauce and finely sliced vegetables to make a flavoursome and satisfying pasta dish; perfect for a quick supper.

Serves 4–6

2 carrots, peeled and cut into matchsticks
1 leek, cut into matchsticks
2 celery sticks, cut into matchsticks
150ml/¼ pint/⅔ cup vegetable stock
225g/8oz smoked trout fillets, skinned and cut into strips
200g/7oz cream cheese
150ml/¼ pint/⅔ cup fish stock
15ml/1 tbsp chopped fresh dill or fennel
225g/8oz/2 cups long curly fusilli or other dried pasta shapes
salt and ground black pepper
fresh dill sprigs, to garnish

1 Put the carrot, leek and celery matchsticks into a pan and add the vegetable stock. Bring to the boil and cook quickly for 4–5 minutes, until most of the stock has evaporated. Remove from the heat and add the smoked trout.

2 Put the cream cheese and fish stock into a pan over medium heat, and whisk until smooth. Add the dill or fennel and salt and ground black pepper to taste.

3 Cook the fusilli in a pan of salted boiling water according to the instructions on the packet. When the pasta is tender, but still firm to the bite, drain it thoroughly, and return it to the pan.

4 Add the sauce, toss lightly and transfer to a serving bowl. Top with the cooked vegetables and trout. Serve immediately, garnished with the dill sprigs.

Cook's Tip
Once regarded as poor man's smoked salmon, smoked trout is a delicious treat in its own right. It is often sold as skinned fillets, but you can also occasionally find them sold whole.

Farfalle with Tuna

Canned tuna is good value for money, is very versatile for weekday suppers, and mixed with pasta one can will easily stretch to feed four people.

Serves 4

400g/14oz/3½ cups dried farfalle
600ml/1 pint/2½ cups passata (bottled strained tomatoes)
8–10 black olives, cut into rings
175g/6oz can tuna in olive oil

1 Cook the pasta in a large pan of lightly salted boiling water according to the instructions on the packet.

2 Gently heat the passata and add the olive rings. Drain the tuna and flake with a fork. Add the tuna to the sauce with abou 60ml/4 tbsp of the pasta water used for cooking the pasta. .

3 Drain the pasta thoroughly and transfer it into a large, warmed serving bowl. Pour the tuna sauce over the top and toss lightly to mix. Serve immediately.

Penne with Cream and Salmon

Supremely quick and easy to make, this dish is also quite elegant and very tasty.

Serves 4

400g/14oz/3½ cups dried penne
115g/4oz smoked salmon, cut intc small strips
25g/1oz/2 tbsp butter
150ml/¼ pint/⅔ cup single (light) cream
salt and ground black pepper

1 Cook the pasta in a large pan of lightly salted boiling water according to the instructions on the packet.

2 Melt the butter in a large pan. Stir in the cream with about a quarter of the salmon, then season with pepper. Heat gently for 3–4 minutes, stirring all the time. Do not allow the sauce to boi

3 Drain the pasta, return to the pan and toss in the sauce. Serve topped with the remaining salmon.

Fusilli Energy 348kcal/1455kJ; Protein 15.9g; Carbohydrate 31.4g, of which sugars 4.5g; Fat 18.5g, of which saturates 10.3g; Cholesterol 45mg; Calcium 74mg; Fibre 2.8g; Sodium 822mg
Farfalle Energy 459kcal/1949kJ; Protein 25.2g; Carbohydrate 78.6g, of which sugars 7.8g; Fat 7.1g, of which saturates 1.1g; Cholesterol 22mg; Calcium 53mg; Fibre 4.2g; Sodium 756mg
Penne Energy 459kcal/ 1936kJ; Protein 19.1g; Carbohydrate 65.7g, of which sugars 3.8g; Fat 15.2g, of which saturates 8.2g; Cholesterol 44mg; Calcium 62mg; Fibre 2.6g; Sodium 592mg

nelli with Breadcrumbs

southern Italy, especially cily and Calabria, fine, stale readcrumbs are often used stead of grated cheese on asta, making the ideal udget ingredient. Sometimes e breadcrumbs are fried r extra texture.

erves 4
0ml/4 tbsp olive oil
garlic cloves, chopped
225g/8oz fresh, ripe tomatoes, quartered and seeded
10 fresh basil leaves, torn into shreds
115g/4oz/1 cup coarse dried breadcrumbs
30–45ml/2–3 tbsp grated Pecorino or Parmesan cheese
60ml/4 tbsp chopped fresh parsley
450g/1lb/4 cups anelli or other pasta shapes
salt

Pour the oil into a large pan and add the garlic. Fry for about -3 minutes, until the garlic is transparent, then add the omatoes and basil. Stir in salt to taste, then cover and simmer e mixture for 20 minutes on medium heat. Add water if the auce becomes too thick.

Bring a large pan of salted water to the boil. Meanwhile, put e breadcrumbs in a bowl and add the cheese and parsley.

When the tomato sauce is almost ready, add the pasta to the oiling water. Bring it back to the boil, then cook the pasta for 2–14 minutes, until tender, then drain and return to the pan.

Pour over the tomato sauce and toss well. Divide the mixture mong four bowls, sprinkle each portion generously with the readcrumb mixture and serve immediately.

Variations

- *Instead of anelli, you could use maccheroncelli (a thin tubular shape, slightly thinner than a pencil) or pennette (short, thin penne).*
- *Use sweet, sun-ripened tomatoes so the sauce has no trace of the sour flavour that unripe tomatoes tend to impart.*

Bacon and Pumpkin Pasta

The sweet flavour of pumpkin is nicely balanced by the Parmesan in this creamy pasta sauce, while fried garlic breadcrumbs provide a welcome crunch.

Serves 4
800g/1¾lb fresh pumpkin flesh, cut into small cubes
300g/11oz dried tagliatelle
65g/2½oz/5 tbsp butter
1 onion, sliced
115g/4oz rindless smoked back bacon, diced
15ml/1 tbsp olive oil
2 garlic cloves, crushed
75g/3oz/1½ cups fresh white breadcrumbs
150ml/¼ pint/⅔ cup single (light) cream
50g/2oz/⅔ cup freshly grated Parmesan cheese
freshly grated nutmeg
30ml/2 tbsp chopped fresh flat leaf parsley
15ml/1 tbsp chopped fresh chives
salt and ground black pepper
sprigs of flat leaf parsley, to garnish

1 Bring two pans of lightly salted water to the boil. Place the pumpkin cubes in one pan and the pasta in the other. Cook for 10–12 minutes, stirring both pans several times.

2 Meanwhile, heat one-third of the butter in a separate large pan. Fry the onion and bacon for 5 minutes.

3 Melt the remaining butter with the oil in a frying pan. Add the garlic and breadcrumbs. Fry gently until the crumbs are golden brown and crisp. Drain on kitchen paper, spoon into a dish and keep warm for topping the pasta.

4 Drain the pumpkin and add it to the onion and bacon mixture, with the cream. Heat without stirring until bubbles appear on the surface and the cream is just below boiling point.

5 Drain the pasta, add to the pan and heat through. Stir in the Parmesan, nutmeg, chopped parsley, chives and seasoning.

6 Spoon into a warmed bowl or individual pasta bowls, sprinkle with the garlic breadcrumbs and garnish with the sprigs of flat leaf parsley. Serve immediately.

nelli Energy 650kcal/2748kJ; Protein 22g; Carbohydrate 107.7g, of which sugars 6.5g; Fat 17.6g, of which saturates 4.1g; Cholesterol 11mg; Calcium 230mg; Fibre 5.1g; Sodium 354mg
acon and Pumpkin Energy 691kcal/2897kJ; Protein 23.8g; Carbohydrate 76.6g, of which sugars 8.1g; Fat 34.2g, of which saturates 18.1g; Cholesterol 83mg; Calcium 293mg; Fibre 4.8g; Sodium 834mg

Spaghetti Carbonara

This Italian classic with pancetta and a garlic-and-egg sauce that cooks around the hot spaghetti is popular worldwide. It makes a great last-minute supper. For a more economical version, use smoked bacon instead of pancetta.

Serves 4

30ml/2 tbsp olive oil
1 small onion, finely chopped
1 large garlic clove, crushed
8 slices pancetta or rindless smoked streaky (fatty) bacon, cut into 1cm/½in pieces
350g/12oz dried spaghetti
4 eggs
90–120ml/6–8 tbsp crème fraîche
60ml/4 tbsp freshly grated Parmesan cheese, plus extra to serve
salt and ground black pepper

1 Heat the oil in a large pan, add the onion and garlic and fry gently for about 5 minutes until softened. Add the pancetta or bacon to the pan. Cook for 10 minutes, stirring often.

2 Meanwhile, cook the spaghetti in a large pan of lightly salted boiling water for 10–12 minutes.

3 Put the eggs, crème fraîche and grated Parmesan in a bowl. Stir in plenty of black pepper, then beat together well.

4 Drain the pasta thoroughly, transfer it into the pan with the pancetta or bacon and toss well to mix. Turn off the heat under the pan, then immediately add the egg mixture and toss thoroughly so that it cooks lightly and coats the pasta.

5 Season to taste, then divide the pasta among four warmed bowls and sprinkle with ground black pepper. Serve the pasta immediately, with extra grated Parmesan handed around separately in a bowl.

Variation
Instead of beating the eggs with crème fraîche, use double (heavy) cream or sour cream, if you prefer.

Tortellini with Ham

This is a very easy recipe that can be made quickly from storecupboard ingredients. It is therefore ideal for an after-work supper, especially for hungry kids after school.

Serves 4

250g/9oz meat-filled tortellini
30ml/2 tbsp olive oil
¼ large onion, finely chopped
115g/4oz cooked ham, diced
150ml/¼ pint/⅔ cup passata (bottled strained tomatoes)
100ml/3½fl oz/scant ½ cup double (heavy) cream
about 90g/3½oz/generous 1 cup freshly grated grano padano cheese
salt and ground black pepper, to taste

1 Cook the pasta in a large pan of salted water, until tender, according to the instructions on the packet.

2 Meanwhile, heat the oil in a large pan, add the onion and cook over low heat, stirring frequently, for about 5 minutes until softened. Add the diced ham to the pan and cook, stirring occasionally, until it darkens.

3 Add the passata to the pan. Stir well, then add salt and pepper to taste. Bring to the boil, lower the heat and simmer the sauce for a few minutes, stirring occasionally, until it has reduced in quantity slightly.

4 Stir the cream into the sauce until it comes back to a simmer. Drain the pasta well and add it to the sauce.

5 Add a handful of grated grano padano to the pan. Stir to combine well and taste for seasoning. Serve in warmed bowls, topped with the remaining grano padano.

Cook's Tip
Passata (bottled strained tomatoes) is handy for making quick sauces, but for a more economical version you can make your own in the summer with a glut of homegrown tomatoes.

Carbonara Energy 708kcal/2966kj; Protein 30.7g; Carbohydrate 66.6g; of which sugars 4.2g; Fat 37.5g; of which saturates 15.5g; Cholesterol 261mg; Calcium 250mg; Fibre 2.8g; Sodium 824mg
Tortellini Energy 373kcal/1549kJ; Protein 17.4g; Carbohydrate 10.9g, of which sugars 3.5g; Fat 29.2g, of which saturates 14.8g; Cholesterol 79mg; Calcium 302mg; Fibre 1g; Sodium 1025mg

paghetti with Rocket Pesto

his is the pesto for real ocket lovers. It is sharp and eppery, and delicious for a ummer pasta meal with a ass of chilled dry white ine. If you make double uantities the pesto will eep, covered, in the efrigerator for 2–3 days

erves 4

garlic cloves
)ml/6 tbsp pine nuts
2 large handfuls rocket (arugula), total weight about 150g/5oz, stalks removed
50g/2oz/⅔ cup Parmesan cheese, freshly grated
50g/2oz/⅔ cup Pecorino cheese, freshly grated
90ml/6 tbsp extra virgin olive oil
400g/14oz fresh or dried spaghetti
salt and ground black pepper
freshly grated Parmesan and Pecorino cheese, to serve

Put the garlic and pine nuts in a blender or food processor nd process until finely chopped.

Add the rocket, Parmesan and Pecorino, oil and salt and epper to taste and process for 5 seconds. Stop and scrape own the side of the bowl. Process for 5–10 seconds more until smooth paste is formed.

Cook the spaghetti in a pan of salted boiling water according the packet instructions.

Turn the pesto into a large bowl. Just before the pasta is ready, ir one or two ladlefuls of the cooking water into the pesto.

Lightly drain the pasta, so you retain some of the cooking quid, transfer it into the bowl of pesto and toss well to mix. erve immediately, with the grated cheeses offered separately.

Variation
To temper the flavour of the rocket (arugula) and make the pesto milder, add 115g/4oz/½ cup ricotta or mascarpone cheese to the pesto in step 4 and mix before adding the water.

Minty Courgette Linguine

Sweet, mild courgettes and refreshing mint are a great combination and are delicious with pasta. Dried linguine has been used here but you can use any type of pasta you like. Couscous also works well in place of pasta.

Serves 4

450g/1lb dried linguine
75ml/5 tbsp garlic-infused olive oil
4 small courgettes (zucchini), sliced into rounds
1 small bunch of fresh mint, roughly chopped
salt and ground black pepper

1 Cook the linguine in plenty of salted, boiling water according to the instructions on the packet.

2 Meanwhile, heat 45ml/3 tbsp of the oil in a large frying pan and add the courgettes. Fry for 2–3 minutes, stirring occasionally, until they are tender and golden.

3 Drain the pasta lightly, retaining some of the liquid, and transfer to the frying pan and toss with the courgettes.

4 Stir in the chopped mint. Season with salt and pepper, drizzle over the remaining oil and serve immediately.

Cook's Tip
To make garlic oil, add several whole cloves to a bottle of olive oil and leave to infuse (steep) for about 2 weeks before using.

Variations
- *For a more creamy version of this dish, add a few good spoons of crème fraîche, instead of the remaining oil, and put the pan back on low heat for a couple of minutes to heat through, stirring gently.*
- *Alternatively, you can fry some finely chopped shallots with the courgettes (zucchini) in regular olive oil rather than garlic-infused oil. Varying the oil flavour can bring a new slant to this dish. Try lemon-infused oil for a more delicate flavour.*

paghetti with Pesto Energy 314kcal/1322kJ; Protein 15.4g; Carbohydrate 43.5g, of which sugars 3.6g; Fat 10.3g, of which saturates 3.4g; Cholesterol 14mg; Calcium 176mg; Fibre 2.7g; Sodium 216mg
linty Linguine Energy 536kcal/2261kJ; Protein 16.2g; Carbohydrate 86.3g, of which sugars 5.8g; Fat 16.4g, of which saturates 2.3g; Cholesterol 0mg; Calcium 86mg; Fibre 4.4g; Sodium 7mg

Broccoli and Chilli Spaghetti

The contrast between the hot chilli flakes and the mild gentle taste of broccoli is delicious and goes perfectly with spaghetti. For add extra flavour and texture, sprinkle the spaghetti and broccoli with toasted pine nuts and grated or shaved Parmesan cheese just before serving.

Serves 4

350g/12oz dried spaghetti
450g/1lb sprouting broccoli, cut into small florets, and including any leaves
150ml/¼ pint/⅔ cup garlic-infused olive oil
1 fat red chilli, seeded and finely chopped
salt and ground black pepper

1 Bring a large pan of lightly salted water to the boil. Add the spaghetti and broccoli florets with any leaves, and cook for 8–10 minutes, until both are tender. Drain thoroughly.

2 Using the back of a fork, crush the broccoli roughly, taking care not to mash the spaghetti strands at the same time.

3 Meanwhile, warm the oil and finely chopped chilli in a small pan over low heat and cook very gently for 5 minutes.

4 Pour the chilli and oil over the spaghetti and broccoli and toss together to combine. Season to taste.

5 Divide between four warmed bowls and serve immediately.

Cook's Tip
Cooking the spaghetti and broccoli in the same pan helps the pasta to absorb more of the vegetable's flavour and vitamins. To retain more of the nutrients, reserve a small amount of the cooking water and pour over the dish before tossing together.

Variation
Exclude the chilli for a tangy, but less spicy dish.

Pasta with Sowly Cooked Onions, Cabbage, Parmesan and Pine Nuts

This is an unusual, but quite delicious, way of serving pasta. Cavolo nero, a Tuscan black cabbage, is a close relative of curly kale.

Serves 4

25g/1oz/2 tbsp butter
15ml/1 tbsp extra virgin olive oil, plus more for drizzling (optional)
500g/1¼lb Spanish onions, halved and thinly sliced
5–10ml/1–2 tsp balsamic vinegar
400–500g/14oz–20oz cavolo nero, spring greens (collards), curly kale or Brussels sprout tops, finely shredded
400–500g/14–20oz dried pasta, such as penne or fusilli
75g/3oz/1 cup freshly grated Parmesan cheese
50g/2oz/½ cup pine nuts, toasted
salt and ground black pepper

1 Heat the butter and olive oil together in a large pan. Stir in the onions, cover and cook very gently, stirring occasionally, for about 20 minutes, until very soft.

2 Uncover the pan, and continue to cook gently, until the onions have turned golden yellow. Add the balsamic vinegar and season well, then cook for a further 1–2 minutes. Set aside.

3 Blanch the cavolo nero, or other greens, in boiling, lightly salted water for about 3 minutes. Drain well and add to the onions, then cook over low heat for 3–4 minutes.

4 Cook the pasta in lightly salted water for 8–12 minutes, until just tender. Drain, then add to the pan of onions and greens and toss thoroughly to mix. Season and stir in half the Parmesan. Transfer the pasta to warmed plates. Sprinkle the pine nuts and Parmesan on top and serve with olive oil for drizzling over.

Variation
To make a delicious pilaff, cook 250g/9oz/1¼ cups brown basmati rice and use in place of the pasta.

Broccoli and Chilli Energy 396kcal/1678kJ; Protein 17.3g; Carbohydrate 68.3g, of which sugars 6g; Fat 7.9g, of which saturates 0.8g; Cholesterol 0mg; Calcium 114mg; Fibre 5.6g; Sodium 24mg
Pasta with Onions Energy 662kcal/2780kJ; Protein 25.7g; Carbohydrate 87.6g, of which sugars 13.5g; Fat 25.7g, of which saturates 8.4g; Cholesterol 32mg; Calcium 494mg; Fibre 8.3g; Sodium 269mg

'asta with Aubergines

his Sicilian recipe is aditionally made from fried ıbergines, but cooking them the oven gives a lighter sh.

erves 4

medium aubergines (eggplants), about 225g/8oz each, diced small
5ml/3 tbsp olive oil
75g/10oz dried macaroni
50g/2oz/²⁄₃ cup grated Pecorino cheese
salt and ground black pepper
shredded fresh basil leaves, to garnish
crusty bread, to serve

For the tomato sauce

30ml/2 tbsp olive oil
1 onion, finely chopped
400g/14oz can chopped tomatoes or 400g/14oz passata

Soak the diced aubergine in a bowl of cold salted water r 30 minutes. Preheat the oven to 220°C/425°F/Gas 7.

Make the sauce. Heat the oil in a large pan, add the onion d cook gently for about 3 minutes until softened. Add the matoes, with salt and pepper to taste. Bring to the boil, lower e heat, cover and simmer for about 20 minutes. Stir the sauce d add a few spoonfuls of water from time to time, to prevent from becoming too thick. Remove from the heat.

Drain the aubergines and pat dry. Spread out in a roasting n, add the oil and toss to coat. Roast for 20–25 minutes, rning the aubergines occasionally so that they brown evenly.

Cook the pasta in a large pan of rapidly boiling salted water r 10–12 minutes or until al dente. Reheat the tomato sauce.

Drain the pasta thoroughly and add it to the tomato sauce, th half the roasted aubergines and half the Pecorino. Toss to ix, then taste for seasoning.

Spoon the pasta and sauce mixture into a warmed large rving dish and top with the remaining roasted aubergines. rinkle the shredded fresh basil leaves over the top, followed the remaining Pecorino. Serve immediately, with crusty bread.

Spicy Tomato Orecchiette

All pasta shapes work well in this incredibly fiery pasta dish, but orecchiette are particularly suitable, since their blandness and chewy texture act as a perfect foil for the hot sauce. The region that created this recipe, Basilicata, is famous for its use of chilli, which locals eat in large quantities and intensity without any obvious ill-effects.

Serves 4

150ml/¼ pint/²⁄₃ cup olive oil
3 garlic cloves
4 whole dried red chillies
60ml/4 tbsp tomato purée (paste)
400g/14oz dried orecchiette

1 Bring a large pan of salted water to the boil.

2 Heat the oil in a different very large pan. Add the garlic and chillies and fry over low to medium heat for 3–4 minutes, until the garlic is soft and golden brown and the chillies are very shiny and swollen. Do not let either burn.

3 Scoop the garlic and chillies out of the oil with a slotted spoon. Put the garlic and chillies in a food processor or blender and add the tomato purée. Process until smooth, then stir back into the oil remaining in the pan.

4 Add the pasta to the pan of boiling water. Cook for about 12–14 minutes until just tender, then drain.

5 Transfer the pasta into the pan containing the garlic and chilli mixture. Toss over the heat until the pasta is evenly coated with the sauce, then serve immediately.

Cook's Tips

- *For a milder flavour, use fewer chillies.*
- *The garlic, chilli and tomato purée (paste) can be pounded together in a large mortar using a pestle and then the oil incorporated to achieve more or less the same effect as with a food processor.*

sta with Aubergines Energy 506kcal/2126kJ; Protein 15g; Carbohydrate 61g, of which sugars 9g; Fat 24g, of which saturates 5g; Cholesterol 12mg; Calcium 178mg; Fibre 7g; Sodium 144mg
icy Orecchiette Energy 577kcal/2424kJ; Protein 12.7g; Carbohydrate 76g, of which sugars 5.2g; Fat 26.8g, of which saturates 3.7g; Cholesterol 0mg; Calcium 32mg; Fibre 3.3g; Sodium 39mg

Pappardelle with Tapenade

This home-made pasta is well worth the effort, but obviously bought dried pasta can easily be substituted if you need a really quick supper dish.

Serves 4

275g/10oz/2½ cups plain (all-purpose) flour
1.5ml/¼ tsp salt
3 eggs
45ml/3 tbsp sun-dried tomato purée (paste)

For the sauce

115g/4oz/⅔ cup pitted black olives
75ml/5 tbsp capers
5 drained anchovy fillets
1 red chilli, seeded and chopped
60ml/4 tbsp fresh basil
60ml/4 tbsp fresh parsley
150ml/¼ pint/⅔ cup olive oil
4 ripe tomatoes, skinned, seeded and chopped
salt and ground black pepper
flat leaf parsley or basil, to garnish
Parmesan cheese shavings, to serve

1 To make the pasta, sift the flour and salt into a bowl and make a well in the centre. Lightly beat the eggs with the tomato purée and pour the mixture into the well.

2 Mix the ingredients together using a round-bladed knife. Turn out on to a work surface and knead for 6–8 minutes until the dough is very smooth and soft, working in a little more flour if it becomes sticky. Wrap in foil and chill for 30 minutes.

3 To make the sauce, put the olives, capers, anchovies, chilli, basil and parsley in a food processor or blender with the oil. Process briefly until the ingredients are finely chopped.

4 Roll out the dough very thinly on a floured surface. Sprinkle with a little flour, then roll up like a Swiss roll (jelly roll). Cut across into 1cm/½in slices. Unroll the pasta strips and lay out on a clean dish towel for about 10 minutes to dry out.

5 Bring a large pan of salted water to the boil. Add the pasta and cook for 2–3 minutes. Drain, return to the pan, add the olive mixture, tomatoes, salt and black pepper, then toss gently over medium heat for about 1 minute until heated through. Garnish with parsley or basil and serve with Parmesan shavings.

Rigatoni with Pork

This is an excellent meat sauce using minced pork. Here it is served with rigatoni, but you could serve it with spaghetti.

Serves 4

1 small onion
½ carrot
½ celery stick
2 garlic cloves
25g/1oz/2 tbsp butter
30ml/2 tbsp olive oil
150g/5oz minced (ground) pork
60ml/4 tbsp dry white wine
400g/14oz can tomatoes
a few fresh basil leaves
400g/14oz/3½ cups dried rigator
salt and ground black pepper
Parmesan cheese shavings, to serv

1 Chop all the fresh vegetables finely, either in a food processo or by hand. Heat the butter and oil in a large pan until just sizzling, add the chopped vegetables and cook over medium heat, stirring frequently, for 3–4 minutes.

2 Add the minced pork and cook for 2–3 minutes, breaking up any lumps in the meat with a wooden spoon. Lower the heat and cook for a further 4–5 minutes, stirring frequently, then stir in the dry white wine.

3 Mix the tomatoes, whole basil leaves, salt and plenty of pepper in to the pan. Bring to the boil, then lower the heat, cover and simmer for 40 minutes, stirring from time to time.

4 Cook the pasta according to the instructions on the packet. Just before draining it, add a ladleful or two of the cooking water to the sauce. Stir well, then taste the sauce for seasoning

5 Drain the pasta, add it to the pan of sauce and toss well. Serve immediately, sprinkled with basil and Parmesan shavings.

Variation

To give the sauce a more intense flavour, soak 15g/½oz dried porcini mushrooms in 175ml/ 6fl oz/¾ cup warm water for 15–20 minutes, then drain, chop and add with the meat.

Pappardelle with Tapenade Energy 577kcal/2424kJ; Protein 12.7g; Carbohydrate 76g, of which sugars 5.2g; Fat 26.8g, of which saturates 3.7g; Cholesterol 0mg; Calcium 32mg; Fibre 3.3g; Sodium 39
Rigatoni with Pork Energy 537kcal/2265kJ; Protein 20.2g; Carbohydrate 79.6g, of which sugars 8.3g; Fat 16.5g, of which saturates 5.7g; Cholesterol 38mg; Calcium 46mg; Fibre 4.5g; Sodium 85mg

›paghetti Bolognese

'his is a much-loved family ›ish, and can also be a great udget meal, made with ninced beef, cooked for an our so that the flavour is eep and satisfying and, dded to spaghetti, will go long way.

erves 6–8

0ml/2 tbsp olive oil
onion, finely chopped
garlic clove, crushed
ml/1 tsp dried mixed herbs
.25ml/¼ tsp cayenne pepper
350–450g/12oz–1lb minced (ground) beef
400g/14oz can plum tomatoes
45ml/3 tbsp tomato ketchup
15ml/1 tbsp sun-dried tomato paste
5ml/1 tsp Worcestershire sauce
5ml/1 tsp dried oregano
450ml/¾ pint/1¾ cups beef or vegetable stock
45ml/3 tbsp red wine
400–450g/14oz–1lb dried spaghetti
salt and ground black pepper
grated Parmesan cheese, to serve

Heat the oil in a medium pan, add the onion and garlic and ɔok over low heat, stirring frequently, for about 5 minutes until ɔftened.

Stir the mixed herbs and cayenne in to the pan and cook for –3 minutes more. Add the minced beef and cook gently for ɔout 5 minutes, stirring frequently and breaking up any lumps the meat with a wooden spoon.

Stir in the canned tomatoes, ketchup, sun-dried tomato paste, Vorcestershire sauce, oregano and plenty of black pepper.

Pour in the stock and red wine and bring to the boil, stirring. :over the pan, lower the heat and leave the sauce to simmer ›r 30 minutes, stirring occasionally.

Cook the pasta according to the instructions on the packet.)rain well and divide among warmed bowls. Taste the sauce ıd add a little salt if necessary.

Spoon the sauce on top of the pasta and serve sprinkled with little Parmesan cheese.

Stuffed Pasta Shells

This makes an excellent dinner party starter for six, or a vegetarian main course for four, in which case you should fill 20 shells.

Serves 6

18 large pasta shells for stuffing
25g/1oz/2 tbsp butter
1 small onion, finely chopped
275g/10oz fresh spinach leaves, trimmed, washed and shredded
1 garlic clove, crushed
1 sachet of saffron powder
fresh nutmeg
250g/9oz/1 cup ricotta cheese
1 egg
1 x quantity Basic Tomato Sauce (see page 9)
about 150ml/¼ pint/⅔ cup dry white wine or vegetable stock
100ml/3½fl oz/scant ½ cup double (heavy) cream
50g/2oz/⅔ cup grated Parmesan cheese
salt and ground black pepper

1 Bring a large pan of salted water to the boil. Add the pasta shells and cook for 10 minutes. Drain the shells, half fill the pan with cold water and place the shells in the water.

2 Melt the butter in a pan, add the onion and cook gently, stirring, for about 5 minutes until softened. Add the spinach, garlic and saffron, then grate in plenty of nutmeg and salt and pepper. Stir well, increase the heat to medium and cook for 5–8 minutes, stirring, until the spinach is wilted and tender.

3 Increase the heat and stir until the water boils away and the spinach is dry. Transfer the spinach to a bowl, stir in the ricotta and beat in the egg. Preheat the oven to 190°C/375°F/Gas 5.

4 Purée the tomato sauce in a blender or food processor, pour it into a measuring jug and make it up to 750ml/1¼ pints/3 cups with wine or stock. Stir in the cream, and taste for seasoning.

5 Spread half the sauce over the bottom of six individual gratin dishes. Remove the pasta shells from the water and fill them with the spinach and ricotta mixture, using a teaspoon. Arrange three shells in the centre of each dish, spoon the remaining sauce over them, then cover with the grated Parmesan. Bake in the oven for 10–12 minutes until bubbling, then serve.

›aghetti Bolognese Energy 396kcal/1682kJ; Protein 30.2g; Carbohydrate 62.3g, of which sugars 8.8g; Fat 2.8g, of which saturates 0.6g; Cholesterol 43mg; Calcium 43mg; Fibre 4.8g; Sodium 82mg
:uffed Pasta Shells Energy 358kcal/1505kJ; Protein 11.6g; Carbohydrate 43.3g, of which sugars 7.7g; Fat 16.7g, of which saturates 5.6g; Cholesterol 20mg; Calcium 56mg; Fibre 2.9g; Sodium 542mg

Pasta Pie

This is an excellent family supper, children absolutely love it. Made mostly from storecupboard ingredients, it makes a low-cost standby meal at short notice.

Serves 4

30ml/2 tbsp olive oil
1 small onion, finely chopped
400g/14oz can tomatoes
15ml/1 tbsp sun-dried tomato purée (paste)
5ml/1 tsp dried mixed herbs
5ml/1 tsp dried oregano or basil
5ml/1 tsp sugar
175g/6oz/1½ cups dried rigatoni
30ml/2 tbsp freshly grated Parmesan cheese
30ml/2 tbsp dried breadcrumbs
salt and ground black pepper

For the white sauce
25g/1oz/2 tbsp butter
25g/1oz/¼ cup plain (all-purpose) flour
600ml/1 pint/2½ cups milk
1 egg

1 Heat the olive oil in a large frying pan and cook the onion over low heat, stirring, until softened. Stir in the tomatoes. Fill the empty can with water and add it to the tomato mixture, with the tomato purée, herbs and sugar.

2 Add salt and pepper to taste and bring to the boil, stirring. Cover the pan, lower the heat and simmer, for 10–15 minutes. Preheat the oven to 190°C/375°F/Gas 5, and cook the pasta according to the instructions on the packet.

3 Meanwhile, make the white sauce. Melt the butter in a pan, add the flour and cook, stirring, for 1 minute. Whisk in the milk a little at a time. Bring to the boil and cook, stirring, until the sauce is smooth and thick. Season, then remove from the heat.

4 Drain the pasta and transfer into a baking dish. Pour the tomato sauce into the dish and stir well to mix with the pasta. Beat the egg into the white sauce, then pour over the pasta and tomato mixture. Level the surface and sprinkle with grated Parmesan and breadcrumbs.

5 Bake for 15–20 minutes until the topping is golden brown and bubbling. Allow to stand for about 5–8 minutes before serving.

Macaroni Cheese

This pasta dish is always a family favourite, but this rich and creamy version is a deluxe macaroni cheese, with the addition of a little blue cheese giving it extra flavour. It goes well with either a tomato and basil salad or a leafy green salad.

Serves 4

250g/9oz/2¼ cups macaroni
50g/2oz/¼ cup butter
50g/2oz/½ cup plain (all-purpose) flour
600ml/1 pint/2½ cups full-fat (whole) milk
100ml/3½fl oz/scant ½ cup double (heavy) cream
100ml/3½fl oz/scant ½ cup dry white wine
100g/4oz/1 cup grated Gruyère or Emmenthal cheese
50g/2oz Gorgonzola cheese, crumbled
75g/3oz/1 cup freshly grated grano padano cheese
salt and ground black pepper, to taste

1 Preheat the oven to 180°C/350°F/Gas 4. Cook the macaroni according to the instructions on the packet.

2 Meanwhile, gently melt the butter in a pan, add the flour and cook, stirring, for 1–2 minutes.

3 Add the milk a little at a time, whisking vigorously after each addition. Stir in the cream, then the dry white wine. Bring to the boil. Cook, stirring constantly, until the sauce thickens. Remove from the heat.

4 Add the Gruyère or Emmenthal, Gorgonzola and about a third of the grated grano padano cheese to the sauce. Stir well to mix in the cheeses, then taste for seasoning and add salt and black pepper if necessary.

5 Thoroughly drain the macaroni and transfer it into a baking dish. Pour the sauce over the pasta and mix well, then sprinkle the remaining grano padano over the top.

6 Place in the preheated oven and bake for 25–30 minutes or until golden brown. Serve immediately.

Pasta Pie Energy 444kcal/1870kJ; Protein 17.4g; Carbohydrate 56g, of which sugars 14.3g; Fat 18.4g, of which saturates 7.8g; Cholesterol 77mg; Calcium 320mg; Fibre 3g; Sodium 279mg
Macaroni Cheese Energy 743kcal/3104kJ; Protein 30.3g; Carbohydrate 52.1g, of which sugars 8.9g; Fat 45.4g, of which saturates 27.8g; Cholesterol 123mg; Calcium 673mg; Fibre 0.4g; Sodium 593mg

Turkey Lasagne

This easy-to-make baked pasta dish is delicious made with cooked turkey left over from a roast dinner mixed with broccoli florets in a creamy cheese sauce.

Serves 4

30ml/2 tbsp light olive oil
1 onion, chopped
2 garlic cloves, finely chopped
450g/1lb cooked turkey, diced
225g/8oz/1 cup mascarpone
30ml/2 tbsp chopped tarragon
300g/11oz broccoli florets
115g/4oz no pre-cook lasagne verdi

For the sauce

50g/2oz/¼ cup butter
30ml/2 tbsp plain (all-purpose) flour
600ml/1 pint/2½ cups full-fat (whole) milk
75g/3oz/1 cup freshly grated grano padano cheese
salt and ground black pepper, to taste

1 Preheat the oven to 180°C/350°F/Gas 4. Heat the oil in a pan and cook the onion and garlic until softened but not coloured.

2 Remove from the heat and stir in the diced turkey, mascarpone and tarragon and season with salt and pepper.

3 Blanch the broccoli for 1 minute, then drain and rinse under cold water. Drain well and set aside.

4 To make the sauce, melt the butter in a pan, stir in the flour and cook for 1 minute, still stirring. Remove from the heat and gradually stir in the milk.

5 Return to the heat and bring the sauce to the boil, stirring constantly. Simmer for 1 minute, then add 50g/2oz/⅔ cup of the grano padano and seasoning to taste.

6 Spoon a layer of the turkey mixture into a large, shallow ovenproof dish. Add a layer of broccoli and cover with sheets of lasagne. Coat with cheese sauce.

7 Repeat these layers, finishing with a layer of sauce on top. Sprinkle with the remaining cheese and bake for 35–40 minutes.

Mushroom and Courgette Lasagne

This is a perfect main-course lasagne for vegetarians wanting a budget meal.

Serves 6

450g/1lb courgettes (zucchini)
50g/2oz/¼ cup butter
1 onion, finely chopped
450g/1lb/6 cups chestnut mushrooms, thinly sliced
2 garlic cloves, crushed
6–8 non-pre-cook lasagne sheets
50g/2oz/½ cup grated Parmesan

For the tomato sauce

60ml/4 tbsp olive oil
1 onion, chopped
1 carrot, chopped
2 x 400g/14oz cans tomatoes
15ml/1 tbsp tomato purée (paste)
5ml/1 tsp dried basil

For the white sauce

40g/1½oz/3 tbsp butter
40g/1½oz/⅓ cup flour
900ml/1½ pints/3¾ cups milk
salt and ground black pepper

1 To make the tomato sauce, heat 30ml/2 tbsp olive oil in a pan, add the onion and carrot and fry until soft. Place in a food processor with the tomatoes, tomato purée and dried basil, and blend to a purée. Preheat the oven to 190°C/375°F/Gas 5.

2 Slice the courgettes. Heat the remaining olive oil and half the butter in a large pan. Cook the courgette slices over medium heat for 5–8 minutes, until lightly coloured on both sides. Remove from the pan with a slotted spoon and transfer to a bowl and season. Repeat with the remaining courgettes.

3 Melt the remaining butter in the pan, and cook the onion for 3 minutes. Add the chestnut mushrooms and garlic and cook for 5 minutes, then add to the fried courgettes.

4 For the white sauce, melt the butter in a pan, stir in the flour then gradually whisk in the milk. Bring to the boil, stirring, until the sauce is thickened. Season to taste.

5 Spread half of the tomato sauce in a shallow ovenproof dish. Add half the vegetable mixture, spreading it evenly. Top with one-third of the white sauce, then half the lasagne sheets. Repeat these layers, top with the remaining white sauce and sprinkle with Parmesan. Bake for 30–45 minutes, until golden.

Turkey Lasagne Energy 673kcal/2819kJ; Protein 49.4g; Carbohydrate 44.3g, of which sugars 11g; Fat 34.4g, of which saturates 18.4g; Cholesterol 142mg; Calcium 471mg; Fibre 2.5g; Sodium 409mg
Mushroom Lasagne Energy 421kcal/1757kJ; Protein 15.5g; Carbohydrate 32.9g, of which sugars 15g; Fat 26.2g, of which saturates 12.4g; Cholesterol 49mg; Calcium 346mg; Fibre 3.8g; Sodium 310mg

Indian Mee Goreng

This is a truly international dish combining Indian, Chinese and Western ingredients. It is a delicious and nutritious treat for lunch or supper.

Serves 6

450g/1lb fresh or 225g/8oz dried egg noodles
60–90ml/4–6 tbsp vegetable oil
150g/5oz firm tofu
2 eggs
30ml/2 tbsp water
1 onion, sliced
1 garlic clove, crushed
15ml/1 tbsp light soy sauce
30–45ml/2–3 tbsp tomato ketchup
15ml/1 tbsp chilli sauce, or to taste
1 large cooked potato, diced
4 spring onions (scallions), shredded
1–2 fresh green chillies, seeded and thinly sliced (optional)
salt and ground black pepper

1 Bring a large pan of water to the boil, add the fresh or dried egg noodles and cook according to the packet instructions. Drain the noodles and immediately rinse them under cold water to halt cooking. Drain again and set aside.

2 Heat 30ml/2 tbsp of the oil in a large frying pan. Cut the tofu into cubes and cook until brown, then lift it out with a slotted spoon and set aside.

3 To make the omelette, beat the eggs with the water and seasoning. Add to the oil in the frying pan and cook without stirring until set. Flip over, cook the other side, then slide out of the pan, roll up and slice thinly.

4 Heat the remaining oil in a wok or large frying pan and cook the onion and garlic for 2–3 minutes. Add the drained noodles, soy sauce, ketchup and chilli sauce. Toss well over medium heat for 2 minutes, then add the diced potato.

5 Reserve a few spring onions to garnish, and stir the rest into the noodles with the chilli, if using, and the tofu.

6 Stir in the sliced omelette. Serve immediately on warmed plates, garnished with the remaining spring onion.

Sichuan Noodles

This tasty vegetarian dish combines egg noodles with plenty of fresh vegetables in a rich, nutty sauce, with just a hint of chilli.

Serves 4

225g/8oz dried egg noodles
½ cucumber, sliced lengthways, seeded and diced
4–6 spring onions (scallions)
a bunch of radishes, about 115g/4oz
225g/8oz mooli (daikon), peeled
60ml/4 tbsp groundnut (peanut) oil or sunflower oil
2 garlic cloves, crushed
45ml/3 tbsp toasted sesame paste
15ml/1 tbsp sesame oil
15ml/1 tbsp light soy sauce
5–10ml/1–2 tsp chilli sauce
15ml/1 tbsp rice vinegar
120ml/4fl oz/½ cup chicken stock or water
5ml/1 tsp sugar, or to taste
salt and ground black pepper
roasted cashew nuts, to garnish (optional)

1 Bring a large pan of water to the boil, add the noodles and cook according to the packet instruction. Drain and rinse them under cold water. Drain again and set aside.

2 Sprinkle the cucumber with salt, leave for 15 minutes, rinse well, then pat dry on kitchen paper. Place in a large salad bowl.

3 Cut the spring onions into fine shreds. Cut the radishes in half and slice finely. Coarsely grate the mooli, using a mandolin or a food processor. Add the vegetables to the cucumber and toss.

4 Heat half the oil in a wok or large frying pan and stir-fry the noodles for about 1 minute. Transfer to a large serving bowl.

5 Heat the remaining oil in the wok or frying pan and add the garlic to flavour the oil.

6 Stir in the sesame paste, sesame oil, soy and chilli sauces, vinegar and chicken stock or water. Add a little sugar and season. Warm over low heat.

7 Pour the sauce over the noodles and toss well. Garnish with cashew nuts, if using, and serve with the vegetables.

Indian Mee Goreng Energy 421kcal/1772kJ; Protein 13.7g; Carbohydrate 59g, of which sugars 4.2g; Fat 16.2g, of which saturates 3.2g; Cholesterol 85mg; Calcium 165mg; Fibre 2.7g; Sodium 416mg
Sichuan Noodles Energy 499kcal/2088kJ; Protein 11.8g; Carbohydrate 60.3g, of which sugars 7.1g; Fat 25g, of which saturates 5.3g; Cholesterol 23mg; Calcium 85mg; Fibre 4.5g; Sodium 510mg

Noodles with Yellow Bean Sauce

Yellow bean sauce adds a distinctive Chinese flavour to this wonderfully simple dish of spicy vegetables and noodles. This recipe is ideal for early summer.

Serves 4

150g/5oz thin egg noodles
200g/7oz baby leeks, sliced lengthways
200g/7oz baby courgettes (zucchini), halved lengthways
200g/7oz sugarsnap peas
200g/7oz peas
15ml/1 tbsp sunflower oil
5 garlic cloves, sliced
45ml/3 tbsp yellow bean sauce
45ml/3 tbsp sweet chilli sauce
30ml/2 tbsp sweet soy sauce
cashew nuts, to garnish

1 Cook the noodles according to the packet instructions, drain thoroughly and set aside.

2 Steam the leeks, courgettes and both types of peas over a pan of simmering water. Cook the vegetables for 5 minutes, then remove and set aside.

3 Pour the water from the pan and wipe dry with kitchen paper. Pour the sunflower oil into the pan and place over medium heat. Add the sliced garlic and stir-fry for 1–2 minutes.

4 Add the yellow bean, sweet chilli and soy sauces into the wok. Stir to mix with the garlic, then add the steamed vegetables and the noodles and toss together to combine. Cook for 2–3 minutes, stirring frequently, until heated through.

5 Divide the vegetable noodles among four warmed serving bowls and sprinkle over the cashew nuts to garnish.

Cook's Tip
Yellow bean sauce is made from fermented yellow beans and has a marvellous texture and spicy, aromatic flavour. However, be very careful not too add too much, because it is very salty – and if you overdo it, the final flavour of the dish will be spoiled.

Thai Noodles with Chicken

This dish combines soft, boiled noodles and crisp deep-fried ones.

Serves 4

250ml/8fl oz/1 cup coconut cream
15ml/1 tbsp magic paste
5ml/1 tsp Thai red curry paste
450g/1lb chicken thigh meat, chopped into small pieces
30ml/2 tbsp dark soy sauce
2 red (bell) peppers, finely diced
600ml/1 pint/2½ cups chicken stock
90g/3½oz fresh rice noodles

For the garnishes
vegetable oil, for deep-frying
90g/3½oz fine dried rice noodles
2 pickled garlic cloves, chopped
small bunch fresh coriander (cilantro), chopped
2 limes, cut into wedges

1 Pour the coconut cream into a large frying pan, bring to the boil and boil, stirring, for 8–10 minutes, until the milk separates and an oily sheen appears on the surface. Add the magic paste and red curry paste and cook, stirring, for 3–5 seconds.

2 Add the chicken and toss. Stir in the soy sauce and peppers and stir-fry for 3–4 minutes. Pour in the stock. Bring to the boil, then lower the heat and simmer for 10–15 minutes.

3 Meanwhile, make the garnishes. Heat the oil in a pan to 180°C/350°F. Break all the fine dried noodles in half, then divide them into four portions. Add one portion at a time to the hot oil. They will puff up on contact. As soon as they are crisp, lift the noodles out and drain on kitchen paper.

4 Bring a pan of water to the boil and cook the fresh noodles until tender. Drain, divide among four dishes, then spoon the curry sauce over. Top each bowl with fried noodles. Sprinkle with pickled garlic and coriander. Serve with lime wedges.

Cook's Tip
Magic paste is made from garlic, coriander (cilantro) and white pepper and is available from Asian stores.

Noodles Yellow Bean Energy 354kcal/1487kJ; Protein 14.6g; Carbohydrate 46.4g, of which sugars 13g; Fat 13.5g, of which saturates 2.7g; Cholesterol 11mg; Calcium 76mg; Fibre 6.8g; Sodium 1008mg
Thai Noodles Energy 433kcal/1830kJ; Protein 17.7g; Carbohydrate 62.7g, of which sugars 8.8g; Fat 14.2g, of which saturates 3g; Cholesterol 43mg; Calcium 115mg; Fibre 2.9g; Sodium 965mg

Rosemary Risotto

This is risotto has a subtle and complex flavour. Filling and quite rich, it only requires a simple side salad.

Serves 4

400g/14oz can borlotti beans
30ml/2 tbsp olive oil
1 onion, chopped
2 garlic cloves, crushed
275g/10oz/1½ cups risotto rice
175ml/6fl oz/¾ cup white wine
900ml–1 litre/1½–1¾ pints/3¾–4 cups hot chicken stock
60ml/4 tbsp mascarpone
65g/2½oz/scant 1 cup freshly grated grano padano cheese, plus extra, to serve (optional)
5ml/1 tsp chopped fresh rosemary
salt and ground black pepper

1 Drain the beans, rinse under cold water and drain again. Purée about two-thirds of the beans fairly coarsely in a food processor or blender. Set the remaining beans aside.

2 Heat the oil in a large pan and gently fry the onion and garlic for 6–8 minutes until very soft. Add the rice and cook over medium heat for a few minutes, stirring constantly, until the grains are thoroughly coated in oil and are slightly translucent.

3 Pour in the wine. Cook over medium heat for 2–3 minutes, stirring all the time, until the wine has been absorbed. Add the stock a ladleful at a time, waiting for each quantity to be absorbed before adding more, and continuing to stir.

4 When the rice is three-quarters cooked, stir in the bean purée. Continue to cook, adding stock until the rice is tender.

5 Add the reserved beans, mascarpone, grano padano and rosemary. Season to taste. Stir, then cover and leave to stand for about 5 minutes. Serve with extra grano padano.

Cook's Tips

Arborio rice is the best type of rice to use for making a risotto because it has shorter, fatter grains than other short grain rices for a creamier risotto.

Risotto with Parmesan

This is perhaps the simplest of all risotto recipes.

Serves 3–4

1 small onion, chopped
65g/2½oz/5 tbsp butter
275g/10oz/1½ cups risotto rice
120ml/4fl oz/½ cup white wine
1 litre/1¾ pints/4 cups hot beef or chicken stock
75g/3oz/1 cup Parmesan cheese, grated
salt and ground black pepper

1 Fry the onion in half the butter. Add the rice, coat with butter and pour in the wine. Cook until the wine evaporates then add the stock gradually, stirring each time until absorbed.

2 Repeat, stirring, until the rice is cooked, stir in the remaining butter and Parmesan cheese, season and serve.

Oven-baked Porcini Risotto

This easy risotto does not require you to stand over it.

Serves 4

25g/1oz/½ cup dried porcini mushrooms, soaked in 750ml/1¼ pints/3 cups boiling water
30ml/2 tbsp garlic-infused olive oil
1 onion, finely chopped
225g/8oz/generous 1 cup risotto rice
salt and ground black pepper

1 Drain the soaked porcini through a sieve (strainer) lined with kitchen paper, reserving the soaking liquor. Rinse and pat dry.

2 Preheat the oven to 180°C/350°F/Gas 4. Heat the oil in a roasting pan on the stove and add the onion. Cook for 2–3 minutes. Add the rice and stir for 2 minutes, then add the mushrooms. Mix in the mushroom liquor, season, and cover.

3 Bake in the oven for 30 minutes, stirring occasionally, until all the stock has been absorbed and the rice is tender. Divide between warm serving bowls and serve immediately.

Rosemary Risotto Energy 479kcal/1991kJ; Protein 12.8g; Carbohydrate 56.3g, of which sugars 1.1g; Fat 19.9g, of which saturates 12.3g; Cholesterol 53mg; Calcium 248mg; Fibre 0.2g; Sodium 305mg
Risotto with Parmesan Energy 531kcal/2220kJ; Protein 20g; Carbohydrate 74.6g, of which sugars 5.2g; Fat 14g, of which saturates 5.6g; Cholesterol 23mg; Calcium 287mg; Fibre 6.4g; Sodium 569mg
Porcini Risotto Energy 258kcal/1074kJ; Protein 4.5g; Carbohydrate 46.1g, of which sugars 0.9g; Fat 5.8g, of which saturates 0.8g; Cholesterol 0mg; Calcium 15mg; Fibre 0.3g; Sodium 1mg

Barley Risotto with Roasted Squash

This healthy risotto is made with nutty-flavoured pearl barley, which is complemented by leeks and roasted squash.

Serves 4

200g/7oz/1 cup pearl barley
1 butternut squash, peeled, seeded and cut into chunks
10ml/2 tsp chopped fresh thyme
60ml/4 tbsp olive oil
25g/1oz/2 tbsp butter
4 leeks, cut into fairly thick diagonal slices
2 garlic cloves, chopped
175g/6oz/2½ cups brown cap (cremini) mushrooms, sliced
2 carrots, coarsely grated
about 120ml/4fl oz/½ cup vegetable stock
30ml/2 tbsp chopped fresh flat leaf parsley
50g/2oz/⅔ cup grano padano cheese, grated
45ml/3 tbsp pumpkin seeds, toasted, or chopped walnuts
salt and ground black pepper

1 Rinse the barley, then cook it in simmering water, keeping the pan part-covered, for 35–45 minutes, or until tender. Drain. Preheat the oven to 200°C/400°F/Gas 6.

2 Place the squash in a roasting pan with half of the thyme. Season with pepper and toss with half the oil. Roast, stirring once, for 30–35 minutes, until the squash is tender.

3 Heat half the butter with the remaining olive oil in a large frying pan. Cook the leeks and garlic gently for 5 minutes.

4 Add the mushrooms and remaining thyme, then cook until the mushroom liquid evaporates and they begin to fry.

5 Stir in the carrots and cook for about 2 minutes, then add the barley and most of the vegetable stock. Season well and part-cover the pan. Cook for a further 5 minutes. Pour in the remaining stock if the mixture seems dry.

6 Stir in the parsley, the remaining butter and half the cheese, then stir in the squash. Add seasoning to taste and serve immediately, sprinkled with the toasted pumpkin seeds or walnuts and the remaining cheese.

Garlic Chive Rice with Mushrooms

A mixture of fresh mushrooms combines with rice and garlic chives to make a tasty accompaniment to meat or fish dishes.

Serves 4

350g/12oz/generous 1¾ cups long grain rice
60ml/4 tbsp groundnut (peanut) oil
1 small onion, finely chopped
2 green chillies, seeded and chopped
25g/1oz garlic chives, roughly chopped
15g/½oz fresh coriander (cilantro) sprigs, with the stalks retained
600ml/1 pint/2½ cups hot vegetable or mushroom stock
250g/9oz mixed mushrooms, wiped clean and thickly sliced
50g/2oz cashew nuts, fried in 15ml/1 tbsp olive oil until golden brown
salt and ground black pepper

1 Wash and drain the rice in a sieve (strainer). Heat half the oil in a pan and cook the onion and chillies over low heat, stirring occasionally, for 10–12 minutes until soft.

2 Set half the garlic chives aside. Cut the stalks off the coriander and set the leaves aside. Purée the remaining chives and the coriander stalks with the stock in a food processor or blender.

3 Add the rice to the onions and fry gently for 4–5 minutes. Pour in the stock mixture, then season to taste. Bring to the boil, then stir and reduce the heat to very low. Cover and cook for 15–20 minutes, or until the rice has absorbed all the liquid.

4 Remove from the heat and lay a clean dish towel over the pan, under the lid, and press on the lid to wedge it firmly in place. Leave to stand for a further 10 minutes.

5 Heat the remaining oil and cook the mushrooms for about 5–6 minutes, then add the remaining garlic chives and cook for another 1–2 minutes.

6 Stir the mushroom mixture and coriander leaves into the rice. Adjust the seasoning, then transfer to a warmed serving dish. Serve sprinkled with the cashew nuts.

Barley Risotto Energy 398kcal/1670kJ; Protein 9.1g; Carbohydrate 52.8g, of which sugars 7.7g; Fat 18.1g, of which saturates 2.4g; Cholesterol 0mg; Calcium 121mg; Fibre 5g; Sodium 21mg
Garlic Chive Rice Energy 535kcal/2227kJ; Protein 11g; Carbohydrate 74.7g, of which sugars 1.9g; Fat 21g, of which saturates 3g; Cholesterol 0mg; Calcium 37mg; Fibre 1.8g; Sodium 41mg

Thai Rice

This is soft, fluffy rice dish is perfumed with fresh lemon grass and limes, and is ideal as a light supper dish or to accompany fried fish.

Serves 4

2 limes
1 lemon grass stalk
225g/8oz/generous 1 cup brown long grain rice
15ml/1 tbsp olive oil
1 onion, chopped
2.5cm/1in piece of fresh root ginger, peeled and finely chopped
7.5ml/1½tsp coriander seeds
7.5ml/1½ tsp cumin seeds
750ml/1¼ pints/3 cups vegetable stock
60ml/4 tbsp chopped fresh coriander (cilantro)
spring onion (scallion) green, toasted coconut strips and lime wedges, to serve

1 Pare the limes using a canelle knife (zester) or grate them using a fine grater, taking care to avoid cutting the bitter pith. Set aside the rind. Finely chop the lower portion of the lemon grass stalk and set aside.

2 Rinse the rice in plenty of cold water until the water runs clear. Transfer into a sieve (strainer) and drain thoroughly.

3 Heat the olive oil in a large pan. Add the onion, ginger, spices, lemon grass and lime rind and fry gently over low heat for about 2–3 minutes.

4 Add the drained rice and cook for 1 minute, then pour in the stock and bring to the boil. Reduce the heat to very low and cover the pan.

5 Cook the rice gently for 30 minutes, then check it. If it is still crunchy, cover the pan and leave for 3–5 minutes more. Remove the pan from the heat.

6 Stir in the fresh coriander, fluff up the grains of rice, cover and leave to stand for about 10 minutes. Garnish the rice with spring onion green and toasted coconut strips, and serve with lime wedges, if you like.

Risi e Bisi

Use good quality ham in this classic Italian risotto; you only need a small amount, and the overall flavour of the dish will be greatly improved.

Serves 4

75g/3oz/6 tbsp butter
1 small onion, finely chopped
275g/10oz/1½ cups risotto rice
about 1 litre/1¾ pints/4 cups simmering chicken stock
150ml/¼ pint/⅔ cup white wine
225g/8oz/2 cups frozen peas
115g/4oz cooked ham, diced
salt and ground black pepper
50g/2oz/⅔ cup freshly grated grano padano cheese, to serve

1 Melt 50g/2oz/4 tbsp of the butter in a large heavy pan until foaming. Add the onion and cook gently for about 3 minutes, stirring, until softened. Have the hot stock ready in separate pan

2 Add the rice to the onion mixture. Stir until the grains start to swell, then pour in the wine. Stir until the wine stops sizzling and most of it has been absorbed, then pour in a little hot stock, with salt and pepper to taste. Stir continuously, over low heat, until all the stock has been absorbed.

3 Add the remaining stock, a little at a time, allowing the rice to absorb all the liquid before adding more, and stirring constantly. Add the peas after about 20 minutes. After 25–30 minutes, the the risotto should be moist and creamy.

4 Gently stir in the diced cooked ham and the remaining butter. Heat through until the butter has melted, then taste for seasoning and adjust as necessary.

5 Transfer the risotto to a warmed serving bowl. Grate or shave grano padano over the top and serve the rest separately.

Cook's Tips
Frozen peas are cheaper than fresh peas, and are available all year round. They are frozen immediately after being picked, which helps to preserve their sweet taste and freshness.

Thai Rice Energy 234kcal/992kJ; Protein 4.3g; Carbohydrate 47.2g, of which sugars 1.8g; Fat 4.5g, of which saturates 0.8g; Cholesterol 0mg; Calcium 30mg; Fibre 1.8g; Sodium 6mg
Risi e Bisi Energy 545kcal/2268kJ; Protein 19.3g; Carbohydrate 61.9g, of which sugars 1.9g; Fat 21.6g, of which saturates 12.8g; Cholesterol 69mg; Calcium 184mg; Fibre 2.7g; Sodium 597mg

ice Tortitas

ke miniature Spanish ortillas, or Italian frittatas, ese flavoursome little rice ancakes are cheap to make, nd are delicious eaten hot, raight from the pan. Serve em either plain or with omato sauce for dipping. hey also make a great coop for any soft vegetable p, such as hummus, uacamole, baba ganoush, hini or mustard dip.

Serves 4

30ml/2 tbsp olive oil
115g/4oz/1 cup cooked long grain white rice
1 potato, grated
4 spring onions (scallions), thinly sliced
1 garlic clove, finely chopped
15ml/1 tbsp chopped fresh parsley
3 large (US extra large) eggs, beaten
2.5ml/½ tsp paprika
salt and ground black pepper

Heat half the olive oil in a large frying pan and stir-fry the rice, ith the potato, spring onions and garlic, over high heat for minutes, until golden.

Transfer the rice and vegetable mixture into a bowl and stir in e parsley and eggs, with the paprika and salt and pepper to ste. Mix well to combine thoroughly.

Heat the remaining oil in the frying pan and drop in large oonfuls of the rice mixture, leaving room for spreading.

Cook the tortitas for 1–2 minutes, then carefully flip them ver and cook the other side for a further 1–2 minutes until ey are evenly browned all over.

Drain the tortitas on kitchen paper and keep hot while ooking the remaining mixture. Serve the tortitas hot.

Variation
Try using sweet potato instead of ordinary potato in this recipe, and substitute cinnamon for the paprika, for a warming, slightly sweet alternative.

Indian Pilaff with Peas

This fragrant, versatile rice dish can be served on its own or with a range of other Indian dishes, including several meat and vegetable curries, a yogurt dish, and chutneys. Garnish the pilaff with chopped fresh mint and coriander, if you like, or with roasted chilli and coconut.

Serves 4

350g/12oz/1¾ cups basmati rice
6–8 cardamom pods
30ml/2 tbsp vegetable oil and a little butter
1 cinnamon stick
4 cloves
1 onion, halved lengthways and sliced
25g/1oz fresh root ginger, peeled and grated
5ml/1 tsp sugar
130g/4½oz fresh peas, shelled, or frozen peas
5ml/1 tsp salt

1 Rinse the rice and put it in a bowl. Cover with plenty of water and leave to soak for 30 minutes. Drain thoroughly.

2 Crush the cardamom pods slightly with the flat blade of a large knife, or in a mortar and pestle, to bruise the pods. This allows the fragrant taste of the seeds inside to flavour the pilaff. Heat the oil and butter, in a heavy pan.

3 Stir the cinnamon stick, cardamom and cloves into the melted oil and butter. Add the onion, ginger and sugar, and fry until golden.

4 Add the peas, followed by the rice, and stir for 1 minute to coat the rice in the buttery oil.

5 Pour in 600ml/1 pint/2½ cups water with the salt, stir once and bring the liquid to the boil.

6 Reduce the heat and allow the mixture to simmer for about 15–20 minutes, until all the liquid has been absorbed.

7 Turn off the heat, cover the pan with a clean dish towel and the lid, and leave the rice to steam for a further 10 minutes. Spoon on to a serving dish or serve it straight from the pan.

ce Tortitas Energy 185kcal/776kJ; Protein 6.8g; Carbohydrate 17.6g, of which sugars 1.2g; Fat 10.4g, of which saturates 2.1g; Cholesterol 143mg; Calcium 56mg; Fibre 1.3g; Sodium 63mg
dian Pilaff with Peas Energy 451kcal/1880kJ; Protein 8.9g; Carbohydrate 75.7g, of which sugars 2.6g; Fat 12.2g, of which saturates 5.4g; Cholesterol 0mg; Calcium 28mg; Fibre 1.8g; Sodium 328mg

Aubergine Pilaff with Cinnamon

This wonderful rice dish combines a range of spices and herbs with tomatoes and aubergines. Eat it on its own with a green salad, or serve with barbecued meat.

Serves 4-6

2 large aubergines (eggplants), peeled lengthways in stripes, then cut into bitesize chunks
30–45ml/2–3 tbsp olive oil
30–45ml/2–3 tbsp pine nuts
1 large onion, chopped
5ml/1 tsp coriander seeds
30ml/2 tbsp currants, soaked in warm water for 5–10 minutes and drained
10–15ml/2–3 tsp sugar
15–30ml/1–2 tbsp cinnamon
15–30ml/1–2 tbsp dried mint
1 small bunch of fresh dill, finely chopped
3 tomatoes, skinned, seeded and finely chopped
350g/12oz/generous 1¾ cups basmati rice, rinsed and well drained
sunflower oil, for deep-frying
900ml/1½ pints/3¾ cups water
juice of ½ lemon
salt and ground black pepper, to taste
fresh mint sprigs and lemon wedges, to serve

1 Place the aubergine chunks in a bowl of salted water. Cover with a plate to keep them submerged, and soak for 30 minutes.

2 Meanwhile, heat the olive oil in a heavy pan, stir in the pine nuts and cook until they turn golden. Add the onion and soften it, then stir in the coriander seeds and currants. Add the sugar, cinnamon, mint and dill and stir in the tomatoes.

3 Stir in the rice, then pour in the water, season and bring to the boil. Lower the heat and partially cover the pan, then simmer for 10–12 minutes, until most of the water has been absorbed. Turn off the heat, and leave, covered, for 15 minutes.

4 Heat enough sunflower oil for deep-frying in a deep-sided pan. Drain the aubergines and squeeze them dry, then fry in batches. When they are brown, lift out and drain.

5 Transfer the rice into a bowl and add the aubergine and lemon juice. Garnish with mint and serve with lemon wedges.

Bulgur Wheat Pilaff

This hearty dish can be made with rice or bulgur wheat, and includes a combination of vegetables, dried fruit and nuts. Serve it with a dollop of thick, creamy yogurt and some melted butter as a substantial lunch dish.

Serves 4–6

350g/12oz/2 cups coarse-grain bulgur wheat, rinsed and drained
25g/1oz butter
2 carrots, cut into matchsticks
75g/3oz/¾ cup blanched almonc
30–45ml/2–3 tbsp pine nuts
30–45ml/2–3 tbsp pistachio nuts, shells removed and roughly chopped
175g/6oz/1 cup soft dried dates, roughly chopped
a handful of fresh coriander (cilantro), chopped
about 25g/1oz/2 tbsp ghee or butter, melted (optional)
salt, to taste
thick and creamy natural (plain) yogurt, to serve

1 Put the bulgur into a bowl, pour over enough boiling water t cover it by 2.5cm/1in, and give it a quick stir. Cover the bowl and leave the bulgur to steam for about 25 minutes, until it has soaked up the water and doubled in volume.

2 Meanwhile, melt the butter in a wide, heavy pan, add the carrots and fry for about 10 minutes, until tender and golden. Toss in the nuts and cook for a further minute, or until they giv off a nutty aroma and begin to colour.

3 Add the dates and, if they look dry, pour in 15–30ml/1–2 tbs water. Transfer the bulgur into the pan and toss until everything is mixed. Turn off the heat, cover the pan with a dish towel and lid, and leave to steam for 5–10 minutes. Stir the coriander through the bulgur, and pour over the ghee or butter. Serve immediately with a dollop of yogurt.

Cook's Tip
Look for soft and succulent whole dates, which usually come from Iran or Iraq, rather than blocks of hard ones, or use soft dried figs or apricots instead.

Aubergine Pilaff Energy 369kcal/1539kJ; Protein 6.1g; Carbohydrate 52.2g, of which sugars 11g; Fat 15.2g, of which saturates 1.8g; Cholesterol 0mg; Calcium 38mg; Fibre 2.7g; Sodium 8mg
Bulgur Wheat Pilaff Energy 412kcal/1719kJ; Protein 9g; Carbohydrate 54g, of which sugars 23.4g; Fat 19.1g, of which saturates 3.9g; Cholesterol 11mg; Calcium 71mg; Fibre 3.4g; Sodium 74m

piced Vegetable Couscous

nis tasty, satisfying getarian main course is eap and easy to make and n be prepared with any mber of seasonal getables such as spinach, eas, or baby corn.

erves 6

ml/3 tbsp olive oil
arge onion, finely chopped
garlic cloves, crushed
ml/1 tbsp tomato purée (paste)
5ml/½ tsp ground turmeric
5ml/½ tsp cayenne pepper
nl/1 tsp ground coriander
nl/1 tsp ground cumin
225g/8oz cauliflower florets
225g/8oz baby carrots
1 red (bell) pepper, seeded and diced
225g/8oz courgettes (zucchini), sliced
400g/14oz can chickpeas, drained and rinsed
4 beefsteak tomatoes, skinned and sliced
45ml/3 tbsp chopped fresh coriander (cilantro)
450g/1lb/2⅔ cups couscous
50ml/3½ tbsp sunflower oil
salt and ground black pepper, to taste
fresh coriander sprigs, to garnish

Heat 30ml/2 tbsp olive oil in a large pan, add the onion and rlic and cook until soft. Stir in the tomato purée, turmeric, yenne, ground coriander and cumin. Cook for 2 minutes.

Add the cauliflower, carrots and pepper, with enough water to me halfway up the vegetables. Bring to the boil, then lower e heat, cover and simmer for 10 minutes. Add the courgettes, ickpeas and tomatoes and cook for 10 minutes. Stir in the sh coriander and season. Keep hot.

To cook the couscous, bring about 475ml/16fl oz/2 cups water the boil in a large pan. Add the remaining olive oil and a nch of salt. Remove from the heat.

Add the couscous. Allow to swell for 2 minutes, then add the nflower oil and heat through, stirring to separate the grains.

Turn the couscous out on to a warm serving dish, and spoon e cooked vegetables on top, pouring over any liquid. Garnish th coriander and serve immediately.

Couscous-stuffed Baked Peppers

Colourful red, yellow or orange peppers are softened in boiling water before being filled with a delicious mixture of couscous, apricots and pine nuts.

Serves 4

4 (bell) peppers
75g/3oz/½ cup couscous
75ml/2½fl oz/⅓ cup boiling vegetable stock
15ml/1 tbsp olive oil
10ml/2 tsp white wine vinegar
50g/2oz ready-to-eat dried apricots, chopped
75g/3oz feta cheese, cubed
3 ripe tomatoes, skinned, seeded and chopped
45ml/3 tbsp toasted pine nuts
30ml/2 tbsp chopped fresh parsley
salt and ground black pepper
fresh flat leaf parsley, to garnish
green salad, to serve

1 Preheat the oven to 190°C/375°F/Gas 5. Halve the peppers lengthways, then remove the core and seeds. Place the peppers in a large heatproof bowl and pour over boiling water to cover. Leave to stand for 3 minutes, then drain and set aside.

2 Meanwhile, put the couscous in a small bowl and pour over the stock. Leave to stand for about 5 minutes until all the liquid has been absorbed.

3 Using a fork, fluff up the couscous, then stir in the oil, vinegar, apricots, feta cheese, tomatoes, pine nuts and parsley, and season to taste with salt and ground black pepper.

4 Fill the peppers with the couscous mixture, gently packing it down using the back of a spoon. Place the peppers, filling side up, in a shallow, ovenproof dish, then pour 150ml/¼ pint/⅔ cup near-boiling water around them. Bake for 20 minutes, until the peppers are tender and the topping is browned, and serve with a crisp green salad.

Cook's Tips
Avoid using green (bell) peppers for this dish because they can become bitter during cooking; red ones are sweeter.

iced Couscous Energy 419kcal/1749kJ; Protein 12.9g; Carbohydrate 61.8g, of which sugars 11.8g; Fat 14.8g, of which saturates 1.9g; Cholesterol 0mg; Calcium 87mg; Fibre 6.7g; Sodium 178mg
ked Peppers Energy 303kcal/1266kJ; Protein 33.7g; Carbohydrate 33.6g, of which sugars 17g; Fat 15.8g, of which saturates 3.9g; Cholesterol 13mg; Calcium 105mg; Fibre 4.3g; Sodium 285mg

Couscous with Dried Fruit

This simple yet delicious dish can be served as a course on its own, or to accompany a spicy tagine or roasted or grilled meat or poultry.

Serves 6

500g/1¼lb/3 cups couscous
600ml/1 pint/2½ cups warm water
5ml/1 tsp salt
pinch of saffron threads
45ml/3 tbsp sunflower oil
75g/3oz/½ cup dried dates
115g/4oz/½ cup ready-to-eat dried apricots
30ml/2 tbsp olive oil
a little butter
75g/3oz/generous ½ cup seedless raisins
115g/4oz/⅔ cup blanched almonds, cut into slivers
75g/3oz/½ cup pistachio nuts
10ml/2 tsp ground cinnamon mixed with 45ml/3 tbsp caster (superfine) sugar

1 Put the couscous in a bowl. Mix together the water, salt and saffron and stir it into the couscous. Leave for 10 minutes. Add the sunflower oil and, using your fingers, rub it through the grains. Set aside. Preheat the oven to 180°C/350°F/Gas 4.

2 Chop the dates and slice the apricots into slivers. In a heavy pan, heat the olive oil and butter and stir in the dates, apricots, raisins, most of the almonds and pistachio nuts.

3 Cook until the raisins plump up, then transfer the nuts and fruit into the couscous and toss together to mix. Place the couscous into an ovenproof dish and cover with foil. Cook in the oven for about 20 minutes, until heated through.

4 Toast the reserved slivered almonds. Pile the hot couscous in a mound on a large serving dish and sprinkle with the cinnamon and sugar in stripes down the mound. Sprinkle the toasted almonds over the top and serve hot.

Cook's Tip
Although saffron is expensive, a little goes a long way, and it is useful for adding both flavour and colour to dishes.

Casablancan Couscous

This delicious summer dish is packed with seasonal vegetables. Serve with yogurt and bread for a stunning vegetarian dinner-party dish.

Serves 6

3 red onions, peeled and quartered
2–3 courgettes (zucchini), halved lengthways and cut into chunks
2–3 red, green or yellow (bell) peppers, seeded and quartered
2 aubergines (eggplants), cut into 6–8 long segments
2–3 leeks, trimmed and cut into long strips
2–3 sweet potatoes, peeled, halved lengthways and cut into strips
4–6 tomatoes, quartered
6 garlic cloves, crushed
25g/1oz fresh root ginger, sliced
a few large fresh rosemary sprigs
about 150ml/¼ pint/⅔ cup olive oil
10ml/2 tsp clear honey
500g/1¼lb/3 cups medium couscous
600ml/1 pint/2½ cups warm water
45ml/3 tbsp sunflower oil
about 25g/1oz/2 tbsp butter, softened and diced
salt and ground black pepper, to taste, plus a pinch of salt
thick natural (plain) yogurt, to serve

1 Preheat the oven to 200°C/400°F/Gas 6. Arrange all the vegetables in a roasting pan. Tuck the garlic, ginger and rosemar around the vegetables. Pour the olive oil and honey over the vegetables, add salt and pepper, and roast, turning occasionally, for 1½ hours until they are tender and slightly caramelized.

2 When the vegetables are nearly ready, put the couscous in a bowl. Stir a pinch of salt into the water, then pour it over the couscous, stirring to make sure it is absorbed evenly. Leave to stand for 10 minutes, then, using your fingers, rub the sunflower oil into the grains and break up any lumps. Transfer into an ovenproof dish, dot the butter over the top, cover with foil and heat in the oven for about 20 minutes.

3 To serve, fork the melted butter into the couscous and fluff it up, then pile it on a large dish and shape into a mound with a pit at the top. Spoon some vegetables into the pit and arrange the rest around the dish. Pour the oil left in the roasting pan over the couscous. Serve with yogurt.

Couscous with Fruit Energy 567kcal/2367kJ; Protein 11.9g; Carbohydrate 71.5g, of which sugars 27.9g; Fat 27.7g, of which saturates 3g; Cholesterol 0mg; Calcium 94mg; Fibre 3.3g; Sodium 79m
Casablancan Couscous Energy 607kcal/2531kJ; Protein 11.3g; Carbohydrate 81.3g, of which sugars 22.2g; Fat 28.3g, of which saturates 5.7g; Cholesterol 9mg; Calcium 115mg; Fibre 9.2g; Sodium 76r

lixed Bean and Aubergine Tagine

eans are not only cheap, ey are also a good source f protein. This is perfect for cold winter's day.

erves 4

)0g/14oz can red kidney beans,
)0g/14oz can black-eyed beans (peas) or cannellini beans
5ml/5 tbsp olive oil
aubergine (eggplant), about 350g/12oz, cut into chunks
celery sticks, finely chopped
onion, thinly sliced
garlic cloves, crushed
-2 fresh red chillies, seeded and chopped
30ml/2 tbsp tomato purée (paste)
5ml/1 tsp paprika
2 large tomatoes, roughly chopped
2 bay leaves
300ml/½ pint/1¼ cups vegetable stock
15ml/1 tbsp each chopped mint, parsley and coriander (cilantro)
salt and ground black pepper
fresh herb sprigs, to garnish

For the mint yogurt

150ml/¼ pint/⅔ cup natural (plain) yogurt
30ml/2 tbsp chopped fresh mint
2 spring onions (scallions), finely chopped

Drain, rinse and drain both types of beans. Heat 60ml/4 tbsp f the oil in a large frying pan or cast-iron tagine base. Add the ubergine chunks to the pan and cook, stirring, for 4–5 minutes. emove and set aside. Preheat the oven to 160°C/325°F/Gas 3.

Add the remaining oil to the tagine base or frying pan, then dd the celery and onion and cook, stirring, for 4–5 minutes, ntil softened. Add the crushed garlic and chopped red chillies nd cook for a further 5 minutes, stirring frequently, until the nion is golden and has softened.

Add the tomato purée and paprika to the onion mixture and ook for 1–2 minutes. Add the chopped tomatoes, aubergine, eans, bay leaves and stock, then season to taste. Cover the gine base with the lid or, transfer to a casserole. Place in the ven and cook for 1 hour.

Meanwhile, mix together the yogurt, mint and spring onions. st before serving, add the fresh mint, parsley and coriander to e tagine and lightly mix through the vegetables.

Garnish with fresh herb sprigs and serve immediately with the int yogurt and some couscous or brown rice.

Mixed Bean and Tomato Chilli

This warming dish is based on common storecupboard ingredients, making it an ideal end-of-the week supper dish when you have eaten everything in the refrigerator.

Serves 4

1 fresh red chilli
1 x 400g/14oz can chopped tomatoes
2 x 400g/14oz cans mixed beans, drained and rinsed
a large handful of fresh coriander (cilantro) or flat leaf parsley
120ml/4fl oz/½ cup sour cream
salt and ground black pepper
finely sliced red or green chilli, to garnish (optional)
French bread and grated Cheddar cheese, to serve

1 Seed and thinly slice the chilli, then put it into a pan. Add the tomatoes and mixed beans and simmer gently on medium heat for about 5 minutes.

2 Finely chop the fresh coriander. Set some aside for the garnish and add the remainder to the tomato and bean mixture. Stir to mix all the ingredients together.

3 Bring the mixture to a gentle boil, then reduce the heat to low, cover, and simmer gently for 10 minutes. Stir the mixture occasionally as it cooks, and add a dash of water if the sauce starts to dry out. Season to taste with salt and black pepper.

4 Ladle the chilli into warmed individual bowls and top with a spoonful of sour cream. Sprinkle with coriander and serve immediately with warmed French bread and cheese.

Variation
To turn this bean chilli into a delicious baked fajita dish, roll the warm beans with a little grated cheese in tortillas. Place the wraps side by side in an ovenproof dish, sprinkle liberally with grated cheese and bake in a medium oven until the cheese has melted. Serve with dollops of sour cream, and sliced jalapeño chillies, and a tomato and red onion salsa.

xed Bean Tagine Energy 209kcal/890kJ; Protein 16.6g; Carbohydrate 33.9g, of which sugars 9.4g; Fat 1.9g, of which saturates 0.5g; Cholesterol 1mg; Calcium 173mg; Fibre 12.3g; Sodium 62mg
xed Bean Chilli Energy 309kcal/1302kJ; Protein 16.7g; Carbohydrate 43.7g, of which sugars 14.1g; Fat 8.7g, of which saturates 4.2g; Cholesterol 18mg; Calcium 193mg; Fibre 12.4g; Sodium 202mg

Braised Beans and Lentils

Easy to make, and very economical, this dish requires little effort. It is important, however, to soak the pulses for at least 12 hours, or overnight, for this recipe.

Serves 4

200g/7oz/generous 1 cup mixed beans and lentils, soaked overnight in water
150ml/¼ pint/⅔ cup extra virgin olive oil
1 large onion, finely chopped
2 garlic cloves, crushed
5 or 6 fresh sage leaves, chopped
juice of 1 lemon
3 spring onions (scallions), thinly sliced
60–75ml/4–5 tbsp chopped fresh dill
salt and ground black pepper

1 Drain the pulse mixture, rinse it thoroughly under cold water and drain again. Put the mixture in a large pan. Cover with cold water, bring to the boil, and cook for about 1½ hours, by which time the beans and lentils will be quite soft and tender.

2 Strain the beans, reserving 475ml/16fl oz/2 cups of the cooking liquid. Return the bean mixture to the clean pan.

3 Heat the oil in a frying pan and fry the onion until light golden. Add the crushed garlic and chopped sage. As soon as the garlic becomes aromatic, add the mixture to the beans.

4 Stir the reserved liquid into the bean and onion mixture, then add plenty of seasoning, bring the mixture to the boil then reduce the heat and simmer for 15 minutes.

5 Stir in the lemon juice, taste and add salt and black pepper as needed, then spoon into warmed serving bowls. Top each bowl with a sprinkling of sliced spring onions and a generous amount of chopped dill, and serve.

Cook's Tip
If you prefer, use canned beans and lentils instead of dried, and omit the cooking stage in step 1.

Lentil, Tomato and Cheese Salad

Brown lentils are pefect in this frugal salad.

Serves 6

200g/7oz/scant 1 cup brown lentils, soaked for 3 hours
1 red onion, chopped
1 bay leaf
60ml/4 tbsp extra virgin olive oil
75ml/6 tbsp fresh parsley, choppe
250g/9oz cherry tomatoes, halved
250g/9oz feta cheese

1 Drain the lentils, place in a pan of cold water, with the onion and bay leaf. Boil for 10 minutes, then simmer for 20 minutes.

2 Drain the lentils, discard the bay leaf and transfer into a bowl. Toss with olive oil and season. When cool, add the parsley and tomatoes. Add the cheese, transfer to a large dish, and serve.

Lentil Casserole with Mushrooms

Lentils make a good partner for stronger flavours, such as the powerful anis used here.

Serves 4

30ml/2 tbsp olive oil
1 large onion, sliced
2 garlic cloves, finely chopped
250g/9oz/3 cups mushrooms
150g/5oz/generous ½ cup brown lentils, soaked overnight
4 tomatoes, cut in eighths
1 bay leaf
25g/1oz/½ cup chopped parsley
30ml/2 tbsp anis spirit or anisette
salt, paprika and black pepper

1 Heat the oil in a large, flameproof casserole. Add the onion and fry gently, with the garlic, for 5 minutes, until softened.

2 Slice the mushrooms and add to the onion and garlic. Continue cooking, stirring gently, for a couple of minutes, until the mushrooms soften.

3 Add the lentils, tomatoes and bay leaf with 175ml/6fl oz/¾ cu water. Simmer, covered, for 30–40 minutes until the lentils are soft, and the liquid has evaporated. Stir in the parsley and anis. Season to taste with salt, paprika and black pepper.

Braised Beans Energy 428kcal/1,788kJ; Protein 13.4g; Carbohydrate 37.7g, of which sugars 4.3g; Fat 26g, of which saturates 3.7g; Cholesterol 0mg; Calcium 62mg; Fibre 3.7g; Sodium 24mg
Lentil Salad Energy 324kcal/1352kJ; Protein 15.8g; Carbohydrate 21.9g of which sugars 3.7g; Fat 19.9g, of which saturates 7.1g; Cholesterol 29mg; Calcium 188mg; Fibre 2.7g; Sodium 619mg
Lentil Casserole Energy 212kcal/892kJ; Protein 11.5g; Carbohydrate 23.2g, of which sugars 4.8g; Fat 7g, of which saturates 1g; Cholesterol 0mg; Calcium 64mg; Fibre 5.8g; Sodium 21mg

ʒraised Lentils with Carrots

ɜrve this simple dish of
ntils flavoured with fragrant
ıge with grilled, broiled or
ırbecued meats. They are
so good on their own
ɜrved simply with a dollop
f yogurt seasoned with
-ushed garlic, salt and
ɜpper, and lemon wedges
ır squeezing.

erves 4–6

75g/6oz/$1\frac{3}{4}$ cup green lentils, rinsed and picked over to remove grit
5–60ml/3–4 tbsp olive oil
1 onion, cut in half lengthways, in half again crossways, and sliced along the grain
3–4 plump garlic cloves, roughly chopped and bruised with the flat side of a knife
5ml/1 tsp coriander seeds
a handful of dried sage leaves
5–10ml/1–2 tsp sugar
4 carrots, sliced
15–30ml/1–2 tbsp tomato purée (paste)
salt and ground black pepper, to taste
1 bunch of fresh sage or flat leaf parsley, to garnish

Bring a pan of water to the boil and add in the lentils. Lower e heat, partially cover the pan and simmer for 10 minutes. rain and rinse well under cold running water.

Heat the oil in a heavy pan, stir in the onion, garlic, coriander ɜeds, sage and sugar, and cook until the onion begins to colour. ɔss in the carrots and cook for 2–3 minutes.

Add the lentils and pour in 250ml/8fl oz/1 cup water, to cover. ir in the tomato purée and cover the pan.

Cook the lentils and carrots for about 20 minutes, until most the liquid has been absorbed. Season with salt and pepper to ste. Garnish with the fresh sage or flat leaf parsley, and serve ɔt or at room temperature.

Cook's Tip
Dried sage has a distinctive and powerful flavour, and needs to be used sparingly. Fresh sage is not as strong..

Creamy Puy Lentils

Wholesome lentils are filling, nutritious, and very good value for money. A poached egg is the perfect companion to the creamy lentils.

Serves 6

250g/9oz/generous 1 cup Puy lentils
1 bay leaf
30ml/2 tbsp olive oil
4 spring onions (scallions), sliced
2 large garlic cloves, chopped
15ml/1 tbsp Dijon mustard
finely grated rind and juice of 1 large lemon
4 plum tomatoes, peeled and diced
6 eggs
60ml/4 tbsp crème fraîche
salt and ground black pepper
30ml/2 tbsp chopped fresh flat leaf parsley, to garnish

1 Put the Puy lentils and bay leaf in a large pan, cover with cold water, and slowly bring to the boil. Reduce the heat and simmer, partially covered, for about 25 minutes, or until the lentils are tender. Stir the lentils occasionally and add more water, if necessary. Drain.

2 Heat the oil in a frying pan and cook the spring onions and garlic for 1 minute. Add the mustard, lemon rind and juice, tomatoes and seasoning, then mix together and cook gently for 1–2 minutes until the tomatoes are heated through. Add a little water if the mixture becomes too dry.

3 Meanwhile, poach the eggs in a pan of lightly salted, barely simmering water for 4 minutes, adding them one at a time.

4 Stir the lentils and crème fraîche into the tomato mixture, remove the bay leaf, then heat through for 1 minute.

5 Divide among six serving plates. Top each portion with a poached egg, and sprinkle with parsley.

Variation
For an extra depth of flavour, cook the Puy lentils in good quality chicken stock instead of water.

aised Lentils Energy 166kcal/696kJ; Protein 7.6g; Carbohydrate 21.1g, of which sugars 6.7g; Fat 6.2g, of which saturates 0.9g; Cholesterol 0mg; Calcium 38mg; Fibre 4g; Sodium 22mg
eamy Puy Lentils Energy 281kcal/1179kJ; Protein 17.2g; Carbohydrate 22.8g, of which sugars 3g; Fat 14.2g, of which saturates 4.9g; Cholesterol 202mg; Calcium 71mg; Fibre 4.5g; Sodium 84mg

Bulgur Wheat and Lentil Pilaff

Bulgur wheat is a very useful storecupboard ingredient. It will keep for weeks in an airtight jar, it has a lovely nutty taste and texture, and only needs soaking before serving in a salad.

Serves 4

115g/4oz/½ cup green lentils
115g/4oz/⅔ cup bulgur wheat
5ml/1 tsp ground coriander
5ml/1 tsp ground cinnamon
15ml/1 tbsp olive oil
225g/8oz rindless streaky (fatty) bacon rashers (strips), chopped
1 red onion, chopped
1 garlic clove, crushed
5ml/1 tsp cumin seeds
30ml/2 tbsp roughly chopped fresh parsley
salt and ground black pepper

1 Soak the lentils and bulgur wheat separately in cold water for 1 hour, then drain. Transfer the lentils into a pan.

2 Stir in the coriander, cinnamon and 475ml/16fl oz/2 cups water. Bring to the boil, then simmer until the lentils are tender and the liquid has been absorbed.

3 Meanwhile, heat the olive oil and fry the bacon pieces until crisp. Remove and drain on kitchen paper.

4 Add the red onion and garlic to the oil remaining in the pan and fry for 10 minutes until soft and golden brown.

5 Stir in the cumin seeds and cook for 1 minute more. Return the crisped bacon to the pan.

6 Stir the drained bulgur wheat into the cooked lentils, then add the mixture to the frying pan. Season with salt and pepper and heat through. Stir in the parsley and serve.

Cook's Tip
Use Puy lentils rather than green lentils, if you have them. You can also use a tin of green lentils if you wish, in which case you won't need to precook them.

Brown Lentils and Rice

This is an ancient classic and a great favourite in the Middle East. It is often served during Lent among the Christian communities, and as such is a typically frugal and economical dish, suitable for a time of fasting.

Serves 4–6

225g/8oz/1 cup brown lentils, rinsed
45–60ml/3–4 tbsp olive oil or ghee
2 onions, finely chopped
5ml/1 tsp sugar
5ml/1 tsp ground coriander
5ml/1 tsp ground cumin
225g/8oz/generous 1 cup long grain rice, well rinsed
sea salt and ground black pepper
5ml/1 tsp ground cinnamon, to garnish

For the crispy onions
sunflower oil for deep-frying
2 onions, halved lengthways and sliced with the grain

1 Bring a pan of water to the boil and toss in the lentils. Boil rapidly for 10–15 minutes, until the lentils are tender but still firm. Drain and refresh under cold water.

2 Heat the oil or ghee in a heavy pan and cook the onions with the sugar for 3–4 minutes, until they begin to turn golden. Add the spices and cook for 1–2 minutes, then add the lentils and rice, tossing to coat the grains in the spicy onion mixture.

3 Add water to just cover the lentils and rice, and bring to the boil. Reduce the heat and simmer gently for about 15 minutes, until the water has been absorbed. Turn off the heat, cover the pan with a clean dish towel, followed by the lid, and leave the rice and lentils to steam for a further 10 minutes.

4 Meanwhile, prepare the crispy onions. Heat the oil in a deep frying pan and deep-fry the onions until brown and crisp, then drain on kitchen paper.

5 Turn the rice into a serving dish, season and fluff with a fork. Sprinkle a little cinnamon over the rice and and spoon the onions on top. Serve immediately with yogurt, or with any meat, poultry or fish dish.

Bulgur Wheat Pilaff Energy 411kcal/1717kJ; Protein 13.7g; Carbohydrate 58.3g, of which sugars 7g; Fat 14.3g, of which saturates 1.8g; Cholesterol 0mg; Calcium 68mg; Fibre 5g; Sodium 9mg
Brown Lentils and Rice Energy 411kcal/1717kJ; Protein 13.7g; Carbohydrate 58.3g, of which sugars 7g; Fat 14.3g, of which saturates 1.8g; Cholesterol 0mg; Calcium 68mg; Fibre 5g; Sodium 9mg

ɛed Lentil Purée with Baked Eggs

his unusual dish is thought › have originated in the 'oorish areas of medieval ›ain. It makes an excellent ıd economical vegetarian ıpper. For an extra Spanish ıvour add some thinly sliced ·een pepper to cook with ıe lentils and leeks, if you ish, and sprinkle a little ıerry over the top of the ıke before cooking. If you ·efer, bake the purée and ʒgs in one large baking dish.

Serves 6

450g/1lb/2 cups red lentils
3 leeks, thinly sliced
10ml/2 tsp coriander seeds, lightly crushed
15ml/1 tbsp chopped fresh coriander (cilantro)
30ml/2 tbsp chopped fresh mint
15ml/1 tbsp red wine vinegar
1 litre/1¾ pints/4 cups hot vegetable stock
4 eggs
sea salt and ground black pepper
fresh parsley, chopped, to garnish

Put the lentils in a large pan. Add the sliced leeks, coriander ·eds, the chopped fresh coriander and mint, then pour in the ıegar and stock.

Put the pan on high heat and bring to the boil, then lower the ·at and simmer for 30–40 minutes or until the lentils are ›oked and have absorbed all the liquid.

Preheat the oven to 180°C/350°F/Gas 4. Season the lentil and ·ek mixture with plenty of salt and black pepper and mix well.

Divide the lentil mixture between four lightly greased baking ·shes, and spread evenly.

Using the back of a spoon, make a hollow in the lentil mixture each dish. Break an egg into each hollow.

Cover the dishes with foil and bake for 10–15 minutes or ıtil the eggs are set. If you prefer your egg yolks to be runny, ›ok until the whites are just set.

Sprinkle each bake with plenty of chopped fresh parsley and rve immediately.

Egg and Lentil Curry

Eggs are an excellent addition to vegetarian curries and, combined with lentils, make a substantial and extremely tasty curry.

Serves 4

75g/3oz/½ cup green lentils
750ml/1¼ pints/3 cups stock
6 eggs
30ml/2 tbsp olive oil
3 cloves
1.5ml/¼ tsp black peppercorns
1 onion, finely chopped
2 green chillies, finely chopped
2 garlic cloves, crushed
2.5cm/1in piece of fresh root ginger, peeled and chopped
30ml/2 tbsp curry paste
400g/14oz can chopped tomatoes
2.5ml/½ tsp sugar
2.5ml/½ tsp garam masala

1 Wash the lentils under cold running water, checking for small stones. Put the lentils in a large, heavy pan with the stock. Cover and simmer gently for about 15 minutes or until the lentils are soft. Drain and set aside.

2 Cook the eggs in boiling water for 10 minutes. Remove from the boiling water and set aside to cool slightly. When cool enough to handle, peel and cut in half lengthways.

3 Heat the olive oil in a large frying pan and fry the cloves and peppercorns for about 2 minutes. Add the onion, chillies, garlic and ginger and fry the mixture for a further 5–6 minutes, stirring frequently.

4 Stir in the curry paste and fry for a further 2 minutes, stirring constantly. Add the chopped tomatoes and sugar and stir in 175ml/6fl oz/¾ cup water. Simmer for about 5 minutes until the sauce thickens, stirring occasionally. Add the boiled eggs, drained lentils and garam masala. Cover the pan and simmer for a further 10 minutes, then serve.

Cook's Tip
You can substitute red lentils for the green. Red lentils disintegrate when cooking, which will give a smoother curry.

·d Lentil Purée Energy 470kcals/1985kJ; Fat 9.1g, of which saturates 2.2g; Carbohydrate 65.8g, of which sugars, 4.2g; Fibre 6.95g; Sodium 424mg
g Curry Energy 238kcal/997kJ; Protein 14.6g; Carbohydrate 14.2g, of which sugars 4.1g; Fat 14.4g, of which saturates 3.1g; Cholesterol 285mg; Calcium 60mg; Fibre 1.9g; Sodium 121mg.

Lentil and Nut Loaf

For a vegetarian or budget alternative at a special celebration, such as Christmas dinner, serve this with all the trimmings, including a tasty vegetarian gravy. Garnish with fresh cranberries and flat leaf parsley for a festive effect.

Serves 6

115g/4oz/½ cup red lentils
115g/4oz/1 cup hazelnuts, skinned
115g/4oz/1 cup walnuts
1 large carrot, coarsely chopped
2 celery sticks, coarsely chopped
1 large onion, coarsely chopped
115g/4oz/1½ cups fresh mushrooms, coarsely chopped
50g/2oz/¼ cup butter, plus extra for greasing
10ml/2 tsp mild curry powder
30ml/2 tbsp tomato ketchup
30ml/2 tbsp vegetarian Worcestershire sauce
10ml/2 tsp salt
1 egg, beaten
60ml/4 tbsp chopped fresh parsley
150ml/¼ pint/⅔ cup water
fresh flat leaf parsley and cranberries, to garnish (optional)

1 Cover the lentils with cold water and soak for 1 hour. Grind the nuts in a food processor, then place them in a large bowl. Put the carrot, celery, onion and mushrooms in the food processor and process until finely chopped.

2 Heat the butter in a pan. Add the vegetables and fry gently, stirring occasionally, for 5 minutes. Stir in the curry powder and cook for 1 minute more. Remove from the heat and set aside.

3 Drain the lentils and stir them into the ground nuts. Add the vegetables, ketchup, vegetarian Worcestershire sauce, egg, salt, chopped parsley and water.

4 Preheat the oven to 190°C/375°F/Gas 5. Grease a 1kg/2¼lb loaf tin (pan) and line with baking parchment or foil. Press the mixture into the tin.

5 Bake for 1–1¼ hours, until just firm, covering the top with foil if it starts to burn. Leave to stand for 15 minutes, turn out, and peel off the paper. Serve immediately, garnished with parsley and cranberries, if you like.

Sausage and Bean Casserole

This casserole is the perfect choice for a winter's evening, and stretches out a small amount of meat with the beans to go much further.

Serves 6

150g/5oz/⅔ cup each dried black-eyed, pinto and cannellini beans
15ml/1 tbsp olive oil
6 rindless smoked streaky (fatty) bacon rashers (strips)
6 large country pork sausages
3 large carrots, halved
3 large onions, halved
1 small garlic bulb, separated into cloves
4 bay leaves
2 fresh thyme sprigs
15–30ml/1–2 tbsp dried green peppercorns
300ml/½ pint/1¼ cups unsalted vegetable stock or water
300ml/½ pint/1¼ cups red wine
sea salt and ground black pepper
thyme sprigs, to garnish

1 Bring a large pan of unsalted water to the boil. Add the beans and boil vigorously for 30 minutes. Drain and set aside.

2 Pour the olive oil into a large heavy casserole, then lay the bacon rashers on top. Add the whole sausages and the halved carrots and onions.

3 Peel but do not slice the garlic cloves, then press them into the mixture with the bay leaves, fresh thyme sprigs and the dried peppercorns. Spoon the cooked, drained beans over the top of the mixture.

4 Pour in the stock or water and wine. Cover the casserole and bring the liquid to the boil over medium heat. Reduce the heat to the lowest setting and cook for 4–6 hours, stirring periodically and topping up the liquid if necessary.

5 Stir the mixture and season before serving, garnished with thyme. Serve from the casserole, accompanied by a green salad.

Variation
Replace half the stock with red wine if you have some to spare.

Lentil Loaf Energy 410kcal/1703kJ; Protein 11.9g; Carbohydrate 16.5g, of which sugars 5.2g; Fat 33.5g, of which saturates 6.6g; Cholesterol 49mg; Calcium 81mg; Fibre 3.6g; Sodium 222mg
Sausage and Bean Casserole Energy 410kcals/1714kJ; Fat, 20.5g, of which saturates 6.7g; Carbohydrate 33.8g, of which sugars 5.4g; Fibre 7g; Sodium 467mg

ʒroad Beans with Bacon

.eep a bag of frozen broad eans in the freezer so that ou can quickly make this ısty satisfying dish.

erves 4

0ml/2 tbsp olive oil
small onion, chopped
1 garlic clove, chopped
50g/2oz pancetta or smoked bacon lardons
225g/8oz broad (fava) beans
5ml/1 tsp pakrika
15ml/1 tbsp sweet sherry
sea salt and ground black pepper

Heat the oil in a frying pan and cook the onion, garlic and acon over high heat until softened.

Add the broad beans and paprika and fry for 1 minute. Add ıe sherry, cover the pan and cook until the beans are tender. eason to taste with salt and black pepper, and serve.

tewed Beans

)elicious hot or cold, this is very adaptable dish that ın be made with canned or ·ied beans, or fresh beans ·hen they are in season. If sing dried beans, soak them vernight in cold water, boil fresh water for 5 minutes, ıen rinse and use as fresh.

Serves 4

45–60ml/3–4 tbsp olive oil
3 cloves garlic, peeled and crushed
2 or 3 leaves fresh sage
400g/14oz can cannellini beans, drained
200g/7oz canned tomatoes, strained
sea salt and ground black pepper

Put the oil in a pan and gently fry the garlic and sage.

When the oil is golden brown, add the beans and season with pinch of ground black pepper.

Stir the mixture together thoroughly, then add the strained ›matoes. Simmer gently for a further 20 minutes. Check and djust the seasoning to taste, then serve.

Polenta and Beans

Polenta and beans, a peasant-food staple, is a real frugal standby. The incorporation of the stewed beans and their sauce into the polenta makes for a tasty dish. It is often served with a sprinkling of grated Pecorino cheese.

Serves 6

400g/14oz/2⅔ cups dried borlotti or cannellini beans, soaked overnight and drained
50g/2oz/⅓ cup lard, white cooking fat or fatty pancetta, cubed
1 carrot, finely chopped
1 celery stick, finely chopped
1 onion, finely chopped
450g/1lb ripe tomatoes, peeled, seeded and coarsely chopped
300g/11oz/2⅓ cups coarse or medium-grade polenta flour
sea salt and ground black pepper
freshly grated Pecorino cheese and extra virgin olive oil, to serve

1 Rinse the soaked beans. Put them in a large pan and cover with plenty of water. Bring to the boil and boil hard for about 5 minutes, then drain and rinse again. Return the beans to the pan, cover with fresh water, bring to the boil, and boil gently for 45 minutes, or until softened. Drain away most of the water.

2 In a separate pan, fry the lard, white cooking fat or pancetta with the carrot, celery and onion for 10 minutes, until softened.

3 Add the tomatoes and stir together. Simmer until thickened and glossy, then season to taste.

4 Drain and add the boiled beans, stir to mix and simmer while you cook the polenta.

5 Bring 2 litres/3½ pints/9 cups water to the boil in a large pan. Add a large pinch of salt, then trickle the polenta flour into the boiling water in a steady stream, whisking constantly. Turn the heat to medium-low. Using a strong wooden spoon, stir the polenta constantly for about 40 minutes.

6 Add the beans and their sauce, reserving a little to serve, if you wish, and continue to cook for a further 10 minutes. Serve sprinkled with cheese and a drizzle of olive oil.

·oad Beans Energy 139kcal/577kJ; Protein 6.8g; Carbohydrate 8.2g, of which sugars 1.6g; Fat 9g, of which saturates 1.9g; Cholesterol 8mg; Calcium 38mg; Fibre 3.9g; Sodium 163mg
ewed Beans Energy 160kcal/669kJ; Protein 6.3g; Carbohydrate 14.6g, of which sugars 2.7g; Fat 8.9g, of which saturates 1.3g; Cholesterol 0mg; Calcium 19mg; Fibre 5.1g; Sodium 425mg
lenta and Beans Energy 458kcal/1926kJ; Protein 20.2g; Carbohydrate 70.4g, of which sugars 5.8g; Fat 11.1g, of which saturates 3.6g; Cholesterol 8mg; Calcium 82mg; Fibre 12.9g; Sodium 26mg

Refried Beans

In this classic Mexican dish the beans are not actually fried twice, but they are cooked twice, first boiled to tenderize, then fried in lard. If the only refried beans you've tried have been the canned ones, you may have found them quite bland. These, however, are superb. If you prefer not to cook in lard, use olive oil instead.

Serves 4

115g/4oz/⅔ cup dried kidney beans, soaked overnight
25g/1oz/2 tbsp lard
2 onions, finely chopped
5ml/1 tsp ground cumin
5ml/1 tsp ground coriander
3 garlic cloves, crushed
small bunch of fresh coriander (cilantro) sprigs
50g/2oz feta cheese
salt

1 Drain the beans, rinse and place in a pan with plenty of cold water. Bring to the boil, boil hard for 10 minutes, then reduce the heat and simmer for 1–1½ hours, until tender. Drain.

2 Melt the lard in a large frying pan. Add the onions, cumin and ground coriander. Cook gently over low heat for about 30 minutes or until the onions caramelize and become soft.

3 Add a ladleful of the soft, cooked beans. Fry them for only a few minutes simply to heat. Mash the beans into the onions as they cook, using a fork or a potato masher. Continue until all the beans have been added, a little at a time, then stir in the garlic.

4 Lower the heat and cook the beans to form a thick paste. Season with salt and spoon into a warmed serving dish.

5 Add the fresh coriander sprigs, crumble the feta cheese on top, then serve immediately while warm.

Cook's Tip

Refried beans are often served as a side dish to accompany chilli con carne, in which case you should leave out the feta cheese, and use grated mature (sharp) Cheddar instead.

Tagine of Butter Beans, Cherry Tomatoes and Olives

Serve this hearty butter bean dish with grills or roasts, particularly fish. It is substantial enough to be served on its own, with a leafy salad and fresh, crusty bread. For added flavour and richness you could add diced chorizo with the onion.

Serves 4

115g/4oz/⅔ cup butter (lima) beans, soaked overnight
30–45ml/2–3 tbsp olive oil
1 onion, chopped
2–3 garlic cloves, crushed
25g/1oz fresh root ginger, peeled and chopped
pinch of saffron threads
16 cherry tomatoes
generous pinch of sugar
handful of fleshy black olives, pitted
5ml/1 tsp ground cinnamon
5ml/1 tsp paprika
small bunch of flat leaf parsley
salt and ground black pepper

1 Rinse the beans and place them in a large pan with plenty of water. Bring to the boil and boil for about 10 minutes, then reduce the heat and simmer gently for 1–1½ hours until tender. Drain the beans and refresh under cold water.

2 Heat the olive oil in a heavy pan. Add the onion, garlic and ginger, and cook for about 10 minutes, or until softened but not browned. Stir in the saffron threads, followed by the cherry tomatoes and a sprinkling of sugar.

3 As the tomatoes begin to soften, stir in the butter beans. When the tomatoes have heated through, stir in the olives, ground cinnamon and paprika.

4 Season to taste with salt and ground black pepper, sprinkle the fresh parsley over, and serve immediately.

Variation

If you are in a hurry, use two 400g/14oz cans butter (lima) beans for this tagine. Rinse the beans well before adding.

Refried beans Energy 160kcal/669kJ; Protein 6.3g; Carbohydrate 14.6g, of which sugars 2.7g; Fat 8.9g, of which saturates 1.3g; Cholesterol 0mg; Calcium 19mg; Fibre 5.1g; Sodium 425mg
Tagine of Butter Beans Energy 146kcal/615kJ; Protein 7.4g; Carbohydrate 16.2g, of which sugars 3.8g; Fat 6.3g, of which saturates 0.9g; Cholesterol 0mg; Calcium 62mg; Fibre 6g; Sodium 16mg

Braised Brown Beans with Red Onion Salad

Traditionally a peasant dish with its origins in ancient Egypt, foul medames is a popular staple dish in the Middle East. It is generally served for breakfast or as part of a mezze spread, with bowls of thinly sliced red onion and parsley.

Serves 4–6

250g/9oz/1 ¼ cups dried broad (fava) beans, soaked overnight
30–45ml/2–3 tbsp olive oil
2 cloves garlic, crushed
5–10ml/1–2 tsp cumin seeds, dry roasted and crushed
juice of 1 lemon
sea salt and ground black pepper

To serve

1–2 red onions, halved lengthways, halved again crossways, and finely sliced with the grain
bunch of fresh flat leaf parsley, roughly chopped

1 Drain the beans and place them in a deep pot filled with water. Bring the water to the boil, reduce the heat and simmer the beans for about 1 hour, until they are tender but not soft or mushy.

2 When the beans are almost cooked, prepare the red onion and parsley accompaniments and pile each one into a small bowl ready for serving.

3 Drain the beans and, while they are still warm, transfer them into a large serving bowl and add the olive oil, garlic and cumin. Squeeze in the lemon juice, season with salt and pepper and mix well to combine the ingredients.

4 Serve the warm beans, accompanied by the bowls of red onion, and parsley, to which everyone helps themselves.

Variation
Foul medames are also often served with crumbled feta cheese as well as the dishes of onions and parsley.

Borlotti Beans

This is a great favourite in Turkey, where the markets sell meaty, pinkish borlotti beans in their dappled pods just for preparing this dish. In poor homes, where meat may be served infrequently, dishes made from borlotti beans and aubergines make a regular appearance.

Serves 4

175g/6oz/scant 1 cup dried borlotti beans, soaked in cold water overnight
45–60ml/3–4 tbsp olive oil
2 red onions, cut in half lengthways, in half again crossways, and sliced along the grain
4 garlic cloves, chopped
400g/14oz can tomatoes
10ml/2 tsp sugar
1 bunch each of fresh flat leaf parsley and dill, coarsely chopped
4 ripe plum tomatoes
salt and ground black pepper
1 lemon, cut into quarters, to serve

1 Drain the beans, transfer them into a pan and fill the pan with plenty of cold water. Bring to the boil and boil for 1 minute, then lower the heat and partially cover the pan. Simmer the beans for about 30 minutes, or until they are tender but not soft or mushy. Drain, rinse well under cold running water and remove any loose skins.

2 Heat the oil in a heavy pan and stir in the onions and garlic. When they begin to soften, add the canned tomatoes, sugar and half the herbs. Toss in the beans, pour in 300ml/½ pint/1 ¼ cups water and bring to the boil. Lower the heat and partially cover the pan, then simmer for about 20 minutes, until most of the liquid has evaporated away.

3 Meanwhile, bring a small pan of water to the boil, drop in the plum tomatoes for a few seconds, then plunge them into a bowl of cold water. Peel off the skins and coarsely chop the tomatoes.

4 Add the tomatoes to the beans with the rest of the herbs – reserving a little for the garnish. Season and cook for a further 5–10 minutes. Serve hot or at room temperature, with lemon wedges for squeezing over.

Braised Brown Beans Energy 200kcal/846kJ; Protein 13.6g; Carbohydrate 27.3g, of which sugars 1.5g; Fat 4.8g, of which saturates 0.7g; Cholesterol 0mg; Calcium 65mg; Fibre 9.4g; Sodium 12mg
Borlotti Beans Energy 266kcal/1119kJ; Protein 12.4g; Carbohydrate 34.4g, of which sugars 14.4g; Fat 9.8g, of which saturates 1.5g; Cholesterol 0mg; Calcium 103mg; Fibre 10.6g; Sodium 33mg

Cod and Bean Stew

Beans help to make the costly cod go further in this delicious, richly spiced and filling fish stew.

Serves 8

1 large red (bell) pepper
45ml/3 tbsp olive oil
4 rashers (strips) streaky (fatty) bacon, roughly chopped
4 garlic cloves, finely chopped
1 onion, sliced
10ml/2 tsp paprika
5ml/1 tsp smoked paprika
large pinch of saffron threads or 1 sachet powdered saffron, soaked in 45ml/3 tbsp hot water
400g/14oz can haricot (navy) beans, drained and rinsed
600ml/1 pint/2½ cups fish stock
6 large plum tomatoes, quartered
350g/12oz fresh skinned cod fillet, cut into large chunks
45ml/3 tbsp chopped fresh coriander (cilantro), plus a few sprigs to garnish
salt and ground black pepper
crusty bread, to serve

1 Preheat the grill (broiler) and line the pan with foil. Halve the pepper, remove the seeds and place the halves, cut side down, in the grill pan and cook under the hot grill for 10–15 minutes, until the skin is charred.

2 Put the pepper into a plastic bag, seal and leave for about 10 minutes to steam. Remove from the bag, peel off the skin and discard. Chop the pepper into large pieces.

3 Heat the oil in a pan, then add the bacon and garlic. Fry for 2 minutes, then add the onion. Cover and cook for 5 minutes until the onion is soft. Stir in the paprika and smoked paprika, the saffron and its soaking water, and salt and pepper to taste.

4 Stir in the drained and rinsed beans and add just enough stock to cover. Bring to the boil and simmer, uncovered, for about 15 minutes, stirring to prevent sticking. Stir in the chopped pepper and tomato quarters. Drop in the chunks of cod and push in to the sauce.

5 Cover and simmer for 5 minutes. Stir in the chopped fresh coriander. Serve in warmed soup plates or bowls, garnished with the coriander sprigs. Eat with lots of crusty bread.

Halibut and Tomato Curry

The chunky cubes of white fish contrast beautifully with the rich red spicy tomato sauce, in which they are cooked, and taste just as good as they look.

Serves 4

60ml/4 tbsp lemon juice
60ml/4 tbsp rice wine vinegar
30ml/2 tbsp cumin seeds
5ml/1 tsp turmeric
5ml/1 tsp chilli powder
5ml/1 tsp salt
750g/1lb 11oz thick halibut fillets, skinned and cubed
60ml/4 tbsp sunflower oil
1 onion, finely chopped
3 garlic cloves, finely grated
30ml/2 tbsp finely grated fresh root ginger
10ml/2 tsp black mustard seeds
2 x 400g/14oz cans chopped tomatoes
5ml/1 tsp sugar
chopped coriander (cilantro) and sliced green chilli, to garnish
basmati rice and pickles, to serve

1 Mix together the lemon juice, vinegar, cumin seeds, turmeric, chilli powder and salt in a shallow glass bowl. Add the cubed fish and turn to coat evenly. Cover and put in the refrigerator to marinate for 25–30 minutes.

2 Meanwhile, heat a large pan over high heat and add the oil. When hot, add the onion, garlic, ginger and mustard seeds. Reduce the heat to low and cook very gently for 10 minutes, stirring occasionally.

3 Add the tomatoes and sugar to the pan, bring to a boil, reduce the heat, cover and cook gently for 15–20 minutes, stirring occasionally.

4 Add the fish and its marinade to the pan, stir gently to mix, then cover and simmer gently for 15–20 minutes, or until the fish is cooked through and flakes easily with a fork.

5 Ladle the curry into shallow individual bowls. Sprinkle with fresh coriander and green chillies to garnish.

6 Serve with basmati rice and pickles, and if you wish to add a tang, drizzle over some natural (plain) yogurt if you like.

Cod and Bean Stew Energy 181kcal/757kJ; Protein 14.4g; Carbohydrate 13.4g, of which sugars 6g; Fat 8.1g, of which saturates 1.8g; Cholesterol 28mg; Calcium 59mg; Fibre 4.6g; Sodium 388mg
Halibut Curry Energy 335kcal/1409kJ; Protein 41.9g; Carbohydrate 8.4g, of which sugars 8.1g; Fat 15.2g, of which saturates 2.1g; Cholesterol 66mg; Calcium 73mg; Fibre 2.2g; Sodium 622mg

Smoked Haddock with Cabbage

his simple and colourful ish of smoked haddock erved with grilled tomatoes nd sautéed shredded abbage makes a healthy and elicious family meal. If Savoy abbage is not available, use nother green variety.

erves 4

Savoy cabbage
75g/1½lb undyed smoked haddock fillet
300ml/½ pint/1¼ cups full-fat (whole) milk
½ onion, peeled and sliced in rings
2 bay leaves
½ lemon, sliced
4 white peppercorns
4 ripe tomatoes
50g/2oz/¼ cup butter
30ml/2 tbsp wholegrain mustard
juice of 1 lemon
salt and ground black pepper
30ml/2 tbsp chopped fresh parsley, to garnish

Cut the cabbage in half, remove the central core and thick bs, then shred the cabbage. Cook in a pan of lightly salted oiling water, or steam over boiling water for about 10 minutes, ntil just tender. Leave in the pan or steamer until required.

Meanwhile put the haddock in a large, shallow pan with the ilk, onion and bay leaves. Add the lemon and peppercorns. ring to simmering point, cover and poach until the fish flakes asily when tested with the tip of a sharp knife. This will take –10 minutes, depending on the thickness. Take the pan off the eat and set aside until needed. Preheat the grill (broiler).

Cut the tomatoes in half horizontally, season them to taste ith salt and pepper and grill (broil) until lightly browned. Drain e cabbage, refresh under cold water and drain again.

Melt the butter in a shallow pan, add the cabbage and toss ver the heat for 2 minutes. Mix in the mustard and season to iste, then transfer the cabbage into a warmed serving dish.

Drain the haddock. Skin and cut the fish into four pieces. lace on top of the cabbage with some onion rings and omato halves. Pour on the lemon juice, then sprinkle with fresh arsley and serve immediately.

Salmon Baked with Potatoes

In this simple, elegant dish, pepper-crusted salmon fillets are baked on a bed of potatoes and onions braised in thyme-flavoured vegetable or fish stock. Salmon is not a particularly economical fish, but if you buy the fillets when on offer at the supermarket, or from frozen, it can sometimes be a good budget buy.

Serves 4

675g/1½lb waxy potatoes, thinly sliced
1 onion, thinly sliced
10ml/2 tsp fresh thyme leaves, plus extra to garnish
450ml/¾ pint/scant 2 cups vegetable or fish stock
40g/1½oz/3 tbsp butter, finely diced
4 salmon fillets, each about 150g/5oz, skinned
30ml/2 tbsp olive oil
15ml/1 tbsp black peppercorns, crushed
salt and ground black pepper, to taste
mangetouts (snow peas) or sugar snap peas, to serve

1 Preheat the oven to 190°C/375°F/Gas 5. Layer the potato and onion slices in a shallow baking dish, such as a lasagne dish, seasoning each layer with salt and pepper and sprinkling with a little fresh thyme.

2 Pour the stock over the layers, dot with butter, cover the dish with foil and place in the oven.

3 Bake the potatoes for 40 minutes then remove the foil and bake for a further 20 minutes, or until they are almost cooked.

4 Meanwhile brush the salmon fillets with olive oil and coat with crushed black peppercorns, pressing them in to the flesh, if necessary, with the back of a spoon.

5 Place the salmon on top of the potatoes, cover with foil and bake for 15 minutes, or until the salmon is opaque, removing the foil for the last 5 minutes.

6 Garnish with fresh thyme sprigs and serve accompanied by mangetouts or sugar snap peas.

noked Haddock Energy 319kcal/1340kJ; Protein 36.1g; Carbohydrate 14.2g, of which sugars 13.7g; Fat 13.1g, of which saturates 7.3g; Cholesterol 90mg; Calcium 146mg; Fibre 4.2g; Sodium 1512mg
almon Energy 517kcal/2160kJ; Protein 33.4g; Carbohydrate 28.4g, of which sugars 3.1g; Fat 30.8g, of which saturates 9g; Cholesterol 96mg; Calcium 47mg; Fibre 1.9g; Sodium 147mg

Seafood Pie

A well-made fish pie is perfect comfort food at any time of the year, and is particularly good made with a mixture of whatever fish is reasonably priced on the day.

Serves 4–5

450g/1lb haddock or cod fillet
225g/8oz smoked haddock or cod
150ml/¼ pint/⅔ cup milk
150ml/¼ pint/⅔ cup water
1 slice of lemon
1 small bay leaf
a few fresh parsley stalks

For the sauce

25g/1oz/2 tbsp butter
25g/1oz/¼ cup flour
5ml/1 tbsp lemon juice, or to taste
45ml/3 tbsp chopped fresh parsley
ground black pepper, to taste

For the topping

450g/1lb cooked potatoes, mashed with 25g/1oz/2 tbsp butter

1 Preheat the oven to 190°C/375°F/Gas 5. Rinse the fish, cut it into bitesize pieces and put into a pan with the milk, water, lemon, bay leaf and parsley stalks. Bring slowly to the boil, then simmer gently for 15 minutes until tender.

2 Strain and reserve 300ml/½ pint/1¼ cups of the cooking liquor. Leave the fish until cool, then flake the flesh and discard the skin and bones. Set aside.

3 To make the sauce, melt the butter in a heavy pan, add the flour and cook for 1–2 minutes over low heat stirring constantly. Then gradually add the reserved cooking liquor, stirring well to make a smooth sauce.

4 Simmer the sauce gently for 1–2 minutes, then remove from the heat and stir in the flaked fish, chopped parsley and lemon juice. Season to taste with ground black pepper.

5 Turn into a buttered 1.75-litre/3-pint/7½-cup ovenproof dish, cover with the mashed potato for the topping and dot with the butter. Cook the pie in the oven for 20 minutes, until golden brown and crunchy on top. Remove from the oven and serve immediately on warmed plates accompanied by green vegetables or a crispy salad.

Creamy Fish and Mushroom Pie

Fish pie is a healthy and hearty dish for a hungry family. To help the fish go further, mushrooms provide both flavour and bulk.

Serves 4

225g/8oz/2½ cups mixed wild and cultivated mushrooms, trimmed and quartered
675g/1½lb cod or haddock fillet, skinned and diced
600ml/1 pint/2½ cups hot milk
900g/2lb floury potatoes, peeled and cut into quarters
25g/1oz/2 tbsp butter
150ml/¼ pint/⅔ cup milk
salt and ground black pepper
freshly grated nutmeg

For the sauce

50g/2oz/4 tbsp unsalted (sweet) butter
1 medium onion, chopped
½ celery stick, chopped
50g/2oz/½ cup plain (all-purpose) flour
10ml/2 tsp lemon juice
45ml/3 tbsp chopped fresh parsley

1 Preheat the oven to 200°C/400°F/Gas 6. Butter an ovenproof dish, sprinkle the mushrooms in the bottom, add the fish, and season with salt and pepper and a little grated nutmeg.

2 Pour on the hot milk, cover and cook in the oven for around 20 minutes. Using a slotted spoon, transfer the fish and mushrooms to a 1.5-litre/2½-cup/6¼-cup baking dish. Pour the poaching liquid into a jug (pitcher) and set aside.

3 Cover the potatoes with cold water, add a good pinch of salt and boil for 20 minutes. Drain and mash with the butter and milk. Season well.

4 To make the sauce, melt the butter in a pan, add the onion and celery, and fry until soft but not coloured. Stir in the flour, then remove from the heat.

5 Slowly add the reserved liquid, stirring until absorbed. Return to the heat, stir and simmer to thicken. Add the lemon juice and parsley, season, then pour into the baking dish. Top the dish with the mashed potato and return to the oven for 30–40 minutes until golden brown. Serve immediately.

Seafood Pie Energy 336kcal/1413kJ; Protein 35.1g; Carbohydrate 24.3g, of which sugars 0.9g; Fat 11.6g, of which saturates 6.7g; Cholesterol 87mg; Calcium 45mg; Fibre 1.7g; Sodium 587mg
Creamy Fish Pie Energy 622kcal/2605kJ; Protein 43g; Carbohydrate 60g, of which sugars 12g; Fat.25g, of which saturates 15g; Cholesterol 120mg; Calcium 289mg; Fibre 6g; Sodium 366mg

Lemon Salmon Loaf

This frugal fish loaf is made using canned salmon. Served with the lemony cucumber sauce it is perfect as a light summer lunch or supper.

Serves 4–6
115g/4oz/2 cups fresh white breadcrumbs
150ml/¼ pint/⅔ cup milk
2 eggs, beaten
400g/14oz can salmon
75g/3oz celery, chopped
grated rind and juice of 1 lemon
salt and ground black pepper

For the sauce
1 cucumber, peeled, and chopped
25g/1oz/2 tbsp butter
15ml/1 tbsp flour
rind and juice of ½ lemon
1 egg yolk

1 Put the breadcrumbs in a large bowl, pour in the milk and add the beaten eggs. Mix well to combine, then leave to stand for 10 minutes. Preheat the oven to 180°C/350°F/Gas 4, and grease a 450g/1lb loaf tin (pan) with butter.

2 Drain the salmon, put in a bowl and flake with a fork. Add to the breadcrumb mixture with the chopped celery, grated lemon rind and juice. Season with salt and pepper and mix well. Transfer to the prepared loaf tin and bake for 1 hour. Leave the loaf in the tin to cool slightly.

3 Make the sauce. Place the cucumber pieces in a small pan, cover with cold water and simmer until just tender. Using a slotted spoon, remove the cucumber and set it aside. Pour the cooking liquid into a measuring jug (cup). Add enough water to make up the liquid to 300ml/½ pint/1¼ cups.

4 Melt the butter in same pan. Stir in the flour using a wooden spoon. Cook, stirring constantly, for 1 minute, then gradually add the reserved cooking liquid, stirring until it boils and thickens. Add the lemon rind and juice and cooked cucumber to the pan.

5 Stir a little of the hot sauce into the egg yolk. Pour back into the pan and heat gently, without boiling. Season to taste. Turn the salmon loaf on to a serving dish. Serve warm, in slices, with the warm cucumber sauce on the side.

Fish Curry with Shallots and Lemon Grass

This is a thin fish curry made with salmon fillets. It has wonderfully strong, aromatic flavours, and should ideally be served in small bowls with plenty of crusty bread or plain boiled rice.

Serves 4
450g/1lb salmon fillets
500ml/17fl oz/2¼ cups fish or vegetable stock
4 shallots, finely chopped
2 garlic cloves, finely chopped
2.5cm/1in piece fresh root ginger, finely chopped
1 lemon grass stalk, outer leaves discarded and the remainder very finely chopped
2.5–5ml/½–1 tsp dried chilli flakes, according to taste
15ml/1 tbsp Thai fish sauce
5ml/1 tsp light muscovado (brown) sugar

1 Remove the skin from the salmon fillets, then place in the freezer for about 30–40 minutes to firm up the flesh slightly.

2 Remove the salmon from the freezer and use a sharp knife to cut the fish into 2.5cm/1in cubes, removing any remaining bones as you do so.

3 Pour the fish or vegetable stock into a pan and bring it slowly to the boil. Add the chopped shallots, garlic, ginger, lemon grass, dried chilli flakes, Thai fish sauce and sugar.

4 Bring the stock back to the boil, stir well to ensure the ingredients are thoroughly mixed, then reduce the heat and simmer gently for about 15 minutes.

5 Add the fish pieces to the stock, bring back to the boil, then turn off the heat. Leave the curry to stand for 10–15 minutes, until the flish cubes are tender. Serve in small bowls.

Variation
You could use monkfish instead of salmon for this recipe.

Salmon Loaf Energy 265kcal/1109kJ; Protein 20g; Carbohydrate 19.1g, of which sugars 2.8g; Fat 12.3g, of which saturates 4.2g; Cholesterol 130mg; Calcium 152mg; Fibre 1g; Sodium 596mg
Fish Curry Energy 218kcal/910kJ; Protein 23.4g; Carbohydrate 3.1g, of which sugars 2.7g; Fat 12.6g, of which saturates 2.2g; Cholesterol 56mg; Calcium 51mg; Fibre 0.8g; Sodium 322mg

Japanese Salmon and Bean Stew

The addition of fresh salmon to this Asian stew helps to make it an extremely nourishing dish, as well as a delicious winter warmer. The canned beans are an added energy boost and eke out the pricier fish.

Serves 2

150g/5oz salmon fillet, skinned and any bones removed, sliced into 1cm/½in thick strips
2.5cm/1in fresh root ginger, peeled, to garnish
400g/14oz canned black-eyed beans (peas) in brine
50g/2oz fresh shiitake mushrooms, stalks removed
1 small carrot, peeled
½ mooli (daikon), peeled
60ml/4 tbsp water
15ml/1 tbsp shoyu (Japanese soy sauce), or soy sauce
7.5ml/1½ tsp mirin or dry sherry
salt

1 Place the salmon strips in a colander, sprinkle with sea salt and leave for 1 hour. Wash away the salt and cut the salmon strips into 1cm/½in cubes. Par-boil in a pan of rapidly boiling water for 30 seconds, then drain. Rinse under cold running water to prevent them from cooking further.

2 Slice the ginger for the garnish thinly lengthways, then stack the slices and cut them into thin threads. Soak in cold water for about 30 minutes, then drain well.

3 Drain the can of black-eyed beans into a medium pan. Reserve the liquid. Chop the mushrooms, carrot and mooli into 1cm/½in cubes as close to the same size as possible.

4 Put the salmon, and vegetables into the pan containing the liquid from the beans. Add the beans, 60ml/4 tbsp water and 1.5ml/¼ tsp salt. Bring to the boil. Reduce the heat and cook for 6 minutes or until the carrot is cooked.

5 Add the shoyu or soy sauce and cook for a further 4 minutes. Add the mirin or sherry and remove the pan from the heat.

6 Leave the stew to rest for 1 hour. Reheat gently to serve warm or serve cold, garnished with the ginger threads.

Smoked Trout Risotto

Risottos are a great way of making more expensive ingredients stretch further and create a filling meal.

Serves 4

30ml/2 tbsp olive oil
1 medium onion, finely chopped
400g/14oz/2 cups risotto rice
1.2 litres/2 pints/5 cups hot fish stock
150ml/¼ pint/⅔ cup white wine
45ml/3 tbsp crème fraîche
45ml/3 tbsp grated grano padano cheese, plus extra, to serve
350g/12oz smoked trout, chopped
60ml/4 tbsp chopped fresh chervil
salt and ground black pepper

1 Heat the oil in a large, heavy pan. Add the chopped onion and fry it gently over low heat for about 5 minutes until softened. Add the rice to the pan and stir well with a wooden spoon to coat each grain thoroughly in oil.

2 Cook over low heat for 2–3 minutes until the rice has turned translucent. Keep the stock bubbling in a second pan.

3 Pour the white wine over the rice in the pan, stirring constantly. Continue to stir for 1–2 minutes until all the wine has been absorbed. Keeping the pan simmering over medium heat, add the hot stock, a ladleful at a time, stirring all the time.

4 Add another ladleful of stock to the rice when the previous quantity has been absorbed, and continue in this way until all the stock has been used up. This will take around 20 minutes.

5 Remove the pan from the heat and stir in the crème fraîche and the grated grano padano cheese.

6 Add three-quarters of the chopped smoked trout and the chopped chervil. Season to taste with plenty of salt and ground black pepper and stir well to mix. Cover the pan and leave to stand for about 2 minutes.

7 Divide the risotto among four warmed serving plates, top with the remaining smoked trout and garnish with fresh chervil sprigs. Serve immediately with extra grated cheese.

Japanese Stew Energy 387kcal/1633kJ; Protein 33.7g; Carbohydrate 43.5g, of which sugars 5.6g; Fat 9.9g, of which saturates 1.9g; Cholesterol 38mg; Calcium 70mg; Fibre 8.2g; Sodium 589mg
Trout Risotto Energy 656kcal/2741kJ; Protein 34.5g; Carbohydrate 81.5g, of which sugars 1.3g; Fat 18.2g, of which saturates 6.9g; Cholesterol 55mg; Calcium 184mg; Fibre 0.2g; Sodium 1772mg

'rout Burgers

hese home-made fish urgers really are a treat for .l the family. They provide ıe ideal way of persuading hildren to eat fish, and :clude hidden veg too. Cook ıe chilled burgers on the arbecue, if you prefer.

lakes 6

50g/12oz trout fillet, skinned
50ml/¼ pint/⅔ cup milk
50ml/¼ pint/⅔ cup hot fish stock
spring onions (scallions), sliced
50g/12oz cooked potatoes
5ml/1 tsp tartare sauce
1 egg, beaten
50g/2oz/1 cup fresh white breadcrumbs
60ml/4 tbsp semolina
salt and ground white pepper

To serve

120ml/4fl oz/½ cup mayonnaise
45ml/3 tbsp drained canned corn
1 red (bell) pepper, seeded and finely diced
8 burger buns
vegetable oil, for shallow-frying
salad leaves
4 ripe tomatoes, sliced

Place the trout in a frying pan with the milk, stock and spring nions. Simmer for 5 minutes, or until the fish is cooked. Lift out of the pan and set it aside. Strain the stock into a bowl, eserving the spring onions.

Mash the potatoes and stir in the tartare sauce, egg and readcrumbs. Flake the trout and add the reserved spring nions. Fold into the potato mixture and season to taste.

Divide the potato mixture into eight and shape into burgers, sing your hands. Coat thoroughly in the semolina and pat ıem into shape. Chill in the refrigerator for 1 hour.

Meanwhile, in a bowl, mix the mayonnaise with the corn ernels and diced red pepper.

Heat the oil in a frying pan and fry the burgers for about 0 minutes, turning once. To serve, split open the buns and oread a little of the mayonnaise over each half. Fill with a few alad leaves, a couple of tomato slices and then add a fish urger on top, replace the tops of the buns and serve.

Hake with Lemon Sauce

This healthy dish is perfect on its own as a light lunch, or serve with steamed new potatoes for a more substantial main course.

Serves 4

500g/1¼lb fresh spinach, trimmed
4 x 200g/7oz fresh hake steaks
30ml/2 tbsp flour
75ml/5 tbsp olive oil
175ml/6fl oz/¾ cup white wine
3–4 strips of pared lemon rind

For the egg and lemon sauce

2.5ml/½ tsp cornflour (cornstarch)
2 large (US extra large) eggs, at room temperature
juice of ½ lemon
salt and ground black pepper

1 Place the spinach leaves in a large pan with just the water that clings to the leaves after washing. Cover and cook over medium heat for 5–7 minutes, then drain and set aside.

2 Dust the fish with the flour. Heat the oil in a large frying pan, add the fish and sauté gently for 2–3 minutes on each side. Pour in the wine, and add the lemon rind and some seasoning. Lower the heat and simmer for a few minutes, then add the spinach, and let it simmer for 3–4 minutes more. Remove from the heat.

3 To make the sauce, mix the cornflour to a paste with a little water. Beat the eggs in a bowl, then add the lemon juice and the cornflour mixture and beat until smooth. Gradually beat in a ladleful of the liquid from the fish pan, then beat for 1 minute. Add a second ladleful in the same way, and continue until all of the liquid is incorporated.

4 Pour the sauce over the fish and spinach, and return the pan to the hob. Allow to cook gently for 2–3 minutes, then serve.

Cook's Tip

Spinach can have a gritty texture if it is not washed properly. The best way to wash it is to soak the leaves in a full sink of cold water, until the grit sinks to the bottom, then lift out and drain in a colander. Repeat if necessary.

'rout Burgers Energy 497kcal/2080kJ; Protein 19.5g; Carbohydrate 45.7g, of which sugars 6.9g; Fat 27.5g, of which saturates 3.8g; Cholesterol 47mg; Calcium 93mg; Fibre 2.9g; Sodium 400mg
ake Energy 441kcal/1,839kJ; Protein 43.6g; Carbohydrate 10.6g, of which sugars 2.3g; Fat 22.1g, of which saturates 3.5g; Cholesterol 141mg; Calcium 273mg; Fibre 2.9g; Sodium 413mg

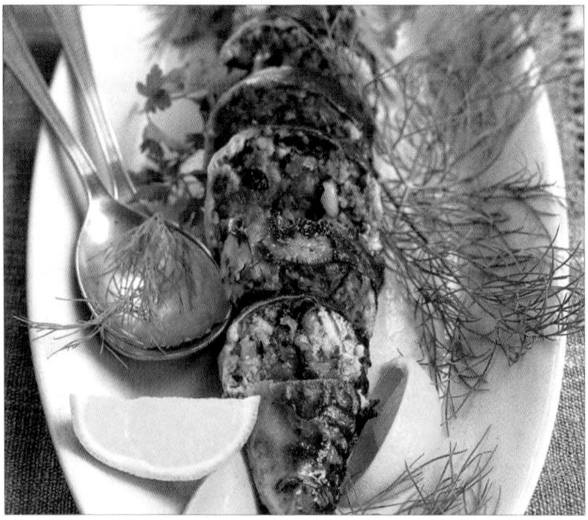

Mackerel Stuffed with Nuts

In this Turkish dish, the fish is massaged to empty it of flesh keeping the skin intact, so that it can then be stuffed to resemble the whole fish once more. Although fiddly to prepare, it is an inexpensive and impressive dish.

Serves 4

1 large, fresh mackerel, scaled and thoroughly washed and gutted
30–45ml/2–3 tbsp olive oil
4–5 shallots, finely chopped
30ml/2 tbsp pine nuts
30ml/2 tbsp blanched almonds, finely slivered
45ml/3 tbsp walnuts, chopped
15–30ml/1–2 tbsp currants, soaked in warm water, then drained
6–8 ready-to-eat dried apricots, finely chopped
5–10ml/1–2 tsp ground cinnamon
5ml/1 tsp ground allspice
2.5ml/½ tsp ground cloves
2.5ml/½ tsp chilli powder
5ml/1 tsp sugar
1 small bunch each of flat leaf parsley and dill, finely chopped
juice of 1 lemon
plain (all-purpose) flour
sunflower oil, for shallow-frying
salt and ground black pepper
parsley and dill fronds, and lemon wedges, to serve

1 Using a rolling pin, gently bash the fish on both sides, to smash the backbone. With your hands, massage the skin to loosen it from the flesh – don't pummel it too hard or the skin will tear.

2 Working from the tail end towards the head, squeeze the loosened flesh out of the opening below the gills. Remove any bits of bone from the loosened flesh, then rinse and set aside.

3 Fry the shallots in the olive oil until soft. Add all the nuts then the currants, apricots, spices, chilli and sugar. Mix in the fish flesh and cook through for 2–3 minutes, then add the herbs and lemon juice and season with salt and pepper.

4 Lift up the empty mackerel skin and push the filling through the opening, shaking the sack a little to jiggle the filling down towards the tail until plump. Toss in flour and fry until the skin begins to turn brown and buckle. To serve, cut the fish crossways into slices and arrange on a dish in a fish shape. Surround with dill and parsley and serve with lemon wedges.

Grilled Mackerel with Spicy Dhal

Oily fish like mackerel are essential as part of a balanced diet and are good value for money. Here they are complemented by tamarind-flavoured dhal, chopped fresh tomatoes, onion salad and flat bread.

Serves 4

4 mackerel or 8 large sardines
fresh red chilli slices and finely chopped coriander (cilantro), to garnish
flat bread and tomatoes, to serve

For the dhal
250g/9oz/1 cup red lentils, or yellow split peas (soaked overnight)
30ml/2 tbsp sunflower oil
2.5ml/½ tsp each mustard seeds, cumin seeds, fennel seeds, and fenugreek or cardamom seeds
5ml/1 tsp ground turmeric
3–4 dried red chillies, crumbled
30ml/2 tbsp tamarind paste
5ml/1 tsp soft brown sugar
30ml/2 tbsp chopped fresh coriander (cilantro)
salt and ground black pepper

1 For the dhal, rinse the lentils, drain them well and put them in a large pan. Pour in 1 litre/1¾ pints/4 cups water and bring to the boil. Lower the heat, partially cover the pan and simmer the lentils for about 30–40 minutes, stirring occasionally, until they are tender and soft.

2 Heat the oil in a wok or shallow pan. Add the mustard seeds, then cover and cook for a few seconds, until they pop. Remove the lid, add the rest of the seeds, with the turmeric and chillies and cook for a few more seconds.

3 Stir in the lentils, with salt to taste. Mix well, then stir in the tamarind paste and sugar. Bring to the boil, then simmer for 10 minutes, until thick. Stir in the chopped fresh coriander.

4 Meanwhile, clean the fish then heat a ridged griddle pan or the grill (broiler) until very hot. Make six diagonal slashes on either side of each fish and remove the head if you like.

5 Season inside and out, then cook for 5–7 minutes on each side, until the skin is crisp. Serve with the dhal, flat bread and tomatoes, garnished with chilli and coriander.

Mackerel with Nuts Energy 520kcal/2154kJ; Protein 20.2g; Carbohydrate 13.7g, of which sugars 10.1g; Fat 43.1g, of which saturates 5.5g; Cholesterol 40mg; Calcium 86mg; Fibre 3.1g; Sodium 53mg
Grilled Mackerel Energy 586kcal/2453kJ; Protein 43.3g; Carbohydrate 36.5g, of which sugars 2.8g; Fat 30.6g, of which saturates 5.7g; Cholesterol 81mg; Calcium 72mg; Fibre 3.6g; Sodium 121m

lackerel with Rhubarb Sauce

ackerel are really at their ost plentiful in early ımmer, just when rhubarb growing strongly. The rtness of rhubarb offsets e richness of the oily fish perfection.

erves 4

whole mackerel, cleaned
5g/1oz/2 tbsp butter
onion, finely chopped
)ml/6 tbsp fresh white breadcrumbs
5ml/1 tbsp chopped fresh parsley
finely grated rind of 1 lemon
freshly grated nutmeg
1 egg, lightly beaten
melted butter or olive oil, for brushing
sea salt and ground black pepper

For the sauce

225g/8oz rhubarb (trimmed weight), cut in 1cm/½in lengths
25–50g/1–2oz/2–4 tbsp caster (superfine) sugar
25g/1oz/2 tbsp butter
15ml/1 tbsp chopped fresh tarragon (optional), to garnish

Ask the fishmonger to bone the mackerel, or do it yourself: ›en out the body of the fish, turn flesh side down and run ›ur thumb firmly down the backbone – when you turn the fish ver, the bones should lift out in a complete section.

Melt the butter in a pan and cook the onion gently for -10 minutes, until softened but not browned. Add the eadcrumbs, parsley, lemon rind, salt, pepper and grated ıtmeg. Mix well, and then add the beaten egg to bind.

Divide the mixture among the four fish, wrap the fish over ıd secure with cocktail sticks (toothpicks). Brush with melted ıtter or olive oil. Preheat the grill (broiler) and cook under edium heat for about 8 minutes on each side.

Meanwhile, make the sauce: put the rhubarb into a pan with 5ml/2½fl oz/⅓ cup water, 25g/1oz/2 tbsp of the sugar and the ıtter. Cook over low heat until the rhubarb is tender. Taste and ld extra sugar if necessary, but it should be quite tart.

Serve the stuffed mackerel with the hot rhubarb sauce, ırnished with a little of the fresh tarragon.

Brandade of Smoked Mackerel

This French dish made with salt cod is supremely soothing. The right kind of salt cod is often difficult to find so this version uses smoked mackerel.

Serves 6

450g/1lb peppered smoked mackerel fillets, with skin on
225ml/7½fl oz/scant 1 cup milk
225ml/7½fl oz/scant 1 cup water
sprig of fresh thyme
1 bay leaf
450g/1lb floury potatoes, peeled
150ml/¼ pint/⅔ cup half olive and half sunflower oil
15ml/1 tbsp horseradish sauce
30ml/2 tbsp wholegrain mustard
45ml/3 tbsp chopped fresh parsley
15ml/1 tbsp chopped tarragon
ground black pepper
grilled or fried toast fingers and olive oil, to serve

1 Place the smoked mackerel fillets in a large pan with the milk and water, thyme and bay leaf. Bring almost to the boil, then remove from the heat and allow the fillets to cool in the liquid.

2 Meanwhile, in a separate pan, boil the potatoes for about 20 minutes until tender, then mash well. Keep warm. Strain the liquid from the mackerel and reserve. Remove the skin from the fish and flake the flesh.

3 Heat the oils in a pan until a piece of day-old bread sizzles when added. Add a spoonful of fish and beat well. Use a deep pan and an electric beater on slow speed.

4 Keep adding the fish, spoonful by spoonful, over medium heat, beating until it has all been added. Be careful to avoid splashes, but once two large spoonfuls have been added to the oil there should be no problem.

5 Stir in the horseradish, mustard and herbs, then beat in the mashed potato. Beat in enough of the reserved cooking liquid to give a smooth, creamy consistency, suitable for spreading.

6 Season well with ground black pepper. Pile the brandade into a dish and drizzle with a little olive oil before serving warm with freshly made toasts.

ıckerel with Rhubarb Energy 728kcal/3034kJ; Protein 48.2g; Carbohydrate 27.5g, of which sugars 9.8g; Fat 48g, of which saturates 14.3g; Cholesterol 193mg; Calcium 129mg; Fibre 1.8g; Sodium 398mg
andade Energy 467kcal/1927kJ; Protein 11.7g; Carbohydrate 1.1g, of which sugars 1.1g; Fat 46.2g, of which saturates 14.8g; Cholesterol 63mg; Calcium 32mg; Fibre 0g; Sodium 144mg

Mackerel with Onions

Perhaps more than most fish, mackerel is best cooked within hours of being caught. When buying, look for really fresh fish with bright eyes and bluish-green tinges on the skin. In this recipe, which is popular around the coast of Britain, the sweetness of the onions and the sharpness of the wine vinegar perfectly complement the oily flesh of the mackerel.

Serves 2

2 mackerel, cleaned
15ml/1 tbsp oil
1 large onion, very thinly sliced
1 garlic clove, finely chopped or crushed
1 bay leaf
150ml/¼ pint/⅔ cup medium apple juice or cider
30ml/2 tbsp wine vinegar
15ml/1 tbsp finely chopped fresh parsley or coriander (cilantro)
salt and ground black pepper

1 Scale and gut the fish, if necessary. Dry on kitchen paper and then make two or three shallow slashes down each side of each mackerel.

2 Heat the oil in a frying pan, add the mackerel and cook over medium heat for about 5–8 minutes on each side or until just cooked through. Lift out and keep warm.

3 Add the onion, garlic and bay leaf to the pan, cover and cook gently for 10–15 minutes, stirring occasionally, until soft and beginning to brown. Remove the lid, increase the heat and continue cooking until the onions are golden brown. Add the apple juice or cider and vinegar.

4 Boil the onions until the mixture is well reduced, thick and syrupy. Remove from the heat, stir in the parsley or coriander, and season to taste. Remove the bay leaf. Place a fish on warmed plates, and serve with the onions.

Cook's Tip

To serve this dish cold, flake the cooked fish, discarding the skin and bones, cover with the onion mixture and leave to cool.

Mackerel with Ratatouille

Make this colourful dish during the summer when peppers and tomatoes are better value for money. Ratatouille is rather like a chunky vegetable stew, with a lovely tangy flavour. This version is particularly lemony, to offset the richness of the mackerel.

Serves 4

2 large mackerel, filleted, or 4 fillets
plain (all-purpose) flour, for dusting
salt and ground black pepper
lemon wedges, to serve

For the ratatouille

1 large aubergine (eggplant), slice
90ml/6 tbsp olive oil
1 large onion, chopped
2 garlic cloves, finely chopped
1 large courgette (zucchini), sliced
1 red and 1 green (bell) pepper, seeded and chopped
800g/1¾lb ripe tomatoes, roughly chopped
1 bay leaf

1 To make the ratatouille, sprinkle the aubergine slices with salt and leave to stand in a colander for 30 minutes.

2 Heat 15ml/1 tbsp of the olive oil in a large flameproof casserole. Gently fry the onion until it softens and colours slightly. Add the garlic, then the courgette and peppers and stir-fry. Add the tomatoes and bay leaf, partially cover and simmer until the tomatoes just soften.

3 Rinse off the salt from the aubergine. Using kitchen paper, squeeze the slices dry, then cut into cubes.

4 Heat 15ml/1 tbsp of the olive oil in a frying pan until smoking. Add the aubergine cubes a handful at a time and cook, stirring over high heat until the cubes are brown on all sides. Stir into the tomato sauce.

5 Cut each mackerel fillet into three, then dust the filleted side with flour. Heat 60ml/4 tbsp of the oil in a frying pan and fry the fillets, floured sides down, for 3 minutes. Turn and cook for a further minute, then slip the fillets into the tomato sauce and simmer, covered, for 5 minutes. Check the seasoning, adjusting i necessary, before serving either hot or cold.

Mackerel with Onions Energy 451kcal/1876kJ; Protein 30.5g; Carbohydrate 15.9g, of which sugars 13.5g; Fat 29.9g, of which saturates 5.6g; Cholesterol 80mg; Calcium 87mg; Fibre 2.4g; Sodium 98m
Mackerel with Ratatouille Energy 544kcal/2260kJ; Protein 28.4g; Carbohydrate 22.9g, of which sugars 17.9g; Fat 38.2g, of which saturates 6.9g; Cholesterol 68mg; Calcium 78mg; Fibre 6.3g; Sodium 104m

ɜaked Sardines with Tomatoes

erved with chunks of crusty read to mop up the elicious sauce, and a crisp reen salad, this simple dish all you need for a tasty, atisfying meal. Sardines are a ery economical fish, so look ut for them in your local shmongers or supermarket vhen in season. Whole ackerel, another great udget fish, and anchovies an also be prepared and ooked this way.

Serves 4

8 large sardines, scaled, gutted and thoroughly washed
6–8 fresh thyme sprigs
juice of ½ lemon
2 x 400g/14oz cans chopped tomatoes, drained of juice
60–75ml/4–5 tbsp olive oil
4 garlic cloves, smashed flat
5ml/1 tsp sugar
1 bunch of fresh purple or green basil
salt and ground black pepper
lemon wedges, to serve

Preheat the oven to 180°C/350°F/Gas 4.

Lay the prepared sardines side by side in a shallow, ovenproof sh, place a sprig of fresh thyme between each one and queeze the lemon juice over them.

In a large bowl, mix the drained tomatoes, olive oil, smashed arlic and sugar. Season to taste with salt and pepper and stir most of the fresh purple or green basil leaves, then tip the ixture over the sardines.

Place the dish in the preheated oven and bake, uncovered, for oout 25 minutes until the fish is cooked through.

Sprinkle the remaining basil leaves over the top and serve hot, ith lemon wedges for squeezing.

Cook's Tip

During the summer, if you have a glut, you can use fresh tomatoes instead of canned. Simply replace the can with 4–5 medium-sized fresh tomatoes, skinned and diced.

Marinaded Sardines

This unusual dish is packed with flavour and is an ideal make-ahead dish for a summer dinner party or al fresco meal. Serve with roasted summer vegetables and flatbread to mop up the marinade.

Serves 4

12–16 sardines, cleaned
seasoned plain (all-purpose) flour, for dusting
90ml/6 tbsp olive oil
salt and ground black pepper
roasted red onion, green (bell) pepper and tomatoes, to garnish

For the marinade

1 onion, sliced
1 garlic clove, crushed
3–4 bay leaves
2 cloves
1 dried red chilli, seeded and chopped
5ml/1 tsp paprika
120ml/4fl oz/½ cup wine or sherry vinegar
120ml/4fl oz/½ cup dry white wine

1 Cut the heads off the sardines and split each of them along the belly. Turn the fish over so that the backbone is uppermost. Press down along the backbone to loosen it, then carefully lift out the backbone and as many of the remaining little bones as possible. Close the sardines up again and dust them with seasoned flour.

2 Heat 30ml/2 tbsp of the olive oil in a frying pan and fry the sardines for 2–3 minutes on each side. With a metal spatula, remove the fish from the pan to a plate and allow to cool, then pack them in a single layer in a large shallow dish.

3 To make the marinade, add the remaining olive oil to the oil in the frying pan. Fry the onion and garlic for 5–10 minutes until translucent. Add the bay leaves, cloves, chilli and paprika, with pepper to taste. Fry for another 1–2 minutes.

4 Stir in the vinegar, wine and a little salt. Allow to bubble up, then pour over the sardines to cover the fish completely.

5 When cool, cover and chill overnight or for up to three days. Serve garnished with the onion, pepper and tomatoes.

ıked Sardines Energy 219kcal/915kJ; Protein 11.7g; Carbohydrate 7.3g, of which sugars 7.3g; Fat 16.2g, of which saturates 3.1g; Cholesterol 0mg; Calcium 57mg; Fibre 2g; Sodium 78mg
ırinaded Sardines Energy 353kcal/1467kJ; Protein 23.7g; Carbohydrate 4.2g, of which sugars 1g; Fat 26g, of which saturates 5.1g; Cholesterol 0mg; Calcium 124mg; Fibre 0.3g; Sodium 129mg

Sicilian Spaghetti with Sardines

This is a traditional dish from Sicily, which uses ingredients that are common to many parts of the Mediterranean, and which together make an economical supper.

Serves 4

12 fresh sardines, cleaned and boned
250ml/8fl oz/1 cup olive oil
1 onion, chopped
25g/1oz/¼ cup dill sprigs
50g/2oz/½ cup pine nuts
25g/1oz/2 tbsp raisins, soaked in water
50g/2oz/½ cup fresh breadcrumbs
450g/1lb dried spaghetti
flour for dusting
salt

1 Wash the sardines and pat dry on kitchen paper. Open them out flat, then cut in half lengthways.

2 Heat 30ml/2 tbsp of the oil in a pan, add the chopped onion and fry until softened and golden. Add the dill sprigs and cook gently for a minute or two.

3 Add the pine nuts and raisins and season with salt. Dry-fry the breadcrumbs in a frying pan until golden. Set aside.

4 Cook the spaghetti in boiling, salted water according to the instructions on the packet, until al dente. Heat the remaining oil in a pan. Dust the sardines with flour and fry in the hot oil for 2–3 minutes. Drain on kitchen paper.

5 Drain the spaghetti and return to the pan. Add the onion mixture and toss well to combine.

6 Transfer the spaghetti mixture to a serving platter and arrange the fried sardines on top. Sprinkle with the toasted breadcrumbs and serve immediately.

Variation

You can also use mackerel fillets for this recipe if you prefer or if sardines are not available.

Pasta Sardine Bake

Pappardelle is perfect for this Sicilian recipe. If you can't find it, any wide pasta will do instead.

Serves 6

2 fennel bulbs, trimmed
large pinch of saffron threads
12 sardines, backbones and heads removed, cut into pieces
60ml/4 tbsp olive oil
2 shallots, finely chopped
2 garlic cloves, finely chopped
2 fresh red chillies, seeded and finely chopped
4 drained canned anchovy fillets
30ml/2 tbsp capers
75g/3oz/¾ cup pine nuts
450g/1lb pappardelle
30ml/2 tbsp grated Pecorino cheese
salt and ground black pepper

1 Preheat the oven to 200°C/400°F/Gas 6. Cut the fennel bulbs in half and cook them in a pan of lightly salted boiling water with the saffron threads for about 10 minutes, until tender. Drain, reserving the cooking liquid. Dice the fennel.

2 Toss the sardines pieces in seasoned flour. Heat the olive oil in a pan, add the shallots and garlic and cook until lightly coloured. Add the chillies and sardines and cook for 3 minutes. Stir in the fennel and cook gently for 3 minutes with a little of the reserved fennel water.

3 Add the anchovies and cook for 1 minute; stir in the capers and pine nuts. Simmer for 3 minutes more, then turn off the heat and set aside.

4 Pour the reserved fennel liquid into a pan and top it up with enough water to cook the pasta. Bring the water to the boil, add salt, and cook the dried pasta for about 12 minutes; fresh pasta until it rises to the surface of the water. When the pasta is just tender, drain it lightly, retaining a little liquid.

5 Grease a shallow ovenproof dish and put in a layer of pasta, then make a layer of the sardine mixture. Repeat the layers, finishing with the fish. Sprinkle over the Pecorino; bake for 15 minutes, until the top is bubbling and golden. Serve while hot, with a green salad if you wish.

Sicilian Spaghetti Energy 819kcal/3453kJ; Protein 48g; Carbohydrate 101g, of which sugars 11g; Fat 28g, of which saturates 6g; Cholesterol 0mg; Calcium 205mg; Fibre 7g; Sodium 285mg
Pasta Bake Energy 597kcal/2512kJ; Protein 41.3g; Carbohydrate 57.3g, of which sugars 4.1g; Fat 24.2g, of which saturates 5.4g; Cholesterol 6mg; Calcium 214mg; Fibre 4g; Sodium 303mg

ʼalt Cod Fritters

ʼ you can get it, salt cod is a
ʼery economical ingredient.
ʼarlic mayonnaise is the
ʼraditional accompaniment to
ʼhese Portuguese fritters.

ʼerves 6

ʼ50g/1lb salt cod
ʼ00ml/½ pint/1¼ cups milk
ʼ spring onions (scallions), chopped
ʼ00g/1¼lb floury potatoes, cooked
30ml/2 tbsp extra virgin olive oil
30ml/2 tbsp chopped fresh parsley
juice of ½ lemon, to taste
2 eggs, beaten
60ml/4 tbsp plain (all-purpose) flour
90g/3½oz/1⅓ cups dry white breadcrumbs
vegetable oil, for shallow-frying
salt and ground black pepper
lemon wedges, garlic mayonnaise and salad, to serve

ʼ Soak the salt cod in cold water for 24–36 hours, changing the ʼater five or six times. The cod should swell as it rehydrates and ʼ tiny piece should not taste too salty when tried. Drain well.

ʼ Poach the cod very gently in the milk with half the spring ʼnions for 10–15 minutes, or until it flakes easily. Remove the ʼod and flake it with a fork into a bowl, discarding bones and ʼin. Drain the cooked potatoes, and mash thoroughly.

ʼ Add 60ml/4 tbsp mashed potato to the flaked cod and beat ʼith a wooden spoon. Work in the olive oil, then gradually add ʼe remaining potato. Beat in the remaining spring onions and ʼe parsley. Season with lemon juice and pepper to taste – the ʼixture may need a little salt. Beat in one egg, then chill in the ʼefrigerator until firm.

ʼ Shape the mixture into 12–18 small round cakes. Coat them ʼ flour, then dip them in the remaining egg and coat with the ʼeadcrumbs. Chill until ready to fry.

ʼ Heat about 2cm/¾in depth of oil in a large, heavy frying pan. ʼdd the fritters and cook over a medium-high heat for about ʼ minutes. Turn them over and cook for a further 4 minutes on ʼe other side, until evenly crisp and golden. Drain on crumpled ʼtchen paper, then serve immediately with the garlic ʼayonnaise, lemon wedges and salad leaves.

Fish Cakes

Fish cakes are a steadfast favourite everywhere, and as these are baked in the oven, they're very easy to make. Serve the fish cakes with a quick homemade tartare sauce (see Cook's tip), buttered potatoes and a sliced cucumber salad to make a complete supper. Salmon and cod are not cheap, but these are so tasty that you can feed six people.

Serves 6

450g/1lb cod or plaice fillet
225g/8oz salmon fillet
175g/6oz smoked salmon
30ml/2 tbsp finely chopped onion
40g/1½oz/3 tbsp melted butter
3 eggs
25g/1oz/¼ cup plain (all-purpose) flour
salt and white pepper
quick homemade tartare sauce, cucumber salad and buttered new potatoes, to serve.

1 Place the cod or plaice and salmon fillets in a shallow dish, and sprinkle with 15ml/1 tbsp salt to draw out some of the moisture. Leave to rest for 10 minutes, then pat dry with kitchen paper.

2 Place the cod and salmon, with the smoked salmon, in a food processor. Add the onion, butter, eggs and flour and pulse until smooth; season with salt and pepper and spoon into a bowl.

3 Preheat the oven to 190°C/375°F/Gas 5. Lightly grease a 23 x 33cm/9 x 13in baking tray. With damp hands, form the fish mixture into 18 slightly flattened, round patties, and place them on the prepared tray.

4 Bake the fish cakes in the preheated oven for 30–35 minutes, until they are cooked through and lightly browned. Serve immediately with tartare sauce, cucumber salad and potatoes.

Cook's Tip

To make tartare sauce mix chopped capers and baby gerkins into 45ml/3 tbsp mayonnaise. Add lemon juice, chopped dill or chives, and salt and pepper to taste, stir together and serve.

ʼalt Cod Fritters Energy 653kcal/2721kJ; Protein 32.7g; Carbohydrate 28.1g, of which sugars 4.2g; Fat 46.4g, of which saturates 7.6g; Cholesterol 178mg; Calcium 123mg; Fibre 1.4g; Sodium 472mg
ʼsh Cakes Energy 407kcal/1700kJ; Protein 48.5g; Carbohydrate 5.5g, of which sugars 0.6g; Fat 21.4g, of which saturates 7.9g; Cholesterol 259mg; Calcium 64mg; Fibre 0.3g; Sodium 1029mg

Kedgeree

Of Indian origin, kedgeree came to England via the colonial expats of the British Empire. It quickly became a popular dish using smoked fish for breakfast or high tea. This is a good budget dish when serving a group of people, either at the beginning or end of the day.

Serves 4–6

450g/1lb smoked haddock
300ml/½ pint/1¼ cups milk
175g/6oz/scant 1 cup long grain rice
pinch of grated nutmeg and cayenne pepper
50g/2oz/¼ cup butter
1 onion, peeled and finely chopped
2 hard-boiled eggs, shelled
salt and ground black pepper
chopped fresh parsley, to garnish
lemon wedges and wholemeal (whole-wheat) toast or a green salad, to serve

1 Poach the haddock in the milk, made up with just enough water to cover the fish, for about 8 minutes, or until just cooked. Skin the haddock, remove all the bones and flake the flesh with a fork. Set aside.

2 Bring 600ml/1 pint/2½ cups water to the boil in a large pan. Add the rice, cover tightly with a lid and cook over low heat for about 25 minutes, or until all the water has been absorbed by the rice. Season with salt and a grinding of black pepper, and the nutmeg and cayenne pepper.

3 Meanwhile, heat 15g/½oz/1 tbsp butter in a pan and fry the onion until soft and transparent. Set aside. Roughly chop one of the hard-boiled eggs and slice the other into neat wedges.

4 Stir the remaining butter into the rice and add the flaked haddock, onion and the chopped egg. Season to taste and heat the mixture through gently (this can be done on a serving dish, covered, in a low oven if more convenient).

5 To serve, pile up the kedgeree on a warmed dish, sprinkle generously with parsley and arrange the wedges of egg on top. Put the lemon wedges around the base and serve hot with toast for breakfast, or with a green salad for supper.

Smoked Fish Soufflé

The fluffy savoury soufflé comes from French cuisine, and was made in grand English kitchens by 19th-century chefs. Soufflés are a great way to use up a glut of eggs.

Serves 4

225g/8oz smoked haddock fillet
300ml/½ pint/1¼ cups milk
2 bay leaves (optional)
40g/1½oz/3 tbsp butter, plus extra for greasing
40g/1½oz/5 tbsp plain (all-purpose) flour
55g/2oz mature (strong) Cheddar cheese, grated
5ml/1 tsp English (hot) mustard
4 egg yolks
5 egg whites
ground black pepper

1 Put the fish into a pan just large enough to hold it in a single layer, and add the milk and bay leaves, if using. Heat slowly until the milk is very hot, with small bubbles rising to the surface, but not boiling. Cover and simmer very gently for 5–8 minutes until the fish is just cooked.

2 Lift out the fish with a slotted spoon, reserving the cooking liquid, and remove any bones.

3 Discard the bay leaves and break the fish up into flakes. Preheat the oven to 190°C/375°F/Gas 5 and grease a 20cm/8in soufflé dish with butter.

4 Melt the butter in a pan, stir in the flour and cook gently for 1 minute, stirring. Remove from the heat and gradually stir in the reserved cooking liquid. Cook, stirring constantly until the sauce thickens and comes to the boil.

5 Remove from the heat. Stir in the cheese, mustard, pepper and fish. Beat in the egg yolks, one at a time. Whisk the egg whites until stiff. Stir a little egg white into the sauce then use a large metal spoon to fold in the rest.

6 Pour the mixture into the prepared dish and cook in the hot oven for about 40 minutes until risen and just firm to the touch. Serve immediately.

Kedgeree Energy 399Kcal/1668kJ; Protein 28.9g; Carbohydrate 38g, of which sugars 2.2g; Fat 14.6g, of which saturates 7.6g; Cholesterol 181mg; Calcium 62mg; Fibre 0.5g; Sodium 974mg
Fish Soufflé Energy 325kcal/1356kJ; Protein 24.4g; Carbohydrate 11.4g, of which sugars 3.8g; Fat 20.3g, of which saturates 10.7g; Cholesterol 272mg; Calcium 247mg; Fibre 0.3g; Sodium 706mg

;moked Haddock Flan

The flan is another recipe in vhich a moderate amount of .sh is bulked out with more :conomical ingredients.

;erves 4

'or the pastry

!25g/8oz/2 cups plain (all-purpose) flour
inch of salt
15g/4oz/1½ cups cold butter
old water, to mix

For the filling

2 pale smoked haddock fillets
600ml/1 pint/2½ cups full-fat (whole) milk
3–4 black peppercorns
sprig of fresh thyme
150ml/¼ pint/⅔ cup double (heavy) cream
2 eggs
200g/7oz potatoes, peeled and diced
ground black pepper

Preheat the oven to 200°C/400°F/Gas 6. To make the pastry, ›ut the flour, salt and butter into the food processor bowl and ›rocess until the mixture resembles fine breadcrumbs.

! Pour in a little cold water and continue to process until the ıixture forms a ball. If this takes longer than 30 seconds add a lash or two more water. Take the pastry ball out of the food ›rocessor, wrap it in clear film (plastic wrap) and leave it to rest ı a cool place for about 30 minutes.

ɜ Roll out the pastry and use it to line a 20cm/8in flan tin (pan). rick the base of the pastry all over with a fork then bake blind ı the preheated oven for 20 minutes.

ɬ Put the haddock fillets in a pan with the milk, peppercorns ıd thyme. Poach for 10 minutes. Remove the fish from the pan sing a slotted spoon and flake into small chunks.

Whisk the cream and eggs together in a large bowl, then ʌhisk in the cooled poaching liquid.

Arrange the flaked fish and diced potato in the base of the astry case, and season to taste with black pepper. Pour the ·ream mixture over the top. Bake for 40 minutes, until lightly rowned on top and set. Serve immediately, cut into wedges.

Salmon Quiche

There are so many ways of making smoked salmon stretch a bit further. Here it forms the filling for a quiche made with potato pastry.

Serves 6

115g/4oz floury potatoes, diced
225g/8oz/2 cups plain (all-purpose) flour, sifted
115g/4oz/½ cup butter, diced
½ egg, beaten
10ml/2 tsp chilled water
chopped fresh dill, to serve

For the filling

6 eggs, beaten
150ml/¼ pint/⅔ cup full cream (whole) milk
300ml/½ pint/1¼ cups double (heavy) cream
30–45ml/2–3 tbsp chopped fresh dill
30ml/2 tbsp drained bottled capers, chopped
275g/10oz smoked salmon, cut into bitesize pieces
salt and ground black pepper

1 Cook the potatoes in a large pan of lightly salted boiling water for 15 minutes or until tender. Drain and return to the pan. Mash the potatoes until smooth and set aside to cool.

2 Place the flour in a bowl and rub or cut in the butter to form fine crumbs. Beat in the potatoes and egg. Bring the mixture together, adding chilled water if needed.

3 Roll the pastry out on a floured surface to a 28cm/11in round. Use the pastry to line a deep, 23cm/9in round, loose-based, fluted quiche pan. Trim the edges. Chill for 1 hour. Preheat the oven to 200°C/400°F/Gas 6. Place a baking sheet in the oven to heat it.

4 Make the filling. In a bowl, beat the eggs with the milk and cream. Stir in the dill and capers and season with pepper. Add in the salmon and stir to combine.

5 Remove the pastry case (pie shell) from the refrigerator, prick the base well and pour the mixture into it.

6 Bake on the baking sheet for 35–45 minutes. Serve warm with mixed salad leaves and some more dill.

ıddock Flan Energy 734kcal/3064kJ; Protein 23.8g; Carbohydrate 58.4g, of which sugars 8.2g; Fat 46.8g, of which saturates 27.9g; Cholesterol 225mg; Calcium 280mg; Fibre 2.3g; Sodium 636mg
lmon Quiche Energy 679kcal/2825kJ; Protein 23.3g; Carbohydrate 34.1g, of which sugars 2.7g; Fat 51.1g, of which saturates 28.9g; Cholesterol 317mg; Calcium 142mg; Fibre 1.4g; Sodium 1070mg

Prawn and New Potato Stew

New potatoes with plenty of flavour, such as Jersey Royals, Maris Piper or Nicola, are essential for this effortless seasonal stew that bulks out the prawns. Use fresh prawns if they are on special offer, otherwise use good-quality frozen ones as they will usually be much more economical and taste almost as good as fresh ones.

Serves 4

675g/1½lb small new potatoes, scrubbed
15g/½oz/½ cup fresh coriander (cilantro)
1 dried red chilli
15ml/1 tbsp olive oil
1 garlic clove
400g/14oz can chopped tomatoes
300g/11oz frozen cooked peeled prawns (shrimp), thawed and drained

1 Cook the new potatoes in lightly salted, boiling water for 15 minutes, until tender. Drain and return to the pan.

2 Meanwhile, finely chop the coriander and crumble the dried chilli. Heat the oil in a large pan and fry the garlic for 1 minute.

3 Add the chopped tomatoes to the pan, together with the chilli, coriander and 90ml/6 tbsp water. Bring to the boil, reduce the heat, cover and simmer gently for 5 minutes.

4 Stir in the prawns and the cooked new potatoes and heat briefly until they are warmed through. Be careful not to overcook the prawns or they will quickly shrivel, becoming tough and tasteless.

5 Spoon the stew into shallow bowls and serve sprinkled with the remaining coriander, torn into pieces.

6 Serve the prawn stew with crusty bread and a crisp green salad, or steamed seasonal vegetables.

Cook's Tip
You can use fresh scampi instead of prawns if available.

Prawn, Tomato and Potato Omelette

This simple dish makes a delicious lunch when served with a fresh leafy green salad, or a healthy light meal when served with steamed seasonal vegetables. You can also cook it in advance and then wrap it up when cool for a summer picnic or a packed lunch. The sweet prawns are cooked gently inside the omelette, which helps them to stay tender and succulent.

Serves 4

200g/7oz potatoes, peeled and diced
30ml/2 tbsp olive oil
1 onion, finely sliced
2.5ml/½ tsp paprika
2 large tomatoes, peeled, seeded and chopped
200g/7oz frozen peeled raw prawns (shrimp), thawed
6 eggs
2.5ml/½ tsp baking powder
pinch of salt

1 Cook the potatoes in a pan of salted boiling water for about 10 minutes or until just tender. Drain and set aside to steam dr

2 Meanwhile, pour the oil into a 23cm/9in frying pan which car safely be used under the grill (broiler). Place over medium heat. Add the onion slices and stir well to coat evenly in the oil. Coo for 5 minutes until the onions begin to soften. Sprinkle over the paprika and cook for 1 minute more.

3 Stir the tomatoes in to the onions, then add the cooked potatoes. Stir gently to mix. Increase the heat and cook for 10 minutes, or until the mixture has thickened and the potatoe have absorbed the flavour of the tomatoes. Remove from the heat and stir in the prawns.

4 Preheat the grill (broiler). Beat the eggs in a bowl, and stir in the baking powder and salt. Pour the mixture into the pan and mix thoroughly to combine.

5 Cover and cook the omelette for 8–10 minutes until the bottom has set, then finish under the hot grill so that the top becomes firm and golden. Cut the cooked omelette into slices and serve it straight away, or cool for eating later.

Prawn Stew Energy 218kcal/924kJ; Protein 16.9g; Carbohydrate 30.4g, of which sugars 5.4g; Fat 4.1g, of which saturates 0.7g; Cholesterol 146mg; Calcium 84mg; Fibre 2.9g; Sodium 171mg
Prawn Omelette Energy 247kcal/1031kJ; Protein 19.6g; Carbohydrate 10.8g, of which sugars 3.1g; Fat 14.5g, of which saturates 3.3g; Cholesterol 383mg; Calcium 93mg; Fibre 1.2g; Sodium 211m

Baked Prawns with Feta

Tangy, salty feta cheese provides the perfect contrast to the sweet, succulent prawns in this simple baked dish. If you use frozen prawns rather than fresh you will find this a more economical dish. Serve with a green salad and fresh bread for a light lunch.

Serves 4

75ml/5 tbsp olive oil
1 onion, chopped
½ red (bell) pepper, seeded and cubed
675g/1½lb ripe tomatoes, peeled and roughly chopped
generous pinch of sugar
2.5ml/½ tsp dried oregano
450g/1lb raw tiger prawns (jumbo shrimp), thawed if frozen and peeled (with the tail shells intact)
30ml/2 tbsp finely chopped fresh flat leaf parsley
75g/3oz feta cheese, cubed
salt and ground black pepper

1 Heat the oil in a frying pan, add the onion and sauté gently for a few minutes until translucent. Add the cubed red pepper and cook, stirring occasionally, for 2–3 minutes more.

2 Stir in the chopped tomatoes, sugar and oregano, then season to taste with salt and pepper. Cook gently over low heat for about 15 minutes, stirring occasionally, until the sauce reduces slightly and thickens.

3 Preheat the oven to 180°C/350°F/Gas 4. Stir the prawns and chopped parsley into the tomato sauce, transfer into a baking dish and spread evenly.

4 Sprinkle the cheese cubes on top, then bake for 30 minutes. Serve hot with a fresh green salad.

Cook's Tip

- *When tomatoes are not in season, substitute fresh ones with 2 x 400g/14oz cans chopped tomatoes, drained of their juices.*
- *Tiger prawns can be expensive, so either buy them when they are on offer, or use frozen ones.*

Octopus and Pasta Bake

This slow-cooked combination of octopus and pasta in a spicy tomato sauce makes a tasty supper dish.

Serves 4

2 frozen octopus, total weight about 675–800g/1½–1¾lb, thawed and cleaned well
150ml/¼ pint/⅔ cup olive oil
2 large onions, sliced
3 garlic cloves, chopped
1 fresh red or green chilli, seeded and thinly sliced
1 or 2 bay leaves
5ml/1 tsp dried oregano
1 piece of cinnamon stick
2 or 3 allspice berries (optional)
175ml/6fl oz/¾ cup red wine
30ml/2 tbsp tomato purée (paste) diluted in 300ml/½ pint/1¼ cups water
225g/8oz/2 cups dried penne or small macaroni-type pasta
300ml/½ pint/1¼ cups warm water
300ml/½ pint/1¼ cups boiling water
ground black pepper
45ml/3 tbsp finely chopped fresh flat leaf parsley, to garnish (optional)

1 Cut the octopus into large pieces and place in a pan over low heat. Cook gently; they will release liquid, and turn scarlet. Keep turning the pieces until the liquid has evaporated.

2 Add the olive oil to the pan and sauté the octopus pieces for 4–5 minutes. Add the onions and cook for 4–5 minutes more, stirring constantly until they start to turn golden. Stir in the garlic, chilli, bay leaf or leaves, oregano, cinnamon stick and allspice, if using. As soon as the garlic becomes aromatic, pour in the wine and let it bubble for a few minutes.

3 Add the tomato purée and some black pepper, cover and cook gently for 1½ hours, or until the octopus is perfectly soft. Stir occasionally and add a little hot water if needed.

4 Preheat the oven to 160°C/325°F/Gas 3. Bring the octopus mixture to the boil, and then add the boiling water. Stir in the pasta, then transfer to a large roasting dish and level the surface. Bake in the oven for 30–35 minutes, stirring occasionally and adding a little hot water if the mixture starts to look dry. Sprinkle the parsley on top, if using, and serve.

Baked Prawns Energy 308kcal/1,282kJ; Protein 24.8g; Carbohydrate 10g, of which sugars 9.1g; Fat 19g, of which saturates 4.8g; Cholesterol 233mg; Calcium 194mg; Fibre 2.9g; Sodium 504mg
Octopus Bake Energy 637kcal/2,669kJ; Protein 38.9g; Carbohydrate 52.9g, of which sugars 10.2g; Fat 28.5g, of which saturates 4.2g; Cholesterol 81mg; Calcium 108mg; Fibre 3.6g; Sodium 25mg

Fried Squid with Split Pea Purée

Medium-sized squid work well for this recipe, although the tender baby squid add a lovely crispness to the texture, which contrasts well with the smooth purée.

Serves 4

225g/8oz/1 cup white beans or yellow split peas
1.5 litres/2½ pints/6¼ cups cold water
1 onion, finely chopped
50g/2oz/½ cup plain (all-purpose) flour
4 medium frozen squid, thawed, total weight about 900g/2lb
2 or 3 shallots, finely chopped
75ml/5 tbsp sunflower oil
60–75ml/4–5 tbsp virgin olive oil
juice of ½ lemon
salt and ground black pepper
15ml/1 tbsp finely chopped fresh parsley, to garnish

1 Soak the beans or split peas in enough cold water to cover for 1 hour. Drain, rinse several times, then drain again. Pour the measured water in to a large, heavy pan. Add the beans or split peas, bring to the boil and skim away any scum.

2 Add the onion and simmer, uncovered, for 1 hour or more, depending on the age of the peas, stirring occasionally, until soft.

3 Season the flour with salt and ground black pepper and then toss the squid in it until each is evenly coated.

4 Purée the pea mixture in a food processor while it is still hot, as it will solidify if you allow it to cool. The purée should be smooth, with the consistency of thick cream. Add salt to taste.

5 Heat the sunflower oil in a large frying pan. When it is hot enough to sizzle, add the squid bodies, without letting them touch each other. Cook until pale golden all over. Add the tentacles and cook until crisp.

6 Spread the pea mixture on individual plates in a thin layer and let it cool a little. Sprinkle the chopped shallots over the top, then drizzle with the olive oil and lemon juice. Place the fried squid on top. Grind a little pepper over the top, add the chopped parsley and serve.

Spicy Squid Stew

Another recipe to make the most of the inexpensive squid, this hearty stew is is a South American recipe, and is ideal on a cold evening, served with plenty of fresh crusty bread or steamed rice. The potatoes disintegrate to thicken and enrich the sauce, making a warming, comforting main course.

Serves 6

600g/1lb 6oz frozen squid, thawed
45ml/3 tbsp olive oil
5 garlic cloves, crushed
4 fresh jalapeño chillies, seeded and finely chopped
2 celery sticks, diced
500g/1¼lb small new potatoes scrubbed, scraped or peeled and quartered
400ml/14fl oz/1⅔ cups dry white wine
400ml/14fl oz/1⅔ cups fish stock
4 tomatoes, diced
30ml/2 tbsp chopped fresh flat leaf parsley
salt
cooked white rice or warmed tortillas, to serve

1 Clean the squid under cold water. Pull the tentacles away from the body. The squid's entrails will come out easily.

2 Remove the cartilage from inside the squid body cavity and discard it. Wash the body thoroughly under cold running water.

3 Pull away the membrane that covers the body. Cut the tentacles from the head, discarding the head and entrails. Leave the tentacles whole but discard the hard beak in the middle. Cut the body into thin rounds.

4 Heat the oil, add the garlic, chillies and celery and cook gently over low heat for about 5 minutes.

5 Stir in the potatoes, then add the wine and stock. Bring to the boil, then simmer, covered, for 25 minutes.

6 When the potatoes are tender, remove the pan from the heat and stir in the squid, tomatoes and parsley. Cover the pan and leave to stand so that the squid cooks very gently in the residual heat. Serve immediately with white rice or tortillas.

Fried Squid Energy 735kcal/3080kJ; Protein 49g; Carbohydrate 50g, of which sugars 5g; Fat 39g, of which saturates 6g; Cholesterol 506mg; Calcium 81mg; Fibre 7g; Sodium 271mg
Spicy Squid Stew Energy 247kcal/1041kJ; Protein 17.6g; Carbohydrate 17.4g, of which sugars 3.8g; Fat 7.8g, of which saturates 1.3g; Cholesterol 225mg; Calcium 48mg; Fibre 2g; Sodium 136mg

quid Stuffed with Rice and Ham

lam and raisins contrast
onderfully with the subtle
avour of the squid. The
uffed squid make a perfect
ain course with boiled rice.

erves 4

frozen squid, about 275g/10oz each, thawed
small onion, chopped
garlic cloves, chopped
0g/2oz dry-cured ham diced
5g/3oz/scant ½ cup long grain rice
0ml/2 tbsp raisins, chopped
30ml/2 tbsp finely chopped parsley
½ small (US medium) egg, beaten
plain (all-purpose) flour, for dusting
250ml/8fl oz/1 cup white wine
1 bay leaf
salt and ground black pepper
30ml/2 tbsp chopped fresh parsley, plus extra, to garnish

For the tomato sauce

90ml/6 tbsp olive oil
1 onion, finely chopped
2 garlic cloves, chopped
200g/7oz can tomatoes
salt and cayenne pepper

Make the tomato sauce. Heat 30ml/2 tbsp oil in a large, ameproof casserole. Add the onion and garlic and cook over a entle heat. Add the tomatoes and cook for 10 minutes. Season ith salt and cayenne pepper.

To prepare the squid, use the tentacles to pull out the body. ut off the tentacles, discard the eyes and everything below. op out the spine. Chop the fin flaps and rinse the bodies.

Heat the remaining oil in a pan and gently fry the onion and arlic together. Add the ham and squid tentacles and stir-fry. Off ne heat stir in the rice, chopped raisins and parsley. Season well nd add the egg to bind the ingredients.

Spoon the mixture into the squid bodies, then close with a nall poultry skewer. Pat dry with kitchen paper, dust with flour nd fry the squid in the oil, turning until coloured on all sides.

Arrange the squid in the tomato sauce. Add the wine and bay af. Cover and simmer for 30 minutes, turning if the sauce does ot cover the squid completely. Serve the squid sliced into rings, urrounded by the sauce and garnished with parsley.

Potato and Mussel Salad with Shallot and Chive Dressing

Shallot and chives in a creamy dressing add bite to this salad of potato and sweet mussels. Serve with a bowl of watercress and plenty of wholemeal bread.

Serves 4

675g/1½lb salad potatoes
1kg/2¼lb mussels, scrubbed and beards removed
200ml/7fl oz/ scant 1 cup dry white wine
15g/½oz flat leaf parsley, chopped
salt and ground black pepper
chopped fresh chives, to garnish
watercress sprigs, to serve

For the dressing

105ml/7 tbsp mild olive oil
15–30ml/1–2 tbsp white wine vinegar
5ml/1 tsp Dijon mustard
1 large shallot, very finely chopped
15ml/1 tbsp chopped fresh chives
45ml/3 tbsp double (heavy) cream
pinch of caster (superfine) sugar (optional)

1 Cook the potatoes in boiling, salted water for 15–20 minutes, or until tender. Drain, cool, then peel. Slice the potatoes into a bowl and toss with 30ml/2 tbsp of the oil for the dressing.

2 Discard any open mussels that do not close when tapped. Bring the white wine to the boil in a large, heavy pan. Add the mussels, cover and boil vigorously, shaking the pan occasionally, for 3–4 minutes, until the mussels have opened. Discard any mussels that have not opened after 5 minutes' cooking. Drain and shell the mussels, reserving the cooking liquid.

3 Boil the reserved cooking liquid until reduced to about 45ml/3 tbsp. Strain this over the potatoes and toss to mix.

4 For the dressing, whisk together the remaining oil, 15ml/1 tbsp vinegar, the mustard, shallot and chives. Add the cream and whisk again to form a thick dressing. Adjust the seasoning, adding more vinegar and/or a pinch of sugar to taste.

5 Toss the mussels with the potatoes, and mix in the dressing and parsley. Sprinkle with chives and serve with watercress.

quid with Rice Energy 344kcal/1449kJ; Protein 28.9g; Carbohydrate 25.5g, of which sugars 4.2g; Fat 9.6g, of which saturates 1.5g; Cholesterol 298mg; Calcium 104mg; Fibre 1.8g; Sodium 701mg
otato and Mussel Salad Energy 512kcal/2132kJ; Protein 13g; Carbohydrate 31g, of which sugars 4g; Fat 34g, of which saturates 8g; Cholesterol 49mg; Calcium 57mg; Fibre 2g; Sodium 287mg

Mussel and Rice Pilaff

This Greek recipe looks and tastes spectacular.

Serves 4

1.6kg/3½lb mussels, cleaned
2 onions, thinly sliced
350ml/12fl oz/1½ cups dry white wine
450ml/¾ pint/scant 2 cups hot water
150ml/¼ pint/⅔ cup olive oil
5–6 spring onions (scallions), chopped
2 garlic cloves, chopped
large pinch of dried oregano
200g/7oz/1 cup long grain rice
45ml/3 tbsp finely chopped fresh flat leaf parsley
45–60ml/3–4 tbsp chopped dill
salt and ground black pepper

1 Discard any mussels that are broken or open. Place the remainder in a large pan with one-third of the onion slices, half the wine and 150ml/¼ pint/⅔ cup of the hot water. Cover and cook over high heat for about 5 minutes, shaking occasionally, until the mussels open. Discard any that stay closed. Shell most, but keep a dozen or so whole for garnish. Strain the liquid through a sieve (strainer) and reserve.

2 Heat the oil in a deep, heavy pan, add the remaining onion and spring onions, and sauté over medium heat until golden. Stir in the garlic and oregano. As soon as the garlic becomes aromatic, add the rice and stir to coat the grains well with oil.

3 After a few minutes, add the remaining wine, stirring until it has been absorbed, then add the remaining 300ml/½ pint/1¼ cups water, the reserved mussel liquid and the chopped parsley.

4 Season with salt and pepper, then cover and cook gently over low to medium heat for about 5 minutes, stirring occasionally.

5 Add the mussels, including those in their shells. Stir in half the chopped dill, making sure that you keep the mussels in their shells intact. If necessary, add a little more hot water.

6 Cover and cook gently for 5–6 minutes, or until the rice is cooked. Sprinkle the remaining dill on top and serve with a green or cabbage salad and black olives.

Mussel Risotto

Fresh root ginger and coriander add a distinctive flavour to this dish, while the green chillies give it heat.

Serves 3–4

900g/2lb fresh mussels
250ml/8fl oz/1 cup white wine
30ml/2 tbsp olive oil
1 onion, chopped
2 garlic cloves, crushed
1–2 fresh green chillies, seeded and finely sliced
2.5cm/1in piece of fresh root ginger, grated
275g/10oz/1½ cups risotto rice
900ml/1½ pints/3¾ cups simmering fish stock
30ml/2 tbsp chopped fresh coriander (cilantro)
30ml/2 tbsp double (heavy) cream
salt and ground black pepper

1 Scrub the mussels, discarding any that do not close when sharply tapped. Place in a large pan. Add 120ml/4fl oz/½ cup of the wine and bring to the boil. Cover the pan and cook the mussels for 4–5 minutes until they have opened, shaking the pan occasionally. Drain, reserving the liquid and discarding any mussels that have not opened. Shell most of the mussels, reserving a few in their shells. Strain the mussel liquid.

2 Heat the oil and fry the onion and garlic for 3–4 minutes until beginning to soften. Add the chillies. Continue to cook over low heat for 1–2 minutes, stirring frequently, then stir in the ginger and fry gently for 1 minute more.

3 Add the rice and cook over medium heat for 2 minutes, stirring, until the rice is coated in oil and becomes translucent. Stir in the reserved cooking liquid from the mussels. When this has been absorbed, add the remaining wine and cook stirring, until absorbed. Now add the hot fish stock, a little at a time, making sure each addition is absorbed before adding the next.

4 When the rice is about three-quarters cooked, stir in the mussels. Add the coriander and season with salt and pepper. Continue adding stock to the risotto until it is creamy and the rice is tender. Remove from the heat, stir in the cream, cover and rest for a few minutes. Decorate with the reserved mussels and serve immediately.

Mussel and Rice Pilaff Energy 405kcal/1686kJ; Protein 15.7g; Carbohydrate 33.3g, of which sugars 3.3g; Fat 19g, of which saturates 2.7g; Cholesterol 43mg; Calcium 93mg; Fibre 1.5g; Sodium 265mg
Mussel Risotto Energy 439kcal/1833kJ; Protein 17.2g; Carbohydrate 56.6g, of which sugars 1.4g; Fat 11.3g, of which saturates 3.5g; Cholesterol 37mg; Calcium 159mg; Fibre 0.2g; Sodium 146mg

ʼlouclade

ʼhis is a traditional dish of ɿussels cooked with shallots, ,arlic and saffron.

ʼerves 6

kg/4½lb fresh mussels, scrubbed and beards removed
50g/9oz shallots, finely chopped
ʼ00ml/½ pint/1¼ cups white wine
ʼenerous pinch of saffron strands (about 12 strands)
5g/3oz/6 tbsp butter
celery sticks, finely chopped
5ml/1 tsp fennel seeds, crushed
2 large garlic cloves, finely chopped
250ml/8fl oz/1 cup fish or vegetable stock
1 bay leaf
pinch of cayenne pepper
2 large egg yolks
150ml/¼ pint/⅔ cup double cream
juice of ½–1 lemon
30–45ml/2–3 tbsp chopped fresh parsley
salt and ground black pepper

Discard any mussels that do not shut when tapped sharply. ʼlace half the shallots with the wine in a pan and bring to the ʼoil. Add half the mussels and cover, then boil for 1 minute, ʼhaking the pan once. Remove the mussels, discarding any that ʼemain closed. Repeat with the remaining mussels.

ʼ Remove the top half-shell from each mussel. Strain the ʼooking liquid and stir in the saffron, then set aside.

ʼ Melt 50g/2oz/4 tbsp of the butter in a heavy pan. Add the ʼemaining shallots and celery and cook over low heat, stirring ʼccasionally, for 5–6 minutes, until softened. Add the fennel ʼeeds and half of the garlic, then cook for 2–3 minutes.

ʼ Pour in the reserved mussel liquid, bring to the boil, simmer ʼr 5 minutes then add the stock, bay leaf and cayenne. Season ʼo taste, then simmer, uncovered, for 5–10 minutes.

ʼ Beat the egg yolks with the cream, then whisk in a ladleful of ʼhe hot liquid followed by the juice of ½ lemon. Whisk this back ʼnto the sauce. Cook over a very low heat, without allowing it ʼo boil, for 5–10 minutes until thickened. Stir the remaining ʼarlic, butter and parsley into the sauce, add the mussels and ʼnore lemon juice to taste. Reheat for 60 seconds and serve.

Crab Bake

The addition of a splash of dry gin brings an extra dimension to this creamy, cheesy baked crab dish. Serve hot with plain boiled rice or fresh crusty bread.

Serves 2

225g/8oz cooked white crab meat
juice of ½ lemon
15ml/1 tbsp chopped fresh herbs, such as parsley, chives and dill
20ml/4 tsp gin
5ml/1 tsp smooth Dijon mustard
5ml/1 tsp wholegrain Dijon mustard
60ml/4 tbsp grated hard cheese, such as Cheddar
ground black pepper

For the béchamel sauce
1 small onion
3 cloves
½ bay leaf
300ml/½ pint/1¼ cups milk
25g/1oz/2 tbsp butter
25g/1oz/¼ cup plain (all-purpose) flour

1 Make an infusion for the béchamel sauce: stud the onion with the cloves, then put it into a small pan with the milk and bay leaf. Bring to the boil, allow to stand for 15 minutes, and strain.

2 Preheat the oven to 180°C/350°F/Gas 4 and butter two medium gratin dishes. Toss the crab meat in the lemon juice. Divide it between the dishes and add a pinch of herbs to each. Sprinkle each dish with 5ml/1 tsp gin and some pepper.

3 Melt the butter for the sauce in a pan, stir in the flour and cook over low heat for 1–2 minutes. Gradually add the infused milk, stirring constantly to make a smooth sauce. Simmer over low heat for 1–2 minutes.

4 Blend the béchamel sauce with the two mustards and use to cover the crab. Sprinkle the cheese on top, and bake in the oven for 20–25 minutes, or until bubbling. Serve immediately.

Cook's Tip
Fresh crab meat gives the best flavour to this dish, but for a more economical option you could use canned crab, drained.

ʼlouclade Energy 300kcal/1248kJ; Protein 15g; Carbohydrate 7g, of which sugars 4g; Fat 23g, of which saturates 12g; Cholesterol 149mg; Calcium 93mg; Fibre 1g; Sodium 441mg
ʼrab Bake Energy 224kcal/936kJ; Protein 17.4g; Carbohydrate 9.6g, of which sugars 4.5g; Fat 11.9g, of which saturates 7.4g; Cholesterol 73mg; Calcium 282mg; Fibre 0.4g; Sodium 489mg

Chargrilled Chicken

An imaginative marinade can make all the difference to the sometimes bland flavour of chicken. This garlicky marinade, with mustard and chilli, gives tender chicken a real punch. Give the chicken plenty of time to absorb the flavours before cooking.

Serves 6

1½ chickens, total weight about 2.25kg/5lb, jointed, or 12 chicken pieces
2 red or green (bell) peppers, quartered and seeded
5 ripe tomatoes, halved horizontally
salt and ground black pepper
lemon wedges, to serve

For the marinade

90ml/6 tbsp extra virgin olive oil
juice of 1 large lemon
4 garlic cloves, crushed
2 fresh red or green chillies, seeded and chopped
5ml/1 tsp French mustard
5ml/1 tsp dried oregano

1 Beat together the oil, lemon juice, garlic, chilli, mustard, oregano and seasoning in a large bowl.

2 Add the chicken pieces, coating thoroughly in the marinade. Cover with clear film (plastic wrap) and chill for 4–8 hours.

3 Prepare the barbecue or preheat a grill (broiler). When the barbecue or grill is hot, lift the chicken pieces out of the marinade and place them on the grill rack. Add the pepper pieces and the tomatoes to the marinade and set aside for 15 minutes. Grill the chicken pieces for 20–25 minutes.

4 Turn the chicken pieces over and cook for 20–25 minutes more. Meanwhile, thread the peppers on two metal skewers. Add them to the grill rack, with the tomatoes, for the last 10 minutes of cooking. Serve with the lemon wedges.

Cook's Tip

If you are jointing the chicken yourself, divide the legs into two and make slits in the deepest part of the flesh. This will help the marinade to be absorbed.

Chicken Fricassée

Traditionally made with chicken, rabbit or veal, this fricassée dish has a wonderfully rich and flavoursome sauce that is further enhanced with cream and fresh herbs. The meat is seared in fat, then braised in stock until tender.

Serves 4

25g/1oz/2 tbsp butter
30ml/2 tbsp sunflower oil
1.2–1.3kg/2½–3lb chicken, jointed
45ml/3 tbsp plain (all-purpose) flour
250ml/8fl oz/1 cup dry white win
600ml/1 pint/2½ cups boiling chicken stock
1 bouquet garni
5ml/1 tsp lemon juice
225g/8oz/3 cups button (white) mushrooms, stalks trimmed
20 small onions or shallots, peelec
75ml/2½fl oz/⅓ cup double (heavy) cream
45ml/3 tbsp chopped fresh parsle
salt and ground black pepper

1 Preheat the oven to 180°C/350°F/Gas 4. Melt half the butter with the oil in a large frying pan. Add the chicken pieces and cook on high heat, turning occasionally, until lightly browned all over. Using a slotted spoon or tongs, transfer the chicken pieces to a large casserole, leaving the juices behind.

2 Stir the flour into the pan juices, then blend in the wine and stock. Add the bouquet garni and the lemon juice. Bring to the boil, stirring, until the sauce thickens. Season and pour over the chicken. Cover the casserole and cook in the oven for 1 hour.

3 Clean the frying pan, then add the remaining butter and heat gently until melted. Add the mushrooms and onions or shallots and cook for 5 minutes, turning frequently until they are lightly browned. Transfer into the casserole with the chicken.

4 Cook for 1 hour more, until the chicken is cooked and tende Remove the chicken and vegetables to a warm serving dish.

5 Add the cream and 30ml/2 tbsp of the parsley to the sauce and whisk to combine. Check the seasoning and adjust if necessary, then pour the sauce over the chicken and vegetables. Sprinkle the fricassée with the remaining parsley and serve.

Chargrilled Chicken Energy 760kcal/3,156kJ; Protein 61.7g; Carbohydrate 11.1g, of which sugars 10.8g; Fat 52.2g, of which saturates 13.3g; Cholesterol 313mg; Calcium 40mg; Fibre 3.1g; Sodium 235mg
Chicken Fricassé Energy 613kcal/2563kJ; Protein 53.1g; Carbohydrate 36.4g, of which sugars 17.9g; Fat 25g, of which saturates 11.1g; Cholesterol 196mg; Calcium 128mg; Fibre 5.3g; Sodium 396mg

evilled Chicken

highs are an economical ay to buy chicken, and ese spicy skewers are a ry tasty. Serve with a crisp af salad and pitta bread.

erves 4
ml/4 tbsp olive oil
garlic cloves, finely chopped
finely grated rind and juice of 1 lemon
10ml/2 tsp crumbled dried red chillies
8 boneless chicken thighs, skinned and each cut into 3 or 4 pieces
salt and ground black pepper
flat leaf parsley leaves, to garnish
lemon wedges, to serve

In a shallow dish, combine the oil, garlic, lemon rind and juice, ied chillies and seasoning. Add the chicken pieces and turn to oat thoroughly in the marinade. Cover and place in the frigerator for at least 4 hours, or overnight.

When ready to cook, thread the marinated chicken on to ght oiled skewers and cook under a pre-heated grill (broiler) r 6–8 minutes, turning frequently. Garnish with parsley and rve with lemon wedges.

piced Coconut Chicken

ou need to plan ahead in rder to make this luxurious icken curry. Serve with rice Indian breads.

erves 4
6kg/3½lb chicken drumsticks
0ml/2 tbsp sunflower oil
0ml/14fl oz/1⅔ cups coconut milk
-6 large green chillies, halved
ml/3 tbsp coriander (cilantro)
lt and ground black pepper
tural (plain) yogurt, to drizzle

For the marinade
8–12 cardamom pods
15ml/1 tbsp grated fresh root ginger
10ml/2 tsp finely grated garlic
105ml/7 tbsp natural (plain) yogurt
2 frsh green chillies, seeded and chopped
5ml/1 tsp ground cumin
5ml/1 tsp ground coriander
5ml/1 tsp turmeric
finely grated rind and juice of 1 lime

Make the marinade. Crush the cardamom pods, and extract e seeds. Place the seeds in a blender with the ginger, garlic, lf the yogurt, green chillies, cumin, coriander, turmeric and lime nd and juice. Process, season and transfer to a large glass bowl.

Add the chicken to the marinade and toss to coat evenly. over the bowl and marinate in the refrigerator for 6–8 hours, overnight if time permits.

Heat the oil in a large pan over low heat. Remove the chicken om the marinade. Add the chicken to the pan and brown all er, then add the coconut milk, remaining yogurt, the marinade d green chillies and bring to a boil.

Reduce the heat and simmer, uncovered for 30–35 minutes. neck and adjust the seasoning, if needed. Chop the coriander d stir it in, ladle into warmed bowls and serve immediately, izzled with the yogurt if you like.

Baked Mediterranean Chicken

This colourful and versatile chicken dish is a classic dish from the Mediterranean, which can have an infinite number of variations. Cubed ham can replace the bacon, but the fat the latter gives off adds flavour to the dish as well as character.

Serves 4
5ml/1 tsp paprika
4 chicken portions
45ml/3 tbsp olive oil
150g/5oz smoked bacon lardons, or diced pancetta
1 large onion, chopped
2 garlic cloves, finely chopped
1 green (bell) pepper
1 red (bell) pepper
450g/1lb tomatoes or 400g/14oz canned tomatoes
30ml/2 tbsp chopped fresh parsley
salt and ground black pepper
boiled rice, or crusty sourdough bread, to serve

1 Rub paprika and salt into the chicken portions. Heat 30ml/2 tbsp oil in a large frying pan. Put in the chicken portions, skin side down, and fry gently.

2 Heat 15ml/1 tbsp oil in a flameproof casserole and add the bacon or pancetta.

3 When the bacon or pancetta starts to give off fat, add the chopped onion and garlic, frying very gently until soft.

4 Remove and discard the stalks and seeds from the peppers and chop the flesh into bitesize pieces.

5 Spoon off a little fat from the top of the chicken pan, if necessary, then add the peppers, pushing them into the spaces between the chicken portions, and cook gently.

6 When the onions are soft, stir in the tomatoes and season to taste with salt and pepper. Transfer the chicken pieces into the casserole, and stir in the cooked peppers.

7 Cover the casserole tightly and simmer over low heat for 15 minutes. Check the seasoning, stir in the chopped parsley and serve with rice or bread, if you like.

evilled Chicken Energy 320kcal/1339kJ; Protein 42.1g; Carbohydrate 0.3g, of which sugars 0.2g; Fat 16.7g, of which saturates 3.2g; Cholesterol 210mg; Calcium 34mg; Fibre 0.5g; Sodium 183mg
iced Coconut Chicken Energy 706kcal/2935kJ; Protein 48.1g; Carbohydrate 15.8g, of which sugars 15.6g; Fat 50.4g, of which saturates 12.8g; Cholesterol 240mg; Calcium 91mg; Fibre 1.5g; Sodium 305mg
editerranean Chicken Energy 462kcal/1947kJ; Protein 46.9g; Carbohydrate 41.3g, of which sugars 24.5g; Fat 13.4g, of which saturates 4.5g; Cholesterol 118mg; Calcium 156mg; Fibre 9.2g; Sodium 133mg

Chicken Pot-au-feu

This rustic recipe has a lovely white wine and herb-scented sauce. Buying a whole chicken is much more economical than buying it already in portions.

Serves 4

1 chicken, about 2.25kg/5lb
1 parsley sprig
15ml/1 tbsp black peppercorns
1 bay leaf
25g/1oz/2 tbsp butter
15ml/1 tbsp olive oil
300g/11oz shallots, cut in half if large
200ml/7fl oz/scant 1 cup dry white wine
300g/11oz baby carrots
175g/6oz baby leeks, washed and trimmed
800g/1¾lb baby new potatoes
120ml/4fl oz/½ cup double (heavy) cream
salt and ground black pepper
mashed potatoes, to serve

1 Joint the chicken into eight pieces and place the carcass in a large stockpot. Add the parsley sprig, peppercorns, bay leaf and the trimmings from the leeks. Cover with cold water and bring to the boil. Simmer for 45 minutes, then strain.

2 Meanwhile, melt the butter with the olive oil in a frying pan, then add the chicken pieces, season, and brown all over. Lift out the chicken pieces on to a plate and add the shallots to the pan. Cook over low heat for 20 minutes, stirring occasionally, until softened, but not browned.

3 Return the chicken to the pan and add the wine. Scrape up any juices from the bottom of the pan, then add the carrots, leeks and potatoes with enough of the stock to cover. Bring to the boil, cover, and simmer for 20 minutes. Stir in the cream.

4 Serve the chicken immediately on warmed serving plates, with mashed potatoes, if you like.

Cook's Tips

Any left-over stock can be kept in the refrigerator to be used in other recipes, such as soups or stews.

Ethiopian Chicken

This long-simmered Ethiopian stew contains hard-boiled eggs, which soak up the flavour of the aromatic spices. Nourishing and warming, it is perfect for the dark winter months. Serve with boiled rice or flatbreads, and thinly sliced red onion rings.

Serves 4

30ml/2 tbsp vegetable oil
2 large onions, chopped
3 garlic cloves, chopped
2.5cm/1in piece fresh root ginger, peeled and finely chopped
175ml/6fl oz/¾ cup chicken stock
400g/14oz can chopped tomatoes
seeds from 5 cardamom pods
2.5ml/½ tsp ground turmeric
large pinch of ground cinnamon
large pinch of ground cloves
large pinch of grated nutmeg
1.3kg/3lb chicken, cut into 8–12 portions
4 hard-boiled eggs
cayenne pepper or hot paprika, to taste
salt and ground black pepper
roughly chopped fresh coriander (cilantro) and finely sliced onion rings, to garnish
flatbread or rice, to serve

1 Preheat the oven to 180°C/350°F/Gas 4. Heat the oil in a large, heavy pan, add the onions and cook for 10 minutes until softened. Add the garlic and ginger and cook for 1–2 minutes.

2 Add the stock and the chopped tomatoes to the pan. Bring to the boil and cook, stirring frequently, for about 10 minutes, until it has thickened, then season to taste.

3 Transfer the mixture to a ceramic cooking pot and stir in the cardamom seeds, turmeric, cinnamon, cloves and nutmeg.

4 Add the chicken in a single layer, pushing the pieces down into the sauce so they are completely coated. Cover the dish with the lid, place in the oven and cook for 1 hour.

5 Remove the shells from the eggs, and prick with a fork. Add to the sauce and cook for 30–45 minutes more, until the chicken is cooked. Season with cayenne pepper or hot paprika. Garnish with coriander, black pepper and onion rings and serve with warmed flatbreads or rice.

Chicken Pot-au-feu Energy 309kcal/1304kJ; Protein 33.2g; Carbohydrate 30.7g, of which sugars 9.2g; Fat 6.7g, of which saturates 1.7g; Cholesterol 98mg; Calcium 79mg; Fibre 7.7g; Sodium 143mg
Ethiopian Chicken Energy 388kcal/1629kJ; Protein 54.6g; Carbohydrate 13g, of which sugars 9.6g; Fat 13.4g, of which saturates 2.8g; Cholesterol 13mg; Calcium 81mg; Fibre 2.5g; Sodium 311mg

rème Fraîche Chicken

ıicken thighs are better lue for money than breast ets, and it takes only a few oments to remove the skin.

erves 4

ml/1 tbsp sunflower oil
6 boneless chicken thighs, skin removed and cut into 3 or 4 pieces
60ml/4 tbsp crème fraîche
1 small bunch of fresh coriander (cilantro), roughly chopped
salt and ground black pepper

Heat the oil in a large frying pan, add the chicken and cook about 6 minutes. Stir in the crème fraîche and allow it to bble for 1–2 minutes.

Add the coriander to the chicken. Season to taste, and serve th rice, and steamed seasonal green vegetables.

ragrant Chicken Casserole

ıis is an aromatic dish that ll be a treat for all the nses. Serve with rice.

erves 4

ml/5 tbsp extra virgin olive oil
5kg/3½lb chicken, jointed
arge onion, peeled and chopped
250ml/8fl oz/1 cup red wine
30ml/2 tbsp tomato purée (paste)
1 cinnamon stick
3 or 4 whole allspice berries
2 bay leaves
salt and ground black pepper
boiled rice, to serve

Brown the chicken in the oil on all sides. Lift out, set aside and ep warm. Add the chopped onion to the hot oil in the same n and cook until translucent. Return the chicken to the pan.

Pour over the wine and cook for 2–3 minutes, until it has duced. Add the tomato purée with 450ml/¾ pint/2 cups hot ater, the cinnamon, allspice, bay leaves, salt and pepper.

Cover the pan and cook gently for 1 hour or until the chicken tender. Serve with rice.

Chicken Casserole

This is a very simple and economical dish to prepare and cook, and with its strong Mediterranean undertones it is also packed with colour and flavour. It is delicious served with fried potatoes or plain boiled rice.

Serves 4

75ml/5 tbsp extra virgin olive oil
1 chicken, about 1.6kg/3½lb, jointed
3 or 4 shallots, finely chopped
2 carrots, sliced
1 celery stick, roughly chopped
2 garlic cloves, chopped
juice of 1 lemon
300ml/½ pint/1¼ cups hot chicken stock
30ml/2 tbsp chopped fresh flat leaf parsley
12 black or green olives
salt and ground black pepper
fried potatoes, to serve

1 Preheat the oven to 180°C/350°F/Gas 4. Heat the olive oil in a wide flameproof casserole and brown the chicken pieces on both sides. Lift them out and set them aside.

2 Add the shallots, carrots and celery to the oil remaining in the casserole and sauté them for a few minutes.

3 Stir the garlic into the sautéed vegetables. As soon as it becomes aromatic, return the chicken to the pan and pour the lemon juice over the mixture. Let it bubble for a few minutes, scraping up any residue on the bottom, then add the stock and season with salt and pepper.

4 Cover the casserole and bake in the oven for 1 hour, turning the chicken pieces over occasionally as the sauce reduces.

5 Remove the casserole from the oven and stir in the chopped fresh parsley and black or green olives.

6 Re-cover the casserole and return it to the oven for about 30 minutes more. Check that it is cooked by piercing with a sharp knife. The juices should run clear.

7 Serve the chicken immediately, with crispy fried potatoes.

eme Fraîche Chicken Energy 222kcal/927kJ; Protein 26.8g; Carbohydrate 0.7g, of which sugars 0.6g; Fat 12.4g, of which saturates 5.4g; Cholesterol 148mg; Calcium 43mg; Fibre 0.6g; Sodium 120mg
agrant Chicken Energy 767kcal/3,195kJ; Protein 53.3g; Carbohydrate 32.5g, of which sugars 2.9g; Fat 47.7g, of which saturates 11.8g; Cholesterol 264mg; Calcium 51mg; Fibre 2.6g; Sodium 206mg
icken Casserole Energy 726kcal/3,008kJ; Protein 54.9g; Carbohydrate 3.8g, of which sugars 3.5g; Fat 54.5g, of which saturates 13.1g; Cholesterol 289mg; Calcium 55mg; Fibre 1.9g; Sodium 435mg

Curried Chicken and Rice

This one-pot meal is perfect for a relaxed dinner party.

Serves 4

60ml/4 tbsp vegetable oil
1.5kg/3–3½lb chicken thigh fillets, cut into small pieces
4 garlic cloves, finely chopped
5ml/1 tsp garam masala
450g/1lb/2⅔ cups jasmine rice, rinsed and drained
10ml/2 tsp salt
1 litre/1¾ pints/4 cups chicken stock
30ml/2 tbsp fresh coriander (cilantro), to garnish

1 Heat the oil in a casserole. Add the chicken and brown on all sides. Add the garlic and garam masala, stir well to coat the chicken, then stir in the drained rice and the salt.

2 Stir in the stock, then cover and bring to the boil. Reduce the heat to low and simmer for 10 minutes, until the rice is cooked and tender. Lift off the heat, leaving the lid on, and leave to stand for about 10 minutes. Transfer to a platter. Sprinkle with the coriander and serve immediately.

Barbecued Chicken

In this simple recipe, chicken pieces are marinated then cooked on a barbecue.

Serves 4

5 garlic cloves, chopped
30ml/2 tbsp ground cumin
7.5ml/1½ tsp ground cinnamon
5ml/1 tsp paprika
juice of 1 lemon
30ml/2 tbsp olive oil
1.3kg/3lb chicken thighs
salt and ground black pepper
pitta bread and salad, to serve

1 In a bowl, combine the garlic, cumin, cinnamon, paprika, lemon juice, oil, and salt and pepper. Add the chicken and leave to marinate for at least 1 hour.

2 When the barbecue is ready, place the chicken on the grill, and cook, turning every few minutes, until the juices run clear. Serve with warmed pitta bread and salad.

Spicy Chicken Jambalaya

This classic Creole dish is great for a low-cost supper, served with a simple salad.

Serves 6

225g/8oz skinless, boneless chicken thigh portions
175g/6oz piece smoked gammon
30ml/2 tbsp olive oil
1 large onion, peeled and chopped
2 garlic cloves, crushed
2 sticks celery, diced
2.5ml/½ tsp dried thyme
5ml/1 tsp mild chilli powder
2.5ml/½ tsp ground ginger
10ml/2 tsp tomato purée (paste)
2 dashes of Tabasco sauce
750ml/1¼ pints/3 cups boiling chicken stock
300g/11oz/1½ cups easy-cook (converted) rice
115g/4oz chorizo sausage, sliced
30ml/2 tbsp chopped fresh flat leaf parsley, plus extra, to garnish
salt and ground black pepper

1 Preheat the oven to 180°C/350°F/Gas 4. Cut the chicken int 2.5cm/1in cubes and season. Trim any fat off the gammon or bacon, then cut the meat into 1cm/½in cubes.

2 Heat 15ml/1 tbsp of the olive oil in a pan, add the onion anc fry gently for about 5 minutes, until beginning to colour. Stir in the garlic, celery, thyme, chilli powder and ginger and cook for about 1 minute. Transfer the mixture to a large ovenproof dish.

3 Heat the remaining 15ml/1 tbsp olive oil in the pan, add the chicken pieces and fry until lightly browned. Add the chicken tc the ovenproof dish with the gammon or bacon cubes.

4 Add the tomato purée and Tabasco sauce to the stock and. pour into the dish, cover and cook in the oven for 45 minutes.

5 Add the rice to the dish. Cover and cook for 20–30 minutes or until the rice is almost tender and most of the stock has been absorbed. Stir in the chorizo and cook for a further 15 minutes, or until heated through. Stir in the chopped parsley then taste and adjust the seasoning.

6 Remove from the oven and leave to stand for 10 minutes. Fluff with a fork, then serve, garnished with parsley.

Curried Chicken Energy 719kcal/3012kJ; Protein 56.7g; Carbohydrate 90.1g, of which sugars 0.3g; Fat 13.9g, of which saturates 1.9g; Cholesterol 140mg; Calcium 57mg; Fibre 0.6g; Sodium 1107mg
Barbecued Chicken Energy 313kcal/1315kJ; Protein 52.7g; Carbohydrate 0.9g, of which sugars 0g; Fat 11g, of which saturates 2.3g; Cholesterol 219mg; Calcium 20mg; Fibre 0g; Sodium 188mg
Chicken Jambalaya Energy 384kcal/1617kJ; Protein 21.2g; Carbohydrate 48.6g, of which sugars 2.9g; Fat 13g, of which saturates 3.6g; Cholesterol 43mg; Calcium 57mg; Fibre 1.1g; Sodium 630mg

:hicken and Split Pea Koresh

oresh is a hearty Persian sh usually made with lamb, ut here it has been ansformed to a lighter ıicken and vegetable stew.

erves 4

)g/2oz/¼ cup green split peas
5–60ml/3–4 tbsp olive oil
large or 2 small onions, chopped
)0g/1¼lb boneless chicken thighs
nl/1 tsp ground turmeric
2.5ml/ ½ tsp ground cinnamon
1.5ml/¼ tsp grated nutmeg
500ml/17fl oz/2¼ cups chicken stock
2 aubergines (eggplants), diced
8–10 ripe tomatoes, diced
2 garlic cloves, crushed
30ml/2 tbsp dried mint
salt and ground black pepper
fresh mint leaves, to garnish
boiled rice, to serve

Put the split peas in a bowl, pour over cold water to cover, ıen leave to soak for about 4 hours. Drain well.

Heat a little of the oil in a pan, add two-thirds of the onions ıd cook for about 5 minutes. Add the chicken and cook until ɔlden brown on all sides.

Add the soaked split peas to the chicken mixture, then the ırmeric, cinnamon, nutmeg and stock. Cook over medium-low ɛat for about 40 minutes, until the split peas are tender.

Heat the remaining oil in a pan, add the aubergines and maining onions and cook until lightly browned. Add the ɔmatoes, garlic and mint. Season with salt and pepper.

Just before serving, stir the aubergine mixture into the chicken ıd split pea stew. Garnish with fresh mint leaves and serve ith boiled rice.

Variation
To make a traditional lamb koresh, use 675g/1½lb stewing lamb in place of chicken. Add to the onions, pour over water to cover and cook for 1½ hours, then proceed as above.

Chicken Biryani with Saffron Milk

Easy to make and very tasty, this fairly mild curry is bursting with flavours and is ideal for a family supper or relaxed dinner party.

Serves 4

10 whole green cardamom pods
275g/10oz/1½ cups basmati rice, soaked and drained
2.5ml/½ tsp salt
2–3 whole cloves
5cm/2in cinnamon stick
45ml/3 tbsp vegetable oil
3 onions, sliced
4 boneless chicken thighs
5ml/1 tsp ground cumin
5ml/1 tsp ground coriander
1.5ml/¼ tsp ground cloves
2.5ml/½ tsp ground black pepper
1.5ml/¼ tsp hot chilli powder
3 garlic cloves, chopped
5ml/1 tsp fresh ginger, chopped
juice of 1 lemon
4 tomatoes, sliced
30ml/2 tbsp chopped fresh coriander (cilantro)
150ml/¼ pint/⅔ cup natural (plain) yogurt, plus extra to serve
4–5 saffron threads, soaked in 10ml/2 tsp hot milk
150ml/¼ pint/⅔ cup cold water
toasted flaked (sliced) almonds and coriander (cilantro) sprigs, to garnish

1 Preheat the oven to 190°C/375°F/Gas 5. Remove the seeds from half the cardamom pods and grind in a mortar and pestle. Set them aside. Bring a pan of water to the boil and add the rice, salt, whole cardamom pods, cloves and cinnamon stick. Boil for 2 minutes, then drain, leaving the whole spices in the rice.

2 Heat the oil in a frying pan and cook the onions until softened and browned. Add the chicken and the ground spices, including the ground cardamom seeds. Mix well, then add the garlic, ginger and lemon juice. Stir-fry for 5 minutes.

3 Transfer the chicken mixture to a casserole and arrange the tomatoes on top. Sprinkle on the fresh coriander, spoon the yogurt evenly on top and cover with the drained rice. Drizzle the saffron milk over the rice and pour over the water. Cover tightly and bake for 1 hour.

4 Transfer to a warmed serving platter. Garnish with toasted almonds and coriander and serve with extra yogurt.

ıicken Koresh Energy 324kcal/1359kJ; Protein 32.4g; Carbohydrate 20.4g, of which sugars 12.6g; Fat 13.1g, of which saturates 2.5g; Cholesterol 131mg; Calcium 61mg; Fibre 6.2g; Sodium 136mg
ıicken Biryani Energy 536kcal/2243kJ; Protein 31.3g; Carbohydrate 74.2g, of which sugars 14.6g; Fat 13g, of which saturates 2.1g; Cholesterol 105mg; Calcium 163mg; Fibre 3.6g; Sodium 139mg

Creamy Chicken with Dumplings

This lovely dish of poached chicken breast in a creamy sauce, topped with light herb and potato dumplings, makes a hearty and warming meal.

Serves 6

1 onion, chopped
300ml/½ pint/1¼ cups vegetable stock
120ml/4fl oz/½ cup white wine
12 chicken thighs, boned and skinned
300ml/½ pint/1¼ cups double (heavy) cream
15ml/1 tbsp chopped tarragon

For the dumplings

225g/8oz potatoes, boiled and mashed
115g/4oz/1 cup self-raising (self-rising) flour
175g/6oz/1¼ cups suet
30ml/2 tbsp chopped fresh herbs
50ml/2fl oz/¼ cup water
salt and ground black pepper

1 Place the onion, stock and wine in a deep-sided frying pan. Add the chicken and simmer for 20 minutes, covered. Remove the chicken, cut into chunks and reserve the stock.

2 Strain the stock and discard the onion. Reduce the stock by about one-third. Remove from the heat, then stir in the cream and tarragon and reheat gently, stirring, until just thickened. Stir in the chicken and season to taste.

3 Preheat the oven to 190°C/375°F/Gas 5. Spoon the mixture into a 900ml/1½-pint/3¾-cup ovenproof dish.

4 Mix together the potatoes, flour, suet and herbs and stir in the water. Knead to make a soft dough. Divide into six and shape into balls with floured hands. Place on top of the chicken mixture and bake uncovered for 30 minutes, until the dumplings are cooked through and golden on top. Serve immediately.

Cook's Tip
Make sure that you do not reduce the sauce too much before it is cooked in the oven, as the dumplings absorb a lot of the liquid as they cook.

Chicken and Mushroom Bake

A delicious and moist combination of chicken, vegetables and gravy topped with crunchy slices of potato.

Serves 4–6

15ml/1 tbsp olive oil
8 chicken thighs, boned and cut in half
1 leek, finely sliced into rings
50g/2oz/¼ cup butter
25g/1oz/¼ cup plain (all-purpose) flour
475ml/16fl oz/2 cups milk
5ml/1 tsp wholegrain mustard
1 carrot, very finely diced
225g/8oz/3 cups button (white) mushrooms, finely sliced
900g/2lb potatoes, finely sliced
salt and ground black pepper

1 Preheat the oven to 180°C/350°F/Gas 4. Heat the oil in a large pan. Fry the chicken for 5 minutes until browned. Add the leek and fry for a further 5 minutes.

2 Melt half the butter in the pan. Sprinkle the flour over and stir in the milk. Cook over low heat until thickened, then stir in the mustard. Add the carrot, mushrooms and salt and black pepper.

3 Cover the base of a 1.75-litre/3-pint/7½-cup ovenproof dish with potato slices. Spoon one-third of the chicken mixture over. Cover with another layer of potatoes. Repeat layering, finishing with a layer of potatoes. Top with the remaining butter in knobs. Bake for 1½ hours in the oven, covering the dish with foil after 30 minutes. Serve immediately.

Simple Fried Chicken

The quickest and simplest of chicken dishes, this makes the most of the delicate flavour of chicken breasts.

Serves 4

4 skinless chicken breast fillets
seasoned flour, for dusting
75g/3oz/6 tbsp butter

1 Pound the chicken with a rolling pin to flatten, and dredge in the flour. Heat the butter in a large frying pan until foaming, then fry the chicken on both sides until golden. Serve immediately.

Creamy Chicken Energy 552kcal/2299kJ; Protein 28.2g; Carbohydrate 26.5g, of which sugars 2.6g; Fat 37.4g, of which saturates 21g; Cholesterol 121mg; Calcium 83mg; Fibre 1.3g; Sodium 80mg
Chicken Bake Energy 358kcal/1510kJ; Protein 31g; Carbohydrate 33.6g, of which sugars 7.8g; Fat 12.1g, of which saturates 6g; Cholesterol 92mg; Calcium 130mg; Fibre 3.1g; Sodium 192mg
Fried Chicken Energy 311Kcal/1302kj; Fat 17.1g; of which saturates 10.2g; Carbohydrate 3g; Fibre 01g; Sodium 120mg

:hicken and Mushroom Pie

'ersatile and delicous, hicken pie is a classic family ıvourite that will be enjoyed ime after time. It is an ideal vay to use up left-over roast hicken, but if you don't have ny then use chicken wings nd thighs, which have a good avour and are better value han chicken breast portions.

erves 6

0g/2oz/¼ cup butter
50ml/8fl oz/1 cup hot chicken stock
0ml/4 tbsp single (light) cream
onion, coarsely chopped
2 carrots, sliced
2 celery sticks, coarsely chopped
50g/2oz fresh (preferably wild) mushrooms, quartered
450g/1lb cooked chicken, cubed
50g/2oz/½ cup frozen peas
beaten egg or milk, to glaze
salt and ground black pepper

For the pastry
250g/9oz/2¼ cups plain (all-purpose) flour
1.5ml/¼ tsp salt
115g/4oz/½ cup cold butter, diced
65g/2½oz/⅓ cup white vegetable fat (shortening), diced
90–120ml/6–8 tbsp chilled water

To make the pastry, sift 225g/8oz/2 cups of the flour and the ılt into a bowl. Rub in the butter and white vegetable fat until ıe mixture resembles breadcrumbs. Sprinkle with about 90ml/ tbsp chilled water and mix until the dough holds together.

Gather the dough into a ball and flatten it into a round. Wrap ı clear film (plastic wrap) so that it is airtight and chill in the efrigerator for at least 30 minutes.

Preheat the oven to 190°C/375°F/Gas 5. To make the filling, ıelt half the butter in a heavy pan over low heat. Add in the emaining flour and cook until bubbling, stirring constantly. Add ıe stock and whisk over medium heat until the mixture boils. :ook for 2–3 minutes, then whisk in the cream. Season to taste ith salt and ground black pepper, and set aside.

Heat the remaining butter in a frying pan, add the onion and arrots and cook over low heat for about 5 minutes. Add the elery and mushrooms and cook for a further 5 minutes, until ıey have softened. Add the cooked chicken and peas and stir.

Add the chicken mixture to the hot cream sauce and stir to ıix. Taste and adjust the seasoning if necessary. Spoon the ıixture into a 2.5-litre/4-pint/10-cup oval baking dish.

Roll out the pastry on a floured surface to a thickness of bout 3mm/⅛in. Cut out an oval 2.5cm/1in larger all around ıan the dish. Lay the pastry over the filling. Seal, then trim off ıe excess pastry. Crimp the edge of the pastry with your ngers to seal all round the pastry edge.

Press together the pastry trimmings and roll out again. Cut ut mushroom shapes with a sharp knife and stick them on to ıe pastry lid with a little of the beaten egg. Glaze the lid with eaten egg or milk, then cut several slits in the pastry to allow ıe steam to escape.

Bake the pie in the preheated oven for about 30 minutes, ntil the pastry has browned. Serve hot.

Chicken and Leek Pie

This recipe will make one large pie, or you can make smaller versions to create four individual pies.

Serves 4

15g/½oz/1 tbsp butter
1 leek, thinly sliced
2 eggs
225g/8oz skinless chicken breast fillets, finely chopped
small handful of fresh parsley or mint, finely chopped
beaten egg or full-fat (whole) milk, to glaze
salt and ground black pepper

For the pastry
225g/8oz/2 cups plain (all-purpose) flour
1.5ml/¼ tsp salt
115g/4oz/½ cup cold butter, diced
65g/2½oz/1/3 cup white vegetable fat (shortening), diced
90–120ml/6–8 tbsp chilled water

1 To make the pastry, sift the flour and the salt into a bowl. Rub in the butter and fat until the mixture resembles breadcrumbs. Sprinkle with 90ml/6 tbsp chilled water and mix until the dough holds together. If it is too crumbly, add a little more water.

2 Gather the dough into a ball and flatten it into a round. Wrap in clear film (plastic wrap) and chill for 30 minutes.

3 Preheat the oven to 200°C/400°F/Gas 6. Roll out the pastry on a lightly floured surface to a thickness of about 3mm/⅛in. Cut out a circle large enough to line the pie dish, or tartlet tins (muffin pans). Cut out the remaining pastry into a lid or lids.

4 To make the filling, melt the butter in a small pan, add the leek and cook gently for about 5 minutes, stirring, until soft.

5 Beat the eggs in a bowl and stir in the chicken, herbs and seasoning. Add the leek and its juices, mix and spoon into the pastry case. Brush the edges of the pastry with egg and place the lid on top, pressing the edges together to seal them. Brush the top with egg or milk and make a two slits in the centre.

6 Put into the hot oven and cook for about 30 minutes, until golden brown and cooked through.

hicken Pie Energy 600kcal/2501kJ; Protein 23.7g; Carbohydrate 38.8g, of which sugars 3.7g; Fat 40g, of which saturates 21.8g; Cholesterol 132mg; Calcium 92mg; Fibre 2.7g; Sodium 226mg
hicken and Leek Energy 588kcal/2459kJ; Protein 23.4g; Carbohydrate 48.4g, of which sugars 2.1g; Fat 34.9g, of which saturates 11.7g; Cholesterol 157mg; Calcium 133mg; Fibre 3.4g; Sodium 496mg

Bacon, Chicken and Leek Pudding

Old-fashioned suet puddings are a wonderful way to make a small amount of meat go much further, and this one is bursting with flavour. Serve with seasonal vegetables.

Serves 4

200g/7oz unsmoked rindless bacon
400g/14oz skinless boneless chicken, preferably thigh meat
2 medium leeks, finely chopped
30ml/2 tbsp finely chopped fresh parsley
120ml/4fl oz/1½ cups chicken or vegetable stock
butter for greasing
ground black pepper

For the pastry

175g/6oz/1½ cups self-raising (self-rising) flour
75g/3oz/½ cup shredded suet (US chilled, grated shortening)

1 Cut the bacon and chicken into bitesize pieces. Mix in a bowl with the leeks and half the parsley. Season with black pepper.

2 Sift the flour into another large bowl and stir in the suet and the remaining parsley. Stir in sufficient cold water to make a soft dough. On a lightly floured surface, roll out the dough to a circle measuring about 33cm/13in across. Cut out one quarter of the circle (starting from the centre), roll up and reserve.

3 Butter a 1.2-litre/2-pint/5-cup heatproof bowl. Use the dough to line the bowl, pressing the cut edges together to seal them and allowing the pastry to overlap the top of the bowl slightly.

4 Spoon the bacon and chicken mixture into the lined bowl. Pour the chicken or vegetable stock over the bacon mixture making sure it does not overfill the bowl.

5 Roll out the reserved pastry into a circle and lay it over the filling, pinching to seal them well. Cover with baking parchment (pleated in the centre to allow the pudding to rise) and then a large sheet of pleated foil, tucking the edges under to seal.

6 Steam over boiling water for 3½ hours. Uncover the pudding, slide a knife around the sides and turn out on to a warmed plate. Serve piping hot with seasonal vegetables.

Roast Chicken with Herb Stuffing

Nothing beats a tender roast chicken for Sunday lunch. Traditional accompaniments include roast potatoes, bread sauce and vegetables.

Serves 6

1 large chicken, about 1.8kg/4lb
15g/½oz/1 tbsp butter
30ml/2 tbsp vegetable oil
6 rashers (strips) of streaky (fatty) bacon
1 small onion, sliced
1 small carrot, sliced
bunch of parsley and thyme
half a glass of white wine
salt and ground black pepper

For the stuffing

1 onion, finely chopped
50g/2oz/¼ cup butter
150g/5oz/2½ cups fresh white breadcrumbs
15ml/1 tbsp fresh chopped parsle
15ml/1 tbsp fresh chopped mixed herbs, such as thyme, marjoram and chives
finely grated rind and juice of ½ lemon
1 small egg, lightly beaten

1 Make the stuffing: fry the onion in the butter over low heat for a few minutes. Remove from the heat, and mix in the breadcrumbs, herbs and lemon rind. Add the lemon juice, beaten egg and a generous amount of salt and pepper.

2 Spoon the stuffing into the neck cavity of the chicken, without packing it in too tightly,. Weigh the stuffed chicken and work out the cooking time, allowing 20 minutes per 450g/1lb plus 20 minutes. Spread the breast with the butter, then put the oil into a roasting pan and lay the bird in it. Season and lay the bacon rashers over the top of the bird. Scatter the onion slices and carrot in the bottom of the pan, with the bunch of herbs.

3 Place in the oven. After 20 minutes, baste the chicken, add the white wine, and cover with foil, reduce the oven to 180°C/350°F/Gas 4 and return to the oven until cooked. Test by inserting a knife into the thigh: if the juices run clear, it is cookec Transfer to a serving dish and allow it to rest for 15 minutes.

4 Carve the chicken. Serve on heated plates with the herb stuffing, the warmed up juices from the pan, and any other accompaniments you like.

Bacon Pudding Energy 535kcal/2236kJ; Protein 28.2g; Carbohydrate 39.4g, of which sugars 2.9g; Fat 31.3g, of which saturates 14.8g; Cholesterol 86mg; Calcium 111mg; Fibre 4g; Sodium 999mg
Roast Chicken Energy 562kcal/2342kJ; Protein 40.9g; Carbohydrate 23.2g, of which sugars 2.7g; Fat 34.5g, of which saturates 11.9g; Cholesterol 216mg; Calcium 72mg; Fibre 1.5g; Sodium 381m

3aked Chicken with Fennel

'his simple dish is perfect as make-ahead meal. It ombines succulent chicken ieces with garlic, shallots nd the aniseed flavour of ennel, and is served in a elicious creamy herb sauce.

erves 4

.6–1.8kg/3½–4lb chicken, cut into 8 pieces or 8 chicken thighs or 4 chicken legs
50g/9oz shallots, peeled
garlic bulb, separated into cloves and peeled
60ml/4 tbsp olive oil
45ml/3 tbsp tarragon vinegar
45ml/3 tbsp white wine or vermouth (optional)
5ml/1 tsp fennel seeds, crushed
2 bulbs fennel, cut into wedges, feathery tops reserved
150ml/¼ pint/⅔ cup double (heavy) cream
5ml/1 tsp redcurrant jelly
15ml/1 tbsp tarragon mustard
30ml/2 tbsp chopped fresh parsley
salt and ground black pepper, to taste

Place the chicken pieces, shallots and all but one of the garlic oves in a flameproof dish or roasting pan. Add the oil, vinegar nd wine or vermouth, if using, and fennel seeds. Season with epper, then marinate for at least 2–3 hours.

Preheat the oven to 190°C/375°F/Gas 5. Add the fennel to ne chicken, season with salt and stir to mix.

Cook the chicken in the oven for 50–60 minutes, stirring once r twice. The chicken juices should run clear, not pink, when the nick thigh meat is pierced with a skewer.

Transfer the chicken and vegetables to a serving dish and over to keep them warm. Skim off some of the fat from the asting pan and bring the cooking juices to the boil, then pour the cream. Stir, then whisk in the redcurrant jelly followed by ne mustard. Check the seasoning.

Chop the remaining garlic clove with the feathery fennel tops nd mix with the chopped parsley. Pour the sauce over the nicken and sprinkle the chopped garlic and herb mixture over ne top. Serve immediately.

Chicken Thighs with Cabbage

This meal is cooked in one pot and is particularly associated with central and northern Portugal. Its cooking method makes it ideal for serving to large numbers of people. The combination of meat with chickpeas and cabbage provides a nourishing dish.

Serves 4

105ml/7 tbsp olive oil
1 onion, chopped
100g/3¾oz/generous ½ cup diced bacon
1 sausage, diced
3 carrots, diced
2 garlic cloves, chopped
2 bay leaves
2 thyme sprigs
8 black peppercorns
8 chicken thighs or 4 chicken legs
1 cabbage
250g/9oz/1½ cups cooked chickpeas
sea salt

1 Heat the olive oil in a large pan. Add the chopped onion and cook over low heat, stirring occasionally, for 5 minutes, until softened and translucent.

2 Increase the heat to medium, add the bacon, sausage, carrots, garlic, bay leaves, thyme sprigs and peppercorns and cook, stirring constantly, for a few minutes more.

3 Add the chicken to the pan, pour in enough water just to cover and season with salt. Bring just to the boil, then lower the heat, cover and simmer gently for 40 minutes.

4 Remove the chicken and keep warm. Reserve the cooking liquid but remove and discard the bay leaves and thyme sprigs.

5 Meanwhile, prepare the cabbage. Cut in half and cut out the central hard part, then separate the leaves and cut into large slices. Steam in lightly salted boiling water for about 10 minutes until tender. Drain well.

6 Mix the cabbage with the chickpeas, then add the reserved cooking liquid. Heat through and blend well, then serve the chicken with the vegetables.

ıked Chicken Energy 568kcal/2349kJ; Protein 24.3g; Carbohydrate 6.5g, of which sugars 5.3g; Fat 49.6g, of which saturates 19.4g; Cholesterol 163mg; Calcium 76mg; Fibre 2.9g; Sodium 112mg
ıicken Thighs Energy 456kcal/1894kJ; Protein 19.6g; Carbohydrate 23.6g, of which sugars 10.5g; Fat 32g, of which saturates 7g; Cholesterol 55mg; Calcium 126mg; Fibre 6.4g; Sodium 643mg.

Seville Chicken

Oranges and almonds are favourite ingredients in southern Spain, especially around Seville, where the orange and almond trees are a familiar sight. This is a great weekend supper treat.

Serves 4

1 orange
8 chicken thighs
plain (all-purpose) flour, seasoned with salt and pepper
45ml/3 tbsp olive oil
1 large Spanish (Bermuda) onion, roughly chopped
2 garlic cloves, crushed
1 red (bell) pepper, sliced
1 yellow (bell) pepper, sliced
115g/4oz chorizo, sliced
50g/2oz/½ cup flaked (sliced) almonds
225g/8oz/generous 1 cup brown basmati rice
about 600ml/1 pint/2½ cups chicken stock
400g/14oz can chopped tomatoes
175ml/6fl oz/¾ cup white wine
generous pinch of dried thyme
salt and ground black pepper
fresh thyme sprigs, to garnish

1 Pare a thin strip of peel from the orange and set it aside. Peel the orange, then cut it into segments, working over a bowl to catch the juice. Dust the chicken thighs with seasoned flour.

2 Heat the oil in a large frying pan and fry the chicken pieces on both sides until nicely brown. Transfer to a plate. Add the onion and garlic to the pan and fry for 4–5 minutes until the onion begins to brown. Add the red and yellow peppers and fry, stirring occasionally, until slightly softened.

3 Add the chorizo, stir-fry for a few minutes, then sprinkle over the almonds and rice. Cook, stirring, for 1–2 minutes.

4 Pour in the chicken stock, tomatoes and wine and add the orange strip and thyme. Season well. Bring to simmering point, stirring, then return the chicken pieces to the pan.

5 Cover tightly and cook over very low heat for 1–1¼ hours until the rice and chicken are tender. Just before serving, add the orange segments and allow to cook briefly to heat through. Garnish with fresh thyme and serve.

Malaysian Fried Chicken with Turmeric and Lemon Grass

In this famous fried chicken dish, which is eaten everywhere in Malaysia and Singapore, the chicken is first cooked with spices and other flavourings to ensure that the flavours thoroughly penetrate the meat, then simply deep-fried to give the pieces an irresistibly crisp, golden skin. If you can't find kecap manis, use the same quantity of dark soy sauce mixed with 15ml/1 tbsp soft brown or muscovado sugar.

Serves 4

2 shallots, chopped
4 garlic cloves, chopped
50g/2oz fresh root ginger or galangal, peeled and chopped
25g/1oz fresh turmeric, chopped
2 lemon grass stalks, chopped
12 chicken thighs or drumsticks or 6 whole chicken legs, separated into drumsticks and thighs
30ml/2 tbsp kecap manis
salt and ground black pepper
vegetable oil, for deep-frying
fragrant rice and a green salad, to serve

1 Using a mortar and pestle or food processor, grind the shallots, garlic, ginger or galangal, turmeric and lemon grass to a paste. Place the chicken pieces in a heavy pan or earthenware pot and smear with the spice paste. Add the kecap manis and 150ml/¼ pint/⅔ cup water.

2 Bring to the boil, reduce the heat and cook the chicken for about 25 minutes, turning it from time to time, until the liquid has evaporated. The chicken should be dry, with the spices sticking to it. Season with salt and pepper.

3 Heat enough oil for deep-frying in a wok. Fry the chicken pieces in batches until golden brown and crisp. Drain them on kitchen paper and serve hot with rice and a green salad.

Cook's Tip
Watch the chicken carefully towards the end of cooking to make sure the spicy coating does not burn.

Seville Chicken Energy 861kcal/3598kJ; Protein 65.3g; Carbohydrate 67.1g, of which sugars 17.1g; Fat 34g, of which saturates 5.6g; Cholesterol 155mg; Calcium 172mg; Fibre 6.3g; Sodium 453mg
Malaysian Chicken Energy 396Kcal/1639kJ; Protein 27g; Carbohydrate 1.5g, of which sugars 1.1g; Fat 31.3g, of which saturates 6.8g; Cholesterol 150mg; Calcium 38mg; Fibre 0.2g; Sodium 358mg

ʀoasted Duck with Potatoes

ɴow that duck is a more ommonly farmed bird, it is ɔften as easy to find one that ꞩ reasonably priced, and as he meat is so flavoursome nd rich, a little can go a long vay. The rich flavour of duck ombined with these weetened potatoes makes n excellent treat for a inner party or special ɔccasion. Serve with steamed reen vegetables.

Serves 4

1 duck, giblets removed
60ml/4 tbsp light soy sauce
150ml/¼ pint/⅔ cup fresh orange juice
3 large floury potatoes, cut into chunks
30ml/2 tbsp clear honey
15ml/1 tbsp sesame seeds
salt and ground black pepper
steamed pak choi, or other leafy green vegetable, to serve

Preheat the oven to 200°C/400°F/Gas 6. Place the duck in a oasting pan. Prick the skin well.

2 Combine the soy sauce and orange juice and pour over the uck. Cook in the oven for 20 minutes.

3 Place the potato chunks in a bowl, stir in the honey and toss o mix well. Remove the duck from the oven and spoon the otatoes all around and under the bird.

4 Roast for 35 minutes, then remove from the oven. Toss the otatoes in the juices and turn the duck over. Put the pan back n the oven and cook for a further 30 minutes.

. Remove the duck from the oven and carefully scoop off the xcess fat, leaving the juices behind.

6 Sprinkle the sesame seeds over the potatoes, season and turn he duck back over, breast side up, and cook for a further 0 minutes. Remove from the oven and keep warm.

7 Pour the excess fat from the roasting pan and simmer the uices on the stove to reduce. Slice the duck and serve with the otatoes and juices, with steamed pak choi.

Duck Legs with Red Cabbage

This Christmas dish from Germany is often served with potato dumplings (page 146) or mashed potato.

Serves 4

8 duck legs
15ml/1 tbsp oil
10ml/2 tsp tomato purée (paste)
200l/7fl oz/scant 1 cup red wine
salt and ground white pepper
chopped fresh parsley, to garnish
potato dumplings, to serve (recipe page 146) or mashed potato

For the red cabbage

3 onions
60g/2½oz lard
1 red cabbage, finely sliced
100ml/3½fl oz/scant ½ cup red wine vinegar
15ml/1 tbsp sugar
2 bay leaves
3 pieces star anise
1 cinnamon stick
200ml/7fl oz/1 cup apple juice
2 apples, chopped
30ml/2 tbsp redcurrant jelly
5ml/1 tsp cornflour (cornstarch)

1 To make the cabbage, chop two of the onions, melt the lard in a large pan and fry the onion for 2 minutes. Add the cabbage, vinegar, sugar, bay leaves, spices and apple juice, bring to the boil, cover and simmer for 30 minutes.

2 Stir in the apples and redcurrant jelly and cook for a further 45 minutes, adding more apple juice if necessary. Towards the end of the cooking time, blend the cornflour with water and stir into the cabbage. Preheat the oven to 200°C/400°F/Gas 6.

3 While the cabbage is cooking, place the duck legs in a roasting pan, season, add a cup of water and roast in the oven for 20 minutes. Reduce the temperature to 160°C/325°F/Gas 3 and cook for a further 40 minutes, basting from time to time.

4 When the legs are cooked, lift them out and keep them warm. Add the remaining onion, chopped, and the tomato purée to the pan and fry over high heat for 3–4 minutes. Deglaze the pan with the wine and cook for another 2 minutes.

5 Serve the duck legs with the sauce poured over, garnished with parsley and accompanied by the red cabbage. Serve with potato dumplings or mashed potato.

oasted Duck Energy 806kcal/3341kJ; Protein 20.8g; Carbohydrate 32.3g, of which sugars 6.4g; Fat 66.8g, of which saturates 17.9g; Cholesterol 0mg; Calcium 53mg; Fibre 2.1g; Sodium 403mg
uck Legs Energy 958kcal/3961kJ; Protein 20.7g; Carbohydrate 32.7g, of which sugars 28.5g; Fat 79.8g, of which saturates 22.8g; Cholesterol 12mg; Calcium 122mg; Fibre 5.1g; Sodium 146mg

Duck with Rice

This classic duck and rice recipe comes from the north coast of Peru, where the best accompaniment is said to be a very cold beer.

Serves 4

1kg/2¼lb duck leg joints
bunch fresh coriander (cilantro)
vegetable oil, for frying
1 medium onion, finely chopped
2 garlic cloves, crushed or sliced
2 medium red (bell) peppers, sliced
5ml/1 tsp ground cumin
1 whole fresh red chilli
250g/9oz/2 cups frozen peas
500g/1¼lb long grain rice
salt

1 Pierce the skin of the duck joints all over with a fork, wash and dry with kitchen paper.

2 Put the coriander leaves in a blender or food processor with 500ml/17fl oz/generous 2 cups water and blend to a purée.

3 Heat a little oil in a large pan and, when very hot, fry the duck pieces, moving them around until browned on all sides. Remove from the pan and set aside on a plate.

4 Reduce the heat to medium, add the onion and garlic to the pan and fry until softened and golden brown.

5 Return the duck to the pan with the coriander purée and sliced peppers. Season with salt and cumin and pour in 500ml/17fl oz/generous 2 cups water.

6 Increase the heat and bring to the boil, place the whole red chilli on top, reduce the heat and simmer, covered, for about 20 minutes. Keeping the chilli whole means you gain all the flavour without the fierce heat.

7 When the duck is cooked, add the peas and rice. Keep the heat at medium-high for 15 minutes, until the rice is partially cooked, then remove and reserve the whole chilli. Reduce the heat, stir the rice gently and simmer on low heat, covered, for a further 10 minutes until the liquid is absorbed. Serve the rice, with the reserved chilli for anyone who wants it.

Slow-cooked Duck Legs

This unusual dish combines the traditional partnership of duck and orange with exotic spices, fragrant lemongrass, fiery chilli and chunks of sweet, juicy pineapple to create a taste sensation. Serve simply with steamed rice and wedges of lime for squeezing over.

Serves 4

4 duck legs
4 garlic cloves, crushed
50g/2oz fresh root ginger, peeled and finely sliced
2 lemon grass stalks, trimmed, cut into 3 pieces and crushed
2 dried whole red Thai chillies
15ml/1 tbsp palm sugar (jaggery)
5ml/1 tsp five-spice powder
30ml/2 tbsp nuoc cham or tuk trey (see Cook's Tip)
900ml/1½ pints/3¾ cups fresh orange juice
salt and ground black pepper
1 lime, cut into quarters, to serve

1 Place the duck legs, skin side down, in a large heavy pan or flameproof clay pot. Cook them on both sides over medium heat for about 10 minutes, until browned and crispy. Transfer them to a plate and set aside.

2 Stir the garlic, ginger, lemon grass and chillies into the fat left in the pan, and cook until golden. Add the sugar, five-spice powder and nuoc cham or tuk trey.

3 Stir in the orange juice and place the duck legs back in the pan. Cover the pan and gently cook the duck for 1–2 hours, until the meat is tender and the sauce has reduced.

4 Season to taste and serve immediately, accompanied by lime wedges to squeeze over it.

Cook's Tips

- *Nuoc cham is a Vietnamese chilli dipping sauce. It can be bought in Asian stores and larger supermarkets.*
- *Tuk trey is a Cambodian marinade made from fish sauce, vinegar, lime juice, sugar and garlic, sold in Asian stores.*

Duck with Rice Energy 981kcal/4083kJ; Protein 33.2g; Carbohydrate 116.9g, of which sugars 10.5g; Fat 39.1g, of which saturates 7.9g; Cholesterol 75mg; Calcium 72mg; Fibre 4.6g; Sodium 122mg
Duck Legs Energy 280kcal/1181kJ; Protein 31g; Carbohydrate 23.8g, of which sugars 23.8g; Fat 10g, of which saturates 2g; Cholesterol 165mg; Calcium 48mg; Fibre 0.4g; Sodium 250mg

Stir-fried Duck with Noodles

he rich flavour and tender exture of duck makes it deal for quick cooking, but ou need to remove the fatty kin, as there is not time for t to render down and crisp n this recipe.

Serves 4
50g/9oz fresh sesame noodles
skinless duck breast fillets, sliced
3 spring onions (scallions), cut into strips
2 celery sticks, cut into matchstick strips
1 fresh pineapple, peeled, cored and cut into strips
300g/11oz mixed vegetables, such as carrots, (bell) peppers, beansprouts and green cabbage, shredded or cut into strips
90ml/6 tbsp plum sauce

1 Cook the noodles in a pan of boiling water for 3 minutes, or ccording to the instructions on the packet. When the noodles re tender, drain in a colander.

2 Meanwhile, heat a wok. Add the duck to the hot wok and tir-fry for about 2 minutes, until crisp. If the duck yields a lot of at, drain off all but 30ml/2 tbsp.

3 Add the spring onions and celery to the wok and stir-fry for minutes more. Use a draining spoon to remove them from he wok and set aside. Add the pineapple strips and mixed egetables, and stir-fry for 2 minutes.

4 Add the cooked noodles and plum sauce to the wok, then eplace the duck, spring onion and celery mixture.

5 Stir-fry the duck mixture for about 2 minutes more, or until he noodles and vegetables are hot and the duck is cooked hrough. Serve immediately.

Cook's Tips
Fresh sesame noodles can be bought from supermarkets or Asian stores. If they aren't available, use dried. Cook according to the instructions, and add a little sesame oil to the water.

Turkey Fajitas

Turkey is an economical substitute for chicken in these traditional Mexican fajitas.

Serves 4
15ml/1 tbsp olive oil
15ml/1 tbsp sunflower oil
1 onion, cut into thin wedges
4 turkey breast fillets, cut into strips
1 red (bell) pepper, sliced
5ml/1 tsp ground cumin
generous pinch of cayenne pepper
2.5ml/½ tsp ground turmeric
175ml/6fl oz/¾ cup passata (bottled strained tomatoes)
120–175ml/4–6fl oz/½–¾ cup chicken stock
115g/4oz/½ cup rice, cooked
8 large tortillas, warmed
sour cream, to serve

For the salsa
1 shallot, roughly chopped
1 small garlic clove
½ green chilli, seeded and sliced
small bunch of fresh parsley
5 tomatoes, peeled and chopped
10ml/2 tsp olive oil
15ml/1 tbsp lemon juice
30ml/2 tbsp tomato juice
salt and ground black pepper

For the guacamole
1 large ripe avocado
2 spring onions (scallions), finely chopped
15–30ml/1–2 tbsp fresh lime or lemon juice
generous pinch of cayenne pepper
15ml/1 tbsp chopped fresh coriander (cilantro)

1 Make the salsa. Chop the shallot, garlic, chilli and parsley in a blender or food processor. Spoon into a bowl. Stir in the chopped tomatoes, olive oil, lemon juice and tomato juice. Season and cover with clear film (plastic wrap) and chill.

2 Make the guacamole. Scoop the avocado flesh into a bowl. Mash with the other ingredients, cover and chill.

3 Heat the oils in a frying pan and fry the onion until soft. Add the turkey and pepper and fry until browned. Stir in the cumin, cayenne and turmeric, then add the passata and stock. Bring to the boil, then simmer for 5–6 minutes until the turkey is cooked.

4 Stir the rice into the turkey and cook for 1–2 minutes and season to taste. Spoon a little of the turkey and rice mixture on to each warmed tortilla. Top with salsa, guacamole and sour cream and roll up. Or let everyone assemble their own.

Stir-fried Duck Energy 455Kcal/1927kJ; Protein 28.3g; Carbohydrate 69g, of which sugars 22.6g; Fat 11g, of which saturates 1.4g; Cholesterol 110mg; Calcium 81mg; Fibre 5.7g; Sodium 143mg
Turkey Fajitas Energy 485kcal/2044kJ; Protein 26g; Carbohydrate 67.4g, of which sugars 15.3g; Fat 14.2g, of which saturates 3.8g; Cholesterol 60mg; Calcium 118mg; Fibre 4g; Sodium 53mg

Turkey Meatballs

Turkey is a great economical food, and in this dish, minced turkey is shaped into small balls and simmered with rice in a richly flavoured tomato sauce, creating a one-pot meal in itself.

Serves 4

white bread loaf, unsliced
30ml/2 tbsp milk
1 garlic clove, crushed
2.5ml/½ tsp caraway seeds
225g/8oz minced (ground) turkey
1 egg white
350ml/12fl oz/1½ cups near-boiling chicken stock
400g/14oz can chopped tomatoes
15ml/1 tbsp tomato purée (paste)
90g/3½oz/½ cup easy-cook (converted) rice
salt and ground black pepper
15ml/1 tbsp chopped fresh basil, to garnish (optional)

1 Using a serrated knife, remove the crusts from the bread and cut into cubes. Place the bread in a mixing bowl and sprinkle with the milk, then leave to soak for about 5 minutes.

2 Add the garlic clove, caraway seeds, turkey, and salt and pepper to the bread and mix together well.

3 Whisk the egg white until stiff, then fold, half at a time, into the turkey mixture. Chill in the refrigerator for 30 minutes.

4 Preheat the oven to 190°C/375°F/Gas 5. Pour the stock into a large ovenproof dish. Add the tomatoes and tomato purée, cover with a lid and cook for 30 minutes.

5 Meanwhile, shape the turkey mixture into 16 small balls. Stir the rice into the tomato mixture, then add the turkey balls.

6 Cook for a further 30 minutes, or until the turkey balls and rice are cooked. Serve immediately.

Variations
You could make these meatballs using any type of minced (ground) meat, including chicken, pork, beef and lamb.

Stuffed Pancakes with Turkey

This festive dish is a wonderful way of using left-over roast turkey.

Makes 6–8

15g/½oz/1 tbsp butter
2.5ml/½ tsp sunflower oil
1 small onion, finely chopped
50g/2oz/½ cup small chestnut mushrooms, quartered
50g/2oz/¼ cup wild rice, cooked
75g/3oz/¾ cup cranberries
25ml/1½ tbsp sugar
60–75ml/4–5 tbsp water
275g/10oz cooked turkey, cubed
150ml/¼ pint/⅔ cup sour cream
30ml/2 tbsp freshly grated grano padano cheese
salt and ground black pepper

For the pancakes
175g/6oz/1½ cups plain (all-purpose) flour
1 egg
350ml/12fl oz/1½ cups milk
oil, for frying

1 Preheat the oven to 190°C/375°F/Gas 5. Make the pancakes. Sift the flour and a pinch of salt into a bowl. Beat in the egg and milk to make a smooth batter.

2 Heat a little oil in a frying pan, pour in about 30ml/2 tbsp of the batter and tilt to cover the bottom of the pan. Cook until the underside is a pale brown colour, then flip the pancake over and cook the other side briefly. Slide it out of the pan and cook five to seven more pancakes in the same way.

3 Heat the butter and sunflower oil in a separate frying pan and fry the onion for 3–4 minutes, until soft. Add the mushrooms and fry for 2–3 minutes, until they are a pale golden colour. Put the cooked rice in a bowl and add the onions and mushrooms.

4 Put the cranberries in a pan and add the sugar and water. Cover and simmer for 10 minutes. Transfer to a bowl with 45ml/3 tbsp of the cooking liquid. Add the rice mixture and 60ml/4 tbsp of the sour cream. Season to taste.

5 Fold the pancakes in four and spoon the stuffing into one of the pockets. Arrange in a lightly greased baking dish. Mix the remaining sour cream with the grano padano and spoon over the top. Bake for 10 minutes to heat through, then serve.

Turkey Meatballs Energy 187kcal/797kJ; Protein 18.2g; Carbohydrate 26.6g, of which sugars 3.9g; Fat 1.7g, of which saturates 0.5g; Cholesterol 32mg; Calcium 44mg; Fibre 1g; Sodium 212mg
Stuffed Pancakes Energy 305kcal/1279kJ; Protein 19.1g; Carbohydrate 29.4g, of which sugars 7.6g; Fat 13g, of which saturates 5.5g; Cholesterol 71mg; Calcium 157mg; Fibre 1g; Sodium 120mg

Turkey and Corn Stew

Turkey is a very popular meat in South America, especially in the north of Peru, where this recipe comes from. Normally a dish like this, which quickly fries the meat, would be prepared with the tender breast meat. Turkey is an economical meat in many other parts of the world too, and is also a low-cost substitute for chicken. It also has a low fat content.

Serves 4

6 corn cobs
90ml/6 tbsp vegetable oil
500g/1 ¼lb skinless turkey breast fillet, cut into 2cm/¾in cubes
1 medium onion, finely chopped
2 garlic cloves, sliced or crushed
2 red chillies, seeded, blended to a purée in 60ml/4 tbsp water
500ml/17fl oz/generous 2 cups chicken stock
salt
chopped fresh parsley, to garnish
white rice, to serve

1 First, strip the kernels from the corn on the cob; hold each cob at one end and use a sharp knife to cut downwards to the other end, releasing the kernels as you cut. Put the kernels in batches in a blender or food processor and blend to a paste.

2 Heat the oil in a large pan and fry the turkey over high heat for 8–10 minutes, until golden on all sides. Stir in the onion and garlic, reduce the heat slightly and cook until the onion is golden and starting to caramelize.

3 Add the chilli purée and cook for 3 minutes, then pour in the chicken stock. Bring to the boil and simmer for 20 minutes. Season to taste with salt.

4 Add the puréed corn to the turkey and simmer for a further 15 minutes, until the sauce has thickened. Garnish with parsley and serve the turkey stew with white rice.

Variation
You can use the same amount of chicken thigh fillets for this recipe, if turkey is not available.

Italian Turkey Steaks with Lime

Citrus fruits such as limes, bergamots and grapefruit grow profusely all over the Italian region of Calabria, and this dish from the area reflects this. Served with tomato wedges, dressed with oil, salt and torn basil leaves.

Serves 4

600g/1lb 6oz turkey steaks
10ml/2 tsp dried oregano
3 ripe limes, 2 juiced and 1 sliced into wedges
75ml/5 tbsp extra virgin olive oil
1 garlic clove
sea salt and ground black pepper

1 Place the turkey steaks between sheets of clear film (plastic wrap) and beat them with a meat mallet or rolling pin until they are as thin as possible.

2 Spread them out in a shallow dish and sprinkle with the oregano. Drizzle with the lime juice and half the olive oil and season with salt and pepper. Cover and leave to marinate at room temperature for about 1 hour.

3 Lift the turkey slices out of the marinade and pat them dry with kitchen paper.

4 Pour the remaining olive oil into a frying pan. Add the garlic and cook over high heat. When it sizzles, add as many of the turkey slices as the pan will hold in a single layer. Fry quickly, for only 1–2 minutes on each side, until cooked through.

5 Transfer the turkey to heated plates and keep hot while cooking the remaining slices.

6 Divide the juices in the pan among the turkey slices, spooning them over the top. Garnish with lime wedges and serve.

Variations
Instead of turkey steaks, try escalopes (US scallops) of chicken or veal, or thin slices of monkfish. Add finely grated lime rind to the marinade for extra flavour.

Turkey Stew Energy 472kcal/1980kJ; Protein 34g; Carbohydrate 42g, of which sugars 15.9g; Fat 19.8g, of which saturates 2.4g; Cholesterol 61mg; Calcium 24mg; Fibre 2.5g; Sodium 461mg
Italian Steaks Energy 310kcal/1294kJ; Protein 32.9g; Carbohydrate 0.1g, of which sugars 0.1g; Fat 19.8g, of which saturates 3.4g; Cholesterol 92mg; Calcium 17mg; Fibre 0.1g; Sodium 82mg

Turkey Croquette Potatoes

These deliciously crisp patties of smoked turkey will become a firm favourite.

Serves 4

450g/1lb potatoes, peeled
3 eggs
30ml/2 tbsp milk
175g/6oz smoked turkey rashers (strips), finely chopped
2 spring onions (scallions), sliced
115g/4oz/2 cups fresh white breadcrumbs
vegetable oil, for deep-fat frying

For the sauce

15ml/1 tbsp olive oil
1 onion, finely chopped
400g/14oz can tomatoes, drained
30ml/2 tbsp tomato purée (paste)
15ml/1 tbsp chopped fresh parsley
salt and ground black pepper

1 Cut the potatoes into even pieces and boil for 20 minutes or until tender. Drain and then return the pan to low heat for a couple of minutes to evaporate the excess water.

2 Mash the potatoes with two eggs and the milk. Season well with salt and pepper. Stir in the turkey and spring onions. Chill in the refrigerator for 1 hour.

3 Meanwhile, to make the sauce, heat the oil in a frying pan and fry the onion for 5 minutes until softened. Add the tomatoes and purée, stir and simmer for 10 minutes. Stir in the parsley, season to taste and keep the sauce warm until needed.

4 Remove the potato mixture from the refrigerator and divide into eight pieces. Shape each piece into a sausage shape and dip in the remaining beaten egg and then the breadcrumbs.

5 Heat the vegetable oil in a deep-fat fryer to 175°C/330°F and deep fry the croquettes for 5 minutes, or until golden and crisp. Serve immediately, accompanied with the sauce.

Cook's Tip

Test the oil temperature by dropping a cube of bread into it. If it sinks, rises and sizzles in 10 seconds, the oil is ready to use.

Turkey Schnitzel

Schnitzel is a pounded-flat, crisp-coated, fried steak of chicken or veal, which originated from Austria and is now a traditional Jewish dish eaten all over the world. Today it is often made with turkey and is therefore a good budget meal, served with shredded cabbage.

Serves 4

4 skinless turkey breast fillets, each weighing about 175g/6oz
juice of 1 lemon
2 garlic cloves, chopped
plain (all-purpose) flour, for dusting
1–2 eggs
15ml/1 tbsp water
about 50g/2oz/½ cup matzo meal
paprika
a mixture of vegetable and olive oil, for shallow-frying
salt and ground black pepper
lemon wedges, shredded white cabbage, tomatoes and peas, to serve (optional)

1 Lay each piece of meat between two sheets of baking parchment and pound with a mallet or the end of a rolling pin until it is about half its original thickness and fairly even.

2 In a bowl, combine the lemon juice, garlic, salt and pepper. Coat the meat in it, then leave to marinate.

3 Meanwhile, arrange three wide plates or shallow dishes in a row. Fill one plate or dish with flour, beat the egg and water together in another and mix the matzo meal, salt, pepper and paprika together on the third.

4 Working quickly, dip each fillet into the flour, then the egg, then the matzo meal. Pat everything in well, then arrange the crumbed fillets on a plate and chill for at least 30 minutes, and up to 2 hours.

5 In a large, heavy frying pan, heat the oil until it will turn a cube of bread dropped into the oil golden brown in 30–60 seconds. Carefully add the crumbed fillets (in batches if necessary) and fry until golden brown, turning once. Remove and drain on kitchen paper. Serve immediately with lemon wedges and a selection of vegetables.

Turkey Croquettes Energy 404kcal/1698kJ; Protein 19.4g; Carbohydrate 47g, of which sugars 7.7g; Fat 16.7g, of which saturates 2.4g; Cholesterol 73mg; Calcium 93mg; Fibre 3.3g; Sodium 315mg
Turkey Schnitzel Energy 368kcal/1546kJ; Protein 45.4g; Carbohydrate 14.7g, of which sugars 0.6g; Fat 14.6g, of which saturates 2.3g; Cholesterol 170mg; Calcium 27mg; Fibre 0.5g; Sodium 125mg

ˈurkey Filo Bundles

ˌfter the Christmas or ˈhanksgiving meal, we often ɴd up with lots of leftovers. ˈhese delicious filo pastry arcels are a marvellous way f using up the turkey.

erves 6

50g/1lb cooked turkey, cut into small chunks
115g/4oz/1 cup Brie, cut into small cubes
30ml/2 tbsp cranberry sauce
30ml/2 tbsp chopped fresh parsley
9 sheets filo pastry, 45 x 28cm/18 x 11in each, thawed if frozen
50g/2oz/¼ cup butter, melted
green salad, to serve
salt and ground black pepper, to taste

Preheat the oven to 200°C/400°F/Gas 6. In a bowl, mix ɔgether the turkey, diced Brie, cranberry sauce and chopped arsley. Season with salt and pepper.

Cut the filo sheets in half widthways and trim to make 18 ʇuares. Layer three pieces of pastry together, brushing them ʼith a little melted butter so that they stick together. Repeat ʼith the remaining filo squares to give six pieces.

Divide the turkey mixture among the pastry squares, making eat piles in the centre of each piece. Gather up the pastry to ɴclose the filling in small bundles.

Place the parcels on a baking sheet, brush with a little melted utter and bake for 20 minutes, or until the pastry is crisp and ɔlden. Serve hot or warm with a green salad.

Variations

- *To make ham and Cheddar bundles, replace the turkey with cubed cooked ham and use Cheddar cheese in place of the Brie. A fruit-flavoured chutney would make a good alternative to the cranberry sauce, if you like.*
- *To make chicken and Stilton bundles, use diced cooked chicken in place of the cooked turkey and white Stilton instead of Brie. Replace the cranberry sauce with mango chutney.*

Turkey Patties

Minced turkey is very good value for money and makes deliciously light patties, which are ideal for summer meals and are especially popular with children. The recipe is a tasty variation on the classic beef burger.

Serves 6

675g/1½lb minced (ground) turkey
1 small red onion, finely chopped
grated rind and juice of 1 lime
small handful of fresh thyme leaves
15–30ml/1–2 tbsp olive oil
salt and ground black pepper, to taste

1 Mix together the minced turkey, chopped onion, lime rind and juice, thyme and seasoning in a large bowl. Use your hands to make sure everything is thoroughly combined.

2 Cover the bowl with clear film (plastic wrap) and chill for up to 4 hours to allow the flavours to blend, then divide the mixture into six equal portions and shape into round patties.

3 Preheat a griddle pan. Brush the patties with oil, then place them on the pan and cook for 10–12 minutes.

4 Turn the patties over, brush with more olive oil and cook for 10–12 minutes on the second side, or until cooked through.

5 Serve the patties immediately with bread rolls, salad and chips (French fries), if you like.

Variation

- *During the summer, when fresh herbs are at their best, try using fresh oregano, parsley or basil in place of thyme.*
- *Use minced (ground) chicken in place of the turkey.*
- *In the colder months, instead of frying the patties, and serving as burgers, try poaching them in chicken stock instead. When the patties are cooked, reduce the stock if necessary, stir in a little cream, and serve the patties and the sauce with rice or mashed potatoes, accompanied by redcurrant jelly or cranberry sauce, for a Swedish-style winter meal.*

ɪrkey Filo Bundles Energy 307kcal/1286kJ; Protein 24.8g; Carbohydrate 23.1g, of which sugars 4g; Fat 13g, of which saturates 8.1g; Cholesterol 78mg; Calcium 99mg; Fibre 1g; Sodium 199mg
ɪrkey Patties Energy 141kcal/592kJ; Protein 27.7g; Carbohydrate 1.2g, of which sugars 0.6g; Fat 2.8g, of which saturates 0.6g; Cholesterol 64mg; Calcium 23mg; Fibre 0.1g; Sodium 57mg

Beef Patties with Onions and Peppers

These burgers are a firm family favourite. They are easy to make, delicious and because minced beef is such an economical cut, they represent very good value for money. Try adding other vegetables, such as sliced red peppers, broccoli or mushrooms, depending on what you have in the refrigerator. Serve the burgers with salad and bread.

Serves 4

500g/1½lb lean minced (ground) beef
4 onions, 1 finely chopped and 3 sliced
30ml/2 tbsp garlic-flavoured olive oil
2–3 green (bell) peppers, seeded and sliced lengthways into thin strips
salt and ground black pepper
crisp green salad and bread, to serve

1 Place the minced beef, chopped onion and 15ml/1 tbsp of the garlic-flavoured oil in a bowl and combine. Season well and form into four large or eight small patties.

2 Heat the remaining oil in a large non-stick pan, then add the patties and cook on both sides until browned. Sprinkle over 15ml/1 tbsp water and add a little seasoning.

3 Cover the patties with the sliced onions and peppers. Sprinkle in another 15ml/1 tbsp water and a little seasoning, then cover the pan. Reduce the heat to low and braise for 20–30 minutes.

4 When the onions are turning golden brown, remove the pan from the heat. Serve the patties with the onions and peppers, a green salad and bread.

Cook's Tip

To make the burger mixture go further, try adding a handful of canned beans, or some cooked lentils at step 1, and increasing the seasoning as needed.

Spaghetti with Meatballs

For a great introduction to the charm of chillies, this simple pasta dish is hard to beat. Adults and children alike will love the gentle heat of the sweet and spicy tomato sauce.

Serves 4

350g/12oz lean minced (ground) beef
1 egg
60ml/4 tbsp roughly chopped fresh flat leaf parsley
2.5ml/½ tsp crushed dried red chillies
1 slice white bread, crusts remove
30ml/2 tbsp milk
about 30ml/2 tbsp olive oil
300ml/½ pint/1¼ cups passata (bottled strained tomatoes)
400ml/14fl oz/1⅔ cups beef stoc
5ml/1 tsp sugar
350–450g/12oz–1lb dried spaghetti
salt and ground black pepper
shavings of grano padano cheese, to serve

1 Put the beef in a bowl. Add the egg, with half the parsley and half the crushed chillies. Season with plenty of salt and pepper.

2 Tear the bread into pieces and place in a bowl. Moisten with the milk. Leave to soak for a few minutes, then squeeze out the milk and crumble the bread over the meat. Mix everything together with a wooden spoon, then use your hands to knead the mixture so that it becomes smooth and quite sticky.

3 Wash your hands, rinse them under the cold tap, then pick up small pieces of the mixture and roll them to make about 20–30 small balls. Place on a tray and chill for 30 minutes.

4 Heat the oil in a large non-stick frying pan. Cook the meatballs in batches until browned on all sides.

5 Meanwhile, pour the passata and stock into a pan. Heat gentl then add the remaining chillies and the sugar, and season. Add the meatballs and simmer for 20 minutes.

6 Cook the pasta until tender. Drain and transfer into a warme bowl. Pour over the sauce and toss gently. Sprinkle with the remaining parsley and shavings of grano padano before serving.

Beef Patties Energy 431kcal/1789kJ; Protein 27.9g; Carbohydrate 21.1g, of which sugars 17.2g; Fat 26.6g, of which saturates 9.6g; Cholesterol 75mg; Calcium 60mg; Fibre 4.4g; Sodium 110mg
Spaghetti Energy 598kcal/2517kJ; Protein 30.7g; Carbohydrate 71.8g, of which sugars 6.7g; Fat 22.9g, of which saturates 7.5g; Cholesterol 101mg; Calcium 61mg; Fibre 3.1g; Sodium 301mg

:hilli Con Carne

'resh green and dried red hillies add fire to this classic 'sh of tender beef cooked in spicy tomato sauce.

erves 6

25g/8oz/1¼ cups dried black beans
00g/1¼lb braising steak
0ml/2 tbsp vegetable oil
onions, chopped
garlic clove, crushed
fresh green chilli, finely chopped
15ml/1 tbsp paprika
10ml/2 tsp ground cumin
10ml/2 tsp ground coriander
400g/14oz can chopped tomatoes
300ml/½ pint/1¼ cups beef stock
1 dried red chilli, crumbled
5ml/1 tsp hot pepper sauce
1 fresh red (bell) pepper, seeded and chopped
salt and ground black pepper, to taste
boiled rice, to serve

Put the beans in a large pan. Add cold water to cover, bring ɔ the boil and boil vigorously for 10 minutes. Drain, transfer ıto a bowl, cover with cold water and soak for 8 hours.

Preheat the oven to 150°C/300°F/Gas 2. Cut the braising :eak into small dice. Heat the vegetable oil in a large, ameproof casserole. Add the onion, garlic and green chilli and ɔok gently for 5 minutes, then transfer the mixture to a plate.

Increase the heat to high, add the diced meat to the casserole ıd brown on all sides. Stir in the paprika, ground cumin and round coriander.

Add the tomatoes, beef stock, dried chilli and hot pepper auce. Drain the beans and add them to the casserole, with ıough water to cover. Bring to simmering point, cover and ɔok in the oven for 2 hours. Stir occasionally and add extra 'ater, if necessary.

Season the casserole with salt and pepper to taste and add ıe chopped red pepper. Replace the lid, return the casserole ɔ the oven and cook for 30 minutes more, or until the meat ıd beans are tender. Sprinkle over the fresh coriander and ərve with boiled rice.

Mexican Spicy Beef Tortilla

This dish ekes out a small amount of beef with rice and tortillas to make a delicious layered bake that is great value for money.

Serves 4

15ml/1 tbsp oil
1 onion, chopped
2 garlic cloves, crushed
350g/12oz braising steak, cubed
225g/8oz/2 cups cooked rice
beef stock, to moisten
3 large wheat tortillas
salt and ground black pepper

For the salsa picante
2 x 400g/14oz cans tomatoes
2 garlic cloves, halved
1 onion, quartered
1 red chilli, seeded and chopped
5ml/1 tsp ground cumin
2.5–5ml/½–1 tsp cayenne pepper
5ml/1 tsp chopped fresh oregano

For the cheese sauce
50g/2oz/¼ cup butter
50g/2oz/½ cup flour
600ml/1 pint/2½ cups milk
115g/4oz/1 cup grated Cheddar cheese

1 First make the salsa picante. Place the tomatoes, garlic, onion and chilli in a blender or food processor and process until smooth. Pour into a pan, add the spices and oregano, and season with salt.

2 Boil for 1–2 minutes, then lower the heat, cover and simmer for 15 minutes until reduced to a thick sauce. Preheat the oven to 180°C/350°F/Gas 4.

3 Make the cheese sauce. Melt the butter in a pan and stir in the flour. Cook for 1 minute. Add the milk, stirring, until it thickens. Stir in all but 30ml/2 tbsp of the cheese and season.

4 Heat the oil in a pan and fry the onion, garlic and meat until browned. Stir in the rice and stock to moisten. Season to taste.

5 Pour about one-quarter of the cheese sauce into the base of a round ovenproof dish. Add a tortilla and then spread over half the salsa followed by half the meat. Repeat, then add half the remaining cheese sauce and the final tortilla. Top with the last of the cheese sauce and sprinkle with the remaining cheese. Bake for in the oven for 15–20 minutes until golden on top.

hilli Con Carne Energy 331kcal/1387kJ; Protein 29.1g; Carbohydrate 26.6g, of which sugars 8.5g; Fat 12.7g, of which saturates 3.9g; Cholesterol 48mg; Calcium 70mg; Fibre 8g; Sodium 70mg
exican Tortilla Energy 907kcal/3802kJ; Protein 43.8g; Carbohydrate 106.5g, of which sugars 15.1g; Fat 34.8g, of which saturates 18.3g; Cholesterol 114mg; Calcium 514mg; Fibre 4.1g; Sodium 598mg

Beef and Lentil Balls

Mixing lentils with the minced beef boosts the fibre content of these meatballs and adds to the flavour.

Serves 8

15ml/1 tbsp olive oil
2 onions, finely chopped
2 celery sticks, finely chopped
2 large carrots, finely chopped
400g/14oz lean minced (ground) beef
200g/7oz/1 cup brown lentils
400g/14oz can plum tomatoes
30ml/2 tbsp tomato purée (paste)
2 bay leaves
300ml/½ pint/1¼ cups beef stock
175ml/6fl oz/¾ cup red wine
30–45ml/2–3 tbsp Worcestershire sauce
2 eggs
2 handfuls fresh parsley, chopped
sea salt and ground black pepper
mashed potatoes, to serve

For the tomato sauce

4 onions, finely chopped
2 x 400g/14oz cans tomatoes
60ml/4 tbsp dry red wine
3 fresh dill sprigs, finely chopped

1 Make the tomato sauce. Combine the onions, tomatoes and red wine in a pan. Bring to the boil, lower the heat, cover, and simmer for 30 minutes. Purée in a food processor.

2 Make the meatballs. Heat the oil in a large heavy pan and cook the onions, celery and carrots for 5–10 minutes until softened. Add the beef and cook until lightly browned.

3 Add the lentils, tomatoes, tomato purée, bay leaves, beef stock and wine. Mix well and bring to the boil. Lower the heat and simmer for 20–30 minutes until the liquid has been absorbed. Remove the bay leaves, then stir the Worcestershire sauce into the beef and lentil mixture.

4 Remove the pan from the heat and add the eggs and parsley. Season with salt and pepper and mix well, then leave to cool. Meanwhile, preheat the oven to 180°C/350°F/Gas 4.

5 Shape the beef mixture into balls with your hands. Arrange in an ovenproof dish and bake for 25 minutes. Meanwhile, reheat the tomato sauce. Just before serving, stir in the chopped dill. Pour the sauce over the meatballs and serve with mash.

Cannelloni Stuffed with Meat

This classic Italian main course is a rich and substantial dish, which takes quite a long time to prepare, but can be made a day ahead up to the baking stage.

Serves 6

15ml/1 tbsp olive oil
1 small onion, finely chopped
450g/1lb minced (ground) beef
1 garlic clove, finely chopped
5ml/1 tsp dried mixed herbs
120ml/4fl oz/½ cup beef stock
1 egg
45ml/3 tbsp white breadcrumbs
150g/5oz/1⅔ cups grated Parmesan cheese
18 cannelloni tubes
salt and ground black pepper

For the tomato sauce

30ml/2 tbsp olive oil
1 small onion, finely chopped
½ carrot, finely chopped
1 celery stick, finely chopped
1 garlic clove, crushed
400g/14oz can plum tomatoes
a few sprigs of fresh basil
2.5ml/½ tsp dried oregano

For the white sauce

50g/2oz/¼ cup butter
50g/2oz/½ cup flour
900ml/1½ pints/3¾ cups milk
nutmeg

1 Heat the olive oil in a medium frying pan and cook the finely chopped onion over low heat, stirring occasionally, for about 5 minutes until softened.

2 Add the minced beef and garlic and cook gently for about 10 minutes, stirring and breaking up any lumps with a wooden spoon. Add the mixed herbs, and salt and pepper to taste, then moisten with half the stock.

3 Cover the pan and simmer for 25 minutes, stirring from time to time and adding more stock as the mixture reduces. Spoon into a bowl and leave to cool.

4 Make the tomato sauce. Heat the olive oil in a medium pan, add the vegetables and garlic and cook over medium heat, stirring frequently, for about 10 minutes. Add the tomatoes. Fill the empty can with water, add to the pan, then stir in the herbs and salt and pepper. Simmer for 25–30 minutes, stirring occasionally. Purée the sauce in a blender or food processor.

5 Add the egg, breadcrumbs and 90ml/6 tbsp of the grated Parmesan to the meat and stir well to mix. Taste for seasoning.

6 Spread a little tomato sauce over the base of a baking dish. With a teaspoon, fill the cannelloni tubes with the meat and place in a single layer in the dish. Pour the remaining tomato sauce over the top. Preheat the oven to 190°C/375°F/Gas 5.

7 Make the white sauce. Melt the butter in a small pan, add the flour and cook, stirring, for 1–2 minutes. Add the milk a little at time, whisking vigorously continuously. Season with salt and pepper, and add a little grated nutmeg.

8 Bring the sauce to the boil and cook, stirring, until smooth and thick. Pour the sauce over the cannelloni, then sprinkle with the remaining Parmesan. Bake for 40–45 minutes until the pasta tubes are tender when pierced with the tip of a knife. Serve after leaving to stand for 10 minutes.

Beef Lentil Balls Energy 272kcals/1154kJ; Fat, total 9.3g; saturated fat 2.9g; polyunsaturated fat 0.8g; monounsaturated fat 4.2g; Carbohydrate 22.65g; sugar, total 9g; starch 11.5g; Fibre 4.5g; Sodium 155mg **Cannelloni** Energy 455kcal/1905kJ; Protein 25.5g; Carbohydrate 41.7g, of which sugars 6.4g; Fat 21.8g, of which saturates 7.8g; Cholesterol 76mg; Calcium 203mg; Fibre 1.6g; Sodium 571mg

ᐧastitsio

ᐧacaroni in a cheese sauce is
ᐧyered with cinnamon and
ımin-spiced minced beef to
ake a creamy Greek
ersion of lasagne.

erves 4–6

25g/8oz/2 cups macaroni
ᐧml/2 tbsp olive oil
large onion, finely chopped
garlic cloves, crushed
50g/1lb minced (ground) steak
ᐧ0ml/½ pint/1¼ cups beef stock
10ml/2 tsp tomato purée (paste)
5ml/1 tsp ground cinnamon
5ml/1 tsp ground cumin
15ml/1 tbsp chopped fresh mint
50g/2oz/¼ cup butter
40g/1½oz/⅓ cup plain (all-purpose) flour
120ml/4fl oz/½ cup milk
120ml/4fl oz/½ cup natural (plain) yogurt
175g/6oz/1½ cups grated mature Cheddar cheese
salt and ground black pepper

Bring a large pan of lightly salted water to the boil. Add the acaroni and cook for 8 minutes, or according to the structions on the packet, until al dente. Drain, rinse under cold ater and drain again. Preheat the oven to 190°C/375°F/Gas 5.

Heat the oil in a frying pan, add the onion and garlic and cook about 8–10 minutes until soft. Add the minced steak and stir til browned. Stir in the stock, tomato purée, cinnamon, cumin d mint, with salt and pepper to taste. Cook gently for about)–15 minutes until the sauce is thick and flavoursome.

Melt the butter in a pan. Stir in the flour and cook, stirring, for minute. Remove the pan from the heat and gradually stir in e milk and yogurt. Return the pan to the heat and cook gently 5 minutes. Stir in half the cheese and season with salt and pper. Stir the macaroni into the cheese sauce.

Spread half the macaroni mixture over the base of a large atin dish. Cover the layer of macaroni with the meat sauce d top with the remaining macaroni.

Sprinkle the remaining cheese over the top and bake for minutes or until golden brown on top. Let the pastitsio stand 10 minutes before serving.

Beef and Aubergine Casserole

Easy to make but with an exotic taste, this slow-cooked combination of a cheaper cut of beef and aubergines in a rich tomato sauce would make an excellent main course for a dinner party. Use good-quality beef and cook it slowly, so it is tender.

Serves 4

60ml/4 tbsp olive oil
1kg/2¼lb good-quality stewing steak or feather steak, sliced in 4 thick pieces
1 onion, chopped
2.5ml/½ tsp dried oregano
2 garlic cloves, chopped
175ml/6fl oz/¾ cup white wine
400g/14oz can chopped tomatoes
2 or 3 aubergines (eggplants), total weight about 675g/1½lb
150ml/¼ pint/⅔ cup sunflower oil
45ml/3 tbsp finely chopped parsley
salt and ground black pepper

1 Heat the olive oil in a large pan and brown the pieces of meat on both sides. Add the onion to the pan and sauté until translucent. Add the oregano and the garlic, then, as soon as the garlic becomes aromatic, return the meat to the pan and pour in the wine. Cook for a few minutes, then add the tomatoes, and enough water to cover the meat. Bring to the boil, lower the heat, cover and cook for about 1 hour, until tender.

2 Meanwhile, slice the aubergines into 2cm/¾in thick rounds, then slice each round in half. Heat the sunflower oil and fry the aubergines in batches over high heat, turning them as they become golden. Drain on kitchen paper and season to taste.

3 Season the meat, then add the aubergine pieces and shake the pan to distribute them evenly. From this point, do not stir the mixture as the aubergines will be quite fragile.

4 Add a little hot water so that the aubergines are just submerged, cover and simmer for 30 minutes more, or until the meat is very tender.

5 Sprinkle the parsley over the top and simmer for a few more minutes before transferring to a serving dish. Serve with hot toasted pitta bread and a fresh green or mixed salad.

stitsio Energy 532kcal/2226kJ; Protein 31g; Carbohydrate 40g, of which sugars 6g; Fat 29g, of which saturates 14g; Cholesterol 97mg; Calcium 313mg; Fibre 3g; Sodium 401mg
ef Casserole Energy 838kcal/3479kJ; Protein 59.2g; Carbohydrate 8.3g, of which sugars 7.6g; Fat 60.2g, of which saturates 14.4g; Cholesterol 145mg; Calcium 44mg; Fibre 4.6g; Sodium 175mg

Madras Beef Curry with Spicy Rice

After long, gentle simmering, this curry has a rich consistency and a beautiful depth of flavour.

Serves 4

30ml/2 tbsp vegetable oil
25g/1oz/2 tbsp butter
675g/1½lb stewing beef, cubed
1 onion, chopped
7 green cardamom pods
2 green chillies, finely chopped
5ml/1 tsp grated fresh ginger
2 garlic cloves, crushed
15ml/1 tbsp Madras curry paste
10ml/2 tsp ground cumin
7.5ml/1½ tsp ground coriander
150ml/¼ pint/⅔ cup beef stock
salt

For the rice

225g/8oz/1 cup basmati rice
15ml/1 tbsp sunflower oil
25g/1oz/2 tbsp butter
1 onion, finely chopped
1 garlic clove, crushed
1 cinnamon stick
1 red (bell) pepper, diced
1 green (bell) pepper, diced
300ml/½ pint/1¼ cups beef stock

1 Heat half the vegetable oil with half the butter in a large pan. When it is hot, fry the meat, until browned on all sides.

2 Heat the remaining vegetable oil and butter and fry the onion for 3–4 minutes until lightly browned. Add three cardamom pods then stir in the chillies, ginger and garlic. Fry for 2 minutes. Stir in the curry paste, 5ml/1 tsp each of ground cumin and coriander, then return the meat to the pan. Stir in the stock. Season with salt, bring to the boil, then simmer for 1–1½ hours.

3 Meanwhile, put the rice in a bowl and cover with boiled water. Soak for 10 minutes, drain and rinse under cold water.

4 Heat the sunflower oil and butter in a heavy pan and fry the onion and garlic for 3–4 minutes until softened Stir in the remaining ground cumin, coriander, cardamom pods and the cinnamon stick. Fry for 1 minute, then add the diced peppers.

5 Add the rice and the chicken stock. Bring to the boil, then reduce the heat, cover, and simmer for about 8–10 minutes until tender and all the liquid has been absorbed. Spoon the spicy rice into a bowl and serve immeditately with the curry.

Rich Beef Stew

Marmalade adds a zesty and sweet note to this hearty beef stew, made with tender chunks of slow-cooked stewing beef, red wine and mushrooms. It makes an excellent family meal served with mashed potatoes.

Serves 4

900g/2lb stewing beef
50g/2oz/½ cup flour
2.5ml/½ tsp paprika
30ml/2 tbsp vegetable oil
225g/8oz onions, chopped
50g/2oz/¼ cup butter
100g/3¾oz button (white) mushrooms, quartered
2 garlic cloves, crushed
15ml/1 tbsp bitter marmalade
300ml/½ pint/1¼ cups good-quality red wine
150ml/¼ pint/⅔ cup beef stock
salt and ground black pepper

1 Preheat the oven to 180°C/350°F/Gas 4. Cut the meat into 2.5cm/1in cubes. Season the flour with salt, black pepper and the paprika, spread it on a tray and coat the meat in it.

2 Heat a large pan, add the vegetable oil and brown the meat. Do this in batches if your pan is small.

3 Transfer the meat to a casserole. Brown the onions in the original pan, adding a little butter if they seem too dry. Add to the casserole. Keeping the pan hot, add the rest of the butter and brown the mushrooms then transfer to the casserole.

4 Add the rest of the ingredients to the casserole and bring to the boil, stirring to combine the marmalade and evenly distribute the meat and mushrooms. Cover the casserole and place in the preheated oven for about 3 hours, until the meat is tender. Serve with creamy mashed potatoes.

Cook's Tip

Stewing steak is very good value for money, and a little goes a long way. It requires slow cooking over low heat to achieve a meltingly tender consistency and for its full flavour to be properly realised, and is best paired with strong flavours.

Madras Beef Curry Energy 717kcal/2984kJ; Protein 44.2g; Carbohydrate 53.8g, of which sugars 7.1g; Fat 36g, of which saturates 14.2g; Cholesterol 125mg; Calcium 41mg; Fibre 1.8g; Sodium 189mg
Rich Beef Stew Energy 544kcal/2276kJ; Protein 53.3g; Carbohydrate 17.1g, of which sugars 6.2g; Fat 24.1g, of which saturates 10.4g; Cholesterol 177mg; Calcium 53mg; Fibre 1.5g; Sodium 242mg

ll-in-one-pot Beef Stew

his one-pot stew makes a ow-cost alternative to a tandard Sunday roast and is ess hassle as the beef, being raised, can sit and wait until ou are ready to eat. Because he vegetables are cooked vith the meat, you also don't ave to worry about cooking eparate accompaniments, so is also good for a meal to ome home to.

Serves 8

25g/1oz/2 tbsp butter, softened
25g/1oz/¼ cup flour
1.6kg/3½lb silverside (pot roast), boned and rolled
450g/1lb small onions, peeled
450g/1lb carrots, peeled and halved
8 celery sticks, quartered
12 small potatoes
30ml/2 tbsp chopped fresh parsley
salt and ground black pepper

Make a beurre manié by combining the butter and flour horoughly. This will be used to thicken the sauce.

Put the joint of beef in a large pan, pour in enough cold water o cover and put on the lid. Bring to the boil, then reduce the eat, cover and simmer for 2 hours, topping up with boiling vater if necessary.

After 2 hours add the prepared vegetables to the pan and immer for a further 30 minutes, until the vegetables are just ooked. Test by inserting the point of a knife into them.

Remove the beef and vegetables from the pan, arrange on a erving dish and keep warm. Boil the stock hard to reduce until ou have about 350ml/12fl oz/1½ cups of the cooking liquor eft. Transfer this into a clean pan, season with salt and ground lack pepper if necessary, and bring to the boil. Whisk in the eurre manié to thicken it and add the chopped fresh parsley.

When you are ready to eat, pour the thickened sauce over e beef and vegetables, retaining some to pass round the table a separate jug (pitcher).

Serve the meat in thick slices, accompanied by a generous erving of the vegetables.

Beef and Chickpea Stew

This aromatic stew combines aubergines, chickpeas and left-over meat with a subtly spiced tomato sauce to create a taste sensation. It is often made with cold roast beef, but you can use any meat, and even stuffing, left over from a Sunday roast.

Serves 4

2 small aubergines (eggplants)
90ml/6 tbsp olive oil
1 large onion, chopped
3 garlic cloves, finely chopped
400g/14oz can plum tomatoes
1 fresh, or bottled, red (bell) pepper, seeded and sliced
400g/14oz cooked beef, cubed, or mixed turkey, ham, or any other left-over meat
250ml/8fl oz/1 cup meat stock
2.5ml/½ tsp ground cumin
2.5ml/½ tsp ground allspice
pinch of ground cloves
2.5ml/½ tsp cayenne pepper
400g/14oz can chickpeas, drained and rinsed
salt and ground black pepper
chopped fresh mint, to garnish

1 Cut the aubergines into cubes and put them into a colander. Sprinkle with 10ml/2 tsp salt, turning the cubes over with your hands. Leave to drain for about 1 hour. Rinse, then squeeze them dry using kitchen paper.

2 Meanwhile put 30ml/2 tbsp oil in a wide flameproof casserole and fry the onion and garlic until soft. If using the fresh pepper, add it to the casserole and stir-fry until softened.

3 Add the tomatoes and the bottled red pepper, if using, the meat, stock, cumin, allspice, ground cloves and cayenne pepper. Season to taste and simmer gently while you fry the aubergine.

4 Heat 45ml/3 tbsp oil over high heat in a large frying pan. Fry the aubergine, in batches if necessary, until they are brown on all sides. (If you need to add more oil, add it to an empty pan, and reheat to high heat, before adding more cubes.)

5 Add the fried aubergine together with the chickpeas to the casserole and bring back to a simmer, adding more stock to moisten, if necessary – the dish should be almost solid. Check the seasonings, garnish with mint and serve.

ll-in-one-pot Stew Energy 875kcal/3656kJ; Protein 89.8g; Carbohydrate 38.5g, of which sugars 16.7g; Fat 41.1g, of which saturates 17.7g; Cholesterol 231mg; Calcium 121mg; Fibre 6.3g; Sodium 358mg
eef Stew Energy 483kcal/2018kJ; Protein 32.1g; Carbohydrate 23.7g, of which sugars 7.4g; Fat 29.6g, of which saturates 6.7g; Cholesterol 58mg; Calcium 74mg; Fibre 8.3g; Sodium 297mg

Slow Baked Beef with Potato Crust

This recipe makes the very most of the delicious taste and tender texture of braising beef by marinating it in red wine and topping it with a cheesy potato crust.

Serves 4

675g/1½lb stewing beef, diced
300ml/½ pint/1¼ cups red wine
slice of orange peel
30ml/2 tbsp olive oil
2 onions, cut into chunks
2 carrots, cut into chunks
1 garlic clove, crushed
225g/8oz/3 cups button (white) mushrooms
150ml/¼ pint/⅔ cup beef stock
45ml/3 tbsp cornflour (cornstarch)
salt and ground black pepper

For the crust

450g/1lb potatoes, grated
30ml/2 tbsp creamed horseradish
50g/2oz/½ cup grated mature (sharp) Cheddar cheese

1 Place the diced beef in a non-metallic bowl. Add the red wine and orange peel and season with black pepper. Mix the ingredients together and then cover and marinate in the refrigerator for at least 4 hours or overnight if possible. Preheat the oven to 160°C/325°F/Gas 3.

2 Drain the beef, reserving the marinade. Heat 30ml/2 tbsp of the oil in a large casserole and cook the meat, in batches, for 5 minutes to seal. Add the onions, carrots and garlic and cook for 5 minutes. Stir in the mushrooms, marinade and beef stock.

3 Mix the cornflour with water to make a smooth paste. Stir into the pan. Season, cover and cook in the oven for 1½ hours.

4 Make the crust 30 minutes before the end of the cooking time. Blanch the grated potato in boiling water for 5 minutes. Drain well and then squeeze out all the extra liquid.

5 Stir in the remaining oil, the horseradish and the cheese, then sprinkle evenly over the surface of the beef.

6 Increase the oven temperature to 200°C/400°F/Gas 6 and cook the dish for a further 30 minutes so that the cheesy pototo topping is crispy and slightly browned.

Stuffed Cabbage Rolls

These tasty, nutritious stuffed cabbage leaves can be found in some form or other in many North European, Scandinavian and Eastern European countries, with variations that reflect seasonal local ingredients. This version, served with lingonberry conserve is a Swedish recipe.

Serves 6–8

1 Savoy cabbage
100g/3¾oz/¾ cup long grain rice
100ml/3½fl oz/scant ½ cup water
15g/½oz/1 tbsp butter
1 large Spanish (Bermuda) onion, chopped
250g/9oz minced (ground) beef
1 egg, beaten
2.5ml/½ tsp chopped fresh thyme leaves
5ml/1 tsp salt
ground black pepper
melted butter for brushing
boiled new potatoes, tossed in butter and chopped parsley, and lingonberry conserve or redcurrant jelly, to serve

1 Cut the base off the cabbage, and separate the leaves. Cook in a large pan of boiling salted water for 1 minute, then drain and refresh under cold running water. Cut out the hard centre of each leaf in a 'V' shape. Set the leaves aside.

2 Put the rice and water in a pan, bring to the boil then simmer for 10–12 minutes until the rice is tender. Drain well, rinse under cold running water and leave to cool. Preheat the oven to 200°C/ 400°F/Gas 6.

3 Melt the butter in a pan, add the onion and fry until softened and slightly golden. Put the minced beef in a large bowl and break up with a fork. Add the onion, cooled rice, beaten egg, thyme, and salt and pepper to season. Use your hands to thoroughly mix the ingredients.

4 Put 30ml/2 tbsp of the mixture into each leaf and wrap into parcels. Brush the parcels with melted butter and place in an ovenproof dish. Bake for about 40 minutes until soft.

5 Serve the cabbage rolls with boiled new potatoes and lingonberry conserve or redcurrant jelly.

Slow Baked Beef Energy 630kcal/2632kJ; Protein 45.9g; Carbohydrate 40.1g, of which sugars 10.8g; Fat 26.9g, of which saturates 10.2g; Cholesterol 111mg; Calcium 152mg; Fibre 4.2g; Sodium 308mg
Stuffed Cabbage Rolls Energy 169kcal/702kJ; Protein 9.2g; Carbohydrate 16.1g, of which sugars 5.2g; Fat 7.6g, of which saturates 3.3g; Cholesterol 47mg; Calcium 49mg; Fibre 1.8g; Sodium 51mg

Pot-roasted Brisket

This Jewish meat dish ncludes kishke, a heavy, dumpling, which is added to the pot. With the potato, it ıelps an economical cut of oeef go even further.

Serves 6–8

5 onions, sliced
3 bay leaves
–1.6kg/2¼–3½lb beef brisket
1 garlic head, broken into cloves
4 carrots, thickly sliced
5–10ml/1–2 tsp paprika
500ml/17fl oz/2¼ cups beef stock
4 potatoes, peeled and quartered
salt and ground black pepper

For the kishke
90cm/36in sausage casing (or cooking-strength plastic wrap)
250g/9oz/2¼ cups plain (all-purpose) flour
120ml/4fl oz/½ cup semolina or couscous
10–15ml/2–3 tsp paprika
1 carrot, grated and 2 carrots, diced (optional)
250ml/8fl oz/1 cup rendered chicken fat
30ml/2 tbsp crisp, fried onions
½ onion, grated and 3 onions, thinly sliced
3 garlic cloves, chopped
salt and ground black pepper

1 Preheat the oven to 180°C/350°F/Gas 4. Put one-third of the onions and a bay leaf in an ovenproof dish, then top with the orisket. Sprinkle over the garlic, carrots and the remaining bay eaves, sprinkle with salt, pepper and paprika, then top with the emaining onions. Pour in enough stock to almost fill the dish, and cover with foil. Cook in the oven for 2 hours.

2 Meanwhile, make the kishke. In a bowl, combine all the ngredients and stuff the mixture into the casing, leaving enough pace for it to expand. Tie into sausage-shaped lengths.

3 When the meat has cooked for about 2 hours, add the kishke and potatoes to the pan, re-cover and cook for a further hour, or until the meat and potatoes are tender.

4 Remove the foil and increase the oven temperature to 200°C/400°F/Gas 6. Move the onions away from the top of the meat to the side of the dish and return to the oven for a urther 30 minutes, or until the meat, onions and potatoes are beginning to brown and become crisp. Serve hot or cold.

Grilled Lamb with Flatbread

In this popular kebab recipe pieces of lamb are wrapped in home-made flatbread with red onion, parsley and a squeeze of lemon.

Serves 6

2 onions, grated
7.5ml/1½ tsp salt
2 garlic cloves, crushed
10ml/2 tsp cumin seeds, crushed
900g/2lb boneless shoulder of lamb, cut into bitesize pieces

For the flatbreads
225g/8oz/2 cups strong white bread flour
50g/2oz/½ cup wholemeal (whole-wheat) flour
5ml/1 tsp salt
200ml/7fl oz/scant 1 cup lukewarm water

To serve
1 large red onion, sliced thinly
1 bunch of fresh parsley, chopped
2–3 lemons, cut into wedges

1 Sprinkle the grated onions with the salt and leave to weep for 15 minutes. Place a sieve (strainer) over a bowl, tip in the onions and press down to extract the juice. Discard the onions, then mix the garlic and cumin seeds into the onion juice and toss in the lamb. Cover and leave to marinate for 3–4 hours.

2 Meanwhile, prepare the breads. Sift the flours and salt into a bowl. Make a well in the middle and gradually add the water, drawing in the flour from the sides. Using your hands, knead the dough until firm and springy – add a little more flour if sticky.

3 Divide the dough into 24 pieces and knead each one into a ball. Place on a floured surface and cover with a damp cloth. Leave to rest for 45 minutes while you get the barbecue ready. Just before cooking, roll each ball of dough into a wide, thin circle. Dust with flour and cover with a damp dish towel.

4 Thread the meat on to metal skewers and cook on the barbecue for 2–3 minutes on each side. At the same time, cook the flatbreads on a hot griddle or other flat pan, flipping them over as they begin to go brown and buckle. Pile up on a plate.

5 Slide the meat off the skewers on to the flatbreads. Sprinkle onion and parsley over each pile and squeeze lemon juice over.

ot-roasted Brisket Energy 781kcal/3271kJ; Protein 44.2g; Carbohydrate 74g, of which sugars 12.7g; Fat 36.4g, of which saturates 14.4g; Cholesterol 113mg; Calcium 124mg; Fibre 5g; Sodium 124mg
rilled Lamb Energy 433kcal/1821kJ; Protein 34.3g; Carbohydrate 37.1g, of which sugars 4.4g; Fat 17.5g, of which saturates 7.9g; Cholesterol 114mg; Calcium 83mg; Fibre 2.5g; Sodium 460mg

Lamb Kebabs

Designed to use up day-old pitta bread, this dish needs no other accompaniment.

Serves 4

500g/1¼lb/2¼ cups lean minced (ground) lamb
5ml/1 tsp paprika
10ml/2 tsp ground sumac
2 onions, finely chopped
1 fresh green chilli, finely chopped
4 garlic cloves, crushed
1 bunch flat leaf parsley, chopped
12 plum tomatoes
30ml/2 tbsp butter
5ml/1 tsp dried oregano
4 pitta cut into bitesize chunks
225g/8oz/1 cup natural (plain) yogurt
salt and ground black pepper

For the tomato sauce
30ml/2 tbsp olive oil
1 onion, finely chopped
2 garlic cloves, finely chopped
1 fresh green chilli, finely chopped
5–10ml/1–2 tsp sugar
400g/14oz can chopped tomatoes

1 Put the lamb into a bowl with the paprika, 5ml/1 tsp sumac, the onions, chilli, garlic and chopped parsley. Knead well to form a smooth paste, cover and chill for about 15 minutes.

2 To make the sauce, heat the oil in a pan, stir in the onion, garlic and chilli and cook until they begin to colour. Add the sugar and tomatoes and cook for 30 minutes until thick. Season, remove from the heat and keep warm.

3 Light the barbecue or preheat the grill (broiler). Shape the kebabs by moulding them around four metal skewers with damp hands. Cook the kebabs on the hot barbecue or grill, for 6–8 minutes, turning once. Thread the tomatoes on to four skewers, and cook those until charred.

4 Fry the pitta chunks in the butter until golden-brown all over. Sprinkle with a little sumac and the oregano, then arrange on a serving dish. Sprinkle a little of the tomato sauce over the bread and spoon half the yogurt on top.

5 Slip the lamb off the skewers, cut into pieces, and arrange on the bread with the tomatoes. Sprinkle with salt, sumac and oregano, and Serve with the remaining sauce and yogurt.

Sumac-spiced Burgers with Relish

The sharp-sweet red onion relish works well with these Middle Eastern-style burgers.

Serves 4

25g/1oz/3 tbsp bulgur wheat
500g/1¼lb lean minced (ground) lamb
1 small red onion, finely chopped
2 garlic cloves, finely chopped
1 green chilli, seeded and finely chopped
5ml/1 tsp ground cumin seeds
2.5ml/½ tsp ground sumac
15g/½oz chopped fresh parsley
30ml/2 tbsp chopped fresh mint
olive oil, for frying
salt and ground black pepper

For the relish
2 red (bell) peppers, halved
2 red onions, cut into 5mm/¼in thick slices
75–90ml/5–6 tbsp virgin olive oil
350g/12oz cherry tomatoes, chopped
½–1 fresh red or green chilli, seeded and finely chopped
30ml/2 tbsp chopped mint
30ml/2 tbsp chopped parsley
15ml/1 tbsp chopped oregano
2.5–5ml/½–1 tsp each ground toasted cumin and sumac, mixed together
juice of ½ lemon
caster (superfine) sugar, to taste

1 Pour 150ml/¼ pint/⅔ cup hot water over the bulgur wheat and leave to stand for 15 minutes, then drain.

2 Place the bulgur in a bowl and add the minced lamb, onion, garlic, chilli, cumin, sumac, parsley and mint. Mix together thoroughly, then season with 5ml/1 tsp salt and plenty of black pepper. Form the mixture into eight burgers and set aside while you make the relish.

3 Grill (broil) the peppers, until the skin chars and blisters. Peel off the skin, dice and place in a bowl. Brush the onions with oil and grill until browned. Add the onions, tomatoes, chilli, mint, parsley, oregano and half of the cumin and sumac mixture to the peppers. Stir in 60ml/4 tbsp oil and 15ml/1 tbsp of the lemon juice and salt, pepper and sugar to taste. Set aside.

4 Heat a frying pan over high heat and grease with olive oil. Cook the burgers for about 5–6 minutes on each side. Serve immediately with the relish.

Lamb Kebabs Energy 642kcal/2688kJ; Protein 35.2g; Carbohydrate 52.8g, of which sugars 24.1g; Fat 33.9g, of which saturates 15.1g; Cholesterol 121mg; Calcium 253mg; Fibre 6.3g; Sodium 456mg
Sumac-spiced Burgers: Energy 537kcal/2228kJ; Protein 27.2g; Carbohydrate 19g, of which sugars 13.4g; Fat 39.6g, of which saturates 11.1g; Cholesterol 96mg; Calcium 83mg; Fibre 4.2g; Sodium 105m

Moussaka

This is a traditional eastern lediterranean dish, popular n both Greece and Turkey.

Serves 4

50ml/¼ pint/⅔ cup olive oil
large onion, chopped
–3 garlic cloves, finely chopped
75g/1½lb minced (ground) lamb
5ml/1 tbsp plain (all-purpose) flour
00g/14oz can chopped tomatoes
30ml/2 tbsp chopped mixed parsley, marjoram and oregano
salt and ground black pepper
450g/1lb aubergines (eggplants), thinly sliced

For the topping

300ml/½ pint/1¼ cups yogurt
2 eggs
25g/1oz feta cheese, crumbled
25g/1oz/⅓ cup Parmesan, grated

Heat 45ml/3 tbsp of the oil in a large, heavy pan. Fry the onion and garlic until softened, but not coloured. Add the lamb nd cook over high heat, stirring often, until browned.

2 Stir in the flour until mixed, then stir in the tomatoes, herbs nd seasoning. Bring to the boil, reduce the heat and simmer ently for 20 minutes.

3 Meanwhile, heat a little of the remaining oil in a large frying an. Add as many aubergine slices as can be laid in the pan, then ook until golden on both sides. Continue frying the aubergines n batches, adding oil as necessary.

4 Preheat the oven to 180°C/350°F/Gas 4. Arrange half the ubergine slices in a large, shallow ovenproof dish. Top with bout half of the meat and tomato mixture, then add the emaining aubergine slices. Spread the remaining meat mixture ver the aubergines.

Beat together the yogurt and eggs, then mix in the crumbled eta and grated Parmesan cheeses, pour the mixture over the neat and spread it evenly.

6 Transfer the moussaka to the preheated oven and bake for 35–40 minutes, or until golden and bubbling. Serve with a imple, mixed leaf green salad.

Shepherd's Pie

Economical and comforting this classic pie is sure to be a hit. You could add some finely chopped celery and frozen peas if you want to add some extra vegetables.

Serves 4

30ml/2 tbsp oil
1 onion, finely chopped
1 carrot, finely chopped
115g/4oz mushrooms, wiped and chopped
500g/1¼lb/2¼ cups lean minced (ground) lamb
300ml/½ pint/1¼ cups chicken stock or water
15ml/1 tbsp plain (all-purpose) flour
bay leaf
10–15ml/2–3 tsp Worcestershire sauce
15ml/1 tbsp tomato purée (paste)
salt and ground black pepper

For the topping

675g/1½lb potatoes, boiled
25g/1oz/2 tbsp butter
45ml/3 tbsp hot milk
15ml/1 tbsp chopped tarragon

1 Heat the oil in a large pan, add the onion, carrot and mushrooms and cook, stirring occasionally, until browned. Stir the lamb into the pan and cook, stirring to break up the lumps, until lightly browned.

2 Blend a few spoonfuls of the stock or water with the flour, then stir this mixture into the pan. Stir in the remaining stock or water and bring to a simmer, stirring.

3 Add the bay leaf, Worcestershire sauce and tomato purée, then cover and cook very gently for 1 hour, stirring occasionally. Uncover the pan towards the end of cooking to allow any excess water to evaporate, if necessary.

4 Preheat the oven to 190°C/375°F/Gas 5. Gently heat the potatoes for a couple of minutes, then mash with the butter, milk and seasoning, to taste.

5 Add the tarragon and seasoning to the mince, then pour into a pie dish. Cover the mince with an even layer of potato and mark the top with the prongs of a fork. Bake for about 25 minutes, until golden brown.

Moussaka Energy 588kcal/2444kJ; Protein 37.9g; Carbohydrate 14.8g, of which sugars 3.7g; Fat 40.9g, of which saturates 18.2g; Cholesterol 206mg; Calcium 379mg; Fibre 2.4g; Sodium 506mg
Shepherd's Pie Energy 426kcal/1788kJ; Protein 33.9g; Carbohydrate 39.2g, of which sugars 6.3g; Fat 15.9g, of which saturates 5.9g; Cholesterol 0mg; Calcium 66mg; Fibre 3.7g; Sodium 240mg

Lamb and Potato Pies

These tasty individual little pies are made with mutton, which is packed with flavour and much better value for money than lamb. Serve them hot with vegetables and onion gravy, or cold for a packed lunch.

Serves 4

450g/1lb boneless mutton
1 large onion, diced
2 carrots, diced
1 potato, diced
2 celery sticks, diced
1 egg, beaten
salt and ground black pepper

For the pastry

500g/1¼lb/5 cups plain (all-purpose) flour
250g/9oz/generous 1 cup cold butter, diced
pinch of salt
120ml/4fl oz/½ cup chilled water

1 To make the pastry, sieve (strain) the flour into a large bowl and add the salt. Rub the butter into the flour with the fingertips until it resembles coarse breadcrumbs. Mix in enough chilled water to bring the dough together. Turn on to a floured worktop and knead once or twice until smooth. Wrap in plastic wrap, and chill for 20 minutes before using.

2 Trim any fat or gristle from the meat and cut it up into very small pieces. Place in a large bowl and add the diced onion, carrots, potato and celery. Mix well and season to taste.

3 Preheat the oven to 180°C/350°F/Gas 4. Cut a third off the ball of pastry and reserve to make the lids of the pies. Roll out the rest and cut out six circles. Divide the meat mixture between the circles, piling it in the middle of each.

4 Roll out the remaining pastry and cut out six smaller circles, about 10cm/4in across. Lay these on top. Dampen the edges of the pastry bases, bring the pastry up around the meat, pleat it to fit the lid and pinch the edges together.

5 Make a small hole in the top of each pie, brush with beaten egg and slide the pies on to baking sheets. Bake for an hour, then serve hot or cold.

Mutton Hotpot

Cuts of mutton can be quite hard to come by today but it really is worth looking out for. Try your local farmers' market or ask your butcher if he could get it for you. Mutton often has a superior flavour to lamb, although it does require longer, slower cooking. Serve this casserole with steamed leafy greens.

Serves 6

6 mutton chops
6 lamb's kidneys
1 large onion, sliced
450g/1lb potatoes, peeled and thickly sliced
600ml/1 pint/2½ cups hot beef stock
salt and ground black pepper, to taste

1 Trim the mutton chops with a sharp knife leaving a little fat but removing any lumps or gristle or splintered bone.

2 Slice the lamb's kidneys in two horizontally and remove the fat and core with a pair of sharp scissors. Preheat the oven to 180°C/ 350°F/Gas 4.

3 Place three of the chops in a deep casserole and season well with salt and ground black pepper.

4 Add a layer of half the kidneys, then half the sliced onion and finally half of the sliced potatoes. Season lightly.

5 Repeat the process, seasoning as you go and making sure that you finish with an even layer of potatoes.

6 Heat the stock and pour it into the casserole, almost covering everything but leaving the potatoes just showing at the top.

7 Cover and cook in the preheated oven for 2 hours, removing the lid for the last 30 minutes to allow the potatoes to brown.

8 Before serving you may want to remove the mutton bones, which after the long cooking process will have lost all the meat. It improves the flavour of the gravy to cook the hotpot with the bones, but once cooked they can be removed.

Lamb Pies Energy 784kcal/3275kJ; Protein 25.1g; Carbohydrate 74.6g, of which sugars 5.2g; Fat 44.9g, of which saturates 26.1g; Cholesterol 178mg; Calcium 155mg; Fibre 4g; Sodium 345mg
Mutton Hotpot Energy 626kcal/2629kJ; Protein 76.9g; Carbohydrate 23.1g, of which sugars 5g; Fat 25.8g, of which saturates 11.6g; Cholesterol 374mg; Calcium 76mg; Fibre 2g; Sodium 269mg

Lamb Pot Roast

This slow-braised dish of ımb and tomatoes, spiced with cinnamon and stewed with green beans, has a Greek influence. It is good served with warm crusty bread to mop up the delicious juices.

Serves 8
kg/2¼lb lamb on the bone
garlic cloves, chopped
.5–5ml/½–1 tsp ground cumin
5ml/3 tbsp olive oil
juice of 1 lemon
2 onions, thinly sliced
about 500ml/17fl oz/2¼ cups lamb, beef or vegetable stock
75–90ml/5–6 tbsp tomato purée (paste)
1 cinnamon stick
2–3 pinches ground allspice
15–30ml/1–2 tbsp sugar
400g/14oz/scant 3 cups runner (green) beans, cut into 2.5cm/1in lengths
salt and ground black pepper
chopped fresh parsley, to garnish

1 Preheat the oven to 160°C/325°F/Gas 3. Coat the lamb with he garlic, cumin, olive oil, lemon juice, salt and pepper.

2 Heat a flameproof casserole. Sear the lamb on all sides, then ıdd the sliced onions and pour in enough stock to cover the neat. Stir in the tomato purée, spices and sugar. Cover, and ook the casserole in the oven for 2–3 hours.

3 Remove the casserole from the oven and remove the meat, our the stock into a pan. Return the lamb and onions to the asserole, and place back in the oven, to cook, uncovered, for further 20 minutes.

4 Meanwhile, add the beans to the stock and boil until the eans are tender. Slice the meat and serve with onions, the ravy and beans. Garnish with parsley and serve immediately.

Variation
You could substitute sliced courgettes for the runner (green) beans if you prefer. They will take less time to cook than the beans, so check them often during the cooking time.

Spicy North African Lamb with Prunes

This Moroccan-inspired dish is full of contrasting flavours that create a rich, spicy and fruity main course. For best results, use lamb that still retains some fat, as this will help keep the meat moist and succulent during roasting. Serve with couscous and seasonal vegetables.

Serves 4
675g/1½lb lamb fillet or shoulder steaks, cut into chunky pieces
5 small onions
7.5ml/1½ tsp harissa
115g/4oz ready-to-eat pitted prunes, halved
salt and ground black pepper, to taste

1 Preheat the oven to 200°C/400°F/Gas 6. Season the lamb with salt and ground black pepper. Heat a heavy frying pan, preferably non-stick, and cook the lamb on all sides until beginning to brown. Transfer to a roasting pan, reserving any fat in the frying pan.

2 Peel the onions and cut each into six wedges. Toss with the lamb and roast for about 30–40 minutes, until the lamb is cooked through and the onions are deep golden brown.

3 Transfer the cooked lamb and onions back into the frying pan. Mix the harissa with 250ml/8fl oz/1 cup boiling water and add to the roasting pan. Scrape up any residue left in the pan and pour the mixture over the lamb and onions.

4 Stir in the prunes and heat until just simmering. Cover and simmer for 5 minutes, then serve.

Cook's Tip
Cooking meat with dried fruit, such as prunes, is a very traditional North African combination, and the savoury meat and sweet prunes create a lovely depth of flavour. You can substitute ready-to-eat dried apricots, if you wish.

amb Pot Roast Energy 307kcal/1279kJ; Protein 28.4g; Carbohydrate 9.8g, of which sugars 8.5g; Fat 17.4g, of which saturates 6.8g; Cholesterol 103mg; Calcium 39mg; Fibre 1.9g; Sodium 83mg
African Lamb Energy 379kcal/1585kJ; Protein 35g; Carbohydrate 17.7g, of which sugars 15.4g; Fat 19.2g, of which saturates 8.8g; Cholesterol 128mg; Calcium 48mg; Fibre 3.1g; Sodium 151mg

Lamb and Carrot Casserole with Barley

Barley and carrots make natural partners for lamb. In this delicious casserole the barley bulks out the meat and adds to the flavour and texture as well as thickening the sauce. The simple dish is comfort food at its best. Serve with boiled potatoes and green vegetables.

Serves 6
675g/1½lb stewing lamb
15ml/1 tbsp oil
2 onions, sliced
675g/1½lb carrots, sliced
4–6 celery sticks, sliced
45ml/3 tbsp pearl barley, rinsed
lamb stock or water
salt and ground black pepper

1 Trim the lamb of any fat or gristle and cut it into bitesize pieces. Heat the oil in a flameproof casserole, add the lamb and toss until the lamb is browned all over.

2 Add the vegetables to the casserole and fry them briefly with the meat. Add the barley and enough stock or water to just cover, and season to taste.

3 Cover the casserole with foil, and then the lid, and simmer gently or cook in a slow oven, 150°C/300°F/Gas 2 for about 1–1½ hours until the meat is tender.

4 Add extra stock or water during cooking if necessary. Serve immediately with potatoes and vegetables.

5 Alternatively, allow the casserole to cool, then refrigerate or freeze until needed. This will allow the flavours to further mature and develop. Thaw, if necessary, and reheat until piping hot before serving.

Cook's Tip
Using water instead of stock produces a clean taste, but you might prefer the meatier, richer gravy that a good stock gives.

Braised Lamb Shanks with Cannellini Beans

Earthy and substantial, this is the ideal dish for chilly autumn evenings. The beans acquire additional layers of taste when slow-cooked in the rich sauce provided by the meat.

Serves 4–6
4 lamb shanks
45ml/3 tbsp plain (all-purpose) flour
45ml/3 tbsp olive oil
1 large onion, chopped
2 garlic cloves, sliced
1 celery stick, sliced
1 carrot, sliced
2 fresh rosemary sprigs
2 bay leaves
175ml/6fl oz/¾ cup white wine
30ml/2 tbsp tomato purée (paste)
225g/8oz/1¼ cups dried cannellini beans, soaked overnight in water to cover
salt and ground black pepper

1 Preheat the oven to 160°C/325°F/Gas 3. Season the lamb shanks and coat them lightly in flour. Heat the oil in a large flameproof casserole over high heat and brown the meat on all sides. Lift them out and set them aside.

2 Add the onion to the oil remaining in the casserole and sauté stir in the garlic, celery, carrot, rosemary and bay leaves.

3 Put the meat back in the pan and pour the wine slowly over it. Let it bubble and reduce, then stir in the tomato purée diluted in 450ml/¾ pint/scant 2 cups hot water.

4 Drain the beans and add them to the pan with black pepper. Mix well. Cover the casserole, and bake in the oven for 1 hour.

5 Stir in salt to taste and add 150ml/¼ pint/⅔ cup hot water. Cover and cook for 1 hour more, or until tender.

Cook's Tips
This dish will improve with time, so you could make it a day in advance, store in the refrigerator and then reheat.

Lamb Casserole Energy 304kcal/1263kJ; Protein 23.2g; Carbohydrate 13g, of which sugars 11.3g; Fat 18g, of which saturates 7.5g; Cholesterol 84mg; Calcium 53mg; Fibre 3.6g; Sodium 110mg
Lamb Shanks Energy 588kcal/2,465kJ; Protein 43.9g; Carbohydrate 39.9g, of which sugars 6.7g; Fat 26.2g, of which saturates 9.1g; Cholesterol 114mg; Calcium 110mg; Fibre 10.5g; Sodium 161mg

piced Lamb with Tomatoes ınd Peppers

elect lean tender lamb from
ıe leg for this lightly spiced
urry with succulent peppers
ıd wedges of onion. Serve
arm naan or pitta bread, or
ome boiled rice to mop up
ıe tomato-rich juices.

erves 6

5kg/3¼lb boneless lamb, cubed
50ml/8fl oz/1 cup natural (plain) yogurt
0ml/2 tbsp sunflower oil
onions
2 red (bell) peppers, seeded and cut into chunks
3 garlic cloves, finely chopped
1 fresh red chilli, seeded and chopped
2.5cm/1in piece fresh root ginger, peeled and chopped
30ml/2 tbsp mild curry paste
2 x 400g/14oz cans chopped tomatoes
large pinch of saffron strands
800g/1¾lb plum tomatoes, halved, seeded and cut into chunks
salt and ground black pepper

Mix the lamb with the yogurt in a bowl. Cover and chill for ɔout 1 hour. Heat the oil in a large pan. Drain the lamb and ɘserve the yogurt, then cook the lamb in batches until it is olden on all sides. Remove from the pan and set aside.

Cut two of the onions into wedges and add to the oil ɘmaining in the pan. Fry for about 10 minutes, until they begin ɔ colour. Add the peppers and cook for a further 5 minutes. emove the vegetables from the pan and set aside.

Chop the remaining onion. Add it to the pan with the garlic, hilli and ginger, and cook, stirring, until softened. Stir in the curry aste and tomatoes with the reserved marinade. Replace the mb, add seasoning to taste and stir. Bring to the boil, reduce ıe heat and simmer for 30 minutes.

Pound the saffron to a powder in a mortar, then stir in a little oiling water to dissolve it. Add to the curry, together with the nion and pepper mixture. Stir the fresh tomatoes into the pan ıd bring back to simmering point. Cook for 15 minutes more efore serving with warmed bread, or rice.

Lamb Meatballs

These flavoursome meatballs contain an exciting mixture of flavours and textures. Serve with lemon, a salad and some creamy yogurt.

Serves 6

250g/9oz/generous 1 cup lean minced (ground) lamb
1 onion, finely chopped
2 garlic cloves, crushed
10–15ml/2–3 tsp cinnamon
30ml/2 tbsp pine nuts
30ml/2 tbsp currants, soaked in warm water for 5–10 minutes
5ml/1 tsp paprika
2 slices of day-old white or brown bread, processed into crumbs
1 egg, lightly beaten
15ml/1 tbsp tomato ketchup
1 bunch each of fresh flat leaf parsley and dill
60ml/4 tbsp flour
sunflower oil, for frying
salt and ground black pepper
lemon wedges, to serve

1 In a bowl, pound the lamb with the onion, garlic and cinnamon. Knead with your hands then add the pine nuts with the currants, paprika, breadcrumbs, egg and ketchup. Season with salt and pepper.

2 Finely chop the herbs, reserving a few sprigs of parsley for the garnish, and knead into the mixture.

3 Take apricot-size portions of the mixture in your hands and roll into balls. Flatten each ball so that it resembles a thick disc, then coat lightly in the flour.

4 Heat the oil in a heavy pan. Fry the meatballs in batches for 8–10 minutes, turning half way through cooking, until browned on all sides. Remove and drain on kitchen paper and keep warm. When all are cooked, serve hot with lemon wedges.

Variation
For a delicious spicy meatball sandwich, shape the mixture into small balls, cook as above for 5–6 minutes, then tuck the browned meatballs into toasted pitta bread pockets with sliced red onion, finely chopped flat leaf parsley and tahini.

piced Lamb Energy 559kcal/2343kJ; Protein 54.4g; Carbohydrate 20.5g, of which sugars 18.8g; Fat 29.6g, of which saturates 13.5g; Cholesterol 191mg; Calcium 139mg; Fibre 4.6g; Sodium 278mg
amb Meatballs Energy 261kcal/1088kJ; Protein 11.4g; Carbohydrate 15.4g, of which sugars 5.2g; Fat 17.5g, of which saturates 4g; Cholesterol 64mg; Calcium 40mg; Fibre 0.7g; Sodium 129mg

Stuffed Lamb with Glazed Onions

Boning and stuffing a joint of lamb makes it easier to carve and there is less wastage. The glazed onions are a lovely accompaniment.

Serves 6–8

1 celery stick
1 bunch fresh parsley
2.25kg/5lb shoulder of lamb, boned, with bone removed, but reserved for the stock
1 carrot
1 leek
1 onion
1 bunch fresh parsley, chopped
2 garlic cloves, chopped
2–3 rosemary sprigs
60ml/4 tbsp potato flour
salt and ground black pepper

For the glazed onions
25g/1oz/2tbsp butter
675g/1½lb shallots or small onions, peeled
30ml/2 tbsp sugar

1 Tie the celery and bunch of parsley together with string. Put in a large pan with the lamb bone, carrot, leek, onion, and plenty of salt and black pepper. Add water to cover, bring to the boil, then reduce the heat and simmer for 2 hours. Strain, cool and remove the fat from the top of the stock.

2 Preheat the oven to 190°/C350°F/Gas 4. Open out the lamb and spread the chopped parsley, garlic and rosemary over the surface. Season with salt and pepper. Roll up and secure with string. Add enough stock in the pan to cover the base. Roast for 1–1½ hours, basting often with the cooking juices, until tender.

3 To make the glazed onions, melt the butter in a large pan. Add the onions and shake to coat. Cook over low heat for 15–20 minutes until tender. Add the sugar, shaking the pan, and cook for a further 5–10 minutes until slightly caramelized. Set aside and keep warm.

4 When the meat is cooked, remove from the roasting pan, and leave to rest. Add a little of the reserved stock to the roasting pan, and heat to deglaze, then stir in the potato flour and gradually add 800ml/1 pint 7fl oz/3¼ cups of the stock. Cook, stirring, until thickened. Season to taste. Serve the meat in thick slices, accompanied by the onions, and a little drizzle of gravy.

Spiced Pork Roast with Apple and Thyme Cream Sauce

Belly of pork is a budget cut, which, when slowly cooked, makes a tasty and tender roasting joint.

Serves 6

75g/3oz/6 tbsp butter
1 medium onion, finely chopped
3 garlic cloves, crushed
bunch of fresh herbs, chopped
225g/8oz/4 cups breadcrumbs
1 egg, beaten
15ml/1 tbsp oil
pork belly joint, about 1.3kg/3lb
salt and ground black pepper

For the spice paste
25g/1oz/2 tbsp butter, melted
30ml/2 tbsp mild mustard
30ml/2 tbsp chutney
15ml/1 tbsp lemon juice
2 garlic cloves, crushed

For the apple and cream sau
2 cooking apples, peeled and cor
1 medium onion, chopped
2 garlic cloves, crushed
150ml/¼ pint/⅔ cup cider
150ml/¼ pint/⅔ cup stock
300ml/½ pint/1¼ cups single (light) cream

1 Gently melt the butter in a medium pan, then add the finely chopped onion and garlic and cook for 5 minutes, until soft.

2 Add the chopped herbs, breadcrumbs, salt and pepper to th pan and mix well to combine. Cool slightly then mix in the egg Preheat the oven to 150°C/300°F/Gas 2.

3 Spread the stuffing over the meat, then roll it up and tie it with cotton string. In a small bowl, combine the spice paste ingredients, and then liberally brush it over the joint.

4 Brown the meat in the oil in a hot roasting pan on the stove then put in the oven and cook for 3 hours. Halfway through cooking turn the joint and brush with the spicy paste again.

5 To make the apple and cream sauce, put the apples, onion an garlic in a large pan and add the cider and stock. Bring to the boil and simmer for 15 minutes, stir in the single cream and then blend until smooth. To serve, cut the meat into slices and serve with the hot sauce.

Stuffed Lamb Energy 731kcal/3033kJ; Protein 41.9g; Carbohydrate 17.6g, of which sugars 10g; Fat 53.7g, of which saturates 27g; Cholesterol 205mg; Calcium 65mg; Fibre 1.4g; Sodium 178mg
Spiced Pork Roast Energy 814kcal/3409kJ; Protein 73.2g; Carbohydrate 41.9g, of which sugars 12.6g; Fat 39.8g, of which saturates 20.2g; Cholesterol 264mg; Calcium 145mg; Fibre 2.4g; Sodium 581m

tir-fried Pork with Chilli nd Scrambled Egg

his tasty combination of ce, pork and Asian flavours a meal in itself, perfect hen you are in a hurry or r a mid-week supper. Use ork belly for a more conomical verison, if you ish, but with such a small nount of meat you could so use the more expensive let. Add green beans or aby corn if you like.

erves 4

)0g/1¼lb/2½ cups long grain rice
45ml/3 tbsp vegetable oil
1 onion, chopped
15ml/1 tbsp finely chopped garlic
115g/4oz lean pork, cut into small cubes
2 eggs, beaten
30ml/2 tbsp Thai fish sauce
15ml/1 tbsp dark soy sauce
2.5ml/½ tsp caster (superfine) sugar
4 spring onions (scallions), finely sliced, to garnish
2 fresh red chillies, sliced, to garnish
1 lime, cut into wedges, to garnish

Cook the rice according to the instructions on the packet. rain thoroughly. On a work surface, spread the rice out on a ean dish towel to cool.

Heat the oil in a wok or large frying pan. Add the onion and rlic and cook for about 2 minutes, until softened.

Add the pork to the softened onion and garlic. Stir-fry until e pork changes colour and is cooked through.

Add the eggs and cook, stirring all the time, until scrambled to small lumps. Add the drained rice and continue to stir and ss, to coat it with the oil and prevent it from sticking.

Stir the fish sauce, soy sauce and sugar in to the wok, and mix ell. Continue to fry until the rice is thoroughly heated.

Spoon into warmed individual bowls and serve, garnished th sliced spring onions, chillies and lime wedges.

Sweet and Sour Thai-style Pork with Vegetables

The fresh flavours, attractive colours and crisp textures of the fruit and vegetables combined with tender pork in this dish are a treat for the eyes and the stomach. Serve on its own or with some plain egg noodles. You could also serve plain rice as an accompaniment.

Serves 4

175g/6oz lean pork
30ml/2 tbsp vegetable oil
4 garlic cloves, thinly sliced
1 small red onion, sliced
30ml/2 tbsp Thai fish sauce
15ml/1 tbsp sugar
1 red (bell) pepper, seeded and diced
½ cucumber, seeded and very thinly sliced
2 plum tomatoes, cut into wedges
115g/4oz piece fresh pineapple, cut into small chunks
2 spring onions (scallions), cut into short lengths
egg noodles, to serve
coriander (cilantro) leaves and spring onions (scallions), shredded, to serve (optional)
ground black pepper

1 Cut the pork into very thin strips. This is easier to do if you place it in the freezer it for 15 minutes first.

2 Heat the oil in a wok or large frying pan. Add the garlic. Cook over medium heat until golden, then add the pork and stir-fry for 4–5 minutes. Add the onion slices and toss to mix.

3 Add the fish sauce, sugar and ground black pepper to taste. Toss the mixture over the heat for 3–4 minutes more.

4 Stir in the red pepper, cucumber, tomatoes, pineapple and spring onions. Stir-fry for 3–4 minutes more.

5 Meanwhile, cook the egg noodles, following the instructions on the packet. Drain thoroughly.

6 When the pork and vegetables are all piping hot, spoon into serving bowls. Garnish with the fresh coriander and spring onions and serve with the noodles.

r-fried Pork Energy 602kcal/2512kJ; Protein 18.8g; Carbohydrate 101.3g, of which sugars 1.1g; Fat 12.8g, of which saturates 2.2g; Cholesterol 113mg; Calcium 45mg; Fibre 0.2g; Sodium 323mg
ai-style Pork Energy 211kcal/885kJ; Protein 20g; Carbohydrate 12.4g, of which sugars 11.8g; Fat 9.4g, of which saturates 2g; Cholesterol 55mg; Calcium 29mg; Fibre 1.8g; Sodium 68mg

Mexican Pork Casserole

Inspired by South American cooking, a paste or 'mole' of chilli, shallots and nuts is added to this casserole.

Serves 6

25ml/1½ tbsp flour
1kg/2¼lb shoulder of pork, cubed
2 large onions, chopped
2 garlic cloves, chopped
600ml/1 pint/2½ cups white wine
115g/4oz ready-to-eat prunes
115g/4oz ready-to-eat apricots
grated rind and juice of 1 orange
salt and ground black pepper
boiled rice, to serve

For the mole

3 medium-hot dried red chillies
75–90ml/5–6 tbsp olive oil
2 shallots, chopped
2 garlic cloves, chopped
1 fresh green chilli, chopped
10ml/2 tsp ground coriander
5ml/1 tsp mild paprika
50g/2oz/½ cup toasted almonds
2.5ml/½ tsp dried oregano

1 Make the mole. Toast the chillies in a dry pan over low heat for 1–2 minutes, then soak in warm water for 30 minutes. Drain, reserving the water, and discard the stalks and seeds.

2 Heat 30ml/2 tbsp oil in a small frying pan and fry the shallots, garlic, fresh green chilli and ground coriander over medium heat for 5 minutes. Transfer the shallot mixture to a food processor or blender and add the drained chillies, paprika, almonds, oregano, and 45–60ml/3–4 tbsp of the chilli soaking liquid to make a paste. Preheat the oven to 160°C/325°F/Gas 3.

3 Season the flour with salt and black pepper, then coat the pork with it. Heat 60ml/4 tbsp of the olive oil in a casserole and fry the pork, until sealed on all sides. Remove from the pan.

4 Add the onions and garlic to the pan, and fry until golden. Add the wine, 100ml/7 tbsp water, and half the mole paste. Bring back to the boil and bubble for a few seconds, then return the pork to the pan. Cover and cook in the oven for 1½ hours.

5 Increase the oven to 180°C/350°F/Gas 4. Add the prunes, apricots and orange juice. Season, cover and cook for about 30 minutes. Add the remaining mole and orange rind, and serve.

Stewed Pork with Chickpeas and Orange

This healthy and colourful dish is perfect comfort food on a cold winter day. Adding any kind of beans or pulses to a meat dish helps it go further, and adds bulk and flavour to the dish.

Serves 4

350g/12oz/1¾ cups dried chickpeas, soaked overnight in plenty of cold water
75–90ml/5–6 tbsp olive oil
675g/1½lb boneless leg of pork, cut into large cubes
1 large onion, sliced
2 garlic cloves, chopped
400g/14oz can chopped plum tomatoes
grated rind of 1 orange
1 small dried red chilli
salt and ground black pepper, to taste

1 Drain the chickpeas, rinse them under cold water and drain them again. Place them in a large pan. Pour in cold water to cover, cover and bring to the boil. Skim the surface, replace the lid and cook gently for 1–1½ hours, until the chickpeas are soft Drain, reserving the cooking liquid, and set them aside.

2 Heat the olive oil in the clean pan and brown the meat cube in batches. As each cube browns, lift it out with a slotted spoor and put it on a plate.

3 When all the meat cubes have been browned, add the onior to the oil remaining in the pan and sauté until light golden. Stir in the garlic, then as soon as it becomes aromatic, add the tomatoes and orange rind.

4 Crumble in the chilli. Return the chickpeas and meat to the pan, and pour in enough of the reserved cooking liquid to cove Add the black pepper, but not salt at this stage otherwise the beans will become tough.

5 Cover the pan and simmer for 1 hour, or until the meat is tender. Stir occasionally and add more reserved liquid if neede The result should be a moist casserole. Add salt before serving

Mexican Casserole Energy 468kcal/1956kJ; Protein 38.8g; Carbohydrate 17.1g, of which sugars 16.9g; Fat 20.7g, of which saturates 4g; Cholesterol 105mg; Calcium 64mg; Fibre 2.9g; Sodium 134mg
Stewed Pork Energy 663kcal/2,781kJ; Protein 56.7g; Carbohydrate 54.4g, of which sugars 11g; Fat 25.7g, of which saturates 4.9g; Cholesterol 106mg; Calcium 184mg; Fibre 11.8g; Sodium 164m

ork Belly with Five Spices

ılthough five-spice powder a Chinese blend, it has een adopted by Thai cuisine, which a balance of the five avours is also important. ork belly is not only an conomical cut, it is also rich fat and flavour, and so a mall amount of it goes a ng way. After the meat has een braised in the intense ock, it is tender and elicious, and will easily feed our people well, served with oiled rice.

Serves 4

1 large bunch coriander (cilantro) with roots (if possible)
30ml/2 tbsp vegetable oil
1 garlic clove, crushed
30ml/2 tbsp Chinese five-spice powder
500g/1¼lb pork belly, cut into 2.5cm/1in pieces
400g/14oz can chopped tomatoes
150ml/¼ pint/⅔ cup hot water
30ml/2 tbsp dark soy sauce
45ml/3 tbsp nam pla
30ml/2 tbsp sugar
1 lime and boiled rice, to serve

Cut off the coriander roots. Chop five of them finely and eeze the remainder for another occasion. Chop the coriander alks and leaves and set them aside.

Heat the oil in a large pan and cook the garlic until golden rown. Stirring constantly, add the chopped coriander roots and ıen the five-spice powder.

Add the pork and stir-fry until the meat is thoroughly coated spices and has browned. Stir in the tomatoes and hot water. ring to the boil, then stir in the soy sauce, nam pla and sugar.

Reduce the heat, cover the pan and simmer for 20 minutes, ıen remove the lid and cook for a further 10 minutes, or until the liquid has reduced. Stir in the chopped coriander stalks nd leaves, squeeze over the lime juice and serve with rice.

Cook's Tip

Make sure that you buy Chinese five-spice powder, as the Indian variety is made up from quite different spices.

Roast Belly of Pork with Root Vegetables

Nothing quite compares with the rich flavour of belly of pork, particularly when it is slowly roasted in the oven until tender with a crisp layer of crackling.

Serves 4–6

1 small swede (rutabaga), weighing about 500g/1lb 2oz
1 onion
1 parsnip
2 carrots
15ml/1 tbsp olive oil
1.5kg/3lb 6oz piece pork belly, well scored
15ml/1 tbsp fresh thyme leaves or 5ml/1 tsp dried thyme
sea salt flakes and ground black pepper

1 Preheat the oven to 220°C/425°F/Gas 7. Cut the vegetables into 2cm/¾in cubes and stir them with the oil in a roasting pan until evenly coated. Pour in 300ml/½ pint/1¼ cups water.

2 Sprinkle the pork rind with thyme, salt and pepper, rubbing them well into the scored slashes. Place the pork on top of the vegetables with the skin side uppermost.

3 Put the pork and vegetables into the hot oven and cook for 30 minutes, by which time the liquid will have almost evaporated to leave a golden crust in the bottom of the pan.

4 Add 600ml/1 pint/2½ cups cold water to the vegetables in the pan. Reduce the oven to 180°C/350°F/Gas 4, and cook for 1½ hours, or until the pork is tender and the juices run clear when the centre of the meat is pierced with a sharp knife. Check during the final 30 minutes to make sure the liquid has not dried up, and add a little extra water if necessary.

5 If the crackling is not yet crisp enough, increase the oven temperature to 220°C/425°F/Gas 7 and continue cooking for another 10–20 minutes, adding extra water if necessary.

6 With a sharp knife, slice off the crackling. Serve it with thick slices of the pork, some vegetables and the juices spooned over.

ork Belly Energy 581kcal/2405kJ; Protein 20.6g; Carbohydrate 11.6g, of which sugars 11.5g; Fat 50.5g, of which saturates 17.1g; Cholesterol 90mg; Calcium 71mg; Fibre 2.3g; Sodium 1109mg
oast Pork Energy 1014kcal/4194kJ; Protein 39.5g; Carbohydrate 9.4g, of which sugars 7.3g; Fat 91.2g, of which saturates 33.1g; Cholesterol 180mg; Calcium 81mg; Fibre 3.3g; Sodium 202mg

Bacon Chops with Apple and Cider Sauce

Either thick cured bacon or fresh pork chops could be used in this recipe, depending on the cost of what is available. Serve the chops with lots of creamy mashed potatoes and steamed buttered cabbage.

Serves 4

15ml/1 tbsp oil
4 bacon chops
1 or 2 cooking apples
knob (pat) of butter
1 or 2 garlic cloves, finely chopped
150ml/¼ pint/⅔ cup dry (hard) cider
5ml/1 tsp sugar
5ml/1 tsp cider vinegar
15ml/1 tbsp wholegrain mustard
10ml/2 tsp chopped fresh thyme
sprigs of thyme, to garnish
salt and ground black pepper, to taste

1 Heat the oil in a large, heavy frying pan, over medium heat, add the bacon chops and fry for 10–15 minutes, browning well on both sides.

2 Peel, core and slice the apples. Remove the chops from the pan and keep warm. Add the butter and apples to the pan and cook until the juices begin to brown.

3 Add the finely chopped garlic and sugar to the pan, and cook for 1 minute, then stir in the cider, cider vinegar, mustard and chopped thyme. Boil for a few minutes until the liquid has reduced to a saucy consistency, then return the chops to the pan for a final 1–2 minutes, turning once.

4 Season to taste, if necessary, and place the chops and sauce on warmed serving plates. Garnish with thyme and serve.

Cook's Tip

If you make shallow cuts in the fat with a sharp knife, it will stop the chops curling up as they cook. It also helps them cook evenly, and allows the fat to render and crisp.

Sausage and Pepper Stew

Bursting with flavour, this stunning yet simple recipe makes a fabulous brunch or lazy lunch dish. Sausages are a great budget standby, and are popular with adults and children alike. Serve this stew with plenty of warm, crusty bread.

Serves 4

675g/1½lb red and green (bell) peppers
75ml/5 tbsp olive oil
500g/1¼lb spicy sausages (such as Italian garlic sausages, Merguez or Toulouse sausages), sliced into thick chunks
400g/14oz tomatoes, skinned and roughly sliced
5ml/1 tsp dried oregano
150ml/¼ pint/⅔ cup hot water
45ml/3 tbsp chopped fresh flat leaf parsley
salt and ground black pepper, to taste
chopped fresh thyme, to garnish
warm, crusty bread, to serve

1 Halve and seed the peppers and cut them into quarters. Hea the olive oil in a frying pan, add the prepared peppers and saute them over medium heat for 10–15 minutes until they start to brown, then transfer to a large pan.

2 Add the sausages to the frying pan, and fry briefly, turning them frequently, to get rid of the excess fat but not to cook them. As soon as they are brown, remove from the pan with a slotted spoon and drain on kitchen paper.

3 Add the tomatoes, sausages and oregano to the peppers in the pan. Stir in the water and season with salt and pepper, then cover the pan and cook gently for about 30 minutes, until the sausages are cooked through and the sauce has reduced.

4 Mix the fresh parsley into the stew, taste and add seasoning if necessary, then garnish with fresh thyme and serve piping hot, with warm crusty bread.

Cook's Tip

Use ordinary pork sausages if you can't find spicy ones.

Bacon Chops Energy 285kcal/1190kJ; Protein 26.4g; Carbohydrate 6.5g, of which sugars 6.5g; Fat 16.1g, of which saturates 5.4g; Cholesterol 40mg; Calcium 17mg; Fibre 0.8g; Sodium 1340mg
Sausage Stew Energy 573kcal/2,378kJ; Protein 14.8g; Carbohydrate 28.9g, of which sugars 15.9g; Fat 45g, of which saturates 14.7g; Cholesterol 50mg; Calcium 106mg; Fibre 5g; Sodium 1,033mg

Potato, Parsnip and Sausage Bake

This easy-to-make bake combines top-quality sausages, onions, garlic and potatoes to create a warming and sustaining dish that is perfect for a cold winter's day. The addition of some economical and seasonal parsnips makes the dish more substantial, and they also help to soak up all the delicious wine-flavoured juices. Serve with seasonal cabbage or broccoli.

Serves 6

15ml/1 tbsp vegetable oil
2 large onions, chopped
1 large leek, washed and sliced
2 garlic cloves, crushed
8 large pork sausages
2 large potatoes, thinly sliced
2 large parsnips, thinly sliced
1.5ml/¼ tsp fresh sage
150ml/¼ pint/½ cup white wine
150ml/¼ pint/½ cup vegetable or chicken stock
salt and ground black pepper, to taste

1 Preheat the oven to 180°C/350°F/Gas 4. Grease a large shallow ovenproof dish and set aside.

2 Heat the vegetable oil in a frying pan. Add the onions and leeks and cook for about 5–6 minutes, until golden. Add the garlic and cook for a further 1 minute, then remove the mixture from the pan and set aside.

3 Add the sausages to the pan and cook on medium heat, turning from time to time, for 5–6 minutes, until golden.

4 Arrange the sliced potatoes and parsnips in the base of the prepared dish. Spoon the onion and leek mixture on top of the potatoes and parsnips. Season with the salt and pepper and sprinkle with the fresh sage.

5 Mix the white wine and stock together in a jug (pitcher) and then gently pour into the dish. Top with the sausages.

6 Cover and bake for 50 minutes, until most of the stock has been reduced. Remove the cover and return to the oven for about 10 minutes to brown the top. Serve hot, with some seasonal greens for a complete meal.

)ublin Coddle

his simple dish is thought ɔ date back to the early 700s, and was left to bubble ently on the stove for as ng as necessary, while the ouseholders were out orking. The name 'coddle' is ought to come from the ench 'caudle' to cook owly. It combines layers of acon and sausages, and is est with a green vegetable, ıd a glass of Guinness.

Serves 6

6 x 8mm/⅓in thick ham or dry-cured bacon slices
6 best-quality lean pork sausages, cut in half if you wish
4 large onions, thickly sliced
900g/2lb potatoes, peeled and thickly sliced
90ml/6 tbsp chopped fresh flat leaf parsley
salt and ground black pepper, to taste

Cut the ham or bacon into chunks and cook with the usages in a large pan containing 1.2 litres/2 pints/5 cups boiling ater for 5 minutes. Drain, but reserve the cooking liquor.

Place half the onions at the bottom of a casserole, then add ılf the ham or bacon, then half the sausages, followed by half e sliced potatoes.

Season, sprinkle in half the parsley, and then repeat the layers, ishing with a tight layer of potatoes. Slowly pour in just ough of the reserved cooking liquor to cover completely.

Lay a piece of buttered foil or baking parchment on top of e mixture in the pan, then cover with a tight-fitting lid.

Simmer over very low heat for about 1 hour, until the liquid reduced and all the ingredients are cooked. Sprinkle the served parsley over the coddle, and serve.

Cook's Tip

It is important for the flavour of this dish to use good-quality pork sausages, and bacon.

ıblin Coddle Energy 336kcal/1409kJ; Protein 12.7g; Carbohydrate 39.3g, of which sugars 9g; Fat 15.4g, of which saturates 6.2g; Cholesterol 33mg; Calcium 80mg; Fibre 3.6g; Sodium 695mg
tato Bake Energy 451kcal/1879kJ; Protein 14g; Carbohydrate 35.2g, of which sugars 7.5g; Fat 29.2g, of which saturates 10.5g; Cholesterol 44mg; Calcium 61mg; Fibre 2.9g; Sodium 844mg

Lamb's Liver, Onion and Bacon Casserole

The trick when cooking liver is to seal it quickly, then simmer it gently and briefly. Prolonged and/or fierce cooking makes liver hard and grainy. Liver, onions and bacon, served in a rich gravy, is a traditional and nutritious dish that goes back several hundred years, when offal was a much bigger part of the general diet. Boiled new potatoes tossed in butter go well with this casserole.

Serves 4

30ml/2 tbsp sunflower oil
225g/8oz rindless unsmoked back (lean) bacon rashers (strips), cut into pieces
2 onions, halved and sliced
175g/6oz/2⅓ cups chestnut mushrooms, wiped clean and halved
450g/1lb lamb's liver, trimmed and sliced
25g/1oz/2 tbsp butter
15ml/1 tbsp soy sauce
30ml/2 tbsp plain (all-purpose) flour
150ml/¼ pint/⅔ cup chicken stock
salt and ground black pepper, to taste

1 Heat the oil in a frying pan and cook the bacon until crisp. Add the onions to the pan and cook for about 10 minutes, stirring frequently, or until softened. Add the mushrooms to the pan and cook for a further 1 minute.

2 Use a slotted spoon to remove the bacon and vegetables from the pan and set aside.

3 Add the liver to the pan and cook over high heat for about 3–4 minutes, turning once to seal the slices on both sides. Remove the liver from the pan and keep warm.

4 Melt the butter in the pan, add the soy sauce and flour and blend together. Stir in the stock and bring to the boil, stirring until thickened. Return the liver and vegetables to the pan and heat through for 1 minute. Season with salt and planty of ground black pepper to taste, and serve with new potatoes and lightly cooked green beans.

Pan-fried Calf's Liver with Crispy Onions

Calf's liver is a an excellent budget cut, and has a lovely dense flavour, which is beautifully complemented with sweet fried onions and crisp sautéed potatoes. Serve a salad of mixed leaves with plenty of delicate fresh herbs, such as fennel, dill and parsley, to complement the simple flavours of this main course.

Serves 4

50g/2oz/¼ cup butter
4 onions, finely sliced
5ml/1 tsp sugar
4 slices calf's liver, each weighing about 115g/4oz
30ml/2 tbsp plain (all-purpose) flour
30ml/2 tbsp olive oil
salt and ground black pepper
chopped fresh parsley, to garnish
sautéed potatoes, to serve

1 Melt the butter in a large, heavy pan with a lid. Add the onions and mix well to coat with butter. Cover the pan with a lid and cook gently for 10 minutes, stirring occasionally. Stir in the sugar and cover the pan.

2 Cook the onions for a further 10 minutes, or until they are soft and golden. Increase the heat, remove the lid and stir the onions over high heat, until they are deep gold and crisp.

3 Use a draining spoon to remove the onions from the pan, draining off the fat. Keep warm.

4 Meanwhile, rinse the calf's liver in cold water and pat it dry on kitchen paper. Season the flour, put it on a plate and turn th slices of liver in it until they are lightly coated in flour.

5 Heat the oil in a large frying pan, on high heat until smoking, add the liver and cook for just 2 minutes on each side, or until lightly browned and just firm.

6 Arrange the liver on warmed plates, together with the crisp onions. Garnish with chopped fresh parsley and serve with sautéed potatoes.

Liver Casserole Energy 440kcal/1832kJ; Protein 35g; Carbohydrate 14.3g, of which sugars 6.1g; Fat 27.4g, of which saturates 9.4g; Cholesterol 527mg; Calcium 50mg; Fibre 2.1g; Sodium 1259r
Pan-fried Calf's Liver Energy 315kcal/1310kJ; Protein 22.7g; Carbohydrate 11.8g, of which sugars 4.4g; Fat 19.9g, of which saturates 8.5g; Cholesterol 452mg; Calcium 39mg; Fibre 1.3g; Sodium 160n

Lamb's Kidneys and Bacon with Sherry

‹idneys cooked in sherry nake an excellent family upper served with some oiled new potatoes.

Serves 4

2 plump lamb's kidneys
Oml/4 tbsp olive oil
15g/4oz smoked bacon lardons
large onion, finely chopped
2 garlic cloves, finely chopped
30ml/2 tbsp plain (all-purpose) flour
150ml/¼ pint/⅔ cup fino sherry
15ml/1 tbsp tomato purée (paste)
30ml/2 tbsp chopped fresh parsley
salt and ground black pepper, to taste
new potatoes, boiled and buttered, to serve (optional)

Halve and skin the kidneys, then remove the cores. Cut the idneys into cubes.

: Heat half the oil in a large frying pan and fry the bacon until ne fat starts to run. Add the onion and garlic and fry until oftened. Remove the onion and bacon to a plate.

: Add the remaining oil to the pan and divide the kidneys into our batches. Put in one handful, and stir-fry over high heat until ealed. (They should not give off any juice.) Remove to a varmed covered plate and repeat until they are all cooked.

Return the onion and bacon mixture to the pan. Sprinkle with our and cook, stirring gently. Add the sherry and stir until hickened. Add the tomato purée and parsley.

Return the kidneys to the pan, and heat gently. Season well nd serve hot with buttered new potatoes, if you like.

Cook's Tip
Kidneys are packed with goodness as well as flavour, and are extremely good value for money. Look for ones that are firm, with an even colour. Avoid those with a dull surface.

Lamb's Kidneys with Creamy Mustard Sauce

This piquant recipe is simple and flexible, so the exact amounts of the ingredients can be adapted to your taste or what you have in the storecupboard. It would be suitable as a supper dish for two or four, in which case rice and green salad make a good accompaniment.

Serves 4

4–6 lamb's kidneys
butter, for frying
10ml/2 tsp Dijon mustard or other mild mustard, to taste
250ml/8fl oz/1 cup white wine
5ml/1 tsp chopped fresh mixed herbs, such as rosemary, thyme, parsley and chives
1 small garlic clove, crushed
about 30ml/2 tbsp single (light) cream
salt and ground black pepper, to taste
fresh parsley, to garnish

1 Skin the kidneys and slice them horizontally. Remove the cores with scissors, and then wash them thoroughly in plenty of cold water. Drain and dry off with kitchen paper.

2 Heat a little butter in a heavy frying pan and gently cook the kidneys in it for a few minute, until cooked as you like them. Remove the kidneys from the pan and keep warm.

3 Add a spoonful of mustard to the pan with the wine, herbs and garlic. Simmer to reduce by about half, then add enough cream to make a smooth sauce.

4 Return the kidneys to their sauce and reheat gently, without cooking any further, or the kidneys will be tough. Serve garnished with parsley, and with rice or a green salad.

Variation
If you prefer a sauce that has a bit more heat, you can add 5ml/1 tsp English (hot) mustard as well as the Dijon mustard to the creamy sauce.

idneys with Sherry Energy 542kcal/2246kJ; Protein 26g; Carbohydrate 1.1g, of which sugars 1g; Fat 48.3g, of which saturates 25.1g; Cholesterol 566mg; Calcium 29mg; Fibre 0g; Sodium 609mg
dneys with Mustard Energy 138kcal/578kJ; Protein 15.6g; Carbohydrate 0.6g, of which sugars 0.6g; Fat 3.8g, of which saturates 1.7g; Cholesterol 288mg; Calcium 20mg; Fibre 0g; Sodium 140mg

Braised Oxtail

While oxtail requires long, slow cooking to tenderize the meat, the resulting flavour is rich and well worth the effort. Braised oxtail is traditionally served with plain boiled potatoes to soak up the rich gravy, though mashed potatoes would be good too.

Serves 6

2 oxtails, total weight about 1.5kg/3lb 6oz, cut into pieces
30ml/2 tbsp flour seasoned with salt and pepper
45ml/3 tbsp oil
2 large onions, sliced
2 celery sticks, sliced
4 medium carrots, sliced
1 litre/1¾ pints/4 cups beef stock
15ml/1 tbsp tomato purée (paste)
finely grated rind of 1 small orange
2 bay leaves
few sprigs of fresh thyme
salt and ground black pepper
chopped fresh parsley, to garnish

1 Preheat the oven to 150°C/300°F/Gas 2. Coat the pieces of oxtail in the seasoned flour, shaking off and reserving any excess.

2 Heat 30ml/2 tbsp oil in a large flameproof casserole and add the oxtail in batches, cooking quickly until browned all over. Lift out and set aside. Add the remaining oil to the pan, and stir in the onions, celery and carrots.

3 Cook the vegetables quickly, stirring occasionally, until beginning to brown. Tip in any reserved flour then add the stock, tomato purée and orange rind.

4 Heat until bubbles begin to rise to the surface, then add the herbs, cover and put into the hot oven. Cook for 3½–4 hours until the oxtail is very tender. Remove from the oven and leave to stand, covered, for 10 minutes before skimming off the surface fat. Adjust the seasoning and garnish with parsley.

Cook's Tip
This dish benefits from being made in advance. When cooled completely, any fat can be removed before reheating.

Haggis with Clapshot Cake

This is a traditional way of serving haggis, with turnip and potato clapshot – a variation on the traditional accompaniment of neeps and tatties; simply mashed turnips and potatoes.

Serves 4

1 large haggis, approximately 800g/1¾lb in weight
450g/1lb peeled turnip or swede (rutabaga)
225g/8oz peeled potatoes
120ml/4fl oz/½ cup milk
1 garlic clove, crushed with 5ml/1 tsp salt
175ml/6fl oz/¾ cup double (heavy) cream
grated nutmeg
ground black pepper
butter, for greasing

1 Preheat the oven to 180°C/350°F/Gas 4. Wrap the haggis in foil, covering it completely and folding over the edges of the foil. Place the haggis in a roasting pan with 2.5cm/1in water. Heat through in the preheated oven for 30–40 minutes.

2 Slice the turnip or swede and potatoes quite finely. A mandolin or food processor is quite handy for this as both vegetables tend to be difficult to cut finely with a knife.

3 Put the sliced vegetables in a large pan and add the milk and garlic. Stir gently over low heat until the potatoes begin to break down and the liquid thickens slightly.

4 Add the cream and nutmeg and some pepper into the mixture. Stir gently. Slowly bring to the boil, reduce the heat and simmer gently for a few minutes.

5 Butter a deep round 18cm/7in dish or a small roasting pan. Transfer the mixture to the dish or pan. It should not come up too high as it will rise slightly and bubble. Bake in the oven for about 1 hour, or until the top is golden brown.

6 Remove the foil from the haggis, place on a warmed serving dish and bring out to the table for your guests to witness the cutting. Use a sharp knife to cut through the skin, then spoon out the haggis on to warmed plates. Serve with clapshot cake.

Braised Oxtail Energy 341kcal/1426kJ; Protein 30.9g; Carbohydrate 13.6g, of which sugars 7.7g; Fat 18.6g, of which saturates 0.7g; Cholesterol 0mg; Calcium 54mg; Fibre 2.3g; Sodium 203mg.
Haggis Energy 918kcal/3819kJ; Protein 24.9g; Carbohydrate 55.3g, of which sugars 8.5g; Fat 67.9g, of which saturates 30.2g; Cholesterol 244mg; Calcium 180mg; Fibre 3.1g; Sodium 1586mg.

Apple Mash with Black Pudding

n German this dish is known s 'heaven and earth' – neaven for the apple, and earth for the potato. The ecipe comes the central egion of Germany, and is a vinning combination of fruity nd savoury ingredients.

Serves 4

5ml/3 tbsp oil
onions, chopped
00g/1¼lb apples, peeled and diced
juice of 1 lemon
5ml/1 tsp sugar
100g/3½oz/7 tbsp butter
500g/1¼lb floury potatoes, freshly boiled
100g/3½oz bacon lardons, or thick rashers, diced
500g/1¼lb black pudding (blood sausage), cut into fairly thin slices
pinch of freshly grated nutmeg
salt and ground white pepper
15ml/1 tbsp chopped parsley, to garnish

Heat 15ml/1 tbsp oil in a pan over medium heat and cook he onions for 2–3 minutes. Add the apple, lemon juice, sugar nd 15ml/1 tbsp water.

Simmer gently until the apple is soft, and add the butter. Add ne apple mixture to the hot, boiled potatoes and mash ogether. Season with salt, pepper and nutmeg. Keep warm.

Heat the remaining oil in two frying pans over high heat. Fry ne bacon lardons in one for 4–5 minutes until crisp.

Slice the black pudding and fry the slices in the other pan ntil browned on both sides.

Spoon the mash on to four plates, then put the fried black udding on top and sprinkle some bacon cubes over it. Garnish vith chopped parsley, and serve.

Variation
If you don't like black pudding, replace it with mini burgers made from minced (ground) pork, or some sliced sausages.

Pig Cheeks with Caramelized Potatoes

This is another hearty German winter dish, designed to keep out the cold, and made with the very reasonably priced cheeks of a pig. These have lots of flavour, but need long, slow cooking before they become tender.

Serves 4

1kg/2¼lb curly kale
100g/3¾oz/⅔ cup lard, or butter
2 onions, peeled and sliced
300ml/½ pint/1¼ cups chicken stock
15ml/1 tbsp medium-hot mustard
500g/1¼lb smoked pig's cheek
500g/1¼lb smoked pork loin
4 smoked sausages, preferably German
800g/1¾lb small potatoes, peeled
50g/2oz/4 tbsp butter
10ml/2 tsp sugar
chopped parsley, to garnish
salt

1 Trim off the tough stems and ribs of the kale, shred the leaves and blanch for about 5 minutes in boiling salted water, until wilted, then drain.

2 Heat the lard in a large pan and fry the onions gently for 2 minutes. Then stir in the curly kale, chicken stock and mustard. When the stock is bubbling, add the whole pig's cheeks, pork loin and sausages. Cover the pan, reduce the heat and cook for 45–60 minutes, stirring occasionally and adding a little more stock if necessary.

3 Boil the potatoes in a large pan of salted water for about 8–10 minutes, or until tender, and drain.

4 Melt the butter in a large frying pan over medium heat. Stir in the sugar. Then add the potatoes and cook, stirring, for 2–3 minutes, so that the butter and sugar mixture caramelizes and coats the potatoes.

5 Remove the meat from the pan. Slice the pork loin and pig's cheek and serve them with the kale, sausages and the caramelized potatoes, garnished with chopped parsley.

pple Mash Energy 855kcal/3559kJ; Protein 20.8g; Carbohydrate 61g, of which sugars 19.7g; Fat 60.4g, of which saturates 26.7g; Cholesterol 156mg; Calcium 193mg; Fibre 4.9g; Sodium 1767mg
g Cheeks Energy 1374kcal/5732kJ; Protein 61g; Carbohydrate 48g, of which sugars 13g; Fat 106g, of which saturates 47g; Cholesterol 245mg; Calcium 387mg; Fibre 13g; Sodium 849mg

Rabbit Casserole with Juniper

Because rabbit is such a lean meat, casseroling is an ideal way to cook it, helping to keep it really moist and juicy.

Serves 4

900g/2lb prepared rabbit pieces
1 onion, roughly chopped
2 garlic cloves, crushed
1 bay leaf
350ml/12fl oz/1½ cups red wine
2 sprigs of fresh thyme
1 sprig of fresh rosemary
15ml/1 tbsp juniper berries
30ml/2 tbsp olive oil
15g/½oz dried porcini mushrooms
30ml/2 tbsp chopped fresh parsley
salt and ground black pepper

1 Put the rabbit pieces in a glass or ceramic dish with the onion, garlic, bay leaf and wine, thyme and rosemary. Lightly crush the juniper berries and add them to the dish. Toss to combine. Cover and marinate in the refrigerator for 4 hours or overnight, turning the pieces once or twice, if possible.

2 Preheat the oven to 180°C/350°F/Gas 4. Remove the rabbit from the marinade, reserving the marinade, and pat dry with kitchen paper. Heat the oil in a frying pan, add the rabbit pieces and fry for 3–5 minutes, turning to brown all over. Transfer the meat to a casserole.

3 Pour the marinade into the frying pan and bring to the boil. Pour over the rabbit, cover, and cook in the oven for 1 hour.

4 Meanwhile, put the mushrooms in a heatproof bowl and pour over 100ml/3½fl oz/scant ½ cup boiling water. Leave to soak for 1 hour, then drain, reserving the soaking liquid, and finely chop the mushrooms. Pour the soaking liquid from the mushrooms into the casserole. Cook for a further 30–45 minutes.

5 Lift out the rabbit pieces and strain the liquid, discarding the vegetables, herbs and juniper berries. Wipe the dish clean, then return the cooking liquid. Add the mushrooms and season and bubble on the stove top until the sauce is reduced.

6 Return the rabbit to the dish, simmer for 5–8 minutes to warm through, stir in the parsley, and serve.

Rabbit with Apricots

The gamey flavours of rabbit go very well in many dishes, especially those with fruits and berries. Once a staple of the countryside, enjoyed by farmers and hunting parties alike, it is now more widely available from good butchers.

Serves 4

2 rabbits
30ml/2 tbsp plain (all-purpose) flour
15ml/1 tbsp vegetable oil
90g/3½oz streaky (fatty) bacon, cut into thin pieces
10 baby (pearl) onions, peeled but kept whole
200ml/7fl oz/scant 1 cup dry white wine
1 bay leaf
12 ready-to-eat dried apricots
salt and ground black pepper

1 Ask your butcher to joint the rabbits, providing two legs and the saddle cut in two. Sprinkle the flour over a dish, season with salt and ground black pepper and mix well into the flour. Roll the rabbit pieces in it one by one to coat lightly all over, shaking off any excess flour. Set aside.

2 Heat a heavy pan and add the vegetable oil. Brown the rabbit pieces all over then remove from the pan and set aside. Brown the bacon and onions.

3 Place the browned rabbit pieces, bacon and onions in a casserole. Pour the wine into the heavy pan and, over low heat, scrape up all the bits from the base of the pan. Add a little water, bring to the boil and pour over the rabbit in the casserole, adding more water if needed to just cover.

4 Add the bay leaf and bring to the boil. Allow to simmer gently for 40 minutes until the rabbit is tender. Remove the rabbit and onions from the pan and set aside, keeping them warm.

5 Put the apricots into the pan and boil until the cooking liquor thickens slightly. Remove the bay leaf and check the seasoning.

6 Return the rabbit and onions to the pan and heat before serving, or you can purée the apricots in the cooking liquor and pour the resulting rich sauce over the rabbit.

Rabbit Casserole Energy 356Kcal/1483kJ; Protein 32g; Carbohydrate 3.2g, of which sugars 2.3g; Fat 17.5g, of which saturates 6.3g; Cholesterol 163mg; Calcium 30mg; Fibre 0.6g; Sodium 66mg
Rabbit with Apricots Energy 481kcal/2022kJ; Protein 60.2g; Carbohydrate 22.5g, of which sugars 21.4g; Fat 13.8g, of which saturates 6.1g; Cholesterol 223mg; Calcium 153mg; Fibre 3.9g; Sodium 417mg

Marinated Pigeon in Red Wine

Pigeon is another very economical game bird. Stir-fried green cabbage and celeriac purée are delicious with this rich casserole.

Serves 4

4 pigeons, each weighing about 225g/8oz
30ml/2 tbsp olive oil
1 onion, coarsely chopped
225g/8oz/3¼ cups chestnut mushrooms, sliced
15ml/1 tbsp plain (all-purpose) flour
300ml/½ pint/1¼ cups game stock
30ml/2 tbsp chopped fresh parsley
salt and ground black pepper

For the marinade
15ml/1 tbsp light olive oil
1 onion, chopped
1 carrot, peeled and chopped
1 celery stick, chopped
3 garlic cloves, sliced
6 allspice berries, bruised
2 bay leaves
8 black peppercorns, bruised
150ml/¼ pint/⅔ cup red wine vinegar
150ml/¼ pint/⅔ cup red wine
45ml/3 tbsp redcurrant jelly

1 Mix all the ingredients for the marinade in a large dish. Add the pigeons, cover and chill for 12 hours, turning frequently.

2 Preheat the oven to 150°C/300°F/Gas 2. Heat the oil in a large, flameproof casserole and cook the onion and mushrooms for about 5 minutes, or until the onion has softened.

3 Meanwhile, drain the pigeons and strain the marinade into a jug, then set both aside separately.

4 Sprinkle the flour over the pigeons and add them to the casserole, breast-sides down. Pour in the marinade and stock, and add the chopped parsley and seasoning. Cover and cook for 2½ hours. Check the seasoning, then serve the pigeons on warmed plates and ladle the sauce over them.

Variation
If you are unable to buy pigeon, this recipe works equally well with rabbit or hare.

Pigeon and Pease Pudding

Pease pudding, is one of Britain's oldest dishes, dating back to at least the Middle Ages. Originally the peas would have been wrapped in a cloth and cooked in stock.

Serves 4

450g/1lb/2 cups green or yellow split peas, soaked overnight
1 medium onion, diced
1 ham bone
1 thyme sprig
1 parsley sprig
2 mint sprigs
2 bay leaves
50g/2oz/¼ cup butter
2 large eggs, beaten
8 pigeon breasts
30ml/2 tbsp vegetable oil
225g/8oz black pudding, sliced
sea salt and ground black pepper
steamed greens, to serve

1 Drain the soaked peas and place in a large pan. Add the onion, ham bone and enough water to cover the peas. Tie the herbs together with string and add to the pot.

2 Bring to the boil and hold the temperature for 1 minute, then turn the heat down to a gentle simmer. Skim off any scum that has formed and cook for 1 hour, topping up with more water if necessary. When the peas are soft, remove the herbs, and the ham bone and discard. Drain the peas, and purée them with a hand blender, adding the butter, eggs and seasoning.

3 Transfer the pea mixture to a well-buttered 1.2-litre/2-pint/5-cup heatproof bowl. Butter a sheet of foil and cover the bowl, securing with string. Place the bowl in a pan and add water to two-thirds of its height. Cover and bring to the boil then reduce the heat and steam the pudding, for 1 hour.

4 When the pease pudding is nearly done, season the pigeon breasts and fry, skin side down, in the oil, for 2–3 minutes. Turn and cook for a further 1–2 minutes. Remove from the pan and keep warm.

5 Add the black pudding to the pan and cook for 3 minutes on each side. To serve, spoon the pease pudding on to plates, pile the black pudding and pigeon on top and add steamed greens.

Marinated Pigeon Energy 286kcal/1189kJ; Protein 25.6g; Carbohydrate 1.5g, of which sugars 1g; Fat 17.4g, of which saturates 0.9g; Cholesterol 0mg; Calcium 23mg; Fibre 0.8g; Sodium 98mg
Pigeon and Pease Energy 857kcal/3595kJ; Protein 54.8g; Carbohydrate 73g, of which sugars 3.6g; Fat 40.6g, of which saturates 13.3g; Cholesterol 162mg; Calcium 107mg; Fibre 5.7g; Sodium 919mg

Steamed Cauliflower and Broccoli with Breadcrumbs and Eggs

Steamed vegetables are a delicious and healthy accompaniment for any main meal. Here they are given a tasty twist with the addition of an egg and breadcrumb topping. To bake the breadcrumbs, place in a medium oven for 5–8 minutes, watching carefully so that they don't scorch.

Serves 6

500g/1¼lb trimmed cauliflower and broccoli
finely grated rind of ½ lemon
1 garlic clove, crushed
25g/1oz/½ cup wholegrain breadcrumbs, lightly baked or grilled (broiled) until crisp
2 eggs, hard-boiled and shelled
salt and ground black pepper

1 Wash the cauliflower and broccoli and break into medium florets, then place in a steamer over a pan of boiling water and steam for about 12 minutes, or until tender. Alternatively, if you prefer, you can boil the vegetables in a large pan of salted water for 5–7 minutes, until just tender.

2 Drain the vegetables thoroughly in a colander and transfer to a warmed serving dish.

3 While the vegetables are cooking, make the topping. In a bowl, combine the lemon rind, garlic and breadcrumbs.

4 Finely chop the hard-boiled eggs, add to the bowl and mix into the breadcrumb mixture.

5 Season the mixture with salt and black pepper to taste, then sprinkle the chopped egg mixture over the cooked vegetables and serve immediately.

Variation
Fry 115g/4oz chopped pancetta or dry-cured streaky (fatty) bacon with 1 small chopped onion in the butter.

Braised Lettuce and Peas with Spring Onions and Mint

This simple recipe comes from France, and is delicious served with steamed or baked fish, or roast duck. You can use fresh or frozen peas, depending on your preference, and which offers the best value.

Serves 4

50g/2oz/¼ cup butter
4 Little Gem (Bibb) lettuces, halved lengthways
2 bunches spring onions (scallions), trimmed and cut into 5cm/2in lengths
5ml/1 tsp caster (superfine) sugar
400g/14oz shelled peas (about 1kg/2¼lb in pods), or frozen peas, thawed
4 fresh mint sprigs
120ml/4fl oz/½ cup chicken or vegetable stock
salt and ground black pepper
15ml/1 tbsp chopped fresh mint, to garnish

1 Gently melt half the butter in a large pan over low heat. Add the lettuces and spring onions.

2 Turn the vegetables in the butter, then sprinkle in the caster sugar, 2.5ml/½ tsp salt and plenty of black pepper. Cover and cook very gently for about 5 minutes, stirring once.

3 Add the peas and mint sprigs. Turn them in the buttery juices and pour in the stock, then cover and cook over low heat for a further 5 minutes. Uncover and increase the heat to reduce the liquid to a few tablespoons.

4 Stir in the remaining butter and adjust the seasoning. Transfer to a warmed serving dish and sprinkle with the chopped mint. Serve immediately.

Cook's Tip
Frozen peas tend to be much cheaper than fresh peas, and since the peas are frozen very shortly after being picked, they are often fresher too.

Steamed Cauliflower Energy 67kcal/280kJ; Protein 6.2g; Carbohydrate 4.7g, of which sugars 1.4g; Fat 2.7g, of which saturates 0.7g; Cholesterol 63mg; Calcium 62mg; Fibre 2.3g; Sodium 62mg
Braised Lettuce Energy 191kcal/790kJ; Protein 8g; Carbohydrate 13.3g, of which sugars 4.2g; Fat 12.3g, of which saturates 6.9g; Cholesterol 27mg; Calcium 52mg; Fibre 5.7g; Sodium 81mg

Brussels Sprouts with Bacon

tir-frying Brussels sprouts, elps to retain their sweet avour and crunchy texture.

erves 4
50g/1lb Brussels sprouts, trimmed and washed and shredded
30ml/2 tbsp sunflower oil
2 streaky (fatty) bacon rashers (strips), finely chopped
10ml/2 tsp caraway seeds, lightly crushed
salt and ground black pepper

Heat the oil in a wok or large frying pan. Add the shredded prouts and turn quickly over the heat, season to taste with salt nd ground black pepper, then remove and set aside.Use the he same wok or pan to cook the chopped bacon. Stir-fry or 1–2 minutes until golden.

2 Return the seasoned sprouts to the pan containing the bacon nd stir in the caraway seeds. Cook for a further 1–2 minutes, hen serve immediately.

Broad Beans with Cream

hese beans taste wonderful ooked and skinned.

erves 4–6
50g/1lb frozen broad (fava) beans
90ml/6 tbsp crème fraîche
salt and ground black pepper
finely chopped fresh chives, to garnish

1 Bring a large pan of water to the boil and cook the beans for bout 8 minutes, until tender. Drain and rinse under cold water.

2 Make a slit along each bean with the tip of a sharp knife and hen gently squeeze out the kernel with your fingers.

3 Put the skinned beans in a pan with the crème fraîche, eason with salt and pepper to taste, cover and heat through ently. Transfer to a warmed serving dish, sprinkle with the nipped chives and serve immediately.

Braised Cabbage with Chorizo

Salty, flavoursome chorizo really complements the subtle flavour of the cabbage in this simple braised cabbage dish. You need to buy the whole sausage chorizo, rather than the packaged, pre-sliced type. Serve this dish as an accompaniment to simply grilled meat, chicken or fish.

Serves 4
225g/8oz green cabbage, washed and trimmed
50g/2oz/¼ cup butter
5ml/1 tsp coriander seeds
2 garlic cloves, finely chopped
50g/2oz cured chorizo sausage, roughly chopped
60ml/4 tbsp dry sherry or white wine
salt and ground black pepper

1 Shred the cabbage, discarding the stalk. Gently melt the butter in a frying pan over low heat, add the coriander seeds and cook for 1 minute, until they start to give off an aroma.

2 Add the shredded cabbage to the frying pan with the chopped garlic and chorizo. Stir-fry over high heat for about 5 minutes, until the cabbage is tender.

3 Add the sherry or wine, salt and and plenty of pepper to the frying pan. Cover the pan and cook for 15–20 minutes, until the cabbage is tender.

4 Taste to check the seasoning. Adjust if necessary, then transfer to a serving dish and serve immediately.

Variation
Smoked streaky (fatty) bacon makes a good substitute for chorizo sausage in this recipe.

Cook's Tip
A typical Spanish household will have two types of chorizo hanging in the larder. A firm, cured chorizo to be sliced and eaten as a snack or tapas and a softer one for use in cooking.

russels Sprouts with Bacon Energy 131kcal/545kJ; Protein 5.9g; Carbohydrate 4.6g, of which sugars 3.5g; Fat 10g, of which saturates 2g; Cholesterol 8mg; Calcium 30mg; Fibre 4.6g; Sodium 164mg
road Beans with Cream Energy 145kcal/608kJ; Protein 9.3g; Carbohydrate 13.5g, of which sugars 1.8g; Fat 6.3g, of which saturates 0.9g; Cholesterol 0mg; Calcium 88mg; Fibre 7.9g; Sodium 13mg
abbage with Chorizo Energy 163kcal/673kJ; Protein 2.1g; Carbohydrate 4.6g, of which sugars 3.3g; Fat 13.4g, of which saturates 7.8g; Cholesterol 32mg; Calcium 37mg; Fibre 1.3g; Sodium 183mg

Wilted Spinach with Rice

Dill adds its distinctive flavour to this delicious dish.

Serves 4

675g/1½lb fresh spinach, trimmed
105ml/7 tbsp olive oil
1 large onion, chopped
juice of ½ lemon
150ml/¼ pint/⅔ cup water
115g/4oz/generous ½ cup rice
45ml/3 tbsp chopped fresh dill
salt and ground black pepper

1 Wash the spinach. Pat dry and shred coarsely. Heat the olive oil in a large pan and sauté the onion until translucent. Add the spinach and stir for a few minutes to coat it with the oil.

2 As soon as the spinach looks wilted, add the lemon juice and the measured water and bring to the boil.

3 Add the rice and half of the dill, then cover and cook gently for about 10 minutes or until the rice is cooked to your taste. Spoon into a serving dish and sprinkle the sprigs of dill on top.

Courgettes in Rich Tomato Sauce

Serve this colourful dish hot or at room temperature as an accompaniment to fish.

Serves 4

15ml/1 tbsp olive oil
1 onion, chopped
1 garlic clove, chopped
4 courgettes (zucchini), sliced
400g/14oz can tomatoes, drained
2 tomatoes, chopped
5ml/1 tsp vegetable stock powder
15ml/1 tbsp tomato purée (paste)
salt and ground black pepper

1 Heat the oil in a heavy pan and sauté the onion and garlic until softened, stirring occasionally. Add the courgettes and cook for 5 minutes more.

2 Add in the canned and fresh tomatoes, then stir in the vegetable stock powder and tomato purée. Simmer for 15 minutes, until the sauce has thickened and the courgettes are just tender. Season to taste with salt and pepper and serve.

Spiced Greens

Here is a really good way to enliven your greens, excellent for crunchy cabbages but also good for kale or even Brussels sprout tops. Choose whatever leafy greens are in season for the most economical version. This is a very good way of persuading reluctant children to eat up all their healthy green vegetables.

Serves 4

1 medium cabbage, or the equivalent in quantity of other leafy greens
15ml/1 tbsp groundnut (peanut) oil
5ml/1 tsp grated fresh root ginger
2 garlic cloves, grated
2 shallots, finely chopped
2 red chillies, seeded and finely sliced
salt and ground black pepper

1 Remove any tough outer leaves from the cabbage then quarter it and remove the core. Separate and wash the leaves, shake dry, then pile together, roll them up, and finely chop with a sharp knife.

2 Pour the groundnut oil into a large frying pan and as it heats stir in the ginger and garlic. Add the shallots and as the pan becomes hotter add the chillies.

3 Add the shredded greens and toss to mix thoroughly. Cover the pan and reduce the heat to create some steam. Cook for about 3 minutes, shaking the pan occasionally.

4 Remove the lid and increase the heat in order to dry off the steam, season to taste with salt and ground black pepper and serve immediately.

Variation

Reduce the amount of chilli for a milder dish, if you prefer. You could also add a few pinches of warm spices, such as fennel seeds or cumin seeds, both of which go very well with cabbage. You can also add a knob of butter if you wish as the greens cook, to add a little richness and flavour.

Wilted Spinach Energy 337kcal/1392kJ; Protein 7.5g; Carbohydrate 29.6g, of which sugars 5.3g; Fat 20.8g, of which saturates 2.9g; Cholesterol 0mg; Calcium 305mg; Fibre 4.3g; Sodium 238mg
Courgettes in Tomato Sauce Energy 89kcal/370kJ; Protein 4.3g; Carbohydrate 9.2g, of which sugars 8.6g; Fat 4.1g, of which saturates 0.7g; Cholesterol 0mg; Calcium 54mg; Fibre 3.2g; Sodium 235mg
Spiced Greens Energy 77kcal/322kJ; Protein 2.6g; Carbohydrate 9.9g, of which sugars 9.4g; Fat 3.1g, of which saturates 0.5g; Cholesterol 0mg; Calcium 90mg; Fibre 3.9g; Sodium 13mg

Fresh Green Beans with Tomato Sauce

This colourful dish can be served as an appetizer, side dish or light lunch, with thin slices of feta cheese and fresh bread. When the beans are fresh and the tomatoes sweet, this dish has an excellent flavour on its own.

Serves 4

800g/1¾lb green beans, trimmed
150ml/¼ pint/⅔ cup olive oil
1 large onion, thinly sliced
2 garlic cloves, chopped
2 small potatoes, peeled and chopped into cubes
400g/14oz can plum tomatoes, chopped
150ml/¼ pint/⅔ cup hot water
45–60ml/3–4 tbsp chopped fresh parsley
salt and ground black pepper
slices of feta cheese, to serve (optional)

1 If the green beans are very long, cut them in half. Drop them into a bowl of cold water so that they are completely submerged. Leave them to absorb the water for a few minutes.

2 Heat the olive oil in a large heavy pan, add the onion slices and fry until translucent but not coloured.

3 Add the garlic to the pan, then, when it becomes aromatic, stir in the potatoes and cook the mixture for a few minutes.

4 Add the tomatoes and the hot water and cook for 5 minutes. Drain the beans, rinse them and drain again, then add them to the pan with a little salt and pepper to season. Cover and simmer for 30 minutes.

5 Stir in the chopped parsley, with a little more hot water if the mixture looks dry. Cook for 10 minutes more, until the beans are very tender. Serve hot with slices of feta cheese, if you like.

Variation
Use slices of Wensleydale or Cheshire cheese instead of feta.

Slow-cooked Okra with Tomato Sauce

Okra makes a deliciously sweet casserole and, combined with fresh tomatoes, at the height of the summer, it makes a very good accompaniment to poultry or meat. The fibrous insides of okra gives out a unique texture when cooked, which when braised or stewed gives the dish a glutinous result.

Serves 6

675g/1½lb fresh okra, trimmed at the top and washed
150ml/¼ pint/⅔ cup olive oil
1 large onion, sliced
675g/1½lb fresh tomatoes, sliced
2.5ml/½ tsp sugar
30ml/2 tbsp finely chopped flat leaf parsley
salt and ground black pepper

1 Cut off the conical head from each okra pod, without cutting into the body of the okra. Remove the black tip at the other end and rinse the pod.

2 Heat the oil in a large, deep pan or heavy frying pan and fry the onion slices until light golden.

3 Stir in the fresh tomatoes, with the sugar, and salt and ground black pepper to taste. Cook for 5 minutes.

4 Add the okra and shake the pan to distribute them evenly and coat them in the sauce. The okra should be immersed in the sauce, so add a little hot water if necessary.

5 Cook gently for 30–40 minutes, depending on the size of the okra. Shake the pan occasionally, but do not stir. Add the flat leaf parsley just before serving.

Cook's Tip
It is possible to buy frozen okra, which you could also use for this recipe if fresh is not available.

Fresh Green Beans Energy 350kcal/1,448kJ; Protein 6.6g; Carbohydrate 21.9g, of which sugars 13.4g; Fat 26.9g, of which saturates 4g; Cholesterol 0mg; Calcium 121mg; Fibre 7.7g; Sodium 25mg
Slow-cooked Okra Energy 326kcal/1,350kJ; Protein 6.5g; Carbohydrate 14.8g, of which sugars 12.8g; Fat 27.3g, of which saturates 4.3g; Cholesterol 0mg; Calcium 295mg; Fibre 9.1g; Sodium 30mg

Radicchio and Chicory Gratin

Baking seasonal salad vegetables in a creamy sauce creates a dish that is wholesome, warming and sustaining. It is delicious served with grilled meat or seafood, or with a bean or lentil casserole.

Serves 4

2 heads radicchio, quartered lengthways
2 heads chicory (Belgian endive), quartered lengthways
25g/1oz/½ cup drained sun-dried tomatoes in oil, chopped
25g/1oz/2 tbsp butter
15g/½oz/2 tbsp plain (all-purpose) flour
250ml/8fl oz/1 cup milk
50g/2oz/½ cup grated Emmenthal cheese
pinch of freshly grated nutmeg
salt and ground black pepper

1 Preheat the oven to 180°C/350°F/Gas 4. Grease a 1.2-litre/2-pint/5-cup ovenproof dish and arrange the radicchio and chicory quarters in it.

2 Sprinkle over the chopped sun-dried tomatoes and brush the vegetables with oil from the jar. Season to taste and cover with foil. Bake for 15 minutes, then uncover and bake for 10 minutes.

3 To make the sauce, melt the butter in a small pan over medium heat. Add the flour and cook for 1 minute, stirring.

4 Remove from the heat and gradually add the milk, whisking all the time until smooth. Return to the heat and bring to the boil, then simmer for 3 minutes to thicken.

5 Season to taste and add the nutmeg. Pour the sauce over the vegetables and sprinkle with the cheese. Bake for 20 minutes, until the leaves are slightly charred. Serve immediately.

Variation

You could use fennel in place of the radicchio and chicory. Par-boil the fennel before putting it in the ovenproof dish, then continue as in the recipe.

Baked Tomatoes with Mint

This is a dish for the height of the summer when the tomatoes are falling off the vines and are very ripe, juicy, full of flavour and at their cheapest. This tomato dish goes especially well with lamb, but you can also eat it by itself, on top of slices of lightly toasted sourdough bread.

Serves 4

6 large ripe tomatoes
olive oil, for brushing
a few pinches of caster (superfine) sugar
300ml/½ pint/1¼ cups double (heavy) cream
2 sprigs of fresh mint
30ml/2 tbsp grated hard goat's cheese
salt and ground black pepper

1 Preheat the oven to 220°C/425°F/Gas 7. Bring a pan of water to the boil and have a bowl of iced water ready.

2 Cut the cores out of the tomatoes and score a cross at the base of each. Plunge the tomatoes into the pan of boiling water for 10–20 seconds and then transfer straight into the iced water. Leave to cool completely.

3 Put the double cream and mint in a pan and bring to the boil. Reduce the heat and allow to simmer until the quantity has reduced by about half.

4 Peel the cooled tomatoes and slice them thinly. Brush a shallow gratin dish lightly with a little olive oil.

5 Layer the sliced tomatoes in the dish, overlapping slightly, and season to taste with salt and ground black pepper. Sprinkle a little sugar over the top.

6 Pour the reduced cream through a sieve (strainer) over the top of the tomatoes, covering them in an even layer.

7 Sprinkle the grated goat's cheese evenly over the top and bake in the preheated oven for about 15–20 minutes, or until the top is browned and bubbling. Serve immediately straight from the gratin dish.

Radiccio Gratin xx x xxxx xx x xxx xxxx xxxx xx xxx xxx x xxxx xx x xxx xxxx xxxx xx xxx xxx x xxxx xx x xxx xxxx xxxx xx xxx xxx x xxxx xx x xxx xxxx xxxx xx
Baked Tomatoes Energy 443kcal/1831kJ; Protein 5g; Carbohydrate 6.7g, of which sugars 6.7g; Fat 44.1g, of which saturates 27.4g; Cholesterol 113mg; Calcium 123mg; Fibre 1.8g; Sodium 105mg

Onion Cake

erve this simple but elicious dish with sausages, amb chops or any roasted neat, even leftovers from the unday roast. The cooking me will depend on the otatoes and how thinly they re sliced: use a food rocessor or mandolin to nake paper-thin slices. The mound of potatoes will cook down to make a buttery cake.

Serves 6

900g/2lb new potatoes, peeled and thinly sliced
2 medium onions, chopped
115g/4oz/½ cup butter
salt and ground black pepper

Preheat the oven to 190°C/375°F/Gas 5. Lightly butter a 0cm/8in round cake tin (pan) and line the base with a circle f baking parchment.

Arrange some of the potato slices evenly in the bottom of ne tin and then sprinkle some of the onions over them. eason to taste with salt and ground black pepper. Reserve 5g/1oz/2 tbsp of the butter and dot the mixture with tiny ieces of the remaining butter.

Repeat these layers, using up all the ingredients and finishing vith a layer of potatoes at the top. Melt the reserved butter nd brush it over the top.

Cover the potatoes with foil, put in the hot oven and cook or 1–1½ hours, until tender and golden. Remove from the oven nd leave to stand, still covered, for 10–15 minutes.

Carefully turn out the onion cake on to a warmed serving late and serve immediately.

Cook's Tip

If using main crop potatoes rather than new, cook in an earthenware or ovenproof dish. Remove the cover for the final 10–15 minutes to lightly brown the top.

Braised Red Cabbage

Cook this very economical, vibrantly coloured dish in the oven at the same time as a pork casserole or joint of meat for a simple, easy-to-prepare meal that is perfect for a cold winter day. Braised red cabbage is a favourite in northern European countries, where winters are long and fresh vegetables are scarce. This dish freezes well, so make double quantities and store leftovers in the freezer.

Serves 8

675g/1½lb red cabbage
30ml/2 tbsp olive oil
1 onion
2 tart eating apples
375g/13oz raw beetroot (beet)
300ml/½ pint/1¼ cups vegetable stock
60ml/4 tbsp red wine vinegar
salt and ground black pepper

1 Cut the red cabbage into fine shreds, discarding any tough outer leaves and the core, and place in an ovenproof dish. Preheat the oven to 190°C/375°F/Gas 5.

2 Thinly slice the onion, then fry in the olive oil in a frying pan until the onion is soft and golden. Peel, core and slice the apples, and peel and coarsely grate the beetroot.

3 Stir the apple slices, vegetable stock and red wine vinegar into the onions, then transfer to the ovenproof dish.

4 Season with salt and pepper to taste, and cover. Put the dish in the preheated oven and cook for 1 hour. Stir in the beetroot, re-cover the dish and cook for a further 20–30 minutes, or until the cabbage and beetroot are tender.

5 Serve immediately with a roasted joint of meat or a casserole, or on its own with plenty of creamy mashed potatoes.

Variation

If you don't have any beetroot (beets), simply increase the quantity of red cabbage.

nion Cake Energy 272kcal/1133kJ; Protein 3.5g; Carbohydrate 29.5g, of which sugars 5.8g; Fat 16.3g, of which saturates 10.1g; Cholesterol 41mg; Calcium 29mg; Fibre 2.4g; Sodium 135mg
raised Red Cabbage Energy 74kcal/309kJ; Protein 2.1g; Carbohydrate 10g, of which sugars 9.5g; Fat 3g, of which saturates 0.4g; Cholesterol 0mg; Calcium 53mg; Fibre 3.1g; Sodium 38mg

Braised Leeks with Carrots

Sweet carrots and leeks go well together and are good finished with a little chopped mint, chervil or parsley. The braised vegetables end up shiny and sweet, and make a low-cost accompaniment to roast beef, lamb or chicken.

Serves 6

65g/2½oz/5 tbsp butter
675g/1½lb carrots, sliced into chunky rounds
2 fresh bay leaves
pinch caster (superfine) sugar
75ml/5 tbsp water
675g/1½lb leeks, cut into 5cm/2in lengths
120ml/4fl oz/½ cup white wine
30ml/2 tbsp chopped fresh mint, chervil or parsley
salt and ground black pepper

1 Melt 25g/1oz/2 tbsp of the butter in a pan and cook the carrots gently, without allowing them to brown, for 4–5 minutes.

2 Add the bay leaves, seasoning, the sugar and water. Bring to the boil, cover and cook for 10–15 minutes, until the carrots are tender. Uncover, then boil until the juices have evaporated, leaving the carrots moist and glazed.

3 Meanwhile, melt another 25g/1oz/2 tbsp of the remaining butter in a wide pan or deep frying pan that will take the leeks in a single layer. Add the leeks and fry them in the butter over low heat for 4–5 minutes, without allowing them to brown.

4 Add seasoning, a good pinch of sugar, the wine and half the chopped herbs. Heat until simmering, then cover and cook for 5–8 minutes, until the leeks are tender, but not collapsed.

5 Uncover the pan with the leeks and turn them in the buttery juices. Increase the heat, then boil the liquid rapidly until reduced to a few tablespoons.

6 Add the carrots to the leeks and reheat them gently, then swirl in the remaining butter. Adjust the seasoning, if necessary.

7 Transfer to a warmed serving dish and serve sprinkled with the remaining chopped herbs.

Spiced Roasted Pumpkin

This dish makes a good accompaniment to sausages or lamb chops.

Serves 4

30ml/2 tbsp olive oil
5ml/1 tsp fennel seeds, bruised
1 garlic clove, crushed
5ml/1 tsp ground ginger
5ml/1 tsp dried thyme
pinch of chilli powder
1.5kg/3lb 6oz pumpkin, peeled and cut into chunks
75g/3oz/¾ cup mature (sharp) Cheddar cheese, grated
salt and ground black pepper

1 Preheat the oven to 200°C/400°F/Gas 6. Put the oil into a large bowl and mix in the fennel, garlic, ginger, thyme and chilli.

2 Season the pumpkin, toss in the oil until evenly coated, then spread in a single layer on a large baking tray. Cook for about 40 minutes, or until tender and golden brown on the edges.

3 Sprinkle the cheese over the top and return to the oven for 5 minutes more. Serve straight from the baking tray, making sure all the bits of cheese are scraped up with the pumpkin.

Baked Squash with Tomatoes

Acorn or butternut squash can be used in this recipe.

Serves 6

1kg/2¼lb pumpkin or orange winter squash, peeled and sliced
45ml/3 tbsp olive oil
2 x 400g/14oz cans chopped tomatoes
2–3 fresh rosemary sprigs
salt and ground black pepper

1 Preheat the oven to 160°C/325°F/Gas 3. Fry the pumpkin in the oil in batches, until golden brown. Remove them from the pan. Add the tomatoes and rosemary leaves to the pan and cook over medium heat for 10 minutes. Season.

2 Layer the pumpkin and tomato sauce in an ovenproof dish, ending with sauce. Bake for 35 minutes, until tender, then serve.

Braised Leeks Energy 163kcal/677kJ; Protein 3.8g; Carbohydrate 18.5g, of which sugars 16.4g; Fat 6.5g, of which saturates 3.6g; Cholesterol 13mg; Calcium 87mg; Fibre 7.8g; Sodium 85mg
Spiced Pumpkin Energy 171kcal/712kJ; Protein 7.1g; Carbohydrate 8.3g, of which sugars 6.4g; Fat 12g, of which saturates 5g; Cholesterol 17mg; Calcium 238mg; Fibre 3.8g; Sodium 127mg
Baked Squash Energy 94kcal/392kJ; Protein 2.1g; Carbohydrate 7.8g, of which sugars 7g; Fat 6.2g, of which saturates 1.1g; Cholesterol 0mg; Calcium 58mg; Fibre 3g; Sodium 12mg

ꝛoot Vegetable Mash

ʼhis root vegetable dish is xcellent with sausages or n top of shepherd's pie in lace of just potato. Turnips ve an earthy flavour, and ʌwede introduces a sweet ccent. It is also slightly less eavy than mashed potato, ʌhich makes it ideal for a ghter meal or supper.

Serves 4
450g/1lb potatoes, peeled
450g/1lb turnips or swede (rutabaga), peeled
50g/2oz/¼ cup butter
50ml/2fl oz/¼ cup milk
5ml/1 tsp freshly grated nutmeg
30ml/2 tbsp chopped fresh parsley
salt and ground black pepper

Chop the potatoes and turnips or swede into chunks. Place ı a pan and cover with cold water.

Bring to the boil over medium heat, then reduce the heat ɴd simmer until both vegetables are cooked, which will take ɔout 15–20 minutes.

Test the vegetables by pushing the point of a sharp knife into ɴe of the cubes; if it goes in easily and the cube begins to ʙreak apart, then it is cooked.

Drain the vegetables thoroughly in a colander. Return to ɪe pan and allow them to dry out for a few minutes over ɔw heat, stirring occasionally to prevent any from sticking ɔ the base of the pan.

Melt the butter with the milk in a small pan over low heat. ɬash the potato mixture, then add in the milk mixture.

Grate in the nutmeg, add the parsley, mix thoroughly and ɜason to taste. Serve immediately with roast meat or game.

Cook's Tip
Any leftover mash can be thinned to taste with good-quality chicken stock, and heated to make a quick homemade soup.

Carrot and Parsnip Purée

Carrots and parsnips are good value, flavoursome and popular winter vegetables.

Serves 4
350g/12oz carrots
450g/1lb parsnips
15g/½oz/1 tbsp butter
1 small bunch parsley leaves, chopped (optional), plus extra to garnish
pinch of grated nutmeg
salt and ground black pepper

1 Peel the carrots and slice them fairly thinly. Peel the parsnips and cut into bitesize chunks (they are softer and will cook more quickly than the carrots). Boil the two vegetables together, in lightly salted water, until tender.

2 Drain them well and put them through a vegetable mill or food processor with the grated nutmeg, a good seasoning of salt and ground black pepper, and the butter. Purée together and taste for seasoning. Transfer the purée to a warmed serving bowl and sprinkle with freshly chopped parsley.

Creamed Leeks

This dish is delicious with a full roast dinner, or served on its own with some bread as a light lunch or snack. Use young leeks, which will keep their shape and texture.

Serves 4
2 leeks, tops trimmed and washed
50g/2oz/¼ cup butter
200ml/7fl oz/scant 1 cup double (heavy) cream
salt and ground black pepper

1 Split the leeks down the middle then cut across so you make pieces approximately 2cm/¾in square. Wash thoroughly and drain in a colander.

2 Melt the butter in a large pan, then add the leeks, stirring to coat them in the butter, and heat through. They will wilt but should not exude water. Mix in the cream, and allow to bubble and reduce. Season to taste and serve.

oot Vegetable Mash Energy 204kcal/852kJ; Protein 3.4g; Carbohydrate 24.1g, of which sugars 7.2g; Fat 11.2g, of which saturates 6.8g; Cholesterol 27mg; Calcium 78mg; Fibre 3.8g; Sodium 111mg
arrot and Parsnip Purée Energy 92kcal/385kJ; Protein 1.8g; Carbohydrate 14.1g, of which sugars 8.7g; Fat 3.5g, of which saturates 1.8g; Cholesterol 7mg; Calcium 48mg; Fibre 4.9g; Sodium 38mg
reamed Leeks Energy 363kcal/1496kJ; Protein 2.5g; Carbohydrate 3.8g, of which sugars 3.1g; Fat 37.6g, of which saturates 23.3g; Cholesterol 95mg; Calcium 51mg; Fibre 2.2g; Sodium 89mg

Mashed Potato with Cabbage

This is versatile side dish makes a welcome change to standard mashed potatoes, and is a good way to encourage children to eat leafy greens. Since the cabbage is stir-fried rather than boiled or steamed, it retains more of its goodness and has a much more interesting texture.

Serves 4
450g/1lb potatoes
50g/2oz/¼ cup butter
50ml/2fl oz/¼ cup full-fat (whole) milk
30ml/2 tbsp olive oil
450g/1lb cabbage, washed and finely shredded
50ml/2fl oz/¼ cup double (heavy) cream
salt and ground black pepper

1 Peel and chop the potatoes, then place in boiling water and boil for 15–20 minutes,until tender.

2 Return the potatoes to the pan and allow them to dry out for a few minutes over low heat, stirring occasionally to prevent any from sticking to the base of the pan.

3 Melt the butter with the milk in a small pan over low heat. Mash the potato mixture, then add the milk mixture.

4 Heat the olive oil in a large frying pan, add the shredded cabbage and fry for a few minutes.

5 Season to taste. Add the mashed potato to the cabbage, mix well then stir in the cream. Serve immediately.

Cook's Tip
To make this recipe into Bubble and Squeak, heat 30ml/2 tbsp olive oil and a large knob of butter in a heavy frying pan. Add the potato and cabbage mixture into the pan, and squash down as it cooks, so that it 'squeaks'. Keep turning and pushing down the mixture so that bits of it brown, then squash it down again to make a cake. Flip it over and cook the other side, then serve hot, with fried eggs, for breakfast or supper.

Potato Cakes

This is the traditional method of making potato cakes on a griddle or in a heavy frying pan. Commercial versions are available in Scotland as thin, pre-cooked potato cakes, which are often fried with a full breakfast.

Serves 4–6
675g/1½lb potatoes
25g/1oz/2 tbsp unsalted (sweet) butter
about 175g/6oz/1½ cups plain (all-purpose) flour
salt
jam, to serve

1 Peel the potatoes and place in a large pan. Cover with water and bring to the boil. Reduce the heat and simmer over medium heat until tender.

2 Drain the potatoes thoroughly, replacing the pan with the drained poatoes over low heat for a few minutes to allow any moisture to evaporate completely.

3 Mash the potatoes with plenty of salt, then add in the butter and mix thoroughly with a wooden spoon. Leave to cool.

4 Turn out on to a floured work surface and knead in about one-third of its volume in flour to make a pliable dough. Roll out to about 1cm/½in thick and cut into triangles.

5 Heat a dry griddle or heavy frying pan over low heat and cook the potato cakes on it for about 3 minutes on each side until browned. Serve hot with butter and jam.

Cook's Tip
Choose a floury variety of potato for excellent mashed potato. Maris Piper, Golden Wonder and Kerr's Pinks are all good choices, but make use of whatever is available locally.

Variation
Serve with bacon rashers (strips) for a hearty start to the day.

Mashed Potato Energy 183kcal/766kJ; Protein 3.9g; Carbohydrate 24g, of which sugars 7.3g; Fat 8.5g, of which saturates 2.4g; Cholesterol 7mg; Calcium 73mg; Fibre 3.5g; Sodium 24mg
Potato Cakes Energy 1276kcal/5392kJ; Protein 30.4g; Carbohydrate 249.1g, of which sugars 6.7g; Fat 24.1g, of which saturates 13.4g; Cholesterol 53mg; Calcium 282mg; Fibre 14g; Sodium 203mg

›imple Pan-fried Potatoes ınd Onions

"his dish uses left-over ooked potatoes that have ›een boiled in their skins. It nakes a tasty ccompaniment to grilled neat or fish or as a ght meal. For a more ustantial meal you could erve with fried eggs.

Serves 4–6

2 onions, peeled
450–675g/1–1½lb whole cooked potatoes, boiled in their skins
15g/1/2oz/1 tbsp butter
15ml/1 tbsp oil, for shallow frying
salt and ground black pepper

Slice the peeled onions in half, then cut them into crescents cross the grain.

Put the onions in a large pan and scald them briefly in boiling vater. Refresh under cold running water and drain well. Peel and hinly slice the potatoes.

Put the butter and oil into a large, heavy frying pan and heat vell. When the fat is hot, fry the onion until tender.

Add the potato slices to the pan and brown them together, ırning the potato slices so they brown on both sides.

Transfer to a warmed serving dish and season to taste with alt and pepper. Serve while very hot.

Roasted Potatoes, Peppers ınd Shallots

"hese potatoes soak up the ıste and aromas of the hallots and rosemary.

erves 4

00g/1¼lb waxy potatoes
2 shallots
2 yellow (bell) peppers
2 rosemary sprigs
olive oil, enough for greasing and drizzling
salt and ground black pepper
crushed black peppercorns, to garnish

Preheat the oven to 200°C/400°F/Gas 6. Par-boil the otatoes in their skins, then drain and leave to cool. Peel and cut half. Peel the shallots, and cut each pepper lengthways into ight strips, discarding the seeds and pith.

Oil a shallow ovenproof dish. Arrange the potatoes and eppers in alternating rows and stud with the shallots.

Cut the rosemary sprigs into 5cm/2in lengths and tuck among ıe vegetables. Season, pour over the olive oil and roast, ncovered, for 30–40 minutes until all the vegetables are tender.

Turn the vegetables occasionally to brown evenly. Serve nmediately while hot or leave to cool and serve at room emperature, with crushed peppercorns.

Potatoes and Parsnips Baked with Garlic and Cream

This creamy, flavoursome baked dish is the ideal accompaniment to many main course dishes and is particularly good in winter.

Serves 4–6

3 large potatoes or 675g/1½lb, peeled and thinly sliced
350g/12oz parsnips, thinly sliced
200ml/7fl oz/scant 1 cup single (light) cream
105ml/7 tbsp milk
2 garlic cloves, crushed
butter or olive oil, for greasing
about 5ml/1 tsp freshly grated nutmeg
75g/3oz/¾ cup coarsely grated Cheddar cheese
salt and ground black pepper

1 Place the slices of potato and parsnip in a steamer and cook for 5 minutes. Leave to cool slightly.

2 Pour the cream and milk into a medium, heavy pan, add the crushed garlic and bring to the boil over medium heat.

3 Remove the pan from the heat and leave to stand at room temperature for about 10 minutes to infuse (steep).

4 Preheat the oven to 180°C/350°F/Gas 4. Lightly grease a 25cm/10in long, shallow rectangular ovenproof dish with butter.

5 Arrange the potato and parsnip slices in layers in the greased dish, sprinkling each layer of vegetables with a little freshly grated nutmeg, a little salt and plenty of ground black pepper.

6 Pour the infused cream and milk mixture into the dish and then press the sliced potatoes and parsnips down into the liquid. The liquid should come to just underneath the top layer of vegetables. Cover with foil and bake for 45 minutes.

7 Remove the foil and sprinkle the grated cheese over the top. Return the dish to the oven and bake uncovered for a further 20–30 minutes, or until the potatoes and parsnips are tender and the topping is golden brown.

an-fried Potatoes Energy 163kcal/681kJ; Protein 3.4g; Carbohydrate 26.4g, of which sugars 5g; Fat 5.5g, of which saturates 3.3g; Cholesterol 13mg; Calcium 26mg; Fibre 2.6g; Sodium 49mg
oasted Potatoes Energy 192kcal/806kJ; Protein 3.9g; Carbohydrate 31.7g, of which sugars 11.2g; Fat 6.4g, of which saturates 1g; Cholesterol 0mg; Calcium 33mg; Fibre 3.7g; Sodium 20mg
otatoes and Parsnips Energy 1443kcal/6055kJ; Protein 47g; Carbohydrate 161.8g, of which sugars 38.1g; Fat 70.4g, of which saturates 43.1g; Cholesterol 189mg; Calcium 1042mg; Fibre 22.8g; Sodium 755mg

Roasted Sweet Potatoes, Onions and Beetroot in Coconut Milk

The roasted sweet potatoes and beetroot are delicious here with the savoury onions, aromatic coconut, ginger and garlic.

Serves 4

30ml/2 tbsp olive oil
450g/1lb sweet potatoes, peeled and cut into thick strips
4 beetroot, cooked, peeled and cut into wedges
450g/1lb small red onions, halved
5ml/1 tsp coriander seeds, lightly crushed
3–4 small whole fresh red chillies
salt and ground black pepper
chopped fresh coriander (cilantro), to garnish

For the paste

2 large garlic cloves, chopped
1–2 green chillies, chopped
15ml/1 tbsp chopped fresh root ginger
45ml/3 tbsp chopped fresh coriander (cilantro)
75ml/5 tbsp coconut milk
30ml/2 tbsp mild olive oil
grated rind of ½ lime
2.5ml/½ tsp light muscovado (brown) sugar

1 First make the paste. Process the garlic, chillies, ginger, coriander and coconut milk in a food processor, blender or coffee grinder to form a coarse paste.

2 Turn the paste into a small bowl and beat in the oil, lime rind and sugar. Preheat the oven to 200°C/400°F/Gas 6.

3 Heat the oil in a roasting pan in the oven for 5 minutes. Add the sweet potatoes, beetroot, onions and coriander seeds, tossing them in the hot oil. Roast for 10 minutes.

4 Stir in the paste and the whole red chillies. Season well with salt and black pepper, and toss the vegetables to coat them thoroughly with the paste.

5 Roast the vegetables for a further 25–35 minutes, or until the sweet potatoes and onions are fully cooked and tender. Stir two or three times to prevent the paste from sticking. Serve immediately, sprinkled with a little chopped fresh coriander.

Swede Pudding

A traditional Finnish dish served at Christmas time, this baked pudding combines mashed swede with butter and cream to make a delicious vegetable accompaniment to many dishes. The texture of swede is fairly dense, so you will need to cut it into relatively small dice.

Serves 4

1 large swede (rutabaga), diced
40g/1½oz/3 tbsp butter, plus extra for greasing
200ml/7fl oz/scant 1 cup double (heavy) cream
50g/2oz/1 cup fine fresh breadcrumbs
2.5ml/½ tsp grated nutmeg
5ml/1 tsp salt
2 eggs, beaten

1 Put the diced swede in a large pan and cover generously with water. Bring to the boil, lower the heat and simmer for about 20 minutes until tender.

2 Remove the pan from the heat and leave the swede to cool in the water for about 30 minutes. Drain well through a sieve (strainer) and mash the swede.

3 Preheat the oven to 180°C/350°F/Gas 4. Grease a deep, ovenproof dish with butter. Pour the cream into a bowl, add the breadcrumbs, nutmeg and salt and mix together until the ingredients are combined. Add the beaten eggs.

4 Add the cream mixture to the mashed swede and mix together. Spoon the mixture into the prepared dish and dot the surface with the butter. Bake in the oven for about 30 minutes until lightly browned. Serve hot.

Cook's Tips

- *Swede (rutabaga) is generally available throughout the whole winter.*
- *Unlike potato, swede contains no gluten, so it will not turn sticky if puréed in a food processor. The other ingredients can be added to the processing bowl when the swede is blended.*

Roasted Potatoes Energy 176kcal/750kJ; Protein 4g; Carbohydrate 40.4g, of which sugars 14.1g; Fat 1g, of which saturates 0.3g; Cholesterol 0mg; Calcium 116mg; Fibre 5.2g; Sodium 103mg
Swede Pudding Energy 434kcal/1794kJ; Protein 6.3g; Carbohydrate 16.9g, of which sugars 7.4g; Fat 38.5g, of which saturates 22.7g; Cholesterol 185mg; Calcium 123mg; Fibre 2.7g; Sodium 712mg

Turnips in a Spicy Yogurt Sauce

ry to find small turnips as hey have a delicate flavour vith a slightly sweet taste vhich complements the our-hot yogurt sauce. Ghee nriches the dish, but you an use oil instead. Avoid utter as this gets too hot.

erves 4

–6 turnips (about 600g/1¼lb)
75g/10oz potatoes
15g/4oz/½ cup full-fat (whole) natural (plain) yogurt
10ml/2 tsp gram flour, sifted
50g/2oz ghee
1 large onion, finely sliced
10ml/2 tsp ginger paste
1–2 green chillies, finely chopped
5ml/1 tsp ground coriander
2.5ml/½ tsp ground cumin
2.5ml/½ tsp chilli powder
2.5ml/½ tsp ground turmeric
5ml/1 tsp salt or to taste
2.5ml/½ tsp sugar
2.5ml/½ tsp garam masala
30ml/2 tbsp coriander (cilantro) leaves, finely chopped

Peel the turnips and quarter them. Cut each quarter into four mall pieces. Peel and cut the potatoes to the same size as the ırnips. Whisk the yogurt and gram flour together and set aside.

Heat half the ghee over a medium-high heat and brown the ırnips, stirring them frequently, until they have a very light crust.

Drain the turnips on absorbent paper. Brown the potatoes in ne same way and drain.

Add the remaining ghee, and reduce the heat to medium. ry the onion, ginger and green chillies until the onion is golden rown. Add the coriander, cumin, chilli powder and turmeric, nd cook for about a minute. Add the browned vegetables and ne yogurt and flour mixture.

Add the salt, sugar and 50ml/2fl oz/¼ cup water. Reduce the eat to low, cover the pan and cook for 20 minutes, stirring and e-positioning the vegetables three or four times.

Sprinkle the garam masala and coriander leaves in to the pan, ir and remove from the heat. Serve the spiced turnips with ny kind of Indian bread.

Spicy Potatoes with Coriander

The spices in this popular potato dish vary across Lebanon, Syria and Jordan but the recipes invariably include fresh chillies and cumin. The dish can be eaten at room temperature as part of a mezze spread, if you wish, but is also often served hot as an accompaniment to grilled and roasted meat and fish.

Serves 4

350g/12oz new potatoes
60ml/4 tbsp olive oil or 30ml/2 tbsp ghee
3–4 cloves garlic, finely chopped
2 fresh red chillies, seeded and finely chopped
5–10ml/1–2 tsp cumin seeds
bunch of fresh coriander (cilantro), finely chopped
sea salt and ground black pepper
1 lemon, cut into wedges, to serve

1 Steam the potatoes with their skins on for about 10 minutes, until they are cooked but still firm.

2 Drain the potatoes and refresh under cold running water. Peel off the skins and cut the potatoes into bitesize pieces.

3 Heat the oil or ghee in a heavy pan and cook the garlic, chillies and cumin seeds for 2–3 minutes, until they begin to colour. Add the potatoes, turning them to make sure they are coated in the oil and spices, and fry for about 5 minutes.

4 Season the potatoes with salt and pepper and stir in most of the coriander. (If serving the dish at room temperature, leave the potatoes to cool first.)

5 Sprinkle the remaining coriander over the top of the potatoes and serve immediately from the pan together with lemon wedges to squeeze over them.

Cook's Tip

If the dish is to be eaten at room temperature it is preferable to cook the potatoes in olive oil, but ghee is often used instead when they are to be served hot.

ırnips Energy 317kcal/1326kJ; Protein 7.9g; Carbohydrate 39.6g, of which sugars 17g; Fat 15.6g, of which saturates 6.7g; Cholesterol 3mg; Calcium 194mg; Fibre 6.3g; Sodium 61mg.
picy Potatoes Energy 174kcal/723kJ; Protein 2.4g; Carbohydrate 15.5g, of which sugars 1.2g; Fat 11.8g, of which saturates 1.7g; Cholesterol 0mg; Calcium 16mg; Fibre 0.9g; Sodium 12mg

Green Leaf and Fresh Herb Salad

This flavourful salad makes an ideal side dish that goes well with meat and fish.

Serves 4

15g/½oz/½ cup mixed fresh herbs, such as chervil, dill, basil, flat leaf parsley, mint, sorrel, fennel and coriander (cilantro)
350g/12oz mixed salad leaves, such as rocket (arugula), radicchio, chicory (Belgian endive), watercress, baby spinach and oakleaf lettuce
50ml/2fl oz/¼ cup extra virgin olive oil
15ml/1 tbsp cider vinegar
salt and ground black pepper

1 Wash and dry the herbs and salad leaves in a salad spinner, or use two clean, dry dish towels to pat them dry.

2 To make the dressing, blend together the olive oil and cider vinegar in a small bowl and season with salt and ground black pepper to taste. Place the prepared mixed herbs and salad leaves in a large salad bowl. Just before serving, pour over the dressing and toss. Serve immediately.

Cucumber and Shallot Salad

This light, refreshing salad is lovely with Indian food.

Serves 4

1 cucumber, peeled, halved lengthways, seeded and sliced
4 shallots, sliced finely
1–2 green chillies, sliced finely
60ml/4 tbsp coconut milk
5–10ml/1–2 tsp cumin
salt, to taste
1 lime, quartered, to serve

1 Place the cucumber slices in a strainer and sprinkle with salt. Set aside for 15 minutes, rinse and drain. Put the cucumber, shallots and chillies in a bowl. Pour in the coconut milk and toss well. Sprinkle most of the cumin over the top.

2 Just before serving, toss the salad again, season with salt and sprinkle the rest of the cumin over the top. Serve immediately with juicy lime wedges to squeeze over the salad.

Celery and Coconut Salad

Juicy, refreshing and good value, this unusual salad is perfect on a hot sunny day as part of a picnic buffet spread, or as an accompaniment to barbecued meats and spicy dishes. It looks especially appealing served in coconut shell, so take care when splitting the shell and if you manage to end up with intact halves, then use them.

Serves 4

½ fresh coconut
8 long celery sticks, leaves reserved for the garnish
45–60ml/3–4 tbsp thick and creamy natural (plain) yogurt
2 garlic cloves, crushed
5ml/1 tsp grated lime rind
juice of 1 lime
salt and ground black pepper
a few sprigs of fresh flat leaf parsley, to garnish

1 If the coconut is still in its shell, use the tip of a sharp knife to carefully lever away the flesh from the shell. Then peel the brown membrane from the white flesh using a vegetable peeler or a knife. Discard the shell and membrane.

2 Coarsely grate the fresh coconut and then the celery sticks and mix together in a bowl.

3 Mix the yogurt and garlic in a small bowl, add the lime rind and juice and season to taste with salt and pepper.

4 Fold the yogurt and garlic dressing in to the grated celery and coconut, then set aside and leave for 15–20 minutes to let the celery juices weep. Don't leave it for too long, however, or it will become watery.

5 To serve, check for seasoning and add more lime juice, salt and pepper if needed. Spoon into a bowl and garnish with the reserved celery leaves and parsley sprigs. Serve immediately.

Cook's Tip
Fresh coconut can be stored in an airtight container in the refrigerator for up to a week, if you have any left over.

Green Leaf Salad Energy 92kcal/377kJ; Protein 0.7g; Carbohydrate 1.6g, of which sugars 1.6g; Fat 9.2g, of which saturates 1.4g; Cholesterol 0mg; Calcium 26mg; Fibre 0.8g; Sodium 3mg
Cucumber Salad Energy 17kcal/68kJ; Protein 0.7g; Carbohydrate 3.3g, of which sugars 2.7g; Fat 0.1g, of which saturates 0g; Cholesterol 0mg; Calcium 19mg; Fibre 0.7g; Sodium 15mg
Celery Salad Energy 126kcal/521kJ; Protein 2.1g; Carbohydrate 2.9g, of which sugars 2.9g; Fat 11.9g, of which saturates 10.1g; Cholesterol 0mg; Calcium 63mg; Fibre 3.6g; Sodium 69mg

Potato and Olive Salad

This delicious salad is simple nd zesty – the perfect hoice for lunch, as an ccompaniment, or as an ppetizer. Similar in ppearance to flat leaf arsley, fresh coriander has a istinctive pungent, almost picy flavour. It is widely used n India, the Middle and Far ast and in eastern Mediterranean countries. new potatoes are not in season, you can substitute another waxy variety, such as Charlotte potatoes, to keep costs down.

Serves 4

8 large new potatoes
60–90ml/4–6 tbsp chopped fresh herbs, such as coriander (cilantro) and chives
10–15 black olives
45–60ml/3–4 tbsp garlic oil (see Cook's Tip)

Cut the new potatoes into chunks. Put them in a pan, pour in vater to cover and add a pinch of salt.

Bring to the boil, then reduce the heat and cook gently for bout 10 minutes, or until the potatoes are just tender.

Drain the potatoes well and leave in a colander to dry horoughly and cool slightly.

When they are cool enough to handle, chop the potatoes and ut them in a large serving bowl.

Drizzle the garlic oil over the potatoes. Toss well and sprinkle vith the chopped fresh herbs, and black olives.

Chill the salad in the refrigerator for at least 1 hour before erving to allow the flavours to develop.

Cook's Tip
To make your own garlic oil, simply add several whole, peeled garlic cloves to a new bottle of oil, and leave to infuse (steep) for about 2 weeks before using. Store in a cool, dark place.

Cabbage Salad with Lemon Dressing

Fresh, colourful and appetizing for little expense, this simple salad combines very thin shreds of raw cabbage and olives with a zesty lemon and parsley dressing to produce a rather sweet-tasting, unusual salad. It makes a healthier alternative to coleslaw, and can be served with grilled or fried meat, poultry or fish.

Serves 4

1 white cabbage
12 black olives

For the dressing

75–90ml/5–6 tbsp extra virgin olive oil
30ml/2 tbsp lemon juice
1 garlic clove, crushed
30ml/2 tbsp finely chopped flat leaf parsley
salt, to taste

1 Cut the cabbage in quarters, discard the outer leaves and trim off any thick, hard stems as well as the hard base.

2 Lay each cabbage quarter in turn on its side and cut long slices as thin as you can until you reach the central core, which should be discarded.

3 Place the shredded cabbage in a large mixing bowl and add in the black olives. Stir to combine.

4 Make the dressing by whisking the extra virgin olive oil, lemon juice, garlic, chopped parsley and salt to taste together in a bowl until well blended.

5 Pour the dressing over the cabbage and olives, and toss the salad until everything is evenly coated.

Variation
For a creamy mayonnaise coleslaw, reduce the amount of olive oil to 30ml/2 tbsp, and mix in 30ml/2 tbsp mayonnaise and 15ml/1 tbsp natural (plain) yogurt.

otato and Olive Energy 238kcal/998kJ; Protein 4g; Carbohydrate 32.6g, of which sugars 2.9g; Fat 11.1g, of which saturates 1.7g; Cholesterol 0mg; Calcium 49mg; Fibre 3.2g; Sodium 448mg
abbage Salad Energy 208kcal/861kJ; Protein 4g; Carbohydrate 12.9g, of which sugars 12.5g; Fat 15.8g, of which saturates 2.2g; Cholesterol 0mg; Calcium 155mg; Fibre 6.2g; Sodium 303mg

Curried Red Cabbage Slaw

Vibrant and fresh, this stunning, crisp slaw combines red cabbage, red pepper and red onion with a creamy mayonnaise sauce. It is particularly good served with rich meat, such as game or duck.

Serves 6

½ red cabbage
1 red (bell) pepper
½ red onion, halved and then thinly sliced
60ml/4 tbsp red or white wine vinegar or cider vinegar
60ml/4 tbsp sugar
120ml/4fl oz/½ cup Greek (US strained plain) yogurt
120ml/4fl oz/½ cup good quality mayonnaise
1.5ml/¼ tsp curry powder
2–3 handfuls raisins
salt and ground black pepper

1 Cut away the stalk the cut the cabbage into quarters. Use a sharp knife to thinly slice all the cabbage. Deseed the red pepper and cut into thin slices.

2 Put the sliced cabbage, pepper and red onion slices in a large mixing bowl and toss to combine.

3 In a small pan, heat the vinegar and sugar until the sugar has dissolved, then pour over the vegetables. Mix thoroughly and then leave to cool slightly. The warm vinegar will react with the vegetables and slightly soften them.

4 Combine the yogurt and mayonnaise, then mix into the cabbage mixture. Season to taste with curry powder, salt and ground black pepper, then mix in the raisins.

5 Chill the salad in the refrigerator before serving, if you have time. Just before serving, drain off any excess liquid and briefly stir the slaw again. Serve with roasted meat or cold cuts.

Cook's Tip
This salad won't keep for long, so don't make it too far in advance otherwise the cabbage will soften too much.

Turnip Salad in Sour Cream

Raw young tender turnips have a crunchy texture and a tangy, slightly peppery flavour.

Serves 4

2–4 young, tender turnips, peeled
¼ –½ onion, finely chopped
2–3 drops white wine vinegar, or to taste
60–90ml/4–6 tbsp sour cream
salt and ground black pepper

1 Thinly slice or coarsely grate the turnips. Alternatively, slice half the turnips and grate the remaining half. Put in a bowl.

2 Add the onion and vinegar and season to taste with salt and plenty of freshly ground black pepper. Toss together, then stir in the sour cream. Chill well before serving.

Gingered Carrot Salad

This fresh and zesty salad is ideal served alongside simple grilled chicken or fish. Fresh root ginger goes perfectly with sweet carrots, and the tiny black poppy seeds not only add taste and texture, but also make an attractive contrast against the bright orange of the carrots.

Serves 4

350g/12oz carrots
30ml/2 tbsp garlic-infused olive oil or olive oil and half a crushed clove of garlic
2.5cm/1in piece of fresh root ginger, peeled and grated (shredded)
15ml/1 tbsp poppy seeds
salt and ground black pepper

1 Peel the carrots and cut them into fine matchsticks. Put them in a bowl and stir in the oil and grated ginger.

2 Cover and chill for at least 30 minutes, to allow the flavours to develop fully.

3 Season the salad with salt and pepper to taste. Stir in the poppy seeds just before serving.

Curried Slaw Energy 272kcal/1136kJ; Protein 3g; Carbohydrate 27.9g, of which sugars 27.5g; Fat 17.5g, of which saturates 3.4g; Cholesterol 15mg; Calcium 74mg; Fibre 2g; Sodium 120mg
Turnip Salad Energy 48kcal/198kJ; Protein 1.1g; Carbohydrate 4.1g, of which sugars 3.7g; Fat 3.2g, of which saturates 1.9g; Cholesterol 9mg; Calcium 42mg; Fibre 1.4g; Sodium 14mg
Gingered Carrot Energy 103kcal/424kJ; Protein 1.2g; Carbohydrate 7g, of which sugars 6.5g; Fat 7.9g, of which saturates 1.2g; Cholesterol 0mg; Calcium 47mg; Fibre 2.4g; Sodium 23mg

Beetroot with Lemon

Fresh beetroot is economical when in season, and when paired with lemon in this salad, makes a simple but healthy accompaniment to most meat dishes.

Serves 4
450g/1lb small beetroot (beets)
grated rind and juice of ½ lemon
about 150ml/¼ pint/⅔ cup extra virgin olive oil
salt and ground black pepper

1 Put the beetroot in a large pan of salted boiling water and cook for about 30 minutes, until tender. Drain the beetroot and allow it to cool, then gently remove the skin. Slice the beetroot into wedges and place in a large bowl.

2 Add the lemon rind and juice, and the oil to the bowl, then season to taste with salt and ground black pepper. Mix gently in the dressing and serve immediately.

Spinach and Roast Garlic Salad

Tender young spinach leaves are combined with roasted garlic, pine nuts and lemon to create a low-cost salad.

Serves 4
12 garlic cloves, unpeeled
450g/1lb baby spinach leaves
50g/2oz/½ cup pine nuts, lightly toasted
juice of ½ lemon
60ml/4 tbsp olive oil
salt and ground black pepper

1 Preheat the oven to 190°C/375°F/Gas 5. Place the garlic cloves in a roasting pan, drizzle over 30ml/2 tbsp of the olive oil and bake for 15 minutes until the skins are slightly charred.

2 Place the garlic cloves, still in their skins, in a salad bowl. Add the spinach, pine nuts, lemon juice and remaining olive oil.

3 Toss well to mix thoroughly, and season with plenty of salt and ground black pepper to taste. Serve immediately, gently squeezing the softened garlic purée out of the skins to eat.

Grated Beetroot and Yogurt Salad

Spiked with garlic and a pretty shade of pink, this colourful and unusual salad makes an economical yet delicious appetizer scooped on to flatbread or chunks of a warm, crusty loaf. The salad can also be served as an accompaniment to roasted, grilled or fried meat.

Serves 4
4 raw beetroot (beets), washed and trimmed
500g/1¼ lb/2¼ cups thick and creamy natural (plain) yogurt
2 garlic cloves, crushed
salt and ground black pepper
a few fresh mint leaves, shredded, to garnish

1 Put the beetroot in a large pan of salted boiling water and cook for about 30–40 minutes, or until the beetroot is tender, but not too mushy or soft.

2 Drain the beetroot and refresh under cold running water, then peel off the skins and grate the beetroot flesh into a stainless-steel colander.

3 Squeeze the grated beetroot lightly with your fingers, or push gently with a wooden spoon to drain off excess water.

4 In a bowl, beat the yogurt with the garlic and season to taste with salt and black pepper.

5 Add the beetroot to the yogurt mixture, reserving a little to garnish the top, and mix well to combine. Garnish with mint leaves and serve immediately.

Variations

- *To make warm beetroot salad, dice the beetroot and put it in a pan with coriander seeds, sugar and a splash of apple vinegar. Stir-fry for about 5 minutes, until the beetroot is tender, then serve warm with the cooling garlic-flavoured yogurt and garnished with dill.*
- *For a lower-fat version, use fat-free yogurt.*

Beetroot with Lemon Energy 265kcal/1097kJ; Protein 1.9g; Carbohydrate 8.6g, of which sugars 7.9g; Fat 25.1g, of which saturates 3.6g; Cholesterol 0mg; Calcium 23mg; Fibre 2.2g; Sodium 74mg
Spinach and Garlic Energy 238kcal/980kJ; Protein 6.9g; Carbohydrate 6.4g, of which sugars 2.6g; Fat 20.6g, of which saturates 2.3g; Cholesterol 0mg; Calcium 198mg; Fibre 3.6g; Sodium 159mg
Grated Beetroot Energy 95kcal/403kJ; Protein 7.8g; Carbohydrate 14.4g, of which sugars 13g; Fat 1.4g, of which saturates 0.6g; Cholesterol 2mg; Calcium 249mg; Fibre 1.3g; Sodium 137mg

Moroccan Rice Pudding

This comforting dessert, cooked in almond-flavoured milk and flavoured with warming cinnamon, is a simple and delicious alternative to traditional and much-loved rice pudding.

Serves 6

25g/1oz/¼ cup almonds
450g/1lb/2¼ cups short grain rice
25g/1oz/¼ cup sugar
1 cinnamon stick
50g/2oz/¼ cup butter
1.5ml/¼ tsp almond extract
175ml/6fl oz/¾ cup full-fat (whole) milk
175ml/6fl oz/1¾ cup single (light) cream
toasted flaked (sliced) almonds and ground cinnamon, to decorate

1 Put the almonds in a food processor or blender with 60ml/4 tbsp of very hot water. Process until finely chopped, then push through a sieve (strainer) into a bowl. Return to the food processor or blender, add a further 60ml/4 tbsp hot water, and process again. Push through the sieve into a pan.

2 Add 300ml/½ pint/1¼ cups water and bring the mixture to the boil. Add the rice, sugar, cinnamon stick, half the butter, the almond extract, half the milk and half the cream, and mix.

3 Bring to the boil, then simmer, covered, for about 30 minutes, adding more milk and cream as the rice mixture thickens. Continue to cook the rice, stirring, and adding the remaining milk and cream, until the pudding becomes thick and creamy.

4 At the end of the cooking time, taste the rice pudding for sweetness, adding a little extra sugar, if necessary. Pour the rice pudding into a serving bowl and sprinkle with the toasted flaked almonds. Dot with the remaining butter and dust with a little ground cinnamon. Serve the pudding hot.

Variation
Add 2 cardamom pods to the milk mixture in step 2, cook them with the rice, then remove before serving.

Lemon Surpise Pudding

This much-loved dessert probably originated in England in the 1950s, when it appeared in a cookbook under the name of lemon soufflé pudding. It is cheap and easy to make, and is perfect for all the family on a cold day. The surprise is the rich, tangy sauce concealed beneath the light sponge.

Serves 4

50g/2oz/¼ cup butter, plus extra for greasing
grated rind and juice of 2 lemons
115g/4oz/½ cup caster (superfine) sugar
2 eggs, separated
50g/2oz/½ cup self-raising (self-rising) flour
300ml/½ pint/1¼ cups milk
single (light) cream, to serve

1 Preheat the oven to 190°C/375°F/Gas 5. Use a little butter to grease a 1.2-litre/2-pint/5-cup baking dish.

2 Beat the lemon rind, remaining butter and caster sugar in a bowl until pale and fluffy. Add the egg yolks and flour and beat together well. Gradually whisk in the lemon juice and milk (the mixture will curdle, but this is supposed to happen).

3 Fold the egg whites lightly into the lemon mixture using a metal spoon, then pour into the prepared baking dish.

4 Place the dish in a roasting pan and pour in hot water to come halfway up the side of the dish. Bake for 45 minutes until the top is golden. Serve the pudding warm, with a drizzle of cream, if you wish.

Variation
For an orange surprise pudding, use 1 lemon and 1 large orange instead of 2 lemons.

Cook's Tip
Buy unwaxed lemons or scrub the peel thoroughly under hot water to remove the wax before grating.

Moroccan Rice Pudding Energy 443kcal/1847kJ; Protein 8.5g; Carbohydrate 66.6g, of which sugars 6.6g; Fat 15.6g, of which saturates 8.4g; Cholesterol 36mg; Calcium 89mg; Fibre 0.3g; Sodium 72mg
Lemon Pudding Energy 320kcal/1346kJ; Protein 7.1g; Carbohydrate 43.4g, of which sugars 33.8g; Fat 14.5g, of which saturates 8.1g; Cholesterol 126mg; Calcium 139mg; Fibre 0.4g; Sodium 145mg

Coffee and Ginger Pudding

This coffee and ginger topped feather-light sponge is made with breadcrumbs, so it's a great way of making good use of stale bread, rather than throwing it away. Serve with creamy custard or scoops of vanilla ice cream if you wish.

Serves 4

30ml/2 tbsp light muscovado (brown) sugar
25g/1oz/2 tbsp preserved stem ginger, chopped, plus 75ml/5 tbsp ginger syrup
30ml/2 tbsp mild-flavoured ground coffee
25g/1oz/2 tbsp preserved stem ginger, chopped, plus 75ml/5 tbsp ginger syrup
115g/4oz/generous ½ cup caster (superfine) sugar
3 eggs, separated
25g/1oz/¼ cup plain (all-purpose) flour
5ml/1 tsp ground ginger
65g/2½oz/generous 1 cup fresh white breadcrumbs
25g/1oz/¼ cup ground almonds
custard or ice cream, to serve

1 Preheat the oven to 180°C/350°F/Gas 4. Grease and line the base of a 750ml/1¼-pint/3-cup ovenproof bowl, then sprinkle in the muscovado sugar and chopped stem ginger.

2 Put the ground coffee in a small, heatproof bowl. Heat the ginger syrup in a small pan, until almost boiling, then pour into the coffee. Stir well and leave for 4 minutes. Pour through a fine sieve (strainer) into the ovenproof bowl.

3 Beat half the sugar with the egg yolks until light and fluffy. Sift the flour and ground ginger together and fold into the egg yolk mixture with the breadcrumbs and ground almonds.

4 Whisk the egg whites until stiff, then gradually whisk in the remaining caster sugar. Fold into the mixture, in two batches. Spoon into the ovenproof bowl and smooth the top.

5 Cover the bowl with a piece of pleated greased baking parchment to give room for rising, and secure with string. Bake for 40 minutes, or until the sponge is firm to the touch. Turn out and serve immediately.

Sticky Toffee Pudding

Rich, sweet and utterly irresistible, this gooey pudding is sure to be a hit every time you make it.

Serves 6

115g/4oz/1 cup toasted walnuts, roughly chopped
175g/6oz/¾ cup butter
175g/6oz/scant 1 cup light muscovado (brown) sugar
60ml/4 tbsp double (heavy) cream
30ml/2 tbsp lemon juice
2 eggs, beaten
115g/4oz/1 cup self-raising (self-rising) flour
vanilla ice cream or single (light) cream, to serve

1 Grease a 900ml/1½-pint/3¾-cup heatproof bowl and put half the walnuts in the bottom.

2 Heat 50g/2oz/¼ cup of the butter with 50g/2oz/¼ cup of the sugar, the cream and 15ml/1 tbsp lemon juice in a small pan, stirring until smooth.

3 Pour half into the heatproof bowl, then swirl to coat it a little way up the sides.

4 Beat the remaining butter and sugar until fluffy, then beat in the eggs. Fold in the flour, remaining nuts and lemon juice and spoon into the basin.

5 Cover the bowl with baking parchment with a pleat folded in the centre, then tie securely with string. Steam for 1¼ hours, or until a skewer inserted in the centre comes out clean.

6 Just before serving, warm the remaining sauce. Unmould the pudding on to a warm plate and pour over the sauce.

Variation
If you have a few squares of dark chocolate in the storecupboard, chop them into small pieces and add to the nuts at the bottom of the bowl, for a chocolate chip sticky toffee pudding.

Coffee and Ginger Energy 382kcal/1617kJ; Protein 9.7g; Carbohydrate 70.6g, of which sugars 53.5g; Fat 8.9g, of which saturates 1.7g; Cholesterol 171mg; Calcium 93mg; Fibre 1g; Sodium 240mg
Sticky Toffee Energy 606kcal/2523kJ; Protein 7.5g; Carbohydrate 46g, of which sugars 31.6g; Fat 44.9g, of which saturates 20.3g; Cholesterol 152mg; Calcium 122mg; Fibre 1.3g; Sodium 279mg

Hot Chocolate Pudding with Rum Custard

These delicious chocolate puddings are sure to be a hit. For a family dessert, flavour the custard with vanilla.

Serves 6

115g/4oz/½ cup butter
115g/4oz/½ cup light muscovado (brown) sugar
2 eggs, beaten
drops of vanilla extract
45ml/3 tbsp unsweetened cocoa powder, sifted
115g/4oz/1 cup self-raising (self-rising) flour
75g/3oz bitter (semisweet) chocolate, chopped
a little milk, warmed

For the rum custard

250ml/8fl oz/1 cup milk
15ml/1 tbsp caster (superfine) sugar
2 egg yolks
10ml/2 tsp cornflour (cornstarch)
30–45ml/2–3 tbsp rum

1 Lightly grease a 1.2-litre/2-pint/5-cup heatproof bowl or six individual moulds. Cream the butter and sugar until pale and creamy. Gradually blend in the eggs and the vanilla extract.

2 Sift together the cocoa powder and flour, and fold into the egg mixture with the chopped chocolate and sufficient milk to give a soft dropping consistency.

3 Spoon the mixture into the bowl or moulds, cover with buttered baking parchment and tie down. Place in a pan with 2.5–5cm/1–2in water, cover with a lid and bring to the boil. Steam a large pudding for 1½–2 hours and individual puddings for 45–50 minutes, topping up with water if necessary.

4 To make the rum custard, bring the milk and sugar to the boil. Whisk together the egg yolks and cornflour in a heatproof bowl, then pour on the hot milk, whisking constantly.

5 Return the mixture to the pan and stir continuously while it slowly comes back to the boil. Allow the sauce to simmer gently as it thickens, stirring all the time. Remove from the heat and stir in the rum. Turn the puddings out and serve with the custard.

Bread and Butter Pudding with Whiskey Sauce

This traditional dessert is a great way of using up stale white bread. The whiskey sauce is an unusual adult addition, but the pudding can also be served with chilled cream or vanilla ice cream, if you prefer.

Serves 6

8 slices of white bread, crusts removed and buttered
115–150g/4–5oz/⅔–¾ cup sultanas (golden raisins), or mixed dried fruit
2.5ml/½ tsp grated nutmeg
260g/9½oz/1¼ cups caster (superfine) sugar
2 large (US extra large) eggs
300ml/½ pint/1¼ cups single (light) cream
450ml/¾ pint/scant 2 cups milk
5ml/1 tsp of vanilla extract
light muscovado (brown) sugar, for sprinkling (optional)

For the whiskey sauce

150g/5oz/10 tbsp butter
1 egg
45ml/3 tbsp Irish whiskey

1 Preheat the oven to 180°C/350°F/Gas 4. Put four slices of bread, buttered side down, in the base of an ovenproof dish. Sprinkle with the sultanas or mixed dried fruit, some of the nutmeg and 15ml/1 tbsp sugar.

2 Place the remaining four slices of bread on top, buttered side down, and sprinkle again with nutmeg and 15ml/1 tbsp sugar.

3 Beat the eggs, add the cream, milk, vanilla extract and 115g/4oz/generous ½ cup caster sugar, and mix to make a custard. Pour over the bread, and sprinkle light muscovado suga over the top, if you would like to have a crispy crust. Bake for 1 hour, or until the pudding has risen and is brown.

4 Meanwhile, make the sauce: melt the butter in a heavy pan, add the remaining caster sugar and dissolve over low heat.

5 Remove from the heat and add the egg, whisking, then add the whiskey. Serve the pudding in big scoops, with the whiskey sauce poured over the top.

Chocolate Pudding Energy 458kcal/1915kJ; Protein 8.3g; Carbohydrate 49g, of which sugars 31.5g; Fat 25.6g, of which saturates 14.5g; Cholesterol 186mg; Calcium 145mg; Fibre 1.8g; Sodium 302m
Bread Pudding Energy 757kcal/3168kJ; Protein 11.7g; Carbohydrate 82g, of which sugars 65.2g; Fat 40.8g, of which saturates 24.3g; Cholesterol 207mg; Calcium 232mg; Fibre 0.9g; Sodium 472mg

Rhubarb Frushie

A frushie is the old Scots word for a crumble. In this instance the topping is made with coarse rolled oats. Other fruits, such as apple and blackberry, or gooseberries, can be used according to availability.

Serves 4

450g/1lb rhubarb or other fruit
45–60ml/3–4 tbsp water
50g/2oz/¼ cup caster (superfine) sugar or 30ml/2 tbsp redcurrant jelly
squeeze of lemon juice

For the topping

50g/2oz/½ cup plain (all-purpose) flour
25g/1oz/scant ⅓ cup coarse rolled oats
50g/2oz/¼ cup soft brown sugar
50g/2oz/¼ cup butter, softened

1 Preheat the oven to 200°C/400°F/Gas 6. Cook the rhubarb or other fruit with the water, sugar or redcurrant jelly, and lemon juice until soft but not mushy. Transfer to a deep pie dish.

2 Combine all the ingredients for the topping with your fingers until the mixture has a crumb-like texture. Sprinkle the crumble topping evenly over the fruit.

3 Place in the top of the preheated oven and bake for about 20 minutes, or until the top is crunchy and slightly brown. Serve immediately with hot custard, fresh whipped cream or vanilla ice cream, if you like.

Plum Crumble

The crumble is an infinitely versatile and perennially popular dessert. Choose whichever plum is available locally. Serve with hot custard, cream or scoops of vanilla ice cream.

Serves 4

450g/1lb stoned (pitted) plums
50g/2oz/¼ cup light muscovado (brown) sugar
15ml/1 tbsp water
juice of 1 lemon

For the crumble topping

50g/2oz/½ cup plain (all-purpose) flour
25g/1oz/generous ¼ cup coarse rolled oats
50g/2oz/¼ cup light muscovado (brown) sugar
50g/2oz/¼ cup butter, softened

1 Preheat the oven to 200°C/400°F/Gas 6. Place a large pan over medium heat. Put the plums in the pan and add the sugar, water and lemon juice. Mix thoroughly and bring to the boil, stirring continuously until the sugar dissolves.

2 Cook the plums until they are just beginning to soften, then place the fruit with the juices in a deep pie dish.

3 Place the flour, oats, sugar and butter in a bowl and mix with your fingers until the mixture resembles breadcrumbs.

4 Sprinkle the crumble topping evenly over the fruit so that it is a good thickness. Bake in the preheated oven for 20 minutes, or until the top is crunchy and brown.

Scone and Butter Pudding

This simple yet elegant pudding is a good way to use up scones that are slightly stale. Either use home-made, or good quality bought ones. You can use any type of dried fruit, depending on what is in your kitchen; dried berries, such as cranberries or cherries, make a lovely sharp, tangy pudding.

Serves 4

50g/2oz/scant ½ cup sultanas (golden raisins)
50g/2oz/¼ cup ready-to-eat dried apricots, cut into small pieces
50ml/2fl oz/¼ cup whisky
300ml/½ pint/1¼ cups milk
300ml/½ pint/1¼ cups double (heavy) cream
5 egg yolks
50g/2oz/¼ cup caster (superfine) sugar
2 drops vanilla extract
6 scones
75g/3oz/6 tbsp butter
60ml/4 tbsp apricot jam, slightly warmed

1 Place the dried fruit and whisky in a small bowl, cover and leave to soak overnight or for at least 2 hours. Preheat the oven to 200°C/400°F/Gas 6.

2 Whisk the milk, cream, egg yolks, sugar and vanilla extract. Slice the tops off the scones and then slice each into three rounds. Butter each round and then layer with the fruit and custard in buttered ramekins. Set aside for 1 hour.

3 Place the ramekins in a deep baking tin (pan) and pour in enough boiling water to come half way up the ramekins. Bake for 40 minutes until risen slightly and golden-brown in colour.

4 Remove from the oven and brush with the warmed apricot jam. Serve immediately in the ramekins.

Variation

If you don't have any whiskey in the house, use brandy or rum instead. You can also use black tea, if you wish, it will have the same effect as the alcohol and will plump up the fruit.

Rhubarb Frushie Energy 267kcal/1126kJ; Protein 3.2g; Carbohydrate 41.4g, of which sugars 27.3g; Fat 11.1g, of which saturates 6.5g; Cholesterol 27mg; Calcium 141mg; Fibre 2.4g; Sodium 83mg
Plum Crumble Energy 304kcal/1284kJ; Protein 2.9g; Carbohydrate 51.5g, of which sugars 37.4g; Fat 11.1g, of which saturates 6.5g; Cholesterol 27mg; Calcium 53mg; Fibre 2.8g; Sodium 82mg
Scone Pudding Energy 796kcal/3305kJ; Protein 8.1g; Carbohydrate 43.2g, of which sugars 43.2g; Fat 63.9g, of which saturates 37.6g; Cholesterol 399mg; Calcium 178mg; Fibre 0.5g; Sodium 187mg

Rhubarb and Raspberry Almond Crumble

The sharp flavour of rhubarb is beautifully offset by sweet raspberries and a sweet almond crumble topping in this stunning dessert.

Serves 4

675g/1½lb fresh forced rhubarb, cut into chunks
a pinch of ground allspice
225g/8oz/scant 1½ cups caster (superfine) sugar
grated rind and juice of 1 lime
225g/8oz raspberries
custard or clotted cream, to serve

For the topping

115g/4oz/1 cup plain (all-purpose) flour
a pinch of salt
50g/2oz/½ cup ground almonds
115g/4oz/½ cup cold butter
115g/4oz/1 cup blanched almonds, chopped

1 Preheat the oven to 200°C/400°F/Gas 6 and put a baking sheet inside to heat up. Cut the rhubarb into chunks and put in a pan with the allspice, 175g/6oz/scant 1 cup caster sugar, lime rind and juice.

2 Cook over low heat for 2 minutes, stirring occasionally, until the chunks of rhubarb are tender but still hold their shape when probed with a knife. Pour into a sieve (strainer), set over a bowl to catch the juices. Leave to cool. Reserve the juices.

3 To make the topping, put the flour, pinch of salt, ground almonds and butter into a food processor and process until the mixture resembles fine breadcrumbs. Transfer into a bowl and stir in the blanched almonds and remaining sugar.

4 Spoon the rhubarb into a large ovenproof dish, and stir in the raspberries. Sprinkle the almond mixture evenly over the surface, mounding it up a little towards the centre.

5 Place the dish on the baking sheet and bake for 35 minutes until crisp and golden on top. Cool for 5 minutes before serving the crumble with warm custard, or clotted cream, and the reserved rhubarb juices.

Apple and Blackberry Wholemeal Crumble

The pinhead oatmeal in the topping makes this traditional hot dessert especially crunchy and flavoursome. Make it in the autumn when apples are plentiful and cheap. Serve with crème fraîche or ice cream.

Serves 8

900g/2lb cooking apples
450g/1lb/4 cups blackberries
juice of ½ lemon (optional)
175g/6oz/scant 1 cup sugar

For the topping

115g/4oz/½ cup butter
115g/4oz/1 cup wholemeal (whole-wheat) flour
50g/2oz/½ cup soft light brown sugar
50g/2oz/½ cup fine or medium pinhead oatmeal
grated lemon rind (optional)

1 Preheat the oven to 200°C/400°F/Gas 6. To make the crumble topping, rub the butter into the flour, and then add the brown sugar and oatmeal and continue to rub in until the mixture begins to stick together, forming large crumbs. Mix in the grated lemon rind, if using.

2 Peel and core the cooking apples, then slice into wedges. Put the apples, blackberries, lemon juice (if using), 30ml/2 tbsp water and the sugar into a shallow ovenproof dish, about 2 litres/3½ pints/9 cups capacity.

3 Cover the fruit with the crumble topping and sprinkle with a little cold water. Bake for 15 minutes, then reduce the heat to 190°C/375°F/Gas 5 and cook for another 15–20 minutes until crunchy and brown on top.

4 Serve the crumble hot with lashings of custard, crème fraîche or vanilla ice cream.

Variation
Blackcurrants and gooseberries can also be used as a filling.

Rhubarb Crumble Energy 812kcal/3403kJ; Protein 14.2g; Carbohydrate 88.1g, of which sugars 65.1g; Fat 47.4g, of which saturates 16.9g; Cholesterol 61mg; Calcium 345mg; Fibre 7.7g; Sodium 191mg
Apple Crumble Energy 470kcal/1974kJ; Protein 5.1g; Carbohydrate 78.2g, of which sugars 60.3g; Fat 17.2g, of which saturates 10g; Cholesterol 41mg; Calcium 71mg; Fibre 7g; Sodium 128mg

›esame and Banana Fritters

'hese deep fried bananas ·oated in sesame seeds are ıbulously good. If you only ave large bananas, cut them ·p into small chunks.

·erves 4

0g/2oz desiccated (dry unsweetened shredded) coconut
0g/2oz/¼ cup sugar
5ml/1 tsp ground cinnamon
2.5ml/½ tsp baking powder
115g/4oz/1 cup rice flour
30ml/2 tbsp sesame seeds
600ml/1 pint/2½ cups coconut milk
sunflower oil, for frying
6 small bananas, peeled and cut in half lengthways
icing (confectioner's) sugar, to dust

Place the coconut, sugar, cinnamon, baking powder, rice flour, ·esame seeds and coconut milk in a large mixing bowl. Whisk horoughly to form a smooth batter. Cover with clear film plastic wrap) and leave to rest for 30 minutes–1 hour.

. Fill a wok or deep frying pan one-third full of the oil and heat ɔ 180°C/350°F (or until a cube of bread, dropped into the oil, ·rowns in 15 seconds).

: Working in batches, dip the halved bananas into the batter, rain off any excess and gently lower into the oil. Deep-fry for –4 minutes, or until golden.

· Remove the bananas using a slotted spoon and drain well on ·itchen paper. Serve hot or warm, dusted with icing sugar, with coops of vanilla ice cream.

Variation

For apple fritters whisk together a batter of 200g/7oz/1¾ cups self-raising (self-rising) flour, 100ml/3½fl oz/scant ½ cup milk, 5ml/1 tsp baking powder, 40g/1½oz caster (superfine) sugar and pinch of salt. Cut 2 large apples into peeled and cored rings, and deep fry in the same way as the banana friters until crisp and golden. Drain on kitchen paper, dust with icing (confectioner's) sugar, and serve straight away.

Sweet and Spicy Rice Fritters

These delicious little golden balls of rice are scented with sweet, warm spices and will fill the kitchen with wonderful aromas while you're cooking.

Serves 4

175g/6oz cooked basmati rice
2 eggs, lightly beaten
60ml/4 tbsp caster (superfine) sugar
a pinch of nutmeg
2.5ml/½ tsp ground cinnamon
a pinch of ground cloves
10ml/2 tsp vanilla extract
50g/2oz/½ cup plain (all-purpose) flour
10ml/2 tsp baking powder
a pinch of salt
25g/1oz desiccated (dry unsweetened shredded) coconut
sunflower oil, for frying
icing (confectioners') sugar, to dust

1 Place the cooked rice, eggs, sugar, nutmeg, cinnamon, cloves and vanilla extract in a large bowl and whisk to combine. Sift in the flour, baking powder and salt and add the coconut. Mix well until thoroughly combined.

2 Fill a wok or deep frying pan one-third full of the oil and heat to 180°C/350°F (or until a cube of bread, dropped into the oil, browns in 15 seconds).

3 Very gently, drop tablespoonfuls of the mixture into the oil, one at a time, and fry for 2–3 minutes, or until golden. Carefully remove the fritters from the wok using a slotted spoon and drain well on kitchen paper.

4 Divide the fritters into four portions, or simply pile them up on a single large platter. Dust them with icing sugar and serve immediately.

Cook's Tip

Unlike many cakes and cookies, these little fritters are gluten-free, so they make a perfect sweet snack for anyone with a gluten intolerance.

›esame Fritters Energy 407kcal/1696kJ; Protein 4.4g; Carbohydrate 44.3g, of which sugars 21.3g; Fat 23.8g, of which saturates 8.9g; Cholesterol 0mg; Calcium 110mg; Fibre 2.9g; Sodium 172mg
›weet and Spicy Fritters Energy 316kcal/1321kJ; Protein 6.6g; Carbohydrate 45.7g, of which sugars 16.3g; Fat 12.4g, of which saturates 4.8g; Cholesterol 95mg; Calcium 46mg; Fibre 1.3g; Sodium 38mg

Calvados-flamed Bananas

Soft and creamy baked bananas, flamed with calvados, are delicious served with a rich butterscotch sauce. The sauce can be made in advance and the bananas are quickly cooked.

Serves 6

115g/4oz/generous ½ cup sugar
25g/1oz/2 tbsp butter
150ml/¼ pint/⅔ cup double (heavy) cream
6 large slightly underripe bananas
90ml/6 tbsp calvados

1 Place the sugar and 150ml/¼ pint/⅔ cup water in a large pan and heat gently until the sugar has dissolved.

2 Increase the heat and boil the mixture until it turns a rich golden caramel colour.

3 Remove from the heat and carefully add the butter and cream; the mixture will foam up in the pan. Replace over low heat and stir to a smooth sauce, then pour into a bowl and leave to cool. Cover and chill until needed.

4 Prepare the barbecue. Wrap the bananas individually in foil. Position a grill rack over the hot coals. Grill the wrapped bananas over high heat for 10 minutes.

5 Transfer the bananas to a tray, open up the parcels and slit the upper side of each banana skin.

6 Meanwhile, gently warm the calvados in a small pan, then pour some into each banana.

7 Put them back on the barbecue and wait for a few seconds before carefully igniting the calvados with a long match. Serve with the sauce as soon as the flames die down.

Cook's Tip
These bananas can be cooked indoors using a grill (broiler) or by baking them in a hot oven.

Treacle Tart

It is worth taking the time to make your own pastry for this old-fashioned favourite, with its sticky filling and twisted lattice topping.

Serves 4-6

225g/8oz/2 cups plain (all-purpose) flour
115g/4oz/ cup cold butter
cold water, to mix

For the filling

260g/9½oz/generous ¾ cup golden (light corn) syrup
1 lemon
75g/3oz/1½ cups fresh white breadcrumbs

1 Make the pastry by sifting the flour and rubbing the butter in until the mixture resembles fine breadcrumbs. Gradually add 45–60ml/3–4 tbsp water until the dough comes together in a ball. Wrap and chill in the refrigerator for 20–30 minutes.

2 On a lightly floured surface, roll out three-quarters of the pastry to a thickness of 3mm/⅛in. Transfer to a 20cm/8in fluted flan tin (pan) and trim off the overhang. Chill the pastry case (pie shell) for 20 minutes. Reserve the trimmings.

3 Put a baking sheet in the oven and preheat to 200°C/400°F/Gas 6. To make the filling, warm the syrup in a pan until it melts. Grate the lemon rind and squeeze the juice.

4 Remove the syrup from the heat and stir in the breadcrumbs and lemon rind. Leave to stand for 10 minutes, then add more crumbs if the mixture is too thin and moist. Stir in 30ml/2 tbsp of the lemon juice, then spread the mixture evenly in the pastry case.

5 Roll out the reserved pastry and cut into 10–12 thin strips. Twist the strips into spirals, then lay half of them on the filling. Arrange the remaining strips at right angles to form a lattice. Press the ends on to the rim.

6 Place the tart on the hot baking sheet and bake for 10 minutes. Lower the oven temperature to 190°C/375°F/Gas 5. Bake for 15 minutes more, until golden. Serve warm.

Calvados Bananas Energy 359kcal/1501kJ; Protein 1.7g; Carbohydrate 43.7g, of which sugars 41.4g; Fat 17.2g, of which saturates 10.6g; Cholesterol 43mg; Calcium 29mg; Fibre 1.1g; Sodium 33mg
Treacle Tart Energy 437kcal/1837kJ; Protein 4.9g; Carbohydrate 71.2g, of which sugars 35.1g; Fat 16.6g, of which saturates 5.1g; Cholesterol 8mg; Calcium 73mg; Fibre 1.4g; Sodium 445mg

.emon Meringue Tart

his popular tart has a tangy mon custard topped with oft meringue. It is best erved at room temperature.

erves 6

quantity of pastry from Treacle Tart recipe (see opposite)
)g/2oz/½ cup cornflour (cornstarch)
250g/9oz/1¼ cup caster (superfine) sugar
finely grated rind and juice of 2 lemons
2 egg yolks
15g/½oz/1 tbsp butter, diced

For the topping
2 egg whites
pinch of salt

Preheat the oven to 200°C/400°F/Gas 6. Roll out the pastry n a lightly floured surface and use to line a 20cm/8in flan tin ɔan). Prick the base with a fork, line with baking parchment or il and add a layer of baking beans to prevent the pastry rising. ake in the oven for 15 minutes.

Remove the beans and parchment or foil, return to the oven ɔ cook for a further 5 minutes until crisp and golden brown. educe the oven temperature to 150°C/300°F/Gas 2.

To make the lemon filling, put the cornflour into a pan and dd 175g/6oz/¾ cup sugar, lemon rind and 300ml/½ pint/1¼ ıps water. Heat the mixture, stirring continuously, until it comes ɔ the boil and thickens.

Reduce the heat and simmer very gently for 1 minute. emove the pan from the heat and stir in the lemon juice.

Add the egg yolks to the lemon mixture, one at a time, eating after each addition, and then stir in the butter. Transfer e mixture into the baked pastry case and level the surface.

To make the meringue topping, whisk the egg whites until stiff, en whisk in half the remaining sugar. Fold in the rest of the ıgar using a metal spoon. Spread the meringue over the lemon ing. Cook for 20 minutes, until the top is lightly browned. eave to cool slightly, then slice to serve.

Curd Tart

Delicious and inexpensive, this tart made from curd cheese and subtly flavoured with allspice is so good that it is difficult to resist second helpings. Serve for dessert or for a special tea.

Serves 8

90g/3½ oz/scant ½ cup light muscovado (brown) sugar
pinch of ground allspice
3 eggs, beaten
grated rind and juice of 1 lemon
40g/1½oz/3 tbsp butter, melted
450g/1lb/2 cups curd (farmer's) cheese
75g/3oz/scant ½ cup raisins

For the pastry
225g/8oz/2 cups plain (all-purpose) flour
115g/4oz/½ cup chilled butter, diced
1 egg yolk
15–30ml/1–2 tbsp chilled water

1 To make the pastry, sift the flour into a mixing bowl and rub in the chilled butter until the mixture resembles fine breadcrumbs. Stir the egg yolk into the flour mixture and add just enough of the water to bind the mixture together to form a soft dough.

2 Put the dough on a floured surface, knead lightly and briefly, then form into a ball. Roll out the pastry thinly and use to line a 20cm/8in fluted loose-based flan tin (tart pan). Cover with clear film (plastic wrap) and chill for about 15 minutes.

3 Preheat the oven to 190°C/375°F/Gas 5. Mix the sugar with the ground allspice in a bowl, then stir in the eggs, lemon rind and juice, butter, curd cheese and raisins. Mix well.

4 Pour the filling into the pastry case (pie shell), then bake for 40 minutes, or until the pastry is cooked and the filling is lightly set and golden brown. Cut the tart into wedges while it is still slightly warm, and serve with cream, if you like.

Variations
Although it is not traditional, mixed spice (apple pie spice) would make a good substitute for the ground allspice.

ımon Meringue Energy 357kcal/1497kJ; Protein 6.8g; Carbohydrate 42.8g, of which sugars 25.1g; Fat 18.9g, of which saturates 9g; Cholesterol 129mg; Calcium 108mg; Fibre 0.7g; Sodium 137mg
ırd Tart Energy 406kcal/1700kJ; Protein 14g; Carbohydrate 41.4g, of which sugars 20g; Fat 21.7g, of which saturates 12.4g; Cholesterol 159mg; Calcium 110mg; Fibre 1.1g; Sodium 371mg

Bakewell Tart

This tart combines soft puff pastry with jam and a rich almond sponge. Served hot, warm or cold it is absolutely delicious with custard, cream or ice cream.

Serves 4

225g/8oz puff pastry
30ml/2 tbsp raspberry jam
2 eggs, plus 2 egg yolks
115g/4oz/½ cup caster (superfine) sugar
115g/4oz/½ cup butter, melted
50g/2oz/½ cup ground almonds
a few drops of almond extract
grated rind of 1 lemon
icing (confectioners') sugar, for dusting

1 Preheat the oven to 200°C/400°F/Gas 6. Roll out the pastry on a lightly floured surface and use to line an 18cm/7in pie plate. Trim the edge.

2 Re-roll the pastry trimmings and cut out wide strips of pastry. Use these to decorate the edge of the pastry case (pie shell) by twisting them around the rim, joining the strips together as necessary. Prick the pastry case all over with a fork, then spread the jam over the base.

3 Whisk the eggs, egg yolks and sugar together in a bowl until the mixture is thick and pale.

4 Gently stir the melted butter, ground almonds, almond extract and lemon rind into the whisked egg mixture.

5 Pour the mixture into the pastry case and bake for about 30 minutes, or until the filling is just set and is lightly browned. Dust with icing sugar before serving hot, warm or cold.

Cook's Tip
Since this pastry case is not baked blind before being filled, place a baking sheet in the oven while it preheats, then place the tart on the hot sheet. This will ensure that the base of the pastry case cooks right through.

Baked Bananas with Toffee Sauce

Bananas make one of the easiest of all desserts, just as welcome as a comforting winter treat as they are to follow a barbecue. For an extra sweet finishing touch, grate some plain chocolate on the bananas, over the sauce, just before serving. If baking on a barbecue, turn the bananas occasionally to ensure even cooking.

Serves 4

4 large bananas
75g/3oz/scant ½ cup light muscovado (brown) sugar
75ml/5 tbsp double (heavy) crean
4 scoops vanilla ice cream, to serv

1 Preheat the oven to 180°C/350°F/Gas 4. Put the bananas, stil in their skins, in an ovenproof dish and bake for 15–20 minutes, until the skins are very dark, almost black, and the flesh feels so when gently squeezed.

2 Meanwhile, to make the toffee sauce heat the light muscovado sugar in a small, heavy pan with 75ml/5 tbsp water until dissolved. Bring to the boil and add the double cream. Cook for 5 minutes, until the sauce has thickened and is toffee coloured. Remove from the heat.

3 Transfer the baked bananas in their skins to serving plates anc split them lengthways to reveal the flesh.

4 Pour some of the sauce over the bananas and top each one with a scoop of vanilla ice cream. Serve any remaining toffee sauce on the side for people to help themsleves.

Variation
A spicy vanilla butter adds a luxurious finish to this dessert. To make, split 6 green cardamom pods and remove seeds, crush lightly. Split a vanilla pod lengthways and scrape out the tiny seeds. Mix with cardamom seeds, finely grated rind and juice of small orange and 45ml/3 tbsp butter into a thick paste. Place a spoonful inside each baked banana.

Bakewell Tart Energy 417kcal/1753kJ; Protein 8.6g; Carbohydrate 56.1g, of which sugars 36g; Fat 19.9g, of which saturates 1.7g; Cholesterol 215mg; Calcium 78mg; Fibre 0g; Sodium 226mg
Bananas with Toffee Energy 455kcal/1910kJ; Protein 6.9g; Carbohydrate 63.2g, of which sugars 56.6g; Fat 21.1g, of which saturates 12.6g; Cholesterol 53mg; Calcium 215mg; Fibre 0.6g; Sodium 178m

Baked Apples

Baking is a simple and nutritious way of cooking this orchard fruit. Use cooking apples such as Bramley. Serve with warm custard while the apples are still hot.

Serves 4
4 large apples
35g/1½oz/3 tbsp butter
90ml/6 tbsp walnuts, roughly chopped
30ml/2 tbsp sugar
5ml/1 tsp cinnamon

1 Preheat the oven to 180°C/350°F/Gas 4. Remove the core of the apples, then score the skin around the circumference to prevent the skin bursting. Place the apples in a baking dish with a little water.

2 Melt 25g/1oz/2 tbsp of the butter. In a bowl, mix the melted butter with the walnuts, sugar and cinnamon.

3 Divide the filling into four and fill the cavity of each apple. Top each with a knob of the remaining butter and bake for about 20–30 minutes or until the apples are soft but not collapsing. Serve hot with warm custard.

Variation
Use a mixture of chopped almonds and honey in the filling instead of walnuts and sugar.

Summer Berries in Warm Sabayon Glaze

This luxurious combination consists of summer berries under a light and fluffy sauce flavoured with liqueur. The topping is lightly grilled to form a caramelized crust.

Serves 4
450g/1lb/4 cups mixed summer berries, such as strawberries, raspberries, blueberries and black or red currants
4 egg yolks
50g/2oz/¼ cup caster (superfine) sugar
120ml/4fl oz/½ cup liqueur, such as Cointreau
mint leaves, to decorate
icing (confectioners') sugar, sifted, to decorate

1 Arrange the fruit in four heatproof ramekins. Preheat the grill (broiler) to high.

2 Whisk the yolks in a large bowl with the sugar and liqueur. Place over a pan of hot water and whisk constantly until thick, fluffy and pale.

3 Pour equal quantities of the sauce over the summer berries in each dish. Place under the preheated grill for 1–2 minutes until just turning brown.

4 Dust the fruit with icing sugar and sprinkle with mint leaves just before serving. You could also add an extra splash of liqueur.

Blackberry Charlotte

A classic pudding, perfect for early autumn. Serve with lightly whipped cream or home-made custard.

Serves 4
65g/2½oz/5 tbsp unsalted butter
175 g/6oz/3 cups fresh white breadcrumbs
50g/2oz/4 tbsp soft brown sugar
60ml/4 tbsp golden (light corn) syrup
finely grated rind and juice of 2 lemons
50g/2oz walnut halves
450g/1lb blackberries
450g/1lb cooking apples, peeled, cored and finely sliced

1 Preheat the oven to 180°C /350°F/Gas Mark 4. Grease a 450ml/¾-pint/2-cup dish with 15g/½oz/1 tbsp of the butter. Melt the remaining butter and add the breadcrumbs. Sauté them for 5–7 minutes, until the breadcrumbs are a little crisp and golden. Leave to cool slightly.

2 Place the sugar, syrup, lemon rind and juice in a small pan and gently warm them. Add the breadcrumbs. Process the walnuts until they are finely ground and stir in to the breadcrumbs.

3 Arrange a thin layer of blackberries in the dish. Top the berries with a thin layer of breadcrumbs.

4 Add a thin layer of apple, topping it with another thin layer of crumbs. Repeat the process with another layer of blackberries, followed by a layer of crumbs. Continue until you have used up all the ingredients, finishing with a layer of breadcrumbs. The mixture should be piled slightly above the top edge of the dish, because it shrinks during cooking.

5 Bake the charlotte for 30 minutes, until the breadcrumbs are golden and the fruit is soft. Serve warm.

Cook's Tip
Blackberries grow in the hedgerow in early autumn. They can be a little woody fresh, but are sweet and tender when cooked.

Baked Apples Energy 294kcal/1229kJ; Protein 5.3g; Carbohydrate 22.8g, of which sugars 22.2g; Fat 20.9g, of which saturates 6.2g; Cholesterol 21mg; Calcium 66mg; Fibre 4.1g; Sodium 67mg
Summer Berries Energy 235kcal/984kJ; Protein 3.9g; Carbohydrate 27.1g, of which sugars 27.1g; Fat 5.6g, of which saturates 1.6g; Cholesterol 202mg; Calcium 48mg; Fibre 1.3g; Sodium 18mg
Blackberry Charlotte Energy 546Kcal/2294kJ; Protein 8.5g; Carbohydrate 81g, of which sugars 48.2g; Fat 23.1g, of which saturates 9.2g; Cholesterol 35mg; Calcium 133mg; Fibre 6.7g; Sodium 498mg

Tarte Tatin

This French dessert was first made by two sisters who served it in their restaurant in the Loire Valley. A special tarte tatin tin is ideal, but an ovenproof frying pan will do.

Serves 8–10

225g/8oz puff or shortcrust pastry
10–12 large apples
lemon juice
115g/4oz/½ cup butter, cut into pieces
115g/4oz/generous ½ cup caster (superfine) sugar
2.5ml/½ tsp ground cinnamon
crème fraîche or whipped cream, to serve

1 On a lightly floured surface, roll out the pastry into a 28cm/11in round less than 6mm/¼in thick. Transfer to a lightly floured baking sheet and chill.

2 Peel the apples, cut them in half lengthways and core. Sprinkle the apples generously with lemon juice.

3 In a 25cm/10in tarte tatin tin (tart pan), or frying pan, cook the butter, sugar and cinnamon over medium heat until the butter has melted and sugar dissolved, stirring occasionally. Continue cooking for 6–8 minutes, until the mixture turns a medium caramel colour, then remove from the heat and arrange the apple halves in the tin, fitting them in tightly.

4 Return the tin to the heat and simmer over medium heat for 20–25 minutes until the apples are tender and coloured. Set aside to cool slightly. Preheat the oven to 230°C/450°F/Gas 8.

5 Place the pastry on top of the tin and tuck the edges inside the edge around the apples. Pierce the pastry in two or three places, then bake for 25–30 minutes until golden and bubbling. Leave to cool in the tin for 10–15 minutes.

6 To serve, run a sharp knife around edge of the tin to loosen the pastry. Cover with a serving plate and, holding them tightly, invert the tin and plate together (do this carefully, in case any caramel drips). Lift off the tin and loosen any apples that stick with a palette knife. Serve the tart warm with cream.

Apple Pie

There are many variations on this classic all-time-favourite recipe, and it is a great way of enjoying seasonal apples. For a slightly different twist, you could add ground cinnamon or dried cranberries to the filling, if you like. Bake in a traditional metal pie plate so that the pastry base will be perfectly cooked. Serve warm or cold with chilled whipped cream, or vanilla ice cream.

Serves 6

Double quantity of pastry from Treacle Tart recipe, (see page 206)
675g/1½lb cooking apples
115g/4oz/generous ½ cup caster (superfine) sugar
75g/3oz/½ cup sultanas (golden raisins) (optional)
a little grated lemon rind (optional)
a knob (pat) of butter or 15ml/1 tbsp of water
a little milk or beaten egg, to glaze
whipped cream, to serve

1 Roll out two-thirds of the chilled pastry and use to line a 23cm/9in pie plate. Use any trimmings to make a rim of pastry around the top edge of the pie plate.

2 To make the filling, peel, core and slice the apples and arrange half of them on the pastry base, then sprinkle over the sultanas and lemon rind, if using. Top with the caster sugar, the remaining apples and butter or water.

3 Roll out the remainder of the pastry to make a circle about 2.5cm/1in larger than the pie plate.

4 Dampen the pastry edging on the rim and lay the top over the apples, draping it gently over any lumps to avoid straining the pastry. Press the rim well to seal. Pinch the edges with your fingers to make a fluted edge.

5 Brush the pastry lightly with milk or beaten egg and bake the pie in the preheated oven for about 30 minutes, or until the pastry has browned and is crisp, and the fruit is cooked.

6 Serve the pie in thick slices, warm or cold, with vanilla ice cream or whipped cream.

Tarte Tatin Energy 236kcal/986kJ; Protein 1.6g; Carbohydrate 25.8g, of which sugars 17.7g; Fat 15g, of which saturates 6g; Cholesterol 25mg; Calcium 24mg; Fibre 1g; Sodium 141mg
Apple Pie Energy 393kcal/1650kJ; Protein 4.1g; Carbohydrate 56.3g, of which sugars 27.7g; Fat 18.4g, of which saturates 11.4g; Cholesterol 46mg; Calcium 68mg; Fibre 2.5g; Sodium 136mg

ᵃancakes with Caramelized Pears

ᶠ you can find them, use Villiams pears for this recipe ecause they are juicier than nost other varieties. For a eally indulgent breakfast, top he pancakes with a generous poonful of crème fraîche or omage frais.

Serves 4
50g/2oz/¼ cup butter
8 ready-made pancakes
4 ripe pears, peeled, cored and thickly sliced
30ml/2 tbsp light muscovado (brown) sugar

Preheat the oven to 150°C/330°F/Gas 2. Tightly wrap the ancakes in foil and place in the oven to warm through.

: Meanwhile, heat the butter in a large frying pan and add the ears. Fry for 2–3 minutes, until the undersides are golden. urn the pears over and sprinkle with sugar. Cook for a further –3 minutes, or until the sugar dissolves and the pan juices ecome sticky.

Remove the pancakes from the foil. Divide the pears among ne pancakes, placing them in one quarter. Fold each pancake in alf over the filling, then into quarters.

Place two folded pancakes on each plate. Drizzle over any emaining juices and serve immediately.

Cook's Tip
To make your own pancakes take 150ml/¼ pint/⅔ cup milk, top up with water to make 300ml/½ pint/1¼ cups. Sift 225g/8oz/2 cups plain (all-purpose) flour into a large bowl. Make a well in the centre and break 2 eggs into it. With a whisk, stir in the eggs, gradually adding the milk mixture to make a smooth batter. Melt 25g/1oz/2 tbsp butter and whisk in. Leave to stand for 30 minutes and stir before using. Preheat a heavy frying pan. Lightly butter and add a large spoonful of batter to make a pancake about 15–20cm/6–8in across. Cook for a minute or until the underside is golden brown. Repeat.

Baked Caramel Custard

This sophisticated custard has a rich caramel flavour which is wonderful with cream and strawberries.

Serves 6–8
250g/9oz/1¼ cups sugar
10ml/2 tsp vanilla extract
425ml/15fl oz/1¾ cups double (heavy) cream
5 large eggs, plus 2 extra yolks
thick double cream and fresh strawberries, to serve

1 Put 175g/6oz/generous ¾ cup of the sugar in a heavy pan with enough water to moisten the sugar. Bring to the boil, swirling the pan until the sugar is dissolved. Boil for 5 minutes, without stirring, until the syrup turns a dark caramel colour.

2 Quickly pour the caramel into a 1-litre/1¾-pint/4-cup soufflé dish. Swirl to coat the base and sides, then set aside to cool.

3 Preheat the oven to 160°C/325°F/Gas 3. Put the vanilla extract and cream in a pan and bring just to the boil, stirring frequently. Remove from the heat, cover and set aside to cool.

4 In a bowl, whisk the eggs and egg yolks with the remaining sugar for 2–3 minutes until smooth and creamy. Whisk in the cream and strain into the caramel-lined dish. Cover with foil.

5 Place in a roasting pan and pour in just enough boiling water to come halfway up the side of the dish. Bake for about 40–45 minutes until just set. Remove from the roasting pan and leave to cool, then chill overnight.

6 To turn out, run a knife around the edge of the dish, then cover with a serving plate and invert slowly, allowing the caramel to run out. Serve with cream and strawberries.

Variation
Slice the strawberries and marinate them in a little sugar and a liqueur or dessert wine, such as Amaretto or Muscat wine.

ancakes with Pears Energy 544kcal/2274kJ; Protein 7.7g; Carbohydrate 64.9g, of which sugars 42.4g; Fat 29.9g, of which saturates 6.5g; Cholesterol 27mg; Calcium 155mg; Fibre 4.3g; Sodium 144mg
aked Custard Energy 622kcal/2587kJ; Protein 9.6g; Carbohydrate 44.8g, of which sugars 44.8g; Fat 46.4g, of which saturates 26g; Cholesterol 386mg; Calcium 98mg; Fibre 0g; Sodium 103mg

Boston Banoffee Pie

This scrumptious pie is so easy to make. Simply press the wonderfully biscuity pastry into the tin, rather than rolling it out.

Serves 6

115g/4oz/½ cup butter, diced
200g/7oz can skimmed, sweetened condensed milk
115g/4oz/½ cup light muscovado (brown) sugar
30ml/2 tbsp golden (light corn) syrup
2 small bananas, sliced
a little lemon juice
whipped cream, to decorate
5ml/1 tsp grated plain (semisweet) chocolate

For the pastry

150g/5oz/1¼ cups plain (all-purpose) flour
115g/4oz/½ cup butter, diced
50g/2oz/¼ cup caster (superfine) sugar

1 Preheat the oven to 160°C/325°F/Gas 3. In a food processor, process the flour and diced butter until the mixture resembles breadcrumbs. Stir in the caster sugar and mix to form a soft, pliable dough.

2 Press into a 20cm/8in loose-based flan tin (pan). Bake in the preheated for about 30 minutes.

3 To make the filling, place the butter in a pan with the condensed milk, brown sugar and syrup. Heat gently, stirring frequently, until the butter has melted and the sugar has completely dissolved.

4 Bring to a gentle boil and cook for 7–10 minutes, stirring constantly, until it thickens and turns a light caramel colour.

5 Pour the hot caramel filling into the pastry case (pie shell) and leave until completely cold.

6 Sprinkle the banana slices with lemon juice to prevent them from discolouring and arrange them in overlapping circles on top of the filling, leaving a gap in the centre. Pipe a swirl of cream in the centre and sprinkle with the grated chocolate.

Irish Whiskey Trifle

This rich trifle is made with real sponge cake, fresh fruit and rich egg custard, but with Irish whiskey rather than the usual sherry flavouring. For family occasions you could use good-quality tinned fruit.

Serves 8

1 x 20cm/8in trifle sponge (see page 214)
225g/8oz raspberry jam
150ml/¼ pint/⅔ cup Irish whiskey
450g/1lb ripe fruit, such as pears and bananas
300ml/½ pint/1¼ cups whipping cream
blanched almonds, glacé (candied) cherries and angelica, to decorate (optional)

For the custard

450ml/¾ pint/scant 2 cups full-fat (whole) milk
1 vanilla pod (bean) or a few drops of vanilla extract
3 eggs
25g/1oz/2 tbsp caster (superfine) sugar

1 To make the custard, put the milk into a pan with the vanilla pod or extract and bring almost to the boil. Remove from the heat. Whisk the eggs and sugar together lightly. Remove the vanilla pod from the milk. Gradually whisk the milk into the egg mixture.

2 Rinse out the pan, return the mixture to it and stir over low heat until it thickens; do not allow it to boil. Turn into a bowl. Cover with clear film (plastic wrap).

3 Halve the sponge cake horizontally, spread with the raspberry jam and make a sandwich. Cut into slices and use them to line the bottom and lower sides of a large serving bowl. Sprinkle with whiskey.

4 Peel and slice the fruit, then spread it out over the sponge. Pour the custard on top, cover with clear film to prevent a skin forming, and leave to cool. Chill until required.

5 Before serving, whip the cream and spread it over the set custard. Decorate the trifle with the almonds, glacé cherries and angelica, if you like.

Boston Banoffee Pie Energy 608kcal/2547kJ; Protein 6.4g; Carbohydrate 78.5g, of which sugars 58.9g; Fat 32g, of which saturates 20.1g; Cholesterol 82mg; Calcium 169mg; Fibre 1.1g; Sodium 299mg
Irish Whiskey Trifle Energy 710kcal/2959kJ; Protein 12.1g; Carbohydrate 58g, of which sugars 42.6g; Fat 43.2g, of which saturates 14.4g; Cholesterol 171mg; Calcium 194mg; Fibre 2.3g; Sodium 336mg

Autumn Pudding

Although summer pudding is made more often, this pudding is just as easy to make, using autumnal fruit instead of the soft fruits of summer. This is another great recipe for using up stale bread, and if you make the filling from picked blackberries and orchard windfalls, then it's almost free.

Serves 8

1 loaf white bread, 2 or 3 days old, crusts removed and sliced thinly
675g/1½lb/6 cups mixed soft fruit, such as blackberries, autumn raspberries, late strawberries, and peeled and chopped eating apples
115g/4oz/generous ½ cup caster (superfine) sugar

1 Use several slices of bread to line the base and sides of a 900ml–1.2 litres/1½–2 pint/3¾–5 cup pudding bowl or soufflé dish, cutting them so that the pieces fit closely together.

2 Put all the fruit into a wide, heavy pan, sprinkle the sugar over and bring very gently to the boil. Cook for 2–3 minutes, or until the sugar has dissolved and the juices run.

3 Remove from the heat and set aside 30–45ml/2–3 tbsp of the juices. Spoon the fruit and the remaining juices into the bread-lined dish and cover the top with the remaining slices of bread. Put a plate on top of the pudding and weigh it down with a heavy can or jar. Leave in the refrigerator for at least 8 hours.

4 Before serving, remove the weight and plate, cover with a serving plate and turn upside down to unmould the pudding. Use the reserved fruit juice to pour over any patches of the bread that have not been completely soaked by the fruit juices. Serve cold, cut into wedges with cream or crème fraîche.

Rhubarb and Ginger Cups

Extremely quick and easy to whip together, this simple dessert uses ready-made rhubarb compote, but you could use home-made if you prefer. Alternatively, use whole-fruit apricot jam.

Serves 4

12 gingernut biscuits (gingersnaps)
50ml/2fl oz/¼ cup rhubarb compote
450ml/¾ pint/scant 2 cups extra thick double (heavy) cream

1 Put the ginger biscuits in a strong, clean plastic bag and seal tightly. Bash the biscuits with a rolling pin until they are roughly crushed but not smashed to dust.

2 Set aside 30ml/2 tbsp of crushed biscuits and divide the rest among four serving glasses.

3 Spoon the rhubarb compote on top of the crushed biscuits, then top with the thick cream. Place in the refrigerator and chill for about 30 minutes.

4 To serve, sprinkle the reserved crushed biscuits over the trifles and serve immediately.

Meringue Layer Cake with Raspberries

This delicious dessert is made with a basic meringue mixture, and is the perfect way to enjoy raspberries, or any other soft fruit.

Serves 10

4 egg whites
225g/8oz/generous 1 cup caster (superfine) sugar, plus extra, to taste

For the filling

300ml/½ pint/1¼ cups whipping cream
3–4 drops of good quality vanilla extract or 2.5ml/½ tsp liqueur, such as Kirsch or Crème de Framboise
about 450g/1lb/2¾ cups raspberries
icing (confectioners') sugar, for dusting

1 Preheat the oven to 150°C/300°F/Gas 2. Line two baking sheets with non-stick baking parchment and draw two circles: one 23cm/9in in diameter and the other 20cm/8in. Fit a piping (icing) bag with a 1cm/½in star nozzle.

2 Whisk the egg whites until stiff peaks form, using an electric mixer. Keeping the machine running, add half of the sugar, 15ml/1 tbsp at a time. Using a metal spoon, carefully fold in the remaining sugar. Use most of the mixture to pipe inside the circles, then use the remaining meringue mixture to pipe nine miniature meringues on to the surrounding baking parchment.

3 Cook for 50–60 minutes, until lightly coloured and dry (the small ones will take less time). Peel off the parchment and cool.

4 Whip the cream until soft peaks form, sweeten with sugar and flavour with a few drops of vanilla extract or liqueur.

5 Lay the larger meringue on a serving dish. Spread with three-quarters of the cream and raspberries. Add the smaller meringue, spread with the remaining cream, and arrange the small meringues around the edge. Decorate the top with the remaining fruit and dust lightly with icing sugar. Serve quickly, before the fruit starts to bleed and the meringue soften.

Autumn Pudding Energy 261kcal/1112kJ; Protein 7.7g; Carbohydrate 57.5g, of which sugars 27.1g; Fat 1.7g, of which saturates 0.4g; Cholesterol 0mg; Calcium 153mg; Fibre 4.2g; Sodium 398mg
Rhubarb and Ginger Energy 695kcal/2874kJ; Protein 3.6g; Carbohydrate 27.1g, of which sugars 14.1g; Fat 64.3g, of which saturates 39.4g; Cholesterol 154mg; Calcium 98mg; Fibre 0.6g; Sodium 124mg
Meringue Layer Cake Energy 298kcal/1252kJ; Protein 3.2g; Carbohydrate 39.5g, of which sugars 39.5g; Fat 15.3g, of which saturates 9.5g; Cholesterol 39mg; Calcium 55mg; Fibre 1.4g; Sodium 44mg

Lemon Posset

This simple, old-fashioned dessert combines lemon with soft whipped cream and caster sugar for a tangy, flavoursome and utterly irresistible dessert.

Serves 4

600ml/1 pint/2½ cups double (heavy) cream
175g/6oz/scant 1 cup caster (superfine) sugar
grated rind and juice of 2 lemons

1 Pour the cream into a heavy pan. Add the sugar and heat gently until the sugar has dissolved, then bring to the boil, stirring constantly. Add the lemon juice and rind, and stir constantly over medium heat until the mixture thickens enough to coat the back of the spoon.

2 Pour the mixture into four heatproof serving glasses. Cool, then chill in the refrigerator until just set.

3 Serve the posset decorated with a few strands of lemon rind, and with a selection of dessert biscuits (cookies), if you like.

Chocolate and Banana Fool

Simple to make and utterly delicious, this can be made ahead and stored in the refrigerator overnight. Use cold fresh, home-made, or store-bought custard.

Serves 4

115g/4oz plain (semisweet) chocolate, broken into small pieces
300ml/½ pint/1¼ cups custard
2 bananas

1 Put the chocolate pieces in a heatproof bowl and place it over a pan of gently simmering water and leave until melted.

2 Pour the custard into a bowl and gently fold in the melted chocolate. Peel and slice the bananas and stir into the chocolate and custard mixture.

3 Spoon into glasses. and chill for 30 minutes before serving.

Iced Raspberry Trifle

This combination of sponge, sherried fruit, ice cream and mascarpone is sheer indulgence.

Serves 8–10

For the sponge

115g/4oz/½ cup butter
115g/4oz/½ cup light muscovado (brown) sugar
2 eggs
75g/3oz/⅔ cup self-raising (self-rising) flour
2.5ml/½ tsp baking powder
115g/4oz/1 cup ground almonds
15ml/1 tbsp milk

To assemble the trifle

300g/11oz/scant 2 cups raspberries
50g/2oz/½ cup flaked (sliced) almonds, toasted
5ml/1 tsp almond extract
90ml/6 tbsp orange juice
200ml/7fl oz/scant 1 cup sherry
500g/1¼lb/2½ cups mascarpone
150g/5oz/⅔ cup Greek (US strained plain) yogurt
about 250ml/8fl oz/1 cup vanilla ice cream
about 250ml/8fl oz/1 cup raspberry ice cream
30ml/2 tbsp icing (confectioners') sugar

1 Preheat the oven to 180°C/350°F/Gas 4. Grease and line a 20cm/8in round cake tin (pan). Put the butter, sugar, eggs, flour, baking powder, almonds in a bowl and beat with an electric whisk for 2 minutes until creamy. Stir in the milk.

2 Spoon the mixture into the prepared tin, level the surface and bake for about 30 minutes or until just firm in the centre. Transfer to a wire rack and leave to cool. Cut into chunky pieces and place these in the base of a 1.75-litre/3-pint/7½-cup glass serving dish. Spinkle with half the raspberries and almonds.

3 Mix the orange juice with 90ml/6 tbsp of the sherry. Spoon over the sponge. Beat the mascarpone with the yogurt, icing sugar and remaining sherry. Put the trifle and the mascarpone in the refrigerator until you are ready to assemble the trifle.

4 To serve, scoop the ice cream and sorbet into the trifle dish. Sprinkle the raspberries and almonds over the ice cream, saving a few for the top. Spoon over the mascarpone mixture and sprinkle with the reserved raspberries and almonds.

Lemon Posset Energy 917kcal/3801kJ; Protein 2.7g; Carbohydrate 48.5g, of which sugars 48.5g; Fat 80.6g, of which saturates 50.1g; Cholesterol 206mg; Calcium 98mg; Fibre 0g; Sodium 36mg
Chocolate Fool Energy 268kcal/1127kJ; Protein 4.1g; Carbohydrate 42.1g, of which sugars 38.1g; Fat 9.6g, of which saturates 4.9g; Cholesterol 3mg; Calcium 81mg; Fibre 1.4g; Sodium 33mg
Raspberry Trifle Energy 608kcal/2537kJ; Protein 17.2g; Carbohydrate 41.9g, of which sugars 33.7g; Fat 39.4g, of which saturates 18.1g; Cholesterol 134mg; Calcium 357mg; Fibre 2.8g; Sodium 269

Oranges in Syrup

This recipe works well with most citrus fruits – for example, try pink grapefruit.

Serves 6

6 medium oranges, peeled, rind from one shredded
200g/7oz/1 cup sugar
100ml/3½fl oz/scant ½ cup fresh strong brewed coffee

1 Cut each peeled orange crossways into slices, then re-form them, with a cocktail stick (toothpick) through the centre.

2 Put the sugar in a pan and add 50ml/2fl oz/¼ cup water. Heat until the sugar dissolves, then boil until the syrup turns pale gold. Remove from the heat and carefully pour 100ml/3½fl oz/scant ½ cup freshly boiling water into the pan. Return to the heat until the syrup has dissolved in the water. Stir in the coffee.

3 Add the oranges and the shredded rind to the coffee syrup. Simmer for 15–20 minutes, turning the oranges once during cooking. Leave to cool, then chill.

Clementines in Cinnamon Caramel

These clementines are a Christmas treat.

Serves 4–6

8–12 clementines, peeled, rind from one shredded
225g/8oz/1 cup sugar
2 cinnamon sticks
30ml/2 tbsp orange liqueur
25g/1oz/¼ cup pistachio nuts

1 Gently heat the sugar in a pan until it melts and turns a rich golden brown. Immediately turn off the heat. Add 300ml/½ pint/1¼ cups just boiled water to the syrup. Bring slowly to the boil. Add the shredded rind and cinnamon sticks, simmer for 5 minutes. Stir in the orange-flavoured liqueur.

2 Leave the syrup to cool for about 10 minutes, then pour over the clementines. Cover and chill overnight. Serve, sprinkled with the pistachio nuts.

Blackcurrant Fool

The strong flavour and deep colour of blackcurrants makes them especially suitable for fools and ices. The fool can also be used to make an easy no-stir ice cream, if you prefer.

Serves 6

350g/12oz/3 cups blackcurrants
about 175g/6oz/scant 1 cup caster (superfine) sugar
5ml/1 tsp lemon juice
300ml/½ pint/1¼ cups double (heavy) cream

1 Put the blackcurrants into a small pan with 45ml/3 tbsp water, and cook over low heat until soft. Remove from the heat, add the sugar according to taste, and stir until dissolved.

2 Leave to cool, then blend or sieve (strain) to make a purée. Set aside and cool. Add the lemon juice and stir well.

3 Whip the double cream until it is fairly stiff and, using a metal spoon, carefully fold it into the blackcurrant purée, losing as little volume as possible.

4 Turn the mixture into a single large serving dish or six individual serving glasses and leave to set. Chill in the refrigerator until ready to serve.

Variation

To make blackcurrant ice cream, turn the completed fool into a freezerproof container. Cover and freeze (preferably at the lowest setting). Transfer from the freezer to the refrigerator 10–15 minutes before serving to allow the ice cream to soften. Serve with whipped cream and cookies, if you like.

Cook's Tip

Fools are a very good way of using up a glut of seasonal fruit, especially if it has gone past its best and is a bit soft, since it is pulped up and combined with cream. Other fruits that work well include raspberries, gooseberries, and rhubarb.

Oranges in Syrup Energy 191kcal/815kJ; Protein 2g; Carbohydrate 48.5g, of which sugars 48.5g; Fat 0.2g, of which saturates 0g; Cholesterol 0mg; Calcium 93mg; Fibre 2.7g; Sodium 10mg
Clementines Energy 216Kcal/915kJ; Protein 1.7g; Carbohydrate 48.1g, of which sugars 48g; Fat 2.4g, of which saturates 0.3g; Cholesterol 0mg; Calcium 50mg; Fibre 1.2g; Sodium 28mg
Blackcurrant Fool Energy 379kcal/1581kJ; Protein 1.5g; Carbohydrate 35.2g, of which sugars 35.2g; Fat 26.9g, of which saturates 16.7g; Cholesterol 69mg; Calcium 75mg; Fibre 2.1g; Sodium 15mg

Lemon Sorbet

This is probably the most classic sorbet of all. Refreshingly tangy and yet deliciously smooth, it quite literally melts in the mouth. Buy unwaxed lemons for recipes such as this one or scrub before paring.

Serves 6

200g/7oz/1 cup caster (superfine) sugar, plus extra for coating rind to decorate
4 lemons, well scrubbed
1 egg white

1 Put the sugar in a pan and pour in 300ml/½ pint/1¼ cups water. Bring to the boil, stirring until the sugar has just dissolved.

2 Using a swivel vegetable peeler, pare the rind thinly from two of the lemons and put in a pan. Simmer for 2 minutes, then take the pan off the heat. Leave to cool, then chill.

3 Squeeze the juice from all the lemons and add it to the syrup. Strain the syrup into a shallow freezerproof container, reserving the rind. Freeze for 4 hours, until it is mushy.

4 Process the sorbet in a food processor until it is smooth. Lightly whisk the egg white with a fork until it is just frothy.

5 Replace the sorbet in the container, beat in the egg white and return to the freezer for 4 hours, or until it is firm.

6 Cut the reserved lemon rind into fine shreds and cook in boiling water for 5 minutes. Drain, then place on a plate and sprinkle with sugar. Scoop the sorbet into bowls or glasses and decorate with the sugared lemon rind.

Cook's Tip

Sorbets are especially delicious during the summer months, as they are refreshing and tangy. Lemon sorbet is great for cleansing the palate, and makes the ideal dessert after a spicy main meal. It is also cheap and easy to make.

Classic Vanilla Ice Cream

Nothing beats the comforting simplicity of vanilla ice cream, which can be served with all manner of hot desserts or with hot and cold sauces.

Serves 4

1 vanilla pod
300ml/½ pint/1¼ cups semi-skimmed (low-fat) milk
4 egg yolks
75g/3oz/6 tbsp caster (superfine) sugar
5ml/1 tsp cornflour (cornstarch)
300ml/½ pint/1¼ cups double (heavy) cream

1 Using a small knife slit the vanilla pod lengthways. Pour the milk into a heavy pan, add the vanilla pod and bring to the boil. Remove from the heat and leave for 15 minutes to infuse.

2 Lift the vanilla pod up. Holding it over the pan, scrape the seeds out of the pod with a small knife so that they fall into the milk. Set the pod aside and bring the milk back to the boil.

3 Whisk the egg yolks, sugar and cornflour in a bowl until the mixture is thick and foamy. Gradually pour on the hot milk, whisking constantly. Return the mixture to the pan and cook over low heat, stirring all the time. When the custard thickens and is smooth, pour back into the bowl. Cool, then chill.

4 Whip the cream until it has thickened but falls from a spoon. Fold it into the custard and pour into a plastic tub or similar freezerproof container. Freeze for 6 hours, or until firm enough to scoop, beating twice with a fork, or in a food processor. Scoop into dishes, bowls or bought cones and either eat it on its own or with a hot dessert.

Cook's Tips

Don't throw the vanilla pod away after use. Instead, rinse, dry and store in the sugar jar. After a week or so the sugar will take on the wonderful aroma and flavour of the vanilla and will be delicious sprinkled over summer fruits.

Lemon Sorbet Energy 134kcal/570kJ; Protein 0.7g; Carbohydrate 34.9g, of which sugars 34.9g; Fat 0g, of which saturates 0g; Cholesterol 0mg; Calcium 18mg; Fibre 0g; Sodium 12mg
Vanilla Ice Cream Energy 542kcal/2245kJ; Protein 6.8g; Carbohydrate 24.4g, of which sugars 24.4g; Fat 47.1g, of which saturates 27.4g; Cholesterol 309mg; Calcium 160mg; Fibre 0g; Sodium 59mg

Chocolate Ripple Ice Cream

This creamy, dark chocolate ice cream, rippled with swirls of rich chocolate sauce is perfect for every occasion.

Serves 4–6

4 egg yolks
75g/3oz/6 tbsp caster (superfine) sugar
5ml/1 tsp cornflour (cornstarch)
300ml/½ pint/1¼ cups milk
250g/9oz dark (bittersweet) chocolate, broken into squares
25g/1oz/2 tbsp butter, diced
30ml/2 tbsp golden (light corn) syrup
90ml/6 tbsp single (light) cream or cream and milk mixed
300ml/½ pint/1¼ cups whipping cream
wafer biscuits, to serve

1 Put the yolks, sugar and cornflour in a bowl and whisk until thick and foamy.

2 Pour the milk into a pan, bring it just to the boil, then gradually pour it in to the yolk mixture, whisking constantly.

3 Return the mixture to the pan and cook over low heat, stirring constantly, until the custard thickens and is smooth. Pour it back into the bowl and stir in 150g/5oz of the chocolate, until melted. Cover closely, leave it to cool, then chill.

4 Put the remaining chocolate into a pan and add the butter. Spoon in the golden syrup. Heat gently, stirring, until the chocolate and butter have melted. Stir in the single cream or cream and milk mixture. Heat gently, stirring, until smooth, then leave to cool, stirring occasionally.

5 Whip the cream until it has thickened but falls from a spoon. Fold it into the custard and pour into a plastic tub or similar freezerproof container. Freeze for 5 hours, or until firm enough to scoop, beating twice during the 5 hours with a fork, or in a food processor.

6 Add alternate spoonfuls of ice cream and chocolate sauce to a 1.5-litre/2½-pint/6¼-cup plastic container. Freeze for 5–6 hours until firm. Serve with wafers.

Brown Bread Ice Cream

The secret of a good brown bread ice cream is not to have too many breadcrumbs (which makes the ice cream heavy) and, for the best texture and deep, nutty flavour, to toast them until really crisp and well browned. Yeast bread produces a better flavour than soda bread for this recipe. Serve on its own or with chocolate sauce.

Serves 6–8

115g/4oz/2 cups wholemeal (whole-wheat) breadcrumbs
115g/4oz/½ cup light soft brown sugar
2 large (US extra large) eggs, separated
30–45ml/2–3 tbsp Irish Cream liqueur
450ml/¾ pint/scant 2 cups double (heavy) cream

1 Preheat the oven to 190°C/375°F/Gas 5.

2 Spread the breadcrumbs out on a baking sheet and toast them in the oven for about 15 minutes, or until crisp and well browned. Be careful not to let them scorch, if you do – start again, burnt breadcrumbs will spoil the ice cream. Leave to cool.

3 Whisk the sugar and egg yolks together until light and creamy, then beat in the Irish Cream. Whisk the cream until soft peaks form. In a separate bowl, whisk the egg whites stiffly.

4 Sprinkle the breadcrumbs over the beaten egg mixture, add the cream and fold into the mixture with a spoon.

5 Fold the beaten egg whites into the mixture. Turn the mixture into a freezerproof container, cover and freeze.

Cook's Tip
Irish Cream liqueur is made from whiskey and cream. Don't buy a bottle just for the recipe, substitute 30ml/2 tbsp whiskey or brandy instead, or leave it out completely. Rum is sometimes added, which gives the ice cream a Christmas flavour.

Choc Ice Cream Energy 900kcal/3749kJ; Protein 11g; Carbohydrate 74.9g, of which sugars 74.3g; Fat 63.9g, of which saturates 37.8g; Cholesterol 314mg; Calcium 211mg; Fibre 1.6g; Sodium 142mg
Bread Ice Cream Energy 561Kcal/2332kJ; Protein 6g; Carbohydrate 37.3g, of which sugars 23g; Fat 43.6g, of which saturates 25.7g; Cholesterol 179mg; Calcium 84mg; Fibre 0.4g; Sodium 196mg

Victoria Sandwich Cake

Serve this traditional English sponge cake sandwiched together with your favourite jam or preserve. For special occasions, fill the cake with prepared fresh fruit, such as raspberries, sliced strawberries or peach segments, as well as jam and whipped cream.

Serves 8–10

175g/6oz/¾ cup soft butter
175g/6oz/¾ cup caster (superfine) sugar
3 eggs, beaten
175g/6oz/1½ cups self-raising (self-rising) flour, sifted
60ml/4 tbsp raspberry or strawberry jam
150ml/¼ pint/⅔ cup whipped cream or crème fraîche
15–30ml/1–2 tbsp icing (confectioners') sugar, or vanilla sugar, for dusting

1 Preheat the oven to 180°C/350°F/Gas 4. Lightly grease and line the bottom of two 18cm/7in shallow round cake tins (pans) with baking parchment.

2 Place the butter and caster sugar in a bowl and cream together until pale and fluffy. This can be done by hand using a mixing spoon or with a hand-held electric mixer, if you have one, which is far quicker and easier.

3 Add the eggs, a little at a time, beating well after each addition. Fold in half the flour, using a metal spoon, then gently fold in the rest and mix to combine.

4 Divide the cake mixture between the two prepared cake tins and level the surfaces with the back of a spoon.

5 Bake for 25–30 minutes, until the cakes have risen, feel just firm to the touch and are golden brown all over. Turn out and cool on a wire rack.

6 When the cakes are cool, sandwich them with the jam and whipped cream or crème fraîche. Dust the top of the cake with sifted icing sugar or vanilla sugar and serve cut into slices. Store the cake in an airtight container or wrapped in foil.

Carrot Cake

Universally loved, this is one of the most irresistible cakes there is. There are many versions; here poppy seeds add crunch, and orange provides a tangy touch.

Serves 8–10

250g/9oz/2¼ cups plain (all-purpose) flour
10ml/2 tsp baking powder
5ml/1 tsp bicarbonate of soda (baking soda)
2.5ml/½ tsp salt
5ml/1 tsp ground cinnamon
45ml/3 tbsp poppy seeds
225g/8oz/1⅓ cups soft light brown sugar
3 eggs, beaten
finely grated rind of 1 orange
225g/8oz raw carrots, grated
75g/3oz/¾ cup walnut pieces
115g/4oz/½ cup butter, melted

For the icing

150g/5oz/scant 1 cup mascarpon
30ml/2 tbsp icing (confectioners') sugar, sifted

1 Preheat the oven to 180°C/350°F/Gas 4. Grease and line a 1.5-litre/2½-pint/6¼-cup loaf tin (pan) with baking parchment.

2 Sift together the flour, baking powder, bicarbonate of soda, sal and cinnamon into a bowl. Stir in the poppy seeds.

3 Mix together the brown sugar, eggs and orange rind in a separate bowl. Lightly squeeze the excess moisture from the grated carrots and stir the carrots into the egg mixture with anc walnut pieces. Gradually stir the sifted flour mixture into the eg mixture until well combined, then gently fold in the butter.

4 Spoon the mixture into the prepared tin, level the top and bake for 1–1¼ hours, until risen and golden brown and a thin metal skewer inserted into the centre comes out clean, if not, put it back for a further 10 minutes and test again. Remove the cake from the loaf tin and cool on a wire rack. Remove the baking parchment when completely cold.

5 To make the icing, beat the mascarpone with the icing sugar and orange rind. Cover and chill until needed. When ready to serve, beat the icing well, then spread thickly over the top of the cake. Serve cut into slices.

Victoria Cake Energy 3577kcal/14,948kJ; Protein 39.7g; Carbohydrate 377.4g, of which sugars 247.3g; Fat 223.1g, of which saturates 134g; Cholesterol 1101mg; Calcium 924mg; Fibre 5.4g; Sodium 1967r
Carrot Cake Energy 3971kcal/16,641kJ; Protein 76.3g; Carbohydrate 491.9g, of which sugars 294.7g; Fat 202.5g, of which saturates 84.5g; Cholesterol 879mg; Calcium 751mg; Fibre 17.6g; Sodium 992mg

Old-fashioned Treacle Cake

The treacle gives a rich colour and a deep flavour to this easy-to-make cake.

Serves 8–10

75g/3oz/6 tbsp butter, diced, plus extra for greasing
250g/9oz/2 cups self-raising (self-rising) flour
2.5ml/½ tsp mixed (apple pie) spice
25g/1oz/2 tbsp caster (superfine) sugar
150g/5oz/1 cup mixed dried fruit
1 egg
15ml/1 tbsp black treacle (molasses)
100ml/3½fl oz/scant ½ cup full-fat (whole) milk

1 Preheat the oven to 180°C/350°F/Gas 4. Butter a shallow 20–23cm/8–9in ovenproof flan dish or baking tin (pan).

2 Sift the flour and spice into a large mixing bowl. Add the butter and, with your fingertips, rub it into the flour until the mixture resembles fine crumbs. Alternatively you could do this in a food processor. Stir in the sugar and mixed dried fruit.

3 Beat the egg and stir in the treacle and then the milk. Stir the liquid into the flour to make a fairly stiff but moist consistency, adding a little extra milk if necessary.

4 Transfer the cake mixture to the prepared dish or tin with a spoon and level out the surface.

5 Place the cake in the hot oven and cook for about 1 hour until it has risen, is firm to the touch and fully cooked through. To check if the cake is cooked, insert a small skewer in the centre – it should come out free of sticky mixture. Leave the cooked treacle cake to cool completely. Serve it, cut into wedges, straight from the dish.

Variation
Vary the dried fruit you use in this cake, using what you have in the storecupboard – try using chopped ready-to-eat dried apricots and stem ginger, or a packet of mixed dried fruit.

Overnight Cake

This simple thin cake contains no added sugar – the sweetness comes from the dried fruit, and no eggs either. It is at its most delicious eaten on the day it is made, its crust being crisp and flaky while the inside is soft and moist. It makes a great addition to a late breakfast with coffee, but is also delicious eaten with cheese, particularly a white variety such as Cheshire.

Serves 8–10

225g/8oz/2 cups plain (all-purpose) flour
5ml/1 tsp ground cinnamon
5ml/1 tsp ground ginger
115g/4oz/½ cup butter, cut into cubes
115g/4oz/⅔ cup mixed dried fruit
300ml/½ pint/1¼ cups milk
2.5ml/½ tsp bicarbonate of soda (baking soda)
15ml/1 tbsp vinegar
crumbly white cheese, to serve

1 Sift the flour and spices. Add the butter and rub in until the mixture resembles fine breadcrumbs. Stir in the dried fruit and enough milk to make a soft mix.

2 Mix the bicarbonate of soda with the vinegar and, as it froths, quickly stir it into the mixture. Cover the bowl and leave at room temperature for about 8 hours, or overnight – this is where the cake's name comes from.

3 Preheat the oven to 180°C/350°F/Gas 4. Grease a shallow 23cm/9in round cake tin (pan) and line its base with baking parchment. Spoon the cake mixture into the prepared tin and level the surface.

4 Put into the hot oven and cook for about 1 hour or until firm to the touch and cooked through – a skewer inserted in the centre should come out free of sticky mixture. If the top starts to get too brown during cooking, cover it with baking parchment.

5 Leave in the tin to cool for 15–20 minutes, then turn out and cool completely on a wire rack. Serve with slices of crumbly white cheese, if you like.

Treacle Cake Energy 2089kcal/8805kJ; Protein 37.4g; Carbohydrate 343g, of which sugars 152.4g; Fat 72.8g, of which saturates 42.2g; Cholesterol 356mg; Calcium 720mg; Fibre 11.1g; Sodium 676mg
Overnight Cake Energy 2069kcal/8681kJ; Protein 34.7g; Carbohydrate 267.9g, of which sugars 96.5g; Fat 103g, of which saturates 63.6g; Cholesterol 263mg; Calcium 780mg; Fibre 9.5g; Sodium 888mg

Walnut Cake

This moist cake isn't made with low cost ingredients, but because it is so rich it goes a long way.

Serves 10–12

150g/5oz/10 tbsp unsalted (sweet) butter
375g/13oz/generous 1¾ cups caster (superfine) sugar
4 eggs, separated
60ml/4 tbsp brandy
2.5ml/½ tsp ground cinnamon
300g/11oz/2¾ cups walnuts, coarsely chopped
150g/5oz/1¼ cups self-raising (self-rising) flour
5ml/1 tsp baking powder
a pinch of salt

For the syrup

30ml/2 tbsp brandy
2 or 3 strips of pared orange rind
2 cinnamon sticks

1 Preheat the oven to 190°C/375°F/Gas 5. Grease a 35 x 23cm /14 x 9in roasting pan or baking dish that is at least 5cm/2in deep. Cream the butter in a mixing bowl until soft, then add 115g/4oz/generous ½ cup sugar and beat until light and fluffy.

2 Add the egg yolks one by one, beating the mixture after each addition. Stir in the brandy, cinnamon and walnuts using a spoon.

3 Sift the flour with the baking powder and set aside. Whisk the egg whites with a pinch of salt until they are stiff. Fold them into the creamed mixture, alternating with spoonfuls of flour until the whites and the flour have all been incorporated.

4 Spread the mixture in the prepared pan or dish. Bake for about 40 minutes, or until the top is golden and a skewer inserted in the cake comes out clean.

5 Mix the remaining sugar and 300ml/½ pint/1¼ cups water in a small pan. Heat gently, stirring, until the sugar has dissolved. Bring to the boil, lower the heat and add the brandy, orange rind and cinnamon sticks. Simmer for 10 minutes.

6 Slice the cake into 6cm/2½in diamond shapes while hot and strain the syrup over it. Let it cool in the pan to absorb the syrup and soak through. Remove from the pan to serve.

Semolina Cake

This no-bake cake takes very little time to make and uses storecupboard ingredients.

Serves 6–8

500g/1¼lb/2¾ cups caster (superfine) sugar
1 litre/1¾ pints/4 cups water
1 cinnamon stick
250ml/8fl oz/1 cup olive oil
350g/12oz/2 cups coarse semolina
50g/2oz/½ cup blanched almonds
30ml/2 tbsp pine nuts
5ml/1 tsp ground cinnamon

1 Put the sugar, water and cinnamon stick in a heavy pan. Bring to the boil, stirring until the sugar dissolves, then boil without stirring for about 4 minutes to make a syrup. Take off the heat and set aside. Remove and discard the cinnamon stick.

2 Meanwhile, heat the oil in a separate, heavy pan. When it is hot, add the semolina and stir until it turns light brown. Lower the heat, add the almonds and pine nuts, and brown together for 2–3 minutes, stirring continuously.

3 Gradually add the hot syrup to the semolina mixture, stirring continuously. It may spit at this point, so stand well away. Return to low heat and stir until all the syrup has been absorbed.

4 Remove the pan from the heat, cover with a clean dish towel and let it stand for 10 minutes. Scrape the mixture into a 20–23cm/8–9in round cake tin (pan), and set aside. When it is cold, unmould it on to a plate and dust with ground cinnamon. Cut into slices and serve.

Apple and Cinnamon Muffins

These fruity, spicy muffins are quick and easy to make and are perfect for serving for breakfast, or for adding to a lunchbox for a tasty snack.

Makes 6

1 egg, beaten
40g/1½oz/3 tbsp caster (superfine) sugar
120ml/4fl oz/½ cup milk
50g/2oz/¼ cup butter, melted
150g/5oz/1¼ cups plain (all-purpose) flour
7.5ml/1½ tsp baking powder
pinch of salt
7.5ml/1½ tsp ground cinnamon
2 small eating apples, peeled, cored and finely chopped
30ml/2 tbsp demerara (raw) sugar

1 Preheat the oven to 200°C/400°F/Gas 6. Line a large muffin tin (pan) with six paper cases. Put the egg, sugar, milk and melted butter in a bowl, and mix to combine.

2 Sift in the flour, baking powder, salt and 2.5ml/½ tsp ground cinnamon. Add the chopped apple and mix roughly. Spoon the mixture into the prepared muffin cases.

3 To make the topping, mix the demerara sugar with the remaining cinnamon. Sprinkle over the uncooked muffins.

4 Bake for 30–35 minutes until well risen and golden brown on top. Transfer the muffins to a wire rack to cool. Serve warm or at room temperature.

Walnut Cake Energy 563kcal/2,349kJ; Protein 8.5g; Carbohydrate 50.6g, of which sugars 39.2g; Fat 35.3g, of which saturates 10.1g; Cholesterol 108mg; Calcium 114mg; Fibre 1.5g; Sodium 177mg
Semolina Cake Energy 888kcal/3,731kJ; Protein 9.1g; Carbohydrate 133.1g, of which sugars 87.6g; Fat 39.1g, of which saturates 4.9g; Cholesterol 0mg; Calcium 75mg; Fibre 1.9g; Sodium 13mg
Apple Muffins Energy 236kcal/995kJ; Protein 4.3g; Carbohydrate 38.2g, of which sugars 19.1g; Fat 8.5g, of which saturates 4.9g; Cholesterol 51mg; Calcium 74mg; Fibre 1.2g; Sodium 73mg

·Ioney and Spice Buns

'hese golden little buns are ·ragrant with honey and innamon. Though they look ·nore appetizing when ·ooked directly in a bun tin, ·hey tend to rise higher (and re therefore lighter) when ·aked in paper cases.

·1akes 18

50g/9oz/2 cups plain (all-purpose) flour
·ml/1 tsp ground cinnamon
5ml/1 tsp bicarbonate of soda (baking soda)
125g/4½oz/generous ½ cup butter, softened
125g/4½oz/10 tbsp soft brown sugar
1 large (US extra large) egg, separated
125g/4½oz clear honey
about 60ml/4 tbsp milk
caster (superfine) sugar, for sprinkling

Preheat the oven to 200°C/400°F/Gas 6. Grease the holes of bun tin (muffin pan) or, alternatively, line with paper cases.

; Sift the flour into a large mixing bowl with the cinnamon and ·ıe bicarbonate of soda.

Beat the butter with the sugar until light and fluffy. Beat in the gg yolk, then gradually add the honey.

With a large metal spoon and a cutting action, fold in the flour ·ıixture plus sufficient milk to make a soft mixture that will just rop off the spoon.

In a separate, clean bowl whisk the egg white until stiff peaks ·ɔrm. Using a large metal spoon, fold the egg white into the ·ake mixture.

Divide the mixture among the paper cases or the holes in the ·repared tin. Place the tin into the hot oven and cook the buns ·ɔr about 15–20 minutes or until they have risen, are firm to the ·ɔuch and golden brown.

Sprinkle the tops lightly with caster sugar and leave to cool ·ɔmpletely on a wire rack.

Shortbread Rounds

There should always be a supply of shortbread in the cookie jar – it is so moreish.

Makes 24

450g/1lb/2 cups butter
225g/8oz/generous 1 cup caster (superfine) sugar
450g/1lb/4 cups plain (all-purpose) flour
225g/8oz/scant 1½ cups ground rice or rice flour
45ml/1 tsp salt
demerara (raw) sugar, to decorate
caster (superfine) sugar, for dusting

1 Place the butter and sugar in a bowl and cream together until light, pale and fluffy. Sift together the flour, ground rice, or rice flour, and salt, and stir into the butter and sugar with a wooden spoon, until the mixture resembles fine breadcrumbs.

2 Working quickly, gather the dough together with your hand, then put it on a clean work surface. Knead lightly until it forms a ball. Lightly roll into a sausage shape, about 7.5cm/3in thick. Wrap in clear film (plastic wrap) and chill until firm.

3 Preheat the oven to 190°C/375°F/Gas 5. Grease two large baking sheets and line with baking parchment.

4 Pour the demerara sugar on to a sheet of baking parchment. Unwrap the dough and roll it in the sugar until evenly coated. Using a large knife, slice the roll into discs about 1cm/½in thick. Place the discs on to the prepared baking sheets, spacing them well apart. Bake for 20–25 minutes until pale gold in colour.

5 Remove from the oven and sprinkle with golden caster sugar. Leave to cool on the baking sheet for 10 minutes before transferring to a wire rack to cool completely.

Cook's Tip
The rice flour adds a toothsome grittiness and shortness to the dough, which is the quality that distinguishes home-made shortbread from the store-bought variety.

·Ioney Buns Energy 152kcal/639kJ; Protein 1.9g; Carbohydrate 23.6g, of which sugars 13g; Fat 6.3g, of which saturates 3.8g; Cholesterol 26mg; Calcium 30mg; Fibre 0.4g; Sodium 49mg
·hortbread Energy 275kcal/1147kJ; Protein 2.5g; Carbohydrate 32g, of which sugars 10.2g; Fat 15.7g, of which saturates 9.8g; Cholesterol 40mg; Calcium 37mg; Fibre 0.8g; Sodium 115mg

Ginger Snaps

When these cookies are baked their tops craze and crack into an attractive pattern that is characteristic of this traditional family favourite cookie.

Makes 24

115g/4oz/½ cup butter, diced
115g/4oz/generous ½ cup caster (superfine) sugar
115g/4oz/½ cup golden (light corn) syrup
225g/8oz/2 cups plain (all-purpose) flour
10ml/2 tsp ground ginger
5ml/1 tsp bicarbonate of soda (baking soda)

1 Preheat the oven to 180°C/350°F/Gas 4. Line two or three baking sheets with baking parchment.

2 Put the butter, sugar and syrup into a pan and heat gently, stirring occasionally, until the butter has melted and the sugar has dissolved. Remove the pan from the heat and leave to cool slightly.

3 Sift the flour, ginger and bicarbonate of soda and stir into the mixture in the pan to make a soft dough.

4 Shape the dough into about 24 balls and arrange them on the prepared baking sheets, well spaced out. Flatten each ball slightly with a metal spatula.

5 Put one baking sheet into the hot oven and cook for about 12 minutes until golden brown (they burn easily). Leave to cool on the sheet for 1–2 minutes, then using a metal spatula, carefully transfer to a wire rack to crisp up and cool completely.

6 Cook the remaining cookies in the same way. Store in an airtight container for up to a week.

Cook's Tip
Measuring syrup is easier if you dip a metal spoon in very hot water first, then quickly dry it.

Ginger Cookies

These richly spiced cookies packed with chunks of succulent preserved stem ginger are very moreish.

Makes 30

350g/12oz/3 cups self-raising (self-rising) flour
pinch of salt
200g/7oz/1 cup golden caster (superfine) sugar
15ml/1 tbsp ground ginger
5ml/1 tsp bicarbonate of soda (baking soda)
115g/4oz/½ cup unsalted (sweet) butter
90g/3½oz/generous ¼ cup golden (light corn) syrup
1 large (US extra large) egg, beaten
150g/5oz preserved stem ginger in syrup, chopped

1 Preheat the oven to 160°C/325°F/Gas 3. Line three baking sheets with lightly greased baking parchment.

2 Sift the flour into a large mixing bowl, add the salt, caster sugar, ground ginger and bicarbonate of soda and stir to combine all the ingredients thoroughly.

3 Dice the butter and put it in a small, heavy pan with the syrup. Heat gently, stirring, until the butter has melted. Remove from the heat and set aside to cool until just warm.

4 Pour the butter mixture over the dry ingredients, then add the egg and two-thirds of the ginger. Mix thoroughly, then use your hands to bring the dough together.

5 Shape the dough into 30 small balls, For larger cookies you could divide into 20 balls. Place them, spaced well apart, on the baking sheets and gently flatten the balls.

6 Press a few pieces of the remaining preserved stem ginger into the top of each cookie. Bake for about 12–15 minutes until light golden in colour.

7 Remove the cookies from the oven and leave to cool for 1 minute on the sheets, then transfer the cookies to a wire rack to cool completely.

Ginger Snaps Energy 101kcal/424kJ; Protein 1g; Carbohydrate 16.1g, of which sugars 9g; Fat 4.1g, of which saturates 2.5g; Cholesterol 10mg; Calcium 17mg; Fibre 0.3g; Sodium 43mg
Ginger Cookies Energy 108kcal/454kJ; Protein 1.4g; Carbohydrate 18.9g, of which sugars 10g; Fat 3.5g, of which saturates 2.1g; Cholesterol 15mg; Calcium 24mg; Fibre 0.4g; Sodium 38mg

)at Chocolate Chip Cookies

hese crunchy cookies are asy enough for children to nake and are sure to isappear as soon as they are aked.

lakes 20

15g/4oz/½ cup butter, plus extra for greasing
15g/4oz/½ cup soft dark brown sugar
eggs, lightly beaten
45–60ml/3–4 tbsp milk
5ml/1 tsp vanilla extract
150g/5oz/1¼ cups plain (all-purpose) flour
5ml/1 tsp baking powder
pinch of salt
115g/4oz/generous 1 cup rolled oats
175g/6oz plain (semisweet) chocolate chips
115g/4oz/1 cup pecan nuts, chopped

Cream the butter and sugar in a large bowl, until pale and uffy. Add the lightly beaten eggs, milk and vanilla extract, nd beat thoroughly.

Sift in the flour, baking powder and salt, and stir in until well nixed. Fold in the rolled oats, chocolate chips and chopped ecan nuts. Chill in the refrigerator for at least 1 hour.

Preheat the oven to 180°C/350°F/Gas 4. Grease two large aking trays. Using two teaspoons, place mounds of the mixture vell apart on the trays and flatten with a spoon or fork.

Bake the cookies for 10–12 minutes in the preheated oven ntil the edges are just colouring, then cool on wire racks.

:hocolate Chip Brownies

hese chunky chocolate rownies are moist, dark and eeply satisfying. They are so ch that you only need a nall square, and they are elicious with coffee.

erves 6–8

50g/5oz 70% plain (semisweet) chocolate, chopped
20ml/4fl oz/½ cup sunflower oil
215g/7½ oz/scant 1 cup light muscovado (brown) sugar
2 eggs
5ml/1 tsp vanilla extract
65g/2½oz/scant ⅔ cup self-raising (self-rising) flour
60ml/4 tbsp unsweetened cocoa powder
75g/3oz/¾ cup chopped walnuts
60ml/4 tbsp milk chocolate chips

Preheat the oven to 180°C/350°F/Gas 4. Lightly grease a nallow 19cm/7½in square cake tin (pan). Melt the plain nocolate in a heatproof bowl over a pan of simmering water.

Beat together the oil, sugar, eggs and vanilla extract. Stir the melted chocolate, then beat well until evenly mixed.

Sift the flour and cocoa powder into the bowl and fold in noroughly. Stir in the chopped nuts and chocolate chips, then ansfer the mixture into the prepared tin and spread evenly.

Bake for about 30–35 minutes, until the top is firm and crusty. ool in the tin before cutting into squares.

Milk Chocolate Crispy Cookies

These little chocolate-coated cornflake cakes are always a hit with kids, and couldn't be easier to make. They are also a good option for budget bakers who want a treat.

Makes 10

90g/3½oz milk chocolate
15ml/1 tbsp golden (light corn) syrup
90g/3½oz/4½ cups cornflakes
icing (confectioners') sugar, for dusting

1 Line a large baking sheet with baking parchment.

2 Break the chocolate into a large, heatproof bowl and add the syrup. Set the bowl over a pan of gently simmering water and leave until melted, stirring frequently.

3 Put the cornflakes in a strong plastic bag and, using a rolling pin, lightly crush the cornflakes, breaking them into fairly small pieces but not into dust.

4 Remove the bowl from the heat and add in the crushed cornflakes. Mix well, until the cornflakes are thoroughly coated in the chocolate mixture.

5 Place a 6.5cm/2½in round cutter on the paper and put a spoonful of the chocolate mixture in the centre. Pack down firmly with the back of the spoon to make a thick cookie.

6 Gently ease away the cutter, using the spoon to help keep the mixture in place. Continue making cookies in this way until all the mixture has been used up. Chill for 1 hour.

7 Put a little icing sugar in a small bowl. Lift each cookie from the paper and roll the edges in the icing sugar to finish.

Variations
You can use any type of chocolate for these delicious little morsels. Simply subsitute an equal quantity of white or dark (bittersweet) chocolate for the milk chocolate.

at Cookies Energy 207kcal/864kJ; Protein 3.2g; Carbohydrate 22.1g, of which sugars 12g; Fat 12.4g, of which saturates 5g; Cholesterol 32mg; Calcium 30mg; Fibre 1.1g; Sodium 46mg
rownies Energy 611kcal/2559kJ; Protein 8.7g; Carbohydrate 69.7g, of which sugars 59.9g; Fat 35g, of which saturates 9.9g; Cholesterol 66mg; Calcium 80mg; Fibre 2.9g; Sodium 124mg
hocolate Cookies Energy 84kcal/355kJ; Protein 1.4g; Carbohydrate 14.2g, of which sugars 7.2g; Fat 2.8g, of which saturates 1.7g; Cholesterol 2mg; Calcium 21mg; Fibre 0.2g; Sodium 112mg

Malted Oat Cookies

This recipe is packed with slow energy-release oats so a couple of biscuits makes a healthier snack that keeps you full for longer – perfect for children's lunchboxes. Flavoured with malt, these chewy, crisp cookies are full of natural goodness.

Makes 18

175g/6oz/1½ cups rolled oats
75g/3oz/½ cup light muscovado (brown) sugar
1 egg
60ml/4 tbsp sunflower or vegetable oil
30ml/2 tbsp malt extract

1 Preheat the oven to 190°C/375°F/Gas 5. Lightly grease two baking sheets. Mix the rolled oats and sugar in a bowl, breaking up any lumps in the sugar.

2 Beat the egg in a small bowl and add it together with the oil and malt extract to the oats and sugar mixture.

3 Set the mixture aside to soak for 15 minutes, then beat together to combine thoroughly.

4 Using a teaspoon, place small heaps of the mixture well apart to allow room for spreading on the prepared baking sheets.

5 Press the heaps into 7.5cm/3in rounds with the back of a dampened fork to give the cookies a distinctive pattern when baked in the oven.

6 Bake the cookies in the preheated oven for 10–15 minutes, until golden brown. Leave them on the baking sheets for 1 minute to firm slightly. With a metal spatula, transfer to a wire rack and leave to cool.

Variation
For a more indulgent batch of cookies, you could add a couple of handfuls of chopped white chocolate, which would make a lovely addition to the malty flavour.

Crunchy Jumbles

Making up your mind about whether you prefer milk or plain chocolate chips is the perfect excuse for baking another batch of these tasty cookies.

Makes 36

115g/4oz/½ cup butter at room temperature, diced
225g/8oz/1 cup sugar
1 egg
5ml/1 tsp vanilla extract
175g/6oz/1¼ cups plain (all-purpose) flour
2.5ml/½ tsp bicarbonate of soda (baking soda)
pinch of salt
115g/4oz/2 cups crisped rice cereal
175g/6oz/1 cup chocolate chips

1 Preheat the oven to 180°C/350°F/Gas 4. Lightly grease two or three large baking sheets.

2 In a large bowl, beat together the butter and sugar until light and fluffy. Beat in the egg and vanilla extract.

3 Sift the flour, bicarbonate of soda and salt over the mixture and fold in until just mixed.

4 Add the cereal and chocolate chips to the mixture and stir thoroughly to mix. Drop spoonfuls of the dough on to the baking sheets, spacing them well apart to allow room for spreading during baking.

5 Bake the cookies in the oven for 10–12 minutes until golden brown. Leave to firm up slightly on the baking sheet for 1–2 minutes. Use a metal spatula to transfer the cookies to a wire rack to cool completely.

Variation
To make Crunchy Walnut Jumbles, add 50g/2oz/½ cup walnuts, coarsely chopped, with the cereal and chocolate. Alternatively you could try adding different breakfast cereals for different textures and tastes.

Malted Oat Cookies Energy 86kcal/364kJ; Protein 1.6g; Carbohydrate 12.8g, of which sugars 5.7g; Fat 3.6g, of which saturates 0.4g; Cholesterol 11mg; Calcium 9mg; Fibre 0.7g; Sodium 12mg
Crunchy Jumbles Energy 95kcal/398kJ; Protein 0.9g; Carbohydrate 14.2g, of which sugars 9.8g; Fat 4.2g, of which saturates 2.5g; Cholesterol 12mg; Calcium 18mg; Fibre 0.3g; Sodium 31mg

Chewy Flapjacks

lapjacks are about the easiest cookies to make.

Makes 18

250g/9oz/generous 1 cup butter
75g/3oz/⅓ cup light muscovado (brown) sugar
225g/8oz/⅔ cup golden (light corn) syrup
375g/13oz/3¾ cups rolled oats

1 Preheat the oven to 180°C/350°F/Gas 4. Line a 28 x 20cm/11 x 8in shallow baking tin (pan) with baking parchment.

2 Heat the butter, syrup and sugar in a pan until the butter has nelted. Stir in the oats. Transfer into the tin and spread evenly. Bake for 15–20 minutes until firm. Leave the flapjack to cool in he tin, then lift it out in one piece and cut into fingers.

Scotch Pancakes

These are lovely served warm for breakfast.

Makes 8–10

115g/4oz/1 cup plain (all-purpose) flour
5ml/1 tsp bicarbonate of soda (baking soda)
5ml/1 tsp cream of tartar
25g/1oz/2 tbsp butter, diced
1 egg, beaten
about 150ml/¼ pint/⅔ cup milk

1 Sift the flour, bicarbonate of soda and cream of tartar ogether into a bowl. Add the butter and rub it into the flour intil the mixture resembles fine, evenly textured breadcrumbs.

2 Make a well in the centre of the flour mixture, then stir in the egg. Add the milk a little at a time, stirring, until you have a thick batter, you may not need all the milk. Lightly grease a griddle pan or heavy frying pan, then preheat it. .

3 Drop three or four spoonfuls of the mixture on the griddle or frying pan. Cook over medium heat for 2–3 minutes, until bubbles rise to the surface. Turn and cook for a further 2–3 minutes, until golden underneath. Serve with butter and honey.

Scones with Jam and Cream

Scones, often known as biscuits in the US, are thought to originate from Scotland. Serve warm with jam and thick cream.

Makes about 8

450g/1lb/4 cups plain (all-purpose) flour
10ml/2 tsp baking powder
5ml/1 tsp salt
50g/2oz/¼ cup butter, chilled and diced
15ml/1 tbsp lemon juice
about 400ml/14fl oz/1⅔ cups milk, plus extra to glaze
fruit jam and clotted cream or whipped double (heavy) cream, to serve

1 Preheat the oven to 230°C/450°F/Gas 8. Sift the flour, baking powder, and salt into a clean, dry mixing bowl. Add the diced butter and rub it into the flour with your fingertips until the mixture resembles fine, evenly textured breadcrumbs.

2 Whisk the lemon juice into the milk and leave for about 1 minute to thicken slightly, then pour into the flour mixture and mix to form a soft but pliable dough.

3 Knead the dough lightly to form a ball, then roll it out on a floured surface to a thickness of at least 2.5cm/1in. Using a 5cm/2in pastry (cookie) cutter, and dipping it into flour each time, stamp out 12 scones. Place on a floured baking sheet. Re-roll any trimmings and cut out more scones if you can.

4 Brush the tops of the scones lightly with a little milk, then bake in the preheated oven for about 20 minutes, or until they have risen and are golden brown. Remove from the oven and wrap in a clean dish towel to keep them warm and soft until ready to serve. Eat with fruit jam and cream.

Variation

To make cheese scones, add 115g/4oz/1 cup of grated Cheddar cheese to the dough and knead it in well before rolling out on a lightly floured surface and cutting rounds.

Chewy Flapjacks Energy 241kcal/1007kJ; Protein 2.7g; Carbohydrate 29.5g, of which sugars 14.3g; Fat 13.2g, of which saturates 7.2g; Cholesterol 30mg; Calcium 18mg; Fibre 1.4g; Sodium 125mg
Scotch Pancakes Energy 90kcal/379kJ; Protein 2.8g; Carbohydrate 12.1g, of which sugars 1.1g; Fat 3.8g, of which saturates 2.1g; Cholesterol 32mg; Calcium 47mg; Fibre 0.5g; Sodium 36mg
Scones with Jam Energy 170kcal/720kJ; Protein 4.5g; Carbohydrate 29.9g, of which sugars 2.1g; Fat 4.4g, of which saturates 2.6g; Cholesterol 11mg; Calcium 172mg; Fibre 1.2g; Sodium 338mg

Apple Cakes

These delicate little apple cakes can be rustled up in next to no time for eating hot off the griddle, if you have one, or frying pan. The quantities have been kept small because they really must be eaten while still very fresh. To make more, double up on the measures. If you wish you could serve as a dessert with stewed apple.

Makes 8–10

oil, for greasing
155g/4oz/1 cup self-raising (self-rising) flour
small pinch of salt
70g/2½oz/5 tbsp butter, cut into small cubes
50g/2oz/4 tbsp demerara (raw) or light muscovado (brown) sugar
1 small cooking apple, peeled, cored and grated
about 30ml/2 tbsp milk
caster (superfine) sugar, for dusting

1 Preheat a lightly oiled griddle or heavy frying pan over low to medium heat.

2 Sift the flour and salt into a mixing bowl. Add the butter and, with your fingertips, rub it into the flour until the mixture resembles fine breadcrumbs. Alternatively, blend the ingredients in a food processor. Stir in the sugar.

3 Stir the grated apple into the flour mixture with enough milk to make a mixture than can be gathered into a ball of soft, moist dough. Work it slightly to make sure the flour is mixed in well but don't over-work.

4 Transfer to a lightly floured surface and roll out the dough to about 5mm/¼in thick. With a 6–7.5cm/2½–3in cutter, cut out rounds, gathering up the offcuts and re-rolling to make more.

5 Smear a little butter on the hot bakestone or pan and cook the cakes, in batches, for about 2 minutes, then flip over and cook for a further 1–2 minutes on the underside until golden brown and cooked through.

6 As the cakes are cooked, lift them on to a wire rack and dust with caster sugar. Serve warm.

Currant Cakes

This recipe for buttery currant cakes is so simple to make – perfect for an afternoon snack. Serve warm as they are, or buttered and sprinkled with cinnamon.

Makes about 16

250g/9oz/2 cups plain (all-purpose) flour
7.5ml/1½ tsp baking powder
small pinch of salt
125g/4½oz/½ cup butter, cut into small cubes
100g/3¾oz/½ cup caster (superfine) sugar, plus extra for dusting
75g/3oz/½ cup currants
1 egg
45ml/3 tbsp milk

1 Heat the bakestone or a large, heavy frying pan over medium to low heat.

2 Sift the flour, baking powder and salt into a large mixing bowl. Then add the butter and, with your fingertips, rub it into the flour until the mixture resembles fine breadcrumbs. Alternatively, you can process the ingredients in a food processor. Stir in the sugar and currants.

3 Lightly beat the egg and with a round-end knife and a cutting action stir it into the flour mixture with enough milk to gather the mixture into a ball of soft dough.

4 Transfer to a lightly floured surface and roll out to about 5mm/¼in thick. With a 6–7.5cm/2½ –3in cutter, cut out rounds, gathering up the offcuts and re-rolling to make more.

5 Smear a little butter or oil over the hot griddle or pan and cook, in batches, for about 4–5 minutes on each side or until golden brown. Transfer to a wire rack, dust with caster sugar on both sides and serve warm or cooled.

Variations

• *For a change, add a large pinch of ground cinnamon or mixed (apple pie) spice to the flour in step 2.*

Apple Cakes Energy 121kcal/508kJ; Protein 1.4g; Carbohydrate 16.5g, of which sugars 6.9g; Fat 6g, of which saturates 3.7g; Cholesterol 15mg; Calcium 26mg; Fibre 0.6g; Sodium 45mg
Currant Cakes Energy 128kcal/540kJ; Protein 4.1g; Carbohydrate 22.8g, of which sugars 1.3g; Fat 2.9g, of which saturates 1.4g; Cholesterol 29mg; Calcium 66mg; Fibre 0.9g; Sodium 29mg

Marmalade Loaf

Orange marmalade and :innamon give this moist loaf :ake a deliciously warm lavour. It makes a lovely tea-:ime cake, but you can also ;erve it as a dessert, with :hick yogurt or even fresh :ustard, it is sure to go down vell with everyone.

Serves 8

?00g/7oz/1¾ cups plain (all-purpose) flour
;ml/1 tsp baking powder
6.25ml/1¼ tsp ground cinnamon
90g/3½oz/scant ½ cup butter, plus extra for greasing
50g/2oz/¼ cup soft light brown sugar
60ml/4 tbsp chunky orange marmalade
1 egg, beaten
about 45ml/3 tbsp milk
50g/2oz/½ cup icing (confectioners') sugar
about 15ml/1 tbsp warm water
thinly pared and shredded orange and lemon rind, to decorate

Preheat the oven to 160°C/325°F/Gas 3. Butter a 900ml/ ½-pint/3¾-cup loaf tin (pan), then line the base with baking parchment and grease.

2 Sift the flour, baking powder and cinnamon into a mixing bowl, then rub in the butter with your fingertips until the mixture resembles fine breadcrumbs. Stir in the sugar.

3 Mix together the marmalade, egg and most of the milk, hen stir into the bowl to make a soft dropping (pourable) :onsistency, adding a little more milk if necessary.

4 Transfer the mixture to the prepared tin and bake for about ¼ hours until firm to the touch. Leave the cake to cool or 5 minutes, then turn on to a wire rack.

5 Carefully peel off the lining paper and leave the cake on the ack to cool completely.

6 When the cake is cold, make the icing. Sift the icing sugar into bowl and mix in the water a little at a time to make a thick ;laze. Drizzle the icing over the top of the cake and decorate vith the orange and lemon rind.

Split Tin Loaf

Home-made bread is far tastier than store bread, has no additives and is cheaper.

Makes 1 loaf

500g/1¼lb/5 cups strong white bread flour
10ml/2 tsp salt
15g/½oz fresh yeast
300ml/½ pint/1¼ cups lukewarm water
60ml/4 tbsp lukewarm milk

1 Lightly grease a 900g/2lb loaf tin. Mix the yeast with half the lukewarm water in a jug (pitcher). Stir in the remaining water. Sift the flour and salt into a large bowl. Make a well in the centre.

2 Pour the yeast mixture into the centre of the flour and using your fingers, mix in a little flour. Gradually mix in more of the flour from around the edge to form a smooth batter.

3 Sprinkle a little flour over the top of the batter and leave in a warm place to prove for about 20 minutes, until bubbles appear. Mix in the milk and remaining flour to make a firm dough.

4 Place the dough on a floured surface and knead for about 10 minutes until smooth and elastic. Place in a lightly oiled bowl, cover with lightly oiled clear film (plastic wrap) and leave to rise, in a warm place, for 1–1¼ hours, or until nearly doubled in bulk.

5 Knock back the dough and turn out on to a lightly floured surface. Shape it into a rectangle, the length of the tin. Roll up lengthways, tuck the ends under and place seam side down in the prepared tin. Cover and leave to rise, in a warm place, for about 20–30 minutes, or until nearly doubled in bulk.

6 Preheat the oven to 230°C/450°F/Gas 8. Cut a deep central slash the length of the bread; dust with flour. Leave for about 10–15 minutes more then bake for 15 minutes.

7 Reduce the oven to 200°C/400°F/Gas 6 and bake for 20–25 minutes more until golden and it sounds hollow when tapped on the base. Turn out on to a wire rack to cool.

Marmalade Loaf Energy 250kcal/1050kJ; Protein 3.5g; Carbohydrate 38g, of which sugars 19g; Fat 10.4g, of which saturates 6.2g; Cholesterol 48mg; Calcium 56mg; Fibre 0.8g; Sodium 86mg
Split Tin Loaf Energy 1888kcal/8008kJ; Protein 72g; Carbohydrate 387.2g, of which sugars 23.2g; Fat 16g, of which saturates 3.9g; Cholesterol 0mg; Calcium 1376mg; Fibre 16.8g; Sodium 4720mg

Quick Wholemeal Loaves

This quick recipe couldn't be simpler to make – the dough requires no kneading and takes only a minute to mix. The bread freezes well, so make a batch and freeze what you don't need when the bread has completely cooled. Slice the loaves before you freeze them, if you don't eat much bread, then defrost it slice by slice you need it.

Makes 3 loaves

1.4kg/3lb/12 cups wholemeal (wholewheat) bread flour
15ml/1 tbsp salt
15ml/1 tbsp easy-blend (rapid-rise) dried yeast
1.2 litres/2 pints/5 cups warm water (35–38°C)
15ml/1 tbsp muscovado (molasses) sugar

1 Thoroughly grease three loaf tins (pans), each about 21 × 11 × 6cm/8½ x 4½ x 2½in and set aside in a warm place.

2 Sift the flour and salt together in a large bowl and warm slightly to take off the chill.

3 Sprinkle the dried yeast over 150ml/¼ pint/⅔ cup of the water. After a couple of minutes stir in the muscovado sugar. Leave for 10 minutes, until frothy.

4 Make a well in the centre of the flour and whisk in the yeast mixture and remaining water. The dough should be slippery. Mix for about 1 minute, working the sides into the middle. Divide the mixture among the prepared tins.

5 Cover the tins with lightly oiled clear film (plastic wrap) and leave to rise in a warm place, for about 30 minutes, or until the dough has risen by about a third to within 1cm/½in of the top of the tins. Meanwhile, preheat the oven to 200°C/400°F/Gas 6.

6 Bake the loaves in the oven for 40 minutes, or until the tops are crisp and they sound hollow when tapped on the base. Turn out on to a wire rack to cool.

Brown Soda Bread

Soda bread is best eaten on the day of baking, but it slices better if left to cool and 'set' for several hours. It is delicious with good butter, farmhouse cheese and some crisp sticks of celery or a bowl of home-made soup.

Makes 1 loaf

30ml/2 tbsp olive oil
450g/1lb/4 cups wholemeal (whole-wheat) flour
175g/6oz/1½ cups plain (all-purpose) flour
7.5ml/1½ tsp bicarbonate of soda (baking soda)
about 450ml/¾ pint/scant 2 cups buttermilk
5ml/1 tsp salt
sea salt

1 Preheat the oven to 200°C/400°F/Gas 6, and grease a baking sheet. Combine the flours and bicarbonate of soda in a mixing bowl and stir in enough buttermilk to make a soft dough. Turn on to a work surface dusted with wholemeal flour and knead for about 10 minutes until smooth.

2 Form the dough into a circle, about 4cm/1½in thick. Lay the dough circle on the baking sheet and mark a deep cross in the top with a floured knife.

3 Bake for about 45 minutes, or until the bread is browned and sounds hollow when tapped on the base. Cool on a wire rack. If a soft crust is preferred, wrap the loaf in a clean dish towel while cooling.

Cook's Tip

Buttermilk can be cultured easily at home, using a 'buttermilk plant'. Cream 25g/1oz fresh yeast, 25g/1oz sugar and 950ml/2 pints/4 cups of tepid milk gradually. Pour the mixture into a well sterilized jug (pitcher). Cover and put in warm place to ferment. Leave until it smells like buttermilk, strain off the liquid and use. Pour tepid water over the lumps in the strainer to wash. Return to the jug and add more milk or milk and water to make more buttermilk.

Wholemeal Loaves Energy 1466kcal/6235kJ; Protein 59.3g; Carbohydrate 303.4g, of which sugars 15g; Fat 10.3g, of which saturates 1.4g; Cholesterol 0mg; Calcium 180mg; Fibre 42g; Sodium 14mg
Soda Bread Energy 2262kcal/9643kJ; Protein 88.5g; Carbohydrate 465.4g, of which sugars 31.4g; Fat 18.9g, of which saturates 6.5g; Cholesterol 27mg; Calcium 1.37g; Fibre 34.2g; Sodium 2.18g

Pumpernickel

This type of rye bread is from Germany, although no one knows how it got its name. This easy version of the traditional recipe uses cocoa powder to achieve the characteristic colour.

Makes 2 loaves

65g/2½oz unsweetened cocoa powder
7g/¼oz packet easy-blend (rapid-rise) dried yeast
15ml/1 tbsp instant coffee powder
200g/7oz/1¾ cups rye flour
300–400g/11–14oz/2¾–3½ cups strong white bread flour
5ml/1 tsp salt
2.5ml/½ tsp sugar
15ml/1 tbsp caraway seeds
105ml/7 tbsp dark beer
15ml/1 tbsp vegetable oil
90ml/6 tbsp treacle (molasses)
corn meal, for sprinkling

1 Mix the cocoa with 50ml/2fl oz/¼ cup boiling water from the kettle, and set aside. In a large bowl, combine the yeast, coffee, flours, salt, sugar and caraway seeds.

2 Make a well in the flour mixture, then pour in the cocoa, 175ml/6fl oz/¾ cup water, the beer, oil and treacle. Mix well to form a dough. Turn out on to a lightly floured surface and knead for about 10 minutes, or until smooth.

3 Place the dough in a lightly oiled bowl and turn the dough to coat in oil. Cover with a dish towel and leave to rise for 1½ hours, or until doubled in size.

4 Oil a baking sheet and sprinkle with cornmeal. Turn the dough on to a lightly floured surface and punch down.

5 Knead for 3–4 minutes, then divide the dough and shape into two round or oval loaves. Place the loaves on the baking sheet, cover with a clean dish towel and leave to rise in a warm place for 45 minutes, or until doubled in size.

6 Preheat the oven to 185°C/360°F/Gas 4½. Bake the loaves for about 40 minutes, or until they sound hollow when tapped on the base. Leave to cool on a wire rack.

Bakestone Bread

A loaf of bread that is cooked on the hob. Quick and very easy to make, the finished loaf has a soft texture and scorched crust.

Makes 1 loaf

500g/1¼lb/4¼ cups plain (all-purpose) flour
5ml/1 tsp salt
5ml/1 tsp sugar
7g/¼oz packet easy-blend (rapid-rise) dried yeast
150ml/¼ pints/⅔ cup full-fat (whole) milk
15g/½oz/1 tbsp butter, cut into small pieces
5ml/1 tsp oil

1 Put the flour into a large bowl and add the salt, sugar and yeast. Combine the milk with 150ml/¼ pint/⅔ cup water and add the butter. Heat gently until the liquid is lukewarm, then stir into the flour and gather it together to make a dough ball.

2 Transfer on to a lightly floured surface and knead until smooth, firm and elastic. Put the oil in a bowl and turn the dough in it until coated. Cover with cling film (plastic wrap) and leave to rise for 1½ hours, or until doubled in size.

3 Place on to a lightly floured surface and knead (gently this time) just until the dough becomes smooth. Using your hands or a rolling pin, press the dough into a rough circle measuring about 20cm/8in in diameter and 2cm/¾in thick. Leave to stand for 15 minutes to allow the dough to relax.

4 Meanwhile, heat a bakestone or heavy frying pan over low to medium heat. Using a wide spatula and your hands, lift the dough on to the surface and leave it to cook for 20 minutes.

5 Turn the bread over and cook the second side for 20 minutes until firm and browned. Leave to cool on a wire rack.

Cook's Tip
Ensure you use standard plain (all-purpose) flour rather than strong white bread flour to make this bread, or it won't work.

Pumpernickel Energy 1276kcal/5400kJ; Protein 27.3g; Carbohydrate 246.4g, of which sugars 42.4g; Fat 24.3g, of which saturates 8.6g; Cholesterol 5mg; Calcium 395mg; Fibre 9.1g; Sodium 187mg
Bakestone Bread Energy 1928kcal/8179kJ; Protein 52.2g; Carbohydrate 399.8g, of which sugars 18.8g; Fat 24.4g, of which saturates 10.8g; Cholesterol 41mg; Calcium 885mg; Fibre 15.5g; Sodium 2136mg

Pitta Bread

The best pitta bread is always soft, tender and moist and needs to be fresh.

Makes 12

500g/1¼lb/4¼ cups strong white bread flour
7g/¼oz packet easy-blend (rapid-rise) dried yeast
15ml/1 tbsp salt
15ml/1 tbsp olive oil
250ml/8fl oz/1 cup lukewarm water

1 Combine the flour, yeast and salt in a bowl. In a separate bowl, mix the oil and water, then stir in half of the flour mixture, until you have a stiff dough Knead in the remaining flour.

2 Place the dough in a clean bowl, cover with a dish towel and leave in a warm place for at least 30 minutes and up to 2 hours.

3 Knead the dough for 10 minutes, or until smooth. Lightly oil the bowl, place the dough in it, cover again and leave to rise in a warm place for about 1 hour, or until doubled in size.

4 Divide the dough into 12 pieces. With lightly floured hands, flatten each one, then roll out into a round about 20cm/8in and about 5mm–1cm/¼–½in thick. Keep the rolled breads covered with a clean dish towel while you make the remaining pittas so that they do not begin to dry out on the surface.

5 Heat a large, heavy frying pan over medium-high heat. When smoking hot, gently lay one piece of flattened dough in the pan and cook for 15–20 seconds. Carefully turn it over and cook the second side for about 1 minute.

6 When large bubbles start to form on the bread, turn it over again. It should puff up. Using a clean dish towel, press on the bread where the bubbles have formed. Cook for 3 minutes, then remove the pitta from the pan. Repeat with the remaining dough until all the pittas have been cooked.

7 Wrap the pittas in a clean dish towel, stacking them as each is cooked. Serve the pittas warm while they are soft and moist.

Onion and Rosemary Focaccia

This bread is rich in olive oil and has an aromatic topping of red onion, fresh rosemary and coarse salt. Serve with a tomato and basil salad for an inexpensive lunch, or with a bowl of tomato soup.

Serves 4–5

450g/1lb/4 cups strong white bread flour, plus extra for dusting
5ml/1 tsp salt
2.5ml/½ tsp light muscovado (brown) sugar
250ml/8fl oz/1 cup lukewarm water
7g/¼oz packet easy-blend (rapid-rise) dried yeast
60ml/4 tbsp extra virgin olive oil, plus extra for greasing
5ml/1 tsp very finely chopped fresh rosemary, plus 6–8 small sprigs
1 red onion, thinly sliced
coarse salt

1 Sift the flour and salt into a bowl. Set aside. Stir the sugar into the water and sprinkle the yeast over. Set aside in a warm place for 10 minutes, until frothy.

2 Add the yeast, the remaining water, 15ml/1 tbsp of the oil and the rosemary to the flour. Mix together to form a dough, then gather the dough into a ball and knead on a floured work surface for about 5 minutes, until smooth and elastic.

3 Place the dough in a lightly oiled bowl, cover with oiled clear film (plastic wrap) and leave to rise for 1–2 hours in a warm place, until doubled in size.

4 Lightly oil a baking sheet. Knead the dough to form a flat loaf that is about 30cm/12in round or square. Place on the baking sheet, cover with oiled clear film and leave to rise again in a warm place for a further 40–60 minutes.

5 Preheat the oven to 220°C/425°F/Gas 7. Toss the sliced onion in 15ml/1 tbsp of the oil to coat, and then sprinkle over the top of the loaf together with the rosemary and coarse salt.

6 Bake the focaccia for 15–20 minutes, until golden. Cool on a wire rack and eat while still fresh and slightly warm.

Pitta Bread Energy 150kcal/638kJ; Protein 3.9g; Carbohydrate 32.4g, of which sugars 0.6g; Fat 1.5g, of which saturates 0.2g; Cholesterol 0mg; Calcium 59mg; Fibre 1.3g; Sodium 493mg
Foccaccia Energy 496kcal/2094kJ; Protein 11g; Carbohydrate 90.4g, of which sugars 3.8g; Fat 12.5g, of which saturates 1.8g; Cholesterol 0mg; Calcium 167mg; Fibre 4g; Sodium 496mg

Garlic and Herb Bread

This irresistible garlic bread includes plenty of fresh herbs. You can vary the overall flavour according to the combination of herbs you choose.

Serves 3–4

1 baguette or bloomer loaf

for the garlic and herb butter

115g/4oz/½ cup unsalted (sweet) butter, softened

5–6 large garlic cloves, finely chopped or crushed

30–45ml/2–3 tbsp chopped fresh herbs (such as parsley, chervil and a little tarragon)

15ml/1 tbsp chopped fresh chives

salt and ground black pepper, to taste

1 Preheat the oven to 200°C/400°F/Gas 6. Beat the butter with the garlic, herbs, chives and seasoning.

2 Cut the bread into 1cm/½in thick diagonal slices, but be sure to leave them attached at the base so that the loaf stays intact.

3 Spread the garlic and herb butter between the slices evenly, being careful not to detach them, and then spread any remaining butter over the top of the loaf.

4 Wrap the loaf in foil, place in the preheated oven and bake for 20–25 minutes, until the butter is melted and the crust is golden and crisp. Cut the loaf into slices to serve.

Cook's Tip

This loaf makes an excellent addition to a barbecue. If space permits, place the foil-wrapped loaf on the top of the barbecue and cook for about the same length of time as for oven baking. Turn the foil parcel over several times to ensure it cooks evenly.

Variations

Flavour the butter with a little chopped fresh chilli, grated (shredded) lime rind and chopped fresh coriander (cilantro).

Griddle-roasted Flat Breads

These Indian flat breads, called chapattis, are dry-roasted on an iron griddle and are delicious spread with a little melted butter. Serve as part of an Indian meal, or with any kind of dips, appetizers or snacks. Freeze any leftovers.

Makes 16

400g/14oz/3½ cups chapati flour (atta) or fine wholemeal (whole-wheat) flour

5ml/1 tsp salt

250ml/9fl oz/1 cup water

a little extra flour, for dusting

melted butter, for brushing

1 Mix the flour and salt together in a mixing bowl. Gradually add the water, continuing to mix until a dough is formed.

2 Transfer the dough to a flat surface and knead it for 4–5 minutes. When all the excess moisture is absorbed by the flour, wrap the dough in clear film (plastic wrap) and let it rest for 30 minutes. Alternatively, make the dough in a food processor.

3 Divide the dough into two equal parts and pinch or cut eight equal portions from each. Form the portions into balls and flatten them into neat, round cakes.

4 Dust the cakes lightly in the flour and roll each one out to a 15cm/6in circle. Keep the rest covered with a damp cloth.

5 Pre-heat a heavy cast-iron griddle over a medium-high heat. Place a dough circle on it, cook for about 30 seconds and turn it over, using a thin metal spatula.

6 Cook until bubbles begin to appear on the surface and turn it over again. Press the edges down gently with a clean cloth to encourage the chapati to puff up (they will not always puff up, but this does not affect the taste).

7 Cook until the underneath begins to brown. Keep cooked chapatis hot by wrapping them in foil lined with kitchen paper. Brush with a little melted butter, and serve warm and fresh.

Garlic Bread Energy 920kcal/3877kJ; Protein 22.1g; Carbohydrate 135.1g, of which sugars 7.2g; Fat 36.2g, of which saturates 20.8g; Cholesterol 82mg; Calcium 317mg; Fibre 6.3g; Sodium 1714mg
Flat Breads Energy 78kcal/330kJ; Protein 3.2g; Carbohydrate 16g, of which sugars 0.5g; Fat 0.6g, of which saturates 0.1g; Cholesterol 0mg; Calcium 10mg; Fibre 2.3g; Sodium 124mg

Shaped Dinner Rolls

These lovely-looking rolls are perfect for entertaining.

Makes 12

450g/1lb/4 cups strong white bread flour
10ml/2 tsp salt
2.5ml/½ tsp caster (superfine) sugar
7g/¼oz packet easy-blend (rapid-rise) dried yeast
50g/2oz/¼ cup butter
250ml/8fl oz/1 cup lukewarm milk
1 egg, plus 1 yolk
poppy and sesame seeds, for sprinkling

1 Grease two baking sheets. Sift the flour and salt into a bowl and stir in the sugar and yeast. Add the butter and rub in until the mixture resembles breadcrumbs. Make a well in the centre. Add the milk and egg to the well and mix to a dough.

2 Knead on a lightly floured surface for 10 minutes, until smooth and elastic. Place in a lightly oiled bowl, cover with lightly oiled clear film (plastic wrap) and leave to rise in a warm place for 1 hour, or until doubled in size.

3 Turn out on to a lightly floured surface, knock back and knead for 2–3 minutes. Divide into 12 even pieces and shape into rolls.

4 To make plaits: divide a piece of dough into three. Roll each piece to a sausage, pinch together at one end, then plait them. Pinch the ends together and tuck under the plait.

5 To make batons: shape each piece of dough into an oblong and slash the surface of each with diagonal cuts. To make knots: shape each piece of dough into a long roll and tie a knot.

6 Place the rolls on the baking sheets, spaced well apart, cover with oiled clear film and leave to rise, in a warm place, for about 30 minutes. Preheat the oven to 220°C/425°F/Gas 7.

7 Mix the egg yolk with 15ml/1 tbsp water and brush over the rolls. Sprinkle some with poppy seeds and some with sesame seeds. Bake for about 15–18 minutes, until golden. Lift off the sheet and transfer to a wire rack to cool.

Soft Morning Rolls

These rolls are best served warm, as soon as they are baked. They are perfect for breakfast with bacon or jam.

Makes 10

450g/1lb/4 cups plain (all-purpose) white flour, plus extra for dusting
10ml/2 tsp salt
20g/¾ oz fresh yeast
150ml/¼ pint/⅔ cup lukewarm milk
150ml/¼ pint/⅔ cup lukewarm water
30ml/2 tbsp milk, for glazing

1 Grease two baking sheets. Sift the flour and salt together into a large bowl and make a well in the centre. Mix the yeast with the milk, then mix in the water. Add to the centre of the flour and mix together to form a soft dough.

2 Knead the dough lightly in the bowl, then cover with lightly oiled clear film (plastic wrap) and leave to rise, in a warm place, for 1 hour, or until doubled in bulk. Turn the dough out on to a lightly floured surface and knock back.

3 Divide the dough into ten equal pieces. Knead lightly and, using a rolling pin, shape each piece to a flat oval 10 x 7.5cm/4 x 3in or a flat round 9cm/3½in.

4 Transfer to the prepared baking sheets, spaced well apart, and cover with oiled clear film. Leave to rise, in a warm place, for about 30 minutes.

5 Preheat the oven to 200°C/400°F/Gas 6. Press each roll with the three fingers to equalize the air bubbles and help prevent blistering. Brush with milk and dust with flour. Bake in the preheated oven for about 15–20 minutes or until lightly and evenly browned. Dust with more flour and cool slightly on a wire rack. Serve warm.

Cook's Tip
These rolls are ideal for serving with home-made beef burgers.

Shaped Dinner Rolls Energy 157kcal/665kJ; Protein 4.6g; Carbohydrate 32g, of which sugars 1.8g; Fat 2g, of which saturates 1g; Cholesterol 4mg; Calcium 86mg; Fibre 1.2g; Sodium 228mg
Soft Morning Rolls Energy 160kcal/682kJ; Protein 4.7g; Carbohydrate 35.7g, of which sugars 1.4g; Fat 0.8g, of which saturates 0.3g; Cholesterol 1mg; Calcium 81mg; Fibre 1.4g; Sodium 401mg

Crumpets

Home-made crumpets are less doughy than bought ones. Serve toasted.

Makes 10

225g/8oz/2 cups plain (all-purpose) flour
2.5ml/½ tsp salt
2.5ml/½ tsp bicarbonate of soda (baking soda)
5ml/1 tsp fast-action yeast granules
150ml/¼ pint/⅔ cup milk
oil, for greasing

1 Sift the flour, salt and bicarbonate of soda into a bowl and stir in the yeast. Make a well in the centre. Heat the milk with 200ml/7fl oz/scant 1 cup water until lukewarm, and tip into the well of flour.

2 Mix well with a whisk or wooden spoon, beating vigorously to make a thick smooth batter. Cover and leave in a warm place for about 1 hour until the mixture has a spongy texture.

3 Heat a griddle or frying pan. Lightly oil the surface, and the inside of three or four metals rings measuring about 8cm/3½ in in diameter. Place the oiled rings on the griddle and leave for 1–2 minutes until hot. Spoon the batter into the rings to a depth of about 1cm/½ in. Cover on a medium heat for about 6 minutes until set, and bubbles have burst open.

4 Lift off the rings, flip the crumpets over and cook the other side for 1 minute. Cool completely, then toast and butter.

English Muffins

Perfect served warm, split open and buttered for afternoon tea.

Makes 9

450g/1lb/4 cups strong white bread flour
7.5ml/1½ tsp salt
350–375ml/12–13fl oz/1½–1⅔ cups lukewarm milk
2.5ml/½ tsp caster (superfine) sugar
15g/½oz fresh yeast
15ml/1 tbsp melted butter
rice flour or semolina, for dusting

1 Flour a non-stick baking sheet. Lightly grease a griddle. Sift the flour and salt into a large bowl and make a well in the centre. Blend 150ml/¼ pint/⅔ cup of the milk, sugar and yeast together. Stir in the remaining milk and butter or oil.

2 Add to the the flour and beat for 4–5 minutes, until smooth and elastic. Cover with oiled clear film (plastic wrap) and leave to rise in a warm place for 45–60 minutes, until doubled in bulk.

3 Turn out on a floured surface and knock back. Roll out to 1cm/½in thick. Using a 7.5cm/3in cutter, cut out nine rounds. Dust with rice flour or semolina and place on the baking sheet. Cover and leave to rise in a warm place for 20–30 minutes.

4 Warm the griddle over medium heat. Cook the muffins slowly in batches for about 7 minutes on each side, or until golden brown. Transfer to a wire rack to cool.

Chive and Potato Drop Scones

These little scones should be fairly thin, soft, and crisp on the outside. Serve them for tea, or cook them fresh for a weekend breakfast.

Makes 20

450g/1lb potatoes
115g/4oz/1 cup plain (all-purpose) flour
30ml/2 tbsp olive oil, plus extra for brushing
30ml/2 tbsp fresh chives, finely chopped
pinch of salt
ground black pepper

1 Cook the potatoes in a pan of salted boiling water for 20 minutes, until tender, then drain thoroughly.

2 Return the potatoes to the clean pan and mash them well with a potato masher. Alternatively, pass them through a potato ricer. Preheat a griddle or heavy frying pan.

3 Add the flour, olive oil, chives and a little salt and pepper to the mashed potato. Mix to a soft dough.

4 Roll out the dough on a well-floured surface to a thickness of 5mm/¼in and stamp out rounds with a floured 5cm/2in plain cookie cutter. Lightly grease the griddle or heavy frying pan with a little olive oil.

5 Reduce the heat to low, add the scones to the pan, in batches, and cook for about 5 minutes on each side, until golden brown and crisp on the outside.

6 Keep the cooked scones warm while you cook the remaining batches. Serve immediately.

Cook's Tips
Cook the scones over constant low heat and do not try to hurry them or the outsides will burn before the insides are properly cooked through. The easiest way to keep the cooked scones warm is to tuck them into a folded dish towel.

Crumpets Energy 93kcal/393kJ; Protein 3g; Carbohydrate 16.5g, of which sugars 1g; Fat 2.1g, of which saturates 1g; Cholesterol 21mg; Calcium 48mg; Fibre 0.6g; Sodium 21mg
English Muffins Energy 201kcal/852kJ; Protein 6g; Carbohydrate 40.7g, of which sugars 2.6g; Fat 2.7g, of which saturates 1.4g; Cholesterol 6mg; Calcium 117mg; Fibre 1.5g; Sodium 356mg
Chive Scones Energy 45kcal/191kJ; Protein 0.9g; Carbohydrate 8.1g, of which sugars 0.4g; Fat 1.2g, of which saturates 0.2g; Cholesterol 0mg; Calcium 9mg; Fibre 0.4g; Sodium 3mg

Herby Seeded Oatcakes

The addition of thyme and sunflower seeds to this traditional recipe makes these oatcakes an especially good accompaniment to cheese – try them with a strong mature Cheddar, or goat's cheese. You could also dip them into a baked Brie.

Makes 32

rolled oats, for sprinkling
175g/6oz/1½ cups plain wholemeal (all-purpose whole-wheat) flour, plus extra for dusting
175g/6oz/1½ cups fine oatmeal
pinch of salt
1.5ml/¼ tsp bicarbonate of soda (baking soda)
75g/3oz/6 tbsp white vegetable fat (shortening)
15ml/1 tbsp fresh thyme leaves, chopped
30ml/2 tbsp sunflower seeds

1 Preheat the oven to 150°C/300°F/Gas 2. Sprinkle two ungreased, non-stick baking sheets with rolled oats. Set aside.

2 Put the flour, oatmeal, salt and bicarbonate of soda in a bowl and rub in the fat until the mixture resembles fine breadcrumbs. Stir in the thyme.

3 Add just enough cold water (about 90–105ml/6–7 tbsp) to the dry ingredients to mix to a stiff, but not sticky dough.

4 Gently knead the dough on a lightly floured surface until smooth, then cut roughly in half and roll out one piece on a lightly floured surface to make a 23–25cm/9–10in round.

5 Sprinkle sunflower seeds over the dough and press them in with the rolling pin. Cut into triangles and arrange on one of the baking sheets. Repeat with the remaining dough.

6 Bake in the oven for about 45–60 minutes until crisp but not brown. Cool on wire racks.

Variation

These oatcakes are also great sprinkled with sesame seeds.

Cheese and Potato Scones

The addition of creamy mashed potato gives these wholemeal scones a light moist texture and a crisp crust. A sprinkling of cheese and sesame seeds adds the finishing touch.

Makes 9

115g/4oz/1 cup wholemeal (whole-wheat) flour, plus extra for dusting
pinch of salt
20ml/4 tsp baking powder
40g/1½oz/3 tbsp unsalted (sweet) butter
2 eggs, beaten
50ml/2fl oz/¼ cup semi-skimmed (low-fat) milk or buttermilk
115g/4oz/1⅓ cups cooked, mashed potato
45ml/3 tbsp chopped fresh sage
50g/2oz/½ cup grated mature (sharp) Cheddar cheese
sesame seeds, for sprinkling

1 Preheat the oven to 220°C/425°F/Gas 7. Lightly grease a baking sheet.

2 Sift the flour, salt and baking powder into a bowl. Rub in the butter using your fingers until the mixture resembles fine breadcrumbs, then mix in half the beaten eggs and all the milk or buttermilk. Add the mashed potato, sage and half the Cheddar and mix to a soft dough with your hands.

3 Turn out the dough on to a floured surface and knead lightly until smooth. Roll out the dough to 2cm/¾in thick, then stamp out nine scones using a 6cm/2½in fluted cutter.

4 Place the scones on the prepared baking sheet and brush the tops with the remaining beaten egg. Sprinkle the rest of the cheese and the sesame seeds on top and bake for 15 minutes, until golden. Transfer to a wire rack and leave to cool.

Variations

- *Use unbleached self-raising (self-rising) flour instead of wholemeal (whole-wheat) flour and baking powder, if you wish.*
- *Fresh rosemary, basil or thyme can be used in place of the sage.*

Herby Oatcakes Energy 62kcal/259kJ; Protein 1.6g; Carbohydrate 7.7g, of which sugars 0.2g; Fat 3g, of which saturates 0.9g; Cholesterol 0mg; Calcium 6mg; Fibre 0.9g; Sodium 21mg
Cheese Scones Energy 124kcal/517kJ; Protein 4.9g; Carbohydrate 10.5g, of which sugars 0.7g; Fat 7.1g, of which saturates 4g; Cholesterol 57mg; Calcium 60mg; Fibre 1.3g; Sodium 87mg

Wheat Thins

These classic wheat crackers are especially delicious with rich-tasting creamy cheeses.

Makes 18

175g/6oz/1½ cups fine stoneground wholemeal (whole-wheat) flour, plus extra for dusting
pinch of salt
5ml/1 tsp baking powder
50g/2oz/½ cup coarse oatmeal
40g/1½oz/3 tbsp sugar
115g/4oz/½ cup unsalted (sweet) butter, chilled and diced

1 Preheat the oven to 190°C/375°F/Gas 5.

2 Put all the ingredients into a food processor and process until the mixture starts to clump.

3 Alternatively, sift the flour, salt and baking powder into a bowl. Add in the bran remaining in the sieve (strainer) and stir in the oatmeal and sugar. Add the butter and rub in with your fingertips until the mixture resembles breadcrumbs.

4 Transfer on to a lightly floured surface, gather the dough together with your hands and roll out.

5 Stamp out 18 rounds with a 7.5cm/3in cookie cutter. Place on an ungreased baking sheet.

6 Bake in the preheated oven for about 12 minutes until just beginning to colour at the edges.

7 Remove from the oven and leave to cool slightly, before transferring to a wire rack to cool completely.

Cook's Tip
These crackers are perfect for serving with a cheeseboard and look very pretty cut into different shapes. You could make star-shaped crackers for Christmas, or heart-shaped ones for Valentine's Day.

Poppy Seed and Sea Salt Crackers

These attractive little crackers are simple to make and use only economical store-cupboard ingredients. They also keep really well in an airtight container, and are ideal to use as the base of drinks party canapés, or they are tasty enough to be served plain as snacks in their own right.

Makes 20

115g/4oz/1 cup plain (all-purpose) flour, plus extra for dusting
pinch of salt
5ml/1 tsp caster (superfine) sugar
15g/½oz/1 tbsp butter
15ml/1 tbsp poppy seeds
about 90ml/6 tbsp single (light) cream
a little milk, for glazing
sea salt flakes, to decorate

1 Preheat the oven to 150°C/300°F/Gas Mark 2. Sift together the flour, salt and sugar into a large bowl. Add the butter and rub in with your fingertips until the mixture resembles fine breadcrumbs. Stir in the poppy seeds.

2 Gradually mix in just enough single cream to the flour mixture for the dough to stiffen.

3 Turn the dough on to a lightly floured surface and roll out to a 20 x 25cm/8 x 10in rectangle. Cut into 20 squares with a knife.

4 Put the crackers on to one or two ungreased baking sheets and brush lightly with milk. Sprinkle a few flakes of sea salt over each cracker.

5 Bake for about 30 minutes, until crisp but still quite pale. Using a metal spatula, carefully transfer the crackers to a wire rack and leave to cool completely.

Variations
Vary the flavour of these crackers by using other small seeds: for example, celery seeds for sharpness, caraway for piquancy or sesame for a slight sweetness. You could also make the crackers larger and use sunflower seeds.

Wheat Thins Energy 98kcal/408kJ; Protein 1.6g; Carbohydrate 10.6g, of which sugars 2.6g; Fat 5.7g, of which saturates 3.4g; Cholesterol 14mg; Calcium 8mg; Fibre 1.1g; Sodium 73mg
Poppy Seed Crackers Energy 39kcal/164kJ; Protein 0.8g; Carbohydrate 4.8g, of which sugars 0.4g; Fat 2g, of which saturates 1g; Cholesterol 4mg; Calcium 17mg; Fibre 0.2g; Sodium 6mg

Festive Cheese Nibbles

Shape these spicy cheese snacks in any way you wish – stars, crescent moons, triangles, squares, hearts, fingers or rounds. Serve with drinks from cocktails to hot and spicy mulled wines.

Makes 60

115g/4oz/1 cup plain (all-purpose) flour, plus extra for dusting
5ml/1 tsp mustard powder
pinch of salt
115g/4oz/½ cup butter
75g/3oz/¾ cup Cheddar cheese, grated
pinch of cayenne papper
30ml/2 tbsp water
1 egg, beaten
poppy seeds, sunflower seeds or sesame seeds, to decorate

1 Preheat the oven to 200°C/400°F/Gas 6. Lightly grease two baking sheets.

2 Sift the flour, mustard powder and salt into a bowl and rub in the butter until the mixture resembles fine breadcrumbs.

3 Stir in the cheese and cayenne pepper and sprinkle on the water. Add half the beaten egg, mix to a firm dough and knead lightly until smooth.

4 Roll out the dough on a lightly floured surface and cut out a variety of shapes. Re-roll the trimmings and cut more shapes until all the dough has been used up.

5 Place the shapes on the prepared baking sheets and brush with the remaining egg. Sprinkle on the seeds.

6 Bake for 8–10 minutes until puffed and golden. Leave to cool on the baking tray for a few minutes before carefully removing to a wire rack with a metal spatula.

Cook's Tip
Serve these nibbles as they are with pre-dinner drinks, or add them to the cheeseboard at the end of a meal.

Fennel and Chilli Ring Crackers

Based on an Italian recipe, these cookies are made with yeast and are dry and crumbly. Try them with drinks, dips or with a selection of antipasti.

Makes about 30

500g/1lb 2oz/4½ cups type 00 flour, plus extra for dusting
115g/4oz/½ cup white vegetable fat (shortening)
5ml/1 tsp easy-blend (rapid-rise) dried yeast
15ml/1 tbsp fennel seeds
10ml/2 tsp crushed chilli flakes
15ml/1 tbsp olive oil
400–550ml/14–18fl oz/1⅔–2½ cups lukewarm water
olive oil, for brushing

1 Put the flour in a bowl and rub in the fat until the mixture resembles fine breadcrumbs.

2 Add the yeast, fennel seeds and chilli flakes and mix well. Add the oil and enough water to make a soft but not sticky dough. Turn out on to a floured surface and knead lightly.

3 Take small pieces of dough and shape into sausages about 15cm/6in long. Shape into rings and pinch the ends together.

4 Place the rings on a non-stick baking sheet and brush lightly with olive oil. Cover with a dish towel and set aside at room temperature for 1 hour to rise slightly.

5 Meanwhile, preheat the oven to 150°C/300°F/Gas 2. Bake the cookies for 1 hour, until they are dry and only slightly browned. Leave on the baking sheet to cool completely.

Cook's Tip
Type 00 is an Italian grade of flour used for pasta. It is milled from the centre part of the endosperm so that the resulting flour is much whiter than plain (all-purpose) flour. It contains 70 per cent of the wheat grain. It is available from Italian delicatessens and some large supermarkets. If you cannot find it, try using strong white bread flour instead.

Festive Cheese Nibbles Energy 27kcal/113kJ; Protein 0.6g; Carbohydrate 1.5g, of which sugars 0g; Fat 2.1g, of which saturates 1.3g; Cholesterol 8mg; Calcium 13mg; Fibre 0.1g; Sodium 22mg
Fennel Crackers Energy 92kcal/385kJ; Protein 1.6g; Carbohydrate 13g, of which sugars 0.3g; Fat 4.1g, of which saturates 1.5g; Cholesterol 1mg; Calcium 24mg; Fibre 0.5g; Sodium 31mg

;hilli Muffins

'repare for a whole new aste sensation with these abulous spicy muffins.

Aakes 12

I 5g/4oz/I cup self-raising (self-rising) flour
'5ml/I tbsp baking powder
inch of salt
225g/8oz/2 cups fine cornmeal
I 50g/5oz/I ¼ cups grated mature (sharp) Cheddar cheese
50g/2oz/4 tbsp butter, melted
2 large (US extra large) eggs, beaten
5ml/I tsp chilli purée (paste)
I garlic clove, crushed
300ml/½ pint/I ¼ cups milk

I Preheat the oven to 200°C/400°F/Gas 6. Thoroughly grease 2 deep muffin tins (pans) or line the tins with paper cases.

2 Sift the flour, baking powder and salt together into a bowl, ıen stir in the cornmeal and I I5g/4oz/I cup of the grated heese until well mixed. Pour the melted butter into a bowl and tir in the eggs, chilli purée, crushed garlic and milk.

3 Pour on to the dry ingredients and mix quickly and lightly ıntil just combined. Spoon into the muffin tins, sprinkle the emaining grated cheese on top and bake for about 20 minutes, ıntil risen and golden brown. Leave to cool for a few minutes in he tin before transferring to a wire rack. Serve warm.

;heese Muffins

'uffed up and golden these nuffins have a yummy cheese lling and a hint of hot spice.

Aakes 9

'0g/2oz/4 tbsp butter
75g/6oz/I ½ cups plain (all-purpose) flour
I 0ml/2 tsp baking powder
30ml/2 tbsp caster (superfine) sugar
5ml/I tsp paprika
2 eggs
I 20ml/4fl oz/½ cup milk
5ml/I tsp dried thyme
50g/2oz mature (sharp) Cheddar cheese, diced

I Preheat the oven to I90°C/375°F/Gas 5. Lightly grease a ıine-cup muffin tin (pan) or line with paper cases. Melt the ›utter in a pan over low heat. Set aside to cool slightly.

2 Sift together the flour, baking powder, caster sugar, salt and ›aprika into a large mixing bowl.

3 Combine the eggs, milk, melted butter and dried thyme in ınother bowl and beat lightly.

4 Add the milk mixture to the bowl of dry ingredients and stir ghtly with a wooden spoon until just moistened and combined. Do not mix until smooth. Place a heaped tablespoonful of he mixture in each of the prepared muffin cups. Divide the ›ieces of cheese equally among them, then top with another poonful of the mixture, making sure that the cheese is covered.

5 Bake for about 25 minutes, until puffed and golden. Leave to tand for 5 minutes before transferring to a wire rack to cool ightly. Serve while still warm.

Bacon and Cornmeal Muffins

Serve these tasty muffins fresh from the oven for an extra special breakfast. They would also be ideal as part of a weekend brunch menu, served with scrambled eggs or an omelette.

Makes 14

8 bacon rashers (strips)
50g/2oz/¼ cup butter
50g/2oz/¼ cup margarine
I I5g/4oz/I cup plain (all-purpose) flour
I5ml/I tbsp baking powder
5ml/I tsp caster (superfine) sugar
pinch of salt
I75g/6oz/I ½ cups cornmeal
250ml/8fl oz/I cup milk
2 eggs

I Preheat the oven to 200°C/400°F/Gas 6. Lightly grease I4 cups of two muffin tins (pans), or line with paper cases.

2 Remove and discard the bacon rinds, if necessary. Heat a heavy frying pan, add the bacon and cook over medium heat, turning occasionally, until crisp. Remove with tongs and drain well on kitchen paper. When cool enough to handle, chop into small pieces and set aside.

3 Melt the butter and margarine in a pan over low heat, then remove from the heat and set aside.

4 Sift together the flour, baking powder, caster sugar and salt into a large mixing bowl. Stir in the cornmeal, then make a well in the centre.

5 Pour the milk into a small pan and heat gently until just lukewarm, then remove from the heat. Lightly whisk the eggs in a small bowl, then add the lukewarm milk. Stir in the melted butter and margarine.

6 Pour the milk and egg mixture into the centre of the well and stir in the dry ingredients until smooth and well blended.

7 Fold in the bacon. Spoon the batter into the prepared tin, filling the cups halfway. Bake for about 20 minutes, until risen and golden. Transfer to a wire rack and serve while still warm.

;hilli Muffins Energy 208kcal/871kJ; Protein 7.8g; Carbohydrate 22.3g, of which sugars 1.5g; Fat 9.6g, of which saturates 5.4g; Cholesterol 54mg; Calcium 162mg; Fibre 0.7g; Sodium 176mg
;heese Muffins Energy 166kcal/698kJ; Protein 5.1g; Carbohydrate 19.3g, of which sugars 4.4g; Fat 8.1g, of which saturates 4.6g; Cholesterol 60mg; Calcium 93mg; Fibre 0.6g; Sodium 96mg
acon Muffins Energy 176kcal/735kJ; Protein 5.2g; Carbohydrate 16.7g, of which sugars 1.3g; Fat 10g, of which saturates 3.2g; Cholesterol 43mg; Calcium 39mg; Fibre 0.5g; Sodium 203mg

Elderberry Jelly

This country jelly uses wild hedgerow and orchard fruits that would otherwise go to waste were not cost-conscious cooks helping themselves to this free food. It is wonderful with roast meat, as well as spread on toast scones.

Makes about 1.8–2.25kg/4–5lb

1.6kg/3½lb cooking apples or windfalls
900g/2lb elderberries
1.2 litres/2 pints/5 cups water
450g/1lb/2¼ cups sugar to 600ml/1 pint/2½ cups juice, warmed

1 Cut up the cooking apples roughly, without peeling. Sort through the elderberries, removing any damaged berries and stalks. Wash and drain.

2 Put the apples in a large pan with the elderberries and add the measured water. Bring to the boil and cook to a pulp. Allow to cool a little, then strain through a jelly bag.

3 Measure the juice and allow 450g/1lb/2½ cups sugar for each 600ml/1 pint/2 cups. Return the juice and sugar to the rinsed pan and heat gently until the sugar has completely dissolved. Bring to the boil. Boil hard until setting point is reached.

4 Pour into warmed, sterilized jars. When cold, cover, seal and store in a cool, dark place until required. The jam will store well for approximately 6 months.

Blackberry and Apple Jam

This simple recipe is ideal for the late summer and early autumn when a family day out blackberrying can supply the berries, and windfall apples are plentiful.

Makes about 4.5kg/10lb

1.3kg/3lb cooking apples
1.8kg/4lb/16 cups blackberries
2.75kg/6lb/13½ cups sugar, warmed

1 Remove any bad bruises from the cooking apples before weighing, then peel, core and cut them up roughly. Put into a large pan. Add half of the water, bring to the boil and simmer until the apples are soft.

2 Pick over the blackberries, wash them gently and drain well. Pour into a preserving pan with 300ml/½ pint/1¼ cups water and cook gently until tender.

3 Press the cooked berries through a sieve (strainer), then return to the rinsed preserving pan. Add the apples and the warmed sugar to the berries. Stir over low heat until the sugar has completely dissolved, and then bring to the boil. Boil the mixture hard for about 15 minutes, or until setting point is reached (105°C/220°F).

4 Skim if necessary, then pour into warmed, sterilized jars. Cover, seal and store in a cool, dark place until required. The jam will keep well for at least 6 months, if correctly stored.

Raspberry Jam

Universally popular, this delicious jam is perfect with scones and cream, on toast, or as a filling for a sponge cake. It is also the classic filling for Bakewell Tart. Raspberries are low in pectin and acid, so won't set firmly, a soft set is perfect.

Makes about 3.1kg/7lb

1.8kg/4lb/10 ⅔ cups firm raspberries
juice of 1 large lemon
1.8kg/4lb/9 cups sugar, warmed

1 Put 175g/6oz/1 cup of the raspberries into the preserving pan and crush them with a fork.

2 Add the rest of the fruit and the lemon juice, and simmer until soft and pulpy.

3 Add the sugar and stir until dissolved, then bring back to the boil and boil hard until setting point is reached (105°C/220°F), testing after 3–4 minutes (see Cook's Tip).

4 Pour into warmed, sterilized jars. When cold, cover, seal and store in a cool, dark place until required. The jam will store well for 6 months.

Variation

For a slightly stronger flavour, 150ml/¼ pint/⅔ cup redcurrant juice can be used instead of the lemon juice.

Cook's Tips

- *To test if jam or jelly has set, put a spoonful on to a cold saucer. Allow it to cool slightly, then push the surface with your finger. Setting point has been reached if a skin has formed and it wrinkles. If not, boil for longer and keep testing until it sets.*
- *Wash jars in hot, soapy water, rinse and turn upside down to drain before using, then sterilize; see Cook's Tips opposite.*

Elderberry Energy 2585kcal/11,070kJ; Protein 15.1g; Carbohydrate 672g, of which sugars 672g; Fat 1.6g, of which saturates 0g; Cholesterol 0mg; Calcium 843g; Fibre 58g; Sodium 86mg
Blackberry Energy 11,740kcal/50,063kJ; Protein 33.9g; Carbohydrate 3081.3g, of which sugars 3081.3g; Fat 4.9g, of which saturates 0g; Cholesterol 0mg; Calcium 2.29g; Fibre 76.6g; Sodium 227mg
Raspberry Energy 7542kcal/32,220kJ; Protein 34.2g; Carbohydrate 1963.8g, of which sugars 1963.8g; Fat 5.4g, of which saturates 1.8g; Cholesterol 0mg; Calcium 1.40g; Fibre 45g; Sodium 162mg

Blackcurrant Jam

'his jam has a rich, fruity avour and a wonderfully trong dark colour. It is rich ı colour and taste and is deal with scones for tea or oread on croissants for a unday breakfast.

Makes about 1.3kg/3lb
1.3kg/3lb/12 cups blackcurrants
grated rind and juice of 1 orange
475ml/16fl oz/2 cups water
30ml/2 tbsp cassis (optional)
1.3kg/3lb/6½ cups sugar, warmed
knob of butter (optional)

Place the blackcurrants, orange rind and juice and water in a rge heavy pan. Bring the mixture to the boil, reduce the heat nd simmer for 30 minutes.

Add the warmed sugar to the pan and stir over low heat until l the sugar has dissolved.

Bring the mixture to the boil and cook for about 8 minutes, r until the jam reaches setting point (105°C/220°F).

Remove the pan from the heat and skim off any scum from ne surface using a slotted spoon if you wish, or stir in a knob of utter, which will usually disperse most of it. Leave to cool for minutes, then stir in the cassis, if using.

Pour the jam into warmed, sterilized jars, cover and seal. eave the jars to cool completely, then label and store in a ool, dark place.

Cook's Tips
There are two ways to sterilize jars:
- *To sterilize in the oven, stand the containers on a baking sheet lined with kitchen paper. Rest any lids on top. Place in a cold oven, then heat to 110°C/225°F/Gas ¼ and bake for 30 minutes. Leave to cool slightly before filling.*
- *To sterilize in the microwave, half fill the glass containers with water and heat on full power until the water has boiled for one minute. Carefully tip the water out, then drain and leave to dry.*

Garden Jam

This versatile mixed fruit jam uses a range of soft fruits, including blackcurrants, blackberries, raspberries and strawberries. You can use any combination of weights for each type of berry, or leave one or two out, depending on what is available. Make sure you buy these fruits in season to keep costs down.

Makes about 3.6kg/8lb
450g/1lb/4 cups blackcurrants, washed and stalks removed
450g/1lb/4 cups blackberries (or whitecurrants or redcurrants), washed and stalks removed
450g/1lb/2⅔ cups raspberries (or loganberries), washed
450g/1lb/4 cups strawberries, washed and hulled
1.8kg/4lb/9 cups sugar, warmed

1 Put the blackcurrants into a large preserving pan and add 150ml/¼ pint/⅔ cup water. Bring to the boil and simmer until the berries are almost cooked.

2 Add the rest of the fruit and simmer gently, stirring occasionally, for about 10 minutes, or until the fruit is just soft.

3 Add the warm sugar to the pan and stir over low heat until it is completely dissolved.

4 Bring to the boil and boil hard until setting point is reached (105°C/220°F). To test, put a spoonful of jam on to a cold saucer. Cool slightly, then push the surface. It is ready if a skin has formed and it wrinkles to the touch. If not, boil for longer and keep testing, until it sets.

5 Remove any scum from the surface of the jam, if you wish, but be careful not to remove any jam, and pour into warmed, sterilized jars. Cover immediately, leave to cool, then label. Store in a cool, dark place for up to 6 months.

Cook's Tip
Add a knob of butter, if you wish, as suggested in the recipe for Blackcurrant Jam, to disperse any scum.

lackcurrant Energy 5504kcal/23,503kJ; Protein 18.4g; Carbohydrate 1448.7g, of which sugars 1448.7g; Fat 0.1g, of which saturates 0g; Cholesterol 0mg; Calcium 1474mg; Fibre 46.9g; Sodium 122mg
arden Energy 7583kcal/32,328kJ; Protein 23.9g; Carbohydrate 1991.7g, of which sugars 1991.7g; Fat 1.4g, of which saturates 0g; Cholesterol 0mg; Calcium 1.44g; Fibre 31.1g; Sodium 203mg

Damson Jam

Damsons are an economical, often free fruit, and produce a deeply coloured, richly flavoured jam that is delicious on toasted crumpets.

Makes about 2kg/4½lb

1kg/2¼lb damsons or wild plums
1.4 litres/2¼ pints/6 cups water
1kg/2¼lb/5 cups preserving or granulated (white) sugar, warmed

1 Put the damsons in a large pan and pour in the water. Bring to the boil, reduce the heat and simmer until they are soft.

2 Stir in the sugar Bring to the boil. Skim off the stones (pits) as they rise to the surface. Boil to setting point (105°C/220°F).

3 Remove from the heat, leave to cool for 10 minutes, then transfer to warmed, sterilized jam jars. Seal immediately to ensure the jar remains sterile. Leave to cool, then label with the name of the jam and the date. Store in a cool, dark place.

Greengage and Almond Jam

This jam has a lovely rich golden colour.

Makes about 1.3kg/3lb

1.3kg/3lb greengages, stoned (pitted)
juice of 1 lemon
50g/2oz/½ cup blanched almonds, cut into thin slivers
1.3kg/3lb/6½ cups granulated (white) sugar, warmed

1 Put the greengages and 350ml/12fl oz/1½ cups water in a preserving pan with the lemon juice and almond slivers. Bring to the boil, then cover and simmer for 15–20 minutes.

2 Add the sugar and stir over low heat until it has dissolved. Bring to the boil and cook for 10–15 minutes, or until the jam reaches setting point (105°C/220°F). Remove the pan from the heat. Leave to cool for 10 minutes, then stir gently and pour into warmed sterilized jars. Seal, then leave to cool completely before labelling. Store in a cool place.

Sour Cherry Jam

Stunning in colour and taste, this summer jam should be made when sour cherries are in season. This recipe is for a runny conserve, almost a thick sauce rather than a set jam, which is delectable spooned drizzled over yogurt or ice cream. The recipe takes two days, as the fruit has to be macerated in the sugar overnight.

Makes about 2kg/4½lb

1kg/2¼lb/6 cups fresh sour cherries, stalks and stones (pits) removed
juice of 1 lemon
1kg/2¼lb/5 cups sugar

1 Rinse and drain the cherries and put them into a large, heavy pan. Spoon the sugar over them, making sure they are all covered, and leave the cherries to weep overnight.

2 Place the pan over the heat and bring the liquid to the boil, stirring from time to time.

3 Add the lemon juice, reduce the heat, and simmer for about 25 minutes, or until the liquid thickens, bearing in mind that this will be a fairly liquid jam.

4 Leave the jam to cool in the pan and then spoon it into warmed, sterilized jars.

5 Keep in a cool, dry place ready to enjoy with bread, or to spoon over milk and rice puddings. The jam will keep well for up to 6 months,

Cook's Tips

Sour cherries are also called cooking cherries, they are harder and less sweet than the ones that are cultivated for eating and have a short season in the spring. You need to make sure you find the right type for this jam, otherwise it will be too sweet.

Damson Energy 4300kcal/18,360kJ; Protein 11g; Carbohydrate 1133g, of which sugars 1133g; Fat 1g, of which saturates 0g; Cholesterol 0mg; Calcium 660mg; Fibre 16g; Sodium 80mg
Greengage & Almond Energy 5896kcal/25,135kJ; Protein 24.9g; Carbohydrate 1476.3g, of which sugars 1475g; Fat 29.2g, of which saturates 2.2g; Cholesterol 0mg; Calcium 978mg; Fibre 24.5g; Sodium 11
Sour Cherry Energy 4420kcal/18,840kJ; Protein 14g; Carbohydrate 1160g, of which sugars 1160g; Fat 1g, of which saturates 0g; Cholesterol 0mg; Calcium 660mg; Fibre 9g; Sodium 70mg

)ried Apricot Jam

'his richly flavoured jam can
›e made any time of year.

ˈ1akes about 2kg/4½lb
75g/1½lb dried apricots
'00ml/1½ pints/3¾ cups apple juice
juice and grated rind of 2 unwaxed lemons
50g/2oz/½ cup blanched almonds, coarsely chopped
675g/1½lb/scant 3½ cups preserving or granulated (white) sugar, warmed

Put the apricots in a bowl, pour over the apple juice and leave ɔ soak overnight. Pour the apricots and juice into a preserving ›an add the lemon juice and rind, bring to the boil, then and 'mmer for 15–20 minutes until the apricots are soft.

ˈ Add the warmed sugar to the pan and bring to the boil, :irring until the sugar has dissolved. Boil for 15–20 minutes, or ntil setting point is reached (105°C/220°F).

Stir the chopped almonds into the jam and leave to stand for bout 15 minutes, then pour into warmed, sterilized jars. Seal, ıen leave to cool completely. Store in a cool, dark place.

:herries in Eau de Vie

hese potent cherries are
ften served at Christmas.

ˈ1akes about 1.3kg/3lb
50g/1lb generous 3 cups cherries
8 blanched almonds
75g/3oz/6 tsp sugar
500ml/17fl oz/scant 2 cups eau de vie

Wash and stone (pit) the cherries, then pack them into a :terilized, wide-necked bottle along with the blanched almonds. poon the sugar over the fruit, then pour in the eau de vie to over and seal tightly.

: Store for at least 1 month before serving, shaking the bottle ow and then to help dissolve the sugar.

Dried Fig Jam

This delectable home-made winter jam is made with dried figs and pine nuts. Look for plump, succulent dried figs with a springy texture – available in some supermarkets, delicatessens and health food stores. Although technically a jam, this preserve is delicious served with cheese, especially crumbly white cheeses, such as Manchego or Wensleydale, or any creamy goat's cheese.

Makes enough for 3 x 450g/1lb jam jars
juice of 1 lemon
5ml/1 tsp ground aniseed
about 700g/1lb 9oz dried figs, coarsely chopped
45–60ml/3–4 tbsp pine nuts
450g/1lb/2¼ cups sugar

1 Put the sugar and 600ml/1 pint/2½ cups water into a heavy pan and bring to the boil, stirring all the time, until the sugar has completely dissolved.

2 Lower the heat and simmer for 5–10 minutes, until the syrup begins to thicken. Add the lemon juice, aniseed and figs to the sugar syrup and stir to combine.

3 Bring to the boil once more, then lower the heat again and simmer for 15–20 minutes, until the figs are tender.

4 Add the pine nuts and simmer for a further 5 minutes. Leave to cool in the pan before spooning into sterilized jars and sealing. Stored in a cool, dry place, the jam will keep for up to 6 months, and is perfect as a Christmas preserve.

Variation
For a warm spicy version of dried fig jam, replace the aniseed with the scraped out seeds of a vanilla pod, 1 cinnamon stick and 2.5cm/1in piece of fresh ginger, peeled and grated. Add these to the sugar syrup at step 2. Also great served with cheese, this version of the recipe is also good stirred into Greek (US strained plain) yogurt for a healthy breakfast.

ried Apricot Energy 4032kcal/17163kJ; Protein 40.9g; Carbohydrate 955.2g, of which sugars 953.8g; Fat 31.9g, of which saturates 2.2g; Cholesterol 0mg; Calcium 970mg; Fibre 46.2g; Sodium 142mg
herries in Eau de Vie Energy 1479kcal/6142kJ; Protein 9.3g; Carbohydrate 53.5g, of which sugars 52.8g; Fat 14.4g, of which saturates 1.1g; Cholesterol 0mg; Calcium 119mg; Fibre 5.9g; Sodium 8mg
ried Fig Energy 869kcal/3693kJ; Protein 8.4g; Carbohydrate 197.5g, of which sugars 197.5g; Fat 10.5g, of which saturates 0.5g; Cholesterol 0mg; Calcium 492mg; Fibre 13.4g; Sodium 115mg

Oxford Marmalade

The characteristic caramel colour and rich flavour of a traditional Oxford marmalade is obtained by cutting the fruit coarsely and cooking it for several hours before adding the sugar.

Makes about 2.25kg/5lb
900g/2lb Seville (Temple) oranges
1.75 litres/3 pints/7½ cups water
1.3kg/3lb/6½ cups sugar, warmed

1 Scrub the orange skins, then remove the rind using a vegetable peeler. Thickly slice the rind and put in a large pan.

2 Chop the fruit, reserving the pips (seeds), and add to the rind in the pan, along with the water. Tie the orange pips in a piece of muslin (cheesecloth) and add to the pan. Bring to the boil, then cover and simmer for 2 hours. Add more water during cooking to maintain the same volume. Remove the pan from the heat and leave overnight.

3 The next day, remove the muslin bag from the oranges, squeezing well, and return the pan to the heat. Bring to the boil, then cover and simmer for 1 hour.

4 Add the warmed sugar to the pan, then slowly bring the mixture to the boil, stirring until the sugar has dissolved completely. Increase the heat and boil rapidly for about 15 minutes, or until setting point is reached (105°C/220°F).

5 Remove the pan from the heat and skim off any scum from the surface. Leave to cool for about 10 minutes, stir, then pour into warmed, sterilized jars and seal. When cold, label, then store in a cool, dark place for up to 6 months.

Cook's Tips
Traditionalists say that only bitter oranges such as Seville should be used to make marmalade. Although this isn't always true, it is most certainly the case when making Oxford marmalade.

Lemon Curd

This classic tangy, creamy curd is still one of the most popular of all the curds. It is delicious spread thickly over bread and also makes a wonderfully rich, zesty sauce that is delicious spooned over fresh fruit tarts.

Makes about 450g/1lb
3 lemons, washed
200g/7oz/1 cup caster (superfine) sugar
115g/4oz/½ cup unsalted (sweet) butter, diced
2 large (US extra large) eggs
2 large egg yolks

1 Finely grate the lemons and place the rind in a large heatproof bowl. Halve the lemons and squeeze the juice into the bowl. Set over a pan of simmering water and add the sugar and butter. Stir until the sugar dissolves and the butter melted.

2 Put the eggs and yolks in a bowl and beat together with a fork. Pour the eggs through a sieve (strainer) into the lemon mixture, and whisk well until thoroughly combined.

3 Stir the mixture constantly over the heat until the lemon curd thickens and lightly coats the back of a wooden spoon.

4 Remove the pan from the heat and pour the curd into small, warmed, sterilized jars. Cover, seal and label. Store in a cool, dark place, ideally in the refrigerator. Use within 3 months. (Once opened, store in the refrigerator.)

Variation
For orange curd substitute the finely grated rind and juice of 2 Seville oranges for the 3 lemons.

Cook's Tip
It is possible to cook the curd in a heavy pan directly over a low heat. However, you need to watch it really carefully to avoid the mixture curdling. If the curd looks begins to curdle, plunge the base of the pan in cold water and beat vigorously.

Oxford Marmalade Energy 5455kcal/23,275kJ; Protein 16.1g; Carbohydrate 1435g, of which sugars 1435g; Fat 0.9g, of which saturates 0g; Cholesterol 0mg; Calcium 1112mg; Fibre 15.3g; Sodium 123mg
Lemon Curd Energy 1942kcal/8119kJ; Protein 22.5g; Carbohydrate 209.7g, of which sugars 209.7g; Fat 118.8g, of which saturates 66.8g; Cholesterol 1105mg; Calcium 247mg; Fibre 0g; Sodium 895mg

Spiced Apple Mincemeat

This fruity mincemeat is traditionally used to fill little pies at Christmas but it can also be used as a filling for large tarts.

Makes about 1.8kg/4lb

500g/1¼lb tart cooking apples, peeled, cored and finely diced
115g/4oz/½ cup ready-to-eat dried apricots, coarsely chopped
900g/2lb/5½ cups luxury dried mixed fruit
115g/4oz/1 cup whole blanched almonds, chopped
175g/6oz/1 cup shredded beef or vegetarian suet (chilled, grated shortening)
225g/8oz/generous 1 cup dark muscovado (molasses) sugar
grated rind and juice of 1 orange
grated rind and juice of 1 lemon
5ml/1 tsp ground cinnamon
2.5ml/½ tsp freshly grated nutmeg
2.5ml/½ tsp ground ginger
120ml/4fl oz/½ cup brandy

1 Put the apples, apricots, dried fruit, almonds, suet and sugar in a large, non-metallic bowl and stir together with a metal spoon until thoroughly combined.

2 Add the orange and lemon rind and juice, cinnamon, nutmeg, ginger and brandy and mix well. Cover the bowl with a clean dish towel, place in a cool place and leave to stand for 2 days, stirring occasionally.

3 Spoon the mincemeat into cool sterilized jars, pressing down well, and being very careful not to trap any air bubbles. Cover and seal. Store the jars in a cool, dark place for at least 4 weeks before using. Once opened, store in the refrigerator and use within 4 weeks. Unopened, the mincemeat will keep for 1 year.

Cook's Tips

- *If, when opened, the mincemeat seems dry, pour a little extra brandy or orange juice into the jar and gently stir in. You may need to remove a spoonful or two of the mincemeat from the jar to do this.*
- *The flavour of mincemeat improves with age, so it is a good idea to make plenty in January, ready for the next Christmas.*

Poached Plums in Brandy

Bottling plums in a spicy syrup is a great way to preserve the flavours of autumn for the winter months. Serve them with whipped cream or vanilla ice cream.

Makes about 900g/2lb

600ml/1 pint/2½ cups brandy
rind of 1 lemon, peeled in strips
350g/12oz/1¾ cups caster (superfine) sugar
1 cinnamon stick
900g/2lb plums

1 Heat the brandy, lemon rind, sugar and cinnamon in a large pan and heat gently until the sugar dissolves. Add the plums and poach for 15 minutes until soft then pack in sterilized jars.

2 Boil the syrup until reduced by a third, then strain over the plums to cover. Seal the jars and store for up to 6 months.

Forest Berries in Kirsch

Late summer in a bottle, this popular German preserve captures the essence of the season in its rich, dark colour and flavour, perfect for Christmas.

Makes about 1.3kg/3lb

1.3kg/3lb/12 cups mixed prepared summer berries
225g/8oz/generous 1 cup granulated (white) sugar
120ml/4fl oz/½ cup Kirsch

1 Preheat the oven to 120°C/250°F/Gas ½. Pack the fruit loosely into sterilized jars. Cover the jars without sealing and place in the oven for 1 hour, or until the juices start to run.

2 Put the sugar and 600ml/1 pint/2½ cups water in a large pan and heat gently, stirring, until the sugar has dissolved. Increase the heat and boil for 5 minutes. Stir in the Kirsch and set aside.

3 Carefully remove the jars from the oven and place on a dish towel. Use the fruit from one of the jars to top up the rest. Pour the boiling syrup into each jar, making sure no air bubbles remain. Seal, cool, then store in a cool, dark place.

Apple Mincemeat Energy 6071kcal/25.579kJ; Protein 52.2g; Carbohydrate 963.6g, of which sugars 939.7g; Fat 227.3g, of which saturates 92.4g; Cholesterol 144mg; Calcium 1156mg; Fibre 44.4g; Sodium 488mg
Plums in Brandy Energy 3035kcal/12.792kJ; Protein 7.1g; Carbohydrate 444.9g, of which sugars 444.9g; Fat 0.9g, of which saturates 0g; Cholesterol 0mg; Calcium 302mg; Fibre 14.4g; Sodium 39mg
Forest Berries Energy 1517kcal/6487kJ; Protein 19.3g; Carbohydrate 334.1g, of which sugars 334.1g; Fat 3.9g, of which saturates 1.3g; Cholesterol 0mg; Calcium 444mg; Fibre 32.5g; Sodium 52mg

Plum Tomato Jam

This unusual summer jam is rarely available commercially, and it is well worth making at home. Made with slightly unripe or firm plum tomatoes, it is syrupy in consistency, and spooned, rather than spread, on to bread.

Makes enough for 2–3 x 450g/1lb jam jars

1kg/2¼lb firm plum tomatoes
500g/1¼lb/2½ cups sugar
115g/4oz/1 cup whole blanched almonds
8–10 whole cloves

1 Skin the plum tomatoes. Submerge them for a few seconds in a bowl of boiling water, then plunge them straight away into a bowl of cold water.

2 Remove them from the water one at a time and peel off the skins with your fingers or a small knife. Place the skinned tomatoes in a heavy pan and cover with the sugar.

3 Leave them to sit for a few hours, or overnight, to draw out some of the juices, then stir in 150ml/¼ pint/⅔ cup water. The tomatoes should be quite juicy – if not, stir in some more water, you may need up to 300ml/½ pint/1¼ cups.

4 Place the pan over low heat on the stove and stir gently with a wooden spoon for about 5 minutes, until all the sugar has completely dissolved.

5 Bring the syrup to the boil and boil for a few minutes, skimming off any froth, then lower the heat and stir in the almonds and cloves.

6 Simmer gently for about 25 minutes, stirring from time to time to prevent the mixture from sticking to the bottom of the pan and burning, which would spoil the flavour.

7 Turn off the heat and leave the jam to cool in the pan before spooning into sterilized jars and sealing. Store in a cool, dry place. Once opened, store the jar in the refrigerator.

Onion Confit

This jam of caramelized onions in sweet-sour balsamic vinegar is an ideal accompaniment to cheese, bread and salads. It is also excellent with ham, or stirred into creamy mashed potato and eaten with sausages. You can make it with red, white or yellow onions, or a mixture, depending on what is available but yellow onions produce the sweetest result.

Makes about 500g/1¼lb

30ml/2 tbsp olive oil
15g/½oz/1 tbsp butter
500g/1¼lb onions, sliced
3–5 fresh thyme sprigs
1 fresh bay leaf
30ml/2 tbsp light muscovado (brown) sugar, plus a little extra
50g/2oz/¼ cup ready-to-eat prunes, chopped
30ml/2 tbsp balsamic vinegar, plus a little extra
120ml/4fl oz/½ cup red wine
salt and ground black pepper

1 Reserve 5ml/1 tsp of the oil, then heat the remaining oil with the butter in a large pan.

2 Add the onions to the pan, cover and cook gently over low heat for about 15 minutes, stirring occasionally. Season the onions with salt and ground black pepper, then add the thyme, bay leaf and sugar.

3 Cook slowly, uncovered, for a further 15–20 minutes until the onions are very soft and dark. Stir the onions occasionally during cooking to prevent them sticking or burning.

4 Add the prunes, vinegar, wine and 60ml/4 tbsp water to the pan and cook over low heat, stirring frequently, for 20 minutes, or until most of the liquid has evaporated. Add a little more water and reduce the heat if it starts to look dry. Remove the pan from the heat.

5 Adjust the seasoning if necessary, adding more sugar and/or vinegar to taste. Leave the confit to cool then stir in the remaining 5ml/1 tsp olive oil and serve if using straight away, or store in a jar in the refrigerator for use later. Keep refrigerated and use within two to three weeks.

Plum Tomato Jam Energy 948kcal/4016kJ; Protein 11.3g; Carbohydrate 187.1g, of which sugars 186.1g; Fat 22.4g, of which saturates 2g; Cholesterol 0mg; Calcium 204mg; Fibre 6.2g; Sodium 45mg
Onion Confit Energy 678kcal/2827kJ; Protein 7.5g; Carbohydrate 87.9g, of which sugars 76.4g; Fat 35.5g, of which saturates 11g; Cholesterol 32mg; Calcium 161mg; Fibre 9.8g; Sodium 113mg

Apple and Sultana Chutney

Use wine or cider vinegar for this chutney to give it a subtle and mellow flavour. For a mild chutney, add only a little cayenne, for a spicier one increase the quantity to taste. It is perfect with cheese and soda bread.

Makes about 900g/2lb

350g/12oz cooking apples
115g/4oz/⅔ cup sultanas (golden raisins)
50g/2oz onion
25g/1oz/¼ cup almonds, blanched
5ml/1 tsp white peppercorns
2.5ml/½ tsp coriander seeds
175g/6oz/scant 1 cup sugar
10ml/2 tsp salt
5ml/1 tsp ground ginger
450ml/¾ pint/scant 2 cups cider vinegar
1.5ml/¼ tsp cayenne pepper
small fresh red chillies (optional), washed but left whole

1 Peel, core and chop the apples. Wash the sultanas, and finely chop the onion and almonds.

2 Tie the peppercorns and coriander seeds in muslin (cheesecloth), using a long piece of string, and then tie to the handle of a preserving pan or stainless-steel pan.

3 Put the sugar, salt, ground ginger and vinegar into the pan, with the cayenne pepper to taste. Heat gently, stirring, until the sugar has completely dissolved.

4 Add the chopped fruit. Bring to the boil and simmer for 1½–2 hours, or until most of the liquid has evaporated.

5 Spoon into warmed, sterilized jars and place one chilli in each jar, if using. Leave until cold, then cover, seal and label. Store in a cool, dark place for a month to mature before use. It will keep for at least 6 months, if correctly stored.

Cook's Tip
If the sultanas have been in your storecupboard for a while, plump them up in boiling water for 20 minutes before using.

Pear and Walnut Chutney

Pears and walnuts are in season round about the same time, in early autumn. This chutney recipe is ideal for using up hard windfall pears as well as the new season nuts, which are much cheaper at that time of year. Its mellow flavour is excellent served with cheese and oatcakes and also good with dishes made with grains, such as in pilaff or with tabbouleh.

Makes about 1.8kg/4lb

1.2kg/2½lb firm pears
225g/8oz tart apples
225g/8oz onions
450ml/¾ pint/scant 2 cups cider vinegar
175g/6oz/generous 1 cup sultanas (golden raisins)
finely grated rind and juice of 1 orange
400g/14oz/2 cups sugar
115g/4oz/1 cup walnuts, roughly chopped
2.5ml/½ tsp ground cinnamon

1 Peel and core the fruit, then chop into 2.5cm/1in chunks. Peel and quarter the onions, then chop into pieces the same size. Place in a preserving pan with the vinegar.

2 Slowly bring to the boil, then reduce the heat and simmer for 40 minutes, until tender, stirring the mixture occasionally.

3 Meanwhile, put the sultanas in a small bowl, pour over the orange juice and leave to soak.

4 Add the sugar, sultanas, and orange rind and juice to the pan. Gently heat until the sugar has dissolved, then simmer for 30–40 minutes, or until the chutney is thick and no excess liquid remains, stirring frequently.

5 Toast the walnuts in a non-stick pan for 5 minutes, until lightly coloured. Stir into the chutney with the cinnamon.

6 Spoon the chutney into warmed, sterilized jars, cover and seal. Store in a cool, dark place and leave to mature for at least 1 month. Use within 1 year. Once opened, store the jar in the refrigerator and use within 3–4 weeks. Serve the chutney with oatcakes and cheese.

Apple Chutney Energy 1299kcal/5525kJ; Protein 10.9g; Carbohydrate 299.5g, of which sugars 297.7g; Fat 14.9g, of which saturates 1.1g; Cholesterol 0mg; Calcium 254mg; Fibre 10.4g; Sodium 3.97mg
Pear Chutney Energy 3501kcal/14,797kJ; Protein 29.8g; Carbohydrate 705.3g, of which sugars 699.3g; Fat 81.4g, of which saturates 6.4g; Cholesterol 0mg; Calcium 603mg; Fibre 40.7g; Sodium 189mg

Mango Chutney

The sweet, tangy flavour of this classic chutney complements the warm taste of Indian spices perfectly, but it is equally good scooped up on crispy fried poppadums, served with chargrilled chicken, turkey or duck breasts, with potato wedges and sour cream, or spread liberally on slices of cheese on toast.

Makes about 1kg/2¼lb

900g/2lb mangoes, halved, peeled and stoned (pitted)
2.5ml/½ tsp salt
225g/8oz cooking apples, peeled
300ml/½ pint/1¼ cups distilled malt vinegar
200g/7oz/scant 1 cup demerara (raw) sugar
1 onion, chopped
1 garlic clove, crushed
10ml/2 tsp ground ginger

1 Slice the mango flesh into medium-sized chunks and place in a large, non-metallic bowl. Sprinkle with salt and set aside.

2 Meanwhile, cut the apples into quarters, then remove and discard the cores and peel. Chop the flesh roughly.

3 Put the malt vinegar and sugar in a preserving pan and heat gently, stirring occasionally, until the sugar has dissolved. Add the mangoes, apple, onion, garlic and ginger to the pan and slowly bring the mixture to the boil, stirring occasionally.

4 Reduce the heat and simmer gently for about 1 hour, stirring frequently towards the end of the cooking time, until it is reduced to a thick consistency and no excess liquid remains.

5 Spoon the chutney into warmed, sterilized jars, cover and seal. Store in a cool, dark place and allow to mature for at least 2 weeks before eating. Use within 1 year of making.

Cook's Tips
When serving mango chutney with crispy poppadums, also offer a selection of other condiments such as lime pickle, finely chopped fresh onion salad and minty yogurt.

Apple and Leek Relish

Fresh and tangy, this simple relish of leeks and apples is perfect with cold meats.

Serves 4

2 slim leeks, white part only, washed thoroughly
2 large apples
15ml/1 tbsp chopped fresh flat leaf parsley
juice of 1 lemon
15ml/1 tbsp clear honey
salt and ground black pepper

1 Thinly slice the leeks. Peel and core the apples, then slice the flesh thinly. Place the sliced leek and apple into a large serving bowl and add the fresh parsley, lemon juice and honey. Season to taste with salt and ground black pepper.

2 Toss the ingredients thoroughly with two wooden spoons until they are well combined. Leave the bowl to stand in a cool place for about an hour before serving, to allow the flavours to blend together.

Sour Mango Sambal

This sour sambal can made with green mango, as here, or papaya.

Serves 4

5ml/1 tsp shrimp paste
4 fresh red chillies, split and deseeded
7.5ml/1½ tsp salt
juice of ½ lime
5ml/1 tsp sugar
1 green mango

1 In a small, heavy pan, dry-roast the shrimp paste until it is aromatic and crumbly.

2 Using a mortar and pestle or food processor, grind the chillies with the salt to form a paste. Add the shrimp paste and sugar and pound into the spicy paste.

3 Peel and shred the mango, then add to the shrimp paste and moisten with the lime juice. Mix well and serve in little bowls.

Mango Chutney Energy 1401kcal/5997kJ; Protein 8.7g; Carbohydrate 360.7g, of which sugars 356.6g; Fat 2.2g, of which saturates 0.9g; Cholesterol 0mg; Calcium 238mg; Fibre 27.8g; Sodium 1019mg
Apple and Leek Relish Energy 59kcal/252kJ; Protein 1.9g; Carbohydrate 12.5g, of which sugars 11.8g; Fat 0.6g, of which saturates 0.1g; Cholesterol 0mg; Calcium 27mg; Fibre 3.4g; Sodium 4mg.
Sour Mango Sambal Energy 34kcal/143kJ; Protein 1.7g; Carbohydrate 6.5g, of which sugars 6.4g; Fat 0.3g, of which saturates 0.1g; Cholesterol 6mg; Calcium 28mg; Fibre 1g; Sodium 794mg

Corn Relish

When golden corn cobs are in season, try preserving their kernels in this delicious relish. It has a lovely crunchy texture and a wonderfully bright, appetizing appearance. Eat with burgers or in a cheese sandwich.

Makes about 1kg/2¼lb

6 large fresh corn on the cob
½ small white cabbage, weighing about 275g/10oz, very finely shredded
2 small onions, halved and very finely sliced
475ml/16fl oz/2 cups distilled malt vinegar
200g/7oz/1 cup golden granulated sugar
1 red (bell) pepper, seeded and finely chopped
5ml/1 tsp salt
15ml/1 tbsp plain (all-purpose) flour
5ml/1 tsp mild mustard powder
2.5ml/½ tsp turmeric powder

1 Put the corn in a pan of boiling water and cook for 2 minutes. Drain and, when cool enough to handle, use a sharp knife to strip the kernels from the cobs.

2 Put the corn kernels in a pan with the cabbage and onions. Reserve 30ml/2 tbsp of the vinegar, then add the rest to the pan with the sugar.

3 Slowly bring to the boil, stirring occasionally until the sugar dissolves. Simmer for 15 minutes. Add the red pepper and simmer for a further 10 minutes.

4 Blend the salt, flour, mustard and turmeric with the reserved vinegar to make a smooth paste.

5 Stir the paste into the vegetable mixture and bring back to the boil. Simmer for 5 minutes, until the mixture has thickened.

6 Spoon the relish into warmed, sterilized jars, cover and seal. Store in a cool, dark place.

7 Use within 6 months of making. Once opened, store in the refrigerator and use within 2 months.

Lime Pickle

This aromatic Indian pickle is often sold in jars at Asian stores and in supermarkets, but the flavour is better if you make it yourself. Hot, fiery and sour, it is served as an accompaniment to curry.

Serves 8–10

8–10 limes
30ml/2 tbsp salt
150ml/¼ pint/⅔ cup sesame or groundnut (peanut) oil
10–15ml/2–3 tsp brown mustard seeds
3–4 garlic cloves, cut into thin sticks
25g/1oz fresh root ginger, peeled and cut into thin sticks
5ml/1 tsp coriander seeds
5ml/1 tsp cumin seeds
5ml/1 tsp fennel seeds
a handful of fresh or dried curry leaves
10ml/2 tsp ground turmeric
10ml/2 tsp hot chilli powder

1 Put the whole limes in a bowl. Cover with boiling water and leave to stand for 30 minutes.

2 Drain the limes and cut each into quarters. Rub them with salt and put them into a sealed sterilized jar. Leave the limes to cure in the salt for 1 week.

3 Heat the oil in a large frying pan and stir in the mustard seeds. When they begin to pop, stir in the garlic, ginger, spices and curry leaves. Cook gently for a few minutes to flavour the oil, then stir in the lime pieces and the juices from the jar.

4 Reduce the heat and simmer for about 45 minutes, stirring from time to time. Store the pickle in sterilized jars and keep in a cool place for 1–2 months.

Cook's Tips
- *This pickle is delicious served with grilled or fried fish, and spicy stir-fried egg noodles.*
- *You can make it hotter by adding more chilli powder.*
- *Asian stores and markets are often the cheapest place to buy limes in bulk.*

Corn Relish Energy 1479kcal/6291kJ; Protein 20.3g; Carbohydrate 356.7g, of which sugars 275.1g; Fat 6.4g, of which saturates 1g; Cholesterol 0mg; Calcium 307mg; Fibre 15.5g; Sodium 3085mg
Lime Pickle Energy 96kcal/395kJ; Protein 0.3g; Carbohydrate 0.9g, of which sugars 0.6g; Fat 10.1g, of which saturates 1.5g; Cholesterol 0mg; Calcium 25mg; Fibre 0.2g; Sodium 1185mg

English Pickled Onions

These powerful pickles are traditionally served with a plate of cold meats and bread and cheese. They should be stored for at least 6 weeks before eating.

Makes enough for 4 x 450g/1lb jars

1kg/2¼lb pickling (pearl) onions
115g/4oz/½ cup salt
15ml/1 tbsp sugar
750ml/1¼ pints/3 cups malt vinegar
15ml/1 tbsp coriander seeds
5ml/1 tsp brown mustard seeds
5ml/1 tsp allspice berries
2–3 dried red chillies
5cm/2in piece fresh root ginger, finely sliced
2–3 blades mace
5ml/1 tsp black peppercorns
2–3 fresh bay leaves

1 To peel the onions, trim off the root ends, but leave the onion layers attached. Cut a thin slice off the top (neck) end of the onion. Place the onions in a bowl, then cover with boiling water. Leave to stand for 4 minutes, then drain. The skin should then be easy to peel using a small, sharp knife.

2 Place the peeled onions in a bowl and cover with cold water, then drain the water into a large pan. Add the salt and heat slightly to dissolve it, then cool before pouring the brine over the onions. Place a plate inside the top of the bowl and weigh it down slightly so that it keeps all the onions submerged in the brine. Leave to stand for 24 hours.

3 Meanwhile, place the sugar and vinegar in a large pan. Wrap all the remaining ingredients, except the bay leaves, in a piece of muslin (cheesecloth). Bring to the boil, simmer for about 5 minutes, then remove the pan from the heat. Set aside and leave to infuse (steep) overnight.

4 Drain the onions, rinse and pat dry. Pack them into sterilized 450g/1lb jars. Add some or all of the spice from the vinegar, except the ginger slices. The pickle will become hotter if you add the chillies. Pour the vinegar over to cover and add the bay leaves. Seal the jars with non-metallic lids and store in a cool, dark place for at least 6 weeks before eating.

Mixed Vegetable Pickle

This fresh, salad-style pickle doesn't need lengthy storing so makes the perfect choice if you need a bowl of pickle immediately. However, it does not have good storing properties, so only make as much as you need. Serve with cold meats, spiced kebabs or pilaffs.

Makes about 450g/1lb

½ cauliflower head, cut into florets
2 carrots, sliced
2 celery sticks, thinly sliced
¼–½ white cabbage, thinly sliced
115g/4oz/scant 1 cup runner (green) beans, cut into bitesize pieces
6 garlic cloves, sliced
1–4 fresh chillies, whole or sliced
5cm/2in piece fresh root ginger, finely sliced
1 red (bell) pepper, sliced
2.5ml/½ tsp turmeric powder
105ml/7 tbsp white wine vinegar
15–30ml/1–2 tbsp sugar
60–90ml/4–6 tbsp olive oil
juice of 2 lemons
salt

1 Toss the cauliflower, carrots, celery, cabbage, beans, garlic, chillies, ginger and pepper with salt and leave them to stand in a colander over a bowl for 4 hours.

2 Shake the vegetables well to remove any excess juices. Transfer the salted vegetables to a bowl.

3 Add the turmeric, vinegar, sugar to taste, oil and lemon juice. Toss to combine thoroughly, then add enough water to distribute the flavours.

4 Cover the bowl with clear film (plastic wrap) and leave to chill in the refrigerator for at least 1 hour, or until you are ready to serve the pickle.

Cook's Tips

- *If you find the flavour of the chilli too hot, use only half a chilli and chop it into tiny pieces. Make sure you remove the seeds.*
- *Chop the vegetables into small bitesize pieces, and try to ensure they are all roughly the same size.*

English Pickled Onions Energy 109kcal/454kJ; Protein 3.1g; Carbohydrate 24.5g, of which sugars 18.6g; Fat 0.5g, of which saturates 0g; Cholesterol 0mg; Calcium 67mg; Fibre 3.6g; Sodium 8mg
Vegetable Pickle Energy 776kcal/3211kJ; Protein 19.1g; Carbohydrate 42.5g, of which sugars 38.3g; Fat 59.6g, of which saturates 8.7g; Cholesterol 0mg; Calcium 302mg; Fibre 17.8g; Sodium 109mg

Pickled Turnips and Beetroot

This is a fantastic way to use these simple root vegetables. The turnips turn a rich red in their beetroot-spiked brine and look absolutely gorgeous stacked on the shelves in the storecupboard.

Makes about 1.6kg/3½lb

1kg/2¼lb young turnips
3–4 raw beetroot (beets)
about 45ml/3 tbsp coarse sea salt
about 1.5 litres/2½ pints/ 6¼ cups water
juice of 1 lemon

1 Wash the turnips and beetroot, but do not peel them, then cut into slices about 5mm/¼in thick. Put the salt and water in a bowl, stir and leave to stand until the salt has dissolved.

2 Sprinkle the beetroot with lemon juice and place in the bottom of four 1.2-litre/2-pint/5-cup sterilized jars.

3 Top with sliced turnip, packing them in very tightly, then pour over the brine, making sure that the vegetables are covered. Seal the jars and leave for at least 7 days before serving.

Preserved Lemons

These richly flavoured fruits are widely used in Middle Eastern cooking to flavour soups and stews.

Makes about 2 jars

10 unwaxed lemons, washed and cut into wedges
sea salt
about 200ml/7fl oz/scant 1 cup lemon juice or a combination of fresh and preserved juice

1 Press a generous amount of salt on to the cut surface of each lemon wedge.and pack into two 1.2-litre/2-pint/5-cup warmed sterilized jars. To each jar, add 30–45ml/2–3 tbsp sea salt and half the lemon juice, then cover with boiling water. Seal the jars and leave to stand for 2–4 weeks before using.

2 To use, rinse the lemons well, then pull off and discard the flesh. Cut the rind into strips and use in stews and casseroles.

Pickled Red Cabbage

This delicately spiced and vibrant-coloured pickle is an old-fashioned favourite to serve with bread and cheese, it is also good served with with roast duck or goose. In northern England pickled red cabbage was the traditional accompaniment to Lancashire hot-pot.

Makes about 1–1.6kg/ 2¼–3½lb

675g/1½lb/6 cups red cabbage, shredded
1 large Spanish (Bermuda) onion, sliced
30ml/2 tbsp salt
600ml/1 pint/2½ cups red wine vinegar
75g/3oz/6 tbsp light muscovado (brown) sugar
15ml/1 tbsp coriander seeds
3 cloves
2.5cm/1in piece fresh root ginger, peeled and thinly sliced
1 whole star anise
2 fresh bay leaves
4 eating apples

1 Put the cabbage and onion in a bowl, add the salt and mix well until thoroughly combined.

2 Transfer the mixture into a colander over a bowl and leave to drain overnight. The next day, rinse the salted vegetables, drain well and pat dry using kitchen paper.

3 Pour the vinegar into a large pan, add the sugar, spices and bay leaves and bring to the boil. Remove the pan from the heat and set aside to cool.

4 Core and chop the apples, then layer with the cabbage and onions in sterilized preserving jars.

5 Pour over the cooled spiced vinegar. (If you prefer a milder pickle, strain out the spices first.)

6 Seal the jars and store for 1 week before eating, served with bread and cheese or as an accompaniment to roasted duck or goose. Eat within 2 months. Once opened, store in the refrigerator.

Pickled Turnips Energy 338kcal/1442kJ; Protein 14.1g; Carbohydrate 69.8g, of which sugars 66g; Fat 3.3g, of which saturates 0g; Cholesterol 0mg; Calcium 541mg; Fibre 29.7g; Sodium 4278mg
Preserved Lemons Energy 48kcal/198kJ; Protein 2.5g; Carbohydrate 8g, of which sugars 8g; Fat 0.8g, of which saturates 0.3g; Cholesterol 0mg; Calcium 213mg; Fibre 0g; Sodium 13mg
Pickled Red Cabbage Energy 674kcal/2868kJ; Protein 12g; Carbohydrate 161.4g, of which sugars 159.3g; Fat 2g, of which saturates 0g; Cholesterol 0mg; Calcium 405mg; Fibre 23g; Sodium 64mg

Pickled Mushrooms

This method of preserving mushrooms is popular throughout Europe and it is a very good way to use up a glut after a day's foraging for wild varieties. The pickled mushrooms are delicious served with chicken or grilled meat.

Makes about 900g/2lb

500g/1¼lb/8 cups mixed mushrooms such as small ceps, chestnut mushrooms, shiitake and girolles
300ml/½ pint/1¼ cups white wine vinegar or cider vinegar
15ml/1 tbsp salt
5ml/1 tsp caster (superfine) sugar
300ml/½ pint/1¼ cups water
4–5 fresh bay leaves
8 large fresh thyme sprigs
15 garlic cloves, peeled, halved, with any green shoots removed
1 small red onion, halved and thinly sliced
2–3 small dried red chillies
5ml/1 tsp coriander seeds, lightly crushed
5ml/1 tsp black peppercorns
a few strips of lemon rind
250–350ml/8–12fl oz/1–1½ cups extra virgin olive oil

1 Trim and wipe the mushrooms and cut any large ones in half.

2 Put the vinegar, salt, sugar and water in a pan and bring to the boil. Add the bay leaves, thyme, garlic, onion, chillies, coriander seeds, peppercorns and lemon rind and simmer for 2 minutes.

3 Add the mushrooms to the pan and simmer for 3–4 minutes. Drain the mushrooms through a sieve (strainer), retaining all the herbs and spices, then set aside for a few minutes more until the mushrooms are thoroughly drained.

4 Fill one large or two small cooled, sterilized jars with the mushrooms. Distribute the garlic, onion, herbs and spices evenly among the layers of mushrooms, then add enough olive oil to cover by at least 1cm/½in. You may need to use extra oil if you are making two jars.

5 Leave the pickle to settle, then tap the jars on the work surface to dispel any air bubbles. Seal the jars, then store in the refrigerator. Use within 2 weeks.

Dill Pickles

Redolent of garlic and piquant with fresh chilli, salty dill pickles can be eaten on their own or they make an ideal accompaniment to a plate of assorted cheeses and cold meats. They go especially well with salt beef and pastrami, and are often seen as essential in a burger.

Makes about 900g/2lb

20 small, ridged or knobbly pickling (small) cucumbers
2 litres/3½ pints/8 cups water
175g/6oz/¾ cup coarse sea salt
15–20 garlic cloves, unpeeled
2 bunches fresh dill
15ml/1 tbsp dill seeds30ml/2 tbsp mixed pickling spice
1 or 2 hot fresh chillies

1 Scrub the cucumbers and rinse them well in cold water. Leave to dry. Put the measured water and salt in a large pan and bring to the boil. Turn off the heat and leave the pan to cool down to room temperature.

2 Using the flat side of a knife blade or a mortar and pestle, lightly crush each garlic clove, breaking the papery skin.

3 Pack the cucumbers tightly into one or two wide-necked, sterilized jars, layering them with the garlic, fresh dill, dill seeds and pickling spice. Add one chilli to each jar.

4 Pour over the cooled brine, making sure that the cucumbers are completely covered. Tap the jars on the work surface to dispel any trapped air bubbles.

5 Cover the jars with lids and then leave to stand at room temperature for 4–7 days before serving. Store in the refrigerator once opened.

Cook's Tips
- *If you cannot find ridged or knobbly pickling cucumbers, use any small cucumbers instead.*
- *Mixed pickling spices can vary, so check what is in them so you get your preferred blend.*

Pickled Mushrooms Energy 931kcal/3844kJ; Protein 14.5g; Carbohydrate 11.6g, of which sugars 10g; Fat 92.3g, of which saturates 13.4g; Cholesterol 0mg; Calcium 52mg; Fibre 8.8g; Sodium 41mg
Dill Pickles Energy 45kcal/180kJ; Protein 3.1g; Carbohydrate 6.8g, of which sugars 6.3g; Fat 0.5g, of which saturates 0g; Cholesterol 0mg; Calcium 83mg; Fibre 2.7g; Sodium 5908mg

piced Poached Kumquats

hese spicy kumquats go specially well with rich neats, such as roast pork or aked ham, or with punchy oat's milk cheese, where the nild spices help to balance he richness.

Serves 6

450g/1lb/4 cups kumquats, cut in half, seeds discarded
115g/4oz/½ cup caster (superfine) sugar
1 small cinnamon stick
1 star anise

1 Place the fruit in a pan with the sugar, 150ml/¼ pint/⅔ cup vater the cinnamon and star anise. Cook gently, stirring until he sugar has dissolved. Then cover and boil for 8–10 minutes.

2 Spoon them into warm, sterilized jars, seal and label.

Marinated Feta Cheese with Capers

Marinating cubes of feta heese with herbs and spices ives a marvellous flavour. erve on toast or with salad.

erves 6

50g/12oz/2 cups feta cheese
2 garlic cloves
2.5ml/½ tsp mixed peppercorns
8 coriander seeds
1 bay leaf
15–30ml/1–2 tbsp drained capers
fresh oregano or thyme sprigs
olive oil, to cover

1 Cut the feta cheese into cubes. Thickly slice the garlic cloves. Mix the peppercorns and coriander seeds in a mortar and rush lightly with a pestle.

2 Pack the feta cubes into a large preserving jar with the bay eaf, inter-spersing layers of cheese with garlic, crushed eppercorns and coriander, capers and the fresh oregano r thyme sprigs.

3 Pour in enough olive oil to cover the cheese. Close tightly and eave to marinate for two weeks in the refrigerator. Lift out the eta and serve on hot toast, sprinkled with a little of the oil.

Yogurt Cheese in Olive Oil

Sheep's milk is widely used in cheese-making in the eastern Mediterranean, particularly in Greece where sheep's yogurt is hung in muslin to drain off the whey before patting into balls of soft cheese. Here it's bottled in extra virgin olive oil with plenty of chilli and herbs – an appropriate gift for a friend who enjoys Greek cuisine.

Makes 2 450g/1lb jars

750g/10oz/1¼ cups Greek sheep's yogurt
2.5ml/½ tsp salt
10ml/2 tsp crushed dried chillies or chilli powder
15ml/1 tbsp chopped fresh rosemary
15ml/1 tbsp chopped fresh thyme or oregano
about 300ml/½ pint/1¼ cups olive oil, preferably garlic flavoured

1 Sterilize a 30cm/12in square of muslin (cheesecloth) by steeping it in boiling water. Drain and lay over a large plate.

2 Mix the yogurt with the salt and place on to the centre of the muslin. Bring up the sides of the muslin and tie firmly with kitchen string. Hang the bag of yogurt over a large bowl to catch the whey and leave in a cool place for 2–3 days, or until the whey stops dripping.

3 Wash thoroughly and dry two 450g/1lb glass preserving jars or jam jars. Sterilize them by heating them in an oven preheated to 150°C/300°F/Gas 2 for 15 minutes.

4 Mix together the chilli and herbs. Take teaspoonfuls of the cheese and roll into balls with your hands. Lower into the jars, sprinkling each layer with the herb mixture.

5 Pour the olive oil over the soft cheese balls until they are completely covered. Mix gently with the handle end of a wooden spoon in order to blend the flavourings through the olive oil, making sure that you do not break up the cheese balls. Store in the refrigerator for up to 3 weeks.

6 To serve the cheese, spoon out of the jars with a little of the flavoured olive oil and spread on to lightly toasted bread.

piced Kumquats Energy 103kcal/441kJ; Protein 0.8g; Carbohydrate 26.6g, of which sugars 26.6g; Fat 0.1g, of which saturates 0g; Cholesterol 0mg; Calcium 33mg; Fibre 0.9g; Sodium 4mg
Marinated Feta Energy 165kcal/683kJ; Protein 9.3g; Carbohydrate 1.3g, of which sugars 0.9g; Fat 13.6g, of which saturates 8.3g; Cholesterol 41mg; Calcium 211mg; Fibre 0.1g; Sodium 840mg
ogurt Cheese Energy 1331kcal/5488kJ; Protein 24g; Carbohydrate 7.5g, of which sugars 7.5g; Fat 138.2g, of which saturates 33.8g; Cholesterol 0mg; Calcium 563mg; Fibre 0g; Sodium 758mg

Index